Juvenile Delinquency

EDITORIAL ADVISORS

Criminal Justice Series

Juvenile Delinquency

Laura Pinto Hansen

Instructor in Criminal Justice
Department of Sociology, Anthropology, and Criminal Justice
New Mexico Highlands University

Professor Emerita in Criminal Justice
Department of Criminal Justice, Sociology, and Social Work
Western New England University

Aspen Publishing

To contact Customer Service, e-mail customer.service@aspenpublishing.com, call 1-800-950-5259, or mail correspondence to:

Aspen Publishing
Attn: Order Department
1 Wall Street
Burlington, MA 01803

Printed in Canada.

1 2 3 4 5 6 7 8 9 0

ISBN 978-1-5438-5624-8

Library of Congress Cataloguing-in-Publication Data application is in process.

ABOUT ASPEN PUBLISHING

Aspen Publishing is a leading provider of educational content and digital learning solutions to law schools in the U.S. and around the world. Aspen provides best-in-class solutions for legal education through authoritative textbooks, written by renowned authors, and breakthrough products such as Connected eBooks, Connected Quizzing, and PracticePerfect.

The Aspen Casebook Series (famously known among law faculty and students as the "red and black" casebooks) encompasses hundreds of highly regarded textbooks in more than eighty disciplines, from large enrollment courses, such as Torts and Contracts, to emerging electives, such as Sustainability and the Law of Policing. Study aids such as the *Examples & Explanations* and the *Emanuel Law Outlines* series, both highly popular collections, help law students master complex subject matter.

Major products, programs, and initiatives include:

- **Connected eBooks** are enhanced digital textbooks and study aids that come with a suite of online content and learning tools designed to maximize student success. Designed in collaboration with hundreds of faculty and students, the Connected eBook is a significant leap forward in the legal education learning tools available to students.
- **Connected Quizzing** is an easy-to-use formative assessment tool that tests law students' understanding and provides timely feedback to improve learning outcomes. Delivered through CasebookConnect.com, the learning platform already used by students to access their Aspen casebooks, Connected Quizzing is simple to implement and integrates seamlessly with law school course curricula.
- **PracticePerfect** is a visually engaging, interactive study aid to explain commonly encountered legal doctrines through easy-to-understand animated videos, illustrative examples, and numerous practice questions. Developed by a team of experts, PracticePerfect is the ideal study companion for today's law students.
- The **Aspen Learning Library** enables law schools to provide their students with access to the most popular study aids on the market across all of their courses. Available through an annual subscription, the online library consists of study aids in e-book, audio, and video formats with full text search, note-taking, and highlighting capabilities.
- Aspen's **Digital Bookshelf** is an institutional-level online education bookshelf, consolidating everything students and professors need to ensure success. This program ensures that every student has access to affordable course materials from day one.
- **Leading Edge** is a community centered on thinking differently about legal education and putting those thoughts into actionable strategies. At the core of the program is the Leading Edge Conference, an annual gathering of legal education thought leaders looking to pool ideas and identify promising directions of exploration.

DEDICATION

The most logical people I should be thanking are the two children I raised, both now adults. The process can only be described as a sociological experiment, with my examining their every behavior with curiosity and wonder, breaking out the developmental psychology books at every turn. However, since my children's wickedest behavior in childhood was at best, mildly and benignly delinquent (they did have their wild moments), they were not the best research subjects, if I wanted to better understand serious juvenile offending. Nor was this book inspired by my own foolish escapades as an adolescent and young adult.

I only became interested in seriously studying juvenile delinquency, and youth gangs specifically, when in graduate school (University of California, Riverside) I stumbled across a course taught by Kirk Williams, on young violent offenders. This was one of many turning points in the development of my research interests. So instead, I am dedicating this book to all the lost or abandoned children who have ever found themselves stuck in the juvenile justice system, specifically those who have ended up in juvenile detention. It is because of concern for them that I have devoted a good portion of my research career studying the societal problems that lead to juvenile offending, as well as teaching courses focused on juvenile delinquency, youth gangs, and sociology of family. I do so in the hopes of inspiring new cohorts of students and scholars to continue to seek out preventative measures in juvenile offending and prevent youth gang recruitment.

Laura Pinto Hansen, Ph.D.
Instructor in Criminal Justice
Department of Sociology, Anthropology, and Criminal Justice
New Mexico Highlands University

Professor Emerita in Criminal Justice
Department of Sociology, Criminal Justice, and Social Work
Western New England University

Summary of CONTENTS

CONTENTS

CHAPTER TWO

(A BRIEF) HISTORY OF JUVENILE DEVIANCE AND DELINQUENCY 27

CHAPTER THREE

CURRENT TRENDS IN YOUTH DEVIANCE AND CRIME: STATUS AND OTHER MINOR OFFENSES 51

CHAPTER **SIX**

INDIVIDUAL RISKS FOR DEVIANCE AND DELINQUENCY 133

CHAPTER SEVEN

FAMILIES, JUVENILE DEVIANCE, AND DELINQUENCY 169

CHAPTER EIGHT

ENVIRONMENTAL AND COMMUNITY RISKS FOR DEVIANCE AND DELINQUENCY 197

CHAPTER **TEN**

PREFACE

It is only in recent human history that we have acknowledged, through scientific discovery, that children are not simply small adults and that they have unique developmental stages. More importantly, those studying neurology and the brain recently theorized (and rightfully so) that the frontal lobe, the location for decision making, self-monitoring, and self-control, is not fully developed until the age of 25. This means that the arbitrary age of 18, used in the criminal justice system to distinguish between juvenile and adult offenders, is something that no doubt baffles many of us who study juvenile delinquency. However, for the purposes of this book and keeping with legal definitions in the United States, we will be looking primarily at criminal behaviors of those under the age of 18 and their treatment when they are caught by school officials, parental units,[1] law enforcement, and/or juvenile authorities.

This book is somewhat different from other juvenile delinquency books in that it is interdisciplinary, looking at juvenile offending through the scholarly lenses of sociology, criminal justice, and developmental and physiological psychology. It is important to note that whether an individual is treated as a child or as a young adult when they break the law, if they end up in any part of the criminal justice system, including in the juvenile courts, it often has long-term consequences on social and intellectual development, making it difficult, though not entirely impossible, to grow up to be a productive and functioning adult. As Aizer and Doyle's (2015[2]) research found, approximately 40% of juveniles who have served time in juvenile detention will be incarcerated in adult prison by the time they are 25.

Though some detention centers for children in the United States look more like residential homes and have pleasant decors, others are foreboding and sterile. And like what we see in schools, not all staff working in juvenile corrections are adept at dealing with any range of behavior problems, including those that are a result of psychiatric or neurological disorders. Hence, we spend time in this book looking at several options other than zero-tolerance policies and juvenile detention, including

[1] You will note throughout this book that I refer to the adults who are responsible for the minors in their care as "parental units," as currently we cannot assume that all parents are biological or adoptive. There are any number of children in the United States who are being raised by others, including by extended family members (e.g., grandparents). In some cases, it may be family friends or foster parents who are raising the child or adolescent as court-ordered guardians, depending on the circumstances.

[2] Aizer, A., and J. J. Doyle (2015). "Juvenile incarceration, human capital and future crime: Evidence from randomly-assigned judges." *Quarterly Journal of Economics*. Vol. 130, Issue 2. DOI: 10.1093/qje/qjv003.

preventative measures. However, admittedly, the worst juvenile detention center, for some children, is still the best alternative, if their home lives are in complete shambles or if they have committed seriously violent offenses.

Though the language we use in the juvenile justice system is "softer," we should not mistake it for being more lenient. In theory, the juvenile justice system is intended to rehabilitate young offenders. In the adult system, as much as lip service is given to rehabilitation, the primary goal is to punish adult offenders. For students reading this book and taking a course in juvenile delinquency who intend to work with this population in their chosen profession, the intent is to offer insight into how to prevent a juvenile from offending in the first place, by addressing the social problems contributing to delinquency, and when they do offend, finding the best alternative possible other than detention.

We also provide a peek behind the curtain of systems of punishment for juveniles in other countries. As students will no doubt discover, in some countries juveniles are provided with several services to rehabilitate them. In other countries, they will be thrown into prison with adult offenders, left to fend for themselves. If students have taken a course in penology or corrections, they will have an opportunity as well to make comparisons between the adult and juvenile justice systems in the United States. It is important to do so, as an unfortunate number of juvenile offenders will age into an adult prison; more alarming, juveniles who have committed the most horrific of crimes may be sent to the adult criminal justice system. If they are found guilty of their crimes, and depending on the jurisdiction, children as young as 12 can be sent to adult prison, before some of them have even reached puberty.

CHAPTER ORGANIZATION

The textbook chapters are designed to offer the richest reading experience for the different styles of learning students have today, including those with various learning disabilities. The organization of the chapters is as follows:

- **Chapter Objectives** guide the reader to the most important goals of the chapter.
- **Key Terms** define vocabulary that is commonly used in juvenile delinquency and juvenile justice. Instructors will note that we have also included definitions to some words that we cannot assume students are familiar with that are not related to juvenile delinquency, but will help them better grasp their relevance in the course.
- **Chapter Summaries** very briefly give a quick overview of the chapter and direct the student to the more important general information contained in them.

- **Discussion Questions** in this section there are a number of questions related to the content of the chapter. These are intended to be used in class discussions, debates, as homework assignments, and/or short answer responses, essays on exams. In some cases, the questions are intended to encourage students to conduct outside research.
- **In the Media** sections provide recent cases of juvenile delinquency or public responses and moral panics centered on extreme types of delinquent behavior.
- **International Perspectives on Juvenile Justice** offer cross-cultural, cross-national views of the treatment of juvenile offenders, as well as a peek behind the walls of juvenile detention centers in other countries around the world.
- **References and Suggested Readings** at the end of each chapter are not only intended to cite the sources used but to encourage students to research topics further, and give them a start for their research papers in class.

You will note that I have included "trigger warnings" in some chapters. Though we expect students in criminal justice, sociology, and social work to be able to handle the harsh realities of juvenile offenders and criminal offending, I do not want to limit this textbook to those students. In the last several years, I have included a statement in my syllabi that there might be some materials discussed in the course (e.g., juvenile delinquency, child abuse, punishment and corrections) that might be more than unpleasant—they might trigger anxiety in students, particularly those who have been victimized. We cannot talk juvenile offending without diving into the unpleasant and disturbing underbelly of society.

ACKNOWLEDGMENTS

Chapter 1

Photograph. 1950s' teenagers dancing. Copyright © Trinity Mirror / Mirrorpix / Alamy Stock.

Infographic. Teens More Likely to Use E-Cigarettes Than Cigarettes. National Institute on Drug Abuse.

Photograph. Juvenile playing intense video games. Copyright © Tima Miroshnichenko via Pexels.

Photograph. Virtual learning anxiety. Copyright © Ty Lim/iStockphoto.com.

Photograph. Harris County Juvenile Justice Center. WhisperToMe (via Wikimedia Commons).

Photograph. Depiction of police questioning minor on possible underage drinking and DUI. Alcohol and Beverage Control, State of California.

Infographic. Minimum cut-off age of understanding crime consequences. The Times of India.

Graph. Number of Arrests, Youth Ages 0–17. Office of Juvenile Justice and Delinquency Prevention.

Chapter 2

Illustration. Schoolmaster spanking a student. Copyright © Grafissimo/iStockphoto .com.

Photograph. Teenagers cruising. Copyright © Dave Bagnall Collection / Alamy Stock Photo.

Photograph. London youth in the 1960s. Copyright © SCPhotos / Alamy Stock Photo.

Infographic. Violent Crime Trends in Urban Cities, 1994–2000. Copyright © 2002 Jeffrey A. Butts. Reprinted with permission.

Illustration. Stereotypical 1960s' greaser. Copyright © RetroClipArt.

Photograph. Elementary school class in Kenya. Copyright © Cecil Dzwowa/ Dreamstime.com.

Chapter 3

Photograph. Young juveniles sending text messages. Copyright © Monkey Business Images/Dreamstime.com.

Infographic. Underaged drinking patterns by grade, 2019. Copyright © Foundation for Advancing Alcohol Responsibilities. Reprinted with permission.

Chapter 4

Photograph. Juvenile shoplifting. Copyright © Fertnig/iStockphoto.com.

Infographic. Motor vehicle theft and arrest rates, 1960–2014. From A. Dixon and G. Farrell, "Age-period-cohort effects in half a century of motor vehicle theft in the United States," Crime Sci 9, 17 (2020). https://doi.org/10.1186/s40163-020-00126-5. Licensed under CC BY 4.0, https://creativecommons.org/licenses/by/4.0/.

Graph. Most commonly abused drugs, high school seniors (excluding alcohol and tobacco), 2014. National Institute on Drug Abuse, National Institutes of Health.

Infographic. Drug violation arrest rates by age, 2000–2018. Copyright © 2019 Jeffrey A. Butts. Reprinted with permission.

Map. Current State Anti-Bullying Laws and Policies, 2022. U.S. Department of Health and Human Services.

Infographic. Youth Incarceration Rates. Copyright © VoxEU.org, based on data by Neal Hazel (Cross-National Comparison of Youth Justice, London: Youth Justice Board, 2008). Reprinted with permission.

Chapter 5

Infographic. Suicide Rates for Teens Aged 15–19 Years, by Sex—United States, 1975–2015. MMWR Morb Mortal Wkly Rep 2017;66:816. DOI: http://dx.doi.org/10.15585/mmwr.mm6630a6External.

Infographic. Violent Crime by Youth: Time of Day. OJJDP Statistical Briefing Book. Online. Available: https://www.ojjdp.gov/ojstatbb/offenders/qa03301.asp?qaDate=2019. Released on April 18, 2022.

Infographic. QuickStats: Rates of Firearm-Related Deaths Among Persons Aged ≥15 Years, by Selected Intent and Age Group—National Vital Statistics System, United States, 2019. MMWR Morb Mortal Wkly Rep 2021;70:365. DOI: http://dx.doi.org/10.15585/mmwr.mm7010a5. Centers for Disease Control and Prevention (CDC).

Infographic. Number of murder offenders in the United States in 2020, by age. Copyright © 2022 Statista. Licensed under CC BY-ND, https://creativecommons.org/licenses/by-nd/4.0/legalcode.

Infographic. Number of homicide victims in the United States in 2021, by age. Copyright © 2022 Statista. Licensed under CC BY-ND, https://creativecommons.org/licenses/by-nd/4.0/legalcode.

Map. Taiwan. Centers for Disease Control and Prevention (CDC).

Chapter 6

Graph. Arrest trends, youth ages 0–17 (1980–2019). Office of Juvenile Justice and Delinquency Prevention (OJJDP).

Infographic. Plutchik's Emotion Dyads. Copyright © 2013 Simon Whatley. Reprinted with permission.

Photograph. Child displaying aggressive behavior. Copyright © Silvia Jansen/iStockphoto.com.

Illustration. Limbic System. Blausen.com staff (29 August 2014). "Medical gallery of Blausen Medical 2014." WikiJournal of Medicine 1 (2). doi:10.15347/WJM/2014.010. Wikidata Q44276831. ISSN 2002-4436. Licensed under CC BY 4.0, https://creativecommons.org/licenses/by/4.0/.

Illustration. Prefrontal Cortex. Copyright © Database Center for Life Science. Licensed under CC BY-SA 2.1 JP, https://creativecommons.org/licenses/by-sa/2.1/jp/deed.en.

Photograph. French family having a summer dinner party. Copyright © dotshock/Dreamstime.com.

Chapter 7

Photograph. Free-ranging children. Copyright © Lisa DeLong/iStockphoto.com.

Infographic. Cycle of Abuse. Avanduyn (via Wikimedia Commons).

Chapter 8

Table. January 2022 Monthly Child Poverty Rates by Children's Race and Ethnicity. From Zachary Parolin, Sophie Collyer, and Megan A. Curran, "Absence of Monthly Child Tax Credit Leads to 3.7 Million More Children in Poverty in January 2022." Poverty and Social Policy Brief Vol 6, no. 2. Center on Poverty and Social Policy, Columbia University. Access at: www.povertycenter.columbia.edu/publication/monthly-poverty-january-2022. Reprinted with permission.

Photograph. Teenage drug addicts. Copyright © Flickr user Artem (via Wikimedia Commons). Licensed under CC BY-SA 2.0, https://creativecommons.org/licenses/by-sa/2.0/.

Illustration. Comic book sample, 1940s. Wikimedia Commons.

Chart. United States Department of Agriculture (USDA).

Photograph. New York Housing Authority Public Housing, Queens. Copyright © Leonard Zhukovsky/Shutterstock.

Photograph. Robert Taylor Homes, Chicago. Library of Congress.

Photograph. Lapa District, Rio de Janeiro, Brazil. Copyright © Andrei Loan Mendes Brito dos Santos. Licensed under CC BY-SA 4.0, https://creativecommons.org/licenses/by-sa/4.0/deed.en.

Chapter 9

Photograph. Gender-Specific Toys, Sears and Roebuck Catalogue, circa 1950s. www.retrowaste.com.

Infographic. Sex differences in traumatic brain injury (TBI) and substance abuse. From Robin Oliverio, Kate Karelina, and Zachary M. Weil, "Sex, Drugs, and TBI: The Role of Sex in Substance Abuse Related to Traumatic Brain Injuries." Front. Neurol. 11:546775. doi: 10.3389/fneur.2020.546775. Copyright © 2020 Frontiers Media S.A. Licensed under CC BY 4.0, https://creativecommons.org/licenses/by/4.0/.

Graph. Change in Black/White Juvenile Placement Disparity; 2015 vs. 2019. Copyright © 2021 The Sentencing Project. Reprinted with permission.

Graph. Disparity by Race and Gender, Pittsburgh Public Schools, Arrests and Referrals. Copyright © 2020 Pittsburgh Post-Gazette.

Photograph. Stolen Generation Children at Kahlin Compound in Darwin, Northern Territory, Australia, 1921. Peter Spillett Collection/Northern Territory Government, Australia.

Chapter 10

Graph. Shooting Incidents at K–12 Schools (Jan 1970–Jun 2022). Copyright © Center for Homeland Defense and Security (CHDS). Reprinted with permission.

Illustration. Learning Styles. Copyright © VectorMine/Shutterstock.

Graph. School Cyberbullying, 2016 and 2019. Copyright © Cyberbullying Research Center. Reprinted with permission.

Photograph. Arrest chart, Operation Eastbound and Down. City of Riverside, California.

Graph. Dropout Rates by Race, 1996–2016. Copyright © 2017 PEW Research Center.

Illustration. School-to-Prison Pipeline. Rockaway Youth Task Force.

Chapter 11

Graph. U.S. Juvenile Justice Structure and Processes. Office of Juvenile Justice and Delinquency Prevention.

Photograph. Arrest of a juvenile suspect. Office of Public Affairs from Washington, DC (via Wikimedia Commons).

Graph. Juvenile Arrest Records, 1980–2019.

Photograph. Oldest Glenn Mills School, youth detention center for delinquent boys. Copyright © Davidshenbo/Dreamstime.com.

Photograph. Juvenile female being publicly shamed. Copyright © Gagliard iPhotography/Shutterstock.

Infographic. States Reporting Juvenile Recidivism Rates. Copyright © 2017 PEW Research Center.

Infographic. Percent of juveniles in justice system who have experienced childhood trauma, loss, and/or domestic violence. Copyright © 2022 American Academy of Pediatrics.

Map. Belgium. OCHA via Wikimedia Commons. Licensed under CC BY 3.0, https://creativecommons.org/licenses/by/3.0/deed.en.

Chapter 12

Graph. Food Insecurity in the United States, 2020. United States Department of Agriculture (USDA).

Graph. The rise in dual-income families. Copyright © 2017 PEW Research Center.

Photograph. Child throwing a tantrum. Copyright © 2015 Mindaugas Danys (via Wikimedia Commons). Licensed under CC BY 2.0, https://creativecommons.org/licenses/by/2.0/deed.en.

Table. Violent crime in the United States, 2019 (Rates per 100,00 inhabitants). Federal Bureau of Investigation.

Photograph. Shasta Groene, police mugshot. Canyon County Sheriff's Office, Idaho.

Infographic. The Key Drivers of Burnout. U.S. Department of Veterans Affairs.

Illustration. Children are exposed to e-waste toxicants through 4 major pathways. Courtesy of the World Health Organization.

Graph. Number of registered crimes against juveniles in Russia from 2009–2021. Copyright © 2023 Statista. Licensed under CC BY-ND, https://creativecommons.org/licenses/by-nd/4.0/legalcode.

Chapter 13

Illustration. Community Stakeholders in Delinquency Prevention. Office of Juvenile Justice and Delinquency Prevention.

Photograph. Father and daughter shopping. Copyright © Pawel L (via Pexels).

Illustration. Circle of Resilience. U.S. Department of Veterans Affairs.

"Graph. Development over Time for Secondary Outcomes per Group. From Anouk Spruit, Peter Hoffenaar, Claudia van der Put, Eveline van Vugt, Geert Jan Stams, "The effect of a sport-based intervention to prevent juvenile delinquency in at-risk adolescents." Children and Youth Services Review, Vol. 94. Copyright © 2018 Elsevier."

Photograph. Moreno Valley, California. Copyright © 2021 Matt Gush.

Graph. Juvenile Justice Funding (in Millions). From Gary Gately, "Federal Juvenile Justice Funding Declines Precipitously" (February 12, 2015), https://jjie.org. Copyright © 2023 Juvenile Justice Information Exchange. Reprinted with permission.

Photograph. Juveniles playing in juvenile detention center, Department of Corrections, Nakhonsawan, Thailand. Copyright © 2017 Yupa Watchanakit/Shutterstock.

Juvenile Delinquency

Chapter **ONE**

Defining Juvenile Delinquency

> *Juvenile crime is not naturally born in the* [child], *but is largely due either to the spirit of adventure that is in* [them], *to* [their] *own stupidity, or to* [their] *lack of discipline, according to the nature of the individual.*
>
> —Robert Baden-Powell, founder of the Scouting[1] movement, 19th century

Chapter Objectives

- Distinguish differences between juvenile deviance and juvenile delinquency.
- Introduce key definitions of juvenile delinquency.
- Identify the three types of juveniles found in juvenile court custody.
- Identify the confusions in defining the juvenile delinquent, both in societal and legal terms.
- Introduce some of the social and legal consequences of juvenile delinquency.

Key Terms

Congregate care
Detention
Deviance
Evidence-based programs
Foster care
Informal and formal sanctions
Juvenile delinquency
Juvenile justice
Moral panic
Social construct
Status offenses
Stigma
Truancy

[1] We should acknowledge that the Boy Scouts of America (now admitting females since 2018), has in recent decades come under fire for its history of rejecting homosexuals, atheists, and agnostics for leadership roles, as well as for a number of sexual abuse allegations.

INTRODUCTION

Perhaps no greater confusion exists over how to define a criminal than in *juvenile justice* (except perhaps in the laws related to white collar offending). Only within the last 150 years have we recognized that children are distinctly different from adults in physical, mental, and social development. Even more recently—only within the past 50 or so years—have we begun to grasp the unique processes in the juvenile brain and their relationship to developmental milestones. Most notably, only very recent discoveries in physiological psychology have led scientists to recognize that the prefrontal cortex, the center for complex behavioral performance, is not fully developed until age 25 (Arain et al., 2013). Only by following these more recent advances in research have we been able to more fully understand the elements, including brain development, that contribute to *juvenile delinquency.*

DISTINGUISHING BETWEEN DEVIANCE AND CRIMINAL BEHAVIOR

Some of the ambiguity in how we define juvenile delinquency lies in the confusion between *deviance* and criminal behavior. Whether discussing adult or juvenile behavior, when weighing these concepts it is useful to keep this in mind: *All crime is deviance, but not all deviance is crime.* Regardless of whether an act is deviant or truly criminal, however, the *stigma* (a term adopted by Erving Goffman, 1963) may remain with the individual, in this case, the juvenile, long after the act itself. Throughout this book, we will discuss Goffman's and other theories on what contributes to delinquency.

TABLE 1.1. Deviance vs. Crime Explained

Crime	Deviance
Crime refers to the violation of law.	Deviance refers to the violation of social rules, norms, and conventions.
Felonies and misdemeanors are the two major categories of crimes under criminal law.	Deviant behavior is categorized as formal or informal.
Crimes are always punishable by law.	Formal deviance is punishable by law, while informal deviance results in social sanctions and stigma.
Examples: Murder, rape, sexual assault, robbery, and fraud	*Formal deviance examples:* murder, rape, robbery, etc. *Informal deviance examples:* picking nose in public, belching, etc.

In general, people hold one of two opposing views on what constitutes deviance, as opposed to criminal behavior. One community may view certain forms of juvenile deviance or delinquency as simply nuisances, while other communities see the same juvenile behavior as intolerable, so much so that they attempt to suppress many activities of teenagers and young adults. One trend that began a couple of decades ago was to impose curfews in malls to discourage unchaperoned juveniles from loitering later than early evening. Some curfews for minors were imposed because of the fear gang activities might take place in the mall, especially if a community was already plagued by youth gangs. Other curfews are meant simply to discourage boisterous teen behavior that might disturb other shoppers. This is ironic, given that teenagers constitute one of the biggest consumer demographics, and many teens are employed in mall stores. More recently, mall culture has fallen out of favor with teens as a place to hang out (Rhone, 2021). However, as in the example of fights breaking out between juveniles at an Arlington, Texas, mall in 2022 resulting in new curfew rules applying for people under the age of 18 (Broussard, 2022), there has been a reluctance to lift curfews in spite of falling revenues at brick and mortar mall stores.

Sociologists and social psychologists often consider deviance a *social construct.* In some cases, the deviance may even be imaginary, as when societies, often during periods of *moral panic*, identify new forms of deviance to find scapegoats for preexisting social tensions (Victor, 1998). A horrific example of this unfolded in Nazi Germany in the 1930s, leading to the Holocaust and World War II. Imagined deviance perceived in juveniles can result in moral indignation and seemingly senseless prohibitions, leading to exaggerated righteousness that targets teenagers. According to Goode and Ben-Yehuda (1994, pp. 33–39), moral panic has five indicators:

- *Volatility*: The sudden eruption and subsiding of concern about a newly perceived threat to society.
- *Hostility*: Deviants are regarded with intense hostility as enemies of the basic values of the society and attributed with stereotypes of "evil" behavior.
- *Measurable concern*: Concern about the threat is measurable in concrete ways, such as attitude surveys.
- *Consensus*: There is consensus in significant segments of the population that the threat is real and serious.
- *Disproportionality*: Concern about the numbers of moral deviants and the extent of harm that they are perceived to be doing.

Today, we cannot underestimate the role social media plays in spreading moral panic. Moral panics tend to emerge quickly, and never so swiftly as when fear spreads through online social networks. Often-unsubstantiated rumors result in widely shared anxieties about today's juveniles.

Before the age of social media, when teenagers began to emerge as a separate class of specifically targeted pop-culture consumers, moral outrage at the perceived detrimental effects of rock 'n' roll burgeoned. The moral panic was in response to

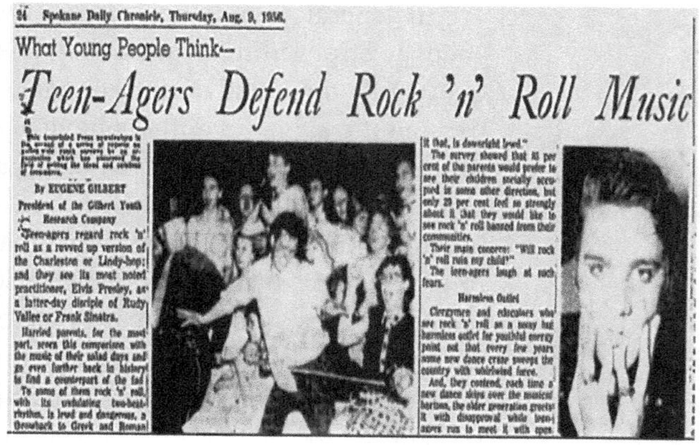

24 Spokane Daily Chronicle, Thursday, Aug. 9, 1956.

What Young People Think—

Teen-Agers Defend Rock 'n' Roll Music

By EUGENE GILBERT

1950s' teenagers dancing (L); newspaper article on rock 'n' roll, 1956 (R).

both the music itself and to the dance styles associated with it. One well-known focus of adult outrage was Elvis "The Pelvis" Presley, who performed with a swiveling dance style. But this source of moral panic did not abate with the 1950s. It continues to emerge in response to teenagers' music preferences, inspired, mostly in conservative circles, by contemporary pop, rock, rap, and hip hop. Guilt by association labels consumers of these music forms, including juveniles, as deviant, even delinquent.

Juvenile deviant behavior does not always lead to a criminal career, and the reaction to perceived deviance is key to this result. Throughout this book we will discuss options for suppressing, diverting, and discouraging deviant and delinquent behaviors in children in efforts to prevent relatively benign behaviors from segueing into crime. Some efforts to suppress deviance and delinquency, unfortunately, are not grounded in *evidence-based programs*. It is important for parents, schools, and law enforcement to view deviance and crime as being on spectrums, rather than simply through the strict dichotomy of good versus bad behaviors. These authorities must understand the shades of gray between the two. Unfortunately, the fear, real or imagined, that less serious "bad" behaviors will lead to the extreme end of the criminal spectrum persists.

Many behaviors or lifestyles pursued by both juveniles and adults may meet disapproval from the general public. Most of these are social or sexual behaviors. For example, tattoos have elicited varying responses throughout human history, on a spectrum from culturally acceptable to deviant. In the United States, tattoos have only recently become fairly commonplace: approximately 35% of the population now has a tattoo, with over half of them having two or more tattoos (Statista Research Department, 2019). However, even today, people who have multiple tattoos are irrationally linked to deviant behavior, most notably by law enforcement (Camacho and Brown, 2018).

Teenagers today get tattoos in greater numbers than ever before. The legal age in the United States to get a tattoo without permission is 18, and some jurisdictions allow juveniles under 18 to get a tattoo with a parent's or guardian's permission. This shift in acceptance serves as an example of how behavior thought to be deviant, but not criminal, will be largely dictated by the dominant culture. Recall that the dominant culture is not necessarily defined by numerical size; the most dominant may, in fact, be the most vocal and powerful.

The definition of deviant behavior is also dictated by where that behavior occurs. What is considered deviant in the United States may not be considered deviant in other countries, and vice versa. Cultural divides, of course, also exist even within the United States. This is evident, for example, in American gun culture, which varies widely throughout the United States, including over norms for age-appropriate firearm use among young juveniles.

Some behaviors considered deviant, even sometimes criminal, in children may be perfectly legal for adults. Two classic examples are alcohol and tobacco use. Even those examples, until recently, were confusing. In the late 1960s, an 18-year-old may have been allowed to purchase alcohol legally in some states, while it might be illegal in others. Until the national minimum drinking age of 21 was established in 1984, the legal drinking age in the United States varied, depending on the state, from 18 to 21.

The National Institute on Alcohol Abuse and Alcoholism (2021) reported that, in 2019, 7 million juveniles and young adults between the ages of 12 and 20 reported drinking alcohol beyond "a few sips" in any given month. Too often, when caught, the juvenile is prosecuted for underaged drinking: adults are rarely charged for providing the alcohol in the first place.

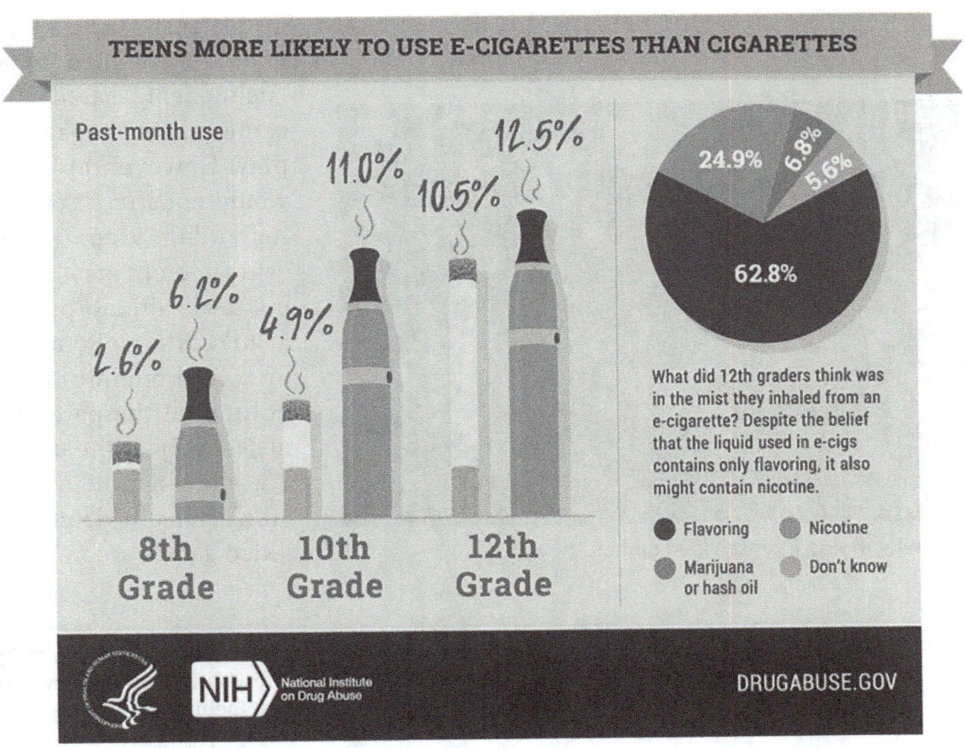

EXHIBIT 1.1 ‖ E-cigarette use among teens

The same pattern applies to smoking. Until recently, states mandated the age at which someone could legally purchase tobacco products. In 2019, President Donald Trump signed an amendment to the Federal Drug and Cosmetic Act raising the legal age from 18 to 21 (U.S. Food and Drug Administration, 2021). Yet today, countless teenagers, some even under 13, consume alcohol and tobacco products, either stolen or illegally procured for their use by adults. Despite this, as the National Institute on Drug Abuse reports (National Institute of Health, 2016), teen tobacco and alcohol use has been on the decline, whereas e-cigarettes have increasingly become a concern.

Even in adult populations, in a number of social and work circles, excessive alcohol consumption and any tobacco use is viewed as being deviant. With the passage of stricter no-smoking rules, at least in the United States, those wishing to smoke have in recent years been banished to designated outdoor smoking areas. Though not universally throughout the United States, and certainly not worldwide, smokers have been stigmatized.

SOCIETAL DEFINITIONS OF DEVIANCE AND JUVENILE DELINQUENCY

There is also a distinction between what society considers to be delinquent behavior and how it is defined legally. For instance, a child that spends considerable time playing violent video games could be defined, in societal terms, as "delinquent," based on the type of video games they choose or are allowed to play. However, by legal definition, we would not arrest a child for simply playing violent video games. As data indicate, violent video game consumption is not the healthiest pursuit for children. If a child criminally misbehaves at school or in the community, fingers will be pointed at the parental units,[2] but not necessarily at the children themselves. We should not jump to the conclusion that children who play violent video games are automatically juvenile

Juvenile playing intense video games.

[2] Throughout this book I will interchangeably use the terms "parental units," parents, and guardians to represent the individuals or the institution responsible for the care and feeding of a child. The term *parental unit* is all-encompassing and can include a grandparent or any relative other than a biological parent who raises a child. It is more expedient than saying "parents and guardians" *ad nauseam*.

delinquents. A number of contradictory studies debate whether playing violent video games results in moral immaturity or aggressive behavior in adolescents (Przybylski and Weinstein, 2019).

In many communities, including in the United States, any form of criminal behavior, even a single incident, can label the juvenile as delinquent. As we will see in examining the legal definitions, this is not necessarily always the case. A child can also be considered guilty by association if their parental units or siblings take part in criminal activity, even if that child has never committed a crime. Among the theories we explore in subsequent chapters are Sutherland's Differential Association Theory (1939), which posits that it is who you socialize with that matters. Becker's Labeling Theory argues that others' perceptions and judgments of a child's behavior may lead the child to conclude that there are no options but to behave criminally, if that is what the world expects, even if the label is false.

Most scholars argue that one criminal act does not make a juvenile delinquent. Though behavior such as shoplifting itself is criminally delinquent, a single criminal act does not make a juvenile a delinquent: only habitual delinquent behavior should be so labeled. This somewhat contradicts legal definitions, as explored in the next section of the chapter, where a juvenile can be legally labeled delinquent after one offense. Definitions of delinquency, between those conceived by society and those grounded in law, can be at times in conflict with one another.

At times, conditions are so extraordinary that we see a decrease in deviance and delinquency, at least in observable acts. The pandemic-related shutdown of in-classroom instruction in early 2020 led, for obvious reasons, to an immediate decline in school-based delinquent offenses. Interestingly, while COVID-19 stay-at-home orders were followed by significant increases in domestic violence among the adult offender population, juvenile domestic violence offending remained relatively stable, with only modest increases among Hispanic and Black juvenile populations (Baglivio et al., 2022). Juvenile domestic violence during the pandemic is speculated to have largely centered on disputes between juveniles and their parental units over school-related issues related to virtual instruction (Baglivio et al., 2022).

Social Class and Delinquency

We cannot discount the importance of social class in what is considered deviant behavior or the consequences of deviant behavior, including crime. By Marxist or neo-Marxist theoretical standards, the definition of crime and delinquency are largely based on social inequalities (Colvin and Pauly, 1983). Linked to this is the divide between those who can afford technology and those who are being left behind. For example, if a child does not have access to a home computer, particularly during stay-at-home orders due to the COVID-19 pandemic, they risk falling behind in school work. This can set them up for failure in the future, both academically and in the workplace, creating structural inequality that can further contribute to delinquency or adult offending.

Teen girls wearing pants to school, 1970s.

A number of studies indicate that children who come from disadvantaged families are more likely to become delinquent. It is not uncommon to see intergenerational offending, as in the case of members of the same family, including juveniles, being involved in gang-related crime, which is more common within poorer neighborhoods. As Westie and Turk noted (1965, p. 456), "Criminologists alone have produced hundreds of studies attempting to determine and explain the relationship between social stratification and the phenomenon of crime." Antisocial behaviors have strong potential for derailing future aspirations, including eventual occupational status (Robins et al., 1962). In the case of juvenile delinquents, criminal behavior may carry over into adulthood, leaving little opportunity to escape poverty or improve job prospects, even though juvenile crime records are generally sealed.

Because wealthier parents and guardians have the resources to prevent it, a child coming from an affluent family and community is less likely to experience long-term effects from their deviant or criminal behavior, as compared to a child from a less financially advantaged family. For example, if a wealthy parent's child becomes addicted to drugs, the child is more likely to be kept out of juvenile custody and placed in rehabilitation instead. We cannot discount the power of having money enough to hire the best legal representation possible in all criminal cases, including those tried in the juvenile court system. We should also take into consideration that it is far easier for wealthy parents and guardians to keep private their child's deviant or criminal behavior, unless the child commits a serious offense that is visible to the community.

Social class is one reason why the actual numbers of juvenile delinquents is uncertain. One of the biggest challenges in studying crime, including juvenile delinquency, is that much of the data comes from police records, rather than from actual crimes committed, a number much more realistically found in victim surveys. In addition, some clever juvenile delinquents may fly under the radar of both their parental units and the police, just as some adult criminals do not get caught (Ozer and Akbas, 2020).

Juveniles who are deviant or delinquent are not completely devoid of morals or value systems. However, a juvenile delinquent may have a set of morals and values that run contrary to those of conventional society. Depending on the form of "delinquency," if enough people agree that the injustices perceived by juveniles are legitimate, changes may be made to policy. An example of this would be the prohibition against females, including teachers, wearing pants in public and private schools, a rule that only changed in most school districts in the 1970s. It then became far more commonplace for females to wear pants, rather than skirts or dresses, to school or work. Prior to the 1970s, any female who showed up to school in pants ran the risk of being sent to the principal's office or sent home to change her clothes.

Social Punishment

Whether discussing juveniles or adults, if the offender is caught and if the behavior is perceived to be deviant, punishment comes by way of *formal* or *informal sanctions*. Formal sanctions are the consequences of breaking rules, regulations, or criminal laws. These can include expulsion from school, arrest, probation, juvenile *detention*,[3] or fines, along with a variety of other ways that a juvenile could be punished for their actions. Informal sanctions are the ways that society and those around us punish us for our behaviors, by condemning them and/or by exclusion. These in turn just might result in further behavior that tries to mask the deviance—in other words, deviants and criminals may actively find ways to not get caught, as they attempt to avoid both formal and informal sanctions.

Unless deviant or criminal behavior comes to the attention of parents, school officials, or law enforcement, the behavior can go on indefinitely. Very few people commit crimes to be arrested, with the exception of those with certain mental health issues and those without homes who are seeking shelter. We should consider a juvenile taken into custody and removed from loved ones and friends to suffer a kind of social death.

We should also consider that juvenile delinquents are not immune to the pressure toward conformity. Social punishment can come from peers, where children who display deviant and antisocial behavior will be shunned by conformists among their friends and others in their age cohort. This in turns narrows the options for a child as far as peer groups they can join. This is one reason why some parental units discourage or even forbid their children from playing with certain children in a neighborhood or school. They fear their child will be influenced by the perceived bad behavior of other children. Most families believe that delinquent behavior is wrong, and in some cases, work to divert their children to more socially accepted peer groups. Other families may not even be aware that the children under their care are associating with deviant or delinquent peers.

Mental Health Issues and Delinquency

We also cannot discount the role that mental health issues play in contributing to deviant or criminal behavior in juveniles. We know that rates of psychiatric disorders are higher in children in the juvenile justice system (Vogel and Messner, 2012;

[3] We should note that detention is not defined the same way in the juvenile justice system as it is in schools. *Detention* in the justice system means that the minor is taken into custody after arrest, adjudication, and sentenced, to be held pre-hearing or to serve time in a juvenile detention center.

Depiction of virtual instruction during COVID-19 pandemic and consequent anxiety.

Wasserman et al., 2004), though there is some question as to whether these mental health issues were preexisting, arose with, or were exacerbated by experiences within the system. Increasingly, a number of behaviors, including drug and/or alcohol addiction, are viewed as public health issues. Particularly in light of the astronomical medical costs associated with illegal (and legal) drug use, public health officials question the validity of incarcerating individuals who suffer from addiction, even if they possessed an illegal drug at the time of their arrest. This applies to both adults and juveniles.

Mental health issues are not the only variables that create interaction effects with delinquency. An interaction effect, in this case, results from a combination of variables that can lead to delinquency. For instance, there is evidence that lower IQ scores, coupled with poor school performance, can result in higher rates in delinquency (Robins et al., 1962). These, of course, are not the only conditions that might lead a child to offend, but they may combine with other factors to ultimately contribute to delinquency. As in the case of adult offenders, we cannot assume that all juvenile delinquents have lower IQs. However, environmental factors, such as poverty or disorganized households, can ultimately affect, in combination, the relationship between IQ, school performance, and delinquency (Ozer and Akbas, 2020).

We will explore further in this book the relationship between mental health issues and delinquency. It will be interesting to learn (although it is too soon to have gathered enough data to come to any conclusions as yet) whether the COVID-19 pandemic, which has resulted in more children experiencing anxiety and other mental health disorders, may in turn contribute to increased delinquency in the short term. At the beginning of the pandemic in early 2020, schools had to turn overnight to online instruction. The data so far indicate that students expressed more status offending, in the form of poor school attendance, cognitive impulsivity, and bullying behaviors—at least in middle-school students, even when controlling for the different forms of instruction, including face-to-face, during 2020–2021 (Walters et al., 2021).

LEGAL DEFINITIONS OF JUVENILE DELINQUENCY

The meaning of juvenile delinquency also varies according to who provides the definition. As we have seen, the label can be thrown around indiscriminately to describe any troublesome behavior found in children or teens. However, laws that dictate juvenile justice are far clearer on what we mean by delinquency.

The most important element in the definition is the meaning of *juvenile*. The legal system in the United States does not base its definition on the individual's mental maturity. After all, some adults behave like children, and conversely, children, due to their circumstances, may very well take on the maturity and responsibilities of adults. However, it would be too confusing for any criminal justice system to decide whether one qualifies as a juvenile or adult on a case-by-case basis, according to emotional and social maturity. Hence the United States Department of Justice (U.S. DOJ, n.d., retrieved from https://www.justice.gov/archives/jm/criminal-resource-manual-38-juvenile-defined), identifies these definitions:

> [a "juvenile" is] *a person who has not attained* [their] *eighteenth birthday, and "juvenile delinquent" is the violation of a law of the United States committed by a person prior to* [their] *eighteenth birthday which would be a crime if committed by an adult. A person over eighteen but under twenty-one years of age is also accorded juvenile treatment if the act of juvenile delinquency occurred prior to* [their] *eighteenth birthday. See 18 U.S.C. § 5031.*

The term delinquency in the juvenile justice system basically means that a minor has been found guilty of a crime in a juvenile court of law. A guilty verdict

Harris County Juvenile Justice Center, Houston, Texas.

is reserved for adult convictions. As in the case of the use of the term delinquency, other terms used in the juvenile justice system are also softer than those used in the adult system. We do not say that a child is incarcerated, but rather "in the custody of the juvenile court system," serving a sentence in detention rather than in jail or prison.

On rare occasions a juvenile is accused of a crime so heinous that district attorneys' offices will demand that they be put on trial in adult court and, if found guilty, serve their time in adult prison. This decision varies from jurisdiction to jurisdiction, with some courts more willing than others to send a juvenile to the adult justice system, particularly in cases of first degree murder. For these juveniles, adult court terms are used.

Juvenile delinquents are classified by the seriousness of their crimes. Those who commit the most disturbing crimes, including murder, are described as young violent offenders. Often, young violent offenders have escalated in their offending, beginning with less serious crimes. As an example, juveniles affiliated with a gang cannot be assumed to be violent offenders; however, the risk is greater that they will evolve in that direction. In Chapter 11 we will explore the factors contributing to violent offending, including influences at home, in the environment, and psychiatric disorders.

Status Offenses

Beyond the obvious examples of alcohol and tobacco use, juveniles are subject to other laws that do not apply to adults. For instance, if an adult did not show up to work one day, failing to call in sick or with another reason, the worst that could

Depiction of police questioning minor on possible underage drinking and DUI.

happen is loss of the job. A person who does this regularly might find themselves in and out of jobs and facing other social and economic consequences, but they would not be placed behind bars. If a child habitually misses school, however, they may very well end up in juvenile custody for a *status offense*.

Status offenses are violations of law committed by juveniles that are not criminal in nature, but can result in referral to juvenile court and possible juvenile detention. The Office of Juvenile Justice and Delinquency Prevention, Department of Justice (OJJDP), identifies the following general types of status offenses: *truancy*, underaged use of alcohol, violation of curfew, running away from home, and general ungovernability (OJJDP, 2015). The main concern is that any one of these risky behaviors can lead to more serious offenses, including those classified as criminal. For example, with underaged use of alcohol, the juvenile risks getting behind the wheel of a car and driving while legally intoxicated, similar to adults who consume too much alcohol.

As the OJJDP (2015) acknowledges, there is no uniform approach to status offenses by individual states. The primary characterizations of status offenders include status offenders who are also delinquents, status offenders who are neglected or abused dependents, or status offenders as a separate legal category (OJJDP, 2015). A neglected or abused juvenile may not be attending classes because their parental units are not actively involved in their education, including failing to get them up in time for school in the morning. Parents might also fear that their abuse and maltreatment will be detected if they send their children off to school. Unfortunately, the great majority of juveniles who have contact with authorities are status offenders and at risk of being arrested or held in custody for noncriminal behavior, whether it is within their control or not (Arthur and Waugh, 2009).

Juvenile Court Custody

In legal terms, juveniles may find themselves under the jurisdiction of juvenile court in three types of situations: the child is mistreated in various ways (e.g., child neglect), the child commits a status offense, or the child commits a crime. Unfortunately, the three categories may overlap. In some jurisdictions, out-of-home care is used as an alternative to juvenile custody, with minors who committed less serious crimes placed in *foster care*. In the United States, over 400,000 children are living in foster care (NCSL, 2020). It is important to note that juvenile offending is not the only reason children are placed in foster care. They may end up there in cases of child maltreatment or when parents are deceased and no family member or suitable guardian has come forward to take responsibility for the child.

Children who are neglected, abandoned, or abused will be protected under the juvenile and family court systems, which may refer them to child protective and social services. The opposite may be true, with child protective services making a referral to the courts, particularly for emergency removal of a child who is in immediate danger. Other alternatives include temporary placement in *congregate care*, which may include residential treatment and short-term supervision by social workers or other specialized personnel (Capacity Building Center for States, 2020). Approximately 55,000 children are in congregate care, living in group homes, residential treatment facilities, psychiatric hospitals, or emergency shelters (NCSL, 2020).

Of course, conceivably a juvenile may face all three situations, as in the example of a minor whose parental units are neglectful, causing the child to fail to attend school and to commit crimes, either to get attention or to survive. This trifecta is particularly difficult for social workers, juvenile probation officers, and detention officers to resolve. Which issue should become the priority? Finding foster placement, getting the child back into school, or punishing the child for the crime or crimes they have committed? The reality is that juvenile detention most likely will be addressed first when a serious crime has been committed, followed by compulsory education provided within detention if the child is not old enough to drop out of school, and the possibility of foster placement upon release from juvenile custody, if release happens before the juvenile is 18.

HOW YOUTH DELINQUENCY DIFFERS FROM ADULT CRIME

By legal definitions, adults commit "crimes," whereas juveniles commit "delinquent acts." To save confusion, throughout this book we will be using the terms crime and delinquent acts interchangeably. In the opinion of Judge LaDoris Cordell, formerly serving on the Superior Court of Santa Clara County in California, where she heard both juvenile and adult cases, juveniles have generally had less life experience, so even if they engage in criminal acts that are as serious as adult crimes, they are "salvageable" and have the potential to become productive members of society (*Frontline*, n.d.). Bridgett Jones, in the same interview, stated, "I think the community understands, or should understand, that the younger a person is, the more likely it is that they can change." (Frontline, n.d., retrieved from https://www.pbs.org/wgbh/pages/frontline/shows/juvenile/bench/different.html).

Not all juvenile offenders are equal. They range from exhibiting mildly deviant behavior to committing serious violent crimes, as we have noted, including homicide. According to Livingstone et al. (2008; Richards, 2011) three primary types of juvenile offender are found in juvenile court systems around the world:

- **Early peaking-moderate offenders**, who begin to exhibit delinquent behavior at pre-adolescence, peaking at about age 14, followed by a decline.
- **Late onset-moderate offenders**, who show no delinquent behavior in their early teen years, but exhibit a gradual increase until around age 16, followed by a decline.

- **Chronic offenders**, who, similar to the adult population of offenders, exhibit an early onset of offending, with a sharp increase over time, continuing to reoffend.

One of the biggest distinctions between juvenile and adult offenders is intent and ability to understand the consequences of criminal behavior. In common law, children are believed to be incapable of committing crimes before the age of seven (HG Legal Resources, n.d.), although this may differ from jurisdiction to jurisdiction; some states have no specified youngest age for intent (National Juvenile Defender Center, n.d.). As much as we would like to put children in neat specific developmental age categories based on age, the reality is that children, teens, and even young adults emotionally and intellectually develop at vastly different rates, often dependent on life experiences.

As an example of the ambiguity of juvenile criminal intent, in 2020, Kaia Rolle, a six-year-old, had her hands ziptied behind her back[4] and was placed in a police cruiser after being arrested for allegedly assaulting a vice principal at her Florida elementary school (Flores and Weisfeldt, 2020). Her classroom offense? She was wearing sunglasses in class and refused to take them off after being asked to do so, resulting in a shouting match with her teacher (Flores and Weisfeldt, 2020). Kaia had a documented sleep disorder, sleep apnea, which her mother stated was the reason for her disruptive behavior in the classroom that day (Flores and Weisfeldt, 2020). In any other context, Kaia's refusal to remove her sunglasses in class would simply be viewed as an act of defiance, and her subsequent alleged attack on the vice principal would be seen as a young child acting out after being understandably upset. It is difficult to prove that Kaia intentionally set out to break the law. In a similar example, in 2021 a Maryland five-year-old boy was detained, handcuffed, and allegedly threatened by police officers when he attempted to leave campus during school hours without permission (Lenthang, 2021).

Since measuring the maturity of juveniles, or adults for that matter, is subjective, the best measure is our understanding of developmental stages in children. However, there is no agreement in the opinions of courts in the U.S. and elsewhere in the world as to the age at which a child understands consequences, as indicated in Exhibit 1.2.

For the most part, adults have easier access to tools needed to commit certain crimes, including weapons and means of escape. In particular, guns are not as readily available, legally or otherwise, to juveniles as to adults. However, this does not mean that juvenile offenders do not have any access to guns, either through the carelessness of adults who do not lock them up in their homes for

[4] The police did not have a pair of handcuffs small enough to conventionally cuff Kaia (Flores and Weisfeldt, 2020).

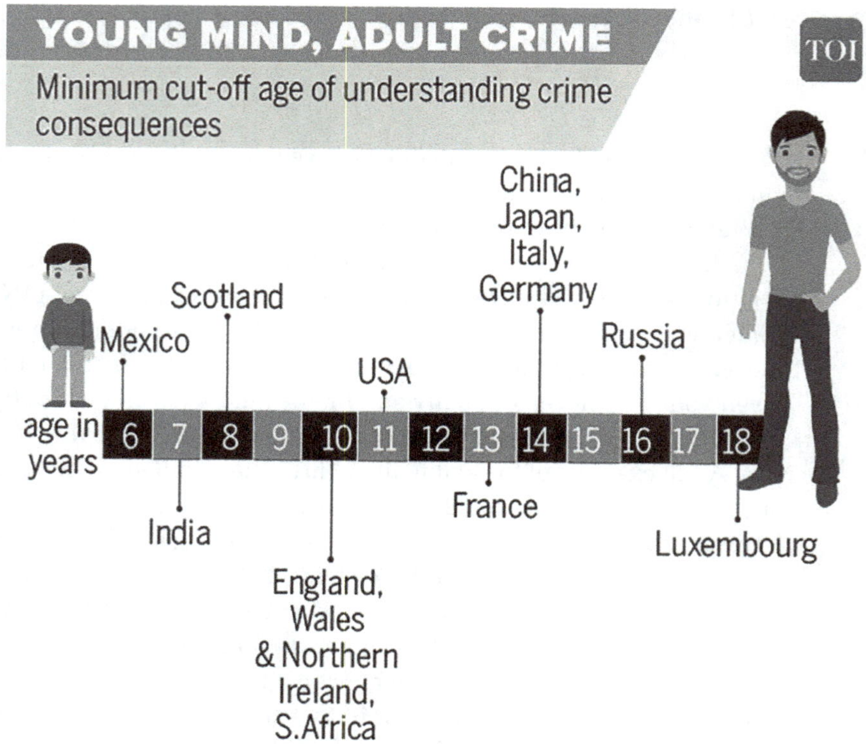

EXHIBIT 1.2 ‖ Worldwide minimum cut-off age of understanding crime consequences

safekeeping or through illegal street purchases, trades, or thefts. Overwhelmingly, violence studies report that firearms are commonly used by juveniles to commit violent crimes in the United States (OJJDP, 2016; OJJDP, 1999). In addition to accidental shootings by juveniles at home, juveniles have perpetrated school shootings, often with premeditation, as in the infamous case of Columbine High School (1999) in Colorado. More recently, in 2021, a Michigan 15-year-old was ordered to stand trial as an adult for killing four fellow students at Oxford High School (Corley, 2021).

As in the case of adults, police officers in the United States, while arresting juveniles, must read them their *Miranda rights*, sometimes called the Miranda warning, as required by the Fifth Amendment of the U.S. Constitution (U.S. Supreme Court, *Miranda v. Arizona*, 384 U.S. 436, 861602, 1966). Juveniles are afforded the same protections under the law as adults before interrogation for a suspected crime. Miranda warning statements may vary from jurisdiction to jurisdiction, but they must convey the same meaning (Miranda Rights, n.d.). However, questions remain as to whether juveniles (or adults) fully understand these rights:

- The right to remain silent.
- The right to have an attorney present during the questioning of a juvenile or an adult.

- If the juvenile suspect or their family cannot afford an attorney, they will be appointed one by the juvenile court.
- Anything said during interrogation while in custody can be used against the suspected juvenile offender, *after* they have been read their Miranda rights.
- If a juvenile suspect has not received notification of these rights during arrest, anything they say cannot be used against them as evidence at their trial.

Juveniles, even when read their Miranda rights, may not understand that they do not have to confess to an alleged crime; they do not need to say anything at all that might incriminate them. Once detained, however, they can legally be denied access to visitors, except for legal counsel, and denied recreation and education (Laird, 2016). The juveniles' only understanding of what it means legally to be arrested and subsequently read their Miranda rights may come from movies and television shows, which do not always accurately portray the realities of arrests or interrogation. (This may also hold true for adults on their first arrest.) Arresting officers, prosecutors, and investigators always assume the suspect's guilt, as they would not advocate for an arrest otherwise, even with the legally assumed innocence of the alleged offender.

It is not uncommon for juveniles to *co-offend*. We will get into greater theoretical detail in Chapter 4 on why co-offending occurs. Briefly stated, during the adolescent years, teens in particular wish to conform with the expectations of the people they hang out with, and they are more susceptible to peer pressure as compared to adults (Richards, 2011). Juveniles (and some younger adults) may commit crimes on a dare or in groups—for example, underaged drinking and

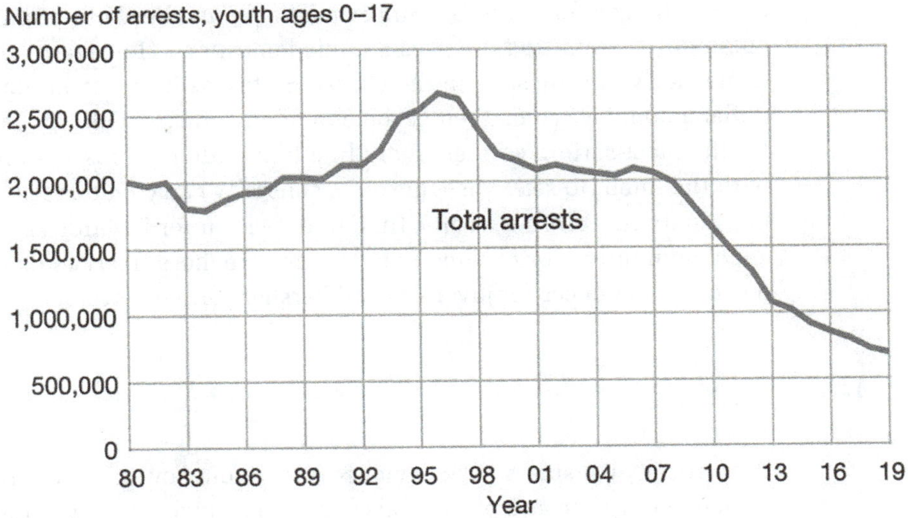

Data source: Analysis of arrest data from the Bureau of Justice Statistics and the National Center for Juvenile Justice.

EXHIBIT 1.3 ‖ Number of Arrests, Youth Ages 0–17

illegal drug use. Young co-offending males are overrepresented in serious criminal activity as compared to females (Lynch, 2002), which we will explore further in Chapter 7, when we examine gender differences in offending.

The good news is, in spite of reports otherwise, juvenile property and violent crime have declined in recent decades. This is reflected in both pre-pandemic reported crimes and numbers of arrests of juveniles for minor and serious offenses (Puzzanchera, 2020). Again, the accuracy of the actual rates of offending depends on whether the reporting agency provides raw numbers or actual rates, typically in terms of crimes per 100,000 residents.

Punishment versus Rehabilitation

Whereas the adult system, for the most part, seeks to punish offenders, the juvenile justice system focuses on redemption and rehabilitation. However, the adult justice system is beginning to come around to thinking that conditions of addiction can contribute to criminal behavior, especially in drug-related crimes. Drug courts have more recently been established in some jurisdictions for offenders facing exclusively drug-related charges. Philosophies toward juvenile detention and adult corrections do change, based on political and public sentiment. For both adults and juveniles, the pendulum continues to swing between philosophies favoring rehabilitation and calls for tougher crime laws.

Misdemeanors versus Felonies

Similar to what we see in the adult population of offenders, juvenile suspects can be charged for a *misdemeanor* or for a *felony*. For both populations, the most commonly committed offenses are misdemeanors. However, definition of a misdemeanor varies by state in the United States, as in the example of the threshold dollar amount at which theft becomes a felony offense. Felony charges are reserved for the most serious crimes, including homicide and possession of illegal drugs with the intent to sell. Misdemeanors generally carry lighter sentences on conviction, including shorter, if any, time in detention for juveniles or probation, fines, and community service. Felony judgments are more likely to come with lengthier detention sentences for juveniles and harsher consequences.

SUMMARY

What society considers to be deviance or delinquency, in either juveniles or adults, is dictated by time and place. It also depends on whatever way the political winds are blowing. Some perceptions of deviance are perennial—for example, listening to forms of music—such as rock 'n' roll in the 1950s and "gangsta" rap (a form of hip hop) in the 1990s—that target juvenile or young adult populations. Others, such as tattoos or marijuana use, have sometimes been viewed as deviant, even criminal, and at other times (and, in the case of recreational use of marijuana, in some states or countries), as acceptable.

There are two types of punishment in cases of juvenile offending. One is informal, involving social sanctions, where the juvenile offender is shunned by their peers or by their peers' parental units, further disadvantaging them as to what type of friends they might have. A child does not necessarily need to be legally labeled a juvenile delinquent to find that they are ostracized in school or in their neighborhood. In many ways, this is a form of banishment or social death. A juvenile who displays troublesome behavior or has been expelled from their school may find themselves in an alternative school where they have no choice but to associate with other troubled juveniles.

The second form of sanction comes from the juvenile justice system and can result in formal punishment. The term "delinquency" can then have different meanings. The use of the word can range from describing juvenile behavior that is troublesome (e.g., loitering) to the criminal offending by young violent offenders. However, use of the term *juvenile delinquent* has stricter legal than social meaning, and refers to offenders convicted of a crime in a juvenile court who committed the crime prior to age 18. As we noted, however, society and courts of law consider some crimes, such as certain types of homicide, so heinous that even a juvenile under 18 at the time of the offense may be referred to the adult court system to stand trial.

Youth delinquency is different from adult offending, though there is some overlap, particularly when looking at adolescents in their mid-to-late teenage years. As noted by Livingstone et al. (2008) and Richards (2011), there are three primary types of juvenile offenders generally found in the juvenile court system: early-peaking-moderate offenders, late onset-moderate offenders, and chronic offenders. Of the three, the last group is most likely to eventually find themselves in the adult criminal justice system.

One of the most notable distinctions between juvenile and adult offenders is in their understanding the consequences of criminal behavior, and in understanding their Miranda rights, once arrested. The age at which an individual is criminally culpable can vary from state to state and from country to country. And whereas adult convictions often seek to incapacitate the offender with probation or jail or prison sentences, juvenile adjudication is more likely to look for rehabilitation and resocialization solutions.

The juvenile and family court systems are not restricted to minors who commit crimes. They may also be called upon to make judgments on the fitness of parental units to care for the children in their custody, including removing children from the home. Minors who have been abandoned, neglected, or have parental units who cannot manage their behavior may be placed in foster or congregative care. These arrangements can be temporary until parental units have successfully petitioned the courts to return their children or wards to their care. They may also be permanent placements until the minor reaches 18.

Juvenile courts also address status offenses, as in the case of children who fail to attend school regularly. However, frequently a juvenile requires attention in more than one area that falls under the umbrella of juvenile courts. A child who needs foster or congregate care may have been accused of status violations and/or committed minor offenses. Juvenile courts and social service agencies must determine which of the issues are the more alarming before settling on the best course of action to prevent further harm to the child, or future offending. The solutions may be different, depending on the willingness of the parental units to cooperate, the jurisdiction, and the temperament of the courts.

IN THE MEDIA

Juvenile "Wickedness"

What we term delinquency in the United States may be labeled something different elsewhere in the world. A more archaic word, "wickedness," is sometimes used instead. Other terms used include "troubled youth," "troublemaker," or even a few leftover terms from the 1950s, like "hoodlum" or "hooligan." As Maitland notes (2016), children are not always as innocent as we make them out to be and, in some cases, parental units may be the last to know when they are misbehaving. Wickedness implies a violation of religious rules and doctrine, beyond general societal-norm violations. But when does wickedness or misbehaving become problematic? When is the child unjustly labeled?

More importantly, and of considerable concern, is when children are targeted as "wicked" because of their minority status. When it became apparent that systematic racial profiling of minority juveniles was happening in Rutherford County, Tennessee, Pastor Vincent Windrow of the Olive Branch Church took to the pulpit in 2021 to alert his congregation to the alarming trend (Ismail, 2021, retrieved from https://www.newschannel5.com/news/pastor-calls-for-systemic-change-following-revelations-in-scathing-rutherford-co-report):

> *We know that in 2016, 10 predominantly Black children were arrested* [at Hobgood Elementary School] *by Murfreesboro Police for not breaking up a fight captured on video. It was a misdemeanor charge, if a charge at all, but some children as young as eight-years-old were handcuffed and taken to a cell. . . . Yes, it's a crisis, but it's a created crisis. Someone manufactured the crisis.*

This raises the question: how culpable is a juvenile who does not actively try to break up a fight that they are not personally involved in, much less when they are eight years old? Pastor Windrow further noted that in such cases, generally one or two juveniles are to blame, yet the criminal justice system can point to its own actions in conducting large-scale arrests as being preventative, "otherwise, someone else will get in that seat and continue this wickedness" (Ismail,

Logo, Murfreesboro Police Department, Tennessee.

2021, retrieved from https://www.newschannel5.com/news/pastor-calls-for-systemic-change-following-revelations-in-scathing-rutherford-co-report). As Pastor Windrow preached to his congregation, "'I'm not talking about hardened criminals; I'm not talking about mobsters or gangsters. . . . We are talking about children [being arrested] . . . such a lack of humanity." (Broden, 2021, retrieved from https://www.dnj.com/story/news/2021/10/26/timeline-rutherford-county-illegal-arrests-and-incarcerations-children/6124000001/).

In a scathing report that came to the attention of Pastor Windrow, the illegal arrest of the ten juveniles was not an isolated incident. Since the 1990s, Rutherford County had habitually illegally arrested and incarcerated juveniles, resulting in a 2017 class-action lawsuit and a $11 million settlement for the affected families (Broden, 2021). Tennessee law strictly prohibits pretrial incarceration for children, except when they have been charged with a violent felony or a weapons offense, or have violated terms of probation (Broden, 2021).

Postscript

The Murfreesboro Police Department reviewed and changed its procedures for handling juvenile cases, including no longer serving juvenile warrants unless they have a court order (Ismail, 2021). Pastor Windrow had personal interest in seeing change in the way juveniles, particularly those who are minorities, are treated by police. Some of the families, whose children were arrested, are congregants in his church (Ismail, 2021).

SOURCES

Broden, S. (2021). A timeline of Rutherford County's history of illegally arresting and jailing minors. *Daily News Journal.* Oct. 26. Retrieved from https://www.dnj.com/story/news/2021/10/26/timeline-rutherford-county-illegal-arrests-and-incarcerations-children/6124000001/.

Ismail, L. (2021). Pastor preaches systematic change following revelations in scathing Rutherford Co. report. News Channel 5, Nashville, TN. Oct. 21. Retrieved from https://www.newschannel5.com/news/pastor-calls-for-systemic-change-following-revelations-in-scathing-rutherford-co-report.

Maitland, K. (2016). *Wicked Children: Murderous Tales from History.* Auckland, NZ: Review Publishing Co., Ltd.

INTERNATIONAL PERSPECTIVES

General Juvenile Delinquency in England

"He was not in a gang" (Slawson, 2021)

In 2021, in spite of stay-at-home recommendations under the pandemic scare before vaccines were readily available in the United Kingdom, London saw an alarming rise of teen homicides. The year 2021 saw a peak exceeding that of 2008, when 28 teen homicides were reported (Metropolitan Police Homicide Report and Guardian Research, 2021; BBC, 2021). The number of teenagers killed in London in 2021 represented nearly one-quarter of all homicides in the city, even though teenagers only make up 8% of the population in London (BBC, 2021).

On December 30, 2021, a 15-year-old was stabbed to death in a park, while a 16-year-old died of injuries sustained in an unrelated stabbing: these were the 29th and 30th teenage homicides in London in 2021 (Slawson, 2021). The vast majority of the victims were non-white (Slawson, 2021). So far, most of the known suspects and those arrested for 2021 teenage stabbings in London have all been teens themselves (Slawson, 2021).

In a press release, Commander Alex Murray, Metropolitan Police Department, London, stated (France, 2021, retrieved from https://www.standard.co.uk/news/crime/london-teen-killings-track-worst-year-b941083.html):

> *My thoughts are with the victims and all those impacted. They are not statistics, not just numbers, they all have families, and they all should have had their lives ahead of them. . . . These devastating losses continue to motivate every single officer at the Met to catch those responsible, bring justice to their families and take weapons off the street.*

As gun prohibition is much stricter in the United Kingdom after the 1968 Firearms Act and its subsequent modifications (U.K. Legislation, 2021), the next weapon of choice became knives, which are even more readily available to teenagers. However, the U.K. also has strict knife possession laws (U.K. Government Services, n.d., retrieved from https://www.gov.uk/buying-carrying-knives):

> *It's illegal* [in the U.K.] *to possess a banned knife or weapon. It's also illegal to:*
>
> - *bring into the UK, sell, hire, lend or give someone a banned knife or weapon*
> - *carry any knife in public without good reason, unless it has a manual folding blade less than 3 inches long*
> - *sell a knife to anyone under the age of 18, unless it has a manual folding blade less than 3 inches long*
> - *use any knife in a threatening way*

There is an extensive list of the types of knives that are prohibited in the U.K., including knives that have been disguised in everyday objects, non-metal knives, swords, telescoping knives, and "knuckle dusters"[5] (U.K. Government Services, n.d).

Whether the weapon of choice is a gun or knife, one cannot assume that teenage homicides are always associated with gang activity. There are a number of examples to indicate this. For one, as the mother of Tamim Ian Habimana, age 15 at the time of his homicide, adamantly claims, her son was not a gang member (Slawson, 2021). In the case of stabbing victim Drekwon Patterson, age 16, his family relocated for safety after he had been previously attacked, with a friend stating that he was not affiliated with any gang (Slawson, 2021). As there is no evidence to the contrary, it cannot be assumed that any of the victims were gang members, even though that possibility may exist in some of the homicide cases.

To put the teenage homicides in perspective, as of 2021, census data for London reported a population of approximately 9.4 million residents (World Population Review, 2021). In comparison, a similarly populated and diverse city in the United States, New York City, with a population of 8.2 million people, witnessed 485 murders in 2021, 4% higher than 2020 numbers (Celona and Balsamini, 2022). According to the NYPD, shooting deaths of juveniles nearly doubled in 2021, as compared to 2019; between January 1 and September 26, 2021, there were 89 shooting victims ages 17 and younger in New York City (Cook, 2021).

SOURCES

British Broadcasting Company (BBC) (2021). London teen homicides: How killing broke 2008 record. Dec. 31. Retrieved from https://www.bbc.com/news/uk-england-london-59239893.

Celona, L., and D. Balsamini (2022). NYC recorded 485 murders in 2021. *New York Post.* Jan. 1. Retrieved from https://nypost.com/2022/01/01/nyc-recorded-485-murders-in-2021/.

Cook, L. (2021). NYC shootings involving children, teens skyrocket at an alarming rate, NYPD data shows. PIX 11. Oct. 12. Retrieved from https://pix11.com/news/local-news/nyc-shootings-involving-children-teens-skyrocket-at-alarming-rate-nypd-data-shows/.

Metropolitan Police, City of London (2021). Statement from Commander Alex Murray regarding teenage homicides. Press release. Dec. 31. France, A. (2021) London "on track" for worst year of teenage killings, police say. Evening Standard. Jun 17. Retrieved from https://www.standard.co.uk/news/crime/london-teen-killings-track-worst-year-b941083.html.

Metropolitan Police Homicide Report and Guardian Research (2021). Graph: In 2021 there were 30 teenage homicides in London, exceeding the 2008 peak. *The Guardian.* Dec. 31. Retrieved from https://www.theguardian.com/uk-news/2021/dec/31/knife-rises-in-london-with-30-teen-homicides-in-2021.

Slawson, N. (2021). "He was not in a gang": Lives and deaths of 30 London teenage homicide victims. *The Guardian.* Dec. 31. Retrieved from https://www.theguardian.com/uk-news/2021/dec/31/knife-rises-in-london-with-30-teen-homicides-in-2021.

[5] A band of metal or other material that can be worn on the fingers and used as a weapon (U.K. Government Services, n.d.).

United Kingdom Government Services (n.d.). Selling, buying, and carrying knives: Basic laws on knives. Retrieved from https://www.gov.uk/buying-carrying-knives.

United Kingdom Legislation (2021). Firearms Act 1968. UK Public General Acts. Jul. 14. Retrieved from https://www.legislation.gov.uk/ukpga/1968/27.

World Population Review (2021). London population. Retrieved from https://worldpopulationreview.com/world-cities/london-population.

CHAPTER DISCUSSION QUESTIONS

1. How is deviance different from crime? Provide some examples of deviance that are not considered criminal behavior.
2. Why is there a disconnect between how society defines delinquency and the strict legal definition?
3. What challenges to preventing juvenile delinquency did the COVID-19 pandemic cause?
4. Why might children placed in foster care be at greater risk for delinquency?
5. Which type of punishment do you believe is more effective in curbing juvenile delinquency, informal or formal sanctions?

GLOSSARY

Congregate care Licensed residential group homes for juveniles.

Detention Synonymous with adult jail or prison; refers to the incarceration of a juvenile offender.

Deviance Behaviors and cultures that run counter to mainstream society. NOTE: All crime is deviance, but not all deviance is crime.

Evidence-based programs Prevention or treatment programs that are designed around studies and data analysis that offer evidence that they are effective.

Foster care Temporary or permanent placement with foster parents that may remain in effect until the juvenile's 18th birthday.

Informal and formal sanctions Forms of punishment that society hands out to an accused deviant or offender. Informal sanctions can include shunning the individual, whereas formal sanctions are used to punish those convicted of a crime.

Juvenile delinquents Term used to refer to juveniles viewed as deviant or criminals. As a legal term, refers to juveniles found delinquent in juvenile court of an offense committed before the juvenile's 18th birthday.

Juvenile justice The courts and agencies that are part of the larger criminal justice system and handle cases of juveniles under 18.

Moral panic A demand for action by a large number of members of society against a threat perceived as being due to deviant behavior by other members. The behavior need not be legally defined as criminal. SEE *Social construct.*

Social construct A rational or irrational idea arising in a society, often with little or no basis in fact. Example: The social construct of race has no basis in biological science. SEE *Moral panic.*

Status offenses Noncriminal acts committed by juveniles, such as violating curfews or truancy. SEE *Truancy.*

Stigma A condition of bearing a negative stereotype or label that is difficult to erase or have forgiven by members of society. In the context of juvenile justice, the term was popularized by sociologist Erving Goffman in *Stigma: Note on the Management of Spoiled Identity* (1963).

Truancy Failure of a juvenile to attend school under compulsory education laws. SEE *Status offenses.*

REFERENCES AND ADDITIONAL SUGGESTED READINGS

Arain, M., M. Haque, L. Johal, P. Mathur, W. Nel, A. Rais, R. Sandhu, and S. Sharma (2013). Maturation of the adolescent brain. *Neuropsychiatric Disorder Treatment.* Vol. 9: 449–461.

Arthur, P. J., and R. Waugh (2009). Symposium Issue: Status offenders and the Juvenile Justice and Delinquency Prevention Act: the exception that swallowed the rule. National Conference on Homeless Youth and the Law. *Seattle Journal of Social Justice.* Spring/Sum. Vol. 555. Retrieved from https://advance-lexis-com.wne.idm.oclc.org/api/document?collection=analytical-materials&id=urn:contentItem:4X48-R680-0198-G00K-00000-00&context=1516831.

Baglivio, M. T., K. T. Wolff, J. A. Reid, S. L. Jackson, and A. R. Piquero (2022). Did juvenile domestic offending change during COVID-19? *Youth Violence and Juvenile Justice.* Jan. Vol. 20, issue 1: 63–79.

Broussard, K. (2022). Arlington mall announces curfew for minors after brawl leads to arrests. *KERA News.* April 21. Retrieved from https://www.keranews.org/business-economy/2022-04-21/arlington-mall-announces-curfew-program-for-minors-after-brawl-ends-in-arrests.

Camacho, J., and W. Brown (2018). The evolution of the tattoo in defiance of the immutable definition of deviance: current perceptions by law enforcement of tattooed arrestees. *Deviant Behavior.* Vol. 39, issue 8: 1023–1041.

Capacity Building Center for States (2020). *Congregate Care in the Age of Family First: Overview.* Washington, DC: Children's Bureau, Administration for Children and Families, U.S. Department of Health and Human Services.

Colvin, M., and J. Pauly (1983). A critique of criminology: Toward an integrated Structural-Marxist Theory on delinquency production. *American Journal of Sociology.* Vol. 89, issue 3: 513–551.

Goffman, E. (1963). *Stigma: Notes on the Management of a Spoiled Identity.* New York, NY: Simon and Schuster, Inc.

Goode, E., and N. Ben-Yehuda (1994). *Moral Panics: The Social Construction of Deviance.* Cambridge, MA: Blackwell.

National Conference of State Legislatures (NCSL) (2020). Congregate care, residential treatment, and group home state legislative enactments, 2014–2019. Q&A. Oct. 30. Retrieved from https://www.ncsl.org/research/human-services/congregate-care-and-group-home-state-legislative-enactments.aspx.

National Institute of Alcohol and Alcoholism (2021). Underage drinking. National Institution of Health. May. Retrieved from https://www.niaaa.nih.gov/publications/brochures-and-fact-sheets/underage-drinking.

Office of Juvenile Justice and Delinquency Prevention (OJJDP) (2015). Literature review: Status Offenders. U.S. Department of Justice. Sep. Retrieved from https://ojjdp.ojp.gov/mpg/literature-review/status-offenders.pdf.

Ozer, M., and H. Akbas (2020). The predictability of IQ on delinquency: A structural equation model (SQM). *International Journal of Criminal Justice Science.* Vol. 15, issue 2: 283–297.

Przbylski, A. K., and N. Weinstein (2019). Violent video engagement is not associated with adolescents' aggressive behaviour: Evidence from a registered report. *Royal Society Open Science.* Feb. 13. London, UK: The Royal Society Publishing. Retrieved from https://royalsocietypublishing.org/doi/full/10.1098/rsos.171474.

Robins, L. N., H. Gyman, and P. O'Neal (1962). The interaction of social class and deviant behavior. *American Sociological Review.* Aug. Vol. 27, issue 4: 480–492.

Rhone, N. (2021). Opinion: Mall culture and teens, already a strained relationship before Lenox curfew. *The Atlanta Journal-Constitution.* Sep. 15. Retrieved from https://www.ajc.com/life/opinion-mall-culture-and-teens-already-a-strained-relationship-before-lenox-curfew/WKIUVN5IUFEITNVPM2DRA7XHOA/.

Statista Research Department (2019). How many tattoos do you have? United States—Number of tattoos in 2019. Dec. 12. Retrieved from https://www.statista.com/statistics/721567/number-of-tattoos-united-states/.

United States Department of Justice (n.d.). 38. "Juvenile" Defined. U.S. Department of Justice Archives. Retrieved from https://www.justice.gov/archives/jm/criminal-resource-manual-38-juvenile-defined.

United States Food and Drug Administration (2021). *Tobacco 21.* Sep. 1. Retrieved from https://www.fda.gov/tobacco-products/retail-sales-tobacco-products/tobacco-21.

Victor, J. (1998). Moral panics and the social construction of deviant behavior: A theory and application to the case of ritual child abuse. *Sociological Perspectives.* Fall. Retrieved from http://pascalfroissart.online.fr/3-cache/1998-victor.pdf.

Vogel, M., and S. F. Messner (2012). Social correlates of delinquency for youth in need of mental health services: Examining the scope conditions of criminological theories. *Justice Quarterly.* Aug. Vol. 29, issue 4: 546–572.

Walters, G. D., L. Runell, and J. Kremser (2021). Social and psychological effects of the COVID-19 pandemic on middle-school students: Attendance options and changes over time. *School Psychology.* Vol, 36, issue 5: 277–284.

Wasserman, G., S. J. Ko, and L. S. McReynolds (2004). *Assessing the Mental Health of Youth in Juvenile Justice Setting.* Report. Washington, D.C.: Department of Justice, Office of Juvenile Justice and Delinquency Prevention.

Westie, F., and A. T. Turk (1965). A Strategy for research on social classes and delinquency. *Journal of Criminal Law, Criminology, and Police Science.* Dec. Vol. 56: 454–462.

Chapter **TWO**

(A Brief) History of Juvenile Deviance and Delinquency

My father kept me busy from dawn to dusk when I was a kid. When I wasn't pitching hay, hauling corn or running a tractor, I was heaving a baseball into his mitt behind the barn . . . if all parents in the country followed his rule, juvenile delinquency would be cut in half in a year's time.

—Bob Feller (1918–2010), Major League Baseball Player

Chapter Objectives

- Review the evolution of definitions of what we mean by juvenile delinquency since the 19th century.
- Provide a brief history of how society changed over time from an agrarian to an industrial economy and the effects of the change on children.
- Review periods in the 20th century when there were moral panics and perceived increases in juvenile deviance and crime.
- Examine how youth culture changed in the mid-20th century, contributing to perceptions of juvenile delinquency.
- Introduce current trends in general perceptions of juvenile delinquency and mental health issues contributing to it.

Key Terms

Autism spectrum
Bipolar disorder
Child maltreatment
Corporal punishment
Incorrigible child
Neurodivergent
Recidivism

INTRODUCTION

How we currently define juvenile delinquency was formulated fairly recently. Despite 6,000 years of civilization marked by written law, considering childhood as a distinct period of life with its own developmental stages, as we noted in Chapter 1, is a fairly new phenomenon. Considering juveniles as occupying a separate, constructed age range has affected definitions of juvenile delinquency and the law's response to it (Hartinger-Sauders, 2008). More recent research has advanced our understanding of juvenile development, learning disorders, and the general mental health of children, with similar effects on contemporary views of deviance and delinquency.

The 19th century gave rise to the term *incorrigible child*, identified as an uncontrollable and dangerously unsocialized child (Soderberg, 2018). Charles Loring Brace, in the First Annual Report of the Children's Aid Society (1854) warned,

> *Let Society beware, when the outcast, vicious, reckless multitude of New York [City] boys, swarming now every foul alley and low street, come to know their power and use it!* (Soderberg, 2018, p. 307)

From the streets of New York City came a new cultural category, the "juvenile delinquent," to describe a member of a population of children who had no adult guidance and were left to their own devices to survive (Soderberg, 2018). There wasn't suddenly an alarming number of such children; rather, children who misbehaved beyond the tolerance of society were being reclassified, requiring new legal classifications as well. More importantly, the Progressive Era of the late 1800s introduced a formal juvenile justice system. Due process for juvenile offenders and protection of children were included in the new system, but regulation was left largely unchanged until the late 20th century (Shichor, 1983).

Not only have definitions of juvenile delinquency evolved, but juvenile justice systems in the United States and elsewhere have been transformed by the classification. The pendulum swings, as in adult corrections, between punitive measures and the desire to reform offenders (Hansen, 2022; Mckee and Rapp, 2014). Either way, the original goals remain to prevent delinquency and, if it nonetheless occurs, to reduce the risk of *recidivism*.

AGRICULTURAL SOCIETY

As this chapter's epigraph implies, rural children were entirely too busy to get into mischief. During the agrarian period of human history (as today), livestock, farms, and fields required work from morning to night, seven days a week. This not only provided a somewhat reliable food supply and income; it was one way that these societies practiced Judeo-Christian values. As Benjamin Franklin rephrased the warning from the King James Bible, *Idle hands are the devil's playground.* That is, those with too much time on their hands may find themselves engaged in immoral behavior. This belief contributed to the American core values of hard work and industry, still instilled in children from an early age in the United States.

Until the advancements of modern medicine, children sadly often died young, sometimes during birth or within the hours or days after. Maternal and infant mortality rates remained high into the early part of the 20th century in the United States. And without contemporary forms of birth control, along with the need for more hands to help out on farms, birth rates were far higher than those in most countries today. Not only did having large numbers of children provide free labor, they provided a built-in surveillance system: siblings working without adult supervision in the fields or house watched out for one another. In addition, extended family groups (e.g., grandparents, aunts, uncles) lived in close proximity, at least before westward expansion; (more recently, today's more transient population is more likely to follow the needs of the labor market). Having extended family nearby often provided additional support and guidance for children, something that is far less common today.

Juveniles were expected from an early age to work on family farms and ranches, taking on a series of age-appropriate chores. This was not intended to be punishment or abuse. Rather, it helped families eke out a livelihood, and it passed on farming and other needed skills to offspring, enabling them to continue the family legacy of farming or ranching. Even today, children in some families who are old enough to work may legally do so in family-run businesses or in minimum wage jobs that contribute to household income. According to Lerman (2000), this particularly holds true in low-income families and those receiving welfare assistance, sometimes to the detriment of juveniles' education, as they may lose sleep and study time as they hold down jobs with nighttime work hours.

Farm and ranch life clearly offered very little time for children to get into mischief, though no doubt some misbehavior did occur. Any type of bad behavior was generally dealt with quickly, as today, both to reign in the child and to serve as a warning to other children in the household or community to behave themselves or suffer the same consequences. The stakes were high. Any deviance or crime committed by juveniles or adults could conceivably reduce agricultural productivity, risking lost profits or, worse yet, jail time for desperately needed extra pairs of hands on a farm or ranch. In some cases, a farm was only able to produce enough to sustain the family, so any lost labor could conceivably result in less food for basic sustenance.

Approximately 90% of the population lived on farms and ranches in the 19th century, compared to the approximately 44% of land devoted to farming at the beginning of the 21st century. Of course, some portion of agriculture today is managed by large corporations. However, according to the U.S. Department of Agriculture, 98% of farms are still family-owned and operated (Whitt, 2021). Under federal law, children of any age can do any type of work on a family-owned farm, with children as young as 10 allowed to work for wages on farms not owned by relatives during harvest season, with parental permission (*APM Reports*, 2019; U.S. Department of Labor, n.d.). In comparison, federal child labor laws in the United States prohibit employment of juveniles under the age of 14 in nonagricultural occupations, restricting the hours and type of labor performed by minors under 16 (U.S. Department of Labor, n.d.). It should be noted that more recently, the Economic Policy Institute has indicated that there are efforts to weaken child labor protections in some states and current restrictions may soon be obsolete if legislation is passed (Sherer and Mast, 2023). This has already come to pass in a number of states in 2023. It is too soon to predict how much more child labor laws will be weakened in other states or at the federal level.

INDUSTRIAL SOCIETY

During the Industrial Age, as cities grew, so did the numbers of people who left the farm to find new opportunities in factories located in urban areas. This was true for both the United States and countries in Western Europe. In turn, the Industrial Age had a direct effect on how and where children were raised, as well as having an effect on types and rates of delinquency.

Once the Industrial Age was in full swing, those children not in school and not working in factories were at loose ends while their parents worked. Women not employed in factories might be engaged in cottage industries, working in the home and thus still not keeping close eyes on their children. Thus came the rise of youth street gangs and the beginnings of juvenile delinquency in urban settings. Charles Dickens, in his novel *Oliver Twist* (Dickens, 1838; 1992), sharply characterized the street gangs of 19th-century London. Dickens's portrayal of the criminal lives of children fending for themselves on the streets came from his own observations of the effects of urbanization and industrialization on impoverished and often homeless juveniles in Victorian England, often falling under the tutelage of criminal adults (Marcus, 1991).

FORMS OF CHILDHOOD EDUCATION

Discussions of education in the United States usually center on public or private schools providing instruction from kindergarten through 12th grade and, for some children, college or trade school. Educating juveniles, however, actually takes place in a much wider context that can include practical technical education provided by family members, employers, or by tradespeople through apprenticeships.

The Industrial Revolution brought about opportunities for juveniles and adults beyond agricultural work. Apprenticeship systems, common in the 18th and 19th centuries both in the United States and elsewhere, helped keep juveniles out of trouble. Apprentices were often little more than indentured servants, given food and shelter in exchange for their unpaid labor. Apprentices, primarily males, could be as young as 10 or 11 and often came from working-class families, though many were orphans raised in foundling homes (Levene, 2008; Childs, 1992). Children taken in as apprentices in charity cases were expected to remain tied to their masters for very long periods and to express eternal gratitude to authority (Levene, 2008). As many as 50% of apprentices failed to complete their service in training, leaving them, again, at loose ends, that could result in unruly, even mob, behaviors (Levene, 2008).

Apprenticeships offered young people some advantages. Some did earn a wage, allowing them to contribute to their households' income as they gained training in semi-skilled or skilled professions (Childs, 1992). For society, this system helped to keep juveniles off the streets and out of trouble. But apprenticeships did not always provide sober, moral environments. Accounts of wayward apprentices in late 18th-century England describe apprentices brought before the courts for a number of offenses, including public drunkenness, running away from their employers, theft, and violence (Levene, 2008). Apprenticeships exist today in some crafts and trades, but they are primarily intended for adults, often following or as part of a period in a trade school.

Children living on remote farms or ranches often received only agricultural training and little or no other education. Compulsory education laws were not imposed until mid-1800s. Even then, instruction rarely went beyond a sixth grade education, received in a schoolhouse where children studying at all levels were taught by one teacher in one room. Education laws were dictated by individual states, and it wasn't until 1918[1] that all states required minors to complete elementary school (Steffes, 2012). Education is relevant in a discussion of juvenile delinquency because, after family life, the primary socialization children receive comes from religious and educational systems. These three social institutions to this day continue to offer the best defense against juvenile delinquency. Formal prekindergarten education, another location for socialization, was nearly nonexistent until the 1960s, motivated by the Head Start program instituted in 1965 and higher rates of maternal employment (Cahan, 1989).

DISCIPLINE IN FAMILIES AND SCHOOLS

In 19th-century America, a number of parenting manuals were published, a genre that continues to proliferate. Meant to guide parents in raising "good children," such manuals included recommendations for punishment, allowing varying

[1] This author's maternal grandmother completed the eighth grade in the early 20th century, then continued on to a girls' finishing school, where she learned the skills needed to run a household, including sewing and cooking. This was pretty typical for girls raised in middle- or upper-class families at the time. By the next generation, in the 1930s, it was a big accomplishment for girls to complete a high school education and unusual for either young men or women to continue on to university.

degrees of leniency. Domestic manuals, coupled with the emergence of juvenile prisons, helped society reimagine the incorrigible child as criminal, rather than simply difficult to raise (Soderberg, 2018). Nineteenth century parents and guardians, particularly in the emerging middle class, consumed these manuals in hopes of not producing a child criminal themselves. Parents, then and now, aware that their children's behavior will reflect favorably or poorly on them, may resort to physical punishment of unwanted behavior.

Children were raised to fear their parents, particularly the wrath of their fathers, an approach that today would be considered psychological abuse. Early parenting manuals even suggested physical management be used to discipline infants before they could speak. Parenting manuals recommended that crying children, including infants, be silenced using escalating physical punishments if they didn't quiet down. Here is an example from a 19th-century parenting book (Soderberg, 2018, p. 315):

> *It may be necessary to add . . . suddenly, but gently, a slap, or a shake just sufficient to render fear the predominant passion. But some rare instances will occur, in which these means will not only not answer the purpose, but serve only to increase the passionate excitement which obtains in the midst of a fit of squalling, or of obstinate, silent resistance to parental authority. In such instances, imitate the practice of physicians. . . . And repeat the slap or ply the rod . . . with the intention to smart. . . .*

Even today parents and experts disagree as to whether an infant or toddler in a tantrum should be ignored or picked up and comforted. The philosophy behind letting children cry without intervention is that it allegedly teaches them to self-regulate their emotions. However, the medical community generally recommends that the duration of time that infants cry should be greatly reduced, with a combination of carrying and massaging the child, rather than leaving them alone for an extended period (Elliott et al., 2002). We should note that very few experts condone physical punishment of crying infants and children. Physical punishment for crying generally only further distresses an infant or toddler, further angering the parent.

Long before there was a juvenile justice system, families provided most of the discipline for their offspring, much of which we would classify as child abuse today. Violence against children as a form of punishment, both at home and in schools, had deep roots in religious beliefs (Finkelstein, 2000). The 17th-century saying "Spare the rod, spoil the child" essentially meant that bad behavior should be beaten out of children, a method of discipline some families use today (Kish, 2018).

Corporal punishment was once commonplace. Parents and schoolmasters were protected by law from prosecution for physical assault and battery of a juvenile when using physical punishment (Cliche, 2007). However, in some countries, including Canada, parents had the right to punish their children only within

Depiction of schoolmaster spanking a student.

reason. "Reason," of course, is subjective. Alarming to some, nineteen U.S. states still allow school corporal punishment, while others, listed in Table 2.1, prohibit the use of physical punishment. The U.S. Supreme Court case *Ingraham v. Wright* (1977) decided that corporal punishment was constitutional, leaving to the states determinations about corporal punishment in public schools, preschool through 12th grade (Gershoff and Font, 2018).

Other forms of corporal punishment include withholding food, forcing a child to miss a meal, or forcing them to eat a noxious substance (e.g., soap), commonly used when children use profanity or talk back to an authority figure. Today the following forms of corporal punishment would also be considered child abuse, even though some were acceptable into the late 20th century (University of Michigan Health, n.d.):

- Spanking, other forms of hitting including slapping
- Pinching or ear pulling
- Forcing a child to remain in a position that is painful or confining them to an uncomfortable space
- Denying a child the use of a bathroom
- Any physical punishment that causes embarrassment or humiliation

In the early 20th century, new systems of discipline emerged in schools, some of which are still in use today. Though corporal punishment remained in some schools and households, other behavioral modification strategies were beginning to be used, such as rewarding good behavior with gold stars or punishing bad behavior by writing a child's name on the chalkboard. These strategies, too, are losing favor in current pedagogy, as they draw attention to children who break

TABLE 2.1. States that Banned Corporal Punishment in Public Schools, in Chronological Order

STATE	YEAR	STATE	YEAR	STATE	YEAR
New Jersey*	1867	Wisconsin	1988	Utah	1992
Massachusetts	1871	Alaska	1989	Illinois	1993
Hawaii	1873	Connecticut	1989	Maryland	1993
Maine	1975	Iowa*	1989	Nevada	1993
District of Columbia	1977	Michigan	1989	Washington	1993
Rhode Island	1977	Minnesota	1989	West Virginia	1994
New Hampshire	1983	North Dakota	1989	Delaware	2003
New York	1985	Oregon	1989	Pennsylvania	2005
Vermont	1985	Virginia	1989	Ohio	2009
California	1986	South Dakota	1990	New Mexico	2011
Nebraska	1988	Montana	1991		

*States where corporal punishment is banned in both public and private schools.

Source: E. T. Gershoff and S. A. Font (2018), Corporal punishment in U.S. schools: Prevalence, disparity of use, and status in state and federal policy, *Social Policy Report* (vol. 30, issue 1), available at https://www.ncbi.nlm.nih.gov/pmc/articles/PMC5766273/.

classroom rules or provide a view of prizes being somehow inequitable for children who do not earn them (Mulvahill, 2019).

Discipline is not simply a means of rewarding good children or punishing wayward children. It is sometimes also intended to be character-building (Kaestle, 1978), leading to children being punished for noncriminal misbehavior. We now know that children who grow up in environments where violence is normative are at *greater* risk for juvenile delinquency. Physically or psychologically abusive punishment can lead to delinquency in children and even to mental health disorders. Chapter 8 goes into greater detail on the roles, beyond punishment, that schools play in contributing to or inhibiting juvenile delinquency.

CHANGING PERCEPTIONS OF JUVENILE CRIME AND DELINQUENCY

The 20th century saw two distinct periods during which teenagers' mores and behavior met with adult disapproval. Unlike the so-called Roaring Twenties and the age of flappers,[2] during which what society saw as wild behavior was restricted to young adults, in the 1950s and 1960s parents' concerns, even alarm, were over their teens. Sometimes driven by the media, parents saw their children as being at risk of deviance and delinquency. Real or imagined, the specter of delinquency often led to efforts at societal and institutional change, rather than attempts to change perceived defects in an individual juvenile's behavior.

1950s: Teenage Rebellion

During the post-WWII era, teenagers and young adults often had more disposable income than ever before. Whereas leading up to WWII, parents and their offspring enjoyed many of the same leisure pursuits and interests, in the 1950s some juveniles adopted value systems apart from the adult mainstream and were consequently labeled rebellious. The emerging youth culture signaled a new norm for teenagers: rebelling against their parents' seemingly rigid rules. The image of a 1950s teen included driving fast automobiles, inventing risqué dance moves, and adopting fashion trends independent of adult styles (Wiseman, n.d.).

The emerging car culture of the 1950s helped shape new definitions of delinquency. Some teenagers, primarily males, cruised the main street of a town on a Saturday night, with no real destination in mind. Adults saw this as a nuisance, even delinquent, but for teenagers in the 1950s and 1960s, cruising was "cool." Though cruising was not criminal behavior per se, some towns and cities made concerted efforts to discourage it.

The teen car culture also included drag or street racing, posing a serious threat not only to the drivers but to bystanders, particularly before safety features, such as seatbelts, became mandatory. Drag racing can be a legitimate organized spectator sport, but in the context of the 1950s, nonprofessional drivers disrupted normal traffic by challenging each other to races, even when they did so on less traveled roads. This perception was exaggerated in movies and the media, where teens were viewed as constantly driving around looking for danger or trouble. Street racing is still popular in some regions today, with drivers subject to citations if they are pulled over by police. In an attempt to curtail drag or street racing, the Jacksonville, Florida, sheriff's department implemented a community-based program, Beat the Heat, to take teenage racing off the streets and onto legitimate race tracks (Sibley, 2001). Another concern in the 1950s, as today, is an association between drag racing on public streets and illegal drug and alcohol use, resulting in impaired drivers (Sibley, 2001).

[2] Flappers were young women who shortened their skirts, bobbed their hair, and in many cases, delayed marriage and motherhood, all of which ran counter to the conventions of the 1920s. They were viewed by some as immoral, when in reality they represented a more independent modern woman.

Teenagers cruising Woodward Avenue, Detroit, Michigan, 1951.

We know now from developmental psychology that a certain amount of rebellion in preteens and teenagers is normal. Teens normatively want to pull away from parental units and begin to explore and express their own viewpoints and inclinations as they move toward adulthood. Some rebellion is fairly benign, such as choosing clothing that while perfectly appropriate streetwear, does not meet with adult approval, particularly when worn in school. Males wearing jeans and white t-shirts to school in the 1950s, into the 1970s, were viewed as potentially delinquent.[3] Other forms of rebellion can be self-sabotaging. Particularly for females, promiscuity in the teenage years, when juveniles often do not fully understand the consequences of their sexual behavior, can disrupt lives with unplanned pregnancies. Though males are also affected by teen pregnancy, it isn't to the same extent as for females. Males, females, and nonbinary and transgender individuals all face the possibility of contracting sexually transmitted diseases as well.

The Newport Academy (2021), a private juvenile residential treatment center, lists the following behaviors as types of rebellion that can lead to more

[3] In the 1950s through the 1970s, jeans and white t-shirts were relatively inexpensive clothing choices, and wearing these items possibly indicated poverty as much as rebellion. As jeans rose in popularity among teenagers, they became increasingly expensive status symbols.

destructive behavior, although in some circles they may be seen as normal parts of growing up:

- Self-defeating behaviors
- Neglecting schoolwork
- Consuming alcohol and drugs
- Breaking rules and/or laws
- Engaging in unhealthy risk-taking, even dangerous activities (the "adrenalin junkie")

1960s and 1970s: Teenage Angst

Whereas rebellious teens in the 1950s were thought by society to have no real cause for their behavior, teens in the 1960s faced social changes that raised legitimate concerns. From the late 1950s to 1975, males in particular felt anxiety over the Vietnam War, more so after the draft was reinstated. Like the engagement in Korea, the Vietnam War, technically a police action, had more ambiguous goals than the nation's earlier participation in the two World Wars. Legally required to register for the draft at 18, many males did enthusiastically anticipate enlisting in the armed forces, drawn by the romance they perceived by previously successful war campaigns. Women did serve during the Vietnam War but in non-combat positions and, like today, they are not required to sign up for selective service when they turn 18 years old, as is the case for males, with some exceptions.

Others reconciled themselves to being drafted, and still others anxiously looked for means to escape the draft, even burning their draft cards in defiance. In 1965, an amendment to the Selective Service Act passed that criminalized the destruction or mutilation of draft cards, with penalties of five years in prison and up to $10,000 in fines (U.S. Supreme Court, *United States v. O'Brien*, 1968). Fear of being sent to Vietnam, coupled with antiwar sentiment, led a number of teenagers and young adults to defy Selective Service orders, in spite of the possibility of being arrested and sentenced to prison. Some went to Canada or other countries to avoid being drafted. Teenage angst was not reserved for American youth, however. Similar rebelliousness and angst occurred simultaneously in the United Kingdom during the 1950s and 1960s, although not associated with Vietnam.

Though females did not face the risk from the draft, a renewed feminist movement, beginning in the 1960s, opened an array of possible paths for women's futures that were not based on marriage and motherhood. In 1960, the median age of marriage for women was 20.3 (as compared to 27.1 today) (Hemez, 2020). Instead of collecting items for their hope chests and trousseaus,[4] females in high school

[4] Hope chests were large wooden boxes that teenage girls would use to start collecting household items (e.g., linens) needed to set up a household once they married. *Trousseau* describes the items that go into a hope chest, including more "grown up" clothing befitting a new bride. Though they had been around for centuries, they became very popular in the United States in the 1950s into the 1970s.

Youth culture, the Ace Café, London, U.K., circa 1960.

increasingly chose curricula that would prepare them for college and careers after they graduated. Until fairly recent decades, however, these careers were primarily limited to secretarial, nursing, teaching, or lower-paying professions still considered more "feminine" in the mid-20th century.

Another major cause for teenaged rebellion was the Civil Rights Movement, which grew more intense in the 1960s. At the height of the movement in the 1960s, children, teenagers, and young adults took part in marches and even violence, in some cases resulting in arrest (U.S. Library of Congress, n.d.). In interviews conducted for the Civil Rights History Project (2009), Freeman Hrabowski reported that in 1963, when he was 12 and still in elementary school, he marched in the Birmingham, Alabama, Children's Crusade to protest school segregation. He was arrested and subsequently spent several days in adult jail (U.S. Library of Congress, n.d.). To social justice and Civil Rights activists, juveniles involved in civil rights protests were viewed as heroic, while conservative members of society and law enforcement saw the juveniles participating in protest marches as delinquents.

The 1960s was also the so-called psychedelic era, when experimentation with illegal drugs spread among teens and young adults. The war on drugs, which began in the 1950s, saw drug use as a crisis of the white, suburban middle class and juveniles as innocent victims that needed to be shielded from illegal drug use (Lassiter, 2015). That view created new classes of juvenile delinquents: users and dealers. Stigmatizing labels, some of which are still used today, invented to describe juveniles (and adults) who used drugs included burnout, dopehead, doper, druggie, junkie, stoner, and others (Addiction Center, 2022).

To add to the rapidly changing social landscape and perceptions of rising delinquency, the Sexual Revolution, from late 1960s to early 1970s, brought new freedoms and anxieties to teens. It is a misconception that teenagers' sexual attitudes became more liberal in the 1960s. Research indicates that sexual attitudes changed little from the 1950s, even as sexual behavior became more prevalent among teens. A study by Caron and Moskey (2002) was conducted in the Northeast, surveying students from the 1950, 1975, and 2000 graduating classes at the same high school. Results showed that the participants from the class of 2000 were much more aware of and had easier access to birth control options (Caron and Moskey, 2002), allowing them to be more sexually active than earlier cohorts, though they were no more liberal in their attitudes toward sex than those who graduated in 1950 or 1975 (Caron and Moskey, 2002).

The 1980s and 1990s

In the 1980s, too, the public perceived a rise in juvenile delinquency. While the juvenile justice system had essentially remained unchanged since the 1970s, by the 1980s the system was seen as too lenient on juvenile offenders (Center on Juvenile and Criminal Justice, 2022; Schwartz et al., 2012). "Get tough on crime" trends throughout the criminal justice system in the 1980s and 1990s responded to these public and political pressures. Juveniles were increasingly sentenced to institutions for even minor offenses and were more frequently transferred to the adult criminal justice system for serious offenses. Juvenile correctional facilities in the United States were increasingly overcrowded and in poor condition (Center on Juvenile and Criminal Justice, 2022).

The focus on punishment for juvenile offenders in this period led to neglect of rehabilitation, before, in the early 21st century, the pendulum swung back away from harsh treatment. Part of this shift in thinking was due to the financial strains on states caused by widespread juvenile (and adult) incarceration (Bonnie et al., 2013). Youth crime also began to drop sharply beginning in the 1990s. In particular, violent crimes overall dropped sharply in large urban areas (Butts and Travis, 2002), reducing pressures for punishment.

Between 1994 and 2000, the number of violent crimes dropped sharply in most of the nation's largest urban areas

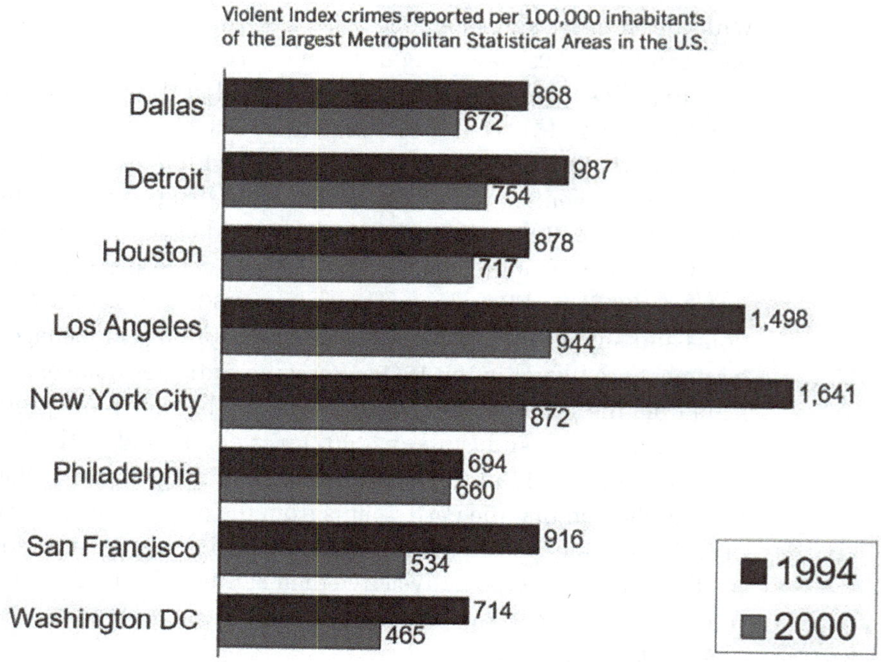

8 of 10 Largest MSAs in U.S.	Violent Index Crimes in 2000
Dallas	22,939
Detroit	33,989
Houston	29,930
L.A.-Long Beach	90,043
New York City	79,485
Philadelphia	33,531
San Francisco	9,195
Washington DC	22,799

Note: 2 of the 10 largest Metropolitan Statistical Areas in the U.S. (Chicago and Boston) did not report sufficient data on "reported crimes" to the FBI in 1994, 2000, or both.

Source: Urban Institute analysis of data from Federal Bureau of Investigation. Annual. *Crime in the United States*. Washington, D.C.: FBI, U.S. Department of Justice.

EXHIBIT 2.1 || Urban violent crime trends, 1994–2000

Current Trends

The past decade saw a further general decline in juvenile delinquency, mirroring the decline in adult offending. Juvenile arrests have increased among females, however, even as juvenile arrests overall have declined. Some of these decreases have been attributed to the dropping U.S. birth rate since 2008 (Morse, 2021). But this is not the whole story. Like any social phenomenon, one variable rarely explains a complex phenomenon like decreased juvenile delinquency. Better diagnoses, at least in more affluent communities, of learning disorders and mental health issues have also contributed to declines in delinquency rates, as children are helped to overcome the frustrations of poor school performance and other problems (see Chapter 8). With better diagnoses came better and earlier intervention strategies.

Rates of anxiety among juveniles are rising, however, in part because it is diagnosed more easily, but also due to the greater number of stressors in modern life. The American Psychological Association (Twenge, 2000) reported that studies indicate that levels of anxiety reported by children today are far greater than levels seen in the 1950s. Anxiety in children and adults is also linked to depression, for which we have far better diagnostic tools today (Anderson and Hope, 2008). Though no single factor is believed to be responsible for juvenile delinquency, some of the mental health variables now identified as contributors are *child maltreatment*, depression, and *bipolar disorder* (Mallet et al., 2009).

It is important to note that before the 1990s, a number of newly identified mental disorders went unrecognized, including the variety of forms of anxiety. Most of the anxiety experienced by juveniles before diagnostic tools were available was often passed off as just part of the pre-teen and teenage experience, such as hormonal changes during puberty. Until fairly recently, pediatricians rarely asked questions during routine exams about juveniles' mental health. Even a diagnosis of *autism spectrum disorder (ASD)* in children is far better understood today than when it was first identified in the 1940s (Evans, 2013). Some of the behaviors exhibited by juveniles and adults who have undiagnosed mental health issues could be misinterpreted as deviance or delinquency.

Neurodivergent is the contemporary designation for individuals on the autism spectrum or diagnosed with attention deficit disorder (ADD), attention deficit hyperactivity disorder (ADHD), or other atypical neurological conditions. Previously, undiagnosed juveniles could easily be labeled delinquent. Recognizing that these individuals have unique cognitive processes requiring professionals with specialized training, including occupational therapy, helps destigmatize these conditions and helps to prevent delinquency by successfully integrating affected juveniles into mainstream school classrooms and society in general (Chin and Patten, 2021; Lurtz and Komarow, 2021).

Along with better diagnosis of conditions that might lead to delinquency, intervention and prevention programs have undergone a number of changes since delinquency was first defined. Instead of hit-or-miss programs and services that may or may not work, never before having been put into practice, pressure (particularly from those financing the intervention or prevention programs) has increased for *evidence-based practices* (EBPs). EBPs require that before launching a juvenile justice program, a pilot program must be conducted to prove that the full program will succeed (Mckee and Rapp, 2014). Increasingly, funding depends on offering evidence and data that support claims that programs and services will truly be beneficial to juveniles and not result in yet further failures in the system. Even with guardrails installed to test out programs before full implementation, as we will see in Chapter 13, one size does not fit all, whether we are talking about individual treatment or general prevention programs.

SUMMARY

Concrete definitions of what it means to be a juvenile and of what delinquent behavior is, particular to juveniles, formed only fairly recently in human history. Not until the late 19th century were children recognized as being distinctly different from adults. The mid-20th century brought about better understanding of developmental psychology. After identifying deviant and criminal behavior in minors as motivated by different forces than those found in adult offenders, a separate juvenile justice system, including forms of punishment, was established.

In the agrarian age, children had little opportunity to get into trouble, much less serious delinquency. They were required to work on their parental units' farms or ranches, contributing to the survival and profit-generating activities of the family. Even today, there are separate labor laws for minors who work in agriculture, allowing them to be employed at a younger age than minors working in nonagricultural businesses.

The Industrial Age changed family dynamics, as people moved to urban centers seeking new opportunities in factories. Children who were left unsupervised, or in some cases, orphaned, either ended up in workhouses or on the streets, giving rise to youth gangs. Those who were more fortunate could seek out apprenticeships, though that did not necessarily prevent delinquency, as some apprentices ran away or took part in criminal activities, including public drunkenness.

Just as the definitions of deviance and delinquency have changed over time, so have the forms of punishment used. Historically, in both households and schools, punishing misbehaving children was used to force them into approved behavior and to frighten and deter other children into obedience.

Corporal punishment, no longer condoned though not prohibited in schools in some states, was once used to control children. A number of these punishments, including spanking and withholding food or water, are now recognized as abusive and as potentially causing psychological harm.

During some periods in the mid-20th century, society perceived teenagers' increasingly rebellious behavior as delinquency. Teenagers were developing their own youth culture, nurtured by a consumer economy that catered to their changing tastes. During these periods, however, teenagers' anxiety rose under the impact of the Vietnam War and the Civil Rights Movement. Teenage boys approaching adulthood were anxious over the draft and being sent to Vietnam, and girls felt the pressure of being given more life course choices than ever before, including the opportunity to delay marriage and children to go to college or pursue a career. In the 1960s, the so-called Sexual Revolution and increasing experimentation with drugs put additional pressures on teens.

One of the most profound changes in how we view delinquency today comes from a better understanding of the juvenile brain and of mental health issues that can contribute to delinquency. Whereas formerly juveniles with neurodivergent conditions might have acted out and been labeled delinquent and subjected to punishment or worse, today therapies and interventions allow them access to normative life choices, including in education and the workplace.

The juvenile justice system has also improved vastly from a century ago. Programs and services must now be evaluated and proven to work. Though not fool-proof, evidence-based programs are our best tools for ensuring that programs and services do the best for the juvenile population they are meant to serve.

IN THE MEDIA

The Outsiders[5]

Contemporary portrayals of juvenile delinquents in movies, television, and other media inevitably depict the most serious juvenile crimes. In television news, about one-third of crime reporting includes juveniles, most focused on homicide and other violent crime (McNamara and Coward Bucher, 2012). Often plots centered on juvenile delinquency follow stereotypical narratives in which a coach, teacher, or social worker works tirelessly to help reform the wayward youth. Not all films or novels about juvenile delinquency have happy endings, however.

The Outsiders (Zoetrope Studios, 1983; trailer available at https://www.youtube.com/watch?v=j4pFHmSuHRQ), a film based on a 1967 novel written by S. E. Hinton when she was still in her teens, depicts Hinton's own experiences as a high school student growing up in Oklahoma. Hinton expressed sympathy for the greaser gang members in her community, who were described as looking like delinquents but who in fact, in her estimation, only looked the part (*The Outsiders* Fan Club, n.d.). The novel was also adapted by Christopher Sergel into a two-act stage play in the 1990s (Dramatic Publishing, n.d.).

The Outsiders takes place in a small town in the 1960s and examines the rivalry between an affluent clique of teens (the "Socials")[6] and a group of economically

[5] This discussion includes no spoilers in case you wish to read the book or see the film yourself.

[6] The term "socials" is often shortened in conversations to "socs," pronounced *soshes*. The term lingers in teen vocabulary today, but usually representing popularity in high school rather than social and economic status.

Stereotypical greaser, 1960s.

disadvantaged teens and young adults (the "Greasers"). The derogatory term *greaser*, used for a subculture of primarily male teenagers and young adults, was derived from their hairstyle, which was slicked back using hair wax or other hair products. The term was first used in the 19th century to describe poor, working-class individuals of Mexican descent (León, 1983) and has historically had racist connotations.

Much as we see in films, an economic divide between privileged teens and those in the working class comes with an associated divide in territories, represented by physical space. Even though these juveniles may attend the same school, economic diversity usually leads to living in differently advantaged neighborhoods. In *The Outsiders*, the greasers come from the so-called "wrong side of the tracks," the poor East Side of Tulsa, whereas the more affluent teens live on the upper-middle- and upper-class West Side.

In the book and film, when the wealthier teens behave delinquently, they are protected from prosecution. Not so for the teens coming from the poor neighborhoods. By the end of the story, two of the younger members of the greasers gang are forced to flee and live on the run after one character, Johnny, defends another, Ponyboy, resulting in the death of a bullying Social.

The film, released in 1983, quickly became a cult classic, and it still resonates with audiences today. Some of its popularity comes from the cast of young actors who went on to Hollywood fame in this and other films, including Tom Cruise, Rob Lowe, and Patrick Swayze. When asked on multiple occasions in interviews through the years why the novel and film are still popular, Hinton has responded that the concept of in-group and out-group conflicts remains, even if the names of the groups change. Teen audiences recognize their own experiences in the characters of the book (*The Outsiders* Fan Club, n.d.). Since its publication, despite its popularity with young readers, the book has been challenged and banned in some schools because of its depictions of violence and supposed "ungodly" themes (Rosenthal, 2014).

SOURCES

De León, A. (1983). *They Called Them Greasers: Anglos Attitudes toward Mexicans in Texas, 1821–1900.* Austin, TX: University of Texas Press.

Hinton, S. E. (1967; 2006). *The Outsiders.* New York City, NY: Viking Press.

Rosenthal, K. (2014). Banned books: Young adult novels. The University of Tulsa, Department of Special Collections and University Archives. Mar 13. Retrieved from http://orgs.utulsa.edu/spcol/?p=3254.

Sergel, C. (n.d.) *The Outsiders*. Book Adaptation. Woodstock, IL: Dramatic Publishing.
The Outsiders Fan Club (n.d.). Interview: S.E. Hinton. Retrieved from http://theoutsidersfan-club.weebly.com/exclusive-interview-with-se-hinton.html.

INTERNATIONAL PERSPECTIVES

General Juvenile Delinquency in Kenya

Most of the research on delinquency we see in this country is conducted on juveniles in the United States, Canada, or Western Europe. However, juveniles' experiences are shaped by cultural contexts, and large sections of the world have yet to be examined for their prevailing definitions and types of juvenile behavior and delinquency (Lansford et al., 2020). This section looks at juveniles and juvenile delinquency issues in Kenya, an African nation.

Studies of Western cultures link lack of adult supervision to delinquency. Routine Activity Theory (Cohen and Felson, 1979), for example, concludes that a parent or guardian's presence helps prevent motivated juvenile offenders from committing crimes. In Kenya, however, juvenile delinquency is also seen as being linked to the nation's colonial past. Until the 1930s, little attention was paid to juvenile delinquency in the country until the effects of urbanization and detribalization on the younger Kenyan population made it apparent that a concerted effort was needed to curb youth crime (Campbell, 2002).

It is expected that adults will be present in schools at all times, including on the school playground. As we noted in this chapter, school attendance continues to be one means by which to keep juveniles occupied. However, the time spent in school varies throughout the world, with some countries allowing very little time for socializing or leisure activities, as compared to countries on the other extreme without compulsory education (Lansford et al., 2020). Kenya has witnessed a rise in juvenile delinquency, explained by some as being due to economic disparity, resulting in poor school attendance. If we consider this phenomenon even in the United States, some adolescents leave school without a degree when they are forced to help support their families financially.

Measurements of delinquency rates often take into account economic conditions. Studies show that much of what has recently happened in the juvenile justice system in Kenya has indeed been affected by economic circumstances. Following an economic decline in the late 1990s, Kenya saw a rise in juvenile delinquency in the 21st century. Some of this is speculated to have been caused by the number of children who left school and ended up on the streets during the crisis because their parents could no longer share the costs of their education with the government (Stockman, 2000). Unlike in the United States, where most funding of schools comes from the federal and state governments, including from property taxes, there are a number of places in the world where parents and guardians have to pay tuition directly to the school. Following the sharp economic downturn, few parents could keep up with the cost of basic necessities, much less their children's education fees.

Kenyan elementary school class.

To alleviate strain on family budgets and, in turn, delinquency problems, the government implemented new educational policies. In 2003, Kenya made elementary education free, and in 2008, it made secondary education free as well (Clark, 2015). Poor quality education persists, however, and illiteracy rates are high, even among those who have attended school (Clark, 2015; Unesco Institute for Statistics, 2022).

Finally, juvenile detention centers in Kenya contrast starkly with those in the United States and elsewhere in the world. Little effort seems to be made to rehabilitate the juveniles housed there. Detention centers are nothing more than placement facilities, with little in the way of social services or meaningful educational opportunities. As Stockman reported (2000), one Kenyan facility holding 200 children had no games, no teachers, and no textbooks.

SOURCES

Clark, N. (2015). Education in Kenya. World Education News and Reviews. Jun 2. Retrieved from https://wenr.wes.org/2015/06/education-kenya#:~:text=In%202003%2C%20the%20government%20of,for%20secondary%20education%20in%202008.

Cohen, L. E., and M. Felson (1979). Social change and crime: A routine activity approach. *American Sociological Review*. Aug., Vol. 44, issue 4: 588–608.

Landsford, J. E., S. Zietz, M. H. Bornstein, K. Deater-Deckard, L. Di Giunta, K. A. Dodge, S. Gurdal, Q. Liu, Q. Long, P. S. Malone, P. Oburu, C. Pastorelli, A. T. Skinner, E. Sorbring, L. Steinberg, S. Tapanya, L. M. Uribe Tirado, S. Yotanyamaneewong, L. P. Alampay,

S. N. Al-Hassan, D. Bacchini, and L. Chang (2020). Opportunities and peer support for aggression and delinquency during adolescence in nine countries. *New Direction for Child and Adolescent Development*, MEDLINE. Sep. 23. Retrieved from https://pubmed-ncbi-nlm-nih-gov.wne.idm.oclc.org/32964604/.

Stockman, F. (2000). Kenya faces obstacles in aiding its poorest children. *Christian Science Monitor.* Vol. 92, issue 84: 7.

Unesco Institute for Statistics (2022). Kenya. Retrieved from http://uis.unesco.org/en/country/ke.

CHAPTER DISCUSSION QUESTIONS

1. Why might physical punishment of minors (or adults) be acceptable in some periods and unacceptable in others?
2. If most minors are no longer working long hours on family farms or ranches, how (beyond school attendance) can they be kept busy and out of trouble today?
3. What historical events occurred in the 1940s and 1950s that might have contributed to the rise of a youth culture separate from adult culture?
4. If you were a parent in the 1950s or 1960s, how might you respond to the social and historical changes that could put your child at risk for deviant or delinquent behavior?
5. Except for the obvious concern for public safety, why were parents generally concerned about the teenage car culture in the 1950s and 1960s?
6. What moral panics in the 1950s and 1960s, not mentioned in this chapter, might have contributed to redefining juvenile delinquency?
7. How have newly defined mental health issues contributed to a better understanding of delinquent behavior?

GLOSSARY

Autism spectrum disorder (ASD) Developmental disability that affects social interactions, communication, learning, and behavior in those diagnosed with ASD. See *Neurodivergent*.

Bipolar disorder Previously labeled manic depression, mental health issue typically marked by periods of mania and unrealistic perceptions of one's abilities, with periods of severe depression.

Child maltreatment Any type of treatment of children that results in physical suffering or psychological harm.

Corporal punishment Physical punishment that includes spanking, withholding food or water, or confinement in an uncomfortable position or place.

Incorrigible child Term used in the late 19th century to describe children who misbehave, do not follow rules, or are unmanageable.

Neurodivergent An individual who possesses unique cognitive processes through which they perceive the world differently or behave differently than the mainstream.

Recidivism Reoffending after being released from custody or during or after probation or parole.

REFERENCES AND ADDITIONAL SUGGESTED READINGS

Addiction Center (2022). Drug and alcohol slang: General drug slang. Retrieved from https://www.addictioncenter.com/drugs/drug-alcohol-slang/.

Anderson, E. R., and D. A. Hope (2008). A review of the tripartite model for understanding the link between anxiety and depression. *Clinical Psychology Review*. Vol. 28: 275–287.

APM Reports (2019). Students on the move: The children in the fields. Aug. 14. Retrieved from https://www.apmreports.org/episode/2019/08/14/the-children-in-the-fields#:~:text=Under%20federal%20law%2C%20children%20of,relatives%20during%20short%2D-term%20harvests.

Bonnie, R. J., R. L. Johnson, B. M. Chemers, and J. A. Schuck, eds. (2013). *Reforming Juvenile Justice: A Developmental Approach*. Washington, D.C.: National Academies Press. Ch. 2.

Butts, J., and J. Travis (2002). *The Rise and Fall of American Youth Violence: 1980 to 2000*. Research report. Washington, D.C.: The Urban Institute.

Cahan, E. D. (1989). Past caring: A history of U.S. preschool and education for the poor, 1820–1965. National Center for Children in Poverty, Mailman School of Public Health. New York City, NY: Columbia University.

Caron, S. L., and E. G. Moskey (2002). Changes over time in teenage sexual relationships: Comparing the high school class of 1950, 1975, and 2000. *Adolescence*. Vol. 37, issue 147: 515–526.

Center on Juvenile and Criminal Justice (CJCJ) (2022). Juvenile justice history.

Childs, M. J. (1992). *Labour's Apprentices: Working-Class Lads in Late Victorian and Edwardian England*. Montreal, Canada: McGill-Queen's University Press.

Chin, Y., and K. Patten (2021). Shifting focus from impairment to inclusion: Expanding occupational therapy for neurodivergent students to address school environments. *American Journal of Occupational Therapy*. May/June Vol. 75, issue 3: 1–7.

Dickens, C. (1838; 1992). *Oliver Twist*. Ware, England: Wordsworth Editions.

Elliott, M. R., S. M. Reilly, J. Drummond, and N. Letourneau (2002). The effect of different soothing interventions on infant crying and parent-infant interaction. *Infant Mental Health Journal*. May/June. Vol. 23, issue 3: 310–328.

Evans, B. (2013). How autism became autism: The radical transformation of a central concept of child development. *History of Human Sciences*. July. Vol. 26, issue 3: 3–31.

Finkelstein, B. (2000). A crucible of contradictions: Historical roots of violence against children in the United States. *History of Education Quarterly*. Vol. 40, issue 1: 1–21.

Gershoff, E. T., and S. A. Font (2018). Corporal punishment in U.S. schools: Prevalence, disparity of use, and status in state and federal policy. Social Policy Report. Vol. 30, issue 1. Available at https://www.ncbi.nlm.nih.gov/pmc/articles/PMC5766273/.

Hartinger-Saunders, R. M. (2008). The history of defining youth: Current implications for identifying and treating delinquent youth. *New York Sociologist*. Vol. 3: 87–106.

Hemez, P. (2020). Distributions of age at first marriage, 1960–2018. *Family Profile*. No. 9. National Center for Family and Marriage, Bowling Green University. Retrieved from https://www.bgsu.edu/ncfmr/resources/data/family-profiles/hemez-distribution-age-first-marriage-fp-20-09.html#:~:text=In%201960%2C%20men's%20median%20age,FP%2D19%2D06).

Kaestle, C. F. (1978). Social change, discipline, and the common school in early nineteenth-century. *Journal of Interdisciplinary History.* Summer. Vol. 9, issue 1: 1–17.

Kish, S. W. (2018). Hold the rod and spare the child. University of Utah Health. Dec. 17. Retrieved from https://uofuhealth.utah.edu/newsroom/news/2018/12/dd-laskey-spanking.php.

Lassiter, M. D. Impossible criminals: The suburban imperatives of America's War on Drugs. *Journal of American History.* June. Vol. 102, issue 1: 126–140.

Lerman, R. I. (2000). Are teens in low-income and welfare families working too much? Urban Institute. Nov. Series B, No. B-25. Retrieved from https://www.urban.org/sites/default/files/publication/62291/309708-Are-Teens-in-Low-Income-and-Welfare-Families-Working-Too-Much-.PDF.

Lurtz, M. R., and A. Komarow (2021). Inclusive financial well-being empowerment model for serving independent, neurodivergent individuals. *Journal of Financial Planning.* Nov. Vol. 34, issue 11: 70–81.

Mallet, C. A., P. A. Stoddard Dare, and M. M. Seck (2009). Predicting juvenile delinquency: The nexus of child maltreatment, depression, and bipolar disorder. *Social Work Faculty Publications.* School of Social Work, Cleveland State University. Retrieved from https://engagedscholarship.csuohio.edu/cgi/viewcontent.cgi?article=1006&context=clsowo_facpub.

Marcus, S. (1991). Homelessness and Dickens. *Social Research.* Spring. Vol. 58, issue 1: 93–106.

McKee, E., and L. Rapp (2014). The current status of evidence-based practice in juvenile justice. *Journal of Evidence-Based Social Work.* Vol. 11, issue 4: 308–317.

McNamara, R. H., and C. Coward Bucher (2012). *Problem Children: Special Populations in Delinquency.* Durham, NC: Carolina Academic Press.

Morse, A. (2021). U.S. births declined during the pandemic. U.S. Census Bureau. Sep. 21. Retrieved from https://www.census.gov/library/stories/2021/09/united-states-births-declined-during-the-pandemic.html#:~:text=The%20number%20of%20U.S.%20births%20has%20been%20declining%20every%20year,on%20average%200.96%25%20a%20year.

Mulvahill, E. (2019). Ways to encourage good behavior without junky prizes or sugary treats: Classroom Ideas. *We are Teachers.* Jan 16. Retrieved from https://www.weareteachers.com/ways-to-encourage-good-behavior/.

Newport Academy (2021). How to deal with a rebellious teen. Sep. 24. Retrieved from https://www.newportacademy.com/resources/restoring-families/rebellious-teen/.

Sherer, J., and N. Mast (2023). Child labor laws are under attack in states across the country: Amid increasing child labor violations, lawmakers must act to strengthen standards. Report, Economic Policy Institute. Mar 14. Retrieved from https://files.epi.org/uploads/263680.pdf.

Shichor, D. (1983). Historical and current trends in juvenile justice. *Juvenile and Family Court Journal.* Vol. 34, issue 3: 61–75.

Sibley, M. (2001). Beat the Heat: A youth program races to keep kids off the street. *Law and Order.* Apr. Vol. 49, issue 4: 60–63.

Soderberg, L. (2018). Writing the criminal child: Antebellum prison records, parenting manuals, and the rise of the incorrigible child. *Journal of Nineteenth-Century Americanists.* Vol. 6, issue 2: 307–334.

Steffes, T. L. (2012). *School, Society, and the State: New Education to Govern Modern America, 1890–1940.* Chicago, IL: University of Chicago Press.

Schwartz, I. M., M. W. Steketee, and J. A. Butts (2012). Business as usual: Juvenile justice during the 1980s. *Notre Dame Journal of Law, Ethics, and Public Policy.* Vol. 5, issue 2: 377–396.

Twenge, J. M. (2000). The Age of Anxiety? Birth cohort change in anxiety and neuroticism, 1952–1993. *Journal of Personality and Social Psychology.* Vol. 79, issue 6: 1007–1021. Available at https://www.apa.org/pubs/journals/releases/psp7961007.pdf.

United States Department of Labor (n.d.). Child labor: Children have rights. Retrieved from https://www.worker.gov/concerns/child-labor-wages/#:~:text=Federal%20child%20labor%20law%20generally,18%20in%20any%20hazardous%20occupation.

United States Department of Labor (n.d.). Parental exemption: Agricultural employment. Retrieved from https://www.dol.gov/general/topic/youthlabor/agriculturalemployment.

United States Library of Congress (n.d.). Youth in the Civil Rights Movement. Civil Rights History Project, 2009. Retrieved from https://www.loc.gov/collections/civil-rights-history-project/articles-and-essays/youth-in-the-civil-rights-movement/.

United States Supreme Court (1968). *United States v. O'Brien.* 391 U.S. 367, No. 232. Decided May 27. Retrieved from https://scholar.google.com/scholar_case?case=12229836877065678192&hl=en&as_sdt=6&as_vis=1&oi=scholarr.

University of Michigan (n.d.). Corporal punishment. Health Library, C.S. Mott Children's Hospital. Ann Harbor, MI. Retrieved from https://www.mottchildren.org/health-library/tm4923.

Whitt, C. (2021). A look at America's family farms. Report, *Farming, Research and Science.* Jul. 29. Washington, DC: U.S. Department of Agriculture.

Wiseman, L. (n.d.). Historiography: Teenage attitudes of the 1950s. Theta Beta, Towson University. *Journal of Historical Studies.* Vol. 21, 13 pp. Retrieved from https://www.oc.edu/uploads/images/documents/Wiseman-Teenage-Attitude-of-the-1950s.pdf.

Chapter **THREE**

Current Trends in Youth Deviance and Crime: Status and Other Minor Offenses

> *If you want to understand the entrepreneur, study the juvenile delinquent. The delinquent is saying with* [their] *actions, "This sucks, I'm going to do my own thing."*
>
> —Yvon Chouinard, American rock climber, founder of outdoor wear company Patagonia

Chapter Objectives

- Compare crime trends in previous decades with current forms of deviance and crime in the juvenile population.
- Distinguish between status offenses and criminal offenses committed by juveniles.
- Identify the forms of racial discrimination that minority juveniles face within the juvenile justice system.
- Outline the more common minor offenses committed by juveniles.

Key Terms

Breach of peace
Co-offend
Curfew
Cyberbullying
Disorderly conduct
Disturbing the peace
Loitering
Miranda Rights
Misdemeanor

INTRODUCTION

Chapter 2 provided a brief introduction to what we mean by delinquency. This chapter will review actual crime trends among juveniles, where available, as reported by researchers and to law enforcement and youth authorities. Of course, in the case of looking at any crime trends, the data are only as good as the quality of what is reported. What the data we do have make clear, however, is that juveniles are both more likely to commit relatively minor offenses and to have higher rates of offending as compared to adults (Tyler, 2015). This is very much in keeping with the at-risk age-group data: primarily males between the ages of 15 and 24.

We do not include a chapter in this textbook devoted solely to the study of juvenile delinquency. That would be a methodology text. However, in this chapter and elsewhere in the book, we will include some discussion of research methodology, plus some of the theoretical approaches to understanding juvenile delinquency. Chapter 4 will shine an interdisciplinary spotlight on current theoretical and observational explanations for the juvenile deviance and delinquent behaviors discussed in this chapter.

We will only briefly make note of any gender differences in offending, though we note that the rates of arrests for female and male juveniles in the justice system are converging (Ehrmann et al., 2019). Chapter 7 will go into greater depth on the differences in the historical and current rates of female[1] and male juvenile offending. Likewise, we will only touch briefly in this chapter on how schools use the concept of delinquency; Chapter 8 will take a closer look at that, with a focus on policy.

As with the adult prison population, minority juvenile delinquents are overrepresented in the juvenile justice system. It is important to note that while Black and Latinx juveniles are more likely to have negative interactions with police, they are also at higher risk for victimization by violent crimes, as indicated by the National Crime Victimization Survey (NCVS) (Tillyer and Tillyer, 2016). Children of color are also more likely to live in poverty, a variable that correlates positively with higher crime and conviction rates. So one side of the debate on how race or ethnicity matters in juvenile delinquency centers on economic circumstances and poorer communities.

[1] As there is far more sensitivity around the subject of nonconforming genders beyond the traditional binary of "female" and "male," crime patterns among those who self-identify as something other than these two will be addressed in Chapter 7. However, crime and arrest statistics still primarily use the traditional gender binary, and we will report those as they are currently identified, though we acknowledge the inaccuracies found there.

CURRENT TRENDS IN JUVENILE CRIMINAL LIFESTYLES AND DEVIANCE

Deviant behavior of juveniles is often mislabeled as delinquency by the media and by the general public, and delinquency can also be passed off as harmless youthful antics, when it should be a concern. Deviance and delinquency tend to stem from selfishness in human nature, which is somewhat normative in children and teens, and from the human desire for self-gratification (Hong et al., 2020). As a result, adolescence becomes a developmental period in which the young person embraces antisocial behaviors, while their friends and families hope and expect such behavior to end as they reach adulthood (Merrin et al., 2018; Moffitt, 2006).

Family and friends can either provide the adolescent with protection or contribute to their deviant behavior. A parent slipping their underaged child a sip of beer is also deviant, and in some cases subject to criminal law and charges of contributing to the delinquency of a minor. In a 2012 study, 20% of juveniles ages 12 to 14 reported that they got alcohol from their parents, and they often report that their first sip was given to them by their parents (Friese et al., 2012).

21st Century Trifecta: COVID-19 Pandemic, Technology, and Social Media

Three notable events over the last couple of decades dramatically changed the habits of juveniles and, in turn, their patterns of deviance. The COVID-19 pandemic led to young people having to spend a number of months in lockdown, beginning in early 2020, before development and distribution of vaccines. This obviously significantly altered the ways in which education could be delivered and limited juveniles' opportunities to socialize or work. This trend was already on the rise, however. A Pew Research Center study (Livingston, 2019) noted that teens were already spending more time sleeping and doing homework and spending their leisure time watching videos and television, rather than socializing with peers. As a result, juveniles spending more time at home had less time to misbehave in public.

Social media has been another significant factor, both before and during the pandemic. COVID-19 accelerated acceptance of social media as an escape, with psychological consequences for preteens, teenagers, and young adults. In a study of juveniles and young adults ages 12 to 20 in a WhatsApp© group during the pandemic, 40% reported feeling more stressed, and both males and females reported they were more likely to become irritated by small, normal irritations, felt like they were a burden, and at times felt lonelier or more left out than in prepandemic times (Sai et al., 2021).

As we all very well know by now, all is not what it seems on social media. Juveniles accessing social media can also create fake online identities, portraying themselves to the world how they would like to be seen, including by expressing

Young juveniles text messaging on cellphones.

toughness and claiming deviant behaviors they may not actually possess or pursue in real life (Hermawati et al., 2021). Fake accounts also provide juveniles, as well as adults, a forum for *cyberbullying* and other cybercrimes, discussed in further detail in Chapter 4. As McCormick (2014) warns, the Internet, by putting information and online access at our fingertips, removes barriers of time and distance: online crimes can be committed from anywhere.

Juveniles are also frequently crime victims online. Criminals who exploit social media, if they possess the skills, can make it difficult to detect clues that lead to the virtual scene of the crime, a computer or cell phone.

The third but not least among the dramatic changes in the lifestyles of juveniles studied here is the smart phone, with its Internet capabilities. For some time now, people under the age of 30 have reported preferring to use text messaging, rather than phone calls, to communicate (Alton, 2017). Juveniles find a number of benefits in using text messaging, including quick communication with their parental units and the ability to receive public service announcements that would not ordinarily reach them. Text messaging has allowed sensitive public service announcements to be transmitted privately, making it useful in sex education and teen pregnancy prevention programs such as the one used by the Healthy Native Youth[2] program serving Native American and Alaskan indigenous teens (Sacca et al., 2021).

Of course, for a greater number of juveniles, their parental units have put great effort into monitoring their children's cell phone use, including using software that prevents them from wandering, aimlessly or not, onto dangerous websites. Children as young as five may have regular access to smart phones, and a reported

[2] For more information on Healthy Native Youth, see https://www.healthynativeyouth.org/.

84.9% of parents monitor their use (LitLab, 2020). But unless an adult confiscates a child's cell phone at night, children conceivably can use them day and night indiscriminately.

In some instances, the immediacy of text messaging has had disastrous results. Michelle Carter, for example, was convicted in Massachusetts of involuntary manslaughter as a youthful offender after she encouraged her boyfriend Conrad Roy, via text messages, to follow through on his threats to commit suicide.[3] As a result of her prompting, he acted on his threats and tragically died in 2014. Carter received a 15-month sentence for her part in Roy's death (Taylor, 2019).

As fast as this textbook is published, youth trends have no doubt already evolved into something unknown today. Some will be harmless, short-lived flirtations with deviance, while others will remain a while. Some might have the potential to lead to juvenile criminal behavior.

COMMON DELINQUENCY: MINOR OFFENSES

We will explain the terms in these next two sections using legal definitions. Remember, however, that definitions, as well as penalties, may differ somewhat from state to state. Also different may be how, depending on the jurisdiction, the types of delinquencies are handled, including options for intervention. The following example of *loitering* illustrates how some legal definitions can be somewhat ambiguous.

Loitering

The act of loitering is when an individual or a group of people hang around somewhere public without taking part in any perceived meaningful activity or without apparent purpose. Loitering is always difficult to assess. For example, does a group of children or teenagers hanging out at a fast food restaurant longer than it takes to eat a meal constitute loitering? From a business perspective, if people are not in and out in a reasonable amount of time, space is being taken up that could be used by new paying customers. Another example might be a group of teens seemingly blocking an entrance to or aisles in a store, in turn potentially discouraging customers from entering or moving freely through the building.

But by definition, when minors loiter, what can seem to adults meaningless activity may serve a very important service: social development through socializing is meaningful, even central, to juveniles' social development. Face-to-face socializing among teens continues to be crucial to adolescent development, as

[3] The telephone number for the National Suicide and Crisis Lifeline is 988. The service is available 24 hours a day, 7 days a week.

studies indicate that online communications can lead to more bullying or predatory behavior, as well as increase existing depression and anxiety (Oprea and Stan, 2012). Students are discouraged from lingering on school campuses after school hours unless they are involved in extracurricular activities. This may leave them with few options for socializing, except at one another's homes, which may be prohibited by parents at work in the after-school hours. If parental units work weekends, evenings, or overnight shifts, their children's face-to-face socializing becomes even more challenging.

Even parents who work from home may seek to curtail children's gatherings there. We saw this during the COVID-19 pandemic, when a great number of adults started working from home. Groups of juveniles socializing, possibly noisily at times, may have been discouraged so as not to interrupt important work calls or Zoom meetings. Where then can juveniles safely and legally congregate without running afoul of the law or their parents?

In addition, unfortunately and alarmingly, racial discrimination intrudes when adults identify who is loitering and who is harmlessly hanging out with friends. In predominantly minority urban neighborhoods, young men of color who hang out together are often profiled as gang-affiliated, whether true or not (Rosenthal, 2001). For example, Chicago implemented vague policies, later challenged in the U.S. Supreme Court in *City of Chicago v. Morales*, that allowed police to disperse groups of loiterers if anyone was suspected of being a gang member, even if no gang activity was discernible (Rosenthal, 2001).

Police who may simply disperse a group of white minors suspected of loitering in more economically advantaged neighborhoods may be more likely to refer Hispanic/Latinx and black youth to authorities under the same circumstances (Claus et al., 2017). Any discrimination between white and minority juvenile suspected offenders is a breach of law itself. Under Title 18, U.S.C., §242 of the United States Code, it is unlawful for law enforcement to "willfully deprive a person of a right or privilege protected by the Constitution or laws of the United States" (U.S. Department of Justice, 2021, retrieved from https://www.justice.gov/crt/deprivation-rights-under-color-law), including the right to peaceably assemble, without prejudice to religion, race, ethnicity, gender, or disability. This includes juveniles.

Disturbing the Peace and Disorderly Conduct

Disturbing the peace charges are also vague and subjective. Often, they will go hand in hand with charges of loitering. Sometimes also referred to as *breach of peace*, the legal definition centers on individuals who are disturbing the tranquility of a public space (Legal Information Institute, 2021). Since a number of public spaces, including urban settings, beaches, and parks, are often boisterous to begin with, such charges must be put in the context of how the behavior affects others at the location. Examples include playing music too loudly, arguing, or fighting.

These offenses in other contexts might not be illegal per se, but they become so when they infringe on the personal rights of others.

Legally juveniles have as much right to hang out in public spaces as anyone else, with the exception of curfew laws. But as one law office notes (Orent Law Offices, 2016), juveniles are not always aware of how their behavior may come across to others or that they might be disturbing others with their behavior, coming across as overly disruptive, or in some cases, threatening. This is also true in a school setting. Disorderly conduct is the most common reason for arrests of students on school grounds (Rivera-Calderón, n.d.).

A disturbing the peace charge can be enhanced, depending on where the offense occurs. Additional punishment is warranted when the offender is not a student or school employee and the offense occurs on school grounds (Legal Information Institute, 2021). For example, if two parents picking up their children from school get into a fight in a carpool lane and start throwing punches, they could be charged with both assault and disturbing the peace.

Disorderly conduct similarly refers to disruptive behavior in public, but it can be a more complex charge. Again, much depends on the particular jurisdiction's legal definition. For example, California Penal Code 626-653.75,[4] Part 1, Chapter 2, classifies the following as disorderly conduct (California Legislative Information, 2021):

- An individual who solicits someone to engage in lewd or immoral behavior in any place open to the public.
- Anyone who solicits or engages in an act of prostitution.
- Individuals who are *panhandling* in public.
- Someone who loiters in or around toilets open to the public with the intent to engage in lewd or unlawful acts (e.g., drug dealing).
- Anyone who is living in a building, structure, vehicle, or place without the owner's permission.
- Public intoxication and/or being under the influence of a controlled substance or drug, so that the individual cannot exercise good judgment on their own safety or the safety of others.
- Someone who is loitering, prowling, or wandering on private property.
- Anyone unlawfully using recording devices to secretly videotape, film, or photograph an individual in a state of full or partial underdress (e.g., fitting rooms at department stores).

In Arizona, however, juveniles are accused of disorderly conduct for an entirely different set of offenses (Orent Law Offices, 2016), illustrating the lack of

[4] Amended by Stats. 2020, Ch 370, §229 (SB 1371), effective January 1, 2021 (California Legislative Information, 2021), retrieved from https://leginfo.legislature.ca.gov/faces/codes_displaySection.xhtml?sectionNum=647.&lawCode=PEN.

consistency in the meaning of the offense from state to state. Arizona includes the following in its definition:

- Failure to regularly attend school
- Graffiti
- Underage drinking
- Traffic violations
- Drug possession, including for distribution
- Assault
- Theft

Both disturbing the peace and disorderly conduct offenses are generally misdemeanors. Even so, the perception of whether these crimes were actually committed in the first place can be subject to interpretation, under a number of possible circumstances.

STATUS OFFENSES

We have already discussed status offenses to some extent in Chapter 1. These offenses are not criminal in nature, but rather arise because the accused person, due to their age, falls under the jurisdiction of juvenile courts and social services. The most common status offense is truancy. But as we have already noted, it is difficult to enforce school attendance if a parental unit is unavailable to take a child to the school campus or is otherwise unwilling to support attendance.

Schools in some states see more chronic absenteeism than others. Truancy is not simply a matter of juveniles wanting to avoid classes and school work. Children experiencing bullying will be less likely to attend school, where they must face their tormentors, even when controlling for other factors, like age, grade level, and number of friends (Owusa et al., 2022).

Other reasons for absenteeism include habitual use of alcohol and/or drugs. Juveniles wandering the streets during school hours may have illicit drug use problems (Chou et al., 2006; Forster et al., 1996). As adolescent drug use has increasingly become a global public health problem in industrialized countries, so has drug-related truancy (Chou et al., 2006). In a Youth Risk Behavior Survey (YRBS) conducted during the COVID-19 pandemic, even in schools with adequate health education programs, 42.9% of secondary school students reported alcohol use and 10.3% reported binge drinking (Parizek, 2021).

Underage drinking is one of the most serious problems affecting adolescent health and the health care system. This is not a new problem, but the age at which children begin drinking has increasingly lowered. *Alcohol use disorder (AUD)*, more commonly known as alcoholism, is used to describe mild to severe problematic alcohol consumption, defined as having impaired ability to stop or control its use, even when facing social or health consequences (National Institute on Alcohol Abuse and Alcoholism, n.d.). AUD is considered a medical and mental health condition, rather than a character flaw.

Alcohol abuse is more difficult to define. The following statistics for the United States come from a 2022 National Center for Drug Abuse study (retrieved from https://drugabusestatistics.org/teen-drug-use/):

- 7.1 million individuals ages 12 to 20 drank in the previous month.
- 25.6% of eighth graders have abused alcohol at least once.
- 61.5% of teens have abused alcohol by twelfth grade.
- 9.15% of all children ages 12 to 17 have used alcohol in the previous month.
- 2.7% of twelfth graders drink alcohol daily.
- 0.4% of eighth graders drink alcohol daily; by tenth grade, 1% drink daily.
- 407,000 teenagers ages 12 to 17 met the criteria for AUD in the previous year.

Most alarming, binge drinking behavior has been on the rise, becoming an increasingly expensive public health issue. By latest Centers for Disease Control and Prevention (CDC) data (Esser et al., 2017), underaged drinking costs the U.S. government approximately $24.3 billion a year, despite multiple laws and school-based alcohol prevention programs (Parizek, 2021; Quigley and Committee on Substance Use and Prevention, 2019). Panchal et al. (2021; Parizek, 2021) found in recent studies that alcohol consumption by adults of legal age increased during the COVID-19 pandemic, with concerns that underage alcohol consumption had likewise increased.

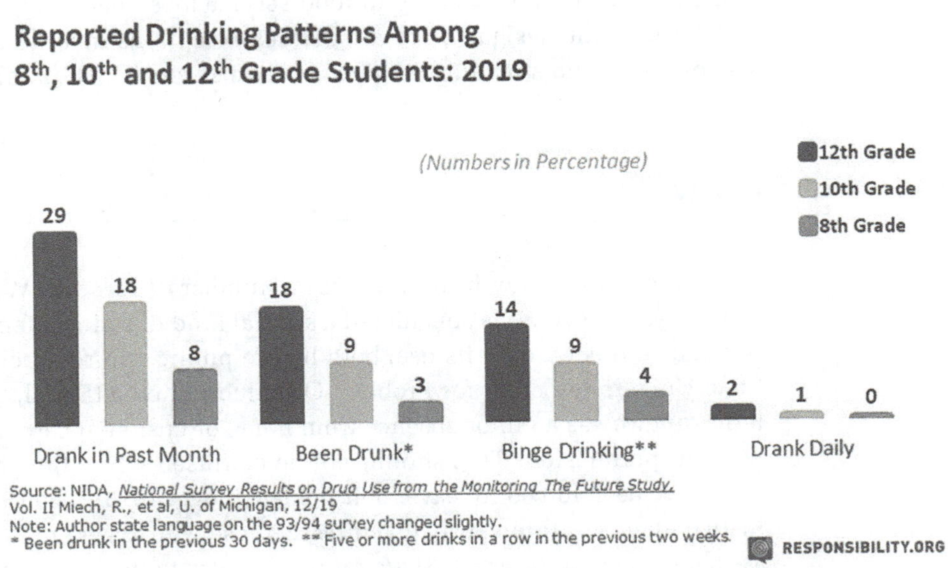

EXHIBIT 3.1 || Underaged Drinking Patterns by Grade, 2019

Curfew violations too can be an ambiguous form of status offending. As reported by the Office of Juvenile Justice and Delinquency Prevention (n.d.; hereafter OJJDP), the original intent of curfew laws in the late 1800s was to decrease crime in the immigrant youth population, making it arguably yet another xenophobic measure targeting non-Western European immigrants in general. Even today, enforcement of curfew laws is seen to be a form of racial profiling more likely to target minority youth. The highest rates of curfew citations are found in inner cities where median family incomes are lowest and the greatest number of Black families live (Sutphen and Ford, 2001). A report by the American Civil Liberties Union (2022; hereafter ACLU), for example, found that arrests for youth curfew violations were disproportionate by race in Minneapolis.

Curfew laws have fallen in and out of favor since the 19th century as a means of supplementing parental control over minor children. We should note that at times of national or community emergencies, including after a natural disaster, adults may also be subject to curfew laws to curtail any opportunistic crimes, including looting, and to clear the streets of unnecessary traffic to ease the work of emergency response teams. WWII brought about renewed interest in curfew laws, as more women aided in the war effort by working in place of male draftees at factories or in other ordinarily male-dominated professions (OJJDP, n.d.). Curfews may also be implemented or more readily enforced when juvenile crime in a community increases, alarming the public (Sutphen and Ford, 2001).

Curfew laws in the United States are set at the discretion of states and local governments. Because of this, the hours during which minors must be at home vary from place to place. Typically curfews require minors to be off the streets between 11 p.m. and 6 a.m., with some jurisdictions allowing less restricted hours during weekends and summers or to accommodate minors working outside the home (OJJDP, n.d.). Especially in food service jobs, teens' scheduled hours may go later than the designated curfew. Other exceptions include going to and from school events and attending religious or civic events (OJJDP, n.d.).

JUVENILE RUNAWAYS

Minors may run away from home for a number of reasons. When juveniles do run away, however, it is considered a special kind of status offense. Though there is some confusion over its use, both by the public and researchers, the Arizona State University Center for Problem-Oriented Policing (Dedel, 2006) defines the term *runaway* as a minor absence from home or custodial care (e.g., foster home) without permission. This should not be confused with "throwaway" juveniles who have been forced to leave their homes (Judge, 2015). The U.S. Department of Justice identifies throwaway juveniles as those who "1) are told to leave home, 2) are abandoned or deserted, 3) are refused reentry to the home after running away, or 4) are unsought by their parents after running away" (Judge, 2015, p. 262; Hammer et al., 2002).

Jeanis et al. (2019) identify five types of runaways:

- **Class 1:** Juveniles with high rates of suspensions and expulsions from school.
- **Class 2:** The "Versatile Expressive" with high levels of criminal and violent behavior.
- **Class 3:** Juveniles who self-medicate with drugs and/or alcohol.
- **Class 4:** The "Survival Strategist" who has low levels of serious criminal offending and whose principal behaviors are nonviolent and non-drug-related offenses.
- **Class 5:** Juveniles who are angry and prone to violent outbursts.

It is important to note that the behaviors found in any one of these classes could be due to mental health issues. As Jeanis et al. (2019) observed, juveniles classified as "versatile expressives" (Class 2) have the highest rate of suicide attempts, followed by those who are angry runaways (Class 5).

In some runaway cases, the child believes that their parental units' rules and standards are tyrannical, whether they are or not. However, in many cases, the child is being psychologically or physically abused by one or more members of their household. Others may find that life in school or in their neighborhoods has become intolerable, even if they are living in a supportive household. In a Florida Department of Juvenile Justice study, the key factor in predicting a child's risk of leaving home are abuse, trauma, antisocial peers, other forms of delinquency, mental health issues, and problems in school (Jeanis et al., 2019). A greater number of children reported missing are runaways and have not been abducted by non-custodial strangers, or someone the child knows other than a parent, a crime exaggerated and sensationalized in the media.

The danger for minors who run away from home or from foster care, with no destination in mind except the streets, is that they can become targets for human trafficking and victimization. In most states, it is a misdemeanor offense to harbor a runaway minor for more than 24 hours, making it additionally challenging for runaways to find safe housing. Though running away from home in itself is not a crime, there can be legal consequences both for the runaway and for their parents or guardians.

LGBTQ2S+[5] youth are at greater risk for running away or being thrown out of their homes. Parental unit tension or rejection of a child's sexual orientation or gender identification often leads to threats and homelessness, with an estimated 20% to 40% of unhoused youth identifying as LGBTQ2S+ (Judge, 2015). Child

[5] LGBTQ2S+ is an all-inclusive initialism standing for lesbian, gay, bisexual, transsexual, queer or questioning, and two spirit communities. The plus sign stands for "all other sexual or gender identifications." "Two spirit communities" refers to some indigenous tribes' recognition and acceptance of people identifying as both male and female. This is not to be confused with intersex individuals, who are born with reproductive or sexual anatomy that does not fit typical definitions of male and female.

abandonment, no matter the circumstances, is illegal. However, unhoused youth have few resources to help them take civil action or press charges against parents, foster parents, or guardians (Judge, 2015).

SUMMARY

Most of the offenses discussed in this chapter are relatively minor and can often be settled between the offender's family and the victim, if one exists, without law enforcement intervention. Other offenses are of greater concern for the potential harm to the juvenile and to others. The status offense of greatest concern is the juvenile runaway.

Minor offenses can be one-and-done events or can escalate into more serious criminal behavior, discussed in the next chapter. In the status offense of truancy,[6] it may be a brief episode, or become a periodically chronic problem. Loitering and other public nuisance laws, along with curfew laws, are less transparent than truancy, with minority juveniles more likely to be targeted with orders to disperse or with citations.

Three major developments in this century have had tremendous but not yet fully understood effects on juvenile delinquency. The COVID-19 pandemic, beginning in early 2020 and extending well into 2022, required that schools put all their courses online, creating a number of issues, from uncertainty over truancy rates to making sure that all students had access to computers to attend virtual classes. In addition, some studies indicate that alcohol consumption increased for the adult and juvenile populations during the pandemic. Alcohol abuse and AUD have continued to be a costly public health issue, with expenditures in the billions of dollars each year on prevention and treatment programs. Other types of juvenile crime, such as loitering, dropped off under the lockdown orders.

The advent of social media and text messaging have also had major impacts on juveniles in the United States, including contributing to new classes of crimes. Harassment and bullying will be discussed further in Chapter 4, along with other cybercrimes committed by juveniles. Access to social media has caused increased levels of depression and anxiety in children and adolescents.

Runaway and throwaway children continue to challenge the juvenile justice system. In many of these cases, parental units have caused the unhousing of these children and may be held legally liable for child abandonment. LGBTQ2S+ youth are particularly vulnerable to becoming unhoused, often because they are kicked out of their homes. The longer they remain on the streets without help or

[6] This author skipped her last class one day in her senior year of high school, after getting into an argument with her then-boyfriend. In spite of her mother working for the school district and trying to intervene on her behalf, she received detention after school, during which she was required to pick up trash on campus. Needless to say, this was indeed a one-and-done incident, as picking up trash on campus was stigmatizing. Everyone knew that you had detention.

intervention, runaway and throwaway minors become increasingly at risk of being exploited and victimized or may victimize others to survive. Misclassifying runaway and throwaway children as criminals, rather than as what they are—at-risk youth—is a major problem.

IN THE MEDIA

Bar Association Admission and Juvenile Arrest Records

To practice law in any given state, future lawyers must pass a bar examination. The New York State Bar Association recently came under fire for a question on its admissions application. Question 26 asks for information on juvenile and adult arrest and criminal records, including citations and tickets, with no follow-up question as to whether an arrest resulted in conviction (Brown, 2022). A copy of the Application for Admission to Practice as an Attorney and Counselor-at-Law in the State of New York is available at https://www.nybarexam.org/admission/B-Bar_Admissions-Questionaire.pdf.[7] New York State Bar Association president, T. Andrew Brown, contends that the question is illegal (Brown, 2022).

However, the bar exam is not the only gatekeeping tool making sure lawyers are well-prepared to practice law. Other barriers may include juvenile arrest and delinquency records. Unsealed juvenile records can result in other discrimination, including in military service and finding housing or employment, depending on the severity of the charges or adjudication (Coleman, 2020).

The content of juvenile arrest and adjudication records can be protected in three ways (Coleman, 2020):

- The individual can request that their records be sealed at age 18 or after they have served their sentence, whichever comes first. Records are not automatically sealed.
- Juvenile records can be expunged, which means that the public cannot access the information. The process by which a juvenile record can be expunged varies from state to state.
- The individual can request that their juvenile record remain confidential, with only limited public access permitted.

The New York State Bar Association is not the only party guilty of asking questions about juvenile and adult arrests. Often employment applications will ask if the applicant has ever been arrested. Unfortunately, the general public, employers included, often fail to distinguish between arrest and conviction records. As Brown (2022) argues, often these questions unfairly discourage minority applicants from

[7] By the time this book is published, the question may have already been modified.

even attempting to enter law school, as they are more likely to have been targeted for citations and arrests, particularly if they grew up in an urban center.

SOURCES

Brown, T. A. (2022). "Bar admission question is illegal and harms diversity." *Bloomberg Law.* Feb 16. Retrieved from https://news.bloomberglaw.com/us-law-week/bar-admission-question-is-illegal-and-harms-diversity.

Coleman, A. R. (2020). "Expunging juvenile records: Misconceptions, collateral consequences, and emerging practices." *Juvenile Justice Bulletin*, Office of Juvenile Justice and Delinquency Prevention (OJJDP). Dec. Retrieved from https://ojjdp.ojp.gov/publications/expunging-juvenile-records.pdf.

INTERNATIONAL PERSPECTIVES

General Juvenile Delinquency in Thailand

Thailand is a popular and exotic destination for Western tourists, to whom it seems to have liberal laws. This could not be further from the truth, however, at least from the standpoint of what laws are on the books. As an example, the consequences of being caught littering in certain designated areas, including popular beaches, can be hefty, at $3,190 and up to a year in jail (Sylvester, 2020). Prohibition on the sale of alcoholic beverages is strictly enforced, along with laws targeting illegal drug use and sales. If caught, the Thailand court and correctional system is unforgiving, no matter one's nationality, and Thailand has a reputation as having some of the harshest prison conditions in Asia (Hansen, 2022).

Traditionally, juvenile cases in Thailand have been decided in committees, rather than in a formal court system. The committees have historically been made up of village elders with little to no formal education or legal expertise (Attayuki, 1977). Many of the decisions made in these committees were based on a religious moral standard, with an eye toward rehabilitating juvenile offenders (Attayuki, 1977). The Instituting Juvenile Courts and Juvenile Procedure Act (B.E. 2494, 1951) moved away from committees (although some are still run by village elders in more rural parts of Thailand) and created a system separate from adult courts (Ukris, 2001).

In Thailand, the lowest age at which one can face criminal charges is eight. Children under that age are not subject to criminal liability. Children ages 8 to 14 cannot be punished, and for juveniles 15 to 17, the courts may consider individual attributes that warrant punishment (Sukpanich, 2012; Ukris, 2001; UNICEF, n.d.). Even for more serious crimes warranting a maximum sentence of five years for juvenile offenders, cases are referred to rehabilitation programs; the children do not enter the justice system (Tongkachok et al., 2021). The intention behind automatic referral to rehabilitation is to remain within international standards, as prescribed by the United Nations and other humanitarian organizations (Tongkachok et al., 2021). For the most serious criminal cases, subject to maximum sentences between 5 and 20 years in prison, the juvenile will be referred to the juvenile court system.

Because of the unique features of the Thai juvenile justice system, statistics for juvenile crimes are a bit hazy. In spite of strict laws, cities in Thailand are plagued with high rates of prostitution and human and drug trafficking, and juveniles are suspected of being both perpetrators and victims in all these types of crimes. Prostitution is illegal in Thailand, but the laws are vague and go largely unenforced, with a number of red-light districts and other sex-focused venues found in urban centers (*World Population Review*, 2022).

Common juvenile offenses seen in the United States are also seen in Thailand and similarly result in time spent in custody; examples include burglary, drug-related offenses, assault, school-related offenses, and public disorder (Sukyirun, 2016). A key focus of delinquency prevention in Thailand, as in the U.S., are urban youth gangs. Thai juveniles view gangs as a way to "fit in," even if that means perpetrating violent crimes (Cohen, 2017).

SOURCES

Attayuki, C. (1977). "Juvenile justice system in Thailand and the United States—A limited comparison." *NCJ.* No. 72118, National Criminal Justice Reference Service. Washington, DC: U.S. Department of Justice, Office of Justice Programs.

Cohen, A. (2017). "Youth gangs, violence, and local culture in Chiang Mai, Northern Thailand." *Journal of Contemporary Ethnography.* Vol. 47, issue 4: 484–507.

Hansen, L. P. (2022). *Introduction to Penology and Corrections.* Bluesprings, MO: Aspen Publishing Company, Inc. Forthcoming.

Sukpanich, T. (2012). "Rising youth crime levels confound justice system." *Bangkok Post.* Jan. 22. Retrieved from https://www.bangkokpost.com/thailand/special-reports/276249/rising-youth-crime-levels-confound-justice-system.

Sukyirun, P. (2016). "Biosocial interaction and juvenile delinquency behaviors of Thai juvenile delinquents." *International Journal of Criminal Justice Science.* Vol. 11, issue 2: 100–113.

Sylvester, P. (2020). "12 Laws in Thailand: How to stay out of jail." *World Nomads.* Feb. 1. Retrieved from https://www.worldnomads.com/travel-safety/southeast-asia/thailand/a-travellers-guide-to-thailands-laws#drug-laws-in-thailand.

Tongkachok, K., A. Samati, and T. Tongkachok (2021). "Restorative juvenile justice system in the southeast border of Thailand." *Psychology and Education.* Vol. 58, issue 2: 2544–2556.

Ukris, D. (2001). Juvenile justice system in Thailand. 118 International Training Course. United Nations Far East Institute for Crime Prevention (UNFEI). Jul. Retrieved from https://www.unafei.or.jp/publications/pdf/RS_No59/No59_22PA_Ukris.pdf.

UNICEF (n.d.). Section 407: Juvenile justice system, Thailand. Legal age limits, State Party Report. Retrieved from https://www.unicef-irc.org/portfolios/documents/446_thailand.htm#:~:text=Thai%20law%20limits%20children's%20criminal,not%20liable%20to%20criminal%20punishment.

World Population Review (2022). Countries where prostitution is legal, 2022. Retrieved from https://worldpopulationreview.com/country-rankings/countries-where-prostitution-is-legal.

CHAPTER DISCUSSION QUESTIONS

1. When does juvenile behavior, some of which is normative for adolescents, cross the line from being merely a nuisance to becoming a criminal act? Examples?
2. Why might the COVID-19 pandemic contribute to increases in underaged drinking and illegal drug use?
3. How have text messaging and social media contributed to minor juvenile offending? Note: More serious juvenile cybercrimes will be discussed in Chapter 4.
4. What in the past few decades has contributed to zero-tolerance policies in schools, to the extent that children as young as five have been handcuffed and arrested for acting up in class?
5. As argued by scholars and policy makers, are minority juveniles more likely to be targeted for citations and arrest because of their race or ethnicity? Or is it a question of targeting poor people in general? Note: This may require doing some research on arrest statistics, both in the adult and juvenile populations.
6. One argument that teenagers make regarding curfew is to ask what prevents them from misbehaving before curfew. Why are juvenile curfew laws necessary?
7. As many juveniles do not understand their Miranda Rights when they are read to them, what other ways could they be protected or prevented from incriminating themselves before or after arrest?

GLOSSARY

Breach of peace When one or more individuals behave in a public space or private home in a way that is disturbing those around them. Examples: Use of obscene or abusive language in a public space, playing loud music late at night, or obstructing vehicular or pedestrian traffic. Synonymous with "disturbing the peace" and violating public peace or order. See *Disorderly conduct.*

Co-offend When two or more individuals participate together in the commission of a crime.

Curfew Remaining outside of the home before or after a designated legal time period (e.g., 11 p.m. to 6 a.m.). Exceptions for juveniles include outside employment that requires being at work outside of curfew hours.

Cyberbullying Use of electronic means, including text messaging, social media, and emails, in order to intimidate, threaten, harass, or embarrass an intended target.

Disorderly conduct Similar to breach of peace violations, disorderly conduct is when an individual behaves in a way that is intended to cause public alarm or create a public nuisance, including fighting or threatening violent behavior.

Examples: public drunkenness, rioting, or a demonstration where participants refuse to disperse once asked by law enforcement to do so. See *Breach of peace*.

Disturbing the peace See *Breach of peace*; *Disorderly conduct*

Loitering Remaining in a public place (e.g., a park or business), seemingly without purpose, for a prolonged amount of time. Not illegal per se, unless posted in a public area.

Miranda Rights A police enforcement procedure, established in 1966 in response to the U.S. Supreme Court decision in *Miranda v. Arizona*. A suspect, including a juvenile, has the legal rights to legal counsel, to have that attorney present during questions, to refuse to answer questions after arrest, and to have an attorney (i.e., public defender) provided if the suspect cannot afford one.

Misdemeanor A punishable offense, varying from state to state, depending on the type of crime, that on average results in less than a year in jail. Misdemeanors, if convicted or adjudicated, are more likely to result in fines, probation, community service, and/or referral to alcohol, substance abuse treatment for both juveniles and adults.

REFERENCES AND ADDITIONAL SUGGESTED READINGS

Alton, L. (2017). "Phone calls, texts, or email?: Here's how Millennials prefer to communicate." *Forbes*. May 11. Retrieved from https://www.forbes.com/sites/larryalton/2017/05/11/how-do-millennials-prefer-to-communicate/?sh=ecd98066d6fd.

American Civil Liberties Union (ACLU) (2022). "Picking up the pieces: A Minneapolis case study." Retrieved from https://www.aclu.org/issues/racial-justice/race-and-criminal-justice/picking-pieces.

Chou, L., C. Ho, C. Chen, and W. J. Chen (2006). "Truancy and illicit drug use among adolescents surveyed via street outreach." *Addictive Behaviors*. Vol. 31: 149–154.

Claus, R. E., S. Vidal, and M. Harmon (2017). "Racial and ethnic disparities in handling juvenile arrests." Research report, U.S. Department of Justice. Document No 250804. Washington, DC: Office of Justice Programs' National Criminal Justice Reference Service.

Dedel, K. (2006). "The Problem with Juvenile Runaways." In *Juvenile Runaways*, Guide No. 37. ASU Center for Problem Oriented Policing. Retrieved from https://popcenter.asu.edu/content/juvenile-runaways-0#:~:text=Juveniles%20run%20away%20from%20home,foster%20care%20or%20group%20homes.&text=%C2%A7%20The%20term%20%22runaway%22%20typically,by%20a%20parent%20or%20guardian.

Ehrmann, S., N. Hyland, and C. Puzzanchera (2019). "Girls in the Juvenile Justice System." Juvenile Justice Statistics, Office of Justice Programs, *National Report Series Bulletin*. April. Washington, DC: U.S. Department of Justice.

Esser, M. B., H. Clayton, Z. Demissie, D. Kanny, and R. D. Brewer (2017). "Current and binge drinking among high school students—United States, 1991–2015." Centers for Disease Control and Prevention (CDC). *Morbidity and Mortality Weekly Report*, Vol. 66, issue 18 (May 12): 474–478.

Flores, R., and S. Weisfeld (2020). "Body camera videos show 6-year-old sobbing and pleading during arrest." CNN. Feb. 26. Retrieved from https://www.cnn.com/2020/02/26/us/body-camera-video-6-year-old-arrested/index.html.

Friese, B., J. W. Grube, R. S. Moore, and V. K. Jennings (2012). "Parents' rules about underage drinking: A qualitative study of why parents let teens drink." *Journal of Drug Education.* Vol. 42, issue 4 (July): 379–391.

Frontline (n.d.). "Juvenile Justice: The reasons for treating juveniles differently." Public Broadcasting Service (PBS), New Mexico. Retrieved from https://www.pbs.org/wgbh/pages/frontline/shows/juvenile/bench/different.html.

Hammer, H., D. Finkelhor, and A. J. Sedlak (2002). *National Incidence Studies of Missing, Abducted, Runaway, and Throwaway Children: Runaway/Throwaway Children: National Estimates and Characteristics.* Office of Juvenile Justice and Delinquency Prevention (OJJDP). Oct. Washington, D.C.: U.S. Department of Justice.

Hermawati, T., R. Setyaningsih, and R. P. Nugraha (2021). "Teen motivation to create fake identity account on Instagram social media." *International Journal of Multicultural and Multireligious Understanding.* Vol. 8, issue 4: 87–98.

HG Legal Resources (n.d.). "Juvenile criminal conduct—At what age are they not liable?" Retrieved from https://www.hg.org/legal-articles/juvenile-criminal-conduct-at-what-age-are-they-not-liable-49366.

Hong, H., Y. Han, and D. H. Lee (2020). "Unselfish motives and deviance: An empirical examination of social concern theory among South Korean adolescents." *Deviant Behavior.* Vol. 41, issue 6: 705–717.

Jeanis, M. N., B. H. Fox, and C. Muniz (2019). "Revitalizing profiles of runaways: A latent class analysis of delinquent runaway youth." *Child and Adolescent Social Work Journal.* Vol. 36, issue 2 (April): 171–187.

Judge, C. (2015). "Thrown away for being gay: The abandonment of LGBT youth and their lack of legal recourse." *Indian Journal of Law and Social Equality.* Vol. 3, issue 2, Article 5 (Spring): 260–280.

Laird, L. (2016). "Miranda for youngsters: Police routinely read juveniles their rights, but do kids really understand them?" *American Bar Association Journal.* Vol. 102, issue 6: 16–18.

Legal Information Institute (2021). "Disturbing the peace." Wex Definitions Team, Cornell Law School. July. Retrieved from https://www.law.cornell.edu/wex/disturbing_the_peace.

Lenthang, M. (2021). "5-year old boy allegedly detained, handcuffed and threatened by police." NBC News. March 27. Retrieved from https://abcnews.go.com/US/year-boy-allegedly-detained-handcuffed-threatened-maryland-police/story?id=76721492.

Livingston, G. (2019). "The way U.S. teens spend their time is changing but differences between boys and girls persist." Pew Research Center. Jan. 20. Retrieved from https://www.pewresearch.org/fact-tank/2019/02/20/the-way-u-s-teens-spend-their-time-is-changing-but-differences-between-boys-and-girls-persist/.

Lynch, J. P. (2002). "Trends in juvenile violent offending: An analysis of victim survey data." *Juvenile Justice Bulletin*, OJJDP. NCJ 191052. Oct. Retrieved from https://www.ojp.gov/pdffiles1/ojjdp/191052.pdf.

Merrin, G. J., J. P. Davis, D. Berry, and D. L. Espelage (2018). "Developmental changes in violent behaviors from early to late adolescence: Associations with parental monitoring and peer deviance." *Psychology of Violence.* Vol. 9, issue 2: 196–208.

Miranda Rights (n.d.). Miranda Rights. Retrieved from http://www.mirandarights.org/index.html.

Moffitt, T. E. (2006). "Life-course persistent versus adolescence-limited antisocial behavior." In *Developmental Psychopathology: Risk, Disorder, and Adaptation*, vol. 3, 2d ed., eds. D. Cicchetti and D. J. Cohen. New York: Wiley.

National Institute on Alcohol Abuse and Alcoholism (NIAAA) (n.d.). "Understanding alcohol use disorder." National Institute of Health. Retrieved from https://www.niaaa.nih.gov/publications/brochures-and-fact-sheets/understanding-alcohol-use-disorder.

Office of Juvenile Justice and Delinquency Prevention (OJJDP) (n.d.). Juvenile justice reform initiatives in the states, 1994–1996. U.S. Department of Justice. Retrieved from https://ojjdp.ojp.gov/sites/g/files/xyckuh176/files/pubs/reform2/ch2_c.html.

Office of Juvenile Justice and Delinquency Prevention (OJJDP) (2016). "Gun violence and youth." *Literature Review*, Model Programs Guide. U.S. Department of Justice. Retrieved from https://ojjdp.ojp.gov/mpg/literature-review/gun-violence-and-youth.pdf.

Office of Juvenile Justice and Delinquency Prevention (OJJDP) (1999). Report to Congress on Juvenile Violence Research. NCJ 176976. U.S. Department of Justice. July. Retrieved from https://ojjdp.ojp.gov/sites/g/files/xyckuh176/files/pubs/jvr/contents.html.

Oprea, C., and A. Stan (2012). "Adolescents' perceptions of online communication." *Procedia—Social and Behavioral Sciences.* Vol. 46: 4089–4091.

Orent Law Offices (2016). "Disturbing the peace—How the Arizona Justice System Looks at the Young Offender." Blog. Jan 28. Retrieved from https://www.orentcriminallaw.com/blog/young-offenders-disturbing-the-peace/.

Owusa, D. N., K. O. Ansah, N. E. Y. Dey, H. O. Duah, P. Agbadi (2022). "Bullying and truancy among school-going adolescents in Timor-Leste: Results from the 2015 global school-based health survey." *Heliyon.* Vol. 8, issue 1: e08797.

Panchal, N., R. Kamal, C. Cox, and R. Garfield (2021). The implications of COVID-19 for mental health and substance use. Kaiser Family Foundation.

Parizek, R. A. (2021). "Health literacy does not protect against underage alcohol use during the COVID-19 pandemic." *Journal of Psychosocial Nursing and Mental Health Services.* Vol. 59, issue 12 (Dec.): Medline.

Puzzanchera, C. (2020). Juvenile arrests, 2018. Juvenile Justice Statistics, *National Report Series Bulletin.* June. Washington, D.C.: U.S. Department of Justice, Office of Justice Programs.

Quigley, J., and the Committee on Substance Use and Prevention (2019). "Alcohol use by youth." *Pediatrics.* Vol. 144, issue 1: 1–6.

Richards, K. (2011). "What makes juvenile offenders different from adult offenders?" Australian Institute of Criminology. *Trends and Issues in Crime and Criminal Justice,* No 409. Updated Aug. 27, 2021.

Rivera-Calderón, N. (n.d.). "Arrested at the schoolhouse gate: Criminal school disturbances law and children's rights at school." National Lawyers Guild. Retrieved from https://www.nlg.org/nlg-review/article/arrested-at-the-schoolhouse-gate-criminal-school-disturbance-laws-and-childrens-rights-in-schools/.

Rosenthal, L. (2001). "Gang loitering and race." *Journal of Criminal Law and Criminology,* Northwestern University School of Law. Vol. 91 (2000–2001): 99–160.

Sacca, L., S. C. Rushing, C. Markham, R. Shegog, M. Peskin, B. Hernandez, A. Gaston, M. Singer, N. Trevino, C. C. Correa, C. Jessen, J. Williamson, and J. Thomas (2021). "Empower sensitive conversations with American Indian and Alaska Native teens." *International Journal of Environmental Research in Public Health.* Vol. 18, issue 17 (Aug. 30): 9126.

Sai, K. G., R. Jalaja, A. Amutha, U. Venkatesan, F. M. Anjana, and R. Unnikrishnan (2021). "Psychological impact of COVID-19 in a social media group." *Journal of Diabetology.* Vol. 12, issue 2 (Jan.): 232–236.

Sutphen, R. D., and J. Ford (2001). "The effectiveness and enforcement of teen curfew law." *Journal of Sociology and Social Welfare.* Vol. 28, issue 1 (March): 55–78.

Taylor, K. (2019). "What we know about the Michelle Carter suicide texting case." *The New York Times.* July 9. Retrieved from https://www.nytimes.com/2019/07/09/us/michelle-carter-i-love-you-now-die.html.

Tillyer, M. S., and R. Tillyer (2016). "Race, ethnicity, and adolescent violent victimization." *Journal of Youth and Adolescence.* Vol. 45: 1497–1511.

Tyler, T. R. (2015). "Why trust matters with juveniles." *American Journal of Orthopsychiatry.* Vol. 85, issue 6, suppl.: S93–S99.

United States Department of Justice (2021). Deprivation of rights under color of law. Civil Rights Division. May 31. Retrieved from https://www.justice.gov/crt/deprivation-rights-under-color-law.

United States Supreme Court (1966). *Miranda v. Arizona*, 384 US 436. June 13. Retrieved from https://www.oyez.org/cases/1965/759.

Chapter **FOUR**

Current Youth Deviance and Crime Trends — Serious Offenses

> *When a juvenile commits a heinous crime, the State can exact forfeiture of some of the most basic liberties, but the State cannot extinguish his* [or her, their] *life and his* [or her, their] *potential to attain a mature understanding of his [or her, their] own humanity.*
>
> — Anthony Kennedy, retired associate justice of the Supreme Court of the United States

Chapter Objectives

- Review the most common serious crimes committed by juveniles.
- Distinguish between forms of stealing committed by juveniles, including theft, burglary, and larceny.
- Highlight juvenile cybercriminals, including digital pirates and cyberbullies.
- Introduce recent and emerging trends in juvenile offending.

Key Terms

Arson
Burglary
Computer hacking
Criminal trespassing
Dark Web
Digital piracy
Embezzlement
Felony
Gang enhancement laws
Intellectual property
Joyride
Kleptomania
Larceny
Megan's Law
Panhandling
Robbery
Sexting
Shoplifting
Theft
Unauthorized snacking
White-collar crime

INTRODUCTION

When considering the differences between minor and serious offenses, severity can be in the eye of the beholder, measured by the size of financial loss or physical injury, or set by legal definition. In this book, the most serious offenses, including criminal assault and homicide, will be covered in Chapter 5 where we discuss the most extreme form of juvenile delinquency: violent offending. This chapter focuses on more common serious crimes committed by juveniles. Juvenile offenders may follow one of two future arcs: continuing their antisocial and criminal behaviors into adulthood or leaving behind their youthful criminal activities as they mature (He et al., 2022). The more violent the offenses when young, the more likely the juvenile is to continue criminal offending, both violent and nonviolent, into adulthood, unless there are successful interventions. We of course cannot discount a third option for the trajectory of juvenile delinquency, particularly for those who are gang-affiliated: a young life ended with a senseless death.

Property and violent crimes committed by minors have been on the decline over the past several decades. Theft, robbery, and burglary, the most common serious offenses committed by juveniles, are the focus of this chapter.

THEFT, ROBBERY, AND BURGLARY

The general legal definition of theft is taking property without permission, with the intent to deprive the victim or victims of the use of their property (Legal Information Institute, n.d.). An example would be stealing someone's mobile phone. The term *larceny* is sometimes interchangeable with theft, depending on state laws, but it is more likely to be associated with physical property, whereas theft can also include *intellectual property*, identity theft, or fraud.

Theft may not be intended to be permanent. Other types of theft are committed where the thief intends to use an item for a limited period of time. Teenagers may steal a car to take it for a *joyride*, for example, intending to return it to the lawful owner or abandoning it somewhere it can be easily found by law enforcement. Persistent stealing can be a sign of serious psychological and emotional problems (American Academy of Child and Adolescent Psychiatry, 2014) no matter how long the thief intends to keep the item they stole.

States distinguish between misdemeanor theft and felony theft on the basis of the value of the stolen property, which can vary from state to state. A number of other types of theft, such as identity theft, are far less likely to be committed by juveniles.

Shoplifting

Shoplifting is not uncommon among teens and may simply be due to impulsivity, the desire to impress deviant peers, or get attention from parental units. In some rare cases, shoplifting behavior is part of a psychiatric disorder, such as *kleptomania*.

Unauthorized snacking at grocery or convenience stores is a common shoplifting offense. An adult or juvenile who in a store helps themselves to a self-serve pastry item or produce, eating it while browsing the aisles with no intention of ever paying for it, has shoplifted. An indication of unauthorized snacking is empty food wrappers hidden on a grocery store shelf. We should note that in most stores, it is perfectly acceptable, though not terribly common, to open a box of something and munch on the contents while shopping, as long as that item is included among other purchases at check out.

Though penalties may vary, most jurisdictions consider unauthorized snacking to be a misdemeanor offense. However, it represents a loss to the store owner, which is commonly passed on in higher prices to customers to offset inventory shrinkage (Hansen, 2020), thus victimizing consumers. Employees, including juvenile workers, are more likely to steal merchandise from their retail employers than are shoppers (Hansen, 2020).

Juvenile shoplifting.

Legal responses to shoplifting vary depending on the value of the item or items stolen; possibilities include arrest, detention by store security, or release to parental custody after the stolen property has been returned. More severe penalties beyond legal consequences may occur in some instances. The Disney Parks in the United States, including Disneyland and Walt Disney World, are notorious for having tight security and pressing charges; they will automatically notify law enforcement in cases of suspected shoplifting (Tan, 2007). Suspects can be banned from ever entering a Disney property again, even if they are not found guilty in a court of law, and they can be subject to trespassing charges if they do try to enter a park (Vu, 2021; Family Vacation Design, n.d.). Admittedly, banning individuals from amusement parks or stores is difficult to enforce.

Embezzlement

We don't ordinarily think of juveniles as being involved with *white-collar crime*. However, employed juveniles may be accused of *embezzlement* if they steal money, typically cash, from their employers. For example, a juvenile working a cash register in the course of their job may steal from the cash drawer, committing embezzlement.

A number of safeguards exist against embezzlement by employees. First, cash registers are now primarily electronic, with records of all sales, and employee productivity is carefully monitored. Even the speed at which employees check out customers is digitally recorded. Second, because customers (except in cash-only businesses)[1] increasingly make fewer cash purchases, using credit cards or debit cards for even small transactions, employees have fewer opportunities to steal cash from store registers.

Embezzlers, including juveniles who steal cash from their workplace, often think that they will be able to covertly replace it undetected once they have the money to do so (Hansen, 2020). In other words, they may view the theft as a temporary, although unauthorized loan from their employer. Others, of course, may have no intention of replacing the stolen money. In a rather elaborate scheme, two Dollar General employees, one of whom was 17 years old at the time, allegedly staged what appeared to be an ordinary store robbery in Mobile, Alabama (Popowski, 2022). Such offenses are challenging for business owners. Much of a business's inventory and cash losses can be attributed to employee theft, making employee/employer relationships difficult or resulting in high employee turnover (Hansen, 2020).

[1] Cash-only businesses may be seen as a bit suspect, as they can be used as laundering operations by organized crime groups (Hansen, 2020). However, to avoid the cost of fees to banks and other credit agencies when accepting credit cards or debit cards for purchases, some smaller businesses may be legitimately cash-only.

Motor Vehicle Theft

The Federal Bureau of Investigation (FBI) identifies motor vehicle theft as stealing or attempting to steal self-propelled vehicles that run on land, including cars, trucks, buses, SUVs, and snowmobiles, without the permission of the owner (FBI, n.d.). It excludes the theft of trains, farm or construction equipment, or watercraft (FBI, n.d.). Rates of motor vehicle theft have dropped since the 1990s, as indicated in Exhibit 4.1.

In the post-WWII years, a common form of motor vehicle theft committed by juveniles and young adults was *joyriding*, a term we introduce earlier in this chapter. In the 1960s, auto manufacturers began to install more security features, as required by the 1968 Motor Vehicle Safety Standard No. 114, including better door and ignition locks (Dixon and Farrell, 2020). In the 1990s, there was an alarming increase in motor vehicle thefts, primarily in urban areas, some of which were associated with gang violence. These included *carjacking*, where drivers were forcibly removed from their vehicle, often at gunpoint. Manufacturers responded again with additional safety features, including requiring ignition keys with RFID chips[2] to start vehicles (City of Portland Crime Prevention Program, 2017).

In 2021 and 2022, a new rash of vehicle thefts began, some perpetrated by juveniles. There has reportedly been a 510% increase in major U.S. cities since the

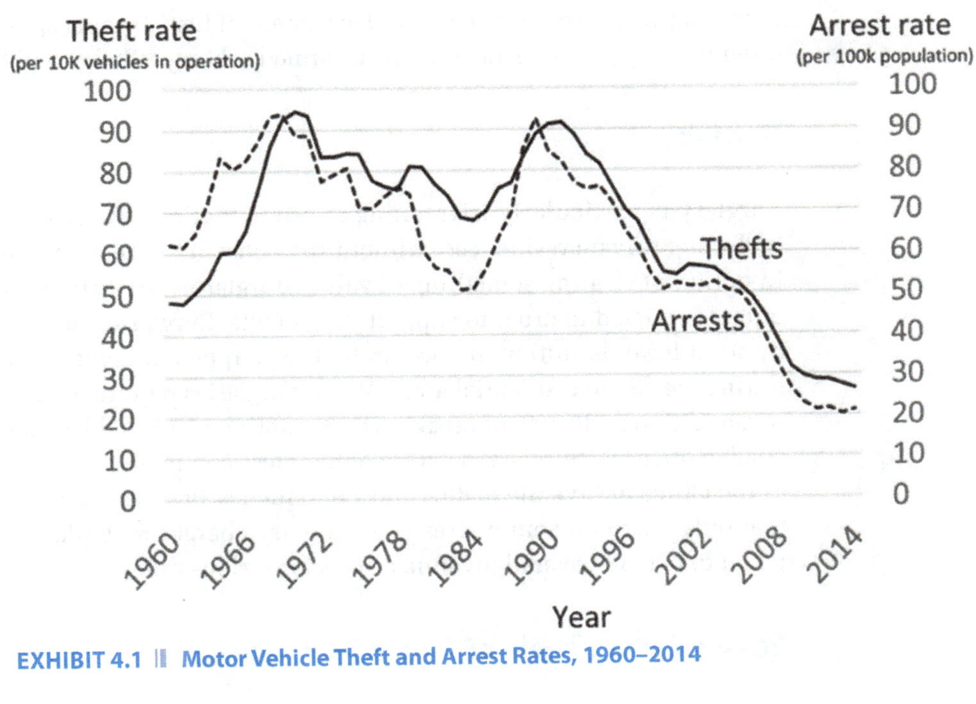

EXHIBIT 4.1 ‖ Motor Vehicle Theft and Arrest Rates, 1960–2014

[2] Radio Frequency Identification or RFID chips include a tracking system meant to discourage theft (IDENTIV, 2021).

onset of the COVID-19 pandemic, attributed to changes in driving habits (Thompson, 2022). In November 2021, an 11-year-old boy was arrested in Chicago on suspicion of being a chronic offender in auto thefts and charged with one felony count of armed aggravated vehicle hijacking (Gallardo, 2021). In incidents involving juvenile offenders in Peoria, Illinois, in February 2022, eight juveniles were taken into custody, accused of aggravated vehicle hijacking, aggravated battery, and entering a running car with a child and adult passenger inside, in addition to three other alleged motor vehicle thefts, including a carjacking (Howell, 2022). Within the same week, three female juveniles in Portage County, Ohio, led police in a chase, allegedly in a stolen car; the driver among them was arrested and charged with theft and operating a vehicle without a license (Bingel, 2022).

Robbery

Robbery is a far more serious offense than theft, even if the value of the items stolen during a theft is greater. In a robbery, items are stolen from victims by force or threat of force if the items are not readily relinquished. Because of the imminent danger of bodily and psychological harm during a robbery, it is a felony offense in most jurisdictions. In robberies, the offender has no intention of ever returning the property to its rightful owner. In an armed robbery the perpetrator carries a weapon, such as a knife, gun, or blunt instrument (HG Legal Resources, n.d.). Alarmingly, according to the U.S. Department of Justice, guns are the weapon most often used by juveniles in committing armed robbery (Sheley and Wright, 2000).

Burglary

Burglary is particularly frightening to crime victims. Burglars enter a building, including private residences, without the consent of the owner, usually with the intention of stealing something of value. Burglaries, like other forms of theft, are often conducted in order to support drug habits. Burglaries can occur day or night, by strict legal definition, but generally they happen at night in commercial areas; during the day in residential areas. When burglaries require forced entry of a building, additional charges of breaking and entering can be added to the list of prosecutable offenses. Burglary is a form of theft less commonly committed by juveniles, as the Office of Juvenile Justice and Delinquency Prevention (OJJDP, n.d.) reported that only 20,700 juvenile arrests on burglary charges took place in 2019, as compared to 696,620 overall juvenile arrests for serious offenses.

Possession and Sale of Stolen Property

Thieves do not always sell the items they steal. Particularly in cases of shoplifting, the stolen property is often intended for personal use. Juveniles who steal property may, however, intend to sell the item or items for cash. Any juvenile or adult who buys or is given these items, wittingly or unwittingly, could be subject to arrest for receiving stolen property.

Sale of stolen property can be a simple transaction between two people, the thief and the buyer. Particularly in a theft associated with organized crime, a broker, commonly called a *fence*, may be involved. Brokers know the items are stolen, but for a percentage of the sale, they find buyers they believe to be trustworthy who will not notify the police. Sometimes a youth gang, organized for criminal activities, may be involved. The black market for stolen goods is murky, and made more so with capability to sell stolen items online.

CRIMINAL TRESPASSING

Criminal trespassing differs from loitering in several ways. Loitering usually takes place in public spaces. Criminal trespassing, on the other hand, is unlawful entry on public or private property, with or without intent to commit a subsequent crime. Criminal trespass can be coupled with loitering, as in the example of teens hanging out in an abandoned building. Unhoused[3] juveniles in search of shelter are a more common example of criminal trespassing.

WEAPONS OFFENSES

As noted above, the most common weapon used by juveniles in committing armed robbery is a hand gun. State laws differ on the age at which firearms can be legally possessed, but U.S. federal law, in the Youth Handgun Safety Act (1993), mandates that all firearms in the home be secured away from minors, and except in a limited number of circumstances, no one under 18 may possess a handgun or have one knowingly sold, delivered, traded, or otherwise transferred to them (U.S. Bureau of Alcohol, Tobacco, and Firearms, 2017; U.S. Senate H.R. 3098, 1993). In some states, including Florida, firearm enhancement statutes may be applied as well, making the penalty for a crime more severe if a weapon was used in its commission (Florida Statutes, 2021, Title XLVI, Ch 790).

Minors can also be charged with weapons possession if they are found to be illegally carrying knives or other objects that can cause bodily harm. Handgun open carry laws in some states apply to adults with specialized gun permits. More

[3] The unhoused or houseless are more commonly called homeless, as well as other more derogatory terms, including vagrants and derelicts. Increasingly, however, it is considered more humane to describe those without permanent shelter, including juveniles, adults, and families without homes, as unhoused or houseless.

recently in some states, a permit is not even required to carry a firearm for qualified individuals, as in the example of more liberalized firearm laws in Texas. A juvenile carrying a weapon, including a knife even for self-defense, can be charged with weapon possession. Like guns, knives are not allowed on school property. Other weapons laws are more ambiguous, with most states having statutes making it illegal to carry a "concealed" or "dangerous" weapon, though a few states do have explicit knife statutes (HG Legal Resources, n.d.b).

GANG-RELATED OFFENSES

A juvenile gang may be peripheral to an adult street gang, just hanging around in the hope of being recruited to join. In other cases, a juvenile may become actively involved in an adult street gang, participating in gang-related crimes, including selling drugs on and off school campuses. The admiring "wanna be" youth may by all appearances, including wardrobe and associates, appear to be part of a gang and may become ensnared in criminal behavior. Youth gangs are covered more extensively in Chapter 5.

Most states will charge offenders under *gang enhancement laws* if the crime is suspected to have been committed as part of gang criminal activity. If the crime is serious enough, and if it is believed to be associated with gang activity, a juvenile suspect may be tried in adult court.

DRUG OFFENSES

A broad range of legal prescription and illegal street drugs are abused by juveniles. We should distinguish between experimenting with and habitual abusive use of drugs. According to Hedden et al. (2015) and the graph found on page 79, alcohol and tobacco are the drugs most commonly experimented with or abused by juveniles, followed by marijuana use.

As a basis of comparison, college students report similar types of illegal drug use, but with the possible introduction of a range of more deadly drugs, including opioids, cocaine, methamphetamine, and fentanyl (National Center for Drug Abuse Statistics, 2022), in their late teens. Distribution and abuse of opioids, including the prescription drug oxycodone, is reaching younger juveniles, however, including middle-school students (Christensen, 2022). In a recent case, a 16-year-old at Bloomfield High School in Connecticut was believed to have overdosed on fentanyl-laced marijuana and to require Narcan, a drug used to counter the effects of opioid overdose (Lenthang, 2022). Overall drug abuse and associated overdose deaths have been on the rise in the past two decades (National Center for Drug Abuse Statistics).

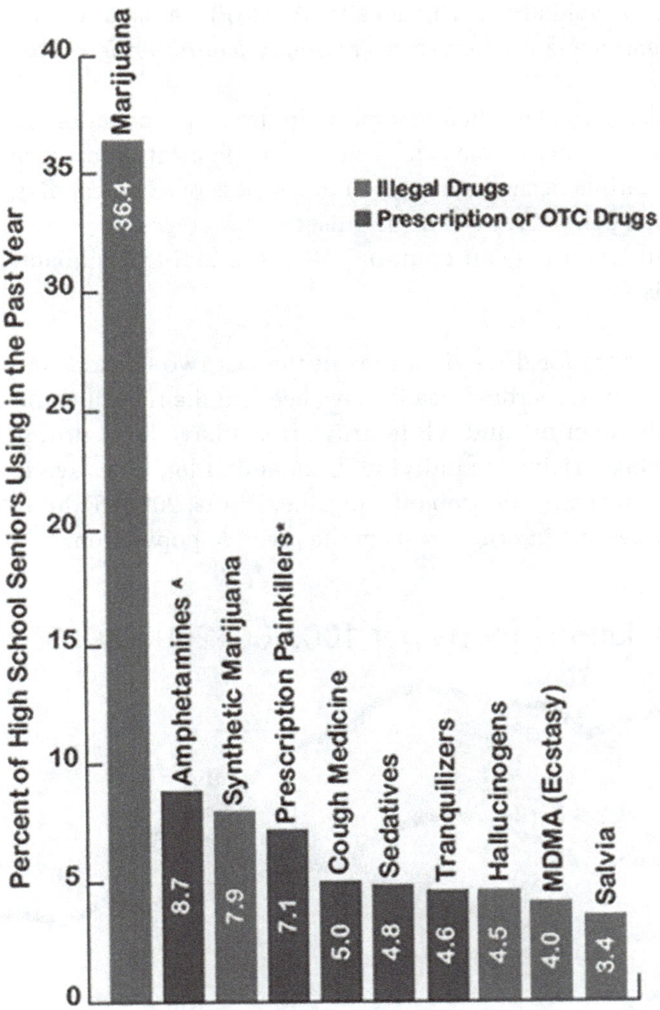

EXHIBIT 4.2 | Most Commonly Abused Drugs, High School Seniors (Excluding Alcohol and Tobacco), 2014

A legal distinction is made between being caught under the influence [e.g., driving under the influence (DUI)], possessing illegal drugs in a quantity that appears to be for personal use, and carrying enough of an illegal drug to be suspected of intending to sell it. Each type of drug case has distinct legal consequences, depending on the charge. Law enforcement and court responses to drug offenses can vary from jurisdiction to jurisdiction, depending on local laws and public sentiment.

In recent years, new laws in some states have legalized medical and recreational marijuana use. As with alcohol, sale of marijuana to anyone under the age of 21 is prohibited, and recreational use by minors is illegal. As the Academy of Child and

Adolescent Psychiatry (2019; hereafter AACAP) warns, however, it can be difficult to detect marijuana use for various reasons (*Healthline Newsletter*, n.d.):

- Dried plants can be rolled to appear similar to a conventional cigarettes.
- Liquid or wax marijuana can be smoked in an electronic cigarette (i.e., vaping).
- Edible marijuana can be disguised in baked goods and candies.
- Marijuana derivatives can be disguised in beverages.
- Oils and tinctures can contain THC,[4] the main psychoactive compound in cannabis.

Arrest rates for drug violations in the last two decades in the United States show that, while overdose deaths have been on the rise, juvenile drug arrests have been on the decline, and while drug arrests have been dropping for juveniles, they have been rising for individuals 25 and older, when we would expect such risk-taking to decline or drop off altogether (Butts, 2019). Exhibit 4.3 illustrates the surprising decline in drug arrests in the juvenile population.

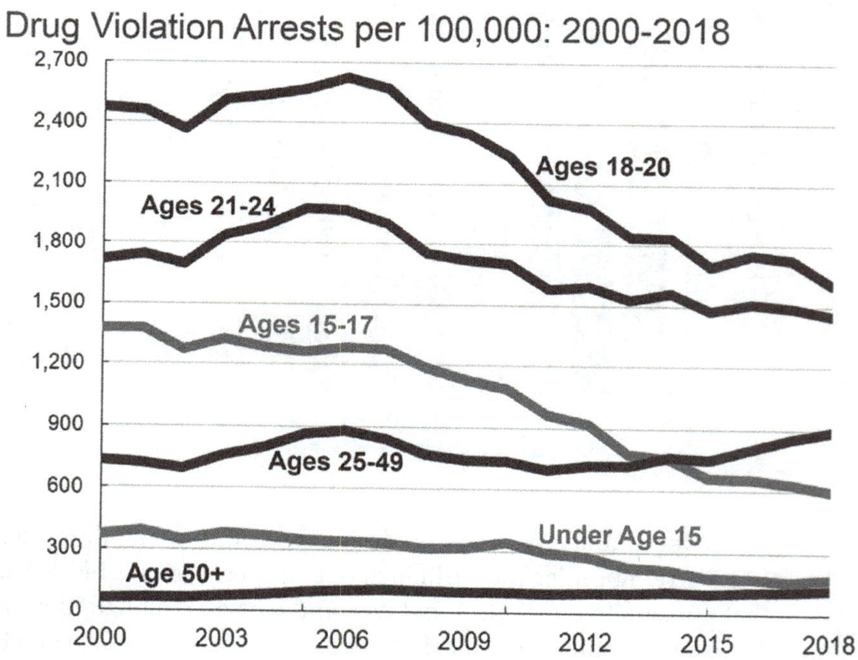

EXHIBIT 4.3 ‖ Drug Violation Arrest Rates, by Age, 2000–2018

---

[4] THC should not be confused with CBD, although they have the same molecular structure and are both found in cannabis. CBD does not provide the same euphoric effects as THC. The two compounds have different effects on the body, and CBD products are more widely legal and available than cannabis products. However, the Federal Drug Enforcement Administration (DEA) and Federal Drug Administration classify both marijuana and CBD as Schedule I drugs (*Healthline Newsletter*, n.d.).

Arrests of juveniles for drug offenses continue to illustrate racial biases, as they have since the war on drugs began in the early 1970s. As early as the 19th century, drug laws have targeted minority groups; one example is charges for opium use among Chinese immigrants to the United States. Black and Latinx juveniles who experience drug offense arrests suffer more long-term effects in their lives and on their adjudication records, as compared to their white counterparts (Ashtiani, 2021).

Special attention, beyond the obvious health concerns, should be paid to smoking by minors. In the United States, tobacco products, including cigarettes and smokeless tobacco, are regulated by both the Bureau of Alcohol, Tobacco, and Firearms, and the U.S. Federal Drug Administration, as they contain addictive chemicals, including nicotine, that can be classified as drugs (Kessler et al., 1997). Until recently, cigarettes could only be sold to individuals 18 years old or older. Federal legislation in 2019 changed the minimum age for tobacco purchase to 21, giving juveniles even less access, in theory, to cigarettes. What is particularly confusing and ambiguous about tobacco laws in the United States, however, is that they set no age limit for possession of tobacco products, and the laws only apply to sales, which are more easily enforced.

Nevertheless, the Centers for Disease Control and Prevention cautions that tobacco use generally is started and established in adolescence, and an estimated 5.6 million current adolescent smokers are predicted to die early from smoking-related illnesses. In 2020, a reported 6.7% of middle-school students and 23.6% of high-school students in the United States used some form of tobacco product (CDC, 2020). Juveniles can be labeled deviant, and in some cases, mislabeled as delinquent, if they smoke cigarettes. Tobacco use is also viewed as a serious public health issue that costs an estimated $300 billion every year in the United States, not for preventive measures, but for treatment of tobacco-related illnesses (CDC, 2021).

VANDALISM

Clinard and Wade (1958, p. 494) defined *vandalism* by minors as "the deliberate defacement, mutilation or destruction of private or public property by a juvenile or group of juveniles not having immediate or direct ownership in the property so abused." Depending on the context, the perception of motive and intention can be subjective. For example, children may jump up and down on a piece of furniture with no intention of breaking it, but their actions may bring about that result. Destruction of property can be perceived as a foolish accident or a deliberate attempt at destruction. A baseball flying through a window, thrown or hit by a neighborhood youngster, can be seen as an unfortunate accident or an intentional act of vandalism. Often when the destruction of property is relatively minor, cost of repairs are negotiated between the juvenile's parental units and the victim without police interference.

Vandalism is a common crime committed primarily by juvenile males. Vandalism can range from minor defacement to destruction of property, and thus straddles the line between being a minor and a serious offense. Because of the financial costs to individuals, businesses, and municipalities for repairs, replacement, and other consequences of vandalism, this book places vandalism among serious juvenile crimes. For example, in Prattville, Alabama, six juveniles ranging in age from 11 to 14 were accused of vandalizing a church, including destroying a piano and other furnishings (Harry, 2021; Ingram, 2021). One of the teens, who was 14 years old at the time of the alleged[5] crime, drove a stolen getaway car, leading the police on a chase through city streets (Ingram, 2021). The teen faces charges of receiving stolen property in the first degree, assault in the first degree, speeding with reckless endangerment, and attempting to elude authorities (Ingram, 2021).

Other common offenses by school-aged children are carving initials into school property, keying cars, tearing down or stealing street signs, and destroying residential mailboxes. Even toilet papering[6] or egging a house or vehicle are considered vandalism, carrying legal consequences if the perpetrators are caught.

Vandalism can also be associated with other criminal behavior. Most notably, juveniles under the influence of alcohol or drugs may lose inhibition and commit other acts of delinquency, including intended or accidental vandalism. Vandalism is also influenced by peer pressure. In a 1970s study of juveniles in an upper-middle-class Chicago suburb, an economic demographic often overlooked in juvenile delinquency studies, the biggest determining factors for the risk for vandalism and other behavioral problems were found to be deficient socialization and inadequate parenting to offset pressure from peers to destroy property (Levin and Kozak, 1979).

Tagging and Graffiti

The most common forms of vandalism committed by juveniles on and off school property are *tagging* and graffiti. Some but not all of this destructive behavior is gang-related. Tagging is specifically intended to mark territory with symbols, initials, or words, whereas graffiti is often subjectively interpreted as art. Like tattoos, graffiti can either be intended, like tagging, to signal or warn off outsiders or to proclaim gang affiliation, or it can be a valid work of artistic expression. An example of this confusion can be found in Iceland, where sanctioned street art in the form of graffiti appears alongside graffiti that is clearly tagging and/or vandalism (Classen, 2007). Removal of unsanctioned tagging and graffiti can be costly for cities.

[5] Note that we use the term alleged, rather than definitively stating that the teens committed the crime. At the time of this writing, this was a new case and the juveniles had not as yet gone to juvenile court.

[6] During this author's high school years in Southern California, having one's house toilet papered was considered a form of flattery and a sign of popularity, much to the chagrin of parental units.

Professional removal of graffiti from private property is likewise expensive and may include additional fees, depending on the location, chemicals used, and cost of travel to and from job sites (Graffiti Solutions, 2021).

Arson

As seen recently in California, New Mexico, and other states in the west, fires can have devastating, long-term results, including subsequent flooding and mudslides. Some fires are natural disasters, as in the example of wildfire or forest fires set off by lightning strikes. More recently, fires have been a result of human activity, only sometimes unintentional. *Arson* is the deliberate, malicious criminal act of setting fire to a building or other flammable materials (Legal Information Institute, n.d.) or setting fire to one's own property with the intention to defraud an insurance company. The Uniform Crime Report (UCR) classifies three types of arson: structural, mobile (e.g., vehicles), and outside (Herniter, 2020). Most fires set by juveniles are extinguished without the need to call emergency responders; however, an estimated 8% to 10% of fires get out of control (Herniter, 2020).

Juveniles who commit arson generally destroy other people's property, as they likely don't own insurable property of their own (other than a vehicle, perhaps, although even those are more likely to be registered and insured in a parent's name). Most states can prosecute if there is unlawful intent to commit arson, with or without the destruction of property; as a federal crime, arson is also defined as a criminal violation resulting in personal injury to another person (Legal Information Institute, n.d.). Juvenile co-offending is also sometimes a factor in arson cases.

In many ways, arson is a violent crime. It has the potential at the very least to kill wildlife, if not humans, particularly if the fire spreads unchecked. Studies have indicated that many arsonists have undergone psychiatric treatment prior to committing arson, meaning that the warning signs may have very well been there (Labree et al., 2010). However, we should note that arsonists are relatively uncommon, and most psychiatrists have little to no contact with them (Perr, 1979).

Juvenile arson risk factors vary. Arson has been little researched. The crime is difficult to investigate, and perpetrators are seldom found. We do know some characteristics of juvenile arsonists, however. In a study of juvenile arsonists, both offending and nonoffending youth reported playing with matches and starting fires (Watt et al., 2015). Juveniles identified as nonoffenders report that they lit fires mostly out of curiosity, boredom, or because their friends set fire to objects or plants (Watt et al., 2015). Habitual and problematic juvenile fire setters are more likely than those who do not start fires to suffer from psychological disorders, anger, frustration, and adverse family events, and to report experiencing more positive emotional responses to the process of setting the fire (Perks et al., 2019; Watt et al., 2015). This pattern is similar in adult arsonists. Female juvenile arsonists are more likely to have set a fire or fires on school property, either accidently or as an impulsive act (Hickle and Roe-Sepowitz, 2010).

JUVENILE SEX OFFENDERS

Young children's normal sexual behaviors differ widely from those of older preteen or teen juveniles. Normal sexual behavior in younger, pre-pubescent children is motivated less by a sexual urge than by curiosity. As Johnson notes (2018), minors display sexual behavior at younger ages today than even a few decades ago, and the onset of puberty occurs earlier in both boys and girls. The gradual lowering of normal puberty onset age ranges has happened over the past 150 years, as a result of better pediatric medical care, better nutrition, and wider food availability (Bellis et al., 2006). However, with earlier puberty onset come public health consequences, among them preteen and teen pregnancies.

When sexual behavior crosses over the line at any age into what is classified as psychologically abnormal, it requires the intervention of mental health care professionals. And in cases where the behavior is criminal, as in the example of rape, attention will come from law enforcement and require juvenile court involvement. Johnson (2018, p. 43) defines abnormal sexual behavior "as behaviors that are developmentally inappropriate, intrusive, or abusive," some of which are criminal. However, some sexual behavior exhibited by juveniles, though outside of what is statistically "normal" by age standards, may still be considered entirely healthy by psychiatric professionals (Murrie, 2012).

There are a number of reasons why juvenile sex offenses are disturbing and result in long-term effects, both for the offender and for the victim(s). First and foremost, sex offenders, whether adult or juvenile, are considered to be the "lepers of the criminal justice system" (Ryan, 2012, p. 11; Geer, 2008, p. 47; Shepherd, 2007, p. 35). Yet a range of crimes can be classified as sex offenses, from indecent exposure (e.g., public urination) to the more serious crimes of rape and sexual assault. Distinctions between severity of crimes is overlooked, however, once the label is applied, particularly in the eyes of the public. Today most states treat adjudicated juvenile sex offenders the same way they treat adults accused and convicted of sex crimes.

The second concern is that, depending on the severity of the crime, juveniles, like adults convicted of sex offenses, are required by law to register as sex offenders. However, this is not always the case for sex offenses committed by minors; the requirement varies by the state. For example, the Maryland Sex Offender Act (1995, amended 2010), depending on the juvenile sex offender's risk of reoffending, requires registration of those convicted of certain types of sex offenses (*Daily Record* Staff, 2015).

The term *Megan's Law* (1996) is used to broadly describe the sex offender registration and notification laws in all states. The law was named after Megan Kanka, who in 1994, at age 7, was raped and murdered by an adult neighbor, Jesse Timmendequas, who had previously served prison time for a sex crime against a child (Ryan, 2012). Since there was no sex offender registry at the time, Megan's family was unaware of his history when Timmendequas moved in across the street (Ryan, 2012). Even in cases where a juvenile has been found to be delinquent or found not guilty by reason of insanity in a sex offense case, the juvenile may be required by law to register as a sex offender. However, several states do not allow information on juvenile sex offenders to be made public (Johnson, 2018). Whether the sex offense is serious or not, juveniles who have been found delinquent in a sex crime will face long-term consequences due to the registry, including housing and employment discrimination.

A third concern is how to navigate the compulsory education needs, in detention, release, or on probation, of juvenile sex offenders who are still too young to drop out of school. Juvenile sex offenders placed in mainstream schools can raise concerns among fellow students and put the offender at risk of reoffending. Another argument, however, points out that offenders placed in schools exclusively for juvenile sex offenders will have little or no possibility of making friends while on school grounds (where juveniles most often meet peers) with non-delinquent classmates (Johnson, 2018).

EMERGING JUVENILE DEVIANCE AND DELINQUENCY TRENDS

Most of the more serious deviance and delinquency trends we see in the juvenile population today can be associated with advances in technology, including the portability of electronic devices, primarily cellphones. Cellular phones with Internet capability, as well as computers, and even smart television sets, have extended the motives and methods by which juveniles can commit delinquent acts.

In the middle of the last century, most discussions of juvenile delinquency centered on wayward girls and hooligan boys, referring to females who were sexually permissive and males who got into criminal mischief. Since the 1950s, greater attention has been given to the psychological reasons that juveniles become delinquent. Gibbens's 1961 report to the World Health Organization indicates that researchers began in the mid-20th century to look at other explanations besides socioeconomic status, turning their attention to better understanding individual personality characteristics. However, with little exception, psychiatric aspects of juvenile deviance and delinquency have been less understood, much less researched, until recent decades. Now, more than ever, researchers and criminal justice practitioners are aware of the relationship between mental health and juvenile delinquency.

Juvenile Cybercriminals

Researchers who focus on *cybercrime* are more likely to study adult rather than juvenile offenders. The exploits of adult cybercriminals could fill many textbooks. However, it is not uncommon for cybercriminals, hackers in particular, to be under the age of 18 (Marcum et al., 2014). The most common forms of cybercrime committed by juveniles are *digital piracy*, online harassment and hacking, cyberbullying, and "*sexting*" or other sexually exploitive behavior (Ciobin, 2021; Dodaj et al., 2020; Lee, 2018; Garcia-Gomez, 2017; Urdis, 2016; Hinduja and Patchin, 2012; Holt et al., 2012; Karaian, 2012).

Whereas the objective of many adult cybercriminals is to defraud individuals (Hansen, 2020), juveniles are more likely to commit cybercrimes for the fun of it, as a challenge, or for thrills. However, for some teens, committing cybercrimes goes beyond recreation. In a 15-month period in 2005 and 2006, a Massachusetts teen managed to hack into the Internet, specifically, telephone providers, to steal personal information, including from celebrities, to broadcast it maliciously and publicly online (Hansen, 2020; U.S. Department of Justice, 2005).

As with adult cybercriminals, one appeal of cybercrime for juveniles is the ability to hide their identity behind a computer screen. These criminals may never see the faces of their victims, unlike in most of the more conventional serious crimes committed by minors (Hansen, 2020). A greater concern for the safety of juvenile cybercriminals is the possibility that they will access the *Dark Web*, a highly encrypted area of cyberspace that is purposely difficult to enter without the right passwords and credentials. Juveniles and adults accessing the Dark Web run the risk of encountering many unsavory characters, including some buying and selling child pornography.

Juvenile hackers do not necessarily operate alone. Although a "lone hacker" works in isolation, "social hackers" co-offend (Hansen, 2020). And unlike conventional crimes, cybercrimes can happen over a long period before they are detected (Hansen, 2020). By the time authorities have caught the perpetrator, whether juvenile or adult, the damage will have been done, and the offenders may have moved on to new forms of cybercrime.

No less alarming have been trends in juvenile *sexting*. Sexting is defined as the transmission or posting of sexually explicit messages and images, including photos, through cell phones, in emails, or on social media (Minor, 2016). In a study of Slovakian adolescents (Holla, 2020), teenagers become motivated to engage in sexting activities in two ways: (1) most frequently, they sext someone they know to seek attention or for entertainment, and (2) they engage in secondary sexting, which is more dangerous, and can involve seeking revenge or retaliation or be out of jealousy. Because sexting has been classified as pornography, when minors are involved, it becomes a prosecutable crime under child pornography laws (Minor, 2016).

Digital Piracy

Piracy is generally associated with sword-wielding attackers on the high seas, wearing eye patches and peg legs, as depicted in movies. But as Hahn (2012, p. 214) notes,[7] "juvenile pirates are not 'The Lost Boys' who live in Neverland and 'don't wanna grow up.'" Piracy today, in the context of juvenile crime, is most commonly associated with cybercrime. It is one form of digital intellectual property theft, where online streaming services, e-books, music, copyrighted videos, and movies are illegally downloaded off the Internet, without purchasing the items.

Some illegal websites are devoted solely to carrying pirated digital content. The extent to which digital piracy continues to be a serious problem is reflected in the associated loss of revenue (Spajic, 2022, retrieved from https://dataprot.net/statistics/piracy-statistics/):

- Pirated video material gets over 230 billion views a year.
- More than 80% of global online piracy can be attributed to illegal streaming services.
- Digital video piracy costs the U.S. economy between $29.2 and $71 billion each year.
- 70,000 jobs a year are lost in the United States due to music piracy.
- Annual global revenue losses from digital piracy in the movie industry are between $40 and $97.1 billion.

According to Lee et al. (2018), 31% of juveniles have illegally downloaded music, movies, and other digital property through the Internet, while 25% of juveniles have uploaded the same types of digital property through blogs and websites without authorization. Juveniles, like adults, are tempted to illegally download copyrighted materials for reasons other than simply low self-control, a cause suggested by Higgins et al. (2008). As Spajic (2022) speculates, the "everyone's doing it" mentality takes digital piracy to be a rather innocuous crime, mistakenly thinking that it is victimless. Juveniles, in particular, may be naïve as to just how much revenue is being stolen virtually each year, not only in the United States but globally.

Cyberbullying

Abusive behavior carried out online is a specialized type of cyber deviance. Cyberbullying is defined as deliberate and repeated aggression carried out against

[7] Though Hahn (2012) is indeed discussing juveniles involved in maritime piracy, this quote is equally applicable to discussions of digital piracy.

specific individuals or groups, using electronic technology (Guo, 2021; Guo, 2016). It can be carried out using text messaging, emails, or through social media posts. The First Amendment of the U.S. Constitution provides for freedom of speech, and subsequent laws, as they relate to electronic mediums, but within reason. It would be impossible and unrealistic to ban all hurtful or unpleasant language used in person or text messages, on social media, or in emails. For children these days, unkind words that used to be tossed around on the playground, in prank calls, or in passed notes at school, are harder to avoid with the omnipresence of social media. It is simply easier today to reach victims with the electronic capability to relay mean-spirited messages and with a wider audience to witness the humiliation.

Incidences of bullying can become so psychologically damaging to the victims, especially juveniles, that a number of mental health issues result, the least of which are anxiety and depression. And hurtful words may be accompanied by threats of bodily harm, whether idle threats or with the potential to be carried out. As such, scholars do not distinguish between cybercrime and cyber deviance, as

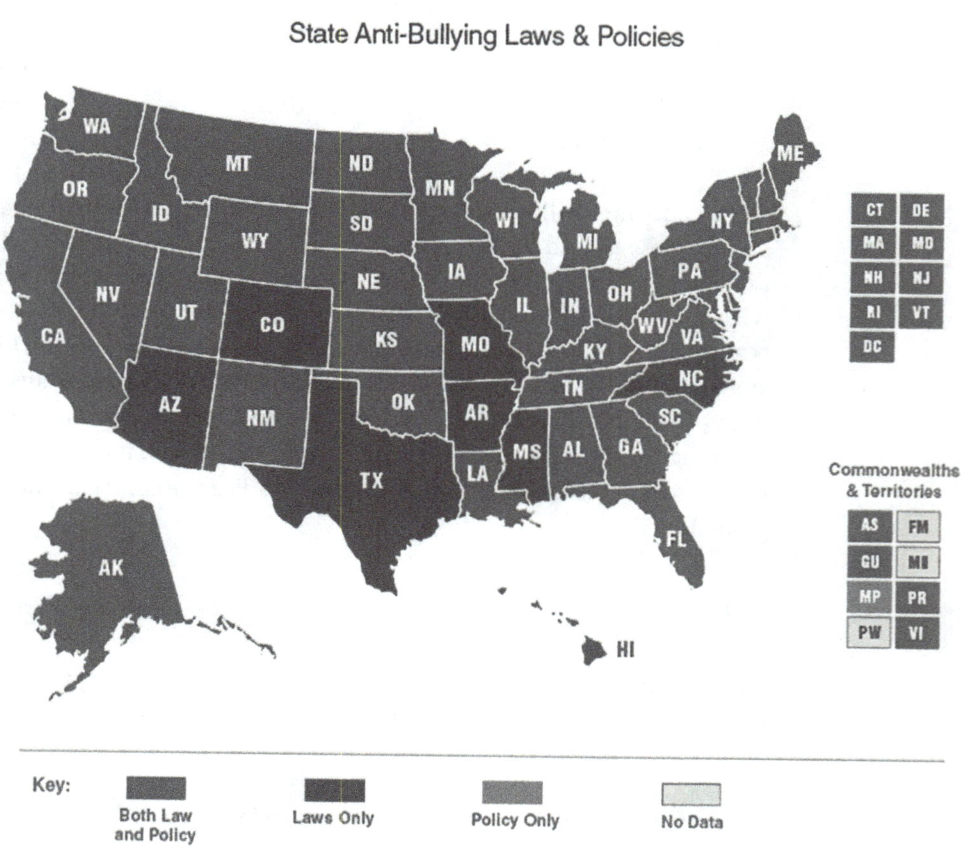

EXHIBIT 4.4 ‖ Current State Anti-Bullying Laws and Policies, 2022

any online harassment can visit irreparable harm on victims who may be without any means of intervention or access to counseling or mental health care.

Though there are no federal laws against cyberbullying, all states have some form of anti-bullying laws. Most states also mandate that schools implement anti-bullying programs and policies (U.S. Department of Health and Human Services, 2022). If cyberbullying crosses the line into "discriminatory harassment, based on race, national origin, color, sex (including sexual orientation and gender identity), age, disability, or religion," it then becomes a civil rights violation (U.S. Department of Health and Human Services, 2021, retrieved from https://www.stopbullying.gov/resources/laws/federal).

Mental Health Disorders

Corresponding with drug and alcohol abuse and other forms of delinquency, increasingly juvenile criminal behavior has become associated with underlying mental disorders. It has been hotly debated as to whether this is a new trend, or if we are now much more knowledgeable about, and have increased capability to diagnose and treat mental health issues in both adults and juveniles. We will more extensively explore theories of mental health disorders and their relationship to juvenile delinquency in Chapter 6. Here, however, we note only that mental disorders are increasingly and disproportionately found among children in the juvenile justice system, the primary referral system for substance use disorders in juveniles (Hartshorn et al.,2015). Disturbingly, juveniles in custody often suffer from a number of psychological, emotional, and social dysfunctions or disabilities, many of which have been left untreated (Office of Juvenile Justice and Delinquency Prevention, 2017).

SUMMARY

Among the many trends in serious juvenile offending, the most concerning is illegal drug and alcohol abuse, which can result in other crimes. Substance abuse is also associated with truancy, a status offense and perhaps the most common juvenile crime, and with vandalism, mostly committed by young males. As in adult offending, a lack of statistics compiled by school officials or through arrest records, self-reports, or victim surveys prevents researchers and criminal justice professionals from assessing the full extent of juvenile offending in minor or serious crimes. In some cases, crimes are concealed due to parental unit intervention before authorities know that juvenile offending has occurred. In other cases, as in the example of cyberbullying, the victims may be too frightened to come forward.

The computer age has allowed bullying juveniles to move online, making it nearly impossible for targeted victims to avoid them. Cyberbullying is nuanced, ranging from mildly hurtful words to threats to do bodily harm. In some cases, cyberbullies have encouraged targeted juveniles to take their own lives. As cyberbullying becomes more prevalent, states and local schools are scrambling to stop it.

Sex offenses too have shifted and multiplied through use of the Internet. Though juveniles are accused of physical rape and sexual assault, the use of cell phones and computers to access the Internet, along with text messaging capabilities, have created new opportunities to commit virtual sex crimes, just as in the adult population. An alarming trend among juveniles involves sexting, where explicit photos or messages are transmitted electronically. Any electronic transmission of child pornography in the United States is illegal, leaving juveniles subject to prosecution for sexting, even if the offense was committed only to flirt or get attention from peers.

Another ongoing challenge in juvenile offending is the rise in diagnoses of mental health issues in the adolescent population. Juveniles in custody are more likely to suffer from some form of mental health disorder though scholars and practitioners debate whether recent increases in diagnoses are due to an actual rise in rates or to better recognition of mental health issues and their contribution to delinquency. This debate also explores whether the mental health issue was present at the time of offending or resulted from being in custody in a juvenile correction facility. In some cases, contact with the juvenile justice system is the first time that a juvenile is recognized to have a mental disability or disorder.

IN THE MEDIA

"Frequent Flyers" in the Juvenile Justice System

Often when a juvenile has been arrested for a serious offense, they have already had numerous encounters with police in their neighborhood or school. When juveniles are repeat offenders, they are often described as "frequent flyers" in the juvenile courts and are seen as being at risk for adult offending once they reach age 18.

Of the many alleged and adjudicated juvenile offenders in the United States, few gain the interest of the media. Some offenders do attract attention, such as perpetrators of heinous crimes, particularly if the offender is a member of a minority group or a repeat offender. Because so much attention goes to repeat offenders with juvenile records, some states are moving to enact three-strike laws that include juvenile records in sentencing decisions. These laws would sentence reoffending adults to prison, in some cases without the possibility of parole, based in some part on their juvenile criminal record. The New Jersey State Supreme Court has hotly debated one such law (Associated Press News, 2022). It is not yet clear how widespread these laws will become.

SOURCE

Associated Press News (2022). "Court: '3 strikes' life sentences can count juvenile crimes." Associated Press. Feb 7. Retrieved from https://apnews.com/hub/juvenile-crime.

INTERNATIONAL PERSPECTIVES

General Juvenile Delinquency in the United Kingdom[8]

In 19th century England, several philanthropic societies emerged to address the problems of poor children (Bradley, 2008). A youth justice system came about later in England and Wales than in the U.S., only established in 1998, where under the Crime and Disorder Act it was formally separated from the adult criminal justice system (Taylor, 2016). Also similarly to the U.S., youth crime rates in the U.K., particularly in London, have fallen in the most recent decade, suggesting that community-based programs to prevent delinquency are working (Clarke, 2021).

Given the general difficulty of obtaining guns of guns in the U.K., knives are most often the weapons used in violent youth crimes. According to Shaw (2019), the overall rates of knife offenses, including possession, have risen sharply since 2016, although rates have remained relatively stable among juveniles aged 10 to 17, despite public perceptions otherwise.

Drug-related offenses in Britain have been steadily climbing in the last couple of years (Clarke, 2021). In a crime victim survey conducted in Wales during stay-at-home orders early in the pandemic, crime declined significantly, excluding fraud and cybercrimes (Office for National Statistics, 2020). The same study showed a 44% increase in drug offenses in May 2020, explained by proactive police investigations. As in the U.S., cybercrime continues to increase in the U.K.

According to juvenile arrest records in the U.K., far fewer adolescents are held in custody than in the U.S. (Wihbey, 2015). Youth incarceration rates in other countries, including England and Wales, have historically been lower than those in the U.S., as demonstrated in Exhibit 4.5.

[8] The United Kingdom consists of four countries: England, Wales, Scotland, and the Republic of Ireland. This section variously refers to the U.K. or to the specific country offering the most pertinent example of the trend discussed.

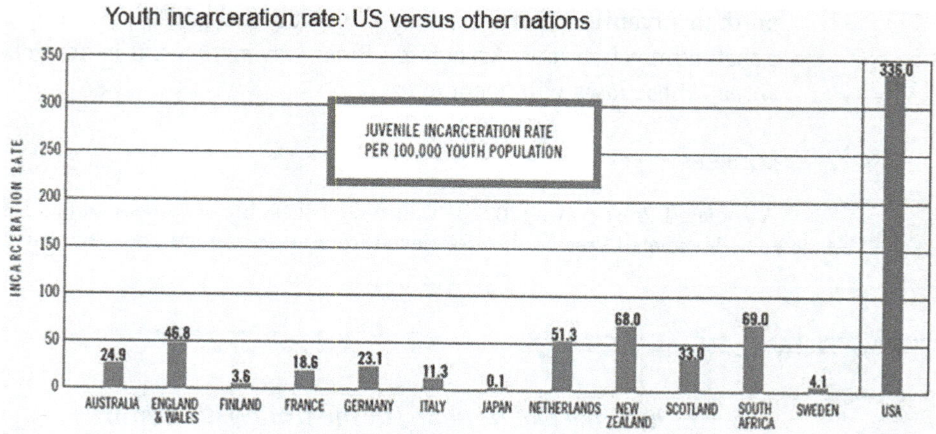

Credit: voxeu.org, based on data from Hazel, Neal, Cross-National Comparison of Youth Justice, 2008

EXHIBIT 4.5 ‖ Youth Incarceration Rates

While the number of children taken into custody in the U.K. has steadily fallen since 2009, the average custodial length has increased, from 11.3 months to 18.6 months (Beard, 2022). As in the U.S., concern continues in the U.K. about racial disparities in who does and doesn't receive time in juvenile detention. The English youth justice system overlooks the realities facing juveniles who offend, and rather than taking a welfare approach, it has been considering deviant behavior criminal at increasingly younger ages (Arthur, 2010).

SOURCES

Arthur, R. (2010). "Protecting the best interests of the child: A comparative analysis of the youth justice systems in Ireland, England and Scotland." *International Journal of Children's Rights.* Vol. 18: 217–231.

Bradley, K. (2008). "Welfare: Juvenile delinquency and the evolution of British juvenile courts c. 1900–1950." History in Focus. Oct. Retrieved from https://archives.history.ac.uk/history-in-focus/welfare/articles/bradleyk.html.

Clarke, N. (2021). "London youth crime have fallen over the last five years." *SW Londoner.* March 17. Retrieved from https://www.swlondoner.co.uk/news/17032021-london-youth-crime-figures-have-fallen-over-the-last-five-years.

Office for National Statistics (2020). Coronavirus and crime in England and Wales, August 2020: Impact of coronavirus (COVID-19) pandemic on crime and people's perceptions of crime during the April and May period of national lockdown. Government office, United Kingdom. Retrieved from https://www.ons.gov.uk/peoplepopulationandcommunity/crimeandjustice/bulletins/coronavirusandcrimeinenglandandwales/august2020.

Shaw, D. (2019). "Reality check: Are more teenagers carrying knives?" *British Broadcasting Corporation News.* Jul 31. Retrieved from https://www.bbc.com/news/uk-46153257.

Wihbey, J. (2015). "Juvenile incarceration and its impact on high school graduation rates and adult jail time." *Journalist's Resource.* Shorenstein Center, Harvard Kennedy School, Harvard University. Feb 4. Retrieved from https://journalistsresource.org/education/juvenile-incarceration-long-term-consequences/.

CHAPTER DISCUSSION QUESTIONS

1. Why are so called "joyrides" by juveniles less frequent today than they were in the 1950s and 1960s? What, besides the COVID-19 pandemic, could explain the increase in carjackings in the past few years?
2. How might authorities distinguish between graffiti as artistic expression and graffiti as vandalism?
3. If no laws clearly criminalize juvenile runaways, why are they sometimes treated like criminals?
4. How has some states' legalization of marijuana for adults complicated enforcement of laws targeting drug use by juveniles?
5. Why do juveniles have more access to guns in the United States, compared to other countries?
6. How can juveniles protect themselves from being bullied at school and online?
7. With diagnoses of mental health issues on the rise among adjudicated juveniles and in the general juvenile population, what services or agencies should assist with therapies and interventions?
8. What obstacles do juveniles face in seeking professional help with mental health issues, including alcohol or drug abuse?

GLOSSARY

Arson Setting a fire deliberately and maliciously, with the intent to destroy property or to defraud an insurance company.

Burglary Illegal entry into a public or private building, with the intention of committing a crime (e.g., theft or vandalism).

Computer hacking Unauthorized use of or entry into computer systems or private networks, often with the intention of stealing information, including personal financial records.

Criminal trespassing Knowingly entering, staying on, and/or refusing to leave private property, without permission of the owner or the individual(s) in control of the property.

Dark Web Subset of the Web that is intended to provide extra encryption and secrecy to users often used to commit cybercrimes.

Digital piracy Illegally downloading content from the Internet or dedicated websites that would otherwise be purchased, including streaming services, movies, games, and music.

Embezzlement Theft of cash, accounts, or material goods from an employer.

Felonies Charges and convictions reserved for more serious crimes, that may be defined differently depending on the state; more likely to result in detention, jail, or prison than misdemeanor charges.

Gang enhancement laws Laws intended to bring stiffer penalties and longer jail or prison sentences for crimes suspected of being gang-related.

Intellectual property Any creative work, including publication, design, symbols, names, and images that are the sole property of the creator and/or the company or organization they are affiliated with.

Joyride Driving a motor vehicle for pleasure recklessly or by theft without the permission of its owner.

Kleptomania A recognized mental health disorder where an individual has a chronic compulsion to steal from others, including by shoplifting.

Larceny General term used to describe theft of personal property.

Megan's Law Federal law (amendment to the Violent Crime Control and Law Enforcement Act of 1994) passed in 1996, named after Megan Kanka, following her rape and murder by a neighbor; the law requires sex offenders to register as such in their communities of residence to alert the public to their presence.

Panhandling Begging for money or food in public, including on public transportation and on the street.

Robbery Unlawfully removing property from a person or place by force or threat of force; armed robbery involves robbery using a weapon, usually a gun.

Sexting Sending sexually explicit messages or photos using text messaging.

Shoplifting Removal of merchandise from a store without paying for it.

Theft General term used for the crime of stealing.

White collar crime One of a broad range of crimes that are committed by employees, including embezzlement, fraud, and falsely reporting work hours and overtime; white-collar crimes can be committed against employers or customers or clients.

REFERENCES AND ADDITIONAL SUGGESTED READINGS

Alton, L. (2017). "Phone calls, texts, or email. Here is how millennials prefer to communicate." *Forbes*. May 11. Retrieved from https://www.forbes.com/sites/larryalton/2017/05/11/how-do-millennials-prefer-to-communicate/?sh=5e150a036d6f.

American Academy of Child and Adolescent Psychiatry (AACAP) (2019). Marijuana and teens. Oct., issue 106. Retrieved from https://www.aacap.org/AACAP/Families_and_Youth/Facts_for_Families/FFF-Guide/Marijuana-and-Teens-106.aspx.

American Academy of Child and Adolescent Psychiatry (AACAP) (2014). "Stealing in children and adolescents." Dec., No 12. Retrieved from https://www.aacap.org/AACAP/Families_and_Youth/Facts_for_Families/FFF-Guide/Children-Who-Steal-012.aspx.

Ashtiani, M. (2021). "The racially disparate effects of drug arrest on high school dropout." *Socius*. Vol. 7 (July). https://doi.org/10.1177/23780231211027097.

Beard, J. (2022). *Youth Custody: Research Brief.* London, ENG: House of Commons Library.

Bellis, M. A., J. Downing, and J. R. Ashton (2006). "Adults at 12? Trends in puberty and their public health consequences." *Journal of Epidemiological Community Health*. Vol. 60, issue 11 (Nov.): 910–911.

Bingel, J. (2022). "3 female juveniles lead deputies on chase in stolen car, Portage County sheriff says." 19 News. Feb 24. Retrieved from https://www.cleveland19.com/2022/02/24/3-female-juveniles-lead-deputies-chase-stolen-car-portage-county-sheriff-says/.

Butts, J. A. (2019). "Older adults responsible for total growth in drug arrests." Research and Evaluation Center, John Jay College of Criminal Justice. Nov 11. Retrieved from https://johnjayrec.nyc/2019/11/11/databits201902/.

Centers for Disease Control and Prevention (CDC) (2021). Economic trends in tobacco. May 25. Retrieved from https://www.cdc.gov/tobacco/data_statistics/fact_sheets/economics/econ_facts/index.htm#:~:text=Smoking%2Drelated%20illness%20in%20the,%24300%20billion%20each%20year%2C%20including%3A&text=More%20than%20%24225%20billion%20for,due%20to%20secondhand%20smoke%20exposure.

Centers for Disease Control and Prevention (CDC) (2020). Youth and tobacco use. Dec 16. Retrieved from https://www.cdc.gov/tobacco/data_statistics/fact_sheets/youth_data/tobacco_use/index.htm.

Christensen, J. (2022). "Middle-school fall prey to fatal fentanyl overdoses." CNN. Feb 18. Retrieved from https://www.cnn.com/2022/02/18/health/fentanyl-fatal-overdoses-middle-schoolers/index.html.

Chui, W. H., and H. C. Chan (2016). "The gendered analysis of self-control on theft and violent delinquency: An examination of Hong Kong adolescent population." *Crime and Delinquency*. Vol. 62, issue 12: 1648–1677.

Cioban, S., A. R. Lazar, C. Bacter, and A. Hatos (2021). "Adolescent Deviance and Cyber-deviance. A systematic literature review." *Frontiers in Psychology*. Oct 12. Retrieved from https://www.frontiersin.org/articles/10.3389/fpsyg.2021.748006/full.

City of Portland Crime Prevention Program (2017). Car theft prevention. Office of Neighborhood Involvement Crime Prevention Program. Summer. Retrieved from https://www.portlandoregon.gov/civic/article/673532.

Classen, T. (2007). *Icepick: Icelandic Street Art*. Corte Madera, CA: Gingko Press, Inc.

Clinard, M. B., and A. L. Wade (1958). "Toward the delineation of vandalism as a sub-type in juvenile delinquency." *Journal of Criminal Law, Criminology, and Police Science*. Vol. 48, issue 5: 493–499.

Corley, C. (2021). "Michigan shooting suspect among thousands of U.S. minors charged as adults yearly." *All Things Considered*, National Public Radio. Dec 4. Retrieved from https://www.npr.org/2021/12/03/1061333484/michigan-school-shooter-is-1-of-thousands-of-u-s-juveniles-charged-as-adults-in-.

Daily Record Staff (2015). Law Digest—Maryland Court of Appeals. Regional Business News, *Daily Record*. Oct 8. Retrieved from https://discovery-ebsco-com.wne.idm.oclc.org/c/lhmm22/viewer/html/YndoLUw1NDkxODI1NURSTUQ=.

Dixon, A., and G. Farrell (2020). "Age-period-cohort effects in half century of motor vehicle theft in the United States." *Crime Science*. Vol. 9, issue 7 (Oct. 1). Open access. Retrieved from https://crimesciencejournal.biomedcentral.com/articles/10.1186/s40163-020-00126-5#citeas.

Dodaj, A., K. Sesar, and S. Jerinic (2020). "A prospective study of high-school adolescent sexting behavior and psychological distress." *Journal of Psychology*. Vol. 154: 111–128.

Family Vacation Design (n.d.). "10 things that will get you banned from Walt Disney World." Retrieved from https://familyvacationdesign.com/10-things-that-will-get-you-banned-from-walt-disney-world/#:~:text=Shoplifting,-The%20shops%20in&text=In%20addition%20to%20uniformed%20security,blend%20in%20with%20the%20crowd.&text=Besides%20being%20one%20of%20the,value%20of%20the%20stolen%20goods.

Federal Bureau of Investigation (FBI) (n.d.). Motor vehicle theft. U.S. Department of Justice. Retrieved from https://ucr.fbi.gov/crime-in-the-u.s/2010/crime-in-the-u.s.-2010/property-crime/mvtheftmain.

Florida Statutes (2021). Weapons and firearms. Title XLVI, Ch 790. Tallahassee, FL: Florida Legislature.

Forster, L. M., M. Tannhauser, and H. M. Barros (1996). "Drug use among street children in southern Brazil." *Drug and Alcohol Dependence.* Vol. 43: 57–62.

Gallardo, M. (2021). "11-year-old boy arrested, considered a 'prolific carjacker.'" ABC 7. Nov 29. Retrieved from https://abc7.com/11-year-old-boy-arrested-for-carjacking-grand-theft-auto-chicago-crime/11282410/.

Garcia-Gomez, A. (2017). "Teen girls and sexual agency: exploring the intrapersonal and intergroup dimensions of sexting." *Media, Culture, and Society.* Vol. 39: 391–407.

Geer, P. (2008). "Justice served? The high cost of juvenile sex offender registry." *Developments in Mental Health Law.* Vol. 27, issue 2 (July): 33–52.

Gibbens, T. C. N. (1961). *Trends in Juvenile Delinquency.* Report. Geneva, Switzerland: World Health Organization.

Graffiti Solutions (2021). "How much should I charge?" Retrieved from https://www.graffitisolutions.com/faq/how-much-should-i-charge.

Guo, S. (2021). "Moderate effects of delinquent peer association, social control, and negative emotion on cyberbullying and delinquency." *School Psychology.* Vol. 36, issue 6: 445–454.

Guo, S. (2016). "A meta-analysis of the predictors of cyberbullying perpetration ad victimization." *Psychology in the Schools.* Vol. 53, No. 4: 432–453.

Hahn, L. (2012). "Juvenile justice and piracy: Prosecutions of juvenile pirates in the United States." *George Mason Law Review.* Vol. 20, issue 1 (2012–2013): 241–274.

Hansen, L. P. (2020). *White Collar and Corporate Crime: A Case Study Approach.* Baltimore, MD: Wolters Kluwer.

Harry, B. (2021). "Juveniles in Morgan County vandalism case found in stolen SUV in Prattville." ABC WAAY 31. Dec 1. Retrieved from https://www.waaytv.com/news/juveniles-in-morgan-county-church-vandalism-case-found-in-stolen-suv-in-prattville/article_d55bebce-7d76-5bae-a149-3b56db8e1b77.html.

Hartshorn, K. J. S., L. B. Whitbeck, and P. Prentice (2015). "Substance use disorder, comorbidity, and arrest among indigenous adolescents." *Crime and Delinquency.* Vol. 61, issue 10: 1311–1332.

He, E., Y. Hongtao, and X. Zhou (2022). "The influence of modernity on juvenile delinquency." *Advances in Social Science, Education and Humanities Research.* Vol. 664: 270–274.

Healthline Newsletter (n.d.). "CBD vs. THC: What's the difference?" Retrieved from https://www.healthline.com/health/cbd-vs-thc#medical-benefits.

Hedden, S. L., J. Kennet, R. Lipari, G. Medley, P. Tice, E. A. P. Coppello, and L. A Kroutil (2015). *Behavioral Health Trends in the United States: Results from the 2014 National Survey on Drug Use and Health.* Washington, D.C.: Substance Abuse and Mental Health Services Administration.

Hermawati, T., R. Setyaningsih, and R. P. Nugraha (2021). "Teen motivation to create fake identity accounts on social media." *International Journal of Multicultural and Multireligious Understanding.* Vol. 8, issue 4 (April): 87–98.

Herniter, M. (2020). "Location, location, location: An analysis of arson risk factors in Pennsylvania cities." *TCNJ Journal of Student Scholarship.* Vol. 22: 1–5.

HG Legal Resources (n.d.). Laws regarding carrying knives. Retrieved from https://www.hg.org/legal-articles/laws-regarding-carrying-knives-31129.

Hickle, K. E., and D. E. Roe-Sepowitz (2010). "Female juvenile arsonists: An exploratory look at characteristics and solo and group arson offences." *Legal and Criminological Psychology*, British Psychological Society. Vol. 15, issue 2: 385–399.

Higgins, G. E., S. E. Scott, and C. D. Marcum (2008). "Digital piracy: An examination of three measurements of self-control." *Deviant Behavior.* July: 440–460.

Hinduja, S., and Patchin, J. W. (2010). "Bullying, cyberbullying, and suicide." *Archives of Suicide Research.* Vol. 14: 206–221.

Holla, K. (2020). "Sexting types and motives detected among Slovak adolescents." *European Journal of Mental Health.* Vol. 15, issue 2: 75–92.

Holt, T. J., A. M. Bossler, and D. C. May (2012). "Low self-control, deviant peer associations, and juvenile cyberdeviance." *American Journal of Criminal Justice.* Vol. 37: 378–395.

Howell, J. (2022). "8 juveniles arrested after various carjackings, motor vehicle thefts over two day span." ABC. Feb 23. Retrieved from https://www.hoiabc.com/2022/02/23/8-juveniles-arrested-after-various-carjacking-motor-vehicle-thefts-over-two-day-span/.

IDENTIV (2021). "What are RFID tags and how are they used?" Feb 12. Retrieved from https://www.identiv.com/community/2021/02/12/what-are-rfid-tags-and-how-are-they-used/.

Ingram, T. (2021). "Juveniles linked to recent Morgan County church vandalism, arrested after chase in stolen vehicle in Prattville. " CBS 42. Nov 10. Retrieved from https://www.cbs42.com/news/crime/juveniles-linked-to-recent-morgan-county-church-vandalism-arrested-after-chase-in-stolen-vehicle-in-central-alabama/.

Johnson, L. D. (2018). "Juvenile sex offenders: Should they go to school with your children or should we create a pedophile academy?" *University of Toledo Law Review.* Vol. 50: 39–66.

JUSTIA US Law (n.d.) 2021 California Code, Part 1, Title 15. Retrieved from https://law.justia.com/codes/california/2021/code-pen/part-1/title-15/.

Karaian, L. (2012). "Lolita speaks: 'Sexting,' teenage girls and the law." *Crime, Media, Culture.* Vol. 8: 57–73.

Kessler, D. A., P. S. Barnett, A. Witt, M. R. Zeller, J. R. Mande, and W. B. Schultz (1997). "The legal and scientific basis for FDA's assertion of jurisdiction over cigarettes and smokeless tobacco." *Journal of the American Medical Association* (JAMA). Vol. 277, issue 5 (Feb.): 405–409.

Labree, W., H. Nijman, H. van Marle, and E. Rassin (2010). "Background and characteristics of arsonists." *International Journal of Law and Psychiatry.* Vol. 33: 149–153.

Lee, B., S. Y. Paek, and R. Fenoff (2018). "Factors associated with digital piracy among early adolescents." *Children and Youth Services Review.* Vol. 86 (Feb.): 287–295.

Lee, B. H. (2018). "Explaining cyber deviance among school-aged youth." *Child Indictors. Research.* Vol. 11: 563–584.

Legal Information Institute (n.d.). Arson. Cornell Law School. Retrieved from https://www.law.cornell.edu/wex/arson.

Lenthang, M. (2022). "Student 16 overdoses on suspected fentanyl-laced marijuana at Connecticut high school, police say." NBC News. Feb 8. Retrieved from https://www.nbcnews.com/news/us-news/16-year-old-student-overdoses-fentanyl-laced-marijuana-connecticut-hig-rcna15302.

Levin, E. M., and C. Kozak (1979). "Drug and alcohol use, delinquency among upper middle class pre- and post-adolescents." *Journal of Youth Adolescence.* Vol. 8, issue 1 (March): 91–101.

Li, D. K. (2019). "Massachusetts high court upholds Carter's convictions for texts encouraging boyfriend's suicide." NBC News. Feb 7. Retrieved from https://www.nbcnews.com/news/us-news/massachusetts-high-court-upholds-michelle-carter-s-conviction-texts-encouraging-n968291.

Marcum, C. D., G. E. Higgins, M. L. Ricketts, and E. Scott (2014). "Hacking in high school: Cybercrime perpetration by juveniles." *Deviant Behavior.* Vol. 35, issue 7: 581–591.

McCormick, L. (2014). "NOTE: The Internet and social media sites: A shift in privacy norms resulting in the exploitation and abuse of adolescents and teens in dating relationships." *Albany Government Law Review.* Vol. 7: 591.

Minor, A. D. (2016). "ESSAY: Sexting prosecutions: Teenagers and child pornography laws." *Howard Law Journal.* Vol. 60: 309.

Murrie, D. C. (2012). "Placing sexual behavior problems in context: What is 'normal' sexual behavior among juveniles?" Ch. 2 in *Juvenile Offenders: A Guide to Evaluation and Treatment for Mental Health Prof*essionals, ed. E. P. Ryan, J. A. Hunter, and D. C. Murrie. Oxford, UK: Oxford University Press.

National Center for Drug Abuse Statistics (n.d.). Drug use among youth: Facts and Statistics. Retrieved from https://drugabusestatistics.org/teen-drug-use/.

Office of Juvenile Justice and Delinquency Prevention (OJJDP) (n.d.). Statistical Briefing Book: Law enforcement and Juvenile crime, most serious offense, 2019. Retrieved from https://www.ojjdp.gov/ojstatbb/crime/qa05101.asp.

Office of Juvenile Justice and Delinquency Prevention (OJJDP) (2017). "Intersection between mental health and the juvenile justice system." *Literature Review,* U.S. Department of Justice. July. Retrieved from https://ojjdp.ojp.gov/mpg/literature-review/mental-health-juvenile-justice-system.pdf.

Perr, I. N. (1979). "Comments on arson." *ASTM International.* Vol. 24, issue 4. Retrieved from https://www.astm.org/jfs10919j.html.

Popowski, A. (2022). "Dollar General employee stages robbery at store, Mobile police say." CBS 42. Jan 28. Retrieved from https://www.cbs42.com/news/crime/dollar-general-employee-stages.

Ryan, E. (2012). "Changing perceptions of juvenile sex offending in society and the legal system." Ch. 1 in *Juvenile Offenders: A Guide to Evaluation and Treatment for Mental Health Prof*essionals, ed. E. P. Ryan, J. A. Hunter, and D. C. Murrie. Oxford, UK: Oxford University Press.

Sacca, Lea, et al. (2021). "Assessment of the Reach, Usability, and Perceived Impact of 'Talking Is Power': A Parental Sexual Health Text-Messaging Service and Web-Based Resource to Empower Sensitive Conversations with American Indian and Alaska Native Teens." *Environmental Research and Public Health.* Vol. 18, issue 17 (Aug.): 9126. Open access at https://www.mdpi.com/1660-4601/18/17/9126.

Sheley, J. F., and J. D. Wright (2000). "High school youth, weapons, and violence: A national survey of weapon-related experiences, behaviors, and concerns—Final Report." NCJRS, Document No. 181053. Feb 18.

Shephard, R. E. (2007). Testimony before the Joint Committee on Healthy Families and Communities, Committee on Education and Labor, the Subcommittee on Crime, Terror, and Homeland Security, and Committee on the Judiciary. U.S. House of Representatives, 110th Congress. Jul 12. Washington, D.C.:U.S. Government Printing Office. Retrieved from https://www.govinfo.gov/content/pkg/CHRG-110hhrg36466/html/CHRG-110hhrg36466.htm.

Spajic, D. J. (2022). "Piracy is back: Piracy statistics for 2022." DataProt. Feb 9. Retrieved from https://dataprot.net/statistics/piracy-statistics/.

Tan, S. (2007). "Some Eden [high school] cheerleaders accused of shoplifting incident happened at Disney World." *Buffalo News.* Apr 4. Retrieved from https://buffalonews.com/news/

some-eden-cheerleaders-accused-of-shoplifting-incident-happened-at-disney-world/article_b4527063-c03a-5e57-9801-7a24514622f8.html#:~:text=Disney%20has%20a%20reputation%20for,can%20file%20the%20appropriate%20report.%22.

Taylor, C. (2016). Review of the Youth Justice System in England and Wales. London, ENG: U.K. Ministry of Justice. May. Retrieved from https://assets.publishing.service.gov.uk/government/uploads/system/uploads/attachment_data/file/577105/youth-justice-review-final-report-print.pdf.

Thompson, M. (2022). "Carjackings soar by up to 500% in US cities." [U.K.] *Daily Mail.* Jan 23. Retrieved from https://www.dailymail.co.uk/news/article-10433381/Carjackings-rise-500-large-cities-disturbing-spikes.html.

Udris, R. (2016). "Cyber deviance among adolescents and the role of family, school, and neighborhood: A cross-national study." *International Journal of Cyber Criminology.* Vol. 10: 127–146.

U.S. Bureau of Alcohol, Tobacco, and Firearms (ATF) (2017). Youth Handgun Safety Act Notice. United States Bureau of Justice. July. Retrieved from https://www.atf.gov/firearms/docs/guide/atf-i-53002-%E2%80%94-youth-handgun-safety-act-notice/download#:~:text=(3)%20Federal%20law%20prohibits%2C,to%20a%20person%20under%2018.

U.S. Department of Health and Human Services (2022). Laws, policies and regulation: State laws. Jan 7. Retrieved from https://www.stopbullying.gov/resources/laws.

U.S. Department of Health and Human Services (2021). Federal law. Oct 6. Retrieved from https://www.stopbullying.gov/resources/laws/federal.

U.S. Department of Justice (2005). "Massachusetts teen convicted for hacking into Internet and telephone service providers and making bomb threats to high schools in Massachusetts and Florida." Press Release, U.S. State Attorney's Office, District of Massachusetts. Sept 8. Retrieved from https://www.justice.gov/archive/criminal/cybercrime/press-releases/2005/juvenileSentboston.htm#:~:text=A%20Massachusetts%20juvenile%20pled%20guilty,high%20schools%20in%20Florida%20and.

U.S. Senate (1993). H.R. 3098—Youth Handgun Safety Act. 103rd Congress (1993–1994). Nov 22. Retrieved from https://www.congress.gov/bill/103rd-congress/house-bill/3098/text#:~:text=3098%20%2D%20103rd%20Congress%20(1993%2D,Congress.gov%20%7C%20Library%20of%20Congress.

Vu, H. (2021). "What happens when you get caught shoplifting at Disneyland?" Law Offices of Hieu Vu. May 28. Retrieved from https://vulawoffice.com/theft/shoplifting-at-disneyland/.

Watt, B. D., K. Geritz, T. Hasan, S. Harden, and R. Doley (2015). "Prevalence and correlates of firesetting behaviours among offending and non-offending youth." *Legal and Criminological Psychology*, British Psychological Society. Vol. 10: 19–36.

Chapter **FIVE**

Young Violent Offenders[1]

Come on now, I want to see blood!

—Unidentified male gang member during a gang initiation ritual[2]

Chapter Objectives

- Review and define the types of violent acts committed by juveniles.
- Identify the characteristics of young violent offenders.
- Explore the phenomenon of juvenile co-offending in violent crimes.
- Evaluate the role of youth gangs in juvenile violent offending.
- Examine the most heinous of violent crimes committed by juveniles, including sexual assault, homicide, and mass and serial killings.

Key Terms

Date rape
Dating abuse
Dating violence
Dating violent offender (DVO)
Electronic dating aggression
Ethnic competition theory
Ghost guns
Hate groups
Hate or bias crimes
Sexual violence
Sibling abuse
Urban violence
White supremacy gangs

[1] **TRIGGER WARNING**: There are a number of sensitive topics discussed in this chapter that might be disturbing to some readers. We recommend that you discuss with your professor or instructor how much or how little of this chapter you will be responsible for.
[2] Cited in L. P. Hansen and M. E. Freitag (2016), "Choreographed Violence in Gang Initiation Rites," Ch. 1 in *Global Perspectives on Youth Behavior, Violence, and Weapons Use*, ed. S. Harding and M. Palasinki (UK: IGI Global), p. 1.

INTRODUCTION

Violent crimes are by far the crimes of greatest concern to law enforcement and the public. Violent crimes can occur during the commission of other crimes or as isolated incidents, such as when a fight breaks out. Quednau (2021) cites as among the causes of violence greed, anger, jealousy, revenge, or pride. Though most violent crimes, particularly those perpetrated by youth, are committed on impulse, others are methodically planned, as we will see in our section on juvenile serial and mass murderers.

Law enforcement often focuses on the most serious crimes, including those committed by young violent offenders. As in the case of all types of offending, we do not always have a clear picture of the extent of violent crimes, as not all such crimes are reported, particularly those committed by juveniles or young adults. For example, if we examine the FBI's National Incident-Based Reporting System (NIBRS) or Uniform Crime Report (UCR) data, which report official crime data, they only list the most serious violent offenses, such as those resulting in serious injury (Lantz, 2020). However, acts of violence range from simple assault, such as shoving someone who remains physically unharmed, to homicide. Violent crimes committed by juveniles and adults include murder, sexual assault, robbery, simple and aggravated assault, and kidnapping (Office of Juvenile Justice and Delinquency Prevention, 2022; hereafter OJJDP).

Of course, there are no good data for how many violent acts might have been committed by juveniles but were thwarted by parental intervention. It is an age-old puzzle: Why do some children become delinquent but, given the same variables, others do not? Research largely ignores this question. We do know that adults' early positive, supportive involvement in children's lives helps prevent both violent and nonviolent delinquency and acts as one of the most important protective factors (Wasserman et al., 2003).

CHARACTERISTICS OF YOUNG VIOLENT OFFENDERS

Several characteristics can be linked to juvenile violent crime. Some are individual risks such as gender, age, history of abuse, and psychiatric disorders. Others are community-level risks, including poverty and an existing culture of violence, such as in neighborhoods plagued by gang activities.

Predictors of Violent Offending

One of the difficulties in identifying a child or teen at risk of committing a violent crime is that underlying psychological or developmental problems often go undiagnosed until a problem has occurred or a crime has been committed. Even then, in some cases, the violent behavior may still not be attributed to existing disorders. In males particularly, some predictors of violent offending, such as oppositional behaviors (e.g., talking back to parental units or teachers), are seen as normal boyish behavior or assertions of masculinity (Sitnick et al., 2019). By far the best predictors of violent offending are gender and age, with late adolescent and young adult males more likely to commit violent crimes compared to females or older males, with crimes occurring most frequently intra-racially among minority males (OJJDP, n.d.). These two variables, of course, are not adequate to predict who is at risk for violent offending.

Strain theories, introduced elsewhere in this book, help explain violent crimes: individuals who are already prone to violence may resort to using it when they cannot reach their goals by other means. A street mugging, for example, with its violence or implicit threat of violence, may be seen by the perpetrator as their only or easiest source of income. Some of the individual stressors that explain violent behavior in juveniles include physical, psychological, or sexual abuse; problems in school; a break-up with or rejection by a romantic partner; and ridicule by friends (Agnew, 2012). Stressors are sometimes more acutely felt by some individuals than others. Using our example of rejection or disappointment, some juveniles will view it as a learning experience, others as a devasting blow to their ego and self-confidence. Much of our perception of stressors is dictated by maturity level or by how we have learned to handle them, often by the examples of others around us.

Physiological explanations exist for violent reactions to life's stressors as well. The human brain is not fully developed until a person reaches their mid-20s, which affects impulsivity. Resorting to violence may indicate an underdeveloped frontal cortex or brain damage from severe head trauma. No matter the explanation, as Agnew notes, "These [perceived] strains upset individuals, creating pressure for corrective action. Some individuals may respond in a violent manner, with violence being used to reduce the strain being experienced, and/or obtain revenge against the source of strain or related targets" (2012, p. 519).

Almost invariably, children who commit violent acts have been victimized by an abusive adult. Approximately 90% of violent young offenders suffer from childhood trauma (Davis, 2011). Some studies characterize the relationship between parents or guardians and young violent offenders as highly contentious and, in some cases, as providing very little support or affection. Many juveniles raised by single mothers describe the relationship with their fathers as more important than their early relationships with their mothers, which may have been severely impaired by divorce or other strains (Yates et al., 1983).

Family dynamics cannot be seen as a controlling factor in violent offending, however. A large number of families today are single-parent, female-headed households (21%, according to the 2020 U.S. Census), often with an absentee father (Hemez and Washington, 2021). Maginnis (1997) contradicts most research that points to young males being at greatest risk for violent offending no matter the household makeup, instead reporting that the greatest indicator of violent crimes in a community is the number of fatherless households. We should note that it is far less common for children to live with their fathers after parents separate (4.5%, based on the 2020 U.S. Census numbers), though the number is greater than in the late 1960s, when divorce became increasingly more prevalent (Hemez and Washington, 2021). However, based on these statistics, we would expect that at least 20% of young males in the United States would be at risk for violent offending, which just isn't the case according to crime and self-reported data.

Differences exist between young female and male violent offenders (see also Chapter 9). Female violent offenders are most likely to be commit crimes against someone with whom they have a relationship, often within the home (Willison, 2016). Young males who commit murder are described as more angry and hostile and as experiencing more paranoia, indicating psychiatric disorders, as compared to nonviolent male juvenile offenders and nonoffending high school students in general (Katz and Marquette, 1996).

One alarming warning sign for the potential for violent offending against others, including homicide, is cruelty to or neglect of animals. As Elkins (2019, retrieved from https://cops.usdoj.gov/html/dispatch/04-2019/animal_cruelty.html) reports, cruelty or neglect toward animals can predict future extreme acts of violence against humans: "Researchers have connected children's abuse of animals to bullying, aggression, school shooting, and sexual abuse. Through these activities, children who feel powerless torment their own victims to gain a sense of control and power for themselves. Moreover, FBI research indicates that most serial killers, school shooters, and mass murderers tortured animals as children."

Though we continue to describe prevention as being a weak link in thwarting juvenile and adult offending, predictors of future violent offending in young children are often noted only in retrospect after a particularly gruesome crime has been committed. As in a number of issues in criminological research, few longitudinal studies are made of early childhood predictors of teen and adult violent offending (Sitnick et al., 2019).

Comparison of Violent Offenders and Nonviolent Offenders

Perhaps the biggest distinction between violent and nonviolent juvenile offenders is that violent offenders, whether male or female, are more likely to be impulsive and to lack remorse (Stephenson et al., 2014). Empathy and sympathy are key, as it is more difficult to distinguish impulsivity as part of a larger psychological disorder at an early age, because children, on the whole, exhibit some propensity for impulsivity.

The development of empathy in early childhood is critical to preventing violent or criminal behavior in adults and children. Adolescents "with higher levels of [the] trait empathy exhibit more prosocial and altruistic behavior, whereas adolescents with lower levels of empathy have been shown to be more aggressive" (Sesso et al., 2021, p. 877). Until juveniles are socialized or mature enough, they may not take the time to process information rationally before acting on their emotions, failing to take into consideration the harm they are doing to others. Violent juvenile offenders who score low on empathy also have higher rates of recidivism, as compared to nonviolent offenders (Bock and Hosser, 2014).

Violent Co-Offending

Juveniles who commit violent crimes often have accomplices. In fact, co-offending juveniles commit more violent offenses than do those acting alone (Lantz, 2020). Two predictors of juvenile violent crime, often detected too late for effective intervention, are undiagnosed antisocial behaviors and the selection of accomplices (Conway and McCord, 2002; Loeber and Hay, 1997; Cairns and Cairns, 1992, 1994; Patterson et al., 1989). Juveniles who co-offend are also more likely to reoffend (Office of Justice Programs, 2005; hereafter OJP).

Here we also see gender differences in co-offending, beyond those we will discuss in Chapter 9. Young male offenders, acting as a group, are associated with more serious injury when they commit violent crimes (Lantz, 2020). This deviates, however, in the context of gang initiation rites, where the prospective new member is ritualistically beaten by existing members. In male gang initiations, the initiate is "beaten in" in a controlled and choreographed ritual, whereas female gang initiations involving violence tend to be more haphazard (Hansen and Freitag, 2016). Male gang members are less likely to set out to seriously injure the recruit, whereas females will resort to hairpulling and other painful torture during initiation (Hansen and Freitag, 2016).

A number of theories help explain violent co-offending. Certainly, those raised in a culture of violence in the home, neighborhood, or both are more likely to see violence as a normal way to deal with frustration or disappointment. Violence then becomes a learned behavior, as suggested by social learning theories in criminology. If we apply Sutherland's differential association theory to violent offending, juveniles associating with those prone to use violence to resolve conflicts will be shunned by deviant peers if they do not likewise resort to violence. In other words, juvenile offenders are affected by the people they choose to associate with or admire, and peer groups or the existence of deviant family members are central to understanding juvenile violent co-offending (Conway and McCord, 2002).

Self-Harm and Violent Offending

Depending on the jurisdiction where the incident takes place, self-harm may be criminalized. Johnson (2021) notes that at least 20 countries in the world consider attempted suicide a crime, including Nigeria, where children as young as seven can be arrested and prosecuted for self-harm. Therapists and psychologists call suicide a permanent solution to a temporary problem and advocate for treating suicidal tendencies as a mental health crisis rather than a criminal act. As Sarah Kline,

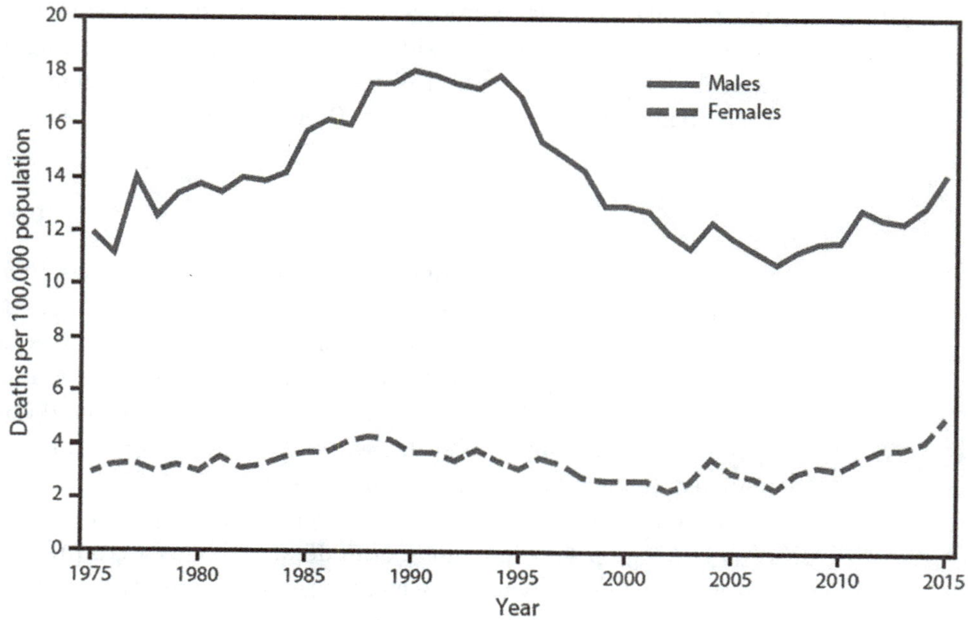

EXHIBIT 5.1: Suicide Rates, Gender Differences, Ages 15-19

co-founder of United for Global Mental Health, states, "Criminalisation of suicide is counterproductive, it does not deter people from taking their own lives. . . . It does deter people from seeking help in a moment of acute crisis and it can prevent people receiving the support they need for their mental health" (Johnson, 2021, retrieved from https://www.theguardian.com/global-development/2021/sep/09/suicide-still-treated-as-a-in-at-least-20-countries-report-finds). Countries that operate under Sharia law criminalize suicide attempts as well.

Though on the federal level in the United States, attempted suicide is no longer classified as a crime, some states still list it as a prosecutable crime (Legal Information Institute, n.d.).[3] Fortunately for the individual, meaningful intervention following an attempted suicide can be lifesaving, even if it also leads to criminal citation. According to the American Academy of Pediatrics (2012), the greatest risk for adolescent suicide is when a firearm is available.

Time of Day

As in the case of adult offending, time of day is a factor in juvenile delinquents' commission of crimes. According to the Office of Juvenile Justice and Delinquency Prevention (OJJDP) of the U.S. Justice Department (OJJDP, 2005), juveniles are most

[3] If you or anyone you know is contemplating suicide, please call the National Suicide Prevention Lifeline immediately at 988 (the new hotline number established in 2022).

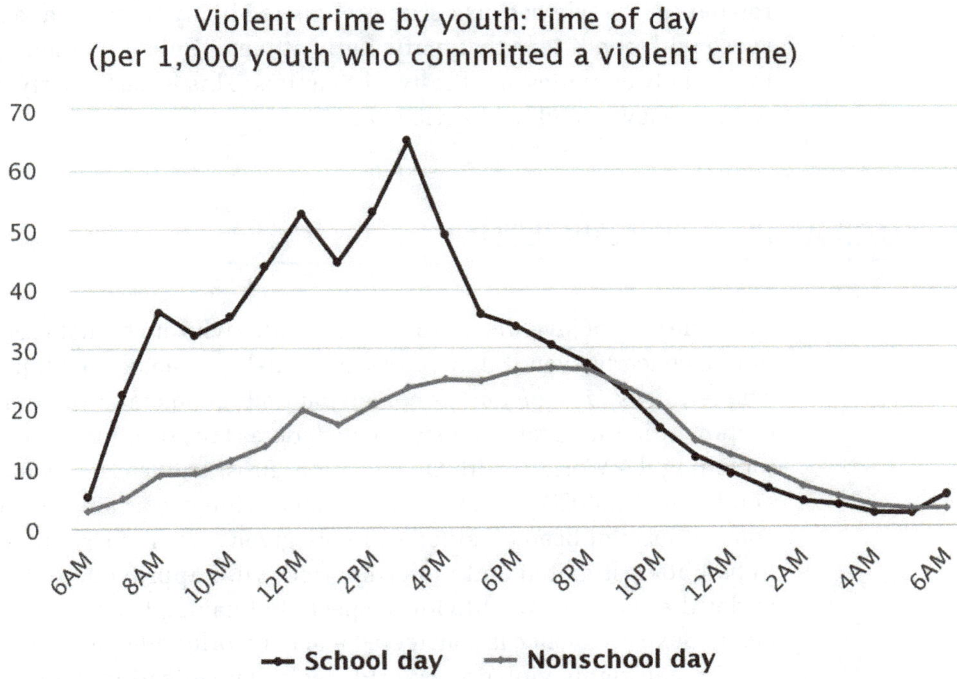

EXHIBIT 5.2 **Violent Crime by Youth: Time of Day** *NOTE: Violent crimes included murder, violent sexual assault, robbery, aggravated assault, simple assault, and kidnapping. Data are from law enforcement agencies in 45 states and the District of Columbia.*

likely to commit violent crimes immediately after the school hours,[4] as demonstrated in Exhibit 5.2.

Exposure to violent victimization of juveniles, on the other hand, is more likely to occur before school. Real or imagined fear of victimization while commuting to school can drive the absentee rates up in more dangerous neighborhoods (Burdick-Will et al., 2019). Students who use public transportation are at risk of victimization, including during their walks to or waits at transit stops (Burdick-Will et al., 2019).

The number of juveniles working while still in school has steadily decreased since the 1990s, putting more adolescents at loose ends and at risk of offending. After-school and summer employment keep adolescents busy, with less time to commit crimes. Whereas in the 1980s over 30% of adolescents ages 16 to 19 held down jobs after school and on weekends, as well as during summer vacations, that figure had dropped to just over 17% by 2021 (Duffin, 2021).

Lifestyle theory also indicates time can be a variable in juvenile crimes. According to Ho et al. (2012, p. 2546), "the opportunity to commit crimes [is]

[4] When this author was in secondary school (middle school and high school), it was not uncommon for rivals to threaten to face each other and fight immediately after school, naming locations off campus where there was less risk of being caught (e.g., alleys).

related to lifestyle because crime events are likely to occur at a special time and space with conditions that particularly attract criminal incidents," and are linked to the daily activities and lifestyle of victims. This is particularly true as applied to online behavior and habits (Ho et al., 2012).

SEXUAL AND DATING VIOLENCE

As in the case of juvenile murderers, juveniles who are sexual predators are of great public concern, even if they represent a small percentage of all juvenile offenders. The term *sexual violence*[5] is somewhat ambiguous, and the definition depends on how it is interpreted by state law, federal law, or international organizations, including the World Health Organization. Broadly, the Centers for Disease Control and Prevention (CDC, 2022) defines sexual violence as any sexual activity where consent has not been obtained or freely given. Rates of sexual violence continue to be underestimated and underreported, with approximately 20% of juveniles under the age of 18 worldwide suspected of having been victimized (Siria et al., 2020). Sexual violence is considered a major worldwide public health issue as well as a human rights violation (World Health Organization, hereafter WHO, 2021), with 30% of women and girls (age 15 and older) reporting having been victimized (United Nations Women, 2022). Sexual violence rates against transgender individuals as reported by the U.S. Office for Victims of Crime (2014) are even higher, with 1 in 2 reporting some form of assault, including hate crimes and intimate partner violence. The International Center for Research on Women (2006) also includes marriages of juvenile females under 18,[6] often followed by domestic and sexual abuse of the child bride, as a form of sexual violence.

Programs in sex education contribute to juveniles' understanding of what sexual violence is and help prevent juvenile sexual offending. According to the National Survey of Family Growth, most teenagers (96% of females and 97% of males) in the United States receive some form of sex education either at home or in school before age 18 (Martinez et al., 2010). However, the curricula vary by region and state and local school rules, so there is no consistency in the type of sex education presented in elementary, middle, or high schools or guarantee that it will include instruction on consent and how to prevent victimization.

[5] If you or someone you know has been a victim of sexual assault, contact the National Sexual Assault Hotline, by chatting online at online.rainn.org or calling (800) 656-4673. Resources, including assistance with Spanish speakers, available at https://www.rainn.org/resources.

[6] Though less common in the United States than in poorer international countries, 44 U.S. states allow marriage under the age of 18 under certain circumstances; 85% of child marriages in the United States involve a girl marrying a significantly older man (Cassidy and Turner, 2021). New York is the latest among six states to ban all marriages of individuals under the age of 18 (Cassidy and Turner, 2021).

Sibling Abuse

"Stranger danger" in the context of sexual violence is a myth. As with any form of abuse, the "stranger danger" tips that children are taught do not adequately prepare them for victimization by people they know. It falsely teaches children and adolescents that they are most likely to be victimized, including molested or raped, by a stranger. In reality, sexual assault is far more likely to occur within intimate partner relationships (WHO, 2021). Child sexual abuse is not always perpetrated by an adult. *Sibling abuse* can include physical, psychological, or sexual abuse, most often when an older sibling abuses a younger one. Sibling sexual abuse, according to the research on the subject, appears to be the most prevalent form of sexual abuse in families, more so than parental incest (Relva et al., 2017; Morrill, 2014).

Sibling abuse goes beyond mere age-appropriate sexual curiosity. The behaviors include exposing younger siblings to pornography, verbal coercion involving physical touch, and sexual intercourse (Tener et al., 2018; Relva et al., 2017). As in the case of parents or guardians who sexually abuse juveniles in their care, sibling sexual abuse often goes unreported and untreated, and as such it is less likely to be researched than other forms of child abuse (Tener et al, 2018). Many parental units, if they become aware of the sibling sexual abuse, will pass it off as either "not serious" or construct their own realities that "it never happened" for fear that disclosure will rupture any imagined "perfect family" image within or outside the family (Tener et al., 2018).

In many cases, even if parental units are aware that the problem exists, they will hide the fact because they are unsure who is the perpetrator or who is the victim. Another reason for concealing sibling sexual abuse is that it can often be mistaken for mutual consent (Relva et al., 2017). Females are more likely to be victimized; one study indicated that 10% of males report having been victimized by one or more siblings, whereas as 15% of females report some sexual experience with a sibling (Relva et al., 2017). However, as in any case of sexual assault, the true extent of the problem is unknown due to underreporting, particularly by males. We also do not know the extent to which a sibling is both perpetrator and victim (Relva et al., 2017).

Dating Violence

We have not yet discussed the phenomenon of interpersonal violence in dating relationships (*dating violent offenders* or DVOs). When intimate partner violence (IVP) or *teen dating violence* occurs in adolescence (ages 15 to 24), including physical, psychological, and sexual violence between two people in an ongoing relationship, it is described as a prevalent, serious social health problem often associated with dating (*dating violence* or *dating abuse*), rather than between cohabitating individuals (Zimmer, 2021; Sjödin et al., 2017). One partner might victimize the other, or they may abuse each other. In the extreme, dating violence can result in assault, rape (*date rape*), or homicide. Those at greatest risk of being victimized are older adolescents with histories of drug use and one or more adverse childhood experiences, while alcohol use predicts higher risk in younger adolescents (Thulin et al., 2021). Intimate partner violence between teenagers is so prevalent that it is estimated that up to two-thirds of youth between ages 12 and 18 are affected by it (Bender et al., 2020).

Not all types of dating abuse involve physical violence, although psychological abuse can lead to physical abuse over time in some cases. The eight types of abuse identified in a dating violence survey conducted in the United States (López-Cepero et al., 2016) include detachment, humiliation, sexual, coercion, physical, gender-based, emotional, and instrumental. Often in these cases the juveniles being targeted, either by strangers or by someone they know, are afraid to tell their parental units.

Of increasing concern are forms of dating violence that take place electronically, either online or by texting. *Electronic dating aggression* can include stalking, harassment, blackmail, and coercion (Thulin et al., 2021). A rash of teenage suicides have occurred following extortion for money over explicit text messages:

- A 16-year-old teenager in Lisbon, New York, was tricked into sending embarrassing photos to someone she met online, reportedly through Facebook. Afterward the blackmailer threatened to send them to classmates and friends and to post them on social media. On March 3, 2021, she took her own life as a result. One month later, just 20 miles down the road, a 15-year-old boy committed suicide under similar circumstances (McClendon, 2022; Benman, 2021).
- A 17-year-old in Michigan was targeted through Instagram in an extortion plot in which he was coerced into taking and sending compromising photos of himself. He died of an apparent suicide on March 25, 2022 (Willetts, 2022).
- In February 2022, an extortionist posing as a girl tricked a California 17-year-old into sending a nude photo of himself, after which the extortionist demanded $5,000 not to expose the photos publicly. The teen killed himself within hours of the request for the nude photo and the blackmail demand (Trujillo, 2022).

A disturbing aspect of these cases is that the extortionists are often adults operating from outside the United States. In the Lisbon, New York, case, the perpetrators were tracked down after a yearlong international search resulting in arrests in Pakistan (McClendon, 2022).

YOUTH GANG VIOLENCE

When discussing gang violence, we cannot, in good conscience, limit our overview to juveniles under the age of 18. Youth gangs are defined as having members from juveniles through young adulthood. However, the United States has no single accepted definition of a youth gang; state and local jurisdictions each develop their own (Howell, 1997). What is universally understood, no matter the gang age range or specific characteristics (e.g., gang name, territory), youth gangs are believed to contribute to much of the violence in a location, particularly in urban settings. Between half and three-fifths of gang members are under age 18, and the FBI believes young gang members are major contributors to crime in a number of U.S. cities and a major contributor to young violent offending (FBI, 2011; OJJDP, n.d.). Even though youth gang members make up a small fraction of the adolescent population in the United States, they account for the majority of violent crimes committed, both as perpetrators and victims (Population Reference Bureau, 2022).

Juvenile Females in Gangs

Though youth gangs are most often male-oriented, increasingly girls with specific risk factors are attracted to gangs (Hansen, 2005). Young female gang membership has been on the rise in recent decades (Hayward and Honeggar, 2014). Most of the risks are attributed to problems at home, including sexual abuse and maltreatment, and gangs are viewed as protection against the powerlessness young females feel in their home lives. For some juvenile females, youth gangs represent a *pseudo-family* to replace their own dysfunctional one (Hansen, 2005). When girls do leave gangs, it is often because they have become pregnant or become involved in the juvenile justice system through arrest or detention, rather than because of any other form of intervention (O'Neal et al., 2014).

The racial makeup of female and male juveniles who join gangs differs. Whereas 10% of young males who join gangs are white, 20% of female gang members are white (Hayward and Honeggar, 2014). The majority of youth gang members, whether female or male, are either Hispanic, Black, or mixed race, with some Asian youth gangs as well. Females who join gangs are more likely than males to have been exposed to physical abuse, including domestic violence (Hayward and Honeggar, 2014; Hansen, 2005; Joe and Chesney-Lind, 1995), suggesting that females join in order to escape their home lives rather than to seek protection on the streets, as is the case with male gang members.

Females are the most likely to be victimized within the context of gang life. Female gang members have been subjected to gang rapes by male gang members, either as part of or outside of gang initiation rituals, and these rapes often go unreported (Nydegger et al., 2017). With few exceptions, there is no gender equality between female and male gang members. Female gang members are more likely to be coerced into intercourse without a condom, resulting in a greater risk of pregnancy and sexually transmitted diseases (Nydegger et al., 2017). There is also often a substantial age difference between sexual partners in gangs, with the females being younger, further exacerbating gender inequality.

Gang Recruitment

Not all neighborhood-oriented youth crews[7] or gangs resort to violence. Many commit petty, nuisance crimes, such as graffiti, and do not present any real threat to the community. However, in the case of more established street gangs, violence is part and parcel of the lifestyle. We should also consider that children as young as elementary school age can be recruited into street gangs, including the more notorious internationally recognized gangs, like MS-13. The majority of youth who identify as gang-affiliated were recruited, on average, around the age of 15; however, they may also be exposed to and tempted by street gangs between the ages of 12 and 14 (National Gang Center, 2015). It is also possible to be in a less traditional gang of juveniles, in which case, recruitment may occur at an even younger age (Sharkey et al., 2022).

In some communities in the United States and elsewhere, it is extremely difficult for male adolescents to avoid joining a gang; in some cases they are made to believe, whether true or not, that their very lives are threatened if they do not join a gang (Welsh, 2017). The fatalist view of death inherent among gang members is clear in the name of a local street gang in Holyoke, Massachusetts: Ready to Die (R2D) (State of Massachusetts, 2019; Hansen, 2014, 2013). In the two western Massachusetts towns of Holyoke and Chicopee, with a combined nine active gangs and 323 known gang members, most violence committed by juveniles and young adults, including simple and aggravated assault, appears to be gang-related (State of Massachusetts, 2019). With combined populations of approximately 96,000 residents, this is a disproportionately high level of gang-related violence.

Juveniles living in gang-infested communities often have a very pessimistic view of their futures. As they see gang members around them either being injured or killed in gang violence, they may have little reason to believe that they themselves will live past their 21st birthdays, doubly so if they belong to a gang. They become fatalistic and pessimistic about their life chances outside of gang life, giving them further reason to believe that they have nothing to lose in committing violent crimes.

Hate Groups and Juvenile Delinquency

Some individuals and groups in the United States are uncomfortable with the country's changing demographics, and this discomfort has resulted in crimes, including violent crimes, against those they perceive to be enemies. A *hate or bias crime* is defined as "an illegal act involving selection based on the perpetrator's bias or prejudice against real or perceived status of the victim." (Näsi et al., 2016, p. 177). These offenses are based on racial, ethnic, national, sexual, gender, or religious animosity. In half the cases, the hate crime offender knew the victim

[7] Juvenile crews are less organized than gangs, are more likely to be neighborhood oriented, and generally do not commit serious offenses, but rather petty crimes, if any at all. Unlike with gangs, someone who moves can join a new crew (Hansen, 2005).

(Rivinius, 2020), with 45% of the cases motivated by either biases against women or perceived LGBTQ2S+ individuals or groups (Kena and Thompson, 2021).

Hate groups have come to the forefront of the news in recent years, and we have seen a rise in hate crimes committed by bands of juveniles under the age of 18 (Godinet and Stotzer, 2017). Juveniles who commit hate crimes have likely been exposed to the influence of adult hate groups. In fact, hate groups, primarily *white supremacy gangs* that identify as racist and xenophobic, actively recruit juveniles and young adults (Blazak, 2001). These groups look for youth, primarily males, who feel overwhelmed by the changing world (Blazak, 2001).

Violent hate group rhetoric and vandalism in the form of alarming graffiti targeting a particular group with disparaging language is considered a prosecutable violent crime. Black churches, synagogues, and mosques have been targeted with graffiti carrying hateful, often frightening and threatening messages, and local law enforcement actively looks for the perpetrators (Hswen, 2022). As a result of the increase in serious consequences, including suicide, due to hateful messaging and postings on social media (some initiated by juveniles), far more acknowledgment has been made in recent years of just how powerful words are in terrorizing the intended target(s).

Crimes committed against those who are perceived to be nonwhite, non-Christian, and/or non-heterosexual, whether true or not, have been steadily rising since the 1990s, in spite of legislation to target and prosecute hate crimes, including the 1968 federal hate crime statue. For example, in the 1990s, attacks against those perceived to be LatinX, Muslim, and/or Arab represented only 5% of assaults, but the number has risen to 25% within the last decade (Rivinius, 2020). Racial and ethnically motivated hate crimes can be attributed to the imagined or real perception of competition over scarce resources, as suggested by *ethnic competition theory* (Van Dyke and Tester, 2014).

The COVID-19 pandemic brought about a backlash against all Asians, not just the Chinese. The virus that causes COVID-19 (coronavirus disease) was first detected in Wuhan, China, leading hate groups and racially biased individuals to falsely conclude that this was a conspiracy against Western countries. Beginning in March 2020, anti-Asian hate hashtags proliferated on social media (Hswen, 2022). Asians and Asian Americans were disproportionately targeted for in-person hate crimes as well. In July 2020, in a particularly horrible case in Brooklyn, New York, males set fire to an 89-year-old Asian woman as she walked in her neighborhood (Hswen, 2022). Unfortunately, anti-Asian sentiment and hate crimes in the United States are not new, just made more visible by social media (Hswen, 2022).

URBAN VIOLENCE

Urban violence plays a role in youth gangs and youth violence in general, with poverty one of the leading causes of this type of offending. In Chicago, for example, more incidents of gun violence take place in the city's poorest neighborhoods. According to Kight and Sykes (2018), the underlying causes of violence in Chicago neighborhoods are historic racial segregation in the city, wealth inequality, the presence of gangs, and law enforcement's inability to solve crimes. Offenders are often left on the streets, able to continue committing more crimes. And even though Illinois has historically had some of the country's toughest gun laws, they have not significantly helped reduce gun violence, at least in Chicago.

For all its notoriety for violent crimes, however, according to the FBI, Chicago ranks 20th in the United States for crimes per 100,000 residents—even Anchorage, Alaska, a seemingly quiet city, ranks higher at 10th place. St. Louis, Missouri, takes first place in violent crimes (*World Population Review*, 2022).

HOMICIDE

With some exceptions, most children who kill have already shown signs of their potential to commit a homicide or have at the very least committed some other seriously violent crime. In some cases, they did not settle for simply murdering their victim; they may have tortured, burned, battered, or raped them as well (Davis, 2011). Juveniles who commit violent crimes, including homicide, are more likely to target children and adolescents due to the size advantage compared to adult targets (Chopin and Beauregard, 2020). In addition, juveniles interact more with other juveniles in their routine activities, giving them greater opportunity to find their victims. With juvenile homicide a "red button issue" for some decades in the United States, when juveniles commit murder, the public wants to know why, even more so when the offender comes from a so-called good home or good family (Heide, 2020). Mothers in particular are often blamed when their child commits a murder or other violent crime (Deegan, 2021). Whether or not it is true in any given case, bad parenting is often blamed.

The long-term outcome for juveniles who commit murder is grim. The juvenile justice system has little motivation to rehabilitate a child who has been convicted of murder (Deegan, 2021). Juvenile homicide offenders who come from disorganized neighborhoods where crime and violence are prevalent are 20 to 22.5 times more likely to be rearrested after time spent in juvenile detention and/or adult prison, and will often reoffend (Heide, 2020). As for the families of adult murderers, those of juvenile homicide offenders are drained of resources and stigmatized for life because of their relationship to the offender (Deegan, 2021). As Deegan (2021, p. 85; Gilmore, 1994, p. 358) writes, "Anybody who has emerged from a family that yielded a murderer must also be formed by the same causes, the same evil, must in some way be responsible for the violence that resulted, must also bear the mark of a frightening and shameful heritage."

Injury of juveniles by firearms, including homicides, is fast becoming the primary source of serious injury in childhood. According to Bender et al. (2020), firearm injuries among adolescents account for 18.7% of all firearm injuries. It is the second leading cause of injury deaths in children from birth to 17 years old; firearms are the cause of death in 87% of all juvenile homicides (Juvenile Justice Information Exchange, 2022). Other statistics contradict this, however, placing firearm-related deaths, including homicide, suicide, or accidents involving guns, first among the leading causes of juvenile death in the United States (Goldstick et al., 2022; American Academy of Pediatrics, 2012).

Given current laws on the purchase of firearms, it is difficult to comprehend how a juvenile can get access to a gun to commit a crime. Under federal law, handgun purchases are prohibited under age 21, and it is prohibited to sell long guns (e.g., rifles) to anyone under 18. The problem is that this prohibition only applies to sales by licensed firearm merchants, and a number of states have no prohibition against long gun ownership by juveniles under 18. This is why gun charges were dropped against Wisconsin teen Kyle Rittenhouse, who at 17 shot three men, killing two, using an AR-15 assault rifle[8] (Richmond, 2021). Gun laws in Wisconsin are somewhat murky. The law reads, "Any person under the age who possesses or goes armed with a dangerous weapon is guilty of a Class A misdemeanor [including any firearm, loaded or unloaded]" (Richmond, 2021, retrieved from https://abcnews.go.com/US/wireStory/explainer-judge-drop-rittenhouse-gun-charge-81285031; Wisconsin State legislation, 948.60 §2a).

As we note elsewhere, juveniles can purchase a gun illegally in several ways. In addition, they can access many legally owned firearms that have not been safely kept locked in their homes.[9] According to the Juvenile Justice Information Exchange (2022), only 46% of parents who own guns keep the gun and ammunition locked away from children. Adults who own firearms cite protection as the primary reason for gun ownership, although rural gun owners are far more likely than urban gun owners to state hunting is their primary reason for owning guns (Igielnik, 2017). Considerable debate divides urban and rural gun owners over the age at which a juvenile should learn gun safety and how to fire a gun.[10] No consensus exists in the United States on when a juvenile is old enough to start training in the use of a firearm (Greenblatt, 2013).

Not all firearm deaths committed by juveniles are homicides. In Kentucky, for example, a five-year-old boy accidentally caused the shooting death of his two-year-old sister (Greenblatt, 2013). In a statement by the American Academy of Pediatrics (2012, retrieved from https://publications.aap.org/pediatrics/article/130/5/e1416/32375/Firearm-Related-Injuries-Affecting-the-Pediatric?autologincheck=redirected), "The

[8] Rittenhouse was found not guilty on all accounts, after claiming self-defense (Sullivan, 2021). Rittenhouse had taken the firearm to a Kenosha protest of the police shooting of Jacob Blake and testified that he was acting as a medic and protecting private property, even though he was not trained or certified in either capacity (Richmond, 2021; Sullivan, 2021).

[9] Gun safety tips for parental units and other adults are available at Safe Kids Worldwide, https://www.safekids.org/tip/gun-safety-tips.

[10] This author, who was raised in a suburb of Los Angeles, California, was eight years old when taught firearm safety and how to fire a 22 rifle and shotgun.

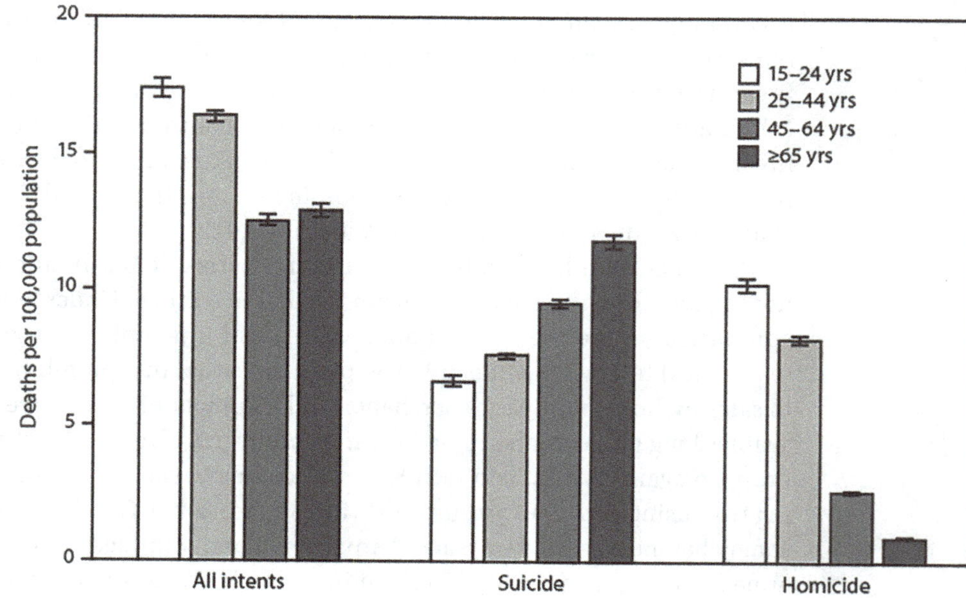

EXHIBIT 5.3 ‖ Rates of Firearm Deaths, by Age and Type, 2019

absence of guns from children's homes and communities is the most reliable and effective measure to prevent firearm-related injuries in children and adolescents." An individual factor for the risk of teen dating violence is access to, and the practice of, carrying a firearm (Bender et al., 2020). Young males, in particular those who have been victimized, are more likely to carry a firearm, including to school, and are more likely to get into physical altercations (Bender et al., 2020).

In recent decades, *ghost guns* have become a growing problem. These are homemade firearms that do not have serial numbers and so cannot be traced back to their owners (State of Illinois, 2022). And as in the case of alcohol, little prevents an adult from legally purchasing a firearm and reselling it illegally to a juvenile. For example, Eric Harris and Dylan Klebold, the two teens who committed the Columbine High School mass shooting, had talked an older friend into purchasing some of the guns used (Marcus, 2022).

Media representations of teen murder suspects are generally false. Unlike the teen killers in the *Scream* movie franchise, juvenile murderers rarely methodically plan homicides. As Gárcia-Baamond et al. (2022, p. 2) state, "the generally badly characterised film image of the typical murderer who creates a plan of action and chooses their victim is ostensibly false in the case of most juvenile homicides." And as Pozueco (2011) noted, media representations, whether in film or the news, only apply in rare, extreme cases, such as serial killers and mass murderers.[11] Juvenile

[11] The difference between serial killers and mass murderers is that serial killers will kill their victims over time and generally in different locations. Mass murderers kill a number of individuals in one location at one time.

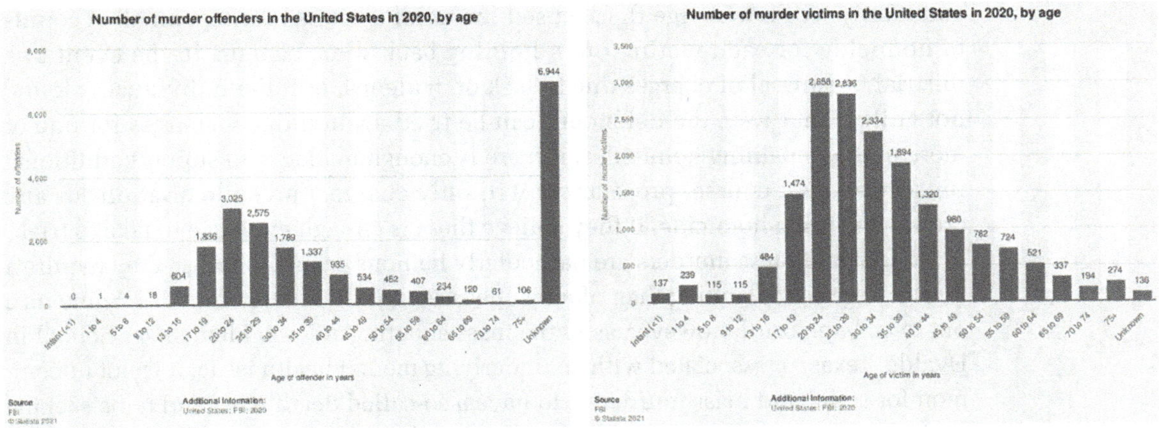

Exhibit 5.4 | **Number of Murder Offenders, U.S., 2020, by Age (L), Number of Murder Victims, U.S., 2020 by Age (R)**

homicide offenders are also stereotyped as social misfits, with histories of arson, bedwetting, and animal cruelty (Deegan, 2021). As Davis (2011) notes, in spite of media accounts, there is no epidemic of "mini-murderers."

Juveniles make up a small fraction of those who commit homicide in the United States. Rarer yet is the juvenile sexual homicide offender, who kills a victim to silence them following a sexual assault (Chopin and Beauregard, 2020). In the vast number of cases of sexual assault and torture, with sadistic behavior ending in murder, the offender, if known, is 20 or older (Statista Research Department, 2021a), while the victims are likely to be between the ages of 20 and 29 (Statista Research Department, 2021b). And though juvenile males are overwhelmingly more likely to commit a homicide, juvenile females are not exempt from committing murders. (See the "In the Media" section of this chapter for an example.)

Though small in numbers, juveniles who kill are not a new phenomenon. The fact that historical accounts of young murderers predate mass media, movies, and violent video games dispels the common myth that all violent juveniles who commit homicide have watched one too many horror films or come from a single-parent household (Davis, 2011). The motivations leading juveniles to commit homicide are universal and timeless: anger, rape and murder fantasies, revenge, jealousy, resistance by the victim during an attempted rape, and an escalation of violence (Chopin and Beauregard, 2020).

Serial Killers and Mass Murderers

There is no legal code in the United States addressing serial killings or mass murders. Individuals accused of such crimes are charged based on the number of murders committed, whether in one instance or over time. The only enhancement to charges is for crimes classified as terrorist acts or associated with gang activity. Prosecutors commonly will not charge the accused for serial or mass murders on all accounts of homicide for each victim, often holding back some charges in the event of a mistrial, dismissal of charges due to lack of evidence, or if the individual is found not guilty. That way, the defendant can be tried again on new charges for one or more of the remaining homicides, if there is enough evidence to support additional prosecution. Of course, prosecutors will only charge a juvenile or adult for any crime, including homicide, if they believe there is enough evidence to take to trial.

Serial and mass murders are particularly heinous crimes, because they require a greater degree of planning than often is the case in individual homicides. Some turn out to be haphazard, however, as in the mass shooting at Robb Elementary School in Uvalde, Texas, or associated with an underlying mental health issue. It is not uncommon for serial and mass murderers to have a so-called death wish and to be seeking "suicide by cop." In some cases, the perpetrator has a history of attempted suicide.

Some instances of mass murders committed by young offenders include:

- On May 23, 2022, 18-year-old Salvador Ramos, a described loner with few friends, entered an Uvalde, Texas, elementary school after crashing his car, with the alleged[12] motivation to commit a mass murder (Levinson et al., 2022). Ramos barricaded himself in two classrooms and proceeded to open fire with an AR-15 style assault rifle, killing 19 children and two teachers. Before the mass shooting at the elementary school, Ramos had admitted on social media that he had just shot his grandmother and warned that he was headed to the school (Levinson et al., 2022). He allegedly told one of his social media contacts that he was in the habit of throwing dead cats at people's houses (Levinson et al., 2022).
- In February 2018, former Marjory Stone High School student Nikolas Cruz, age 19, entered a Parkland, Florida, school and proceeded to open fire with a semi-automatic rifle, killing 17 people on campus and injuring another 14 people (Chuck et al., 2018). Cruz had recently been expelled from the school for behavior problems (Chuck et al., 2018).
- The Columbine High School mass murder took place in Littleton, Colorado, in April 1999, and resulted in the death of 12 students and 1 teacher and injuries to 20 others on campus that day (FBI, 1999a). The gunmen were Eric Harris, 18, and Dylan Klebold, 17, both students at Columbine, calling themselves the "Trench Coat Mafia." They opened fire and detonated a number of homemade explosive devices. Harris and Klebold ultimately committed suicide at the school immediately after their rampage, before law enforcement could confront them (FBI, 1999b).

Those who commit serial or mass murder, whether adults or juveniles, are predators, but predator offenders represent the smallest number of juvenile

[12] Ramos was killed by Border Patrol officers in the classroom, and as he never was arrested, tried, and convicted, we still describe his crime as "alleged," even though there is overwhelming, undisputed evidence that he was the perpetrator. Ramos had recently legally purchased two assault rifles on his 18th birthday (Levinson et al., 2022).

homicide offenders (Chopin and Beauregard, 2023; 2020). Incidences of mass murder are growing, however, particularly those committed on school grounds. Again, one common denominator of these crimes is the availability of firearms. The juvenile perpetrators of these horrific crimes are often described as having been disenfranchised in school and victims of bullying.

SUMMARY

This chapter contains disturbing, difficult to digest information. Violent crimes are a primary concern for crime fighters, but prevention programs may or may not be effective. With few resources to prevent violent crime, law enforcement often can only respond helplessly to the scene after the fact.

Much of the youth violence we witness today is attributed to gangs, primarily in urban settings, though gang violence can be found in smaller cities as well. In poorer communities where gang violence is prevalent, juveniles are recruited into gangs as young as elementary-school age. Females are also targeted for gang recruitment. However, once they join, females are more likely to be victimized, including by sexual assault and coercion into unsafe sex practices, by much older gang-affiliated males.

Violent crimes, including homicides, are motivated by greed, anger, revenge, or pride, for both juvenile and adult offenders. Juveniles, and in particular, gang members, account for the greater number of violent crimes committed. However, as violent crimes like assault and rape often go unreported, even with substantial victimization surveys, academics, policy makers, and law enforcement do not know the full extent of violent crime.

It is difficult to identify characteristics that would help predict violent offending in juveniles. Part of the problem is that juveniles, by their very nature, can be impulsive. Until the brain has fully developed, particularly the frontal cortex, it often difficult to determine whether pathological impulsivity led a juvenile to commit a violent crime. What we do know is that juveniles and adults who score low on empathy are more likely to act impulsively and commit violent crimes. We also know that juveniles who have been victimized, at home or through bullying, are more likely to resort to violence to resolve conflicts. This applies as well to those raised in an environment of violence, whether in the home or the community.

Juveniles can also commit violent sex crimes, including rape. However, one type of sexual violence that often goes unreported is sibling sexual abuse. Even when parental units are aware of the problem, they often hide it, as they are concerned about shattering their own and the outside world's image of theirs as the perfect family. Despite the stereotype that older relatives or adults perpetrate child sex abuse, researchers fear that sibling sexual abuse of minor children is even more common than adult child abuse.

Of all forms of violent offenses committed by juveniles, homicides are of greatest concern, in part fueled by media interest. Despite an ongoing controversy in the United States over interpretation of Second Amendment rights as they apply to firearm ownership, firearm deaths account for the majority of injuries and deaths of juveniles, whether the perpetrators are juveniles or adults. A number of child advocacy and activist groups point not only to gun ownership but also to adults' failure to store guns safely as primary causes for accidental or intentional injury where guns are involved.

Though they are less frequent than any other form of homicide committed by children, serial and mass murders by juvenile offenders do occur, seemingly at alarming rates. Homicides, including serial and mass murders by juveniles, are rarely planned, but rather can be haphazard, though some planning has to take place to obtain a firearm. Serial and mass murders are often associated with mental health issues, though this is anecdotal, rather than based in research. It is difficult to generalize about juveniles who commit extremely violent crimes, as these still happen infrequently, preventing development of statistical probability or characterizations of these kind of juvenile killers.

IN THE MEDIA

Little Girl Lost: Juvenile Female Killers

Cindy Lee Collier's horrendous childhood was filled with sexual and physical abuse and set her up for a lifetime of misery. She was raped before age 10 (Bovsun, 2017), and when she contracted a venereal disease at 13, resulting in painful menstruation with excessive bleeding, she attempted to take her own life (Davis, 2011). After a series of juvenile crimes, including shoplifting, drug use, and carjacking, Collier was sent to juvenile detention at 14 (*Femme Killers*, 2020; Bovsun, 2017).

In the summer of 1983, Collier, then 15, and her accomplice Shirley Wolf, then 14, who had had a similarly bleak childhood, hatched an elaborate and murderous plan. The two girls planned to run away from the California juvenile facility where they both lived, kill someone, and steal their car for transportation (Davis, 2011; Merriam, 1998). After they successfully escaped the facility, they knocked on a number of doors in a condominium complex to find someone from whom they could steal car keys (*My Crime Library*, n.d). After being turned away by several of the neighbors, they eventually targeted 85-year-old Anna Brackett. After gaining entrance to her home on the pretense that they thought they were being followed and needed to use her phone, Collier and Wolf strangled and stabbed Brackett to death (Davis, 2011). In her diary, Wolf wrote, "Today Cindy and I ran away and killed an old lady. It was lots of fun" (Bovsun, 2017).

The two girls were caught after Brackett's son Carl discovered his mother's body, with at least 28 stab wounds, including one that was 4 inches deep (Bovsun, 2017). Neighbors in the condominium complex identified Collier and Wolf from

Cindy Collier and Shirley Wolf.

their failed attempts to find a victim. Carl, too, recognized the girls. He had been driving to his mother's home to pick her up for bingo, and he remembers spotting the girls hitchhiking on the highway (*Femme Killers*, 2017).

Postscript

Collier and Wolf were eventually arrested, prosecuted, found delinquent[13] in the murder of Anna Brackett, and sentenced to serve time in California Youth Authority facility until their 27th birthdays.

Collier was released from the California Youth Authority after nine years. After her release, she earned a two-year associates degree, and studied law at Pepperdine University School of Law in California (*Femme Killers*, 2017; Merriam, n.d.). She currently has four children and lives in Northern California (Merriam, n.d.).

Wolf assaulted fellow prisoners and eventually stabbed a supervisor at the facility in the face and hand, earning her an additional nine years behind bars in adult prison (Davis, 2011). She was released in 1995 after serving 12 years, and even though she had completed her high school education while in prison, she was subsequently arrested for a variety of crimes (Merriam, n.d.). In 2015 she entered treatment with a counselor, in the hope of finally turning her life around (Merriam, n.d.).

[13] In adult court, an accused person can be found guilty of a crime, whereas in juvenile cases, the accused can be found delinquent.

SOURCES

Bovsun, M. (2017). "Teenage girls brutally murder 85-year-old woman 'just for fun' in 1983." *Daily News*. Aug 20. Retrieved from https://www.nydailynews.com/news/crime/teen-girls-brutally-murder-woman-85-fun-1983-article-1.3426680.

Davis, C. A. (2011). *Children Who Kill: Profiles of Teen and Pre-teen Killers*. London, UK: Allison and Busby.

Femme Killers: Shirley Wolf and Cindy Collier Murder Anna Brackett (2020). Video, Youtube.com. Jul 11. Retrieved from https://www.youtube.com/watch?v=usWPzaLC5k8.

Merriam, J. (n.d.). "Little Girl Lost: A True Story of Shattered Innocence and Murder." Website. Retrieved from https://www.joanmerriam.com/little-girl-lost-1.

Merriam, J. (1998). *Little Girl Lost*. Bemidji, MN: Pinnacle Publishing, LLC.

My Crime Library (n.d.). Cindy Collier and Shirley Wolf teen killers. Retrieved from https://mycrimelibrary.com/cindy-collier-and-shirley-wolf-teen-killers/.

INTERNATIONAL PERSPECTIVES

Violent Youth Crime in Taiwan

Taiwan has received very little attention when it comes to studying youth crime. Since the beginning of this century, concern has been growing there over a perceived rise in violent crimes committed by juveniles.

Map: Taiwan.

Comparing the types of crimes and perceptions of crime in Taiwan with those in the United States, we find the following (Nation Master, 2022):

- People in the United States are 34% more likely to report that they believe that crime has increased in the past three years.
- Crime rates in the United States are four times that of Taiwan.
- The United States has 46% more cannabis use than Taiwan.
- People in the United States are three times more likely to fear being victimized.
- There is six times more violent crime committed in the United States than in Taiwan.
- Intentional homicides are 74 times greater in the United States than in Taiwan.
- The United States has 36 times more prisoners per capita than Taiwan.

According to Textor (2021), in 2020, there were approximately 10,226 recorded young offenders in Taiwan, down from the estimated 30,000 in the 1990s (Lee, 2005). By the early 2000s, there were a number of violent juvenile crimes that caught the attention of the public and the media, including the following (Ho et al., 2012; Huang, 2007; Lee, 2005):

- Two teenagers in 2000 kidnapped and murdered a 15-year-old boy, subsequently attempting to hide the body in a barrel of cement.
- In 2004, five teenagers allegedly cut off the fingers of a policeman.
- In 2005, a 14-year-old girl was raped and murdered in her home when a 16-year-old male discovered her during an attempted robbery.
- Increasing numbers of teenagers took drugs, joined joy-riding gangs, committed sexual abuse, and entered prostitution.
- A growing number of teenagers are believed to be associated with major organized crime groups, or are acting as small-time gangsters themselves.
- Cybercrimes have come to the forefront of crimes committed by Taiwanese juveniles.
- The Taiwanese Criminal Investigation Bureau reported that the number of juvenile criminal suspects rose from 9 in 2001 to 907 in 2010.

Juveniles in Taiwan, particularly those who commit violent crimes, are often associated with gangs, as is the case in the United States. Gang affiliation is one of the biggest predictors of violent offending by juveniles in Taiwan (Lai, 2019). Youth gangs in Taiwan are inevitably tied to organized crime, with juveniles controlled by older gang members higher up in the ranks of gang organization (Duffy, 2004). Though there are no enhancements of charges if a violent crime is committed within the context of gang life, as there are in the United States, a revision of the Taiwanese Firearms Statute (2008) increased penalties for the use of any weapon (including guns, knives, or even explosives) in the commission of crime to up to 50% greater punishment, as compared to cases where no weapon was used (U.S. Library of Congress, 2008).

In Taiwan, juvenile detention is decidedly different from detention in the United States. The deceptive drop in the number of juvenile offenders recorded since the 1990s is attributed to changes in record keeping practices. With a focus on protecting rather than punishing juvenile offenders, Taiwan's juvenile justice system has shifted focus to education, rehabilitation, or as the Taiwanese view it, "redirection" (Lee, 2005). Some juvenile offenders, particularly those with more minor charges, are thus much less likely to become part of the juvenile detention system in Taiwan.

SOURCES

Duffy, M. P. (2004). Introduction. In *Teen Gangs: A Global View*, ed. M. P. Duffy and E. Gillig. Westport, CT: Greenwood.

Ho, L., Y. Lin, and C. Huang (2012). "Influences of Online Lifestyle on Juvenile Cybercrime Behaviors in Taiwan." 2012 International Workshop on Information and Electronics Engineering (IWIEE). *Procedia Engineering*. Vol. 29: 2545–2550.

Huang, J. (2007). "Labor force participation and juvenile delinquency in Taiwan: A time series analysis." *Journal of Family Economic Issues*. Vol. 28: 137–150.

Lai, Y. (2019). "Determinants of importation and deprivation on committed juvenile offenders' violent misconduct: A Taiwanese perspective." *International Journal of Offender Therapy and Comparative Criminology*. Vol. 63, issue 8: 1242–1264.

Lee, C. (2005). "Youth in Trouble—Where Can They Call Home?" M. Hill, trans. *Taiwan Panorama*. May. Retrieved from https://www.taiwan-panorama.com/Articles/Details?Guid=-c9a5a95d-2b0e-4d99-b913-ce58ab7dc1b4&langId=3&CatId=11.

Nation Master (2022). Crime stats: Compare key data on Taiwan and the United States. Retrieved from https://www.nationmaster.com/country-info/compare/Taiwan/United-States/Crime.

Textor, C. (2021). Number of young offenders in Taiwan 2010–2020. Statista. Jan 6. Retrieved from https://www.statista.com/statistics/319872/taiwan-number-of-young-offenders/#:~:text=In%202020%2C%20approximately%2010%2C226%20young%20offenders%20had%20been%20recorded%20in%20Taiwan.

U.S. Library of Congress (2008). Taiwan: Amendment to Firearms Law. Dec 5. Retrieved from https://www.loc.gov/item/global-legal-monitor/2008-12-05/taiwan-amendment-to-firearms-law/.

CHAPTER DISCUSSION QUESTIONS

1. What can be done to help juveniles avoid gang life if they live in a violent neighborhood?
2. Knowing some characteristics of young violent offenders, what interventions, assuming unlimited resources, could be implemented to prevent violent crime?
3. Without citing political reasons, why should a juvenile who has committed a serious violent crime like homicide be held in an adult facility? Why not?
4. In what ways does youth gang life increase the probability of committing a violent crime?

5. What purposes does it serve to have violent gang initiation rituals, including beating an initiate?
6. Why might young females in gangs continue their membership given their greater risk for victimization?
7. Besides the reasons given in this chapter, why might parental units ignore signs that sibling abuse is taking place in their household?
8. Why might there be less attention paid to trends in juvenile crimes in countries like Taiwan?

GLOSSARY

Date rape Nonconsensual intercourse within the context of a dating relationship. See *dating abuse, dating violence.*

Dating abuse Similar to intimate partner violence (IPV), when one or both parties in a dating relationship physically, emotionally, or physically abuse the other. See *date rape, dating violence.*

Dating violence Any form of violence that takes place within the context of a dating relationship. See *dating abuse, date rape.*

Dating violent offender (DVO) A juvenile or adult who commits date rape, violent dating abuse, or any other form of violent crime on a romantic interest or partner. See *date rape, dating abuse, dating violence.*

Electronic dating aggression Targeting a romantic interest or partner with abusive and/or threatening content in emails, text messages, or direct messaging on social media.

Ethnic competition theory The fear by some that a particular racial, ethnic, or religious minority will grow in numbers and create competition for resources, including jobs.

Ghost guns Guns that are homemade, rather than manufactured, including those that can be made with a 3D printer.

Hate or bias crimes Any crime, including violence, vandalism, or threatening language, that is motivated by deep-seated prejudices on the basis of race, ethnicity, religion, gender, or sexual orientation. See *hate groups.*

Hate groups A collective of individuals, often organized and using social media, that advocate hatred or violence against others on the basis of race, ethnicity, religion, gender, or sexual orientation. See *hate or bias crimes.*

Sexual violence Any form of violent act against others that involves sexual abuse, including sexual assault and rape.

Sibling abuse Physical, emotional, and/or psychological abuse of a sibling, generally most often by an older sibling victimizing a younger one. Includes sibling incest and molestation.

Urban violence Refers to the violence witnessed in larger cities, including gang activities, assaults, and gun violence.

White supremacy gangs Any organized hate group that advocates extreme prejudice, and often violence, against anyone perceived to be a racial or ethnic minority and/or non-Christian. As in the example of the Aryan Brotherhood, which are often found in prisons, some white supremacy groups based in the United States and around the world are described as neo-Nazi organizations. See *hate or bias crimes* and *hate groups*.

REFERENCES AND ADDITIONAL SUGGESTED READINGS

Agnew, R. S. (2012). "Strain theory and violent behavior." Ch. 26 in *The Cambridge Handbook of Violent Behavior and Aggression*, ed. D. J. Flannery, A. T. Vazsonyi, and I. D. Waldman. Cambridge, UK: Cambridge University Press.

American Academy of Pediatrics (AAP) (2012). "Firearm-related injuries affecting the pediatric population." Council on Injury, Violence, and Poison Executive Committee. *Pediatrics.* Vol. 130, issue 5: e1416–e1423.

Bender, A. K., E. Koegler, S. D. Johnson, V. Murugan, and R. Wamser-Nanney (2020). "Guns and intimate partner violence among adolescents: A scoping review." *Journal of Family Violence.* Retrieved from https://www.researchgate.net/profile/Vithya-Murugan/publication/343653440_Guns_and_Intimate_Partner_Violence_among_Adolescents_a_Scoping_Review/links/605d2352a6fdccbfea084b6d/Guns-and-Intimate-Partner-Violence-among-Adolescents-a-Scoping-Review.pdf.

Benman, K. (2021). "Another teen suicide blamed on internet blackmail." 7 News. Apr 12. Retrieved from https://www.wwnytv.com/2021/04/12/another-teen-suicide-blamed-internet-blackmail/.

Blazak, R. (2001). "White boys to terrorist men: Target recruitment of Nazi Skinheads." *American Behavioral Scientist.* Vol. 44, issue 6: 982–1000.

Bock, E. M., and D. Hosser (2014). "Empathy as a predictor of recidivism among young adult offenders." *Psychology, Crime, and Law.* Vol. 20, issue 2: 101–115.

Burdick-Will, J., M. L. Stein, and J. Grigg (2019). "Danger on the way to school: Exposure to violent crime, public transportation, and absenteeism." *Sociological Science.* Vol. 6: 118–142.

Cairns, R. B., and B. D. Cairns (1994). *Lifelines and Risks: Pathways of Youth in Our Time.* New York: Cambridge University Press.

Cairns, R. B., and B. D. Cairns (1992). "The sociogenesis of aggressive and antisocial behaviors." *Frameworks and Forecasts: Advances in Criminological Theory.* Vol. 3: 157–191.

Cassidy, P., and T. Turner (2021). "The fight continues to end child marriage in the U.S." UNICEF USA. Aug 25. Retrieved from https://www.unicefusa.org/stories/fight-continues-end-child-marriage-us/38893#:~:text=International%20conversations%20about%20child%20marriage,married%20before%20their%2018th%20birthday.

Centers for Disease Control and Prevention (CDC) (2022). "Fast facts: What is sexual violence?" June 22. Retrieved from https://www.cdc.gov/violenceprevention/sexualviolence/fastfact.html.

Chopin, J., and E. Beauregard (2023). "The unusual case of sexual homicide against males: Comparisons and classifications." *International Journal of Offender Therapy and Comparative Criminology.* Apr. Vol. 67, issue 5: 499–523.

Chopin, J., and E. Beauregard (2020). "Juvenile sexual murderers: Examination and classification of the crime-commission process." *Journal of Forensic Sciences.* Vol. 65, issue 5: 1627–1637.

Chuck, E., A. Johnson, and C. Siemasko (2018). "17 killed in mass shooting at high school in Parkland, Florida." NBC News. Feb 15. Retrieved from https://www.nbcnews.com/news/us-news/police-respond-shooting-parkland-florida-high-school-n848101.

Conway, K. P., and J. McCord (2002). "A longitudinal explanation of the relationship between co-offending with violent accomplices and violent crime." *Aggressive Behavior.* Vol. 28: 97–108.

Davis, C. A. (2011). *Children Who Kill: Profiles of Teen and Pre-teen Killers.* London, UK: Allison and Busby.

Deegan, S. J. (2021). "The meaning of murder: Family members in the lives of juvenile homicide offenders." *British Journal of Criminology.* Vol. 61: 85–103.

Duffin, E. D. (2021). Graph: U.S. teens (16–19) who are enrolled in school and working. Statista. Retrieved from https://www.statista.com/statistics/477668/percentage-of-youth-who-are-enrolled-in-school-and-working-in-the-us/.

Elkins, F. (2019). "Animal cruelty: A serious crime leading to horrific outcomes." U. S. Department of Justice. *Dispatch.* Vol. 12, issue 3 (April). Retrieved from https://cops.usdoj.gov/html/dispatch/04-2019/animal_cruelty.html.

FBI (Federal Bureau of Investigation) (1999a). *Columbine High School* (monograph). Washington, DC: General Accounting Offices (GAO) Publications.

FBI (Federal Bureau of Investigation) (1999b). *Freedom of Information and Privacy Acts: Columbine High School.* Washington, DC: General Accounting Offices (GAO) Publications. Pt. 1.

FBI (Federal Bureau of Investigation) (2011). *National Gang Threat Assessment: Emerging Trends.* Washington, DC: General Accounting Offices (GAO) Publications.

García-Baamonde, M. E., M. Blázquez-Alonso, J. M. Moreno-Manso, E. Guerrero-Barona, and M. Guerrero-Molina (2022). "Youth serial killers: Psychological and criminological profiles." *International Journal of Environmental Research and Public Health.* Vol. 19. Retrieved from https://www.mdpi.com/1660-4601/19/9/5359.

Gilmore, M. (1994). *Shot in the Heart: One Family's History in Murder.* New York: Viking Press.

Godinet, M. T., and R. Stotzer (2017). "Juvenile perpetrators of race/ethnicity-based bias crimes." *Journal of Ethnicity in Criminal Justice.* Vol. 15, issue 1: 21–35.

Goldstick, J. E., R. M. Cunningham, and P. M. Carter (2022). "Current causes of death in children and adolescents in the United States." *New England Journal of Medicine.* Vol. 386 (May): 1955–1956.

Greenblatt, A. (2013). "When it comes to guns, how young is too young?" New England Public Radio (NEPR). May 2. Retrieved from https://www.npr.org/2013/05/02/180607299/when-it-comes-to-guns-how-young-is-too-young.

Hansen, L. L. (2014). *Survey Report, Residents and Agencies—2012–2013, South Holyoke Safe Neighborhood Initiative, Fall 2012.* Holyoke, MA: Holyoke Safe Neighborhood Initiative.

Hansen, L. L. (2013). *Survey Report, First Wave: South Holyoke Safe Neighborhood Initiative, Fall 2012.* Holyoke, MA: Holyoke Safe Neighborhood Initiative.

Hansen, L. L. (2005). "Girl 'Crew' Members Doing Gender, Boy 'Crew' Members Doing Violence: An Ethnographic and Network Analysis of Maria Hinojosa's New York Gangs." *Western Criminology Review.* Vol 6, issue 1:134–144. Retrieved from http://www.westerncriminology.org/documents/WCR/v06n1/article_pdfs/hansen.pdf.

Hansen L. P., and M. E. Freitag (2016). "Choreographed violence in gang initiation rites." Ch. 1 in *Global Perspectives on Youth Behavior, Violence, and Weapons Use*, ed. S. Harding and M. Palasinki. UK: IGI Global.

Hayward, R. A., and L. Honegger (2014). "Gender differences in juvenile gang members: An exploratory study." *Journal of Evidence-Based Social Work*. Vol. 11: 373–382.

Heide, K. M. (2020). "Juvenile homicide offenders look back 35 years later: Reasons they were involved in murder." *International Journal of Environmental Research and Public Health*. Vol. 17, issue 11 (June): 3932.

Hemez, P., and C. Washington (2021). Percentage and number of children living with two parents has dropped since 1968. United States Census Bureau. Apr 12. Retrieved from https://www.census.gov/library/stories/2021/04/number-of-children-living-only-with-their-mothers-has-doubled-in-past-50-years.html.

Ho, L., Y. Lin, and C. Huang (2012). "Influences of Online Lifestyle on Juvenile Cybercrime Behaviors in Taiwan." 2012 International Workshop on Information and Electronics Engineering (IWIEE). *Procedia Engineering*. Vol. 29: 2545–2550.

Howell, J. C. (1997). Youth gangs. Office of Juvenile Justice and Delinquency Prevention Fact Sheet. Office of Juvenile Justice and Delinquency Prevention (OJJDP), Office of Justice Programs, U.S. Department of Justice. FS-72.

Hsu, C. (2010). *Humanitarian Criminology: Theory of Control and Restorative Justice*. Taipei, Taiwan: San Ming Book Inc., Ltd.

Hswen, Y. (2022). "Online hate: The new virus." *American Journal of Public Health*. Vol. 112, issue 4 (April): 545–547.

Igielnik, R. (2017). "Rural and urban gun owners have different experience, views on gun policy." PEW Research Center. Jul 10. Retrieved from https://www.pewresearch.org/fact-tank/2017/07/10/rural-and-urban-gun-owners-have-different-experiences-views-on-gun-policy/.

International Center for Research on Women (2006). "Child marriage and domestic violence." Retrieved from https://www.icrw.org/files/images/Child-Marriage-Fact-Sheet-Domestic-Violence.pdf.

Joe, K. A., and M. Chesney-Lind (1995). "'Just every mother's angel': An analysis of gender and ethnic variations in youth gang membership." *Gender and Society*. Vol. 9, issue 4: 408–431.

Johnson, S. (2021). "Suicide still treated as a crime in at least 20 countries, report finds." *The Guardian*. Sep. 9. Retrieved from https://www.theguardian.com/global-development/2021/sep/09/suicide-still-treated-as-a-in-at-least-20-countries-report-finds.

Juvenile Justice Information Exchange (2022). Youth gun violence section. Resource Hub. Retrieved from https://jjie.org/hub/youth-gun-violence/.

Katz, R. C., and J. Marquette (1996). "Psychosocial characteristics of young violent offenders: A comparative study." *Criminal Behaviour and Mental Health*. Vol. 6, issue 4: 339–348.

Kena, G. and A. Thompson (2021). Hate crime victimization, 2005–2019. NCJ 300954. Bureau of Justice Statistics, U.S. Department of Justice. Sep. Retrieved from https://bjs.ojp.gov/sites/g/files/xyckuh236/files/media/document/hcv0519_1.pdf.

Kight, S. W., and M. Sykes (2018). "The deadliest city. Behind Chicago's segregated shooting sprees." *AXIOS*. Aug 14. Retrieved from https://www.axios.com/2018/08/14/chicago-gun-violence-murder-rate-statistics.

Lantz, B. (2020). "Co-offending group composition and violence: The impact of sex, age, and group size on co-offending violence." *Crime and Delinquency*. Vol. 66, issue 1: 93–122.

Legal Information Institute (n.d.). Suicide. Cornell Law School. Retrieved from https://www.law.cornell.edu/wex/suicide.

Levinson, E., I. Chapman, A. Ross, and S. Prokupecz (2022). "Uvalde school shooting suspect was a loner who bought two assault rifles for his 18th birthday." CNN. May 26. Retrieved from https://www.cnn.com/2022/05/25/us/uvalde-texas-school-shooting-salvador-ramos/index.html.

Loeber, R., and D. Hay (1997). "Key issues in the development of aggression and violence in childhood to early adulthood." *Annual Review of Psychology*. Vol. 48: 371–410.

López-Cepero, H. E. Fabelo, L. Rodríguez-Franco, and F. J. Rodríguez-Díaz (2016). "The Dating Violence Questionnaire: Validation of the Cuestionario de Violencia de Novios using a college sample from the United States." *Violence and Victims*. Vol. 31, issue 3: 438–456.

Maginnis, R. L. (1997). "Single-Parent Families Cause Juvenile Crime." In *Juvenile Crime: Opposing Viewpoints*, ed. A. E. Sadler and S. Barbour. San Diego, CA: Greenhaven.

Marcus, R. (2022). "Why do we let children buy firearms?" Opinion. *Washington Post*. May 27. Retrieved from https://www.washingtonpost.com/opinions/2022/05/27/why-kids-can-buy-guns/.

Martinez, G., J. Abma, and C. Copen (2010). Educating teenagers about sex in the United States. National Center for Health Statistics Data Brief. Center for Disease Control and Prevention (CDC), U.S. Department of Health and Human Services. No. 44 (Sep.). Retrieved from https://www.cdc.gov/nchs/data/databriefs/db44.pdf.

McClendon, J. (2022). "He threatened to post NY teen's naked photos online. Her suicide leads to arrests in Pakistan." *Advance Local Media*. Mar 28. Retrieved from https://www.syracuse.com/crime/2022/03/he-threatened-to-post-ny-teens-naked-photos-online-her-suicide-leads-to-arrests-in-pakistan.html.

Merriam, J. (1998). *Little Girl Lost*. Bemidji, MN: Pinnacle Publishing, LLC.

Morrill, M. (2014). "Sibling sexual abuse: An exploratory study of long-term consequences for self-esteem and counseling considerations." *Journal of Family Violence*. Vol. 29: 205–213.

Näsi, M., M. Aaltonen, and J. Kivivuori (2016). "Youth hate crime offending: The role of strain, social control and self-control theories." *Journal of Scandinavian Studies in Criminology and Crime Prevention*. Vol. 17, issue 2: 177–184.

National Gang Center (2015). *Parents' Guide to Gangs*. Washington, DC: Office of Juvenile Justice and Delinquency, U.S. Department of Justice.

NBC Dallas Fort Worth, Channel 5 (2022). "Texas gunman warned of shooting grandmother, school in private Facebook messages." May 25. Retrieved from https://www.nbcdfw.com/news/national-international/texas-gunman-warned-of-shooting-grandmother-school-in-private-facebook-messages/2977774/.

Nydegger, L. A., W. DiFranceisco, K. Quinn, and J. Dickson-Gomez (2017). "Gender norms and age-disparate sexual relationships as predictors of intimate partner violence, sexual violence, and risky sex among adolescent gang members." *Journal of Urban Health*. Vol. 94: 266–275.

Office for Victims of Crime (2014). Responding to transgender victims of sexual assault. Office of Justice Programs, U.S. Department of Justice. June. Retrieved from https://ovc.ojp.gov/sites/g/files/xyckuh226/files/pubs/forge/sexual_numbers.html.

Office of Justice Programs (OJP) (2005). *Research in Brief: Co-Offending and Patterns of Juvenile Crime*. National Institute of Justice. Washington, DC: U.S. Department of Justice. Retrieved from www.ojp.gov/pdffiles1/nij/210360.pdf.

Office of Juvenile Justice and Delinquency Prevention (OJJDP) (n.d.). *Characteristics and Patterns of At-Risk Juveniles and Factors that Contribute to Violence Committed by or Against Juveniles*. Report to Congress, *Juvenile Violence Research*. Department of Justice Programs. Retrieved from https://ojjdp.ojp.gov/sites/g/files/xyckuh176/files/pubs/jvr/1.html.

Office of Juvenile Justice and Delinquency Prevention (OJJDP) (2022). OJJDP Statistical Briefing Book. Apr 18. Retrieve from https://www.ojjdp.gov/ojstatbb/offenders/qa03301.asp#:~:-text=Violent%20crimes%20by%20youth%20(ages,of%20school%20on%20school%20 days.&text=Note%3A%20Violent%20crimes%20include%20murder,%2C%20simple%20assault%2C%20and%20kidnapping.

O'Neal, E. N., S. H. Decker, R. K. Moule, Jr., and D. C. Pyrooz (2014). "Girls, gangs, and getting out." *Youth Violence and Juvenile Justice*. Vol. 14, issue 1: 1–18.

Patterson, G. R., B. D. DeBaryshe, and E. Ramsey (1989). "A developmental perspective on antisocial behavior." *American Psychology*. Vol. 44: 329–335.

Population Reference Bureau (2022). Summary: Gang Involvement. KidsData. Retrieved from https://www.kidsdata.org/topic/73/gang-involvement/summary.

Pozueco, J. M. (2011). *Psicopatía, Trastorno Metnal y Crimen Violento: Aspectos Clínico-Forenses, Médico-Legales y Criminológicos* [Psychopathy, Mental Disorder: Clinical-Forensic Medico-Legal and Criminological Aspects]. Madrid, Spain: EOS.

Quednau, J. (2021). "How are violent crime rates in U.S. cities affected by poverty?" *The Park Place Economist*. Vol. 28, issue 1. Retrieved from https://digitalcommons.iwu.edu/cgi/viewcontent.cgi?article=1530&context=parkplace.

Relva, I. C., O. M. Fernandes, and M. Alarcão (2017). "Dyadic types of sibling sexual coercion." *Journal of Family Violence*. Vol. 32: 577–583.

Richmond, T. (2021). Explainer: Prosecutors play up Rittenhouse inexperience. Associated Press. Nov 7. Retrieved from https://apnews.com/article/wisconsin-police-chicago-illinois-police-brutality-3df3e885caf039996246a4d9760859d4.

Rivinius, J. (2020). "New research reveals tremendous diversity in hate crime offenders' backgrounds and motivation." National Consortium for the Study of Terrorism and Responses to Terrorism. Department of Homeland Security Emeritus Center of Excellence University of Maryland. Oct 26. Retrieved from https://start.umd.edu/news/new-research-reveals-tremendous-diversity-hate-crime-offenders-backgrounds-and-motivations.

Sesso, G., G. E. Brancati, P. Fantozzi, E. Inguaggiato, A. Milone, and G. Masi (2021). "Measures of empathy in children and adolescents: A systematic review of questionnaires." *World Journal of Psychiatry*. Vol. 11, issue 10: 876–896.

Sharkey, J. D., S. Stifel, and A. Mayworm (2015; 2022). How to help me get out of a gang: Youth recommendations to family, school, community, and law enforcement systems. *OJJDP Journal of Juvenile Justice*. Pp. 64–83. *eScholarship*, University of California Santa Barbara. Retrieved from https://escholarship.org/content/qt2g45f1rx/qt2g45f1rx.pdf.

Siria, S., E. Echeburúa, and P. J. Amor (2020). "Characteristics and risk factors in juvenile sexual offenders." *Psicothema*. Vol. 32, issue 3: 314–321.

Sitnick, S. L., C. Galán, A. Chardée, and D. S. Shaw (2019). "Early childhood predictors of boys' antisocial and violent behavior in early adulthood." *Infant Mental Health Journal*. Vol. 40, issue 1 (Jan.): 67–83.

Sjödin, A., M. Wallinius, E. Billstedt, B. Hofvander, and T. Nilsson (2017). "Dating violence compared to other types of violence: Similar offenders but different victims." *European Journal of Psychology Applied to Legal Context*. Vol. 9, issue 2: 83–91.

State of Massachusetts (2019). *Charles E. Shannon Community Safety Initiative: Holyoke/Chicopee*. Boston, MA: Massachusetts Executive Office of Public Safety and Security.

Statista Research Department (2021a). Murder in the U.S.: Number of offenders in the United States 2020, by age. Statista Research. Oct 7. Retrieved from https://www.statista.com/statistics/251884/murder-offenders-in-the-us-by-age/.

Statista Research Department (2021b). Murder in the U.S.: Number of victims in the United States 2020, by age. Statista Research. Oct 7. Retrieved from https://www.statista.com/statistics/251878/murder-victims-in-the-us-by-age/.

Stephenson, Z., J. Woodhams, and C. Cooke (2014). "Sex differences in predictors of violent juvenile offending." *Aggressive Behavior*. Vol. 40, issue 2 (March-April): 165–177.

Sullivan, B. (2021). "Kyle Rittenhouse is acquitted of all charges in the trial over killing 2 in Kenosha." New England Public Radio. Nov 19. Retrieved from https://www.npr.org/2021/11/19/1057288807/kyle-rittenhouse-acquitted-all-charges-verdict.

Tener, D., E. Lusky, N. Tarshish, and S. Turjeman (2018). "Parental attitudes following disclosure of sibling sexual abuse: A child advocacy center intervention study." *American Journal of Orthopsychiatry*. Jan 25. Retrieved from https://calio.org/wp-content/uploads/2017/08/Parental-Attitudes-Following-Disclosure-of-Sibling-Sexual-Abuse-A-Child-Advocacy-Center-Intervention-Study.pdf.

Thulin, E. J., J. E. Heinze, P. Kernsmith, J. Smith-Darden, and P. J. Fleming (2021). "Adolescent risk of violence and electronic dating abuse: A latent class analysis." *Journal of Youth and Adolescence*. Vol. 50, issue 12 (Dec.): 2472–2486.

Trujillo, D. (2022). "Mother issues warning after teen son dies by suicide over cyber blackmail." NBC Bay Area. Apr 4. Retrieved from https://www.nbcbayarea.com/news/local/mother-issues-warning-after-teen-son-dies-by-suicide-over-cyber-blackmail/2854872/.

Tsai, T. M. (2002). "On Personal Victimization Features and Causes." Thesis, Department of Crime Prevention, Central Police University, Taiwan.

United Nations Women (2022). Facts and figures: Ending violence against women. United Nations. Feb. Retrieved from https://www.unwomen.org/en/what-we-do/ending-violence-against-women/facts-and-figures.

Van Dyke, N., and G. Tester (2014). "Hate crimes on college campuses." *Journal of Contemporary Criminal Justice*. Retrieved from https://www.researchgate.net/profile/Nella-Van-Dyke/publication/269598354_Dangerous_Climates_Factors_Associated_With_Variation_in_Racist_Hate_Crimes_on_College_Campuses/links/56faaa3a08ae8239f6dad24e/Dangerous-Climates-Factors-Associated-With-Variation-in-Racist-Hate-Crimes-on-College-Campuses.pdf.

Wasserman, G. A., K. Keenan, R. E. Tremblay, J. D. Cole, T. I. Herrenkohl, R. Loeber, and D. Petechuk (2003). "Risk and protective factors of child delinquency." *Child Delinquency Bulletin Series*. Office of Juvenile Justice and Delinquency Prevention, Office of Justice Programs, U.S. Department of Justice. April. Retrieved from https://www.ojp.gov/pdffiles1/ojjdp/193409.pdf.

Welsh, E. (2017). "Note and Comment: The path of most resistance: Resisting gang recruitment as a political opinion in Central America's join-or-die gang culture." *Pepperdine Law Review*. Vol. 44: 1083.

Willetts, M. (2022). "Teen under 'extreme pressure' from Instagram extortionist dies by suicide, MI cops say." *Kansas City Star*. Mar 30. Retrieved from https://www.kansascity.com/news/nation-world/national/article259937105.html.

Willison J. (2016). "Characteristics of violent crime committed by female prisoners." *Violence and Victims*. Vol. 31, issue 3: 552–570.

Wisconsin Legislature (n.d.). Chapter 948: Crimes against children. Retrieved from https://docs.legis.wisconsin.gov/statutes/statutes/948/60/2/a.

World Health Organization (WHO) (2021). Violence against women: Key facts. Mar 9. Retrieved from https://www.who.int/news-room/fact-sheets/detail/violence-against-women#:~:-text=Sexual%20violence%20is%20%22any%20sexual,the%20victim%2C%20in%20any%20setting.

World Population Review (2022). Most violent cities in America 2022. Retrieved from https://worldpopulationreview.com/us-city-rankings/most-violent-cities-in-america.

Yates, A., L. E. Beutler, and M. Crago (1983). "Characteristics of young violent offenders." *Journal of Psychiatry and Law*. Vol. 11, issue 2 (June): 137–149.

Zimmer, S. (2021)."Dating violence and victimization." *Salem Press Encyclopedia*. New York: Salem Press.

Chapter **SIX**

Individual Risks for Deviance and Delinquency

By the time I got to high school, I knew what I was gonna do. Mainly because I looked around and saw there wasn't much else I was able to do. I was a criminal. I was a juvenile delinquent.

—Hunter S. Thompson, author and founder of the gonzo journalist movement[1]

Chapter Objectives

- Introduce the most common individual risks for juvenile deviance and delinquency.
- Compare and contrast theories of individual deviance and delinquency.
- Explore a number of mental health issues that can contribute to delinquency.
- Examine a number of types of addictions, including to drugs and alcohol.

Key Terms

Attachment theories
Autism Spectrum Disorder
Bipolar disorder
Bounded rationality
Childhood Separation Anxiety Disorder (CSAD)
Cognitive theories
Developmental disorders
Emotional intelligence
Fight or flight response
Hypomania

[1] Hunter S. Thompson is perhaps best known for his semi-autobiographical book and movie, *Fear and Loathing in Las Vegas*. A gonzo journalist writes as a participant-observer, presenting their own perspectives rather than traditional objective news reporting.

Internet gaming disorder
Life-course theories
Limbic system
Mania
Neurotransmitter
Physiological psychology
Prefrontal cortex
Psychopathology

INTRODUCTION

The theories presented in this chapter and in Chapter 7, where we focus on environmental factors contributing to delinquency, are just that, theories. Some are better substantiated by evidence-based evaluations and rigorous research than others, and some continue to cause controversy and debate in academic and clinical circles. Certainly, we will only scratch the surface of the possible individual risk factors for juvenile offending, but we will explore the more commonly cited ones including a number of mental health issues and disorders.

This chapter focuses on individual risks and thus primarily engages with theories from research in psychology. Many psychological explanations that seem valid in explaining adult criminal behavior can be applied to juveniles as well, but others apply more specifically to juveniles, including theories in developmental psychology—the study of human social and physical development.

As yet, no single theory successfully merges our understanding of psychology and criminology to explain all forms of delinquency. Some individual explanations for deviance and delinquency, however, can be paired with environmental factors; for example, a juvenile genetically predisposed to mental health issues and raised in poverty may be more likely to commit a crime. Our main focus in this chapter will be on developmental psychology, physiological psychology, and mental health disorders.

DEVELOPMENTAL PSYCHOLOGY AND DELINQUENCY

Criminal laws are age-specific, distinguishing the age at which a juvenile becomes an adult. Most of us have met people who are very mature even before they become teenagers and older adults who still act like teenagers, fighting tooth and nail against the normal aging process. This section discusses another aspect of age: what experts in psychology describe as the normal processes of childhood physical and psychological development. In that context, we also highlight extraordinary childhood experiences that can derail normal psychological development.

Age-Crime Curve Approach

One common way to study juvenile crime is to look at how incidences of crime correlate with the minor's age. The *age-crime curve approach* of juvenile deviance and delinquency proposes a sharp increase in the potential for offending between the ages of 15 and 19, with a gradual decline as the individual enters adulthood (Liu, 2015; Sampson and Laub, 2005; Uggen, 2000; Stattin et al., 1989; Farrington, 1986).

The age-crime curve approach complements other developmental and *life-course theories* of juvenile crime—a set of paradigms to explain criminal behavior in juveniles and adults that developed in the 1980s. Within this set of theories, researchers try to figure out when and why minors start offending (onset), why they continue to offend (persistence), and why they might eventually stop offending (desistance) (McGee and Farrington, 2019). We will explore life-course theories further in the next chapter, but for now, these theories should be considered means for understanding the distinction between juvenile and adult criminal behavior.

The Intelligence Quotient (IQ) Gap

Yet another explanation for offending, both in adults and in juveniles, is the gap in intelligence between offenders and non-offenders, measured by IQ. Juvenile delinquents tend to have, on average, lower measurable IQ scores by eight points compared to their non-delinquent peers (Lynam et al., 1993). Higher intelligence

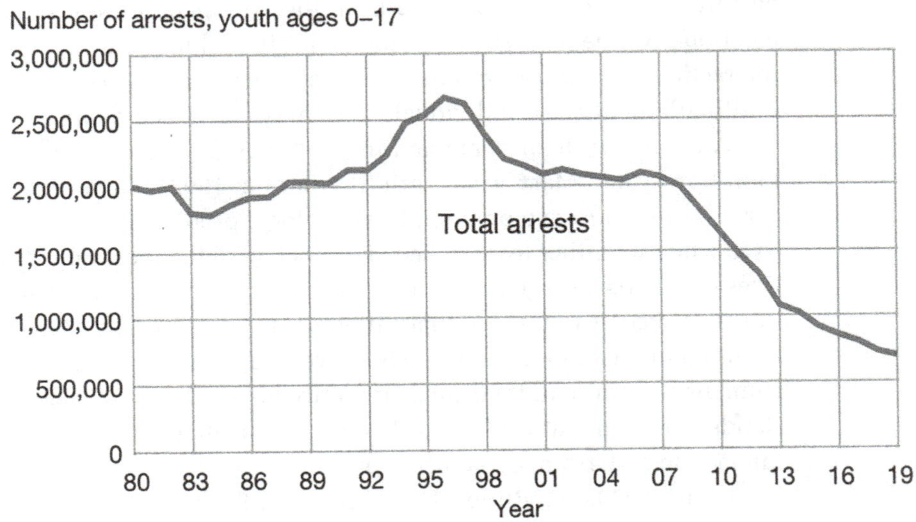

Data source: Analysis of arrest data from the Bureau of Justice Statistics and the National Center for Juvenile Justice.

EXHIBIT 6.1 ‖ Age-Crime Curve Graph: Arrest Trends, Youth Ages 0–17, 1980–2019

reportedly is a protective factor in conventional offending (Jovanovic et al., 2012; Herrnstein and Murray, 2009; Herrnstein and Murray, 1994).

Not everyone agrees that IQ tests can predict risk for criminal behavior. Ozer and Akbas (2020) found no significant relationship between IQ and juvenile offending in their study of 9,944 boys between ages 10 and 18. In their estimation, environmental factors provide a better explanation, as these will have a significant effect on IQ (Ozer and Akbas, 2020). We should also acknowledge that some of the most notorious criminals have had relatively superior IQs, including serial killers Ted Bundy and Jeffrey Dahmer. And as Oleson (2016) proposes, the reason why we see fewer people with higher IQs in juvenile detention and prison is because they are less likely to get caught.

We should caution that IQ tests have been disclaimed and often found to be unreliable measures of true intelligence. A number of ethical issues surround the study of the genetics of intellectual development and race, as well as whether cultural biases are built into IQ tests (Serpico, 2021; Larivée and Gagné, 2007). Historically, cultural and racial biases, particularly toward Blacks taking the exam, have been ignored in the content, administration, and interpretation of IQ tests (Jorgensen, 1973). This has gone largely unchanged, even in the face of evidence that IQ tests are inherently biased (Martschenko, 2018).

Attachment and Separation Anxiety Theories

A number of *attachment theories* propose that a juvenile's emotional disconnect from their family members or school can be an individual risk factor for deviance or delinquency. These address the social rather than cognitive reasons why children may become detached from the very people they should be closest to emotionally. The process of attachment begins at birth and develops on the basis of interactions with those around us. However, some neurological disorders can make it difficult for affected individuals to form strong attachments.

Attachment theory emerged in the 1950s. Two key founding theorists were John Bowby and Mary Ainsworth (Bretherton, 1992). Their theory is grounded in early childhood developmental psychology, predicting certain junctures in our lives when we either learn to become attached to the most important people in our lives or are discouraged from doing so. Attachment theories also consider evolutionary processes, positing that different stages in human evolution changed the meaning of attachment and to whom we attach ourselves as a means of survival. Humans remain with their nuclear family longer than most species on earth, so it stands to reason that we form different types of attachments to the members of our immediate and extended family over time.

In the 1960s, H. Rudolph Schaffer and Peggy Emerson refined Bowby and Ainsworth's attachment theory by identifying specific developmental stages in which attachment is formed and solidified. These stages are identified in Table 6.1.

TABLE 6.1 Stages of Attachment

Stage/Age	Type of Attachment
Asocial (0 to 6 weeks)	Babies prefer human faces, but do not discriminate between people and objects.
Diffuse (6 weeks to 6 months)	Babies show no preference for a specific individual and can be comforted by anyone.
Single strong attachment (7 months to 1 year)	Babies develop strong preference for one person and become afraid of strangers.
Multiple attachments (1 year+)	Babies will begin to show attachment to a number of individuals.

Source: Schaffer and Emerson, 1964.

Schaffer and Emerson (1964) argued that learning theory had dominated psychological theories with few empirical studies on the development of emotional attachment in infants. In particular, Schaffer and Emerson examined the extent to which infants protest being separated from those they love, identified as *childhood separation anxiety disorder* (CSAD) when it is excessive. It is one of the most common forms of childhood anxiety (Feriante and Bernstein, 2021).

Emotional attachment runs both ways. Parental units who have low attachment to their children can inflict childhood trauma by neglecting, or even more seriously, maltreating them. In turn, the child may very well develop feelings of distrust and suspicion when meeting new people. Babies' distrust and difficulty in bonding with parental units may have some basis in the mother's own painful past parent-child relationship, referred to by Frailberg et al. (1975) as the "ghosts in the nursery" (Shieh and Tsai, 2022). We should be careful to not blame mothers for every attachment issue in children. Fathers and father figures can likewise have a powerful influence on how children emotionally attach to others, particularly as they get older. If parental units have not had adequate role models themselves for forming meaningful relationships with others, or their own parents were abusive or neglectful, difficulty in attachment can carry over into the next generation in the absence of self-awareness or intervention.

We also cannot discount other factors mothers might face in bonding with their newborns. In more recent years, we have attained a better understanding of post-partum depression and how it might cause some new mothers to feel physically and emotionally disconnected from their offspring. Thankfully, pharmaceutical and therapeutic solutions can help women who experience post-partum depression.

A number of theorists (Vaughan et al., 2017; Battaglia, 2015; Ehrenreich et al., 2008) identified the following individual factors as playing a role in psychopathological cases of separation anxiety in children (Feriante and Bernstein, 2021, retrieved from https://www.ncbi.nlm.nih.gov/books/NBK560793/):

- Childhood parental loss (by separation, divorce, or death)
- Extended parental absences (e.g., military deployment, incarceration, or immigration for work)
- Diagnosis of an anxiety disorder in a parent (especially panic disorder)
- Parental alcoholism (14% of children of alcoholic parents develop CSAD)
- Parental conflict
- Low parental warmth
- Parental styles that discourage autonomy (e.g., reinforcing avoidance behaviors by removing the child from anxiety-provoking situations)
- Parent co-sleeping with child (demonstrative increased risk of developing anxiety or depressive symptoms)
- Foster care
- Adoption
- Relocation due to occupation
- Maternal smoking
- Maternal alcohol consumption
- Low birth weight
- Female sex (increased prevalence of CSAD in girls, as compared to boys)

Less understood are the effects of sibling separation on delinquency, particularly if a child is put in juvenile placement or detention. Few and limited studies address sibling separation and the feelings of those who remain in the home or are sent to different foster placements (Font and Woo Kim, 2021). Hispanic and Black children are more likely to experience placement instability, moving from one foster home to another, as well as being separated from their siblings while in foster care (Font and Woo Kim, 2021). Researchers advocate for siblings to be placed together in foster care, as separation can present a greater risk that one or more siblings from the same family will become delinquent (Novak and Benedini, 2020).

Besides risks for delinquency, children and adolescents cope with rejection by parental units, peers, or romantic interests by withdrawing—showing a tough exterior and unemotional responses to others, when in actuality they are experiencing inner turmoil. This in turn can exacerbate a number of mental health issues.

Developmental Disorders and Delinquency

Most public and private schools attempt to get children to conform to a standardized model of student behavior. This includes early socialization on how to behave in class and get along with others. This facilitates learning in contexts of having thirty or more students in a classroom. Even children without *developmental disorders* have different learning styles, however, and can become easily frustrated if not presented with alternative ways to master the curriculum. This is doubly difficult without diagnoses and, in many cases, special education, for children and teens with developmental disorders.

Some of the more common developmental disorders seen in juveniles and adults include (Traylor, 2021):

- **Attention Deficit Hyperactivity Disorder (ADHD):** Affects the brain's regulation of behavior.
- **Autism Spectrum Disorder (ASD):** Affects communication, social interaction, and experiences in the world.
- **Cerebral Palsy (CP):** Disorder affecting the brain and spinal cord, affecting movement, muscle tone, and coordination.
- **Intellectual Disability (ID):** Significant cognitive or intellectual impairment that impacts functioning in everyday life.
- **General Learning Disabilities:** Disabilities that affect the brain's ability to receive, process, store, or respond to information.

It is more than likely that deviance and delinquency linked to developmental disorders, particularly those that go undiagnosed, are associated with poor school performance. Juvenile delinquents with developmental disorders are also much more likely to have coexisting psychiatric disorders, as concluded in a study of people who were born with Autism Spectrum Disorder (ASD) (Rutten et al., 2017). As this implies, most of these developmental disorders have a range of behaviors along which the disability prevents the individual from functioning fully in society. The key to how little or how much the disability will affect someone in the long run is early detection. Unfortunately, not all parents or school personnel are necessarily trained or equipped to provide the best interventions available to recognize developmental disabilities and help prevent juvenile delinquency.

EMOTIONAL PSYCHOLOGY AND DELINQUENCY

At a very young age, most children are socialized at home or at school to express emotions productively. However, in some cases, children are taught to suppress their feelings, sometimes to their own psychological and physical detriment. To the extreme, children may be taught at home, usually by the example of an abusive parental unit or sibling, to react in destructive ways, both verbally and physically, depending on their emotions at any given time. *Emotional psychology* examines how people react physically and emotionally to events in their lives and whether the behavior is socially acceptable. Only recently have criminologists begun to link emotions to the decisions made by juvenile delinquents (Piquero, 2017).

The study of emotions is complex, making it difficult to identify a single theory that explains why people react to others and to life events as they do. More than 90 definitions of emotions have emerged from psychology within the last century (Plutchik, 2001). Plutchik (2001; 1982) distilled these to eight basic emotions, with corresponding physiological reactions.

Plutchik's theory posits something like the color wheel in art, with four pairs of opposite emotions (see Exhibit 6.2): Joy and sadness, trust and disgust, fear and anger, surprise and anticipation. It can also be argued that we can swing precariously between two opposing emotions at any given time as events unfold or as we obtain more information about our situation. Those who suffer from undiagnosed or unmedicated *bipolar disorder*, discussed later in this chapter, may find themselves erratically, and to others, seemingly irrationally, swinging between emotional extremes.

The emotion most closely associated with juvenile delinquency is anger. If individuals do not learn to control their angry reactions at an early age, the maladjustment may result in violent behavior, targeted either at themselves or at others. As Roff and Wirt (1985, p. 564) and others have noted, "Aggressive behavior has emerged as the most common problem associated with peer rejection, and childhood aggression has been found to be the strongest behavioral indicator of delinquency and young adult antisocial behavior." (See also Roff and Wirt, 1984; Eron, 1983; Farrington, 1978; Eron et al., 1974; Havighhurst et al., 1962.) Violent crimes certainly can result from uncontrolled anger.

Plutchik's Emotion Dyads

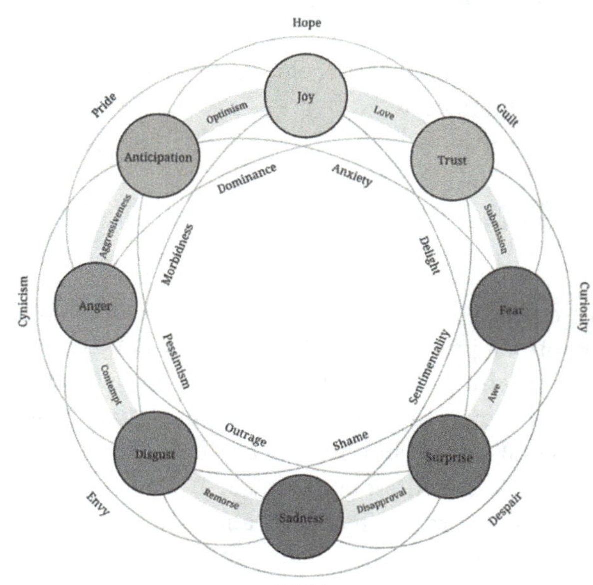

EXHIBIT 6.2 ‖ Plutchik's Emotion Dyads

Aggressive behavior in a child.

Anger management therapy is not limited to adults. It is also an effective tool in treating a child who displays inappropriate anger with the potential for, or experience of, violent behavior. However, as noted elsewhere in this chapter, emotions cannot always be easily controlled with behavioral modification. In some cases, the anger is a symptom of a larger, more serious neurological or psychiatric disorder.

Subjective Experiences

As we often highlight in sociology, people live in their own realities. This is true for children, including the juvenile delinquent. Along with life experiences being subjectively[2] interpreted by individuals, the function of decision making is also limited by what is called *bounded rationality* (Hansen, 2020; Simon, 1990): We may make decisions based on information that is incorrect or incomplete. For example, a youth gang decides to initiate a fight with a rival gang for some perceived slight when, in actuality, the insult was based on rumors and not facts. Individuals, and organizations for that matter, make faulty decisions in everyday life,

[2] To be subjective means to assess information and situations on the basis of one's socialization, experiences, learned prejudices, and biases. To be objective is to look at information and situations without considering one's emotions or personal beliefs or being influenced by the person or persons presenting the alleged facts.

before having all the facts or correct information. Unfortunately, as in the example of gang violence, this can have deadly consequences.

Subjective realities can also be fabricated or manipulated by others. Juveniles are particularly susceptible to the suggestions of others. For example, the victim of child maltreatment may be continually told by their abuser that it is their fault that they are being excessively punished, physically or verbally. If the victim is told enough times that it is their fault, they may very well come to believe it. Well-documented studies, including a survey of 7,347 people conducted by the anti-bullying charity Ditch the Label in the U.K. indicate that children who are bullied at home or elsewhere are more likely to become bullies themselves (Ditch the Label, 2019). Likewise, a child growing up in a household where domestic violence is normalized may take that reality into the world and use violence to settle disputes and disagreements.

Emotional Intelligence

Emotional intelligence (EI) is defined as "the ability to perceive, manage, and reason about emotions and to use this information to guide thinking and behavior adaptively." (Kahn et al., 2016, p. 903). Psychologists debate whether people are born with EI, sometimes described as temperament, or if it develops over time based on life experiences. EI has been linked with the ability to adapt to school, including to instruction and social situations on campus (Kahn et al., 2016). It has also been linked to psychopathology, including unremorseful delinquency (Piquero, 2017; Kahn et al., 2016).

Key components of emotional intelligence (University of Western Alabama, n.d., p. 15) include:

1. **Appraising and expressing emotions in the self and others**: Recognizing or expressing verbal or nonverbal cues about emotion.
2. **Regulating emotion in self and others**: Managing emotions so that all parties are motivated towards a positive outcome.
3. **Using emotions in adaptive ways:** Using emotion and the interpretation of emotions to result in positive outcomes.

How juveniles display their emotions in juvenile court, including demonstrating sincere remorse for the crimes they have committed, can have a profound effect on the outcome. Plus, reoffending can leave the impression that prior sanctions have failed to work as deterrents, giving further credence to a perception that the repeat juvenile offender is not remorseful.

Regulating Emotions

Much of what we know about regulating emotions and preventing delinquency comes from studies in physiological psychology, the topic of our next section. Here we consider the ways we have been socialized into regulating our emotions. No matter what brain chemistry or physiology we might possess, a good portion of how we react to the world has been socialized into us, first by parents and then by every subsequent social encounter, including at school.

Emotional regulation is defined as changes associated with emotions activated independently of the emotions themselves (Lewis and Steiben, 2004; Cole et al., 2004). In other words, depending on how we have been trained, our emotions affect whether reactions elicited by situations and people will be constructively or negatively regulated. Reality TV shows demonstrate that not everyone reacts to challenges in the same way, even if contestants are faced with the same or similar situations. Something that might hurt and anger one person may be completely ignored or laughed off by another.

The ability to regulate one's emotions develops over time and is often learned through interaction with others. Sociologist Charles Horton Cooley believed that individuals develop their self-image and respond to others through the "looking-glass self" (Cooley, 1902). That is, we gauge our own reaction to others, or what we think of ourselves, by how others react to something we do or say. This is part of our subjective reality. As an example, to be successful in educational and work settings, it is necessary to regulate how we react to others when we perceive their behavior to us as mean or unkind. Without such regulation, ordinary situations can escalate into unpleasant or even unproductive and damaging confrontations.

If a child perceives that a rival covets the same toy as they do, they may resort to insults and physical threats to get the toy. How many times have we heard parental units say to their children, "Play nice"? We certainly see these types of confrontations in normal sibling rivalries. Danger lies in emotions that escalate, leading the child to follow through on a threat. Much of what we learn about regulating our own emotions comes not only from what others, primarily adults, teach us, but from trial and error in our interactions with siblings and peers, as we see whether showing our emotions has either the desired or a negative effect on our goals. This learning can lead children to resort to delinquent behaviors to obtain the desired effect or coveted item.

Learning to self-regulate our emotions is crucial to navigating our way through life challenges such as disappointment. Juvenile delinquents often find challenges at school, including remaining motivated to succeed. School failures can result in frustration, and in some cases embarrassment, in front of teachers and peers. Negative emotions, including shame, set students up to adopt avoidance behaviors that can lead to truancy and absenteeism (Alonso-Tapia et al., 2020).

Gender Differences in Emotion Regulation

Though we will cover gender differences in offending extensively in Chapter 9, it is important to note here that there are generally distinct gender differences when it comes to how we are socialized with regard to expressing our emotions.

Traditionally, boys are taught to keep their feelings hidden and in check, unless their masculinity is being challenged, in which case the only emotion they are expected to show is anger. As a result, males tend to have a significantly higher ability to accept their emotional responses, but more difficulty in controlling their impulsive behavior or developing emotional avoidance strategies (Kaur et al., 2022). In contast, those who are identified as females are socialized to be more accepting of their emotional responses, and in turn tend to use more emotion-regulating strategies, including reflection, acceptance, and seeking out emotional support from others (Kaur et al., 2022). For example, when a teenage boy has been rejected by a love interest, they may be conditioned to hide their feelings, never letting on to their peers how much it has hurt them. A teenage girl typically is more likely to seek comfort in discussing the rejection extensively with their friends or close family members.

Cultural differences also affect how we outwardly display our emotions. Infants as young as 11 months can distinguish differences in expression (happy versus angry) in their caregivers (Liu et al., 2021). Understandably, infants show a preference for happy faces, as compared to neutral, frightened, or angry faces, with higher rates of negative physiological responses to the latter (Liu et al., 2021). Children who are frequently exposed to negative emotions in others, even when it is not directed at them, may eventually resort to self-destructive and avoidance behaviors, or lash out themselves at others. In some cases, they may come to exhibit deviant or delinquent behaviors.

PHYSIOLOGICAL PSYCHOLOGY AND DELINQUENCY

How we are socialized into regulating our emotions and behaviors is not solely dependent on those around us. The physiology, or physical structure, and the functioning of the juvenile brain continues to develop into early adulthood, and can affect how individuals perceive the events and people in their lives. It is not simply a stereotype that teenagers seem moodier, as compared to prepubescent juveniles or adults. Behaving in an overly dramatic fashion when faced with otherwise ordinary events is part of the experience of many teenagers. Most outgrow this phase. However, defects in or damages to brain chemistry or physiology can result in inappropriate responses to negative life events, including drug or alcohol abuse or other self-medicating behaviors, and juvenile delinquency.

Emotional Reactivity

Along with hormonal changes brought about by puberty, adolescence is a period when juveniles may be more reactive to events and people in their lives. What might seem unimportant to adults can be blown out of proportion by children

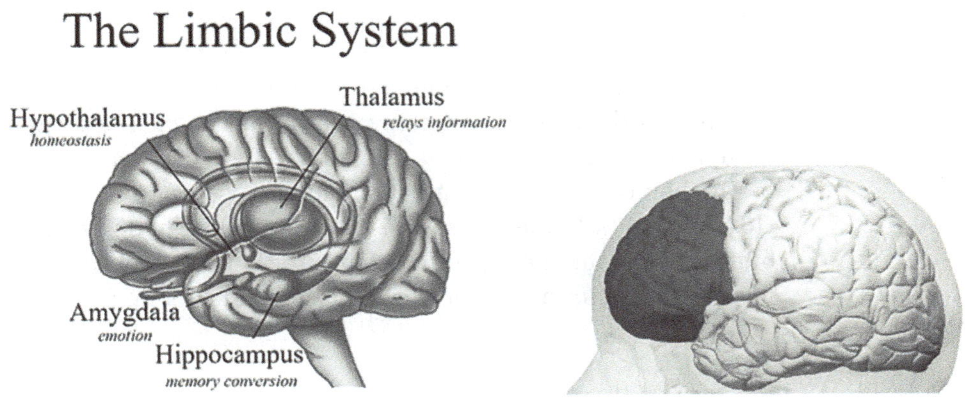

EXHIBIT 6.3 ‖ Limbic System and Prefrontal Cortex

or teens. During adolescence, the parts of the brain that help regulate emotions, including the *limbic system* and the *prefrontal cortex*, undergo changes. The limbic system, made up of the hypothalamus, thalamus, amygdala, and hippocampus, helps to regulate responses to emotional stimuli (Khoo, 2020). The prefrontal cortex, development of which continues into young adulthood, is responsible for processing and maintenance of emotions, decision making, and impulse inhibition (Ahmed et al., 2015; Holt et al., 2008). Damage, abnormality, or underdevelopment of either or both of these systems can result in inappropriate emotional responses and delinquent behavior.

More recent studies indicate that constant exposure to one's own negative emotions can result in changes in brain chemistry and structure. Studies of late teens and young adults indicate that individuals otherwise classified as mentally healthy who report having recently experienced a bad mood are more likely to score higher on the Depression Anxiety Stress Scales (DASS) and experience a decrease in the chemicals in the brain that help regulate emotions (Yeung et al., 2021). *Cognitive theories* support research on changes in brain chemistry when individuals experience stress that can influence how they interpret and remember negative information and increase the risk for depression (Feurer et al., 2020; Disner et al., 2011).

During adolescence, overall rates of depression rise, and gender differences emerge in the symptoms of depression, most notably in places where there is more gender inequality (Salk et al., 2017). However, males are also less likely to report depression. The absence of outward symptoms of depression in males may be due to social conditioning, throwing some statistics on adolescent depression into question. We are only now gaining better understanding of the causes of depression during adolescence, including in deviant or delinquent juveniles. Parental units can be confused about whether depressive symptoms they see in their children are serious enough to seek treatment or professional advice, or are part of juveniles' normal developmental path, particularly in adolescents.

Neurocriminology

A companion to an age-crime approach to studying the criminal behaviors in juveniles is the neurocriminology approach. The methodology has three prongs, with neurological impairment, attention deficit disorders (e.g., ADD, ADHD), and brain chemistry seen as separate focuses in *neurophysiology* (Mostafapoor and Hoseini, 2017). In these cases, researchers look at underlying conditions that are often well beyond the capability of juveniles to deal with or outgrow without pharmaceutical and/or mental health counseling interventions.

SELF-CONTROL THEORIES

Self-control theories can be tied to a number of the topics we discuss in this chapter, including emotional intelligence and regulating emotions. There are a number of ways we can view the role of self-regulation of emotions, or self-control. Particularly in homicide cases, attorneys often see "loss of self-control" as a cornerstone of the defense of violent juvenile and adult offenders, arguing that even a reasonable person can lose self-control given the right circumstances (Buchhandler-Raphael, 2020). Through a criminological theory lens, one of the key elements of loss of self-control is the perception that a criminal act will result in the immediate gratification of desires, in which case, any self-control one may have simply goes out the window (Gottfredson and Hirschi, 1990).

There are conflicting and competing theories as to why children may have low self-control that puts them at risk of delinquency. They coincide with nature versus nurture arguments, where some argue that an individual's temperament and behaviors are a product of genetics and others maintain they are the result of early socialization by parental units and other influential adults, including teachers. More than likely, it is a combination of both factors.

There have been far more studies of environmental factors in influencing self-control. However, some genetic studies support that heredity cannot be discounted as a factor in juvenile offending. In a twins study conducted in the Netherlands (Willems et al., 2018), genetic influences were found to play a considerable part in the levels of self-control witnessed in prepubescent children, meaning that there may be high heritability of low self-control in some individuals.

Other self-control theories focus on the external or nurturing influences on learning how to keep one's emotions in check. Gottfredson and Hirschi (1990) argued that the characteristics of low self-control can be present when there is an absence of any nurturing, discipline, or training by parental units. Self-control is formed in childhood and remains relatively stable over the course of one's lifetime (Gottfredson and Hirschi, 1990). As Sykes and Matza (1957) noted, deviance and delinquency, which are behavior based, have their roots in the values and norms learned from hanging around with other delinquent juveniles. [Some contradictions with social bond theories (Hirschi, 1969) are discussed in the next chapter.] In other words, delinquent behavior, including that resulting from low self-control, often is a product of both individual characteristics and interaction with one's associates, including friends and family.

GENERAL MENTAL HEALTH DISORDERS AND DELINQUENCY

Psychopathology

Whereas juvenile offending with no mental illness present is most often associated with environmental factors, psychopathological reasons can be organic, including brain chemistry, substance use and abuse, and genetics. We define psychopathology as mental or behavior disorders that have manifested in the juvenile due to head trauma, abnormal physiological changes, or an inherited condition. Where psychopathology differs from psychology is in how the former focuses on the origins of the behavior, whereas the latter, particularly in the practice of clinical psychologists and psychiatrists, looks for ways to treat diagnosed mental and behavior disorders.

Anxiety Disorders

Anxiety disorders cover a broad range of mental health conditions, including panic disorder, social anxiety disorders, and general anxiety disorders. As we noted earlier, one of the most common anxieties seen in children is childhood separation anxiety disorder (CSAD) (Rapee et al., 2009; Schaffer and Emerson, 1964). Anxiety disorders are the most prevalent form of psychopathology found in juveniles, who risk carrying them over into adulthood; they can also develop into other disorders, including depression (Vasey et al., 2014; Rapee et al., 2009).

When juvenile delinquents suffer from anxiety disorders, the question always arises: Which came first, delinquency or anxiety? Only recently, after an explosion of research on anxiety disorders in the 1990s, have researchers and mental health professionals realized that anxiety in children is much more common than previously thought (Rapee et al., 2009).

Fight or Flight Response in Anxiety Disorders

Events in our lives evoke both emotional and physiological reactions. Those with anxiety disorders may have a tendency to react strongly to most anxiety-causing situations and to want to run away from them. Using Plutchik's wheel of emotions, we can describe the impulses as follows (Emotional Intelligence Network, n.d.):

- Physiological reactions to joy versus sadness: **Connect or withdraw**.
- Physiological reactions to fear versus anger: **Get small and hide or get big and loud.**
- Physiological reactions to anticipation versus surprise: **Examine closely or jump right in**.
- Physiological reactions to disgust versus trust: **Reject or embrace**.

Known as *fight or flight response*, theorists believe that our responses to a confrontational situation are instinctual and evolutionarily ingrained: doing one or the other is often critical to survival. This response is part of a larger body of research studying the psychological and physiological effects of stress. Given the lag in development of the frontal cortex, juveniles making the decision not to flee a confrontation may end up in a fight.

The instinct to fight is not exclusive to males. In a study of gang initiation (Hansen and Freitag, 2016), while male gang members will throw punches at initiates during "jumping in" rituals, the fight is controlled, stopping after a few blows. Female gang members, however, are more likely to have initiation assaults get out of hand, including not only punches but indiscriminate and painful hair-pulling as well (Hansen and Freitag, 2016). This is further exacerbated by verbal assaults on the initiate from members on the sidelines of the initiation (Hansen and Freitag, 2016).

In cases of extreme stress, individuals may also become frozen, stopping in their tracks. This is another adaptive response that provides time to look or listen for clues on how to proceed, as part of a fight-flight pattern of behavior (Bracha, 2004; Gray, 1988). Potential victims more often do this, and it sometimes happens to juvenile delinquents during the voluntary commission of a crime as the situation dictates, though unwilling participants in delinquency may have a similar response.

Clinical Depression and Delinquency

We should distinguish between infrequent bouts of "the blues" and cases where sadness becomes a chronic state of being. Oyama and Piotrowski (2022) define clinical depression as one of the most common psychiatric disorders that can happen during our lifetimes, with symptoms ranging from a fleeting mood to long-term internal and outwardly expressed sadness. *The Statistical Manual of Mental Disorders* (DSM-5, 2013), published by the American Psychiatric Association, identifies a number of depressive disorders on a spectrum, including the extreme case of clinical depression, also known as a major depressive disorder (Oyama and Piotrowski, 2022).

A number of studies have indicated a connection between delinquency and depression, mostly based on studies of juveniles already in custody. It is understandable that minors who are caught up in either the juvenile justice system or the child welfare system might exhibit symptoms of depression. Fewer studies look to whether a juvenile delinquent was depressed prior to committing a crime, as the diagnosis may not even have come up until after custody, when social workers and mental health professionals may step in.

Again, it is not always clear which occurs first. We can imagine situations where depression leads to self-destructive behavior, including suicide,[3] if there isn't intervention. Attempted suicide may lead to further depression and suicide attempts. Individuals who attempt suicide, even if they are juveniles, are viewed as being selfish, attention-seeking, emotionally weak, and immoral, though these are unfair, and in many cases, false stereotypes that create a double stigma that can prevent or impede recovery and treatment (Sheehan et al., 2017).

Having been caught in deviant or delinquent behavior resulting in punishment or social banishment can be followed by feelings of anger or depression and, in some cases, embarrassment and shame. Researchers know that, oddly enough, the symptoms of depression, including social rejection of others and withdrawal from friends and family, may be a protective factor against further delinquency, steering the juvenile away from delinquent peers (Siennick et al., 2020). Juveniles who are depressed, rather than withdrawing from prosocial peers and turning to antisocial peers, as would be expected, instead resort to general social withdrawal away from all peers, which in itself is unhealthy (Siennick et al., 2020; Hussong et al., 2011).

Bipolar Disorder

Once called manic-depressive disorder, individuals who suffer from a bipolar disorder may experience mood swings, vacillating between manic states with out-of-control kinetic behavior and debilitating depression. The Mayo Clinic reports that bipolar disorder can occur at any age, but symptoms may not be identified as part of this specific mental health issue until the teenage years or early 20s, based on biological changes in the brain or genetics (Mayo Clinic Staff, n.d.a).

There are a number of types of bipolar disorder and not everyone experiences *mania* or *hypomania*. The Mayo Clinic identifies the following as the most common types found (Mayo Clinic Staff, n.d.a):

- **Bipolar I disorder:** There has been at least one manic episode, preceded or followed by hypomania or depression. Mania, in some cases, can result in psychosis.

[3] If you or someone you know is contemplating suicide, and you are in the United States, immediately call the National Suicide Hotline at **988**.

- **Bipolar II disorder:** There has been at least one major depressive episode and at least one hypomanic episode, with no manic episode.
- **Cyclothymic disorder:** There have been at least two years in adults or one year in children and teenagers with a number of episodes of hypomania symptoms, with periods of depressive symptoms that are less severe than major depression.
- **Additional types:** Bipolar or other disorders that have symptoms brought on by certain drug or alcohol consumption or due to a medical condition (e.g., stroke).

The inability to handle day-to-day life during manic or depressive episodes is often characterized by social dysfunction. Some of the mood symptoms found in young juveniles diagnosed with bipolar disorder include social withdrawal, physical and verbal aggression against others, and victimization (Weintraub et al., 2022). Freeman et al. (2009), Morris et al. (2017), and Beyer et al. (2003) found in their studies that individuals who have bipolar disorder, including juveniles, will also have less perceived social support, fewer friends, and more interpersonal conflict, as compared to healthy individuals (Weintraub et al., 2022). They may also lash out in anger at targeted individuals, particularly at caregivers, further socially isolating themselves (Pompili et al., 2014).

International studies have found childhood-onset bipolar disorder to be a common illness across many samples of international juvenile populations, characterized by recurring mood symptoms, social dysfunction, and suicidal thoughts in patients with Bipolar I Disorder (MacPherson et al., 2022). As found in studies of recidivism rates of juvenile offenders who have bipolar disorder, the challenge is getting the patient to comply with taking antimanic medication consistently, as ordered by their physician or psychiatrist (Dailey et al., 2005). As in the case of other failures to take medication (55% of patients with chronic disorders do not follow their doctors' or psychiatrists' instructions) over a long period of time, patients with bipolar disorder will either fail or refuse to take their medication because they are not fully aware of their illness, have concurrent alcohol or drug abuse problems, find that the cost of the medication is prohibitive, and/or have a poor relationship with their psychiatrist (Amador and Johanson, 2000).

The rapper and music producer Ye, formerly known as Kanye West, who was diagnosed with bipolar disorder after a psychiatric emergency in 2016, more recently reported that he periodically stops taking medication because he doesn't like how it makes him feel, and that in his estimation he is more creative while in a manic state without it (Lee, 2022). Unlike Ye, it is a myth that most patients stop taking antimanic drugs because they prefer the manic state to feeling numb while medicated (Lee, 2022; Berman and Boguski, 2020). More often than not, their reasons for not taking the medication were those stated in the previous paragraph. With or without medication, at least in the case of childhood-onset bipolar disorder, the prognosis is that symptoms will worsen upon entering adulthood (MacPherson et al., 2022), further putting the individual at risk of adult offending.

Schizophrenia

Similar to bipolar disorder, the onset of schizophrenia may not be recognized until late teens for males and late 20s to 30s in females (National Alliance on Mental Illness, 2022). Diagnosis in teenagers is difficult, though the symptoms can be present before diagnosis; first signs including a change in friendships, sudden poor performance in school, difficulty with sleep, and irritability, all of which can of course be symptoms of other periodic teenage angst, unrelated to serious mental health issues (National Alliance on Mental Illness, 2022). The symptoms of schizophrenia can mimic those of other mental health issues as well, including bipolar disorder, further confusing diagnoses (Soares-Weiser et al., 2015).

Obvious psychotic symptoms that can be exhibited in individuals with schizophrenia, to varying degrees, include the following (Piotrowski and Tischauser, 2022; Butcher et al., 2020):

- Lack of motivation
- Flattened affect
- Inability to feel pleasure
- Difficulty in speaking
- Withdrawal
- Delusions and hallucinations
- Depression
- Mania
- Paranoia
- Disorganization
- Difficulty paying attention
- Poor working memory
- Inability to process information and make informed decisions.

Psychotic symptoms present in individuals with schizophrenia do not always lead to serious criminal offending. In a study conducted at a high security residential psychiatric hospital, psychotic symptoms were not found to be responsible for every criminal or violent behavior in individuals with schizophrenia (Jones, 2010). Some juveniles had begun offending in advance of the onset of the disease, with criminal behavior more likely associated with trauma in childhood or developmental disorders (Jones, 2010).

In the same family of disorders, *schizoaffective disorder* is not typically seen in children. It can have the combined symptoms of schizophrenia and bipolar disorder, including depression or mania, coupled with hallucinations or delusions (Mayo Clinic Staff, n.d.b). The typical age of onset is between 16 and 30 (National Alliance on Mental Illness, 2022). In children, some of the first symptoms may go undiagnosed or misdiagnosed as some other mental health issue, including attention deficit hyperactivity disorder (ADHD). Few studies examining the onset of schizophrenia, schizoaffective disorder, or bipolar disorder include juveniles under 18 as research subjects (Laursen, 2020). The absence of children who have not been diagnosed with any of these disorders thus does not mean that the typical onset age is set in stone as first appearing only in older adolescence or early adulthood.

There is a much greater risk of substance abuse in teens and adults diagnosed either with schizophrenia or schizoaffective disorder. Substance abuse acts as a form of self-medication, as in other mental health disorders, including anxiety. Within three years of initial diagnosis, males with these disorders are more likely than females to have serious substance abuse issues beyond alcohol and cannabis abuse (Laursen et al., 2020).

Theories of Addiction

One need not be addicted to drugs and/or alcohol to have use of these substances lead to criminal activities in juveniles or adults. Drugs and alcohol, in combination with a still-developing frontal cortex, can result in questionable or risky behavior in children, teenagers, and young adults. It is often difficult, particularly for parental units, to recognize whether their teenage child is developing an addiction to alcohol or if consumption is part of the presumably normal, if illegal, rites of passage for teenagers and young adults. Addiction begins with occasional use and ends with consumption of excessive amounts of drugs or alcohol, to the social and physical detriment of the individual (Winger et al., 2005). For juveniles, full addiction may not occur until they have entered adulthood. It is well-documented that the younger alcohol experimentation and use begins, the more likely it will result in alcohol-related disorders later in adulthood (Baily et al., 2015). Among the consequences of addiction can be deviance or delinquency.

Consumption of illegally obtained prescription drugs or street drugs is of greater concern to parental units and law enforcement, even though underaged drinking is a cause for concern as well. The social reasons for drug and alcohol use, abuse, and addiction will be explored in the next chapter, examining environmental risks for delinquency. Here we examine the individual mechanics of addiction.

Historically, addictions have been viewed as character flaws or moral defects of the addicted individual. Though the behaviors of addicts can reinforce these characterizations, research has come a long way toward more valid explanations for addiction. The stigmatizing term "alcoholism," for example, has been replaced by the less stigmatizing label alcohol use disorder (AUD). Experts today identify two types of addiction, both often requiring therapy in order to recover: chemical and behavioral (Raypole, 2020).

Chemical addictions are now often recognized as medical conditions (other terms used include medical, biomedical, or disease models of addiction). Even the criminal justice system recognizes this, to some extent, with some jurisdictions now having drug courts. A number of studies have indicated a genetic component to chemical addiction, such as neurochemical deficits or imbalances (Matheny, 1998). This can happen when there is too little or too much of a certain *neurotransmitter*. The absence or overabundance of these neurotransmitters can result in negative behaviors, like addiction, or other inappropriate responses to everyday stresses.

Some neurotransmitters in the brain are seen as specifically related to chemical addiction. Dopamine, a neurotransmitter, is proposed to be one of these primary chemicals in the brain associated with addiction (the "Dopamine Hypothesis") (Marco, 2011). Dopamine is activated by natural and artificial rewards, including food, sex, and drugs (Tomkins and Sellers, 2001). Individuals with low levels of dopamine are at risk of becoming addicted to drugs or alcohol, as their systems attempt to replicate the positive feelings by artificially releasing the neurotransmitter.

The recent opioid addiction epidemic has alarmed both law enforcement and health care professionals. Between 1996 and 2001, Purdue Pharma, the maker of OxyContin (which contains the chemical oxycodone, a highly addictive substance), conducted all-expenses-paid symposia nationwide for doctors, promoting the drug as the best pharmaceutical for pain management (Zee, 2009). It was one of the most aggressive marketing campaigns ever pushing for doctors to prescribe a drug. By 2004, OxyContin was the leading drug abused in the United States (Zee, 2009). In a 2002 survey of American households by the National Survey on Drug Use and Health, an estimated 7.6% of adolescents between the ages of 12 and 17 reported nonmedical use of prescription opioids without a doctor's order (Sung et al., 2005; Substance Abuse and Mental Health Services Administration, 2003). High school students primarily used the opioids OxyContin and Vicodin (produced by Abbott) without a prescription; between 1999 and 2001, the two drugs represented the largest increase in emergency room admissions for drug overdoses (Sung et al., 2005).

It is a misconception that nonmedical use of opioids is more likely among juveniles from white-collar, middle-class families. Unlike in the media portrayals, juvenile prescription drug users are in reality more likely to come from lower-income families and to fit a profile similar to abusers of other illegal drugs (Sung et al., 2005). Those addicted to opioids also tend to use multiple drugs, and addiction is more likely to afflict juveniles typically at risk for delinquency, including those living in poverty (Sung et al., 2005).

Even as chemical and medical models of addiction gain traction among health-care professionals, the behavioral model of addiction continues to dominate. Behavioral approaches view drugs and alcohol as enforcers of positive feelings, as when someone uses or abuses either substance to seem more gregarious at a party. Behavioral addiction can be a symptom of impulse-control disorder, a mental health issue in which individuals have difficulty controlling emotions or behavior, including drug or alcohol consumption (Thomas, 2022).

An alternative to both chemical and behavioral explanations is the *biopsychosocial model*. This model takes into consideration both biological or genetic factors, along with social or environmental factors (Skewes and Gonzalez, 2013). The benefit of taking a more holistic approach to addiction is that it recognizes that recovery requires treating both the mind and the body (Skewes and Gonzalez, 2013). How an individual's addiction is labeled will determine the approaches taken to treatment: medical, psychological, or psychiatric. When alcoholism or other addictions are combined with mental illness in the patient, the challenge is knowing which to treat first and foremost.

Addictions in juveniles and adults are not limited to drugs and alcohol. Beyond substance abuse issues, Raypole (2020) identifies seven other common behavioral addictions:

- Shopping addiction
- Exercise addiction
- Food addiction
- Sex addiction
- TV addiction
- Social media addiction
- Gambling addiction, including *Internet gaming disorder*

Granted, most of these behavioral addictions will not lead to juvenile delinquency. However, as with substance abuse addictions, these compulsions are often cloaked in secrecy, causing irritability or anxiety with withdrawal symptoms, and in cases where money is needed to support the habit (e.g., shopping addiction), they can lead to criminal activities, including shoplifting, stealing, and robbery. When there is a sex addiction present, whether in adults or juveniles, it can also lead to criminal behavior, including, in some cases, consumption of child pornography. At the very least, it can lead to risky sexual behavior, making the juvenile vulnerable to pregnancy and/or contracting a sexually transmitted disease.

Post-Traumatic Stress Disorder (PTSD) and Delinquency

The study of post-traumatic stress disorder, more commonly known as PTSD, began in earnest after soldiers returned from Vietnam in the 1960s and 1970s with a number of mental health issues. The disorder was studied for its association with adult crime victims, in particular victims of domestic or interpersonal violence who never saw combat duty. It is only recently that more attention has been paid to pediatric PTSD. According to Grasso et al. (2019, p 113), "Post-traumatic stress disorder (PTSD) is a chronic, often debilitating, condition that affects roughly 5% of the general adolescent population. . . ." and can be seen in higher rates among children in the juvenile justice or child welfare systems. Left untreated, PTSD may cause a number of social impairments that can follow the afflicted individual throughout their childhood and adulthood (Grasso et al., 2019).

PTSD can result in deviant and delinquent behavior. Kerig (2019) defines post-traumatic risk seeking as the "active pursuit of dangerous, self-destructive, or reckless activities following exposure to trauma in order to meet specific behavioral functions" (Modrowski and Kerig, 2019, p. 1962). Substance abuse, for example, has been demonstrated to be associated with juvenile PTSD (Winningham et al., 2019). In addition to substance abuse, juvenile victims of sexual abuse prior to the age of 18, and who suffer from PTSD as a result, are at greater risk for engaging in risky sexual behavior (Hahn et al., 2021).

SUMMARY

This chapter by no means exhausts the list of factors behind juvenile deviance and offending. The theories presented here are, however, the most recently accepted explanations for juvenile crime. Most causes of criminal behavior are found in an individual's psychological makeup. (Wider social causes of criminal offending by juveniles are covered in the next chapter.) The theories in Chapters 6 and 7 are best used in combination when trying to explain why juveniles commit deviant or criminal acts. Despite work of theorists like Gottfredson and Hirschi (1990), finding one general theory to explain juvenile offending is likely an impossible task.

Developmental psychology theories help to explain what can go wrong in early childhood and adolescence and contribute to delinquency. Some of these explanations include developmental disorders due to genetics, in utero conditions, or at birth. Physiological psychology helps us to understand the functions of the brain, including how brain chemistry contributes to risky or criminal behaviors, including addictions. Both theoretical areas also help to explain emotional reactivity and impulsivity disorders.

Behavioral explanations for criminal behavior include self-control theories. These are closely related to developmental and physiological explanations of crime, as children are expected to outgrow impulsive and inappropriate emotional responses to disappointment. When they don't, due to brain chemistry, or as Gottfredson and Hirschi proposed in 1990, because of an absence of nurturing or discipline, it can result in deviance and delinquency in adolescence and adulthood. As we will see in the next chapter, low self-control can be encouraged and rewarded by delinquent peers.

Some criminal behaviors witnessed in adults and juveniles have origins in psychopathology. A number of psychiatric disorders can sometimes result in criminal behavior, including anxiety, depression, and more seriously, bipolar and schizophrenia disorders. We say "sometimes," as a great majority of those suffering from psychological or psychiatric disorders will not offend. However, we see that a large portion of those in the adult and juvenile justice systems suffer from mental health disorders.

The most prevalent factor contributing to juvenile offending is substance abuse. This includes addiction to alcohol and/or prescription or illicit drugs. Addictions have been explained using chemical/medical/genetic models, behavioral models, or a combination, such as the biopsychosocial model. All three models deviate from traditional views of addiction explained by an individual's character or moral flaws. Other currently accepted explanations fall into the category of behavioral theories, which remain in the forefront of theories of delinquency.

Particularly in the case of underage drinking, it is sometimes difficult for a parental unit to recognize whether experimentation is part of normal socialization by peers or a cause for concern. As we noted earlier in this book, even if parental units tolerate, condone, or ignore underage drinking by their children, it is illegal under the age of 21 in the United States, with the exception of states that allow underage drinking as part of legitimate religious practices. The opioid epidemic, especially among juveniles, has caused great alarm recently and resulted in an increase in emergency room admissions due to drug overdoses.

Other factors contributing to juvenile offending that were largely ignored until more recently include PTSD. Initially considered a phenomenon exclusive to military personnel who had been stationed in combat zones, mental health professionals now recognize that adults who have not been exposed to war can also be afflicted with PTSD following stressful or traumatic life experiences, including exposure to domestic or interpersonal violence or other crime victimization. Juvenile PTSD can result in a number of risk-taking behaviors, including sexual promiscuity and alcohol or drug abuse.

IN THE MEDIA

Video Game Addiction and Delinquency

In 2007, Daniel Petric, 16 at the time, shot both his parents in Ohio, wounding his father and killing his mother (Martinez, 2009). His reason? His parents had taken away his *Halo 3* video game, a first-person shooter game (Hawk, 2021; Martinez, 2009). The association between consumption of media violence, including in video games, and aggressive, antisocial behaviors has been well-established in juvenile delinquency research (DeLisi et al., 2012). However, there is less understanding of video game or Internet addiction. Internet gaming disorder (ICD) was added to the International Classifications of Diseases by the World Health Organization (WHO) in 2018, and video game addiction, in general, was formally recognized as a legitimate psychiatric disorder in 2022 (Olson and Williams, 2022; Parmar et al., 2021).

According to Parmar and Lagoy (2021) the tell-tale signs in juveniles and adults that video game use may have become an addiction are:

- Mood changes
- Poor hygiene
- Lack of structure
- Isolation or reduced social behavior
- Procrastination
- Fatigue
- Appetite changes
- Problems at work or academic decline
- Increased conflict with family over video game use

Treatment for video game addiction includes medication commonly used to treat depression and ADHD, cognitive behavioral therapy, and individual and family counseling sessions (Parmer et al., 2021). Given that juveniles frequently play video games together, it can be a difficult addiction to overcome, particularly if the goal is complete abstinence.

Postscript

Petric was sentenced to 23 years in adult prison, even though he was a juvenile at the time of his crime (Martinez, 2009). At the time of his trial, he could have received a sentence of life in prison without the possibility of parole (Martinez, 2009). Jack Thompson, a crusader against violent video games, is currently campaigning for a new trial for Petric, on the argument that Petric was addicted to violent video games (Hawk, 2021).

SOURCES

DeLisi, M., M. G. Vaughn, D. A. Gentile, C. A. Anderson, and J. J. Shook (2012). "Violent video games, delinquency, and youth violence: New evidence." *Youth Violence and Juvenile Justice.* Oct. Retrieved from http://www.sabineduflo.fr/wp-content/uploads/2016/12/jeux-video-violents-et-dc3a9linquance.pdf.

Hawk, J. (2021). "New trial for Petric? Anti-video game activist wants second chance for Brighton man who shot his parents." *Chronicle.* Nov. 13. Retrieved from https://chroniclet.com/news/281679/new-trial-for-petric-anti-video-game-activist-wants-second-chance-for-brighton-man-who-shot-parents/.

Martinez, E. (2009). "Game over for teen who killed mother over video game." *CBS News.* June 17. Retrieved from https://www.cbsnews.com/news/game-over-for-teen-who-killed-mother-over-video-game/.

Olson, P., and L. Williams (2022). "Is video game addiction a real illness?" *Bloomberg.* Mar 19. Retrieved from https://www.bloomberg.com/opinion/articles/2022-03-19/is-video-game-addiction-a-real-illness.

Parmar, R., and J. Lagoy (2021). "Is video game addiction a disorder?" *Psychiatric Times.* Vol. 38, issue 10. Retrieved from https://www.psychiatrictimes.com/view/is-video-game-addiction-a-disorder.

INTERNATIONAL PERSPECTIVES

Juvenile Addiction in France

France is one of many European countries with a more liberal view of juvenile alcohol consumption when compared to the United States. Wine is often served at meals in France to complement the meal, not to get intoxicated. Juveniles are allowed exposure to low-alcohol beverages, like beer and wine, to demystify them. Since children are often attracted to things that are prohibited, including alcohol, it is believed that exposure will make them less tempted.

A few decades ago there was no age minimum on alcohol consumption in France (Salzberg, 2021). Amid growing concern over rising rates of binge drinking and motor vehicle accidents and other alcohol-related injuries, the minimum age for alcohol purchases in France today is 18, with consumption allowed at 16 in the presence of an adult (World Population Review, 2022; Salzberg, 2021). Concern also grew over an increased correlation between alcohol consumption and juvenile crime. In an international study that included France, boys were often under the influence of alcohol and/or drugs when they engaged in delinquent acts, but less so for juvenile females committing crimes (Rocca et al., 2019).

Since alcohol consumption at meals is treated as normative in France, researchers were interested to learn whether the country's adult and juvenile populations were at higher risk for AUD. Reportedly, 7% of adults in France have AUD (Costa et al., 2020). In an early study of alcohol consumption in France that included children in their first year of secondary school (mean age, 11.5), approximately one-fifth (21.9%) of adolescents reported regular alcohol consumption, though those numbers have decreased in more recent years (Bailey et al., 2015). In comparison, in the United States, an estimated 14.5 million cases of AUD are

A French family.

reported among individuals 12 and older—4% of the population (National Institute of Alcohol Abuse and Alcoholism, 2022). The actual numbers may be higher. As of 2019, even before the COVID-19 pandemic, a reported 6.3% of people in the United States, ages 18 and over, admitted to heavy alcohol use (National Institute of Alcohol Abuse and Alcoholism, 2022).

More recently, France has given more attention to other forms of substance addiction than alcohol. As Jeanne et al. (2017) have reported, a number of new drugs have been introduced to French youth in the last 20 years, and their patterns of consumption have changed. The most common substances consumed by juveniles in France continue to be tobacco, alcohol, and cannabis (Jeanne et al., 2017). However, other drugs have become increasingly available to juveniles in France, including performance-enhancing pharmaceuticals, such as Ritalin, which is widely prescribed for ADD and ADHD (Jeanne et al., 2017).

SOURCES

Bailey, J., A. Rouchard, C. Garcia, C. Roehrig, and J-P. Ferley (2015). "Alcohol use in young adolescents. A survey in French secondary schools." *Archives of Pediatric and Adolescent Medicine*. Vol. 22, issue 5: 510–517.

Costa, M., T. Barré, M. Coste, I. Yaya, C. Berenger, M. Tanti, C. Cutarella, M. Mora, P. Poloméni, M. Maynard, D. Teuma, M. Bazin, G. Maradan, P. Rou, and P. M. Carrieri (2020). "Screening and care for alcohol use disorder in France: Expectations, barriers and levers using a mixed-methods approach." *BMC Public Health*. Vol. 20, issue 358. Retrieved from https://bmcpublichealth.biomedcentral.com/articles/10.1186/s12889-020-08495-x#citeas.

Jeanne, G., D. Purper-Ouakil, H. Rigole, and N. Franc (2017). "New patterns of substance use and abuse among adolescents: A knowledge synthesis." *Encephale*. Vol. 43, issue 4 (Aug.): 346–353.

National Institute of Alcohol Abuse and Alcoholism (2022). Alcohol use in the United States. National Institute of Health. March. Retrieved from https://www.niaaa.nih.gov/publications/brochures-and-fact-sheets/alcohol-facts-and-statistics.

Rocca, G., A. Verde, and U. Gatti(2019). "Impact of alcohol and cannabis use on juvenile delinquency: Results from an international multi-city study (ISRD3)." *European Journal on Criminal Policy and Research*. Vol. 25, issue 3 (Sep.): 259–271.

Salzberg, A. (2021). "French Culture: What is the legal drinking age in France and why?" *French Together*. July 19. Retrieved from https://frenchtogether.com/drinking-age-france/#:~:text=The%20legal%20drinking%20age%20in%20France%20is%2018%2C%20or%2016,a%20country%20of%20wine%2Dlovers.

World Population Review (2022). Drinking age by country, 2022. Retrieved from https://worldpopulationreview.com/country-rankings/drinking-age-by-country.

CHAPTER DISCUSSION QUESTIONS

1. Of the theories presented in this chapter, which one is the most compelling explanation for individual juvenile offending? Why?
2. What theories are the least compelling in explaining juvenile deviance or delinquency? Why?

3. In recent years there have been discussions of the role in criminal behavior of chronic traumatic encephalopathy (CTE)—a condition associated with athletes who play contact sports and have suffered from multiple concussions. How might this be a concern in juveniles who play contact sports?
4. What contributes to higher rates of depression and anxiety in juveniles?
5. We ordinarily think of people who are depressed as being unmotivated, but this is a stereotype. Why might a juvenile who is suffering from clinical depression feel compelled to commit a crime, going against this stereotype?
6. Which theory of addiction makes the most sense to you in explaining juvenile offending? Why?
7. Why might parental units turn a blind eye to their child's alcohol or drug addiction, ignoring the symptoms the child might show?
8. Besides the addictions listed in this chapter, can you think of any other possible addictions that might lead to juvenile offending?

GLOSSARY

Attachment theories A number or theories and hypotheses centered on understanding the bonds between people, with a focus on early childhood development.

Autism Spectrum Disorder A broad range of disorders that include symptoms of difficulty with social function and interaction, as well as repetitive behaviors. First signs can be detected as early as infancy, and there can be some associated delays in childhood development.

Bipolar disorder A medical condition typically characterized as having moods alternating between states of elation and depression, though this may not be the case for all individuals with the disorder.

Bounded rationality Herbert A. Simon's theory (1982; 1990) that decisions are made on the basis of imperfect or missing information. Because we often know this to be the case, we run with "good enough" decisions, particularly if we are pressed for time.

Childhood Separation Anxiety Disorder (CSAD) Mental health issue commonly seen in infants and children, where there is a pathological attachment to certain family members and fear of separation.

Cognitive theories A number of theories that focus on the mechanics and patterns of thinking in individuals, including creative processes.

Developmental disorders A number of disabilities related to slowed or abnormal development in children and adults, including physical, learning, language, or behavior deficiencies.

Emotional intelligence Unlike the intelligence quotient (IQ), emotional intelligence measures the ability to put into practice skills of self-awareness, including perceiving and regulating emotions.

Fight or flight response The biological and psychological imperative that individuals face in perceived dangerous or stressful situations, in which the natural instinct is to either stay and fight or run from the threat.

Hypomania Not to be confused with hypermania, hypomania is a milder form of mania that can include abnormally high levels of excitement, happiness, and energy, marked with sleep deprivation, talkativeness, and inflated self-worth. (See *mania*.)

Internet gaming disorder Addiction recognized by the World Health Organization as a condition where individuals' lives are disrupted by excessive time spent playing games on the Internet, and marked by symptoms of withdrawal when they are unable or prohibited from playing.

Life-course theories A multidiscipline approach to studying human development, based in life stages (e.g., infancy, early childhood, etc.).

Limbic system The part of the brain responsible for behavior and emotional responses. The three main parts of the limbic system are the amygdala, cingulate gyrus, and the hippocampus.

Mania Common symptom in bipolar disorder, to varying degrees, with symptoms of exaggerated excitement, and euphoria, marked with episodes of delusions and hyperactivity. (See *Hypomania*.)

Neurotransmitters Chemical substances released in the brain from the nervous system that transmit messages between neurons and from neurons to muscles.

Physiological psychology The branch of psychology that focuses on brain anatomy, including the relationship between physiology and behavior.

Prefrontal cortex The part of the brain that is key to self-regulation, self-control, and conflict resolution. The prefrontal cortex is not fully developed in humans until around the age of 25.

Psychopathology A mental or behavior disorder that is likely to require medical and/or psychiatric intervention to control or resolve.

REFERENCES AND ADDITIONAL SUGGESTED READINGS

Ahmed, S. P., A. Bittencourt-Hewitt, and C. L. Sebastian (2015). "Neurocognitive bases of emotion regulation development in adolescence." *Developmental Cognitive Neuroscience*. Vol. 15 (Oct.): 11–25.

Alonso-Tapia, J., D. M. Abello, and E. Panadero (2020). Regulating emotions and learning motivation in higher education students. *International Journal of Emotional Education.* Vol. 12, issue 2: 73-89.

Amador, X., and A. Johanson (2000). *I Am Not Sick: I Don't Need Help!* Tallinn, EE: ViDA Press.

Bailly, D., A. Rouchard, C. Garcia, C. Roehrig, and J-P. Ferley (2015). "Alcohol use in young adolescents. A survey in French secondary schools." *Archives of Pediatric and Adolescent Medicine.* Vol. 22, issue 5: 510–517.

Battaglia, M. (2015). "Separation anxiety: At the neurobiologial crossroads of adaptation and illness." *Dialogues in Clinical Neuroscience.* Vol. 17, issue 3 (Sep.): 277–285.

Berman, M. R., and M. S. Boguski (2020). "Understanding Kanye West's bipolar disorder: From a presidential bid to Satanic vaccines, could this represent a full-blown manic episode?" *Med Page Today.* Jul 15. Retrieved from https://www.medpagetoday.com/popmedicine/celebritydiagnosis/87581.

Beyer, J. L., M. Kuchibhatla, C. Looney, E. Engstrom, F. Cassidy, and K. R. R. Krishnan (2003). "Social support in elderly patients with bipolar disorder." *Bipolar Disorder.* Vol. 5: 22–27.

Bracha, H. S. (2004). "Freeze, flight, fight, fright, faint: Adaptationist perspectives on Acute Stress Response Spectrum." *CNS Spectrums.* Vol. 9, issue 9: 679–685.

Bretherton, I. (1992). "The origins of Attachment Theory: John Bowlby and Mary Ainsworth." *Developmental Psychology.* Vol. 28, issue 5: 759–775.

Buchhandler-Raphael, M. (2020). "Loss of self-control, dual-process theories and provocation." *Fordham Law Review.* Vol. 88, issue 5: 1815–1874.

Butcher, I., K. Berry, and G. Haddock (2020). "Understanding individuals' subjective experience of negative symptoms of schizophrenia: A qualitative study." *British Journal of Clinical Psychology.* Vol. 59: 319–334.

Dailey, L. F., S. W. Townsend, M. W. Dysken, and M.A. Kuskowski (2005). *Journal of Clinical Psychiatry.* Vol. 66, issue 4 (April): 477–484.

Cole, P. M., S. E. Martin, and T. A. Dennis (2004). "Emotion regulation as a scientific construct: Methodological challenges and directions for child development research." *Child Development.* Vol. 75: 317–333.

Cooley, C. H. (1902). *Human Nature and the Social Order.* New York: Scribner's.

Disner, S. G., C. G. Beevers, E. A. P. Haigh, and A. T. Beck (2011). "Neural mechanisms of the cognitive model of depression." *Nature Reviews Neuroscience.* Vol. 12, issue 8: 467–477.

Ditch the Label (2019). *The Annual Bullying Survey: Annual Benchmark of Bullying in the UK.* London, UK: Ditch the Label.

Ehrenreich, J. T., L. C. Santucci, and C. L. Weiner (2008). "Separation anxiety disorder in youth: Phenomenology, assessment, and treatment." *Psicología Conductual.* Jan 1, Vol. 16, issue 3 (Jan.): 369–412.

Emotional Intelligence Network (n.d.). Plutnik's wheel of emotions: Exploring the emotion wheel. 6 Seconds Organization. Retrieved from https://www.6seconds.org/2020/08/11/plutchik-wheel-emotions/.

Eron, L. D. (1983). "The consistency of aggressive behavior across time and situations." Paper delivered at *Consistency of Aggression and Its Correlates Over 20 Years*, Annual Meeting, American Psychological Association, Anaheim, CA.

Eron, L. D., L. O. Walder, L. R. Hussmann, M. M. Lefkowitz (1974). "The convergence of laboratory and field studies of the development of aggression." In *Determinants and Origins of Aggressive Behavior*, ed. J. deWitt and W. W. Hartup. Foxboro, MA: Moulton Publishing.

Farrington, D. P. (1986). "Age and crime." *Criminal Justice.* Vol. 1: 189–250.

Farringinton, D. P. (1978). "The family background of aggressive youths." In *Aggressive and Antisocial Behaviour in Childhood and Adolescence*, ed. L. Hersove, M. Berger, and D. Shaffer. Oxford, UK: Pergamon.

Feriante, J., and B. Bernstein (2021). "Separation anxiety." The National Center for Biotechnology Information, National Library of Medicine, National Institute of Health. July 26. Retrieved from https://www.ncbi.nlm.nih.gov/books/NBK560793/.

Feurer, C., K. M. James, C. E. Foster, and B. E. Gibb (2020). "Sustained attention and individual differences in adolescents' mood and physiological reactivity to stress." *Journal of Abnormal Child Psychology.* Vol. 48: 1325–1336.

Font, S. A., and H. Woo Kim (2021). "Sibling separation and placement instability for children in foster care." *Child Maltreatment.* April. Retrieved from https://pubmed.ncbi.nlm.nih.gov/33910412/.

Frailberg, S., E. Adelson, and V. Shapiro (1975). "Ghosts in the nursery: A psychoanalytic approach to the problems of impaired infant-mother relationships." *Journal of American Academy of Child Psychiatry.* Vol. 14, issue 3: 387–421.

Freeman, A. J., E. A. Youngstrom, E. Michalak, R. Siegel, O. I. Meyers, and R. L. Findling (2009). "Quality of life in pediatric bipolar disorder." *Pediatrics.* Vol. 123, issue 3: e446–e452.

Gottfredson, M. R., and T. Hirschi (1990). *A General Theory of Crime.* Stanford, CA: Stanford University Press.

Grasso, D. J., C. Doyle, and R. Koon (2019). "Two rapid screens for detecting probable Post-Traumatic Stress Disorder and interpersonal violence exposure: Predictable utility in a juvenile justice sample." *Child Maltreatment.* Vol. 24, issue 1: 113–120.

Gray, J. A. (1988). *The Psychology of Fear and Stress,* 2d ed. Cambridge, UK: Cambridge University Press.

Hahn, C. K., A. M. Hahn, R. M. Simons, and S. J. Caraway (2021). "Women's perceived likelihood to engage in sexual risk taking: Posttraumatic stress symptoms and poor behavioral regulation." *Journal of Interpersonal Violence.* Vol. 36: 11–12.

Hansen, L. L., and M.E. Freitag. (2016). " 'Come on now, I want to see blood!': Choreographed violence in gang initiation rites." Ch. 1 in *Global Perspectives on Youth Behavior, Violence, and Weapons Use,* ed. S. Harding and M. Palasinki. UK: IGI Global.

Hansen, L. P. (2020). *White Collar and Corporate Crime: A Case Study Approach.* Baltimore, MD: Wolters Kluwer.

Havighhurst, R. J., P. H. Bowman, G. P. Liddle, C. V. Matthews, and J. V. Pierce (1962). *Growing Up in River City.* New York: Wiley.

Herrnstein, R., and C. Murray (2009). "The link between cognitive ability and criminal behavior." Ch. 7 in *Key Readings in Criminology,* ed. T. Newburn. Portland, OR: Willan Publishing.

Herrnstein, R., and C. Murray (1994). *The Bell Curve: Intelligence and Class Structure in American Life.* New York: Free Press.

Hirschi, T. (1969). *Causes of Delinquency.* Berkeley: University of California Press.

Holt, D. J., D. Ongur, C. I. Wright, B. Dickerson, and S. L. Rauch (2008). "Neuroanatomical systems relevant to neuropsychiatric disorders." In *Massachusetts General Hospital Comprehensive Clinical Psychiatry,* ed. T. Stern, M. Fava, T. Wilens, and J. Rosenbaum. Amsterdam, NL: Elsevier.

Hussong, A. M., D. J. Jones, G. L. Stein, D. H. Baucom, and S. Boeding (2011). "An internalizing pathway to alcohol use and disorder." *Psychology of Addictive Behaviors.* Vol. 25, issue 3: 390–404.

Jones, R. M., M. Van den Bree, M. Ferriter, and P J. Taylor (2010). "Childhood risk factors for offending before first psychiatric admission for people with schizophrenia: A case-control study of high security hospital admissions." *Behavioral Science and the Law.* Vol. 28: 351–365.

Jorgensen, C. C. (1973). "IQ tests and their educational supporters." *Journal of Social Issues.* Vol. 29, issue 1 (March): 33–40.

Jovanovic, D., M. Novakovic, A. Salamadic, N. Petrovic, and S. Maric (2012). "Analysis of the relationship between intelligence and criminal behavior." *Journal of Health Sciences.* Vol. 2, issue 3: 224–231.

Kahn, R. E., E. Ermer, P. Salovey, and K. A. Kiehl (2016). "Emotional intelligence and callous-unemotional traits in incarcerated adolescents." *Child Psychiatry and Human Development*. Vol. 47: 903–918.

Kaur, A., S. Z. Kailash, K. Sureshkumar, C. Sivabackiya, and N. Rumaisa (2022). "Gender differences in emotional regulation capacity among the general population." *IAIM*. Vol. 9, issue 1: 22–28.

Kerig, P. K. (2019). "Linking childhood trauma exposure to adolescent justice involvement: The concept of posttraumatic risk-taking." *Clinical Psychology Science and Practice*. Jan: e12280. Retrieved from https://www.researchgate.net/profile/Patricia-Kerig/publication/331586409_Linking_Childhood_Trauma_Exposure_to_Adolescent_Justice_Involvement_The_Concept_of_Posttraumatic_Risk-Seeking/links/60e4e8ac299bf1b0319bbebc/Linking-Childhood-Trauma-Exposure-to-Adolescent-Justice-Involvement-The-Concept-of-Posttraumatic-Risk-Seeking.pdf.

Khoo, A. (2020). "The emotional brain." *Young Scientist Journal*. Jul 22. Retrieved from https://ysjournal.com/the-emotional-brain/.

Larivée, S., and F. Gagné (2007). "Les biais culturel de tests de QI: La nature du problem (The cultural biases of IQ tests: The nature of the problem)." *Canadian Psychology*. Vol. 48, issue 4: 221–239.

Laursen, M. F., R. W. Licht, C. U. Correll, T. Kallehauge, A. Christensen, M. Rodrigo-Domingo, and R. E. Nielsen (2020). "Diagnostic stability in children and adolescents with bipolar disorder, a nationwide register-based study." *International Journal of Bipolar Disorders*. Vol. 8, issue 14. Retrieved from https://journalbipolardisorders.springeropen.com/articles/10.1186/s40345-020-0179-3#citeas.

Lee, T. (2022). "We gotta talk about Kanye West: What Kanye West can teach us about bipolar disorder and Black mental health." Podcast. *Into America*, MSNBC. Mar 25. Retrieved fromhttps://www.msnbc.com/podcast/into-america/transcript-we-gotta-talk-about-kanye-west-n1293165.

Lewis, M. D., and J. Steiben (2004). "Emotional regulation in the brain: Conceptual issues and directions for developmental research." *Child Development*. Vol. 75, issue 2 (March/April): 371–376.

Liu, L., M. du Toit, and G. Weidermann (2021). "Infants are sensitive to cultural differences in emotions at 11 months." *Plos ONE*. Vol. 16, issue 9: 1–15.

Liu, S. (2015). "Is the shape of the age-crime curve invariant by sex? Evidence from a national sample with flexible non-parametric modeling." *Journal of Quantitative Criminology*. Vol. 31: 93–123.

Lynam, D., T. Moffitt, and M. Stouthamer-Loeber (1993). "Explaining the relationship between IQ and delinquency: Class, motivation, school failure, or self-control." *Journal of Abnormal Psychology*. Vol. 102, issue 2: 187–196.

MacPherson, H. A., A. Y. Kudinova, E. Schettini, G. A. Jenkins, A. C. Gilbert, S. A. Thomas, and K. L. Kim (2022). "Relationship between cognitive reflexibility and subsequent course of mood symptoms and suicidal ideation in young adults with childhood-onset bipolar disorder." *European Child and Adolescent Psychiatry*. Vol. 31, issue 2: 299–312.

Marco, D. (2011). "The Dopamine Hypothesis of drug addiction and its potential therapeutic value." *Frontiers in Psychiatry*. Vol. 2: 64.

Martschenko, D. (2018). "The IQ test wars: Why screening for intelligence is still so controversial." *The Conversation*. Feb 1. Retrieved from https://theconversation.com/the-iq-test-wars-why-screening-for-intelligence-is-still-so-controversial-81428.

Matheny, J. D. H. (1998). "Strategies for assessment and early treatment with sexually addicted families." *Sexual Addiction and Compulsivity*. Vol. 5: 27–48.

Mayo Clinic Staff (n.d.a). Bipolar disorder: Overview. Retrieved from https://www.mayoclinic.org/diseases-conditions/bipolar-disorder/symptoms-causes/syc-20355955#:~:

text=Although%20bipolar%20disorder%20can%20occur,symptoms%20may%20vary%20over%20time.

Mayo Clinic Staff (n.d.b). Schizoaffective disorder: Overview. Retrieved from https://www.mayoclinic.org/diseases-conditions/schizoaffective-disorder/symptoms-causes/syc-20354504#:~:text=Schizoaffective%20disorder%20is%20a%20mental,such%20as%20depression%20or%20mania.

McGee, T. R., and D. P. Farrington (2019). "Developmental and life-course explanations of offending." *Psychology, Crime and Law.* Vol. 25, issue 6: 609–625.

Modrowski, C. A., and P. K. Kerig (2019). "Investigating the association between posttraumatic risky behavior and offending in adolescents involved in the juvenile system." *Journal of Youth and Adolescence.* Vol. 48: 1952–1966.

Morris, G., K. Walder, S. L. McGee, O. M. Dean, S. J. Tye, M. Maes, and M. Berk (2017). "A model of the mitochondrial basis of bipolar disorder." *Neuroscience and Biobehavioral Research.* Vol. 74 (March), Pt. A: 1–20.

Mostafapoor, M., and S. M. Hoseini (2017). "'Neurocriminology,'" a new approach to the analysis of juvenile violent crime (with emphasis on age-crime curve)." *Faṣlnāmah-i Pizhūhish-i Huqūq-i Kiyfarī.* Vol. 5, issue 19: 127–196. Trans. from Farsi.

National Alliance on Mental Illness (2022). Schizophrenia: Overview. Retrieved from https://www.nami.org/About-Mental-Illness/Mental-Health-Conditions/Schizophrenia.

Novak, A., and K. Benedini (2020). "Sibling separation and self-reported offending: An examination of the association between sibling placement and offending behavior." *Child and Youth Services Review.* Vol. 111 (April): 104830.

Oleson, J. C. (2016). *Criminal Genius: A Portrait of High-IQ Offenders.* Oakland, CA: University of California Press.

Oyama, O., and N. A. Piotrowski (2022). "Depression." In *Magill's Medical Guide*, ed. B. C. Auday, M. A. Buratovich, and G. F. Marrocco. Ipswich, MA: Salem Press.

Ozer, M. M., and H. Akbas (2020). "The Predictability of IQ on delinquency: A structural equation model (SQM)." *International Journal of Criminal Justice Sciences.* Vol. 15, issue 2: 283–297.

Piotrowski, N. A., and L. V. Tischauser (2022). "Schizophrenia." In *Magill's Medical Guide*, ed. B. C. Auday, M. A. Buratovich, and G. F. Marrocco. Ipswich, MA: Salem Press.

Piquero, A. R. (2017). " 'No remorse, no repent': Linking lack of remorse to criminal offending in a sample of adolescent offenders." *Justice Quarterly.* Vol 34, issue 2: 350–376.

Plutchik, R. (2001). "The nature of emotions: Human emotions have deep evolutionary roots, a fact that may explain their complexity and provide tools for clinical practice." *American Scientist.* Vol. 89, issue 4: 344–350.

Plutchik, R. (1982). "A psychoevolutionary theory of emotions." *Social Science Information.* Vol. 21, issues 4–5: 529–553.

Pompili, M., D. Harnic, X. Gonda, A. Forte, G. Dominici, M. Innamrati, K. H. Fountoulakis, G. Serafini, L. Sher, L. Janiri, Z. Rihmer, M. Amore, and P. Girardi (2014). "Impact of living with bipolar patients: Making sense of caregivers' burden." *World Journal of Psychiatry.* Vol. 4, issue 1 (March): 1–12.

Rapee, R. M., C. A. Schniering, and J. L. Hudson (2009). "The brain and behavior in childhood and adolescent anxiety disorders." In *Anxiety Disorders and Adolescents*, 2d ed., ed. W. K. Silverman and A. P. Fields. New York: Cambridge University Press.

Raypole, C.; rev. T. J. Legg (2020). "Types of addiction and how they're treated." *Healthline.* Feb 27. Retrieved from https://www.healthline.com/health/types-of-addiction.

Roff, J. D., and R. D. Wirt (1985). "The specificity of childhood problem behavior for adolescent an and young adult maladjustment." *Journal of Clinical Psychology.* Vol. 41, issue 4 (July): 564–571.

Roff, J. D., and R. D. Wirt (1984). "Childhood aggression and social adjustment as antecedents of delinquency." *Journal of Abnormal Child Psychology.* Vol. 12: 111–126.

Rutten, A. X., R. R. J. M. Vermeiren, and C. Van Nieuwenhuizen (2017). "Autism in adult and juvenile delinquents: A literature review." *Child and Adolescent Psychiatry and Mental Health.* Vol. 11, issue 1: 1–12.

Salk, R. H., J. S. Hyde, and L. Y. Abramson (2017). "Gender differences in depression in representative national samples: Meta-analyses of diagnoses and symptoms." *Psychology Bulletin.* Vol. 143, issue. 8 (Aug.): 783–822.

Sampson, R. J., and J. H. Laub (2005). "A life-course view of the development of crime." *Annals of the American Academy of Political and Social Science.* Vol. 602, issue 12: 12–45.

Schaffer, H. R., and P. E. Emerson (1964). "The development of social attachments in infancy." *Monographs of the Society for Research in Child Development.* Pp. 1–77.

Serpico, D. (2021). "The cyclical return of the IQ controversy: Revisiting the lessons of the resolution on genetics, race and intelligence." *Journal of the History of Biology.* Retrieved from https://doi.org/10.1007/s10739-021-09637-6.

Sheehan, L. L., P. W. Corrigan, and M. A. Al-Khouja. (2017). "Stigma of Suicide: Stakeholder perspectives on the stigma of suicide attempt survivors." *Crisis: The Journal of Crisis Intervention and Suicide Prevention,* Vol. 38, issue 2: 73–81.

Shieh, P., and T. Tsai (2022). "The prediction of perceived parenting style on mother-infant bonding." *Acta Psychologia.* Vol. 226 (June): 103573.

Siennick, S. E., A. O. Widdowson, and M. E. Feinberg (2020). "Youth with co-occurring delinquency and depressive symptoms: Do they have better or worse delinquent outcomes?" *Journal of Youth and Adolescence.* Vol. 49, issue 6: 1260–1276.

Simon, H. A. (1990). "Bounded rationality." In *Utility and Probability,* ed. J. Eatwell, M. Milgate, and P. Newman. New York: Palgrave MacMillan.

Simon, H. A. (1982). *Models of Bounded Rationality.* Cambridge, MA: MIT Press.

Skewes, M. C., and V. M. Gonzalez (2013). "The Biopsychosocial Model of addiction." Ch. 6 in *Principles of Addiction: Comprehensive Addiction Behaviors and Disorders,* Vol. 1, ed. P. Miller. Amsterdam, NL: Elsevier.

Soares-Weiser, K., N. Maayan, H. Bergen, C. Davenport, A. J. Kirkham, S. Grabowski, and E. E. Adams (2015). "First rank symptoms for schizophrenia." In *Cochrane Database of Systematic Reviews.* Cochrane Collaborative. Hoboken, NJ: John Wiley and Sons.

Stattin, H., D. Magnusson, and H. Reichel (1989). "Criminal activity at different ages: A study based on a Swedish longitudinal research population." *British Journal of Criminology.* Vol. 29, issue 4: 368–385.

Substance Abuse and Mental Health Services Administration (2003). *Results from the 2002 National Survey on Drug Use and Health: National Findings.* Rockville, MD: Office of Applied Studies.

Sung, H., L. Richter, R. Vaughan, P. B. Johnson, and B. Thom (2005). "Nonmedical use of prescription opioids among teenagers in the United States: Trends and correlates." *Journal of Adolescent Health.* Vol. 37: 44–51.

Sykes, G. M., and D. Matza (1957). "Techniques of neutralization: A theory of delinquency." *American Sociological Review.* Vol. 22, issue 6: 664–670.

Thomas, S. (2022). "Impulse Control Disorders and substance abuse." American Addiction Centers. Mar 15. Retrieved from https://americanaddictioncenters.org/co-occurring-disorders/impulse-control-disorder.

Tomkins, D. M., and E. M. Sellers (2001). "Addiction and the brain: The role of neurotransmitters in the cause and treatment of drug dependence." *Canadian Medical Association Journal.* Vol. 164, issue 6: 817–821.

Traylor, V. (2021). "What are the 5 developmental disabilities?" New Jersey Developmental Disabilities Council. Oct 2. Retrieved from https://www.njddc.org/5-developmental-disabilities/.

Uggen, C. (2000). "Working as a turning point in life course of criminals: A duration model of age, employment, and recidivism." *American Sociological Review.* Vol. 65, issue 4: 529–546.

University of Western Alabama (n.d.). The Science of Emotions: Exploring the Basics of Emotional Psychology. UWA online. Retrieved from https://online.uwa.edu/wp-content/uploads/2019/04/Science-of-Emotion-Guide-UWA.pdf.

Vasey, M. W., G. Bosmans, and T. H. Ollendick (2014). "The developmental psychopathology of anxiety." In *Handbook of Developmental Psychopathology*, ed. M. Lewis and K. Rudolph. Boston, MA: Springer.

Vaughan, J., J. A. Coddington, A. H. Ahmed, and M. Ertel (2017). "Separation anxiety disorder in school-age children: What health care providers should know." *Journal of Pediatric Health Care.* Vol. 31, issue 4 (July-Aug.): 433–440.

Weintraub, M. J., D. Keenan-Miller, C.D. Schneck, M. F. Borlik, R. L. Suddath, S. E. Marvin, M. K. Singh, K. D. Chang and D. J. Miklowitz (2022). "Social impairment in relation to clinical symptoms in youth at high risk for bipolar disorder." *Early Intervention in Psychiatry.* Vol. 16: 17–25.

Willems, Y. E., C. V. Dolan, C. E. M. van Beijsterveldt, E. L. de Zeeum, D. I. Boomsma, M. Bartels, and C. Finkenauer (2018). "Genetic and environmental influences on self-control: Assessing self-control with the ASEBA Self-Control Scale." *Behavior Genetics.* Vol. 48: 135–146.

Winger, G., J. H. Woods, C. M. Galuska, and T. Wade-Galuska (2005). "Behavioral perspectives on the neuroscience of drug addiction." *Journal of Experimental Analysis of Behavior.* Vol. 84, issue 3 (Nov.): 667–681.

Winningham, R. D., M. R. Buetlich, D. E. Banks, T. C. B. Zapolski, and M. C. Aalsma (2019). "Substance use disorder and posttraumatic stress disorder symptomology on behavioral outcomes among juvenile justice youth." *American Journal on Addictions.* Vol. 28, issue 1 (Jan.): 29–35.

Yeung, M. K., T. L. Lee, A. S. Chan (2021). "Negative mood is associated with decreased working memory in young adults." *Psychophysiology.* Vol. 58, issue 6: e13802.

Zee, A. V. (2009). "The promotion and marketing of OxyContin: Commercial triumph, public health tragedy." *American Journal of Public Health.* Vol. 99, issue 2: 221–227.

Chapter **SEVEN**

Families, Juvenile Deviance, and Delinquency[1]

Every unpunished delinquency has a family of delinquencies.

—Herbert Spencer, 19th century social philosopher

Chapter Objectives

- Building on the individual risks for juvenile delinquency (Chapter 6), introduce the family dynamics that contribute to offending.
- Review family communication patterns and parenting styles that can result in juvenile deviance and delinquency.
- Introduce the factors in child maltreatment that put children and adolescents at risk for mental health issues, addiction, and delinquency.
- Highlight the risks for intergenerational offending.

Key Terms

Attachment theory
Corporal punishment
Emotional security theory
Extended family
Family
Family cohesion
Family stability
Free-range
Gaslighting
Helicoptering
Interaction ritual chains
Interactional theory
Intimate partner violence (IPV)
Nuclear family
Pseudo family
Social anxiety disorder (SAD)
Social bond (and control) theory
Spatial autonomy
Verbal violence

[1] **TRIGGER WARNING**: Several sensitive topics discussed in this chapter might be disturbing to some readers. We recommend that you discuss with your professor or instructor how much or how little of this chapter you will be responsible for.

INTRODUCTION

In the last chapter we discussed the individual risks for deviance and delinquency. This chapter looks at family dynamics, which have just as great an influence on whether a child becomes delinquent. When a family unit experiences malfunction or dysfunction, delinquency seems to be inevitable absent some form of intervention. For example, when couples divorce, the children of the marriage may benefit from or even require counseling. When individual and family risks converge with community risks (the topic of Chapter 8), a child or adolescent may find it nearly impossible to avoid some form of deviance or delinquency, from relatively minor criminal behavior to serious offenses or, in the worst cases, violent offending. Without aggressive intervention, a young delinquent can grow up to be an adult offender.

Throughout this book we have described "parents" as "parental units," as biological or adoptive parents are not always those who rear their children. The legal and sociological definition of *family* is relationships through blood ties, legal adoption, or marriage. *Nuclear family* includes the stereotypical household of two parents and their children. The so-called "normal" family is seen as a myth by most researchers, and seen against this myth, most if not all families have some degree of dysfunction, particularly in contemporary U.S. society. No family is perfect, even if some seem so on the surface. The degree to which a family experiences its own dysfunction, and the nature of that dysfunction, will determine the risk for deviance or delinquency it creates for the juveniles living in it.

The *extended family* consists primarily of all the peripheral blood relatives, including those who live with the nuclear family and/or have the primary job of raising children they did not give birth to. This can include grandparents and great-grandparents, cousins, aunts and uncles, and their offspring, plus those who marry into the family as more distant in-laws. The *pseudo family*, a label which in many ways is an injustice to these types of relationships, are a couple or groups of people who function as a family emotionally and economically, including occupying the same home, but are not related by blood, marriage, or adoption. An example would be a cohabitating but not legally married couple. Pseudo families can be just as invested in household relationships (if not more so, as the ties are voluntary, not legal) as compared to nuclear or extended families, but they are nonetheless at greater risk of dissolving (Graff, 2019). According to the PEW Research Center, adults are more likely to cohabitate without marrying and married couples have higher rates of satisfaction and trust in their partner (Graff, 2019).

Sutherland's theory of differential association helps to explain the effect on juveniles of spending time with family members who are deviant or commit crimes. As we will note again in Chapter 8 on community risks, children growing up in households where deviant or criminal activities occur, no matter what other messages they learn at school, church, or elsewhere in the community, will see the socially unacceptable behavior happening at home as normal, particularly if witnessed continuously from an early age.

Family remains the first and primary source of socialization in childhood. *Interactional theory* (Huijsmans, 2018; Thornberry et al., 2003; Thornberry, 1987) suggests that the importance of parents as the primary source of socialization changes over time, with peers, including siblings who are close in age, becoming more influential in early, middle, and late adolescence as children begin to seek more autonomy and freedom.

PARENTAL UNITS' ATTITUDES

We will continue to use the term parental units in this chapter to describe the person or people with the primary role of caring for a household's children, whether related biologically or through fostering, adoption, or a parent's remarriage. Parental units have profound effects on how their children eventually parent their own children. Often young adults contemplating starting a family will say they do not want to parent as they were parented, but inevitably some elements of that experience will spill over into how they raise their children.

The key family variables that predict delinquency are first, how parental units feel about their children, from pregnancy through the formative years, and second, communication. Ideally, every child born on this planet would be welcomed into a loving, nurturing family unit. The reality is that many are born into families where they are not wanted or to parental units who are ill-equipped to care for them, such as teenage parents or parents suffering from mental health issues. An even more accurate predictor of delinquency due to family dynamics is the extent to which children feel rejected or are poorly supervised, and family management and parenting styles overall (Hoeve et al., 2009; Loeber and Dishion, 1983).

Family Communication Patterns That Contribute to Delinquency

Understanding why patterns of poor communication in families persist, including use of abusive language, shaming, and chronic verbal fighting, requires research into why these patterns emerge in the first place. Yelling at children is now classified as *verbal violence* (see Table 7.1), which erodes self-confidence and potentially leads to social and emotional disorders (Wahyuni et al., 2019), often contributing to delinquency. Randall Collins's (2005) theory of *interaction ritual chains* helps explain how poor communication in families becomes habitual over time. For example, positive rituals, like regular family dinners sharing lively conversation and good humor, reinforce family bonds. Negative rituals, like habitual shouting matches and verbal fighting, emotionally drain individuals (Collins, 2005). Poor communication tends to continue if no one realizes that the constant arguments tend to go nowhere and often escalate. Most of us know of family arguments on certain subjects (e.g., housework) that repeat themselves, with no resolution. A conscious effort is needed to break the cycle of verbal abuse.

TABLE 7.1 Forms of Verbal Violence

Type	Description
1. Rejection of children's opinions or activities	Chronic verbal expression of adults against or disagreeing with what children say or do.
2. Use of language/terms that are not suitable for children/labeling	a) Analyzing/likening children with objects or creatures that are in picture of parents. b) Labeling/giving nicknames to children because of the physical condition of the child (e.g., "fat").
3. Daily language options or expressions that are not suitable for children	Lewd, suggestive language; profanity
4. Excessive anger expressions	Act of saying aloud or yelling insults; shouting at child, cursing at child.
5. Comparing with objects or other children	Comparing a child to ugly or unpleasant objects; comparing a child negatively to a more favored child.
6. Disparaging, demeaning, or threatening children	Telling a child that they are "worthless, unwanted", using language that is intended to hurt the child's feelings, threats of withdrawing affection or threats of physical violence.

Source: Wahyuni et al., 2019, p. 213.

It would make sense to change patterns of confrontations and negative communication in a family. Yelling has negative effects on the body, including raised blood pressure and heart rate, making this form of communication detrimental to physical health as well. Even if children are not directly yelled at, verbal fighting between adults in a household has negative consequences. According to *emotional security theory* (Silva and Calheiros, 2018; Cummings and Davies, 2010), negative interparental communication (e.g., yelling at each other) presents risks for negative outcomes for children and adolescents because it increases their insecurity about their parental units' relationship (i.e., creating fear of divorce) and can undermine the relationship between the parental units and their children (Silva and Calheiros, 2018).

Children begin learning very early about who they can trust and turn to for comfort. *Attachment theory* (Bowlby, 1969) focuses on how long-term relationships are established. Bowlby posits four stages: pre-attachment in early infancy; an indiscriminate phase during which the child shows signs of attachment; the discriminate phase in which the child attaches to the primary caretaker; and finally, at about ten months, the multiple phase, in which the child bonds with multiple caregivers (Cherry, 2019; Bowlby, 1969). If children and adolescents cannot turn to their parents or guardians as sources of security because of fighting and inconsistency in discipline, family communications break down further, and offspring hide misadventures and disappointments (Silva and Calheiros, 2018). All of this can result in delinquency, or at the very least, status offending, like running away from home.

Communication patterns are often passed down from generation to generation, making bad communication habits even harder to break. However, there is a cultural element to the volume at which we speak, where in some families even calling people to the dinner table is done in a raised voice, with no malice intended, while damaging insults can be handed out in a quiet voice in other families.

PARENTING PRACTICES AND DELINQUENCY

Probably the most important parenting practices to prevent delinquency are monitoring children's activities and setting good examples in the home. Parenting practices occupy a continuum, with most parents lenient in some matters and stricter in others. Parental influence, if positive and supportive without stifling the child, can reduce the impact of having deviant or delinquent friends and behaviors (Vitaro et al., 2000). Conversely, parental units who hover excessively over their children and are controlling run the risk of alienating them, and in some cases, juveniles will be driven to find ways to escape these parental units' watchful eye. A number of researchers have found that adults who had parents who are both controlling and *helicoptering* experienced low school engagement in their teen years and had delinquent behavior and/or depression while transitioning from childhood to adulthood (Edwards, 2019; Mak, 1994). Parental rigidity and inflexibility can result in rebellion in the teen years, a developmental stage in which it is perfectly normal to start pulling away from parents. Likewise, children, including adolescents, without adequate parental supervision, influence, or control are at risk for delinquency and, if already involved in the juvenile justice system, for recidivism (Williams-Butler, 2013).

Somewhere toward the other end of the spectrum are parental units who advocate the *free-range* method of raising children. Free-range parenting allows children more freedom, without passing on unfounded fears or the hysteria found in overprotective parenting (Pimental, 2012). Up until the 1980s, this parenting style, though not labeled free-range, is how most children were raised. You may have heard an older adult say, "We played outside in our neighborhood until the street lights came on. Then we had to go home." Free-ranging children are allowed to make mistakes, including at school, and to suffer the consequences, with little parental interference. Children are also allowed *spatial autonomy* in free-range parenting, which allows them to play outside freely, with some limitations, like remaining in the neighborhood or a local park (Little and Rice, 2021). As Morin (2021) advises, free-range parenting should not be confused with neglect, permissiveness, or lack of involvement; it is intended to make children more independent by encouraging self-confidence and self-reliance.

Free-ranging children.

Overprotective parenting has emerged out of media-fueled fears of kidnapping and/or child molestation. With overprotective parenting becoming normative in the United States, families practicing free-range parenting are at risk of being reported to child protective services, as has happened in some cases when parents have allowed their children to play unsupervised at a park and a concerned neighbor has called the police. In some states in recent years, laws have been passed making it illegal to let children play outside without adult supervision, even in their own neighborhoods. States including Oklahoma, Texas, and Colorado are attempting to reverse these laws to protect parental units from being prosecuted for neglect if they practice free-range parenting (Coltrain, 2022; Brooks, 2018).

As we noted, functional parenting styles form a spectrum, with most parents falling somewhere between "helicoptering" and advocating for free-range child-rearing. Again, we should not confuse either extreme of the spectrum of what can be considered to be normal parenting with neglect. Neglect means near-total disregard for the welfare of the child. We will discuss neglect and other forms of child maltreatment later in this chapter.

FAMILY COHESION

How much a nuclear family is intact, bonded to one another, and working toward the same family goals, including socialization, religious upbringing, and education, has an effect on how much risk a child faces for delinquency. It is important to note that a family can be intact without necessarily being a cohesive unit. *Family cohesion* is defined as the extent to which family members are emotionally bonded with one another (Rivera et al., 2008; Olson et al., 1982). Even in the case of divorced parents, successful co-parenting, where there is agreement on visitation rights and parenting styles, can provide considerable protection against delinquency. We also cannot underestimate the role of the extended family in helping to prevent delinquency, including the involvement of grandparents, aunts, and uncles in enforcing positive social values.

During the 1950s and 1960s in the United States, television shows like *Father Knows Best, Leave It to Beaver*, and *The Adventures of Ozzie and Harriet* depicted unrealistic family dynamics. Family disputes were resolved in half hour segments, including commercial interruptions, often with humor and moral lessons thrown in for good measure. When children misbehaved, they were always apologetic and contrite. Traditional gender roles were enforced in the post-WWII era, and situation comedies (sitcoms) and dramadies in the infancy of television portrayed the white middle-class family as the social norm, with little regard for the variety of real families (*American Century*, n.d.). Later sitcoms and dramas began to portray more realistic families (e.g., *Modern Family*), though elements in some of today's television shows and movies present still one view of the American family as the "real" one.

In reality, siblings often do not get along and parental units do not always have the perfect solution or sage advice to offer in any given situation. Family members are not always working toward the same goals. Families often are made up of people with different temperaments, personalities, and expectations, resulting in family conflict, sometimes over the most mundane things, including household chores and, for children, sharing toys.

And certainly, most conflicts are not resolved within a half hour, as depicted in television sitcoms. One only has to experience the stress of a family road trip to appreciate that, as much as a family may appear to be happy and thriving, children act up because of the tedium of travel or repeatedly ask, "Are we there yet?", even as it makes parental units cranky. Even in the best functioning families, conflict and disagreements over a number of important things, including money and parenting styles, give rise to periodic discontent, sometimes even leading to arguments that are beyond repair and, in the extreme, divorce. However, it is for these very reasons that in many cases, divorce is a means by which to restore family harmony in separate households.

One dimension of family cohesion is the extent to which the family remains stable over time. *Family stability* is defined as when the family structure remains relatively intact, whether it is a traditional nuclear family, a step-family, or a single-parent family (Cheng, 2004; Hao and Xie, 2002), and parenting and routines are consistent. Importantly, in communities where children witness violence, family cohesion and stability act as protective variables in preventing delinquency, as well as protection against the possible long-term impact of frequently witnessing violence (e.g., gang activity) (Barr et al., 2012; Matherne and Thomas, 2001).

Another factor in family cohesion is how well families adapt to change. Even in the most stable families, change is inevitable. Parents' careers may include periods of unemployment, parental units may have to work out of town, or frequent moves may occur due to the nature of a parent's work (a common experience in military families). Family cohesion has been found in studies to be a more important variable in preventing delinquency and fostering adaptability. It is the cohesion that provides the flexibility to adapt more easily to change (Clark and Shields, 1996). In our military family example, surprisingly, frequent relocation is not always associated with more stress: "Although moving can be a particularly stressful endeavor, it appears that, for military families, the settling in process may bring a new network of personal and institutional support that provide the family with a larger circle of potential support. . . ." (Sumner et al., 2016, p. 256). So, family cohesion can be enhanced by outside social and emotional support, particularly during stressful times. Also, military families receive material support when they move from post to post.

Social Bond (and Control) Theory

In a number of cases, families of criminals are described as "quiet and nice" or "good neighbors," so we cannot discount the fact that we do not always know what is going on behind closed doors in family households. Hirschi's *social bond (and control theory)* (1969) assumes that juveniles (and adults as well) have natural inclinations toward delinquency, and social bonds help prevent them from giving into these supposed natural proclivities. Attachments (or social bonds) and commitment are not only assumed to be to family, but to schools, the community, and employers, including the acceptance of the societal expectations to behave legitimately. If social bonds break down in any of these social arenas, delinquency can and does occur, at least in theory.

We should caution that there is a generalizability problem with social bonding theories, including Hirschi's. Some researchers suggest that we cannot necessarily assume that male and female juveniles lacking social bonds experience that absence in the same way. More traditional theories of delinquency (Özbay and Özcan, 2008; Smith and Paternoster, 1987) and Hansen's research (2005), for example, indicate that young males may turn to gangs to find the mentoring they feel they are lacking at home, and in particular, to assert their masculinity, often with violent consequences, whereas females seek more familial bonds from their fellow gang members when they join. To some extent, there is also the issue that Hirschi's social bond theory runs counter to his and Gottfredson's theory of self-control, which we introduced in the last chapter. In social bond theory, crime prevention comes from controls outside of one's self; in self-control theory, the crime prevention comes from within.

It is also important to note that historically girls receive more supervision from their families, particularly in the teen years, than boys (Bastug, 2002), making their social bonding experiences different, including with parental units and friends. However, as indicated in Özbay and Özcan (2008), research in both Western and non-Western countries, even with the differences in the ways boys and girls are supervised by parents taken into account, shows that variables associated with social bonding (e.g., social class, attachment to family, community, and family) play equal roles for both sexes in juvenile offending.

DELINQUENT SIBLINGS

Again, noting that whom a juvenile habitually hangs around may present risks for delinquency, it would only be natural to expect that delinquency runs in families. Even in sister-brother pairs, there is high predictability that if an older sibling is delinquent, the younger one will follow suit (Slomkowski, 2003). As a reminder, boys as risk-takers are more likely to be delinquent than girls. Sibling delinquency is a strong indicator for future offending by other children in the household and is suggested to be a target for treatment of delinquency (Walters, 2017). Risk factors in a family that affect one child will have effects on other children in the household. This makes a good argument for treating more than the individual delinquent child: a holistic approach treats all family members for potential risk factors.

There is some discrepancy in research as to whether there is more delinquency found in larger families. Earlier research found that the overcrowded conditions of larger families result in poor role models, parental criminality, sibling delinquency, competition for physical space, and limited emotional resources (Fischer, 1984). More recent research indicates that in full-biological families (i.e., everyone is related by blood), less delinquency is found, as compared to non-full-biological households (e.g., remarriage with stepsiblings), where more delinquency is predicted, regardless of household size (Collier and Mears, 2022).

The age at which delinquency begins appears to relate to having a delinquent sibling, depending on the two siblings' sexes. Huijsmans et al. (2018) conducted a study to determine what effect a sibling's delinquent offending, as compared to the influences of parental units, schools, or peers, has on whether other children in a family eventually commit crimes. They found that a "[s]ibling's delinquency was shown to be positively related to adolescent delinquency in early adolescence only for sister and mixed-sex sibling pairs, but disappeared in later adolescences. In brother pairs, an opposite pattern was observed: sibling delinquency was not related to delinquent behavior in early adolescence, whereas it was in late adolescence."

Depending on the age and sex of siblings, in other words, the influence of a delinquent sibling will not necessarily be felt, at least in offending or potential for co-offending, in childhood, but rather in early or later adolescence. However, Huijsmans et al. (2018) also noted that little research has been done on the effects of delinquent siblings on other family members in adolescence, much less the effect on even younger siblings. Studies do indicate that siblings will influence one another's alcohol and substance abuse during adolescence, partially because they often share friends, some of whom might be delinquent (Whiteman et al., 2013).

SINGLE-PARENT HOUSEHOLDS

Increasingly since the 1970s, we have seen a dramatic rise in single-parent households, the majority of which are headed by women. Single-parent households can result from death, desertion, divorce, or out-of-wedlock births. Since the 1970s, out-of-wedlock births have been on the rise, and by 1990, 64% of Black infants and 18% of white infants were born to unwed mothers, increasing the likelihood that they will live in poverty (Akerlof and Yellen, 1996). Increasingly, the fathers of children conceived out-of-wedlock are reluctant to marry the mother: "If she is not willing to have an abortion or use contraception . . . why should I sacrifice myself to get married?" (quoted in Akerlof and Yellen, 1996). The conditions under which a single-parent household becomes a risk for delinquency are (Kroese et al., 2021):

- Separated or divorced parents
- Death of a parent
- Single family starts at a younger age
- Children grow up only with the biological mother

The consequences of and response to out-of-wedlock pregnancy differ among cultures and according to circumstances. The most stigmatizing is when a teenager who engages in unprotected sex or has contraception fail becomes pregnant. This is less stigmatizing for women in their twenties or thirties, but also less common due to the availability of contraceptives to adult women.[2]

In both cases, depending on the state or country in which the woman lives and her religious or political beliefs, terminating the pregnancy may be an option. Having a child out-of-wedlock thus becomes a choice for many females. Males face choices about whether to marry or to pay child support (Akerlof and Yellen, 1996). In recent years, pregnancy termination has become more restricted in a number of states, more so after the June 24, 2022, U.S. Supreme Court decision overturning *Roe v. Wade* (1973), which had federally protected abortion rights. A number of states had trigger laws[3] in place to prohibit or severely restrict pregnancy termination, even in cases of rape, incest, miscarriage, or risk to the mother's life or health. In addition, even if child support has been court ordered, it is not guaranteed that support will be faithfully paid, much less on time, except where states garnish the father's wages, assuming he is employed. Of course, there are those rare exceptions where females were the primary bread winners and they are ordered to pay child support, if the other parent spends substantial time in the care of their children.

[2] As of this writing, availability of contraception, including the morning-after pill, is being called into question by a number of U.S. states. Even without the 2022 *Dobbs v. Jackson* decision by the Supreme Court, some females have not had equal access to contraception, as some health insurance plans do not cover it.

[3] Trigger laws are legal placeholders in states, activated in the event that the U.S. Supreme Court makes a particular ruling or judgment affecting current state law. They are unenforceable until a new ruling changes the circumstances.

Child support may also be ordered in cases of same-sex couples who dissolve their relationship after having children.

If abortion is not an option, legally or otherwise, the only choice is to carry the baby to term and either put the child up for adoption or raise the child, with or without help from a partner or family. In these cases, the child is at greater risk for delinquency, particularly in the case of teenaged parents. As reported by Coyne et al. (2013), not only are offspring of teenage mothers at risk for delinquency, the teenage mothers themselves are more likely to be convicted of a crime in young adulthood, as compared to women who delay having children until their twenties or later.

It is becoming increasingly more accepted in American society for adults in their thirties or forties with established careers but who have not found a romantic partner (or who choose to remain unmarried) to make the conscious decision to either adopt or have a biological child alone. Not only are women choosing to raise families without a partner; males are increasingly doing the same through surrogacy or adoption. What financial means and emotional support are available to an unwed mother who decides to keep her baby, whether she is a teenager or approaching middle age, will make a difference in her ability to keep her child from becoming delinquent. No matter the age of the parents, or whether one or two parents are present, children who are raised in loving, supportive households with greater financial means are less likely to become delinquent (Kroese et al., 2021; Wright and Wright, 1993). However, the reality is that many women raising children on their own struggle financially, with an estimated 26.8% of single mothers and their children living in poverty (Creamer and Mohanty, 2018).

Divorce and Delinquency

Dysfunctional family dynamics that do not get resolved can lead to intergenerational dysfunction. Children raised in a hostile household, with parental units arguing all the time and no real evidence of affection, are likely to replicate these patterns if and when they find their own romantic partners. Of course, the extent to which this happens is predicated on how much self-awareness and resolve an individual has and their ability to avoid an unhealthy way of functioning in a family. This often takes counseling. In many families, the only way to resolve dysfunction is the divorce of parental units. However, divorce can result in its own consequences for children, even if it is the healthiest choice.

Divorce as a research topic did not gain traction until the 1970s, when more women entered the workforce and gained the economic freedom to leave unhappy marriages. Following divorce research were studies on the role divorce plays in increased risks for delinquency. The common causes of conflict in a household that lead to divorce include:

- Financial problems
- Jealous spouse
- Different parenting styles

- Differences in discipline styles with children
- Conflict with a spouse's friends or family
- Spouses growing apart, when they have married at a young age
- Spouses not perceived as carrying equal weight in household duties

During the course of a divorce or its aftermath, children can be exposed to conflict, hostility, and aggression. Divorce may result in less supervision of children or in weaker attachment to one parent or another. Children of divorced parents are also more likely to end up in poverty or experience financial difficulties. Unlike successful co-parenting, hostility, or worse yet, verbal abuse or physical violence between divorcing or divorced parents can result in maladjustment for children, including depression and risk for delinquency to get attention (Katz and Low, 2004). Substantial research exists on the immediate consequences of divorce on juvenile delinquency, particularly in adolescence, but far fewer studies examine the long-term effects (into adulthood) of divorce on offending; the effects may only be short-term and temporary (Boccio and Beaver, 2019).

Stepparents and Delinquency

We know from divorce statistics that subsequent marriages after divorce are also susceptible to separation or divorce from new spouses. Blended families are less stable, with more conflict with stepparents and/or stepsiblings. There may be feelings of rejection or jealousy, particularly if a stepchild feels neglected by their own parent or the stepparent after remarriage. Studies on stepparents show a risk that stepparents will give preferential treatment to their own biological child.

As found in a number of studies of delinquency, the effect on delinquency of having a stepparent depends on whether the stepchildren are male or female. Males with stepparents are at slightly higher risk for serious offending as compared to females; however, the strongest indicator as to whether a stepchild will become delinquent is the amount of time spent with a parent, biological or not (Tygart, 1990). The effects of an absent natural father and the presence of a stepparent on delinquency varies not only by gender, but by race, socioeconomic status, and neighborhood context (Free, 1991). Not all "broken homes" or reconstituted families with stepparents are equal with regard to the causes or contributors to delinquency, and as we noted above, the effects of changing family dynamics on the risks for juvenile offending may be short-lived (Boccio and Beaver, 2019).

DOMESTIC VIOLENCE AND DELINQUENCY

In this section, we examine the effects on children of witnessing domestic violence and its effect on the risk of delinquency. Domestic violence can include general *interpersonal violence* between parents and children or between siblings; it also includes *intimate partner violence* (IPV) between romantic partners. Unfortunately, unless a child is being abused, they rarely receive services to help with this trauma (Walters, 2018). However, children who witness domestic violence can suffer from similar levels of distress as children who are themselves abused (Walters, 2018).

Despite the lack of services available, substantial research has been done on the relationship between domestic violence and children exposed to it. The violent behavior of parental units has been well-documented to often have detrimental effects on children in the household (Steketee et al., 2021). It is important to distinguish the different ways that children process being witnesses to domestic violence. For some, they internalize the experience, resulting in a number of mental health disorders. Others will externalize their experiences, either in delinquency or by becoming abusers themselves, often carrying this behavior into adulthood. Risks for either internalizing or externalizing the experience of witnessing domestic violence multiply when the child is also the victim of abuse (Moylan et al., 2009).

CHILD MALTREATMENT

Maltreatment is one of the leading causes of delinquency, PTSD, depression, and anxiety in children. Researchers define childhood maltreatment "as any act or failure to act of the primary caretaker of the child which provides a risk of emotional or physical harm for the child" (Hoeboer et al., 2021, p. 2; see also Gilbert et al., 2009). This includes parental units who, though they themselves are not directly abusing the child, are aware that abuse is going on and do little to nothing to stop or prevent it. Some primary caretakers who do nothing to prevent abuse of their children may themselves be victims of the very same tormentors. Parents who do not report abuse can be held criminally liable for child neglect at the least. The definition of what constitutes child maltreatment, however, varies from state to state in the United States.

Child maltreatment can result in a number of psychological disorders, from mild to severe, many of which, if not all, are carried into adulthood, including anxiety and depression. Less commonly understood or studied is the relationship between child maltreatment and *social anxiety disorder* (SAD), characterized by intense fear of the judgment of others (Myers and Llera, 2020; American Psychiatric Association, 2013). If abused children gravitate toward delinquent peers, they may be afraid to *not* be delinquent themselves, for fear that they will be rejected or expelled by the group.

Definition of maltreatment can also vary greatly from culture to culture and from generation to generation. For example, in some households, including in the United States, spanking a child is still considered a perfectly acceptable form of punishment; *corporal punishment* is also still used in schools in some southern states (Gershoff and Lee, 2019). In other households, and in some jurisdictions,

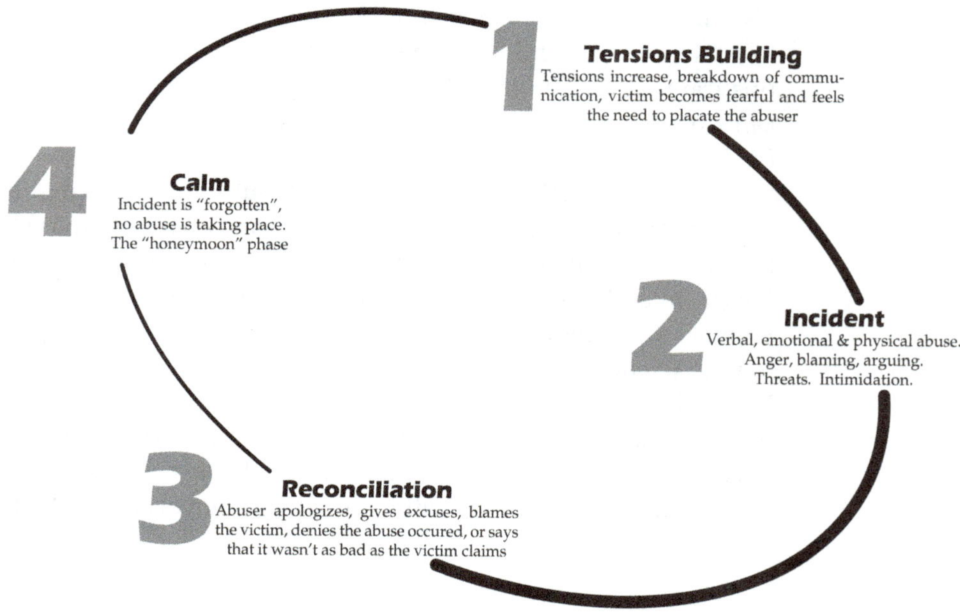

EXHIBIT 7.1 ‖ Cycle of Abuse

spanking is viewed as a form of child abuse, criminally punishable in a court of law. The World Health Organization (WHO) and the International Society for Prevention of Child Abuse and Neglect (ISPCAN) have established that physical force, including spanking, if used in disciplining children, is a form of maltreatment with potential harm to the child's health and well-being; the adage "spare the rod and spoil the child" has lost legitimacy as a parenting strategy (Steketee, 2021).

Historically in the United States, abuse of children took place in the privacy of households. It was so removed from public concern the American Society for the Prevention of Cruelty of Animals (ASPCA) was established in 1866, *before* the Society of the Prevention of Cruelty to Children in 1874. This also indicates a strong cultural belief in preserving parental rights. Even in this century, parental rights are so protected that child maltreatment often goes undetected until the emotional and physical damage is done.

Physical Abuse

Parental physical abuse takes a number of forms. Miller-Perrin and Perrin (2012, p. 19) identify the following as the most common forms of child maltreatment:

- **Legitimate:** A violent act that is culturally condoned (e.g., slapping a child's hand)
- **Legitimate/Expressive:** Violence as catharsis
- **Legitimate/Instrumental:** Physical punishment of children
- **Illegitimate:** A violent act that is culturally condemned (e.g., punching a child in the face)

- **Illegitimate/Expressive:** Most recognized and publicized
- **Illegitimate/Instrumental:** "For the child's own good," but defined by society as abuse.

Whether witnessing physical violence or being victimized themselves, children who grow up in violent households (and communities) have the potential to become violent themselves. There are a number of studies that indicate that early exposure to physical abuse before adolescence results in a greater risk for violent juvenile offending later on, with violence begetting violence (Lansford et al., 2007; Stouthamer-Loeber et al., 2001). Studies are inconclusive as to whether there are long-term effects (Lansford et al., 2007). Physical abuse in childhood, with or without sexual abuse, also results in riskier sexual behavior in both males and females during the teen years (Lansford et al., 2007).[4]

Emotional and Psychological Abuse

Child maltreatment is not limited to physical abuse, as in the example we noted in our earlier discussion of the effects of verbal violence. In fact, as it may very well be more commonplace, we place more focus on the nonphysical forms of child abuse. Emotional neglect is defined as the failure of caretakers to respond to the emotional needs of their children (Hoeboer et al., 2021). Child psychological abuse is identified as repeated patterns of behavior, including verbal, that withhold from the child the love and affection expected in a parent-child relationship or convey to the child that they are worthless, unloved, or unwanted, as well as threats of physical or psychological violence (Miller-Perrin and Perrin, 2012; Hart et al., 2002).

Physical abuse is always accompanied by emotional and psychological abuse. Scholars and practitioners have a difficult time agreeing on distinctions between emotional and psychological abuses (Origins Behavioral Healthcare, 2019; O'Hagan, 1995). In some cases, a parental unit or others will wound a child with their words or actions without ever laying a hand on them; however, there are differing opinions on what type of abuse that is. Therapists in their practices treating juvenile abuse victims have found that even though emotional and psychological abuse may not leave a physical mark on the child, it can result in anxiety, depression, addiction, and delinquency (Origins Behavioral Healthcare, 2019). Several studies have indicated that severe PTSD symptoms are more likely to come from emotional abuse and neglect than from psychological abuse, both for adults and children (Hoeboer et al., 2021).

Recently the term *gaslighting* has been increasingly used in reality television and on social media to describe supposed abuses in relationships. Authentically applied to conditions in which an individual's sense of reality is distorted by their abuser, gaslighting can also include attempts to control the victim by making

[4] We have to assume that this is true for all genders, though in the Lansford et al. study (2007), the researchers only reference the gender binary of male and female.

them feel somehow insane or incompetent (Laderer, 2021; Origins Behavioral Healthcare, 2019). In the case of domestic violence, a physical and/or emotional abuser purposely makes their victim feel the abuse is their fault. Children can be made to feel this way by their abusers and be threatened with further abuse if they report the maltreatment to anyone in the family or to authorities. Worse yet, children are also made to believe that no one, not even trusted adults, will believe that they are being abused.

The risk factors for emotional or psychological abuse in families include (Centers for Disease Control and Prevention, 2022; Miller-Perrin and Perrin, 2012):

- Intergenerational psychological abuse
- Single-parent households
- Social isolation or parent absence
- Financial stress in the family
- Parental unemployment
- Parental use of drugs or alcohol
- Low education of parents

Child Sexual Abuse

As damaging as physical or psychological abuse is for children, perhaps the worst form of child maltreatment is sexual abuse. Even in prisons, convicted child molesters are shunned by their fellow prisoners (Hansen, 2023). Children and adolescents can be sexually abused at home by parental units, close family members, or by siblings. Child sexual abuse is a multifaceted, closeted problem, and even professionals have a difficult time distinguishing between sexual or nonsexual behavior, e.g., in young siblings' mutual exploration of genitalia (Miller-Perrin and Perrin, 2012). In general terms, child sexual abuse is defined by the following conditions, regardless of whether sexual relations are consensual (Finkelhor et al., 1997):

- When there is a large age gap or maturational differences between sexual partners.
- When one of the partners is in a position of authority or in a caregiving relationship with a juvenile.
- When the act is carried out against the juvenile by using violence, threat, or trickery.

To date, we still do not have clear numbers as to the prevalence of child sexual abuse, as the subject of sex continues to be largely taboo in American culture, for all the seemingly open discussions, particularly on social media. However, it is suspected by researchers and therapists alike that child sexual abuse is more widespread worldwide than statistics reveal. We do know that such abuse is more prevalent in some family structures than others.

Strangers can also sexually exploit minors, including through human trafficking, though this is far less prevalent than the media portrays, but this chapter is concerned with abuse within families or by family friends.

Types of sexual exploitation include pornography and prostitution as well as direct sexual abuse. Juvenile females are more likely to experience sexual victimization, but boys who have been abused present a particular challenge because they are less likely to disclose the abuse. They are also more likely to be taught sexual behavior by their abuser, to be concerned that if sexual abuse is detected that their freedoms will be curtailed, and, if they have been abused by another male, to be afraid of losing their masculinity or carrying the stigma of supposed homosexuality (Finkelhor et al., 1997).

Child Maltreatment and Delinquency

We have good evidence from research that any of the forms of child abuse discussed in this section can result in mental health disorders. Children who have been physically or psychologically abused have greater rates of mental health problems in adolescence and experience stunted socioemotional development, tending to lash out verbally or violently at others (Li et al., 2021; Rizvi and Najam, 2014). As we know from Chapter 6 on individual risks for delinquency, mental health disorders in children can result in behavioral, deviant, and/or criminal behavior. Physical abuse is not alone in being a risk for delinquency. Physical punishment has likewise been shown to increase the risk for delinquency, in both boys and girls (Steketee et al., 2021; Farrington et al., 2017). Again, as we noted, there are disagreements as to what types of physical punishment constitute abuse based on cultural differences and state laws.

When children are exposed to interpersonal violence between family members or in their household and are victims of maltreatment as well, there is a greater risk for more violent juvenile offending. The effects of exposure to interpersonal violence can last well into adulthood and can result in intergenerational violent offending (Steketee et al., 2021). It is also not unusual for juveniles who have contact with the juvenile justice system due to delinquency to be involved with the child welfare system. According to Williams-Butler (2013, p. 460), "A substantial proportion of adolescents enter the juvenile justice system with a history of neglect and approximately one-third of these adolescents are still associated with an active child welfare case at the time of initial arrest."

SUMMARY

We started out the beginning of this chapter noting that most families have some form of dysfunction. Relationships in families are generally messy, and there is no such thing as the perfect family. Depending on the extent and type of dysfunction, it can result in damaging individual family members, impacting their risk for delinquency, especially when coupled with individual risks (Chapter 6) and community risks (Chapter 8). The extent to which there are long-term effects of family dysfunction that follow into adulthood, including repeating parental units' patterns of communication and parenting, depends on factors such as the degree of social support, self-awareness, and in some cases, intervention.

The ways families communicate effectively (or not) with one another can have an effect on delinquency as well. If children and adolescents learn that most disputes end in arguments, some of which are loud and can lead to domestic violence, it can ultimately result in their carrying those patterns over into their adult relationships if they do not receive counseling or some other intervention. Unfortunately, children who are exposed to emotional or physical violence, even if they are not directly victimized, often are overlooked by social services and do not receive help coping with their parental units' behavior.

The risk of delinquency is predicated, perhaps first and foremost, by parenting styles. The two extremes, too much permissiveness or too much control, can result in delinquency. Most parents fall somewhere in the middle–permissive in some things, more restrictive in others. In recent years, conceptualizations of conflicting parenting styles have emerged, including the helicopter parent who might stunt their child's ability to develop self-reliance and the free-range parent that allows their child too much autonomy and that might, in some cases, result in offending, though there is little research to indicate this to be the case. These more extreme parenting styles are not necessarily associated with more delinquency, but we do know definitively that neglect contributes to delinquency.

A number of family risks beyond verbal abuse fall under child maltreatment, including physical, emotional and psychological abuse, and, most horrifically, sexual abuse. Physical and sexual abuse are always accompanied by emotional and psychological abuse. Any and all of these put children at risk of being victimized, becoming delinquent, and developing a number of mental health disorders. All too often, children who are in the juvenile justice system are also candidates for child welfare services because of some form of abuse.

IN THE MEDIA

Intergenerational Offending — Fathers and Sons in Prison

In this chapter we have discussed some family dynamics that get passed down from generation to generation. These can be positive, as when parents pass on to children an appreciation for education or the value of hard work. However, negative patterns of communication can also be passed down, as can criminal behavior (e.g., illegal drug use), resulting in greater risk for juvenile offending. When criminal behavior is passed down from generation to generation, the *Crime Reporter* describes this as a "generational curse":

> *Since 2011, Jose Cintron Jr., has lived on the same Pennsylvania cell block as his father, who is 58. Their story is not unusual. . . . According to one*

> *criminologist's analysis of the National Longitudinal Study of Adolescent Health, 5 percent of families account for more than 50 percent of all arrests, Philly.com reports. Many studies have found that people whose parents have committed crimes are at least two times more likely to be perpetrators themselves. Sexual offending runs in families. So does violent crime.* (Criminal Justice News, 2018, retrieved from https://thecrimereport.org/2018/01/25/generational-curse-fathers-in-prison-with-their-sons/)

Children and adolescents who witness their parents' illegal *drug* use are also at greater risk for addiction and juvenile offending, beyond any genetic disposition toward addiction:

> *When Mr. Alvin was growing up [in Singapore], he watched as his father, who he says was an opium addict, fed his drug habit at home. . . . During times when his father [who was] also addicted to alcohol and gambling—did not get his fix and went through withdrawals, his family would have to face his violent outbursts. . . .*
>
> *"I [the son] started glue sniffing, I started taking sleeping pills and I proceeded to marijuana before I even collected my IC (identification card) at 12 years old."* (Abdullah, 2021, retrieved from https://www.channelnewsasia.com/international)

Unfortunately, as we will see in our last chapter on prevention programs, there is little understanding about how to prevent intergenerational offending (Flynn et al., 2017). As Farrington noted (2011) and as reflected in the statistics quoted by the *Crime Reporter*, it is really only a small number of families that account for a considerable quantity of the offenses committed, meaning that intergenerational offending should be targeted for prevention, particularly in the case of juvenile offenders. What we do know is that education is a disruptor of intergenerational poverty, social welfare dependency, and criminal offending (Anderson et al., 2021), though admittedly, as we note elsewhere in this book, this is difficult for many to achieve as college education and even vocational training programs are relatively expensive, at least in the United States.

SOURCES

Abdullah, A. Z. (2021). "IN FOCUS: Breaking the cycle of addiction passing from parent to child." Channel NewsAsia. Jan 13. Retrieved from https://www.channelnewsasia.com/singapore/in-focus-singapore-inter-generational-drug-abuse-636611.

Anderson, S. H., L. S. Richmond-Rakerd, T. E. Moffitt, and A. Caspi (2021). *Psychology and Cognitive Sciences.* Jul 26. Vol. 113, issue 31: e2103896118. Retrieved from https://www.pnas.org/doi/pdf/10.1073/pnas.2103896118.

Crime and Justice News (2018). " 'Generational curse': Fathers in prison with their sons." *The Crime Report.* Jan 25. Retrieved from https://thecrimereport.org/2018/01/25/generational-curse-fathers-in-prison-with-their-sons/.

Farrington, D. P. (2011). "Families and crime." In *Crime and Public Policy*, ed. J. Q. Wilson and J. Petersilia. London, UK: Oxford University Press.

Flynn, C., N. Van Dyke, and K. Gelb (2017). "Intergenerational offending: The case for exploring resistance." *Probation Journal.* Vol. 64, issue 2: 146–154.

INTERNATIONAL PERSPECTIVES

International Approaches to Child Protection

In the United Kingdom, the National Society for the Prevention of Cruelty (NSPCC) reports the following grim statistics, offering a snapshot of just how prevalent child abuse is in the U.K. (Action Against Abuse, n.d.):

- Approximately 50,500 children in the U.K. are at risk for abuse.
- Infants under the age of 1 are at more risk of being killed by someone other than their parents than any other single year age group.
- One in five children in the U.K. have experienced severe maltreatment.
- One in six children in the U.K. ages 11–17 have experienced sexual abuse.
- One in four young adults report that they were severely maltreated while growing up.
- One in six young adults report having been neglected at some point during their childhood.
- One child a week in the U.K. will be killed due to maltreatment.[5]

Attitudes on childrearing, definitions of delinquency, and the need for child protective services, is not consistent throughout the world. According to the Ministry of External Affairs, India (n.d.), child protection laws worldwide are intended, in theory, to protect children from violence, exploitation, abuse, and neglect (Price-Robertson et al., 2014). However, child protection laws differ around the world, based on societal norms, religion, development levels, and legal systems (Ministry of External Affairs, Government of India, n.d.), in spite of the call for a legal ban internationally of all forms of corporal punishment on children by the United Nations (United Nations, n.d.).

Many Muslim countries are ruled legally and religiously by Islamic laws. Unlike the United States, where the criminal justice system is secular, any crime that takes place in an Islamic country is viewed as not only an offense against the state, but as a crime against religious doctrine. When it comes to laws protecting children, there are some key discrepancies in and between Muslim countries. Though the Quran, the written religious authority for Islamic belief, provides clear guidance on the protection of children, local customs and geopolitical dynamics can be contradictory in the application of child protective laws (Hutchinson, et al., 2014).

Inconsistencies with what constitutes child maltreatment versus punishment are not exclusive to Muslim communities. The same can be true for any religion or religious group that inconsistently interprets its scriptures. A number of studies

[5] Comparatively speaking, in the United States, a report of child abuse happens every ten seconds and more than five children a day die from child maltreatment, with 80% of those under the age of four (Action Against Abuse, n.d.).

indicate that parental units who practice more conservative Protestant religions are more likely to use corporal punishment in disciplining their children (Wolf and Kepple, 2019; Fréchette et al., 2015). What Benjamin Shmueli refers to as "conservative-traditional" Judaism allows corporal punishment of children under Jewish law, with the caveat that it should not result in physical injury or violate the rights of the child (Shmueli, 2010; 2014).

The United Nations (n.d.) provides these examples of international legislation aimed at stopping violence against children:

- **Austria:** Every child has the right to protection and care, with consideration of their own interest, according to the Federal Constitutional Act on the Rights of Children, 2011.
- **Ireland:** The Child First Act (2015) explicitly defines harm to children as assault, ill-treatment, and sexual abuse and calls for prohibition of corporal punishment.
- **Kenya:** Kenya's new constitution (2010) includes children's right to be protected from abuses and/or neglect.
- **Mongolia:** The Law on the Rights of the Child of 2016 prohibits corporal punishment and any other form of violence, physical abuse, or psychological abuse taking place in social (e.g., public) settings.
- **Peru:** The Code of Children and Adolescents prohibits torture, cruel or degrading treatment, forced labor, prostitution, trafficking, or the sale of children.
- **Sweden:** The Swedish Penal Code includes an extensive list of prohibitions, including the ban on physical punishment and humiliating treatment of children.

In examining risks for delinquency, we see that the United States is not alone in considering child maltreatment a prime cause of juvenile offending. As we cautioned earlier in this book, international statistics on rates of delinquency are difficult to obtain, and that is the case as well for information on the correlation internationally between child maltreatment and delinquency.

SOURCES

Action Against Abuse (n.d.). Global child abuse statistics. https://actionagainstabuse.wordpress.com/child-abuse-need-to-know/global-child-abuse-statistics/.

Hutchinson, A. J., P. O'Leary, J. Squire, and K. Hope (2014). "Child protection in Islamic Contexts: Identifying appropriate mechanisms and processes using a roundtable methodology." *Child Abuse Review*. Vol. 24, issue 6: 395–408.

Ministry of External Affairs (n.d.), India. "Child protection laws in different countries." Consular, Passport, and Visa Division, Government of India. Retrieved from https://www.mea.gov.in/child-protection-laws-in-different-ccountries.htm.

Price-Robertson, R., L. Bromfield, and A. Lamont (2014). "International approaches to child protection: What can Australia learn?" *Child Family Community Australia*. CFCA Paper No. 23. Australian Institute of Family Studies, Australian Government. Jul. Retrieved from https://aifs.gov.au/cfca/sites/default/files/publication-documents/cfca-paper23.pdf.

Shmeuli, B. (2014). "Corporal punishment of children in Jewish Law." *Jewish Law Annual*. Vol. 18: 137–212.

United Nations (UN) (n.d.). "Legal ban on violence against children." UN Special Representative of the Secretary-General on Violence Against Children. Retrieved from https://violenceagainstchildren.un.org/content/legal-ban-violence-against-children.

Wolf, J. P., and N. J. Kepple (2019). "Individual and county-level religious participation, corporal punishment and physical abuse of children: An exploratory study." *Journal of Interpersonal Violence*. Vol. 34, issue 19: 3983–3994.

CHAPTER DISCUSSION QUESTIONS

1. How might a family that engages in verbal violence find better ways of communicating with children in the household?
2. Even if children are well cared for, why might marital conflict still contribute to delinquency?
3. What challenges might families face today in preventing juvenile delinquency?
4. Which of the following scenarios constitutes child maltreatment? If so, why?
   a. A parental unit sends a child to their room for the rest of the day for misbehaving.
   b. A parental unit tells their child that they are lazy when they don't want to help out with a chore.
   c. A parental unit requires their teenage child to be home by 10 p.m., even if all their friends are able to stay out later.
   d. A parental unit withholds lunch money when they find out their child is spending it on candy at a local store after school.
   e. A parental unit is not often physically affectionate (e.g., hugs) because that's the way they were brought up.
5. Why are children in a household where there is interpersonal violence between adults still at risk for deviance or delinquency, even if the children are left untouched?
6. We know that accurate international crime statistics are difficult to obtain. Why is there even less transparency in many countries on the rates of delinquency and child maltreatment?

GLOSSARY

Attachment theory Focuses on the development of long-term relationships, including with parental units, friends, and romantic partners, that is based in trust that these will be safe and secure relationships.

Corporal punishment Any physical punishment, including spanking.

Emotional security theory Developmental theory that proposes that the quality of relationships in a family will be either supported or undermined by how children are treated by parents and other household members.

Extended family Family members outside of the nuclear family, including grandparents, aunts, uncles, cousins, etc.

Family (legal definition) Individuals who are related by blood, legal adoption, or marriage.

Family cohesion The extent to which a family functions together in all aspects of family life, including communication, values, roles, and expectations, plus how emotionally bonded they are to one another.

Family stability The extent to which there is consistency in structure, activities, and routines in a family.

Free-range parenting Philosophy and style of parenting that allows children and adolescents more freedom, including in their movement and physical space. Example: Allowing children to play at a park close to home without adult supervision. See *Spatial autonomy*.

Gaslighting Form of psychological abuse where the victim is lead to believe by their abuser that they are at fault for any abuse or mistreatment, and in some cases made to believe that they are mentally unstable.

Helicoptering Parenting style where parental units impulsively and consistently monitor their children's every move, chaperoning them and closely supervising all homework assignments and school activities.

Interaction ritual chains Randall Collin's theory that constant negative interaction with others will result in emotional exhaustion. Conversely, positive interaction enforces positive relationships.

Interactional theory Similarly to Sutherland's differential association, proposes the theory that from early childhood, exposure to delinquent peers can result in delinquent behavior, with parental units and home life playing an important role in preventing delinquency.

Interpersonal violence Abuse, aggression, and/or violence that occurs between two or more people, often where there is a close relationship, as in the example of *intimate partner violence* (IPV). See *Intimate partner violence (IPV)*.

Intimate partner violence (IPV) Abuse, aggression, and/or violence between romantic partners. See *Interpersonal violence*.

Nuclear family Immediate family, typically including two adults and children.[6]

Pseudo family Individuals who are not related by blood, legal adoption, or marriage that form a cohesive unit performing all the functions of a nuclear family, including cohabitating and sharing expenses.

[6] We are avoiding using the heteronormative family structures of a father and mother, husband and wife, in this definition, to be more inclusive of less traditional families.

Social anxiety disorder (SAD) A common anxiety disorder where individuals experience fear in or when anticipating social interaction with others, and may continue do anything they can to avoid social situations (avoidance behavior), if not treated.

Social bond (and control) theory Travis Hirschi's 1969 theory proposing that humans are naturally prone to delinquency and that social bonds, including those to family, community, school, etc., plus acceptance of societal norms, values, and culture, prevent people from committing crimes.

Spatial autonomy Where individuals, including children, can exercise freedom in where they go and with whom they interact.

Verbal violence Any form of verbal abuse, including insults, name-calling, and yelling, that can result in psychological and emotional or mental health issues, particularly if there is consistent, ongoing abuse.

REFERENCES AND ADDITIONAL SUGGESTED READINGS

Akerlof, G. A., and J. L. Yellen (1996). Report: An analysis of out-of-wedlock births in the United States. The Brookings Institute. Aug 1. Retrieved from https://www.brookings.edu/research/an-analysis-of-out-of-wedlock-births-in-the-united-states/.

The American Century (n.d.). Television: The ideal American family. Retrieved from https://americancentury.omeka.wlu.edu/exhibits/show/reinforcement-of-gender-roles-/television--the-ideal-american.

American Psychiatric Association (2013). *Diagnostic and Statistical Manual of Mental Disorders, 5th ed.* Arlington, VA: American Psychiatric Publishing.

Barr, S. C., R. Hanson, A. M. Begle, D. G. Kilpatrick, B. Saunders, H. Resnick, and A. Amstadter (2012). "Examining the moderating role of family cohesion on the relationship between witnessed community violence and delinquency in a national sample of adolescents." *Journal of Interpersonal Violence*. Vol. 27, issue 2 (Jan.): 239–262.

Bastug, S. (2002). "Household and family in contemporary Turkey: An historical perspective." In *Autonomy and Dependence in the Family: Turkey and Sweden in Critical Perspective*, ed. R. Lijestrom and E. Ozdalga. London, UK: Swedish Research Institute in Istanbul.

Boccio, C. M., and K. M. Beaver (2019). "The influence of family structure on delinquent behavior." *Youth Violence and Juvenile Justice*. Vol. 17, issue 1: 88–106.

Bowlby, J. (1969). "Attachment and loss." In *Attachment*, vol 1. New York: Basic Books.

Brooks, K. (2018). *Small Animals: Parenthood in the Age of Fear*. New York: Flatiron Books.

Centers for Disease Control and Prevention (CDC) (2022). Violence prevention: Risk and protective factors. Apr 6. Retrieved from https://www.cdc.gov/violenceprevention/childabuseandneglect/riskprotectivefactors.html.

Cheng, T. (2004). "Impact of family stability on children's delinquency: An implication for family preservation." *Journal of Family Social Work*. Vol. 8, issue 1: 47–60.

Cherry, K. (2019). "What is attachment?: The importance of early emotional bonds." *Very Well Mind*. Jul 17. Retrieved from https://www.verywellmind.com/what-is-attachment-theory-2795337.

Clark, R. D., and G. Shields (1996). "Family and delinquency: The interaction between cohesion and adaptability." *Journal of Crime and Justice*. Vol. 19, Iss. 2: 67–82.

Collier, N. L., and D. P. Mears (2022). "Delinquent by the dozen: Youth from larger families engage in more delinquency—Fact or myth?" *Crime and Delinquency*. Apr 25. Sage Journals. https://doi.org/10.1177/00111287221088036.

Collins, R. (2005). *Interaction Ritual Chains*. Princeton Studies in Cultural Sociology. Princeton, NJ: Princeton University Press.

Coltrain, N. (2022). "A kid playing alone doesn't mean they're neglected, new Colorado law states." *News-Tribune*. Mar 31. Retrieved from https://www.brushnewstribune.com/2022/03/31/colorado-reasonable-independence-for-children-neglect/.

Coyne, C. A., N. M. G. Fontaine, N. Långström, P. Lichtenstein, and B. M. D'Onofrio (2013). "Teenage childbirth and young adult criminal convictions: A quasi-experimental study of criminal outcomes for teenage mothers." *Journal of Criminal Justice*. Vol. 41, issue 5 (Sep.-Oct.): 318–323.

Creamer, J., and A. Mohanty (2018). U.S. poverty rate drops to 11.8% in 2018. United States Census Bureau. Sept 10. Retrieved from https://www.census.gov/library/stories/2019/09/poverty-rate-for-people-in-female-householder-families-lowest-on-record.html.

Cummings, E. M., and P. T. Davies (2010). *Marital Conflict and Children: An Emotional Security Perspective*. New York, NY: Guilford Press.

Edwards, J. (2019). Helicopter parenting: Control vs. support makes all the difference. *News*. University Communications, Brigham Young University. Jun 17. Retrieved from https://news.byu.edu/news/helicopter-parenting-control-vs-support-makes-all-difference#:~:text=Further%2C%20the%20researchers%20found%20that,delinquent%20behavior%20and%2For%20depression.

Farrington, D. P., H. Gaffney, and M. M. Ttofi (2017). "Systematic reviews of explanatory risk factors for violence, offending, and delinquency." *Aggression and Violent Behavior*. Vol. 33: 24–36.

Finkelhor, D., S. L. Hamby, D. Moore, and M. A. Straus (1997). "Sexually abused children in a national survey of parents: Methodological issues." *Child Abuse and Neglect*. Vol. 21, issue 1: 1–9.

Fischer, D. G. (1984). "Family size and delinquency." *Perceptual and Motor Skills*. Vol. 58, issue 2: 527–534.

Fréchette, S., M. Zoratti, and E. Romano (2015). "What is the link between corporal punishment and child physical abuse?" *Journal of Family Violence*. Vol. 30, issue 2: 135–148.

Free, M. D. (1991). "Clarifying the relationship between the broken home and juvenile delinquency: A critique of the current literature." *Deviant Behavior*. Vol. 12, issue 2: 109–167.

Gershoff, E. T., and S. J. Lee, eds. (2019). *Ending the Physical Punishment of Children: A Guide for Clinicians and Practitioners*. Washington, D.C.: American Psychological Press.

Gilbert, R., A. Kemp, J. Thoburn, P. Sidebotham, L. Radford, D. Glaser, and H. L. MacMillan (2009). "Recognising and responding to child maltreatment." *The Lancet*. Jan 10, Vol. 373: 167–180.

Graff, N. (2019). Key findings on marriage and cohabitation in the U.S. Pew Research Center. Nov. 6. Retrieved from https://www.pewresearch.org/fact-tank/2019/11/06/key-findings-on-marriage-and-cohabitation-in-the-u-s/.

Hansen, L. L. (2005). "Girl 'crew' members doing gender, boy 'crew' members doing violence: An ethnographic and network analysis of Maria Hinojosa's New York gangs." *Western Criminology Review*. Vol. 6, issue 1: 134–44.

Hansen, L. P. (2023). *Introduction to Penology and Corrections*. Springfield, MO: Aspen Publishing.

Hao, L. X., and G. H. Xie (2002). "The complexity and endogeneity of family structure in explaining children's misbehavior." *Social Science Research*. Vol. 31, issue 1: 1–28.

Hart, S. N., M. R. Brassard, N. J. Binggeli, and H. A. Davidson (2002). "Psychological maltreatment." In *The APSAC Handbook on Child Maltreatment*, ed. J. E. B. Myers, L. Berliner, J. Briere, C. T. Hendrix, C. Jenny, and T. A. Reid. Thousand Oaks, CA: Sage Publications, Inc.

Hirschi, T. (1969). *Causes of Delinquency*. Berkeley, CA: University of California Press.

Hoeboer, C., C. de Roosm, G. E. van Son, P. Spinhoven, and B. Elzinga (2021). "The effect of parental abuse on the severity of PTSD in children and adolescents." *Child Abuse and Neglect*. Vol. 111: e104775.

Hoeve, M., J. S. Dubas, V. I. Eichelsheim, P. H. van der Laan, W. Smeenk, and J. R. M. Gerris (2009). "The relationship between parenting and delinquency: A meta-analysis." *Journal of Abnormal Child Psychology*. Vol. 37, issue 6 (Aug.): 749–775.

Huijsmans, T., V. I. Eichelsheim, F. Weerman, S. J. T. Branje, and W. Meeus (2018). "The role of siblings in adolescent delinquency next to parents, school and peers: Do gender and age matter?" Vol. 5: 220–242. Retrieved from https://link.springer.com/article/10.1007/s40865-018-0094-9.

Katz, L. F., and S. M. Low (2004). "Marital violence, co-parenting, and family-level processes to children's adjustment." *Journal of Family Psychology*. Vol. 18, issue 2 (June): 372–382.

Kroese, J., W. Bernasco, A. C. Liefbroer, and J. Rouwendal (2021). "Single-parent families and adolescent crime: Unpacking the role of parental separation, parental decease, and being born to a single-parent family." *Journal of Developmental and Life-course Criminology*. Vol. 7: 596–622.

Laderer, A. (2021). "How to spot gaslighting: 6 things gaslighters say to manipulate you." *Insider*. Jul 23. Retrieved from https://www.insider.com/gaslighting-examples.

Lansford, J. E., S. Miller-Johnson, L. J. Berlin, K. A. Dodge, J. E. Bates, and G. S. Pettit (2007). "Physical abuse and later violent delinquency: A prospective longitudinal study." *Child Maltreatment*. Vol. 12, issue 3: 233–245.

Li, Q., F. Wang, and J. Ye (2021). "Impact of psychological abuse on children and social skill development." *Aggression and Violent Behavior*. Sep 25: e101667.

Little, S., and A. Rice (2021). "Considering autonomous exploration in healthy environments: Reflections from an urban wildscape." *International Journal of Environmental Research and Public Health*. Vol. 18: e11867.

Loeber, R., and T. Dishion (1983). "Early predictors of male delinquency." *Psychological Bulletin*. Vol. 94, issue 1: 68–99.

Mak, A. S. (1994). "Parental neglect and overprotection as risks in delinquency." *Australian Journal of Psychology*. Vol. 46, issue 2: 107–111.

Matherne, M. M., and A. Thomas (2001). "Family environment as a predictor of adolescent delinquency." *Adolescence*. Vol. 36, issue 144 (Winter): 655–664.

Miller-Perrin, C. L., and R. D. Perrin (2012). *Child Maltreatment: An Introduction*. Los Angeles, CA: SAGE Publications, Inc.

Morin, A. (2021). "The free-range style of parenting." *Very Well Family*. Sep 26. Retrieved from https://www.verywellfamily.com/what-is-free-range-parenting-1095057.

Moylan, C. A., T. I. Herrenkohl, C. Sousa, E. A. Tajima, R. C. Herrenkohl, and M. J. Russo (2009). "The effects of child abuse and exposure to domestic violence on adolescent internalizing and externalizing behavior problems." *Journal of Family Violence*. Vol. 25: 53–63.

Myers, N. S., and S. J. Llera (2020). "The role of child maltreatment in the relationship between social anxiety and dissociation: A novel link." *Journal of Trauma and Dissociation*. Vol. 21, issue 3: 319–336.

O'Hagan, K. P. (1995). "Emotional and psychological abuse: Problems with definition." *Child Abuse and Neglect*. Vol. 19, issue 4 (April): 449–461.

Olson, D. H., C. S. Russell, and D. H. Sprenkle (1982). "The circumplex model of marital and family systems, VI: Theoretical update." *Family Process*. Vol. 22: 69–83.

Origins Behavioral Healthcare (2019). "Is there a difference between emotional abuse and psychological abuse?" Feb. 20. Retrieved from https://www.originsrecovery.com/is-there-a-difference-between-emotional-abuse-and-psychological-abuse/.

Özbay, Ö., and Y. Z. Özcan (2008). "A test of Hirschi's Social Bonding Theory." *International Journal of Offender Therapy and Comparative Criminology.* Vol. 52, issue 2: 134–157.

Pimental, D. (2012). "Criminal child neglect and the 'free range kid': Is overprotective parenting the new standard?" *Utah Law Review*. Vol. 947, issue 2: 947–999.

Rizvi, S. F. I., and N. Najam (2014). "Parental psychological abuse toward children and mental health problems in adolescence." *Pakistan Journal of Medicine*. Vol. 30, issue 2 (Mar.-Apr.): 256–260.

Rivera, F. I., P. J. Guarnaccia, N. Mulvaney-Day, J. Y. Lin, M. Torres, and M. Alegria (2008). "Family cohesion and its relationship to psychological distress among Latino groups." *Hispanic Journal of Behavioral Science*. Vol. 30, issue 3: 357–378.

Silva, C. S., and M. M. Calheiros (2018). "Stop yelling: Interparental conflict and adolescents' self-representations as mediated by their perceived relationships with parents." *Journal of Family Issues*. Vol. 39, issue 7: 2174–2204.

Shmueli, B. (2010; 2014). "Corporal punishment of children in Jewish law." *Jewish Law Annual*. Vol. 18: 137–212.

Slomkowski, C., R. Rende, K. J. Conger, R. L. Simons, and R. D. Conger (2003). "Sisters, brothers, and delinquency; Evaluating social influence in early and middle adolescence." *Child Development*. Vol. 72, issue 1: 271–293.

Smith, A. D., and R. Paternoster (1987). "The gender gap in theories of deviance: Issues and evidence." *Journal of Research in Crime and Delinquency*. Vol. 24: 140–172.

Steketee, M., C. Aussems, and I. H. Marshall (2021). "Exploring the impact of child maltreatment and interparental violence on violent delinquency in an international sample." *Journal of Interpersonal Violence*. Vol. 36: 13–14.

Stouthamer-Loeber, M, R. Loeber, D. L. Homish and E. Wei (2001). "Maltreatment of boys and development of disruptive and delinquent behavior." *Development and Psychopathology.* Vol. 13: 941–955.

Sumner, J., D. Boisvert, and J. P. Andersen (2016). "The effects of stress and social support on externalizing behaviors among children in military families." *Deviant Behavior*. Vol. 37, issue 3: 246–262.

Thornberry, T. P. (1987). "Toward an interaction theory of delinquency." *Criminology.* Vol. 25, issue 4: 863–892.

Thornberry, T. P., A. J. Lizotte, M. D. Krohn, C. A. Smith, and P. K. Porter (2003). "Causes and consequences of delinquency." In *Taking Stock of Delinquency: An Overview of Findings from Contemporary Longitudinal Studies*, ed. T. P. Thornberry and M. D. Krohn. New York: Springer Publishing.

Tygart, C. E. (1990). "Self-reported delinquency and natural parents-stepparent youth relations." *Journal of Divorce and Remarriage*. Vol. 13, issue 4: 89–99.

Vitaro, F., M. Brendgen, and R. E. Tremblay (2000). "Influence of deviant friends on delinquency: Searching for moderator variables." *Journal of Abnormal Child Psychology.* Vol. 28, issue 4 (Aug.): 313–325.

Wahyuni, H., Y. Riyanto, and I. K. Atmadja (2019). "The impacts of verbal violence by family members on children's social emotional aspects." *Advances in Social Science, Education and Humanities Research*. Vol. 387: 210–214.

Walters, A. C. (2018). "The forgotten children: Victims of domestic violence, victims of the system." *Albany Government Law Review*. Vol 12: 286.

Walters, G. D. (2017). "Sibling delinquency as a risk factor for future offending: An exploratory analysis." *Youth Violence and Juvenile Justice.* Vol. 16, issue 4: 343–357.

Whiteman, S. D., A. C. Jensen, and J. L. Maggs (2013). "Similarities in adolescent siblings' substance use: Testing pathways of influence." *Journal of Studies on Alcohol and Drugs.* Vol. 74, issue 1 (Jan.): 104–113.

Williams-Butler, A. (2013). "Adolescent neglect, juvenile delinquency and the risk of recidivism." *Journal of Youth and Adolescence.* Vol. 42: 454–465.

Wright, K. N., and K. E. Wright (1993). *Family Life and Delinquency: A Policymakers' Guide to the Literature.* Office of Juvenile Justice and Delinquency Prevention and National Institute of Justice. Washington, DC: U.S. Department of Justice.

Chapter **EIGHT**

Environmental and Community Risks for Deviance and Delinquency

> *I was a medium-level juvenile delinquent from Newark who always dreamed about doing a movie.*
>
> —Shaquille O'Neal, four-time NBA champion, media personality, actor, producer

Chapter Objectives

- Examine the risk factors for delinquency that are beyond the control of the individual, including neighborhoods.
- Identify the risks for delinquency through association with delinquent peer groups.
- Review community risks, including social inequality, disorganization, and prevalence of firearms and drugs.

Key Terms

Anomie
Differential association
Differential opportunity theory
Informal housing
Relative poverty
Section 8 housing
Slumlord
Social disorganization theory
Strain theory

INTRODUCTION

Many factors other than family are beyond the control of the individual juvenile. This chapter examines factors in the environment that can contribute to delinquency, including social inequalities, peer groups, and neighborhood structures.

Because teenagers were seen as impulsive, irresponsible, and "not as responsible for their actions as adults" (Greenberg, 2011, p. 212) in the early 20th century, leniency was extended to juvenile offenders, even if they were part of a larger delinquent subgroup, with the exception of juveniles of color. Depressions in 1893 and 1929 led to efforts to save jobs for adults by discrediting the capabilities of juveniles (Greenberg, 2011). Mid-20th century research on delinquent subgroups primarily focused on delinquency in the 1950s, when a distinct teenage subculture, separate from adults, emerged. As teenagers age, the consequences for delinquency, particularly if they co-offend with others, become greater, and leniency gives way to expectations that they simply need to grow up and behave more like adults.

Multiple factors contribute to the risk for delinquency, and the impact of broad factors such as environmental ones vary from individual to individual (Shader, 2003). An interesting question is why some children become delinquent and others do not when faced with the same risk factors in the community. Though we will be exploring preventative measures in our last chapter, much of the success at keeping children out of trouble comes from efforts in individual households and schools. In communities with higher risk for delinquency, including poorer neighborhoods, it can be an endless battle to keep juveniles from being attracted to criminal activities.

SOCIAL INEQUALITIES

There are a number of theories that help explain why social inequality leads to crime. The two main views come from functionalist theory and conflict theory. Social psychological and social interaction theories can also help explain social inequality.

Social inequality can result in social class differences in the ability of parental units to supervise their children:

> *Pre-adolescent and early adolescent middle and upper class children are supervised more closely than their working class counterparts and thus come to expect and accept adult authority, while working class youths, who enter unsupervised street life among peers at an early age, have more autonomy to protect, and guard their prerogatives jealously.* (Greenberg, 2011, p. 212)

Greenberg (2011) was making his observations during a period when women were increasingly entering the job market (though women in the working classes have historically participated in the labor force), and we should acknowledge that there was a rise in the number of so-called "latchkey kids"[1] beginning in the late

[1] The term *latchkey kids* was used for the growing number of children from the late 1960s on who, because their mothers worked, were left alone either before or after school, or sometimes both.

1960s. However, with the growing number of women in the workplace, particularly from middle-class households, there was also a subsequent growth in childcare centers for those who could afford them. With self-care beginning, on average, at around eight years old, latchkey kids, no matter the social class, if left home alone after school, are at greater risk for loneliness, stress, obesity, delinquency, and exposure to dangerous situations (Rajalakshmi and Thanasekaran, 2015). When they can do so, parents who both work try to stagger their work schedules to make sure their children are not left alone at home, or at least only for the briefest of periods. However, single parent households and those with no flexibility in their jobs do not have that luxury.

A contemporary functionalist theory or perspective came more recently primarily out of Talcott Parson's body of work in sociology, in the mid-20th century. We should note that functionalist theories, at least outside of studies of deviance, have fallen out of favor and have faced considerable criticism in the past several decades. From a functionalist perspective within criminology, crime delineates what is socially acceptable and what is not.

Emile Durkheim, a key founding father of functionalism and sociology, proposed that acts of deviance and crime demonstrate to the rest of society what bad behavior looks like, confirming moral boundaries (Moynihan, 1998; Durkheim, 1895). We can see this in the type of laws that are passed, as well as in the socialization of children. Parental units often use misadventures of one or more of their children as examples to the rest of the children in the household of what is offensive, including using punishment as a deterrent against further bad behavior.

Conflict theories take a decidedly different view as to why crime and delinquency occur. The basis of conflict is in social-economic stratification, where those who have money and power dictate what should be considered deviance or crime and propose, often through legislation, what behaviors are punishable within the criminal justice system. An often cited example is the 1986 Anti-Drug Act, which made possession and use of crack cocaine a more serious offense than powder cocaine use. The penalty disparity for crack cocaine was one hundred times as stringent compared to convictions for powder cocaine use. In other words, someone who is caught carrying one gram of crack cocaine could be subject to up to five years in prison; the sentence for someone caught with one hundred grams of powder cocaine was no harsher despite the larger amount (Vagins and McCurdy, 2006).

Before the Anti-Drug Act (H.R. 5484) passed, Blacks received sentences that were 11% higher than for whites in similar drug convictions; by 2010, that disparity rose to 49% (Vagins and McCurdy, 2006). As crack cocaine is much cheaper to purchase than powder cocaine, poor people and people of color have been disproportionately prosecuted since the passing of the act, and the focus has shifted from rehabilitation for drug use and abuse to punishment, both for adults and juveniles.

Poverty

Poverty continues to be one of the strongest predictors of crime. Poverty may not mean that people resort to stealing and burglary to illegally obtain luxury goods. Poverty may mean resorting to robbery or shoplifting to survive. For example, in 2019, a woman was caught trying to steal baby formula from a Target store in Springfield Township, Pennsylvania (CBS3 Staff, 2019). Baby formula is used as a cutting agent in the manufacturing of illegal drugs, like methamphetamine, but the woman had an infant and toddler with her at the time of the incident (CBS3 Staff, 2019), so the baby formula could have been intended for them. Law enforcement, however, alleged that the formula would be sold on the black market (CBS3 Staff, 2019). When any food product is shoplifted, it is possible that it may have been stolen out of desperation. Nearly one in five children (17%) live in poverty in the United States—approximately 12.5 million—and they must be housed, clothed, and fed, a good explanation for why basic necessities, not luxury items, are commonly stolen (Parolin et al., 2022).

There is a distinct difference between real poverty and *relative poverty* in the context of delinquency. Juveniles may not know where their next meal is coming from, if their parents will have a job tomorrow, or if there will be a roof over their heads. That is real poverty. Relative poverty means feeling that you have less money, fewer possessions, or a less impressive job than others. In other words, one may be living a very comfortable lifestyle, but can feel "poor" in relation to those who live in the same neighborhood or community.

For example, many people have the misconception that everyone in Beverly Hills, California, is extremely wealthy, but some in Beverly Hills may be living

TABLE 8.1 Monthly Child Poverty Rates by Children's Race and Ethnicity

	SPM CHILD POVERTY RATE (%)			
Children	December 2021	January 2022	Percentage Pt. Change	Percent Change
All	12.1%	17.0%	4.9 p.p.	41.1%
White	7.5%	11.4%	3.9 p.p.	52.3%
Black	19.5%	25.4%	5.9 p.p.	30.4%
Latino	16.8%	23.9%	7.1 p.p.	42.5%
Asian	11.9%	15.1%	3.2 p.p	26.9%

	NUMBER IN POVERTY		
Children	December 2021	January 2022	Increase
All	8,912,000	12,574,000	3,662,000
White	2,750,000	4,189,000	1,438,000
Black	2,175,000	2,837,000	662,000
Latino	3,165,000	4,509,000	1,344,000
Asian	519,000	659,000	140,000

Parolin, Collyer, and Curran (2022), Center on Poverty and Social Policy at Columbia University, Monthly SPM Poverty for January 2022. **Numbers rounded to thenearest thousand.*

in real or imagined poverty, in comparison with other residents. The reality is that some wealthy people live in massive, custom-built homes and others live in ordinary subdivisions adjacent to Beverly Hills. Although these homes are substantial, they are not custom-built. They are indistinguishable from homes built in many other less affluent cities. Beverly Hills even has low-income housing for those who qualify (Low Income Housing, n.d.).

It is likewise a misconception that children growing up in less advantaged households will feel their deprivation equally. For example, one of two siblings growing up in poverty might pursue a career that provides a lucrative income but is always looking over their shoulder, fearful that poverty is still lurking just around the corner, no matter how much money they make or how many possessions they accumulate. The other sibling may have learned to be productively resourceful, even in the face of poverty, choosing a career path where income is not as important (e.g., social work or teaching), as they may believe that no matter what, they will survive. People, including juveniles, live in their own realities and can have completely different perspectives and responses to poverty, even though they may face the same challenges.

One theory that helps explain why juveniles living in real or imagined poverty may feel the need to commit crimes to obtain the things that they desire is that the legitimate means to do so may not be available to some, if not many, people. Juveniles cannot readily get legitimate jobs to help out their families unless they are old enough and have parental permission. Robert K. Merton proposed *strain theory* (1938) to explain patterns of deviance, including crime. The strain is in not being able to achieve the goals society expects of us by normative or legal means. Merton identified five ways in which to reconcile societal goals and available means for achieving them: conformist, ritualist, retreatist, innovator, and rebel. The characteristics of each are summarized in Table 8.2.

In 1985, Robert Agnew presented a revision of Merton's strain theory focused specifically on delinquency. His criticism of Merton's original theory was that it overemphasized monetary and material success (Agnew, 2012). In his revised theory, Agnew also introduced the argument that the origin of the strain was not merely in the inability to achieve societally approved goals, but in the inability to escape from painful or aversive conditions, including some of the consequences of living in poverty (Agnew, 2012; Agnew, 1985). Agnew's study of delinquent boys (1985) found that they were more likely to commit crimes if they were exposed to unfair treatment or criticism by parents and teachers, rather than simply being bored (Agnew, 2012).

We should note that Agnew's views and examples of strain theory may be better suited for individual explanations of deviance. We can acknowledge that in some cases, the source of strain may rest within the individual. However, as strain theories apply to poverty, it can be an epidemic in poorer neighborhoods where the expected societal goals are difficult to achieve, such as finding money to pay for a college education or a job that pays well enough to escape poverty.

TABLE 8.2 Merton's Strain Theory Summary (1938)

Do You Agree with Societal Goals?	Do You Agree With and Have the Means to Achieve Those Goals?	Typology	Response	Juvenile Example
Yes	Yes	Conformist	"If I work really hard, I will get ahead" (e.g., promotion, degree, first home, etc.)	A+ Student
Yes	No	Innovator	"I want what everyone else has, and I don't care how I get it."	Shoplifter
No	Yes	Ritualist	"I really don't care about promotion, but I do have to pay my bills."	Fast food worker
No	No	Retreatist	"I'm going to quit school, stay home, and get wasted."	Drop out
Challenges these	Challenges these	Rebel	"Why am I doing this and is there a better way?"	Gang member

Sources: Merton, 1938; St. Cloud University Informedia Services, 2017, retrieved fromhttps://blog.stcloudstate.edu/ims/2017/02/01/merton-strain-theory/; ShortcutsTV, 2017, retrieved from https://www.youtube.com/watch?v=7HpnxUep2ZU.

Companion explanations of delinquency include *anomie* and *differential opportunity theory.* The anomie theory of delinquency (Merton, 1967) proposes that crimes are committed when juveniles cannot get what they want or cannot achieve their goals by conventional means. More specifically, the ability to achieve these goals is not equally available to everyone. Differential opportunity theory (Cloward and Ohlin, 1960) suggests that the American Dream[2] is a myth and that not everyone finds that hard work results in getting a job that pays well.

[2] The American Dream suggests that if you work hard enough, you can achieve anything. The reality is that no amount of hard work can substitute for advantages found at birth and/or through social networks that provide more opportunities for some and few opportunities for anyone other than the truly exceptional.

For example, of all the talented high school and college athletes, only a very small percentage will end up with a lucrative contract from one of the major teams. According to Hawke (n.d.) and NCAA Research (2020), the chances of becoming a professional athlete are not in *anyone's* favor: only 1% of the top 1% of the best players will succeed. Even if they do have the good fortune of playing professionally for a major team, their careers can be short-lived due to injury or poor performance in the early years of playing.

The chances of playing for an NCAA college team are also slim, no matter how talented a high school athlete may be. In football alone, there are an estimated 1 million high school players, with only 6.5% of them continuing on in college; 1.2% of college football players will be drafted into the NFL (Hawke, n.d.; NCAA Research, 2020). Even fewer of those will continue on to have a successful career in the NFL.

The same odds face aspiring musicians and actors as well, no matter how talented they might be. Yet, becoming a famous sports figure, actor, or musician is a dream of many juveniles hoping to escape poverty. Likewise, parental units living in poverty may falsely believe that fame is readily available to their children and may encourage them to pursue unrealistic dreams. It can result in disappointment for both parental units and adolescents when those dreams are not realized, not to mention the financial and time sacrifices it takes to play a sport or take music or acting lessons, even at the high school level.

Being disillusioned in childhood contributes to juvenile delinquency, as juveniles come to the realization that opportunities are just not there without an adequate education (which is costly), work experience, or the right connections. As adolescents from lower-class, working-class, and in even today middle-class families approach adulthood, many of their fantasies of a pathway to success are squashed by the realities of limited opportunities (Greenberg, 2011).

DELINQUENT SUBCULTURES

When we think of a group of co-offending juvenile delinquents today, we may immediately jump to the conclusion that they must be part of a gang. However, not all delinquent groups are gangs. Delinquent gangs engage in organized criminal behavior. We discussed youth gangs in greater detail in Chapter 5. This section covers how peer groups may form haphazard and disorganized patterns of deviance or delinquent behavior, which have been one of the age-old problems of adolescence. Behaviors include underaged drinking, drug use, sexual experimentation, dangerous driving habits, and joyriding in stolen automobiles (Greenberg, 2011; Bloch and Niederoffer,1958).

Some deviant or delinquent behavior among friends may appear rather harmless, even if potentially destructive, as in our previously mentioned example of toilet-papering a house. Other behavior may rise to serious offending, such as illegal

Teenage drug addicts, Saint Petersburg, Florida.

drug use and distribution. We should note that toilet-papering a house technically involves trespassing, littering, and sometimes vandalism, if the landscape is damaged in any way. We should also note that toilet-papering a house, for teenagers, can be symbolic, either offered as a sign of admiration for a fellow student or as a form of mockery for a despised one. Either way, juveniles are rarely prosecuted for toilet-papering a house, unless there is considerable monetary loss, such as the cost of hiring someone to clean up the mess.

Delinquent subcultures, including gangs, encompass groups of juveniles that reject some, if not all societal expectations, including those of parental units, teachers, religious leaders, or the community at large. As we noted early on in the book, not all deviance is criminal. Some of the hairstyles and clothing choices in the 1960s (long hair on males and miniskirts on females) met with disapproval from more conservative groups and dismay from parental units and school officials. Though these trends might have been prohibited in school at the time, they were by no means criminal. In the case of delinquent subcultures, the behavior goes well beyond deviance and has crossed over into prosecutable crimes.

Some theories about delinquent subgroups in the 1950s and 1960s can be applied to current patterns of delinquency. Values and norms are formed within delinquent subgroups that run counter to the legal system, making it impossible for group members to show any remorse when they have broken the law or reluctance to commit crimes (Cohen and Short, 1958; Sykes and Matza, 1957). Cloward and Ohlin identified three distinct types of subcultures that juvenile delinquents typically belong to (Mackay, 1989; Cloward and Ohlin, 1960):

- **Criminal subcultures**, involved in property crimes
- **Conflict subcultures**, involved in violent crimes
- **Retreatist subcultures**, involved in drug crimes

Today, theorists are more likely to believe that elements of all three delinquent subcultures can exist in individual groups. Some or all members of a clique can partake in one or more of the delinquent subgroups. The best examples of this in juvenile delinquency are youth gangs, whether formed around neighborhood ties or associated with larger, more dangerous organized criminal enterprises.

Differential Association

Edwin Sutherland, a prominent theorist of white-collar crime, is also well-known for his *differential association theory* (Sutherland and Cressey, 1939). The premise of the theory is that beyond any genetic predisposition to criminal behavior (e.g., a mental health issue), criminal behavior, including that of juveniles, is learned. More importantly, criminal behavior will often be learned from the family we are born into and the friends we make—if those family members or friends are deviants or criminals. The nine principles of differential association include (Sutherland and Cressy, 1939):

- Criminals need to be trained as criminals by other people.
- Criminal behavior is learned through both verbal and nonverbal communication.
- Learning to be a criminal happens within close, intimate groups.
- The types of criminal behavior learned include criminal attitudes and rationalization, and the means by which to commit a crime.
- Laws are discriminately viewed within the group, and many of them are deemed unreasonable.
- When there is enough peer pressure to violate the law, a person can become delinquent.
- Association with criminals may vary in frequency, duration of time spent with them, and intensity of interaction.
- Criminal behavior is not simply a matter of imitation; the individual must be motivated and enticed to learn it.
- Criminal behavior cannot merely be explained by general deviant drives or values.

There are a number of examples we can examine to apply differential association theory to juveniles. If we take a look at how a juvenile becomes a frequent consumer of cannabis,[3] it is not a habit that forms overnight, but rather initially learned from others. If a juvenile hangs out with a peer group that uses any cannabis product, including edibles, they may very well be tempted to try it themselves. Howard Becker (1953) outlined the steps by which someone becomes a marijuana user: (1) Learns to smoke it, presumably from others, in a way that will produce the desired effects, (2) learns to recognize the effects, within themselves and by witnessing them in others, connecting the effects with the use of marijuana, and (3) learns to appreciate the effects of marijuana.

[3] Even though cannabis is legal in some states for recreational use, even those states have an age limit of 21 for purchase and consumption. Also, cannabis is still illegal at the federal level, so even where it is legal for adults 21 years and older, it is still illegal for juveniles and adults.

Certainly, in most cases, particularly if drug paraphernalia are used (e.g., pipe, bong) in order to smoke marijuana, more times than not a potential user depends on someone to teach them how to procure the drugs, let alone use them. Today, of course, juveniles are as likely to learn on their own from social media, TikTok, and YouTube videos. Juveniles who actually obtain drug paraphernalia and/or cannabis products would be entering delinquent territory, an even more challenging feat if they live in a jurisdiction where marijuana use is prohibited.

POPULAR CULTURE AND SOCIAL MEDIA INFLUENCES

The influences on deviance and delinquency, or good behavior, for that matter, are not restricted to peer groups or family. We cannot underestimate the influences that popular culture, the media, and social network websites may have on juveniles. However, of the three, social network websites have been the cause of most alarm and moral panic in recent decades, as compared to popular sub cultures such as gangster rap and heavy metal music (Springhall, 1999; Arnett, 1991), which have historically been demonized for contributing to delinquency.

Before rap or heavy metal music, and long before invention of the personal computer, smart phones, or the Internet, parental units were concerned about other forms of media that targeted a juvenile audience. Comic books, in particular, other than "wholesome" ones, raised a moral panic. In fact, progressive psychiatrist and infamous anti-comics crusader, Fredric Wertham (1895–1981), often claimed that

> *comics are an important factor in causing juvenile delinquency. . . . The contents of comics is almost universally one of crime, violence, horror, "emphasis of sexual characteristics which 'can lead to erotic fixations of all kinds,' and 'sadist-masochistic mixture of pleasure and violence.'"* (Thrasher, 1949, pp. 195, 203; also see Wertham, 1948).

However, Wertham used only the most extreme comic books as his examples, ignoring the thousands of comic books that have much milder content (Thrasher, 1949). Hence Wertham's claims were more likely to be based in moral panic than in fact. Wertham's perspective is a particularly curious one, considering that comic books were used in the 1940s to promote anti-Nazi sentiment to support the U.S. war effort, portraying Hitler as a comic book villain (Peters, 2017; Fertig et al., 2017).

Though there are certainly a number of anecdotal stories of how crimes have been inspired by television shows, music, or movies, Helgott (2020) claims that little empirical evidence supports a significant relationship between media consumption and crime. However, earlier studies, including Arnett's study (1991) of the effects on juveniles of listening to heavy metal music, indicate that at least when it comes to musical tastes, there might indeed be a correlation with reckless

Comic book sample, 1940s.

behavior (e.g., driving habits). But which came first? Delinquency or the consumption of music that is not necessarily mainstream and includes lyrics describing criminal behavior?

The Internet offers an environment with open, interactive, and user-generated content. Social media promises plenty of rewards and opportunities for self-expression and identity formation (Bunders and Weerman, 2020). However, there are also inherent risks, including cyberbullying and exposure to harmful content and encouragement of delinquency (Bunders and Weerman, 2020). In Ohannessian and Vannucci's study (2020), juveniles who regularly use social media exhibited more delinquent behavior, with boys who use Facebook regularly and Hispanic adolescents, both male and female, who use Instagram regularly are at an elevated risk for delinquent behavior. However, a reported 75% of adolescents between the ages of 13 and 17 maintain at least one active social media profile, 90% report social media use, and 51% report daily use (American Academy of Child and Adolescent Psychiatry, 2022). This should make us hesitate to jump to the conclusion that all social media use results in greater risk for delinquency. If it did, we would have more evidence that frequent social media use by juveniles leads to delinquency.

Recently a number of news outlets, including those outside the United States (e.g., *People Magazine* and 7 News Australia), have reported the dangers of challenges–hashtags that are linked to dangerous behaviors, including self-harm, and other inappropriate content on the popular social media platform, TikTok (Daoud and Steadman, 2022; Brown, 2022). Among the concerns Brown (2022) cites for parents of juveniles who use TikTok are the following:

- Kids can be targeted by predators.
- It is easy to encounter inappropriate content.
- The conversations around mental health are dangerous.
- The nature of the app might cause kids anxiety.
- Users might become victims of cyberbullying.
- There are privacy concerns over user data on TikTok.

In response to growing concerns from parental units and others, TikTok put new safety features in place in August 2021 (Brown, 2022):

- Accounts for children between ages 13 and 15 will not receive push notifications[4] after 9 p.m.
- For teens ages 16 and 17, push notifications will be disabled after 10 p.m.
- Users between the ages 16 and 17 must actively switch their settings to enable direct messaging. Those under 16 don't have access to direct messages.
- Users under age 16 trying to publish their first video will get a pop-up message to help them better understand their privacy options. They won't be able to publish the video without selecting who will be allowed to see it.

TikTok is not the only example of a social media platform concerning to parental units and in some cases, law enforcement. It is well-established in research that spending considerable time socializing with delinquents presents a greater risk of becoming delinquent (Warr, 2002; Hoeben et al., 2016; Sutherland and Cressey, 1939), in this case, socializing with them online. The age of the juvenile consumer of social media appears to matter. In a study conducted by Bunders and Weerman (2020), younger adolescents, as compared to older adolescents, were found to be more influenced by delinquent online interaction with their peers that ultimately spills out into delinquency offline.

[4] Push notifications are messages sent from a mobile phone app to the user's screen. They provide updates and messages and are intended to motivate the user to take action (e.g., open a phone app to see the latest message on a social network website).

DISORGANIZED COMMUNITIES

Perhaps the most important factor after family contributing to delinquency is the disorganized community. Theories of community disorganization were some of the earliest and most influential addressing ecological issues contributing to delinquency, beginning with *The City* (1967) by Robert E. Parker, Earnest W. Burgess, and Roderick D. McKenzie. The authors focused on urban neighborhood disorganization, using Chicago as the backdrop for their research. Elijah Anderson, in *The Code of the Streets* (1999), proposed that where one grows up can influence behavior and that living in a violent community can result in delinquency. Anderson's social laboratory was Philadelphia:

> *Almost everyone residing in poor inner-city neighborhoods is struggling financially and therefore feels a certain distance from the rest of America, but there are degrees of alienation. . . . Most residents are decent or are trying to be. The same family is likely to have members who are strongly oriented toward decency and civility, whereas other members are strongly oriented toward the street—and all that it implies.* (Anderson, 1999, pp. 35, 36)

Chicago and Philadelphia represent cities with many urban problems, including poverty, juvenile delinquency, and youth gangs.

Social Disorganization Theory

Before the Chicago School studies of community disorganization, *social disorganization theory* was presented as an explanation of crime, including delinquency. Social disorganization was defined by Clifford Shaw and Henry D. McKay in 1942 as the inability of the members of a community, including elected officials, to share the same values or jointly resolve problems within their neighborhoods (Bond, 2015; Bursik, 1988). Conversely, a sense of community can be defined as members feeling like they belong, and that they share a faith that any problems that arise can be resolved with citizens' commitment to doing what is best for the whole community (Cantillon et al., 2003; McMillan and Chavis, 1986). If there is an absence of community cohesion, particularly when it comes to solving problems of delinquency, children in that community are put at risk for criminal offending.

Social disorganization can be found at a local level, including in specific neighborhoods, or it can affect the entire town or city. For example, in Riverside, California, some neighborhoods are plagued with gang violence, while others are untouched. The Casa Blanca neighborhood has historically had to deal with a gang presence, including turf wars, while others like the Canyon Crest neighborhood, which is nearly adjacent to Casa Blanca, goes largely untouched by neighboring gang activities (Office of the Attorney General, State of California Department of Justice, 2020). Within social disorganization theory, there are a number of community variables that specifically correlate with youth violence (Osgood and Chambers, 2003):

- **Residential instability:** The more disorganization within a community, the greater the expectation that juvenile delinquency will also increase.
- **Ethnic diversity:** Social disorganization theory predicts more delinquency in communities with more ethnic diversity that breeds more fear and distrust.
- **Family disruption:** Where there are higher rates of family disruption (e.g. divorce), the expectation is that there will be more delinquency.
- **Economic status:** As noted earlier, there is the expectation that there will be more youth violence in poorer communities.
- **Population density:** The greater the population density (e.g., number of people per square block), the greater the expectation that there will be more youth (and adult) violence.[5]
- **Proximity to urban areas:** Proximity to large cities results in juveniles being exposed to more sophisticated types of criminal behavior.[6]

A once-popular explanation for community and social disorganization is the broken windows theory, proposed by James Q. Wilson and George Kelling in an article published in *The Atlantic Monthly* magazine in 1982. They wrote, "Social psychologists and police officers tend to agree that if a window in a building is broken and left unrepaired, the rest of the windows will soon be broken" (Wilson and Kelling, 1982, retrieved from https://www.theatlantic.com/magazine/archive/1982/03/broken-windows/304465/). The theory was often cited to explain why rundown communities experience more crime.

Broken windows theory has also been associated with Philip Zimbardo, a lead researcher in the controversial Stanford University prison experiment.[7] In 1969, Zimbardo conducted a field study where he abandoned two cars in two very different communities, one a poor, crime-ridden neighborhood in Queens, New York, the other an affluent neighborhood in Palo Alto, California. The license plates of both cars were removed and hoods left up making them appear to be abandoned (Vedantam et al., 2016). The goal of the experiment was to see which vehicle would be vandalized first and how quickly. The car in Queens was vandalized within ten minutes of its abandonment; the car in Palo Alto remained untouched

[5] Though this proposition is included in social disorganization theory, research in both urban and rural areas is inconclusive as to whether population density really is an important variable, when controlling for other conditions (Osgood and Chambers, 2003).

[6] Later versions of social disorganization theory and research include this proposition (Osgood and Chambers, 2003; Heitgerd and Bursik, 1987).

[7] For more information on the Stanford University prison experiment, see https://www.apa.org/topics/forensics-law-public-safety/prison.

for more than a week; vandalism only occurred after Zimbardo smashed the car with a sledgehammer (Wilson and Kelling, 1982).

Vandalism is one of the crimes that juveniles are most often accused of, so it would seem that the broken windows theory would apply to the effects of juvenile delinquency in a community. However, like all theories and hypotheses, it is always good to have a healthy dose of skepticism when weighing their merit. What makes broken windows theory suspect is that a number of subsequent research projects have debunked it:

> *Despite the widespread influence of the 1982 Atlantic Monthly essay, remarkedly little is known about the effects of broken windows. A number of leading researchers in sociology, law, and police studies—including Wesley Skogan at Northwestern, Robert Sampson at Harvard, Stephen Raudenbush at the University of Michican, Anthony Braga at Harvard, and Jeffrey Fagan at Columbia, among others—have compiled datasets from different urban areas to explore the broken windows hypothesis, but the evidence remains, at best, mixed.* (Harcourt and Ludwig, 2005, p. 3)

Social disorganization is not exclusively an urban problem. Though much of the focus of social disorganization in communities has been centered on urban settings, community disruption can also occur in suburbs and rural settings, although rural communities tend to be more conservative, with a "law and order" mentality, and little tolerance is shown for even minor juvenile offending (DeJames, 1980).

There have been a number of rapid changes, both socially and economically, in rural communities that have contributed to perceptions of disorder. Family farms have been disappearing since the 1950s (Tunnell, 2006; U.S. Department of Agriculture, 2005; Deavers and Hoppe, 1992), and juveniles living in rural areas are well aware of seemingly more exciting lives lived elsewhere, thanks to social media. And as idyllic as rural communities may seem, as portrayed in popular culture with depictions of "folksy" people who generally appear happy, the reality is that there is rural poverty, particularly affecting people of color living in these areas, as shown in Exhibit 8.1.

As reported by the United States Department of Agriculture (2022), in 2019, 21% of children under the age of 18 lived in nonurban households functioning below the poverty level, compared to 16.1% in urban households. The same variables that contribute to higher rates of juvenile offending in cities, including levels of ethnic diversity, female-headed households and frequent household moves, also contribute to rural juvenile offending, even though juvenile violent crime is exponentially higher in urban as compared to rural communities (Zuckerman, 2022). Less serious property crimes and vandalism committed by juveniles occur more in rural settings than urban ones, but rural areas do not provide the same types of social services or juvenile justice programs as metro areas–programs that could better address rural delinquency issues (DeJames, 1980).

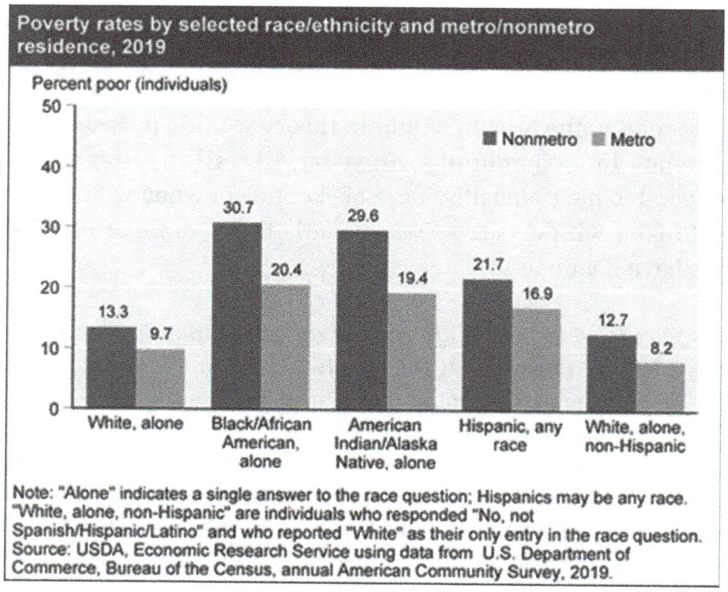

EXHIBIT 8.1 ‖ Urban vs. Nonurban Poverty, 2019

Low Neighborhood Attachment and Percentage of Rental Properties

It is reasonable to assume that the more attachment one has to a particular community, the more likely that the residents will be invested in its well-being. However, there are a number of neighborhood stressors, beyond the conditions of property as noted in broken windows theory, that can negatively affect how we might feel about the community that we live in. Some of these include the presence of prostitution, incidences of public urination, and the visibility of the unhoused (Woldoff, 2002; Skogan, 1990). Important to the discussion of juvenile delinquency, deteriorating neighborhoods also results in more juveniles dropping out of school, a contributor to criminal behavior, as well as more teenage pregnancies (Crane, 1991). Offspring of unmarried teenagers face an additional individual risk for juvenile and adult offending.

The extent to which any of these stressors exist in a neighborhood will affect how people feel about their community. Adults will transfer their own feelings of not belonging to the community to the children in their lives. This in turn can contribute to delinquency, if juveniles likewise do not have a sense of civic pride or respect for their neighbors.

Some of what contributes to neighborhood attachment is the number of rental properties in the community. Though landlords and property managers are increasingly expecting tenants to sign long-term leases to provide rental income stability, month-to-month rental properties are still available in some areas. When tenants do not commit to long-term occupancy, it can contribute to a flux of people moving in and out of a community, with neighbors more likely to remain strangers. And as shown in the documentary, *Homeless: The Motel Kids of Orange County* [California][8] (HBO Documentary Films, 2020), there is even more instability for families living in rental properties with week-to-week terms of occupancy.

The condition of rental properties depends on whether the landlord is present or has hired a conscientious property manager. The so-called "absentee" landlord or *slumlord*, can be a source of a number of problems in urban areas, including crime, blight, and juvenile delinquency (Rephann, 2009). In a broader sense, what matters is how residents view the neighborhood. Woldoff (2002) identified four key conditions, in addition to an absentee landlord, that can diminish feelings for and attachment to a community:

- **Physical disorder:** The extent to which residents take pride in maintaining their rental property, which can include poor housing, presence of abandoned buildings, and empty lots.
- **Social disorder:** The extent to which residents trust the people in their neighborhood, get along with one another (or fight), and can be relied on to keep an eye out for trouble in the neighborhood.
- **Victimization:** The amount and kinds of victimization experienced in the neighborhood.
- **Perception of crime:** To what extent that there is perceived or real presence of crime in a neighborhood, including burglaries, prostitution, and illegal drug sales; how safe residents feel walking alone in their neighborhoods at night.

These do not only impact how adults feel about their neighborhoods, but also how juveniles feel as well.

Public Housing Projects

As part of the New Deal during the Great Depression, the federal housing program began in earnest, intending to provide jobs in construction as well as housing for the poor (National Low Income Housing Coalition, 2019). It was thought that public and low-income housing would offer a solution to inner-city poverty by meeting a basic human necessity (Stoloff, 2004). In the 1960s, housing projects were part of a federal urban renewal plan, intended to eliminate urban neighborhoods where very poor minorities primarily lived ("slums")[9] (Modica, 2009).

Instead, many low-income housing projects became stigmatizing for the people living there, including juveniles. In some cases, they became eyesores on the

[8] Technically these children and their families are not unhoused, as they do have housing, however temporary it might be for some.

[9] The term "slum" refers to a neighborhood that is very poor, overcrowded, and deteriorating. Today the term is considered to be insensitive, offensive, and stigmatizing and is no longer generally used in academic circles.

New York Housing Authority public housing, Queens (L); Robert R. Taylor Homes, Chicago, circa 1988 (R).

urban landscape, as in the example of the Robert Taylor Homes in Chicago, built in 1962. Besides being unimaginative architecturally, the housing project gained notoriety as it became the site of gang violence and associated crimes, including drug dealing, and came to represent failed urban policy (McQuilling and *Sun Times*, 2022; Modica, 2009). Even before the building project in Chicago was completed, the *Chicago Defender* in 1959 described it as a "Jim Crow housing project," as it was designated to primarily house poor Black residents (McQuilling and *Sun Times*, 2022).

As well-meaning as low-income housing opportunities may have initially been in the 1930s, today they are not all equal. During the Depression, large numbers of people were living in either relative or real poverty, placing most everyone in the same boat. Housing projects were not special programs promoting home ownership to low-income families in middle-class neighborhoods, however.[10] They became a program of wholesale warehousing of the poor in substandard rental public housing projects, which had a detrimental effect on children raised there. Conceived with extreme population density resulting in uncomfortably crowded conditions, they became instruments of forced racial segregation.

There are a number of social problems associated with public housing projects in large cities, including urban blight, higher rates of crime, and higher unemployment rates. Of equal concern is the strain placed on the juvenile justice system in areas where there is a high concentration of poverty, combined with the negative consequences for juveniles exposed to violence and drug dealing (Hawes, 2014). According to the U.S. Department of Urban Development (n.d.), 43% of those living in public housing are children.

[10] In 1980, the author's mother was able to purchase a condominium in the affluent community of Irvine, California, because of a lottery for low-income housing in the neighborhood of Woodbridge. Today, it is difficult if not impossible to find affordable housing even for the middle class in Irvine, much less in most communities in Orange County, California. According to Realtor.com (https://www.realtor.com/realestateandhomes-search/Irvine_CA/overview), in March 2022 the median house price in Irvine was $1.3 million.

Neglected or poorly managed public housing or other forms of low-income housing can result in a number of community problems that also trickle down to families. As these are generally higher crime areas, it is more difficult for families to help prevent delinquency. We should also note that those who have been incarcerated for serious crimes are often denied access to public housing, though there are some *Section 8 housing* assistance programs for felons, depending on the state. This may further cause deterioration in families when one or more family member is not allowed to live with their immediate nuclear family. As we present in this book, children of incarcerated parental units and those living in single-parent households are more likely to become delinquent or eventually become adult offenders, if they are not delinquent during childhood.

Public housing projects also tend to be set in desolate places, in some cases without reliable public transportation and where there is little incentive for small or large businesses to establish themselves. This in turn results in fewer job opportunities for both juveniles and adults, further exacerbating the cycle of poverty in these communities. For example, in Holyoke, Massachusetts, the Holyoke Housing Authority owns and operates 821 low-income units (Holyoke Housing Authority, n.d.). The area in and around the housing projects is arguably a food desert, where there is little in the way of larger chain stores offering discount prices on food or job opportunities for residents. The Pioneer Valley Transit Authority (PVTA) in western Massachusetts, which includes the city of Holyoke, has limited public transportation options for residents in smaller communities like Holyoke and nearby Chicopee (PVTA, 2019) to get to more affordable food options or employment opportunities in larger cities like Springfield.

Availability of Drugs

Substance abuse is one key risk factor in juvenile offending. In Chapter 6, we discussed the risks of individual abuse and addiction. Here we review the consequences of ready availability of drugs, a larger community public health issue. There cannot be substance abuse issues for adults or for juveniles unless alcohol and/or drugs, prescribed or not, are available.

Because illegal drug sales are covert, it is difficult to estimate just how available drugs are to juveniles, much less adults. It may only appear on the surface that drug availability is higher in poor urban neighborhoods, when in reality, as noted by Recovery Village (2021), a rehabilitation center in Florida, adolescents can obtain drugs and alcohol a number of ways, as there are illegal substances available to juveniles in most communities, including those with wealthier residents. Perhaps rehabilitation centers offer the best estimates of the availability of drug levels in a community, though their statistics and information are based on juveniles who voluntarily or involuntarily seek treatment for drug and/or alcohol abuse. Rehabilitation centers do not necessarily take into consideration recreational users, particularly those who have not been arrested, in their data, nor do statistics from law enforcement or other government agencies reflect actual numbers.

As we noted in the previous section, one of the problems and criticisms of public housing is the drug dealing and drug use present, often conducted in the open. For communities where public housing is close to schools, this can be an ongoing concern and a challenge for law enforcement, as in the example of Holyoke, Massachusetts (discussed further in Chapter 10, on juvenile delinquency in schools).

Not just the availability of drugs, but the types of illicit drugs sold in a community, present serious challenges. It is also important to note that illicit drugs are not only obtained on the street or in clandestine neighborhood locations. Increasingly, distribution and sales take place on the Internet, including through Craigslist and other sites, resulting in wider availability of illicit drugs, including for juveniles, even though law enforcement monitors these sites (Liu and Bharadwaj, 2020). Illicit drug sales on Craigslist are most likely to take place in wealthier areas where incomes are higher and unemployment lower (Liu and Bharadwaj, 2020).

Illegal drug use and its underground markets are not merely an urban problem, even though they are most often associated with larger cities (Wilkins et al., 2018). In a study of smaller towns and rural areas in New Zealand, where there is greater availability of methamphetamines and more dangerous street drugs sold mostly by gangs and less access to cannabis, consumption of the latter, including by juveniles, is greater (Wilkins et al., 2018). In the United States, alcohol use, inhalant use, and illicit drug use are more prevalent among high-school-aged juveniles who live on farms, as compared to those living in towns or cities (Rhew at al., 2011).

Rural communities have become attractive markets for illicit drugs. There are high rates of substance abuse disorders, largely due to low education attainment, rural poverty, and unemployment, as well as isolation (Rural Health Information Hub, 2020). Historically it has been easier to hide an illicit drug lab in a rural area, though much methamphetamine, a relatively cheap drug, currently comes from Mexican drug cartels (Morris, 2018). To further exacerbate the problem, there is a lack of pediatric mental health care, including substance abuse treatment, available in poorer rural towns (Hodgkinson et al., 2017).

Availability of Firearms

As in the case of the availability of drugs and alcohol for juveniles, we might assume that the level of violence occurring in a community will be higher where there is greater access to firearms. As Yamane (2017, p. 1) explains,

> *The world today is awash in a sea of small arms in the hands of civilians, with the United States leading the way by a considerable margin. . . . Wright (1995, p. 64) observed that there is "nearly one gun for every man, woman, and child in the country."*

Within the last decades of the 20th century, gun violence had a greater impact on juveniles and young adults, with a significant number of juveniles, some as young as nine years old, reporting that they carry a gun outside their home (Sheppard et al., 2000; Kahn et al., 1998). The consequences of carrying a firearm, for adults and juveniles, can be unintentional injury or death.

Firearm availability for juveniles is not limited to illegally obtained weapons. According to Stansfield et al. (2021), countless numbers of studies have indicated that higher levels of legal firearm availability result in higher rates of intimate partner homicide. Likewise, higher rates of licensed firearm dealers in cities are associated with higher rates of intimate partner homicide (Stansfield et al., 2021). What is alarming is that during the first six months of the COVID-19 pandemic there was a surge in firearm-related injuries inflicted by young children on other young children, correlated with an increase in new firearm ownership during the lockdown (Bell et al., 2021).

There has been a concerted effort made by lawmakers recently to reduce juvenile access to firearms, including prosecuting parental units who do not safely store them in the home. A recent example of this includes the prosecution of the parents of 15-year old Ethan Crumbley, the suspect in the fatal shootings at Oxford High School, Detroit, Michigan. The parents had allegedly purchased a semi-automatic gun for their son just days before he opened fire on his classmates in December 2021 (Healy, 2021).

Though the number of students who report carrying a weapon to school, including guns, has decreased in recent decades, in 2019, reportedly 13% of ninth to twelfth graders had carried a weapon on school property, with few measurable differences found by sexual identity or grade level (National Center for Education Statistics 2021). By some estimates, one in 18 teenagers carry a gun at school (Reinberg, 2019). The most common reason juveniles carry a gun to school is fear, with males more likely than females to be armed with a gun (Reinberg, 2019).

SUMMARY

In the last two chapters, we reviewed the individual and family risks for juvenile delinquency. In this chapter, we examined the larger, community-based risks. We also noted that the three can be intertwined, as in the example of the availability to juveniles of drugs and alcohol and individual risks for addiction. Among the key community risks for delinquency are poverty, social inequality, and disorganized neighborhoods.

Though the American Dream is alive and well in the United States, for those living in poverty it can offer false hope for upward mobility. A number of theories help us to understand the relationship between poverty and juvenile delinquency, including strain, anomie, and opportunity theories. Differential association helps us to understand how criminal behavior is learned from deviant or criminal others. When children eventually see that there is little to no way out of poverty, based on their observations of their families and people in their neighborhoods, it can set them up for helplessness, failure, and risk of delinquency.

Poverty can either be real, as in the example of having difficulty keeping a roof over one's head or food on the table, or relative poverty, when we compare what we have to the belongings and successes of those around us. Even children raised in middle-class families are seeing their dreams of upward mobility diminish, as college becomes more expensive, along with the costs of housing and food, as well as rising prices on other necessities. It is doubly difficult for children of poverty, who may unrealistically believe, based on false social media narratives and parental expectations, that they can become the next star athlete or famous musician or actor. When these dreams are not realized, there is greater temptation to turn to crime, as well as risk for mental health disorders.

Another community-based risk for deviance and delinquency is neighborhood disorganization. There are a number of factors that contribute to this, including higher rates of rental properties in some communities, with neighbors moving in and out; absentee and disinterested landlords; and general neighborhood deterioration. The last factor has been explored with broken window theory, though a number of studies have discredited the results of this earlier research. However, there is a good deal of research that indicates that public housing projects, at least historically, are more likely to expose juveniles to visible signs of prostitution, gang-related crimes, and drug dealing.

Other community factors include the availability of drugs, alcohol, and firearms. Of course, like any industry, legal or illegal, supply and demand will drive the availability of any of these. In the United States, firearms have become so readily available that it is estimated that there is a gun for every person living in this country. The true numbers, of course, are higher, taking into consideration the accessibility of guns stolen during the commission of burglary or unregistered guns available for purchase illegally on the streets or on the Internet. For juveniles, availability of drugs, alcohol, and firearms is not limited to large cities. Rural towns and farming communities have likewise had their share of problems associated with these.

IN THE MEDIA

The Link Between Lead Exposure and Delinquency

In this chapter, our focus has been on the social environment in communities that can contribute to delinquency. We should not ignore contributing factors in the physical environment as well, including chemical and mineral hazards. For nearly a century now, we have had a greater understanding of the links between exposure to environmental lead, a dangerous neurotoxin, found in paint, gasoline, food cans, and unregulated water sources, and lower IQs delinquency, and behavioral problems (Gibson et al., 2022; Muller et al., 2018; Hamilton, 1929). In a number of states, including Massachusetts, you cannot sell a home unless you have a licensed lead inspector certify that it is free of possible lead hazards (Commonwealth of Massachusetts, 2022). If lead is present in the paint or elsewhere in the home, it must be removed by a professional, generally at cost to the home seller.

Of particular concern is children living in homes with private well water. Gibson et al. (2022) found that compared to children with access to public water supplies, "those relying on private wells have a 21% higher risk of any delinquency and a 38% increased risk of serious delinquency." Well water is not limited to rural areas. In some cases, as in the example of Wake County, North Carolina, municipalities have excluded homes in primarily densely populated Black communities from access to public water sources, leaving them no choice but to depend on private well water (Gibson et al., 2022).

Exposure to lead is more prevalent within poorer communities like Wake County. Community activists, including the Young Lords and Black Panthers, called attention in the 1960s and 1970s to how lead exposure is unequally distributed, being found primarily in poor minority communities (Muller et al., 2018; Nelson, 2016; Markowitz and Rosner, 2013). The Muller et al. (2018) study found that racial disparities in lead exposure could be found at all income levels, in both urban and rural communities, and that there were income disparities for both Blacks and whites, making poverty a common denominator.

SOURCES

Commonwealth of Massachusetts (2022). Finding and removing lead. Retrieved from https://www.mass.gov/finding-and-removing-lead.

Gibson, J. M., J. M. MacDonald, M. Fisher, and P. J. Cook (2022). "Early life lead exposure from private well water increases juvenile delinquency risk among US teens." *Proceedings of the National Academy of Sciences of the United States* (PNAS). Jan 31. Retrieved from https://www.pnas.org/doi/10.1073/pnas.2110694119.

Hamilton, A. (1929). *Industrial Poisons in the United States*. New York: Macmillan.

Markowitz, G., and D. Rosner (2013). *Lead Wars: The Politics of Science and the Fate of America's Children*. Berkeley: University of California Press.

Muller, C., R. J. Sampson, and A. S. Winter (2018). "Environmental inequality: The social causes and consequences of lead exposure." *Annual Review of Sociology*. Vol. 44, issue 1: 263–282.

Nelson, A. (2016). "Genuine struggle and care: An interview with Cleo Silvers." *American Journal of Public Health*. Vol. 106: 1744–1748.

INTERNATIONAL PERSPECTIVES

"Bad Neighborhoods" in Rio de Janeiro, Brazil

American cities are not alone in having what some term "bad neighborhoods." According to Jensen (2017), there are a number of signs that indicate that a neighborhood is in disorder, and even dangerous, among them,

- Pairs of shoes tied together, thrown over the electric lines.
- Broken shards of glass in parking lots.

- Multiple burned-down or run-down houses.
- A lot of discarded trash in the streets and on sidewalks.
- Shopping carts abandoned on the side of the road.
- Pizza places that won't deliver to homes in the neighborhood.

Of neighborhoods around the world listed as the most dangerous by travel writers, the Lapa district in Rio de Janeiro, Brazil, tops the list (*Independent*, 2016). You would not think so, considering how travel promotion websites encourage visiting the district. Described as the most Bohemian neighborhood in Rio de Janeiro, it is well known for its architecture, including an aqueduct built in 1723, the Arcos da Lapa, and its lively nightlife (Rio.com, n.d.).

The U.S. State Department cautions that Brazil in general has recently witnessed rising crime rates in cities, including violent crime, with assaults common (Bureau of Consular Affairs, 2022). Furthermore, the State Department notes that neighborhoods of *informal housing* (*favelas*) are to be avoided at any time of the day, due to high crime rates there (Bureau of Consular Affairs, 2022). *Favelas* account for a good portion of the drug-trafficking gangs and turf wars in Rio de Janeiro, creating an "ecology of danger" in areas of informal housing (Barcellos and Zaluar, 2014).

There are reports that juveniles are held in detention in Brazil under cruel and allegedly inhumane conditions that contribute to the violence witnessed in Lapa and elsewhere in Rio de Janeiro and other Brazilian cities. Under Brazilian law, juvenile offenders between the ages of 12 and 18 are supposed to be rehabilitated through education or community service, with detention reserved only for

Lapa District, Rio de Janeiro, Brazil.

the most serious crimes; 16- and 17-year-old juveniles can be tried as adults and sent to adult prison (Griffin, 2017).

However, even children accused of minor crimes in Brazil have ended up in juvenile detention, in overcrowded conditions where frequent riots break out and there is little opportunity for education or rehabilitation (Griffin, 2017). A decade ago, researchers in Brazil found a high prevalence of psychiatric disorders, including attention deficit hyperactivity disorder (ADHD), anxiety, and depressive disorders among juvenile offenders in Rio de Janeiro (Candido de Andrade et al., 2011). Seventy percent of juvenile delinquents in the city reported drug abuse and/or dependence; 52% reported alcohol abuse and/or dependence (Candido de Andrade et al., 2011). The problem remains that once released, juveniles who might be on the verge of adulthood will return to their neighborhoods, including Lapa, as hardened criminals and/or with severe mental health issues, further making the neighborhood dangerous not just for tourists but for the adults and juveniles living in them.

SOURCES

Barcellos, C., and A. Zaluar (2014). "Homicides and territorial struggles in Rio de Janeiro favelas." *Revista de Sáude Pública*. Vol. 48, issue 1 (Feb.): 94–102.

Bureau of Consular Affairs (2022). Brazil travel advisory. U.S. Department of State. Apr 18. Retrieved from https://travel.state.gov/content/travel/en/traveladvisories/traveladvisories/brazil-travel-advisory.html.

Candido de Andrade, R., F. Assumpção, I. A. Teixeira, and V. Aparecida da Silva Fonseca (2011). "*Prevalencia de transtornos psiquiatrico em jovens infratores na cidade do Rio de Janeiro, Brasil: Estudo de genero e relacao com a gravidade do delito* [Prevalence of psychiatric disorders in young offenders in the city of Rio de Janeiro (RJ, Brazil): Study of gender and relationship with the severity of the offense]." *Ciência and Saúde Coletiva*. Vol. 16, issue 4: e1678–4561.

Griffin, J. (2017). "Is brutal treatment of young offenders fuelling crime rates in Brazil?" *Guardian*. March. Retrieved from https://www.theguardian.com/global-development/2017/mar/03/brazil-crime-rates-brutal-treatment-young-offenders.

Independent (2016). "Dangerous neighborhoods." Nov. 15. Retrieved from https://www.independent.co.uk/travel/news-and-advice/world-s-most-dangerous-cities-countries-neighbourhoods-mexico-colombia-brazil-naples-johannesburg-a7418186.html.

Jensen, L. (2017). "Bad neighborhood." *Thought Catalog*. Jul. 13. Retrieved from https://thoughtcatalog.com/lorenzo-jensen-iii/2017/07/25-signs-that-youre-in-a-bad-neighborhood/.

Rio.com (n.d.). A neighborhood full of surprises: Lapa. Retrieved from https://www.rio.com/practical-rio/lapa.

CHAPTER DISCUSSION QUESTIONS

1. In what ways do community risks for juvenile delinquency overlap with the individual risks discussed in Chapter 6?
2. How can parental units counteract the negative effects that a disorganized neighborhood might have on their children?

3. In what ways, beyond what is discussed in this chapter, does social inequality contribute to delinquency?
4. If the American Dream is a myth for many, why do so many in American society, across all social economic strata, still believe that if you work hard you can achieve anything?
5. By what means can intergenerational poverty be avoided or eliminated?
6. How might social justice causes and activism help in reducing juvenile delinquency?
7. Why has it been so difficult to get gun legislation passed, including requiring parental units to safely secure firearms in the home?
8. What can communities do to reduce the presence of drugs in their neighborhoods?

GLOSSARY

Anomie Lack of common mores or ethical standards in an individual or group, where social norms deteriorate or disappear altogether.

Differential association Edwin Sutherland's theory that individuals become deviant or criminal when associating with deviant or criminal individuals or groups.

Differential opportunity theory Cloward and Ohlin's theory that proposes that individuals, as well as environmental factors, contribute to whether there are opportunities to commit crimes.

Informal housing Any flimsy, makeshift structure that is unregulated, without consideration for zoning laws or public safety, and used by unhoused or impoverished people as housing.

Relative poverty Feeling of poverty felt by individuals, no matter which community they live in, when they are not as well-off financially or in terms of the possessions they own (e.g., house, car, etc.), when they compare themselves to their neighbors.

Section 8 housing Federally funded voucher program that assists very low-income families, the elderly, and the disabled with rent, typically paying between 30% and 40% of rent, though in some cases the program will pay 100%. See U.S. Department of Housing and Urban Development (HUD) at https://www.hud.gov/topics/housing_choice_voucher_program_section_8.

Slumlord Slang term used to describe an absentee owner of rental property that gives little to no attention to the conditions of their property or the concerns of their tenants.

Social disorganization theory Theory used to describe the conditions in neighborhoods, communities, towns, cities, and rural areas where there is little civic trust or unity and no effective social control for crime, including juvenile delinquency.

Strain theory Robert Merton's theory that if individuals cannot achieve society's goals and expectations (e.g., education, good job) and/or access society's means for reaching those goals, they will find deviant or criminal ways to do so or reject then altogether and become retreatists or rebels.

REFERENCES AND ADDITIONAL SUGGESTED READINGS

Agnew, R. (2012). "Reflection on 'A revised strain theory of delinquency.'" *Social Forces.* Vol. 91, issue 1: 33–38.

Agnew, R. (1985). "A revised strain theory of delinquency." *Social Forces.* Vol. 64, issue 1: 151–167.

Anderson, E. (1999). *The Code of the Streets: Decency, Violence, and the Moral Life of the Inner City.* New York: W.W. Norton.

Arnett, J. (1991). "Heavy metal music and reckless behavior among adolescents." *Journal of Youth and Adolescence.* Vol. 10, issue 6 (Dec.): 573–592.

Becker, H. (1953). "Becoming a marihuana user." *American Journal of Sociology.* Vol. 59, issue 3: 235–242.

Bell, T. M., C. Robbins, and A. Gosain (2021). "The influence of the COVID-19 pandemic on pediatric firearm injuries." *Pediatrics.* Vol. 148, issue 1 (July): e2020049746.

Bloch, H. A., and A. Niederhoffer (1958). *The Gang.* New York: Philosophical Library.

Bond, M. (2015). Criminology: Social disorganization theory explained. LinkedIn. Mar 1. Retrieved from https://www.linkedin.com/pulse/criminology-social-disorganization-theory-explained-mark-bond/.

Brown, M. (2022). "Is TikTok safe for kids?" *Parents.* Jan 28. Retrieved from https://www.parents.com/kids/safety/internet/is-tiktok-safe-for-kids/.

Bunders, D. J., and F. M. Weerman (2020). "Social media and delinquency: Exploring the relation between online and offline interaction with friends and online and offline delinquency." *Kriminologie-Das.* Vol. 2, issue 2. Retrieved from https://www.kriminologie.de/index.php/krimoj/article/view/52/61.

Bursik, R. J. (1988). "Social disorganization and theories of crime and delinquency: Problems and prospects." *Criminology.* Vol. 26, issue 4: 519–551.

Cantillon, D., W. S. Davidson II, J. H. Schweitzer (2003). "Measuring community social organization: Sense of community as a mediator in social disorganization theory." *Journal of Criminal Justice.* Vol. 31, issue 4 (July-Aug.): 321–339.

CBS3 Staff (2019). "Police: Woman arrested for stealing baby formula from Target, man still on the loose after tossing baby at security." CBS3 Philadelphia. Dec 18. Retrieved from https://philadelphia.cbslocal.com/2019/12/18/police-woman-arrested-for-stealing-baby-formula-from-target-man-still-on-loose-after-tossing-baby-at-security/.

Cloward, R. A., and L. E. Ohlin (1960). *Delinquency and Opportunity: A Theory of Delinquent Gangs.* New York: Free Press.

Cohen, A. K., and J. F. Short (1958). "Research in delinquent subcultures." *Journal of Social Issues.* Vol. 14, issue 3 (Aug.): 20–37.

Crane, J. (1991). "The epidemic theory of ghettos and neighborhood effects on dropping out and teenage childbearing." *American Journal of Sociology.* Vol. 96, issue 5 (March): 1226–1259.

Daoud, E., and K. Steadman (2022). "Parents warned of potentially deadly TikTok 'blackout challenge.'" *7 News.* Mar 21. Retrieved from https://7news.com.au/technology/tiktok/parents-warned-of-potentially-deadly-tiktok-blackout-challenge-c-6143424.

Deavers, K. L., and R. A. Hoppe (1992). "Overview of the rural poor in the 1980s." In *Rural Poverty in America*, ed. C. M. Duncan. New York: Auburn House.

DeJames, J. (1980). Issues in rural juvenile justice. Office of Justice Programs, U.S. Department of Justice. Retrieved from https://www.ojp.gov/ncjrs/virtual-library/abstracts/issues-rural-juvenile-justice-juvenile-justice-rural-america-p-4-15#:~:text=Rural%20areas%20lack%20social%20service,the%20rural%20juvenile%20delinquency%20problem.

Durkheim, E. (1895). *Rules of Sociological Method*, 2d ed. Reprint 1982. Ed. S. Lukes, trans. W. D. Halls. New York: Free Press.

Fertig, M., J. Kirby, and W. Eisner (2017). *Take That, Adolf!: The Fighting Comic Books of the Second World War.* Seattle, WA: Fantagraphics.

Greenberg, D. F. (2011). Delinquency and the age structure of society. In *Radical and Marxist Theories of Crime*, P. B. Stretesky and M. J. Lynch. Philadelphia, PA: Routledge Publishers. Pp. 189–223.

Harcourt, B. E., and J. Ludwig (2005). "Broken windows: New evidence from New York City and a five-city social experiment." Public Law and Legal Theory Working Paper No. 93. *University of Chicago Law Review.* Vol. 73. The Law School, University of Chicago. Retrieved from http://www.law.uchicago.edu/academics/publiclaw/index.html.

Hawes, A. (2014). Housing policies contributing to juvenile delinquency. Lexington Fair Housing. Dec 29. Retrieved from https://lexingtonfairhousing.com/wp/wp-content/uploads/2015/03/Housing-Policies-Contributing-to-Juvenile-Delinquency.pdf.

Hawke, A. (n.d.). "Chances of going pro: What is the likelihood of your child making it to the big leagues?" *League Side.* Retrieved from https://leagueside.com/chances-of-going-pro/#:~:text=Take%20football%20for%20instance%2C%20only,will%20make%20it%20to%20NFL.

Healy, J. (2021). "Behind the charges faced by the parents of the Michigan shooting suspect." *New York Times.* Dec 4. Retrieved from https://www.nytimes.com/2021/12/03/us/crumbley-parents-charged-michigan-shooting.html.

Helgott, J. (2020). *Copycat Crime: How Media, Technology and Digital Culture Inspire Criminal Behavior and Violence.* Westport, CT: Praeger.

Heitgerd, J. L., and R. J. Bursik (1987). "Extracommunity dynamics and the ecology of delinquency." *American Journal of Sociology.* Vol. 92, issue 4 (Jan.): 775–787.

Hodgkinson, S., L. Godoy, L. S. Beers, and A. Lewin (2017). "Improving mental health access for low-income children and families in primary care setting." *Pediatrics.* Vol. 139, issue 1 (Jan.): e20151175.

Hoeben, E. M., R. C. Meldrum, and J. T. Young (2016). "The role of peer delinquency and unstructured socializing in explaining delinquency and substance use: A state-of-the-art review." *Journal of Criminal Justice.* Vol. 47: 108–122.

Home Box Office (HBO) Documentaries (2010). *Homeless: The Motel Kids of Orange County.* Jul 26 (release date).

Kahn, L., S. A. Kinchen, B. I. Williams, J. G. Ross, R. Lowry, C. V. Hill, J. A. Grunbaum, P. S. Blumson, J. O. Collins, and L. J. Kolbe (1998). "Youth risk behavior surveillance—United States, 1997." *Morbidity and Mortality Weekly Report CDC Surveillance Summaries.* Vol. 47, issue 3: 1–89.

Liu, J., and A. Bharadwaj (2020). "Drug abuse and the Internet: Evidence from Craigslist." *Management Science.* Vol. 66, issue 5 (May): 1783–2290.

MacKay, P. (1989). "Cloward and Ohlin's theory of delinquent subcultures—revisited." *Police Journal: Theory, Practices, and Principles.* Vol. 62, issue 4 (Oct.): 290–296.

McMillan, D. W., and D. M. Chavis (1986). "Sense of community: A definition and theory." *Journal of Community Psychology.* Vol. 14 (Jan.): 6–23.

McQuilling, M., and *Sun Times* (2022). Robert Taylor Homes. Apr 14. Retrieved from https://halbaronproject.web.illinois.edu/items/show/44.

Merton, R. K. (1967). "Social Structure and Anomie." In *Theories of Deviance*, 4th ed., ed. S. H. Traub and C. B. Little. Itaska, IL: F. E. Peacock.

Merton, R. K. (1938). "Social structure and anomie." *American Sociological Review.* Vol. 3, issue 5: 37–45.

Modica, A. (2009). "Robert R. Taylor Homes, Chicago, Illinois (1959–2005)." *Black Past.* Dec 19. Retrieved from https://www.blackpast.org/african-american-history/robert-taylor-homes-chicago-illinois-1959-2005/.

Morris, F. (2018). "Methamphetamine roils rural towns again across the U.S." *All Things Considered*, New England Public Media, NPR. Oct 25. Retrieved from https://www.npr.org/sections/health-shots/2018/10/25/656192849/methamphetamine-roils-rural-towns-again-across-the-u-s.

Moynihan, D. P. (1998). "Is crime always functional?" In *Taking Sides: Clashing Views on Controversial Issues in Crime and Criminology*, 5th ed., ed. R. C. Monk. New York: McGraw Hill Education.

National Center for Education Statistics (2021). "Students carrying weapons on school property and anywhere and students' access to firearms." *Condition of Education.* U.S. Department of Education Sciences. Retrieved from https://nces.ed.gov/programs/coe/indicator/a13.

National College Athletic Association (NCAA) Research (2020). Estimated probability of competing in college athletes. Apr 8. Retrieved from https://ncaaorg.s3.amazonaws.com/research/pro_beyond/2020RES_ProbabilityBeyondHSFiguresMethod.pdf.

National Low Income Housing Coalition (2019). Public housing history. Oct 17. Retrieved from https://nlihc.org/resource/public-housing-history#:~:text=The%20federal%20public%20housing%20program,result%20of%20powerful%20grassroots%20organizing.

Office of the Attorney General, California (2020). Attorney General Becerra announces takedown of Riverside street gang. Press release, State of California Department of Justice. Jan 17. Retrieved from https://oag.ca.gov/news/press-releases/attorney-general-becerra-announces-takedown-riverside-street-gang.

Ohannessian, C. M., and A. Vannucci (2020). "Social media use and externalizing behaviors in early adolescence." *Youth and Society.* Vol. 53, issue 6: 871–893.

Osgood, D., and J. M. Chambers (2003). Community correlates of rural youth violence. Office of Juvenile Justice and Delinquency Prevention, U.S. Department of Justice. May. Retrieved from https://www.ncjrs.gov/HTML/ojjdp/193591/page1.html#:~:text=Social%20disorganization%20theory%20specifies%20that,strong%20systems%20of%20social%20relationships.

Parker, R. E., E. W. Burgess, and R. D. McKenzie (1967). *The City.* Chicago, IL: University of Chicago Press.

Parolin, Z., S. Collyer, and M. A. Curran (2022). Table 1: January 2022 Monthly Child Poverty Rates by Children's Race and Ethnicity, in "Absence of monthly tax credits lead to 3.7 million more children in poverty in January 2022." *Poverty and Social Policy Brief.* Center on Poverty and Social Policy, Columbia University. Vol. 6, issue 2. Retrieved from https://static1.squarespace.com/static/610831a16c95260dbd68934a/t/620ec869096c78179c7c4d3c/1645135978087/Monthly-poverty-January-CPSP-2022.pdf.

Peters, M. (2017). "A collection of anti-Nazi comic book covers from the 1940s is one of the most relevant books of the year." *Salon*. Aug 17. Retrieved from https://www.salon.com/2017/08/17/a-collection-of-anti-nazi-comic-book-covers-from-the-1940s-is-one-of-the-most-relevant-books-of-the-year/.

Pioneer Valley Transit Authority (PVTA) (2019). Schedule, Holyoke. Retrieved from http://pvta.com/schedules.php.

Rajalakshmi, J., and P. Thanasekaran (2015). "The effects and behaviours of home alone situation by latchkey children." *American Journal of Nursing Science*. Vol. 4, issue 4: 2017–211.

Recovery Village (2021). "Where teens get illicit drugs," ed. C. Renzoni. Oct 20. Retrieved from https://www.therecoveryvillage.com/teen-addiction/drug/how-teens-get-drugs/.

Reinberg, S. (2019). "1 in 18 U.S. teens carries a gun to school: Study." *News*, WebMD.

Rephann, T. J. (2009). "Rental housing and crime: The role of property ownership and management." *The Annals of Regional Science*. Vol. 43, issue 2: 435–451.

Rhew, I. C., J. D. Hawkins, and S. Oesterle (2011). "Drug use and risk among youth in different rural contexts." *Health Place*. Vol. 17, issue 3 (May): 775–783.

Rural Health Information Hub (RHIhub) (2020). "Substance use and misuse in rural areas." Dec. 9. Retrieved from https://www.ruralhealthinfo.org/topics/substance-use.

Shader, M. (2003). Risk factors for delinquency: An overview. Office of Juvenile Justice and Delinquency Prevention (OJJDP), Office of Justice Programs, U.S. Department of Justice. Retrieved from https://www.ojp.gov/pdffiles1/ojjdp/frd030127.pdf.

Sheppard, D., H. Grant, W. Rowe, and N. Jacobs (2000). "Fighting juvenile gun violence." *Juvenile Justice Bulletin*, Office of Juvenile Justice and Delinquency Prevention (OJJDP). Sept. Retrieved from https://www.ojp.gov/pdffiles1/ojjdp/182679.pdf.

Skogan, W. (1990). *Disorder and Decline: Crime and the Spiral Decay in American Cities*. New York, NY: Free Press.

Springhall, J. (1999). *Youth, Popular Culture and Moral Panics: Penny Gaffs to Gangsta-Rap, 1830–1996*. London, UK: MacMillan Press.

Stansfield, R., D. Semenza, and T. Steidley (2021). "Public guns, private violence: The association of city-level firearm availability and intimate partner homicide in the United States." *Preventative Medicine*. Vol. 148 (July): e106599.

Stoloff, J. A. (2004). A brief history of public housing. Jan. Retrieved from https://www.researchgate.net/publication/228789405_A_brief_history_of_public_housing.

Sutherland, E., and D. R. Cressey (1939). *Principles of Criminology*. Reprint 1992. Lanham, MD: AltaMira Press.

Sykes, G. M., and D. Matza (1957). "Techniques of neutralization: A theory of delinquency." *American Sociological Review*. Vol. 22: 664–670.

Thrasher, F. M. (1949). "The comics and delinquency: Cause or scapegoat." *Journal of Educational Sociology*. Vol. 23, issue 4 (Dec.): 195–205.

Tunnell, K. D. (2006). "Socially disorganized rural communities." *Crime, Media, Culture*. Vol. 2, issue 3: 332–337.

U.S. Department of Agriculture (USDA) (2022). Rural poverty and well-being. Mar 7. Retrieved from https://www.ers.usda.gov/topics/rural-economy-population/rural-poverty-well-being/#demographics.

U.S. Department of Agriculture (USDA) (2005). Data available at: http://www.usda.gov.

U.S. Department of Housing and Urban Development (HUD) (n.d.). Public housing: Image versus facts. Office of Policy Development and Research. Retrieved from https://www.huduser.gov/periodicals/ushmc/spring95/spring95.html#:~:text=Public%20housing%20contains%20a%20much,43%20percent%20of%20public%20housing.

Vagins, D. J., and J. McCurdy (2006). *Cracks in the System: Twenty Years of Unjust Federal Crack Cocaine Law.* Washington, D.C.: American Civil Liberties Union (ACLU).

Vedantam, S., C. Benderev, T. Boyle, R. Klahr, M. Penman, and J. Schmidt (2016). "How a theory of crime and policing was born, and went terribly wrong." National Public Radio (NPR). Nov 1. Retrieved from https://www.npr.org/2016/11/01/500104506/broken-windows-policing-and-the-origins-of-stop-and-frisk-and-how-it-went-wrong.

Warr, M. (2002). *Companions in Crime: The Social Aspects of Criminal Conduct.* Cambridge, UK: Cambridge University Press.

Wertham, F. (1948). "The psychopathology of comic books: A symposium." *American Journal of Psychotherapy.* Vol. 2, issue 3 (July): 472–490.

Wilkins, C., J. S. Romeo, M. Rychert, J. Prasad, and T. Graydon-Guy (2018). "Determinants of high availability of methamphetamine, cannabis, LSD and ecstasy in New Zealand: Are drug dealers promoting methamphetamine rather than cannabis?" *International Journal of Drug Policy.* Vol. 61 (Nov.): 15–22.

Wilson, J. Q., and G. L. Kelling (1982). "Broken windows: The police and neighborhood safety." Originally published in *Atlantic Monthly,* Vol. 249, issue 3 (March): 29–38. Retrieved from http://personal.psu.edu/exs44/597b-Comm&Crime/Wilson-Kelling-Broken%20Windows.pdf.

Woldoff, R. A. (2002). "The effects of local stressors on neighborhood attachment." *Social Forces.* Vol. 81, issue 1: 87–116.

Wright, J. D. (1995). "Ten essential observations on guns in America." *Society.* Vol. 32, issue 3: 63–68.

Yamane, D. (2017). "The sociology of U.S. gun culture." *Sociology Compass.* Vol. 11: e12497.

Zuckerman, D. (2022). "Youth violence in rural areas." National Center for Health Research. Retrieved from https://www.center4research.org/youth-violence-rural-areas/.

Chapter **NINE**

Gender Differences and Disparities in Juvenile Offending[1]

> *To me, this world is nothing but evil, and my own evil just happened to come out 'cause of the circumstances of what I was doing.*
>
> —Aileen Wuornos, serial killer, survivor of childhood sexual abuse, prostitute by age 11, discussing trading sexual favors for cigarettes and other treats in elementary school[2]

Chapter Objectives

- Define what we mean by gender and gender differences, including socialization in childhood.
- Focus on how offending by males and by females is similar and how it differs.
- Emphasis on young female offenders as an underrepresented population in research.
- Review how males and females are treated differently (or the same) in the juvenile justice system.
- Identify the risks for the transgender youth population in the juvenile justice system.

---

[1] Though race is not the primary topic of this chapter, we cannot discuss gender without also discussing its intersection with race.

[2] Source: Stockton, 2021, retrieved from https://allthatsinteresting.com/aileen-wuornos#:~:text=The%20Troubled%20Early%20Life%20Of%20Aileen%20Wuornos&text=Aileen%20Wuornos%20found%20prostitution%20early,the%20habit%20on%20her%20own. Wuornos, the subject of the movie *Monster* (Paramount Pictures, 2003), was executed in Florida on October 9, 2002.

Key Terms

Commercialized vice
Dysthymia
Gender
Gender dysphoria
Gender nonconforming
Major Depressive Disorder (MDD)
Major Depressive Episode (MDE)
Statutory rape
Stolen Generation (Australia)
Superpredator
Transgender youth
Waywardness laws

INTRODUCTION

As we note elsewhere in this book, the terms sex and gender are not synonymous. Again, sex is defined by biological markers identified at birth, in the majority of cases, as female or male based on genitalia. Gender in sociology is defined as the role or roles we are expected to play in society, based on our biological sex. We will be discussing characteristics decidedly associated with the female gender and considered "feminine" and characteristics associated with being male or "masculine." To reflect our appreciation and understanding that gender is on a spectrum, we will avoid the classic gender binary of "male" and "female" where possible. However, research on delinquency and crime in general still focuses on this binary, so any statistics as well as research on physiological or psychological differences presented in this chapter will be primarily based on the gender binary used in research, unless otherwise noted, despite all its inaccuracies with regard to today's reality.

Since gender expectations begin at birth in most cases, this means we can expect that children who grow into delinquency will do so differently depending on their sex. There are, of course, outliers who defy gender norms early in their childhood or are raised by parents who believe in gender-neutral child rearing practices. In some cases, particularly in youth gangs, females early on see the advantages that male gang members gain because of their sex and may emulate some of their characteristics, including violence (Hansen, 2005), just as women working in non-traditional positions in business or other male-dominated fields may believe, true or not, that their only way to succeed is by being "tough," countering the expectation that women are the "softer" sex.

Within the last century, what it means to be masculine or feminine has evolved, as social roles in society and within families have begun to blur. Middle-class women began to be freed from stereotypes as homemakers and primary caregivers to children, and increasingly joined the workforce,[3] beginning in the mid-20th century (Goodwin, 2019). This in turn posed a threat to traditional norms for males, where, as Henry L. Minton stated, "[a]s a consequence of this destabilization,

[3] We should note that many working-class women have always worked, often in decidedly feminized professions.

the ideal of manliness shifted from the Victorian veneration of character and emotional restraint to the expression of a 'passionate manhood' through unrestrained primitive instincts (e.g., lust, greed, assertiveness, competitive sports, and militarism)" (Minton, 2000, p. 613). We certainly can see this demonstrated by the rise in the number of mass shootings, including those perpetrated by juvenile males in schools, which are often committed by individuals who feel lost in what it means to be masculine in modernity, which is often exacerbated by mental health issues.

No class of juvenile offenders is more demonized than Black males. As in the adult population, they are overrepresented in the juvenile justice system, along with other minority males and females. Criminologists for the most part believe that what drove increases in juvenile violence, including homicide, in the Black community is the greater availability of firearms and other weapons and poverty, not a new breed of violent teens (Zimring, 2011; Bogert and Hancock, n.d.). The myth of the *superpredator*[4] Black male juvenile has been perpetuated by the media, and in some cases by questionable research data, resulting in generations of Black males being unfairly stigmatized (Bogert and Hancock, n.d.).

With gender roles increasingly blurred, as well as "tough on crime policies" that are often politically motivated, it should come as no surprise that we have seen changes in the rates of offending by juvenile females and males as well as by race, in some cases seeing the gaps closing in arrests. Even so, we still see enough distinct differences between the biological sexes to warrant attention.

EARLY CHILDHOOD DEVELOPMENT, SOCIALIZATION, AND GENDER DIFFERENCES

In our chapter on family characteristics that can contribute to delinquency, we discussed the influence families have on early socialization. In this chapter we shine a spotlight on how both families and society as a whole attempt to socialize children into their expected gender roles from birth. Even hospitals have a habit of placing female babies at birth in pink blankets and male babies in blue, colors that have come to represent the gender binary.[5] Family configuration—single-parent household, two-parent household, guardians, etc.—has a profound effect on how children from early childhood see their roles in life, primarily based on their biological sex. Traditionally "ideal masculinity" has been viewed in boys (and men) as active, adventurous, powerful, and sexually aggressive, while the "ideal

[4] The term *superpredator* was coined by John DiIulio, a political scientist, in a 1995 interview with *The Weekly Standard*, citing that 6% of boys in Philadelphia commit more than half of the serious crimes committed by juvenile males (Bogert and Hancock, n.d.).

[5] This runs counter to the traditional colors of bicycles, where girls had blue bikes and boys had red. It also runs counter to older fashion history: pink was worn by male aristocrats. It wasn't until the 1940s that pink became feminized and blue designated as masculine.

Gender-specific toys, Sears and Roebuck catalog, circa 1950s.

female" is depicted as passive, young, dependent, sexually submissive, and often incompetent and dumb (Goodwin, 2019; Minton 2000). Ironically and tragically, as Minton (2000) points out, these characterizations of girls and women have consequently contributed to their victimization. However, we noted in our introduction that those stereotypes are increasingly being challenged within families, in school, and in the workplace.

Even marketers are moving away from a strict gender binary. Historically, everything from clothing to toys for children was distinctly female or male oriented. Up until very recently when more unisex toys emerged, girls were encouraged to play with toys that were adapted toward heteronormative expectations for marriage, babies, and domesticity, whereas boys were given toys that were masculine and career-oriented, as in the example of toy versions of first-responder uniforms and equipment, or tool boxes intended to imitate those used in manual labor professions or around the house in male-oriented work (e.g., building, repairs).

To a large extent, criminal activities of juveniles were likewise divided between what boys and girls could be expected or allowed to do, based on their sex and gender. Female juvenile offenders are more likely to commit status offenses and nonviolent crimes, as compared to their male counter parts (Mullis, 2004). Even in adult offending, particularly when it comes to gangs and organized crime, it is a "man's world," where females often are victimized or play secondary roles.

For example, male drug dealers are more likely to sell expensive and dangerous drugs in larger quantities, as compared to female drug dealers, who are more likely to sell cheaper, lower level street drugs, like cannabis (where it is still illegal), in smaller quantities, leaving them out of more lucrative illegal drug markets. Even general homicide statistics lean heavily in favor of male offenders. And while both adolescent females and males may be influenced by deviant friends or family, persistent offending by females is more likely to happen because of the influence of a romantic partner (Cauffman and Monahan, 2015).

We cannot discount the difference between the physiology of male and female brains. Universally around the world, researchers find differences between the female and male brains in processing, chemistry, structure, and brain activity (Jantz, 2014). As an example, though we see similarities in girls and boys in genetic risks and neurological abnormalities as they apply to risk for alcoholism, the way by which each transition into the disease is different, based on both psychological and social changes in adolescence, including the increased risk-taking behavior seen in males (Schulte et al., 2009). Again, how much of this is based in different physiology and how much is based in gender expectations is debatable.

It is also important to note that there are differences between girls and boys in both cognitive and social development, which may also help explain a greater risk for offending by juvenile males. Girls generally outperform boys in language development, even if they were preterm at birth and at risk for developmental delays (Tulviste et al., 2020; Cattani et al., 2010; Ment et al., 2003). If we consider that language development provides means for successful conflict resolution, girls may develop these skills to resolve disputes, even if only to verbally abuse victims. In other words, girls are more likely to use their words as weapons; boys are more likely to resort to using their fists. This is additionally supported by the fact that, based both on stereotypes and research to support them, girls and women are more socially expressive and responsive than males, indicating stronger social orientation even in the first year of life (Barbu et al., 2011). At play, girls tend to be more interactive and to play face-to-face with their playmates, while boys are more likely to play side-by-side, even if they are involved in the same play activities, and they tend to talk at each other, rather than to each other.

Whether developmental psychology is taken into consideration when juveniles do end up in the juvenile justice system is a different story. Fortunately, in juvenile court there are often psychological evaluations required for juveniles accused of crimes. However, even though judges do take into consideration a juvenile's age, their ability to control their emotions and behavior, and their lack of maturity, most will only connect any such deviance to juvenile offending, not in the context of normal emotional and psychological development (Berryessa and Reeves, 2020). Few if any of us go through childhood and adolescence without making some questionable choices and decisions, as these are part and parcel of the process of growing into adulthood.

STATISTICS: JUVENILE OFFENDERS BY GENDER

Though over several decades, females have been more represented in the juvenile justice system than in earlier decades, both the number of males and females arrested has declined (Ehrmann et al., 2019).

Ehrmann et al. (2019) note the following changes for female juvenile delinquents:

- Arrests involving girls decreased by more than half (53%) between 2006 and 2015, reaching their lowest point in three decades.
- Delinquency cases and petitioned-status cases involving girls also reached their lowest points since the early 1990s, decreasing 43% and 44%, respectively, from 2006 through 2015.

- After falling 47% since 2006, the number of females in placement in 2015 was at its lowest level since at least 1997.
- Since 2006, the proportion of females remained relatively constant for arrests, delinquency cases, petitioned status cases, and youth in placement.
- Larceny-theft, simple assault, and disorderly conduct accounted for 50% of arrests and 56% of delinquency cases involving girls in 2015.
- Truancy offenses accounted for more than half (55%) of petitioned status offense cases involving females.
- In 2015, delinquency cases involving girls were less likely to be petitioned, adjudicated, or result in out-of-home placement than cases involving boys.

There are contradictory explanations as to why crime is dropping in the juvenile population for both girls and boys. We have alluded to the fact that the birth rate in the United States has been on a steady decline since the 1990s, which would mean fewer juveniles to offend, and that may be one explanation for current downward trends in juvenile offending. However, other explanations may help more to understand the contradictions in juvenile offending data.

One explanation we have not explored as yet are changes in policing over the past decade. Particularly in recent years, with the outpouring of support on both sides of the controversy over defunding police, some departments have struggled to retain or recruit officers. If this is the case, fewer officers means fewer arrests, particularly on minor offenses. However, we have also seen a rise in the number of juvenile females accused of assault over the past few decades. Some of this is a function of violent crimes previously classified as simple assaults committed by juveniles now being classified as aggravated assaults,[6] a more serious charge. Plus, some assault charges are subjective, depending on the perceptions of arresting officers or prosecutors, and often based on the extent of injury to the victim. So as always with statistics, we have to caution that the real numbers, as far as actual offending goes, may be higher and might not be reflected in more recent arrest records. This also helps to explain why we see a rise in some types of juvenile offending in the data, like assaults, while arrests decreased overall.

GENDER DIFFERENCES: JUVENILE OFFENDING

Expectations for gender-specific behavior have never been as evident than in the disparity between girls and boys witnessed in treatment by law enforcement and

[6] When this author was in high school, if females got into physical altercations on campus, no matter how much a fight might escalate, the fight was resolved by sending the offenders to the principal's office to be given after-school detention or suspension. With today's zero tolerance policies in school, the police are more likely to be called in, whether the fight is between boys or girls, which may partially explain why more juvenile females are arrested for assault, leaving the impression that females have somehow become more violent.

the courts when they commit similar offenses. We start our section on gender differences in offending with a brief overview of explanations of why females have been unfairly targeted for noncriminal behavior by the criminal justice system.

Juvenile delinquent females are more likely to receive time in custody for low-level misdemeanor offenses compared to males, as noted in this narrative:

> *. . . [O]ne night when the high school freshman [a female] came home late from prom dress shopping, she decided to shove [her mother] back. Her mother called the police. In a matter of minutes, the 14-year-old went from teenager to juvenile delinquent charged with second-degree assault. . . . The same things she'd done before—not coming home on time, leaving the house without permission—were offenses that landed her back in maximum-security lockup nearly a dozen times over the next two years. . . . [I]f she had been a boy, statistics show it probably would have been different. . . . Once in the system [girls] are often detained longer.* (Green, 2016, retrieved from https://www.baltimoresun.com/news/investigations/bal-juvenile-justice-gender-gap-20161216-story.html)

And as we have noted, there has been extensive research on the causes of male juvenile offending, as compared to research on females. It is unclear as to what extent the risk factors that explain male delinquency can be applied to delinquent females (Zahn et al., 2010). As Sax (2017) cautions, no matter what sex or gender differences there may be based on biology or socialization, each child is unique and complex, but we cannot be blind to the fact that sex and gender are the major ways by which we differentiate individuals, including juvenile delinquents.

What appears to be different in girls, in particular those who frequently run away from home and commit other status offenses, is that they are more likely to be the victims of neglect, sexual, and physical maltreatment (Berlinger and Elliot, 2017; Zahn et al. 2010; Welsh et al., 1995; Feitel et al., 1992; Stiffman, 1989). Ge et al. (1994) also note that girls have more exposure to negative life events, particularly in the home (e.g., stressed parents), making them more sensitive to the effects. As these theorists and others caution, even seemingly minor offending by girls and female adolescents may mask a more serious problem. And while boys make up the majority of juvenile arrests, girls are more likely to be arrested for running away and for prostitution or *commercialized vice* (Sickmund, 2009; Cauffman, 2008; Grisso, 2008). By the 1980s, the typical female juvenile offender was 16 years old, living in a poorer urban area, and likely to be a high school dropout, with a history of sexual and/or physical abuse (Bergsman, 1989), often leaving them with few options beyond running away from home.

Mental Health Similarities and Differences

As with boys, mental health issues in girls is a primary factor in juvenile offending. However, it is important to point out that most juvenile delinquents do not suffer from severe mental illness (Sax, 2017). While the average juvenile offender met the criteria for three psychiatric diagnoses of varying degrees, some girls within the juvenile justice system may have as many as eight (Howie, 2004). How much of this greater number of diagnoses in females can be contributed to societal biases in which mental health issues somehow represent weakness, which contradicts masculine stereotypes, is debatable.

Juvenile females and males follow different paths to abuse of substances such as drugs and alcohol. Some of this is due to biological and social differences, where females have historically been found to begin drinking at a later age with a faster progression to addiction and abuse than males. However, more recent research indicates that the gap is closing between males and females, where the differences in addiction have greatly diminished in recent decades (Oliverio et al., 2020).

In one area of mental health and neurological issues related to substance abuse, we do see a notable difference between males and females. As juvenile males are more likely to play contact sports, they are more susceptible to traumatic brain injuries (TBI). However, traumatic brain injuries are not limited to playing sports; females can also sustain head injuries in childhood or adolescence. There is a distinct difference between males and females in the way they recover from these injuries, particularly in any subsequent substance abuse (Oliverio et al., 2020), as indicated in the diagram. Substance abuse may also lead to sustaining a TBI that would not be classified as a sports injury, since alcohol and/or drug use increases the probability of injury from a motor vehicle accident or a fall from a height (Oliverio et al., 2020; Andelic et al., 2010).

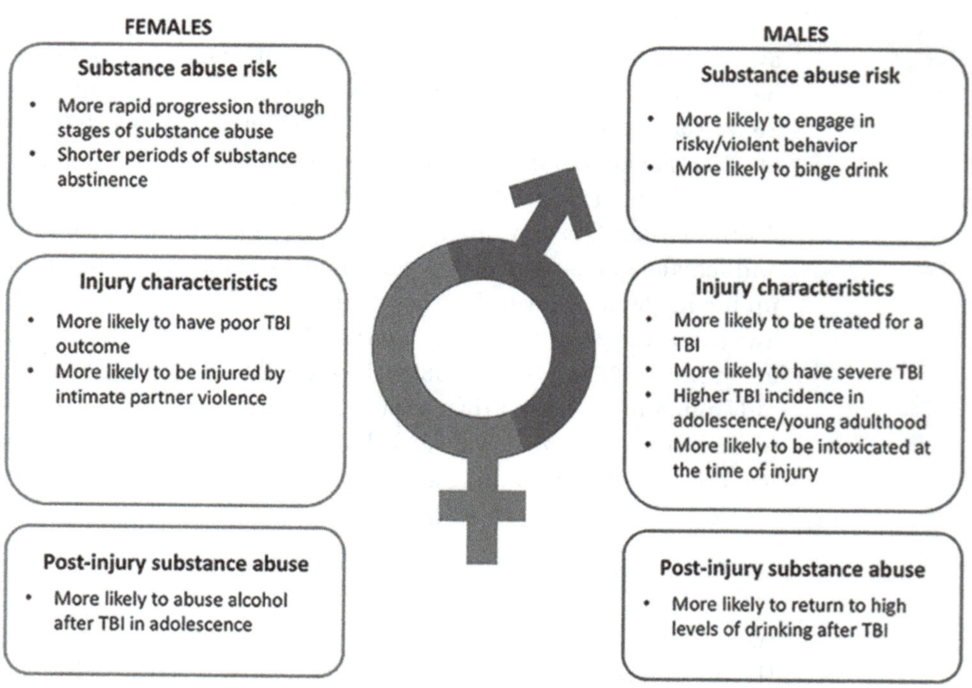

EXHIBIT 9.1 ‖ Sex Differences in Traumatic Brain Injury (TBI) and Substance Abuse

There has also has been an observed increase in female juvenile offenders found to be experiencing *Major Depressive Episodes (MDE)*, along with *Major Depressive Disorder (MDD)* and *dysthymia*, more so than in the male juvenile offender population (Holzer et al., 2017). In other words, girls in the juvenile justice system are more likely to experience persistent and chronic depression. What is important to note is that treatment plans and interventions for female juvenile offenders or potential offenders are often lacking, falling behind the number of programs available for delinquent juvenile males or adult females, even though female juvenile delinquency has been on the rise (Office of Juvenile Justice and Delinquency Prevention, 2018).

Along with depression, we reviewed in Chapter 6 individual risks for offending that may come from other mental health or developmental disorders. An additional condition showing neurological differences in the sexes and risks for offending is in attention deficit hyperactivity disorder (ADHD), where boys are more likely to suffer from flight or fight syndrome, indicative of anxiety disorders, and girls are more likely to have interpersonal relationships fraught with conflict (Cauffman, 2008).

"Wayward" Girls

A number of laws in the United States targeted so called "wayward children" that disproportionately targeted female juveniles. In the 19th century, there was an obsession with controlling noncriminal deviant behavior in juveniles, leading to what we now term as status offenses (Garlock, 1979). Today, we still see female juveniles more likely to be adjudicated for status offenses than males, including running away from home (Mullis, 2004).

Even during the Progressive Era and reformatory age of corrections beginning in the 19th century, incarcerated girls and women were not necessarily treated better than in previously co-ed prisons, nor treated fairly by the juvenile and criminal justice systems. In contemporary criminal justice, except in serious conspiracy offenses, we do not lock up juveniles or adults who might be at risk for offending in advance of actually committing crimes. Under *waywardness laws*, however, girls and women were arrested and punished if they were simply poor or had been disobedient to their parents, one fear being that they may turn to prostitution. Detaining them was hoped to be a way of "reforming" them, even though they hadn't committed any criminal offense (Ryan, 2022). Esther, for example, was referred at age 18 to criminal court and sent to a reformatory home in the early 20th century because her mother complained that she was incorrigible (Spaulding, 1921).

Likewise, girls and women were incarcerated for being gender nonconforming, showing masculine tendencies (e.g., wearing male attire), or lesbianism, in spite of having never committed any crime. The New York State Reformatory for Women was notorious for incarcerating gender nonconforming females. First opened in 1901 in Bedford Hills, it housed females aged 15 to 30 (Ryan, 2022;

Potter, 2004). Juvenile males exhibiting homosexual or transgender tendencies were also targeted by the juvenile justice system, but throughout its history, the juvenile justice system has been used disproportionately to police the sexuality of girls (Myers, 2005).

Sex Offenders

Sex offenders, like murderers, are generally anomalies in juvenile offending. However, when there are juvenile sex offenders, they are treated by the juvenile justice system and psychiatric community as future adult sex offenders, though research contradicts the belief that they will continue offending into adulthood (Ryan, 2016). During adolescence, some will only engage in sexual discussions, and only some will actually engage in sex (Johnson, 2018). Females who are sexually active or are sex offenders run counter to traditional societal expectations of girls and women as passive sex objects. Females as sexual predators is unthinkable to many, more so juvenile female sex offenders.

Though some of the sexual behavior of children and adolescents is considered to be age-appropriate or normal developmentally, some can also be problematic, particularly when it results in the victimization of others. Abnormal sexual behaviors are defined as "behaviors that are developmentally inappropriate, intrusive, or abusive" (Kellogg, 2009, p. 993) and are often linked to victimization, including the perpetrator having been sexually or physically abused themselves (Johnson, 2018; Kellogg, 2009). Unlike other types of juvenile offending, sex offense adjudications are more difficult to leave behind—juvenile sex offenders are more likely to be stigmatized by their conviction, even though in some cases the offense and conviction took place before they had reached puberty (Johnson, 2018).

As much as female juvenile offending is overlooked, girls who are sex offenders are even more widely ignored in research. Their adult counterparts are similarly invisible in research. The reason for this is multifaceted. One, juvenile females are assumed to not commit sex crimes; two, there is the misconception that there are far fewer of them; and three, female sex offenders are viewed as less threatening (Manetsch et al., 2021). However, the victimization data indicates that female and male juveniles reportedly exhibit similar rates of sexual aggression against others (Manetsch et al., 2021; Slotboom et al., 2011). More importantly, the number of female sex offenders is rising (Goodwin, 2019). The lack of attention is attributed to the fact that sexual offenses committed by juvenile and adult females go unnoticed, undetected, or largely ignored by law enforcement (Manetsch et al., 2021; Denov, 2004; Hendriks and Bijleveld, 2004; Vandiver and Kercher, 2004).

Language describing offenders in rape laws is increasingly becoming gender-neutral, at least in some states. This was not always the case. Since the 1970s, more states adopted language that specifies "he or she," as in the example of *statutory rape* laws. We should note that the language in rape laws is still very much nuanced and regional, as in Mississippi, where first-degree forcible rape is defined as "and assault with intent to forcibly ravish any female of previous chaste character" (Miss. Code Ann. §97-3-71, 2018). The danger in this antiquated language is that sexually active female victims of rape, whether they are juveniles or not, will have their credibility called into question. Similarly, in the case of sex crimes in general, it is important to remember that victimization of boys and men is underreported, more so than in the case of female victimization, though that too often also goes unreported.

There are other notable similarities and difference between juvenile male and female sex offenders. Like male offenders, female juveniles are likely to model the type of aggressive behavior that they have witnessed in adults they live with or have close contact with (Mathews et al., 1997). Equally, juvenile male and female sex offenders have the same types of psychological disturbances, with repeated patterns of offending, and with multiple victims (Mathews et al., 1997). However, by far, female juvenile sex offenders have experienced far more pervasive childhood sexual abuse (CSA), childhood trauma, and maltreatment (Plummer and Cossins, 2018; Mathews et al., 1997).

One concern for juvenile sex offenders, whether male or female, is the controversy surrounding the use of a juvenile sex offender registry. At this time, 34 states have some form of juvenile sex offender registry, some of which are private, while others are made public (Interstate Commission for Juveniles, 2021). There are both emotional and rational arguments for having a sex offender registry, including for juvenile offenders. Most would argue that they exist for the safety of the community and as a deterrence. However, others believe that it is punitive, particularly in the case of juvenile offenders. Even the courts disagree as to whether sex offender laws are punitive when applied to juveniles (Klein, 2017). Klein (2017) reports this anecdote, for example:

> *Alexander was seventeen when he was convicted of a sex offense after having sex with his fifteen-year-old girlfriend, who was below Michigan's age of consent of sixteen. Since 2003, Alexander has registered as a sex offender, and his personal information has been readily available on a public internet registry. As a result, he has lost jobs, fallen into poverty, and faced harassment by passersby. His ex-girlfriend's parents even wrote a letter requesting his removal from the registry, but to no avail: Alexander will remain a registered sex offender until 2028.*

Not all sex offenses are comparable in severity, as in the example of underaged juveniles engaging in consensual sex versus the violent crime of rape. But a listing on a sex offender registry, no matter the severity of the crime, is often equally stigmatizing for the offender. Alexander, in our previous example, has had a number of opportunities blocked for him because of his sex offense adjudication and will not be eligible to be taken off the registry until he is 42 years old. By that age, most opportunities to escape poverty have passed people by, including in education and employment, so he may very well be doomed to a lifetime of poverty, perhaps primarily due to his juvenile indiscretion (although we do not know enough about Alexander's life to know what other factors are contributing to his poverty). There is little to no argument that juveniles who are predatory and commit violent sex crimes should be on a registry and receive aggressive psychiatric treatment, if necessary, involuntary commitment to a mental health facility (American Bar Association, 2003).

A secondary concern with juvenile sex offenders, whether they are female or male, is that after they are released from detention they need to fulfil their compulsory education requirements. If they are segregated and placed in a school specifically for sex offenders, they will exclusively attend classes with fellow offenders (Johnson, 2018). Some oppose the creation of special schools for juvenile sex offenders, arguing that the environment will result in the growth of criminal networks, with the possibility of further offending or victimization, even with smaller, better-monitored class sizes (Johnson, 2018).

Violent Female Offenders

We have examined young violent offenders in greater detail in Chapter 5. Here we will primarily address what we know to be differences between young male and female violent offending. We generally think of females, whether juvenile or adult, as being more likely to be victimized compared to males, the reality is that female juveniles can also be involved in violent offending, though not at the same rates as males. In the extreme, they can also be capable of homicide.

Female juveniles get into violent confrontations for a number of reasons. On the surface, it may appear to be over a trivial matter. However, fights break out when attempts to resolve conflicts with conversation or healthy debate fail. The most common reasons girls get into physical fights is jealousy, perceived slight or insult; learned behavior from home, either from parents or siblings; and general antisocial behavior (Ness, 2010). Juvenile males fight to assert dominance. If roughhousing turns into actual assault or an imperative to survive, as in the example of gang violence, males will be more physically aggressive than girls (Sax, 2017).

Much of what we see in female violent offending is associated with gang involvement, covered in Chapter 5. As we have noted elsewhere in this book, juvenile and adult female gang members self-report increasingly turning to violence to settle disputes, including more often carrying firearms than in the past (Hansen, 2005). We saw a steady rise in juvenile female-committed assaults between 1980 and 1998, followed by a slight decrease leading into the 2000s, with a reported 48% decrease in arrests of juvenile females for aggravated assault between 2006 and 2015 (Ehrmann et al., 2019).

However, researchers suspect that the increase in numbers of female violent offending reported between 1980 and 1998 follows from increased numbers of females being arrested due to policy changes, confirmed by comparing Uniform

Crime Report (UCR) statistics with actual rates of victimization found in the National Crime Victims Survey (NCVS) data (Steffensmeier et al., 2006). More alarming, the belief that girls are becoming more aggressive or violent may be due to the fact that more juvenile females are being referred to juvenile court for delinquent or deviant behavior that was largely ignored in the past (Steffensmeier et al., 2005).

We should also caution that much of what we believe about the rates of violent offending, whether committed by juvenile males or females, is influenced by what is reported in the media. As juvenile defendants' identities are protected in the media, except in the most heinous crimes involving homicide, what is reported are high-profile incidents of violence perpetrated by girls (Steffensmeier et al., 2005). An example of media portrayal of girls who commit violent crimes can be seen in news headlines, like in Markowicz's 2015 lead for an article published in the New York Post: "America's girls have a violence problem." This headline paints a picture of all female juveniles being at risk for violent offending, not just in extreme, outlier instances. This is simply not the case.

Another example of how media influences perceptions of girls and female adolescent offending is the 2014 Slender Man[7] case in which two 12-year-old girls, Morgan Geyser and Anissa Weier, stabbed their friend 19 times (Associated Press, 2021), and left her on the side of the road, presumably to die:

> *The girls were in the bathroom stall at the park when they decided to try to knock out Leutner before they killed her. "From what I read on the computer, it is easier to kill people when they are either asleep or unconscious, and it's also easier if you do not look them in the eyes," Weier said. "I kind of . . . banged her head up against the concrete." But the girls lost their nerve. . . . and left the bathroom. Weier said she was the one who suggested taking Leutner into the nearby woods to kill her.* (Yang and Dooley, 2019, retrieved from https://abcnews.go.com/US/investigators-slender-man-case-discuss-chilling-interviews-12/story?id=66320806)

Fortunately, Leutner survived, but this chilling account of her attempted murder by two 12-year-olds, as it was reported in the news, along with other reports of violent female offenders, resulted in the perception that girls are increasingly becoming violent. However, these cases are extremely unusual compared to the more typical forms of violent crimes, primarily simple assaults, that delinquent girls prone to violence commit. It is also important to note that in the Slender Man case, both Geyser and Weier were remanded at sentencing to mental health facilities, after being diagnosed with mental health disorders. Weier received a conditional release in 2021 (Associated Press, 2021).

There is no dispute in whether drug and/or alcohol abuse plays a part in violent offending. More alarming, the increase in prescribing anti-anxiety medications

[7] Slender Man is a fictional character that became viral on the Internet and was allegedly the catalyst for Geyser and Weier's attempted murder of their friend. SEE Biggs, 2014, available at https://techcrunch.com/2014/06/30/the-story-of-slenderman-the-internets-own-monster/

and antidepressants in adolescents has been linked to violent crimes (Hemminki et al., 2016). The concern with these research results is whether this is a circular argument, as a number of juveniles are placed on these types of medications after offending (Hemminki et al., 2016). And violent crimes, including homicide, are more likely to be linked to opioid and other more serious types of drug abuse (Tiihonen et al., 2015).

GAY AND TRANSGENDER OFFENDERS

Up until 1973, the American Psychiatric Association (APA) listed homosexuality as a mental health disorder. It was a milestone for the LGBTQ2S+ community to have the APA finally declare that homosexuality was not a mental illness or sickness. They declared, "We no longer insist on a label of sickness for individuals that insist that they are well and demonstrate no generalized impairment in social effectiveness," supporting civil rights legislation at all levels of government that would assure the same protections to homosexuals that are guaranteed to others (Turner, 2017, retrieved from https://www.hrc.org/news/flashbackfriday-today-in-1973-the-apa-removed-homosexuality-from-list-of-me).

Even with the APA's declaration, 30% of the American population today still believes that homosexuality is deviant and morally wrong and should be treated as a form of delinquency in the juvenile population (Statista Research, 2021). The transgender population is even less understood by the general public. Some of these unfounded beliefs inevitably leak into the criminal justice system, including the juvenile justice system.

Gender dysphoria is a condition in which an individual is born with the biological markers of one sex but identifies with and has a strong desire to live as the gender of the opposite sex. *Transgender males* (individuals born with female biology, but identifying as male) and *transgender females* (individuals born with male biology, but identify as female), represent a population at heightened risk for anxiety and depression. Transgender and *gender-nonconforming* (TGNC) youth are subject to a number of physical and psychosocial challenges that put them at greater risk for attempted or completed suicide (Kimberly et al., 2018). Transgender youth, as well as their adult counterparts, are also a population at greater risk for ridicule and victimization.

There has been much political rhetoric around transgender issues of late, with some states criminalizing gender reassignment therapies for juveniles. Family and immediate community support of transgender youth affects how well they adjust going into adulthood, with or without gender reassignment in adolescence. However, we should caution that in this current political environment, efforts are being made to criminalize any attempts by parental units and/or doctors to assist with gender reassignment, including surgery and hormone therapies, for juveniles. In addition to efforts to prevent gender reassignment, TGNC youth and adults face a number of social barriers associated with transphobia and homophobia (Transformative Justice Law Project of Illinois, n.d.):

- **Barriers to education:** TGNC youth suffer at all levels of education, including being forced to use gendered bathrooms and locker rooms based on biological sex, placing them at risk for harassment and discrimination.
- **Barriers to housing:** TGNC youth and adults are at risk of becoming unhoused due to discrimination. TGNC youth are also often forced to run away from home or foster care.
- **Barriers to employment:** TGNC youth and adults are harassed and discriminated against in the workplace, including in hiring practices.
- **Barriers to medical care:** Most transgender health care is not covered by medical insurance. It is also difficult to find doctors trained in trans-related health care issues.

Any and all of these factors put TGNC juveniles and adults at risk for offending, "with the population over-represented in the criminal legal system due to institutionalized oppression and increased poverty and criminalization" (Transformative Justice Law Project of Illinois, n.d., retrieved from https://www.prisonlegalnews.org/media/publications/Guide%20to%20Criminalization%20of%20Trans%20%26%20Gender%20Non-Conforming%20People%20Transformative%20Justice%20Law%20Proj.%20of%20IL.pdf).

Gay and transgender juveniles continue to be overrepresented in the juvenile justice system. More than 300,000 gay and transgender youth are arrested or detained every year, even though the LGBTQ2S+ youth only represent 5 to 7% of the overall juvenile population (Hunt and Moodie-Mills, 2012).

SUMMARY

Most of the differences that we see between female and male juvenile and adult offending are a function of gender role expectations. As we noted, the definitions of sex and gender should not be confused. Depending on one's biological sex at birth, individuals will be expected to behave in either feminine or masculine ways, a gender binary that is rapidly becoming obsolete with social change. However, the criminal and juvenile justice systems operate primarily on the premise of two sexes, female and male. As with any data, we must always be cautious to look at statistics that point to differences between female and male offenders with some skepticism.

As in other areas of research, juvenile females who commit crimes are largely ignored. However, when they do commit serious violent crimes, the media tends to sensationalize it, and in some cases, to paint a distorted picture of girls becoming more violent. But as much as girls who commit crimes are vilified, there is no other class of youth offenders more stigmatized than Black male juveniles. Members of the urban Black male population have been falsely labeled *superpredators*, causing intergenerational stigma.

Some of the differences we see in female and male juvenile offending is based in biological and social development. For example, girls generally outperform boys in language development, which may explain why females will talk their way out of disputes, rather than turn to physical altercations, which are more likely to happen between males. It is important to note that though judges in juvenile cases will take into consideration the age and maturity of a juvenile in adjudication, they will often look at criminal behavior through a lens specific to juvenile offenders, not necessarily through a developmental stages lens that highlights the fact that that adolescents are known to make questionable choices as part of the process of reaching adulthood.

Arrest rates for both female and male juveniles have steadily decreased in recent decades, with the exception of a rise in arrest rates for females accused of assault. However, for the most part, female juveniles are more likely to be arrested for status offenses, including truancy and running away from home. And females are more likely to receive time in custody for minor juvenile offenses compared to males, even though waywardness laws that targeted females have largely disappeared.

There are some differences as well in mental health issues as they are experienced in males in females, including addiction. Females tend to experiment with drugs and alcohol at a later age than males, but their use of drugs or alcohol become problematic more quickly. We should also note that males and females differ in their experience of recovery from traumatic brain injuries, which in many cases can lead to substance abuse and anger issues, particularly if there are chronic head injuries, as in the example of football players. Females have also become more prone to dysthymia, with girls seen in the juvenile justice system more likely to be diagnosed with chronic depression.

Female juvenile sex offenders are on the most part a rarity, at least based on arrest records. However, as indicated by victims' surveys, girls and boys can be nearly equally sexually aggressive. Both male and female juvenile sex offenders face a lifetime of stigma associated with adjudication for sex crimes. Some form of sex offender registry for juveniles exists in 34 states, a stigma that can result in lost education and job opportunities that haunt the individual for a lifetime. Unfortunately, even though sex registries do indicate the severity of the crime, to the general public they do not ordinarily distinguish between someone adjudicated for statutory rape, even if both parties are juveniles, versus an individual who committed a serious violent sex crime.

As we noted early in the chapter, gender expectations are based on biological sex. We are increasingly becoming aware that the sex and gender link is not the same for everyone. A percentage of the population identifies with the sex opposite what they were born with biologically. Not all gender nonconforming individuals are transgender, however. Gender dysphoria has been detected in children as young as two or three years old, and as part of the LGBTQ+ community, they are at risk for being abused, victimized, and rejected by their families. As a result, juveniles who identify as transgender are not only at risk for a number of mental health issues, including anxiety and depression; they are also at greater risk for committing status and criminal offenses. This is largely due to barriers to education, housing, employment, and medical care, all risks in the general juvenile and adult populations for offending.

IN THE MEDIA

Lost Girls: Racial, Ethnic, and Gender Disparities in the Juvenile Justice System

Studies and statistics time and time again confirm that not only are minority youth more likely to be arrested, as compared to white youth, but they are also more likely than whites to be detained and ultimately incarcerated once arrested, even for the same crimes. The disparity in treatment between minority juvenile offenders and white youth is not simply seen in conventional crimes. Native American and Black youth are more likely to be incarcerated on status offenses (e.g., truancy) or technical violations (e.g., violating curfew while on probation) (Sanders, 2021).

Though Black youth make up approximately 14% of the juvenile population in the United States, Black youth account for 35% of girls arrested and in juvenile facilities; Black males under the age of 18 make up 42% of boys in detention (MST Services, 2021; Sawyer, 2020). Being female and a person of color represents double minority status. In many respects, girls of color technically must navigate three minority statuses, at least in the United States: being female, belonging to a racial or ethnic minority, and being a juvenile. Systemic racism, and to some extent sexism, permeate the criminal justice system, including the juvenile justice system, at every stage—including policing, courts and sentencing, and reentry after incarceration—even more so for minority girls, though as we have indicated, juveniles who are Black males are more likely to be irrationally feared (Sawyer, 2020; Leiber and Fix, 2019). Some states are also quicker to incarcerate minority youth in general, as indicated by Exhibit 9.2.

Green (2016), in her anecdote included earlier in this chapter, notes that the teenage girl who shoved her mother was Black. In Maryland, where the incident took place, Black juvenile females are nearly five times as likely to be referred to the juvenile courts, as compared to white girls—twice the national disparity rates—and to be placed in decrepit, unsafe facilities. In comparison, according to Sentencing Project data (2020), Black and Hispanic or Latina girls nationally are incarcerated at three times the rate of white girls; Native American girls are four times as likely as white girls to be incarcerated. The example in Exhibit 9.3 of the racial and gender gaps in youth arrests and referrals to juvenile court in the Allegheny County, Pennsylvania school systems reveals the glaring disparities.

Black and American Indian Youth Are Disproportionately Incarcerated for Status Offenses, Technical Violations

Youth aged 17 or younger confined in juvenile facilities, per 100,000, by race and offense categories, 2019

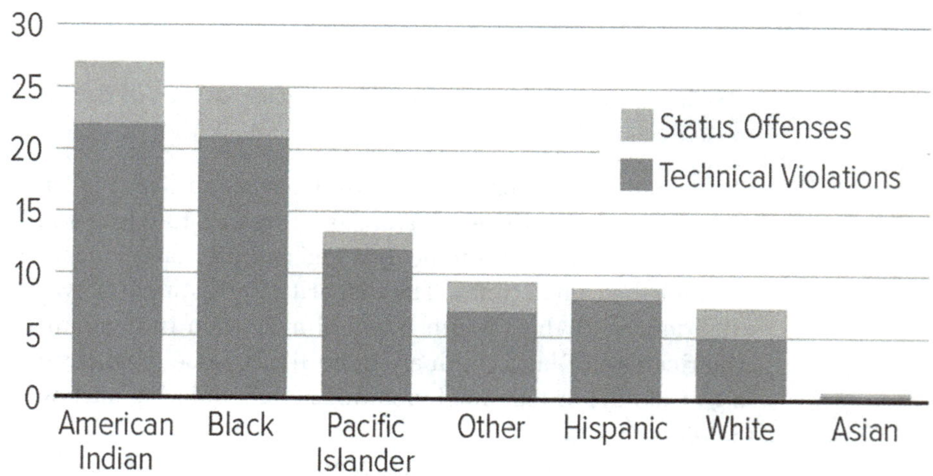

Note: Status offenses are non-delinquent/non-criminal offenses; offenses that are illegal for underage people, but not for adults. They include, but are not limited to curfew violations, running away, and underage drinking. Technical violations are violations of probation, parole, or valid court orders. Examples include failure to participate in a specific program, failure to appear for drug tests or meetings, and failure to pay restitution. "Other" = When collecting the data, OJJDP gave respondents the opportunity to identify race/ethnicity other than the categories listed above and to specify what the "other" race was. The majority of these entries, which account for less than 1 percent of the records, were individuals with multiple race identification. It is not known what proportions of those included in the categories listed above were also of mixed racial/ethnic identity.

Source: Office of Juvenile Justice and Delinquency Prevention (OJJDP)

CENTER ON BUDGET AND POLICY PRIORITIES | CBPP.ORG

EXHIBIT 9.2 ‖ Change in Black/White Juvenile Placement Disparity; 2015 versus 2019

Providing programs and social services to juveniles at risk for delinquency is estimated to save states millions, if not billions, of dollars in the long run, particularly in communities of color and ethnic diversity (Sanders, 2021). In spite of this, just as in the adult offender population, much more funding goes to the back-end of juvenile justice—incarceration—rather than to front-end prevention programs.

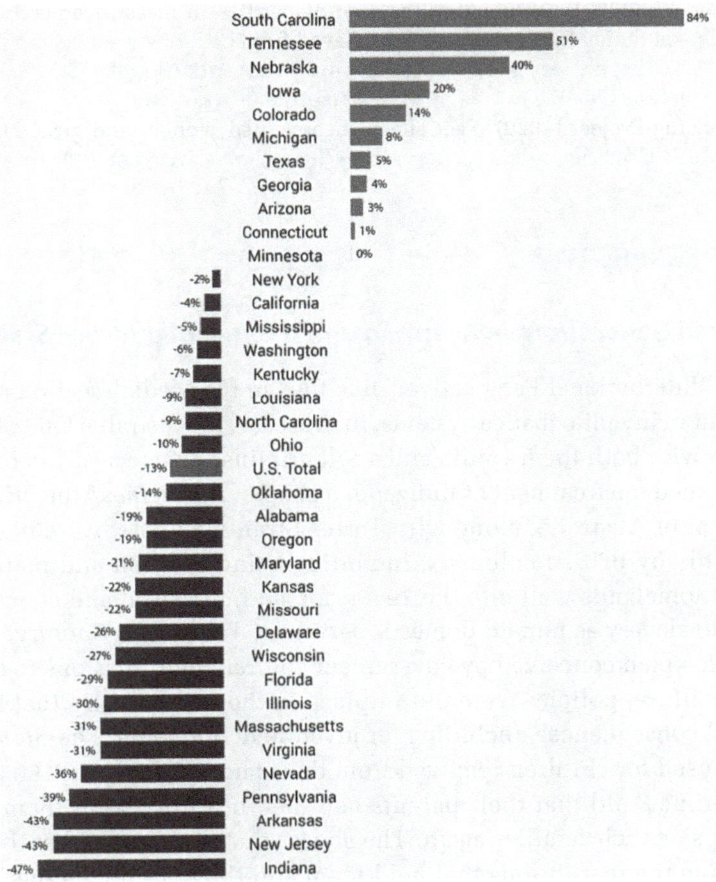

EXHIBIT 9.3 || Changes in Rates of Minority Juvenile Placements, 1997-2018

SOURCES

Green, E. L. (2016). "Lost girls: Young women face harsher punishment in Maryland's juvenile justice system." *Baltimore Sun.* Dec 16. Retrieved from https://www.baltimoresun.com/news/investigations/bal-juvenile-justice-gender-gap-20161216-story.html.

Leiber, M. J., and R. Fix (2019). "Reflections on the impact of race and ethnicity on juvenile court outcomes and efforts to enact change." *American Journal of Criminal Justice.* Vol. 44: 581–608.

Markowicz, K. (2015). "America's girls have a violence problem." *New York Post.* Sep 7. Retrieved from https://nypost.com/2015/09/07/americas-young-girls-have-a-violence-problem/.

Multisystemic Therapy (MST) Services (2021). Racial disparities among juvenile facilities. Apr 28. Retrieved from https://info.mstservices.com/blog/racial-disparities-in-juvenile-facilities#:~:text=The%20Prison%20Policy%20Initiative%20shared,in%20detention%20centers%20are%20Black.

Sanders, C. (2021). "State juvenile justice reforms can boost opportunities, particularly for communities of color." Center on Budget and Policy Priorities. Jul 27. Retrieved from https://www.cbpp.org/sites/default/files/7-27-21sfp.pdf.

Sawyer, W. (2020). "Visualizing the race disparities in mass incarceration." *Briefings*, The Prison Policy Initiative. Jul 27. Retrieved from https://www.prisonpolicy.org/blog/2020/07/27/disparities/?gclid=Cj0KCQjwmuiTBhDoARIsAPiv6L__SQQSqsRghc6LHV5OAG0QbaNttnZh8bvRcGv7t_ta1IhVl9i0LZoaAqMOEALw_wcB.

Sentencing Project (2020). Fact sheet: Incarcerated women and girls. Nov. Retrieved from file:///Users/laurahansen/Downloads/Incarcerated-Women-and-Girls.pdf.

INTERNATIONAL PERSPECTIVES

"Stolen Generation" in Australia and the Juvenile Justice System

This "International Perspective," like the "In the Media" section above, centers on racism in juvenile justice systems, in this case, in Australia. One of the gravest concerns with both the juvenile and adult criminal justice systems in Australia is the continued mistreatment of indigenous people. *Aborigines*,[8] the original native population of Australia, along with Torres Strait islanders, were historically treated horribly by British colonists, including being chained and marched away from their homelands well into the 1960s, forced into prison and concentration camps, or into slavery as unpaid domestic servants (*Welcome to Country*, 2022).

In a plan conceived by government and religious missions to erase the Aboriginal culture, policies were put in place in the 20th century that had far-reaching social consequences, including for juvenile delinquents. The *Stolen Generation*, a term used for children removed from their families between 1905 and 1967, were sometimes told that their parents had died or didn't want them, and they often never saw their families again. The abuses that they suffered at the hands of those running the institutions that held them and the non-indigenous people who fostered them caused trauma that continues to affect subsequent generations today (Korff, 2022).[9] Some of the abuses included being stripped of their indigenous names, called only by a number, and physically punished if they used their native language (Korff, 2022).

As a result of the inferior education that Aboriginal children were given under the child separation policies, they were ill-equipped as adults to help their own children with their school work. Aboriginal children under these policies were expected to become essentially domestic servants or provide manual labor to white families and economic enterprises in Australia. Similar to what we see in the United States after the end of slavery, Aborigines with fewer opportunities for any form of upper mobility out of poverty due to inadequate education and resulting underemployment often turn to juvenile delinquency and adult offending.

---

[8] *Aborigine* is a broad term to describe a member of one of many distinct indigenous groups in Australia, each with unique languages, cultures, and ceremonies (Krishnamoorthi, 2019).

[9] This is similar to the trauma experienced by Native American children who were removed from their families in Canada and the United States and placed in residential schools away from their families and culture.

Stolen Generation children at Kahlin Compound in Darwin, Northern Territory, Australia, 1921.

As in the indigenous populations in Canada and the United States,[10] alcoholism is prevalent in the Aboriginal population of Australia. In a study conducted in the 1970s of Aboriginals and non-Aboriginals in an alcohol withdrawal unit in Australia, though the chronology of drinking patterns were similar, the Aboriginals consumed more alcohol, were less educated, had less vocational achievement, and were often unhoused (Chegwidden and Flaherty, 1977). Nearly 50 years later, Aboriginals remain disproportionately represented among the unhoused and those suffering from alcohol dependency, with equally disproportionate responses from law enforcement and the medical community more often placing them in prisons than treatment centers (Krishnamoorthi, 2019). Hence, poverty is intergenerational among indigenous people in Australia and the Torres Strait, often as a result of the policies put in place over one hundred years ago that still affect them to this day. To put this into perspective, only 1.9% of the college population in Australia, ages 20 to 24, are Aboriginal (Korff, 2020).

As Allam and Murphy-Oates report (2021), over half of the children and adolescents in juvenile custody in Australia are Aboriginal or Torres Strait islanders, and 54% of juveniles in detention between the ages of 10 to 17, including 80% of those aged 10, are Aboriginal. These are grossly disproportionate figures, given that Aboriginal juveniles only make up 6% of the under-18 population in Australia

[10] First Nations in Canada; Native American in the United States.

(Allam and Murphy-Oates, 2021; Ransley and Marchetti, 2018). That means that rates of incarceration of indigenous youth are 22% higher than rates for are non-indigenous youth (Allam and Murphy-Oates, 2021).

Postscript

In the late 1990s, the Australian government attempted to make amends for the injustices that the Aboriginal population faced. Between 1997 and 1999, official apologies were given in all states and territories. It wasn't until 2008, however, that the Australian Parliament, through then-Prime Minister Kevin Rudd, issued a formal apology to the victims of the Stolen Generation policies of the 20th century (Australian Institute of Aboriginal and Torres Strait Islanders Studies, n.d.). However, Australia has a long history of incarcerating indigenous people indefinitely, with restrictions to movement, limitations on their own culture, and language, and forced removal of Aboriginals into missions (Ransley and Marchetti, 2018). Australian Child Protection has been accused of continuing to apply similar so-called protectionist[11] policies, with social workers removing indigenous children from their homes for supposed neglect, with little understanding of the Aboriginal culture (Neubauer, 2014). Just because a child is playing on the streets into the evening hours does not mean they are neglected—Aboriginal children are raised not only by nuclear and extended family members, but by the community as a whole: watchful eyes are everywhere (Neubauer, 2014).

SOURCES

Allam, L., and L. Murphy-Oates (2021). "Australia's anguish: the indigenous kids trapped behind bars." *Guardian*. Jan 17. Retrieved from https://www.theguardian.com/australia-news/2021/jan/18/australias-anguish-the-indigenous-kids-trapped-behind-bars.

Australian Institute of Aboriginal and Torres Strait Islanders Studies (n.d.). "The Stolen Generations." Government of Australia. Retrieved from https://aiatsis.gov.au/explore/stolen-generations.

Berryessa, C. M., and J. Reeves (2020). "The perceptions of juvenile judges regarding adolescent development in evaluating juvenile competency." *Journal of Criminal Law and Criminology*. Vol. 110, issue 3: 551–592.

Chegwidden, M. B., and B. J. Flaherty (1977). "Aboriginal versus non-Aboriginal alcoholics in an alcohol withdrawal unit." *Medical Journal of Australia*. Vol. 1, issue 19: 699–703.

Kellogg, N. D. (2009). *Clinical Report—The Evaluation of Sexual Behaviors in Children*. Itasca, ILL: American Academy of Pediatrics.

Korff, J. (2022). "A Guide to Australia's Stolen Generations." *Creative Spirits*. May 3. Retrieved from https://www.creativespirits.info/aboriginalculture/politics/stolen-generations/a-guide-to-australias-stolen-generations.

Korff, J. (2020). "Aboriginal students in higher studies at University." *Creative Spirits*. May 16. Retrieved from https://www.creativespirits.info/aboriginalculture/education/aboriginal-students-in-higher-studies-at-university.

[11] Protectionist policies were and are intended to subjugate a minority population to a white majority and are considered to be racist, though they are advertised as being "for their own good."

Krishnamoorthi, M. (2019). "The dilemma of disempowerment: How generational trauma impacts alcohol abuse rates in the Australian Aboriginal community." *Humanities and Social Sciences*. Vol. 18 (Spring): 15–20.

Murphy-Oates, L. (2022). "Revisited: How Isaiah survived Australia's juvenile justice system." Produced by E. Leabeater, M. Herbert, and J. Koning; executive production by M. Martignonim, G. Jackson, and L. Murphy-Oates. Podcast, *Guardian*. Jan 3. Retrieved from https://www.theguardian.com/australia-news/audio/2022/jan/04/revisited-how-isaiah-survived-australias-juvenile-justice-system.

Neubauer, I. L. (2014). "Australian child protection accused of repeating sins of 'Stolen Generations.'" *Time Magazine*. Mar 11. Retrieved from https://time.com/19431/australian-child-protection-accused-of-repeating-sins-of-stolen-generations/.

Ransley, J., and E. Marchetti (2018). "Medicalizing the detention of Aboriginal people in the Northern Territory: New/old regime of control?" *Social and Legal Studies*. Vol. 30, issue 1: 104–122.

Welcome to Country (2022). History: Australia's brutal treatment of Aboriginal people. Jan 2. Retrieved from https://www.welcometocountry.org/australias-brutal-treatment-of-aboriginal-people/#:~:text=Neck%20chains%20were%20used%20while,oppression%20continues%20today%20as%20well.

CHAPTER DISCUSSION QUESTIONS

1. Why might female juvenile offenders receive less attention in research?
2. In what ways are girls and boys socialized differently in childhood to prevent juvenile offending?
3. Why is there a continued disconnect between crime reports and the rates of offending by female juvenile delinquents?
4. In what ways did the Waywardness Laws serve to not only punish juvenile delinquency, but to punish deviance as well?
5. Why were girls and women primarily targeted with Waywardness Laws? What equivalent laws might be enforced in the juvenile justice system today?
6. What prevents communities and agencies from spending more time and money on female juvenile offenders?
7. This will take a bit of research. Beyond what we report here, what are some of the more common crimes committed by girls, as they are reported by state and federal agencies?
8. In what ways does the media contribute to misrepresentation of the gender differences between female and male juvenile offending?

GLOSSARY

Aborigines (Australia) Indigenous people of Australia and surrounding islands.

Commercialized vice As defined by the FBI, "the unlawful promotion of or participation in sexual activities for profit, including attempts," including prostitution.

Dysthymia A persistent mental health disorder stemming from depression, where individuals lose interest in daily activities, lack motivation, and chronically experience feelings of hopelessness.

Gender In sociological terms, the roles and identities that individuals are expected to take, based on their biological sex (genitalia). Note: The terms "gender" and "sex" are often confused. Sex refers to the biological markers identified at birth and by secondary sex characteristics that emerge in puberty.

Gender dysphoria The disconnect between the biological sex one is born with and the strong desire to be another gender, which often results in considerable psychological stress. Gender dysphoria can be experienced as early as two or three years of age, more acutely between the ages of four and six

Gender nonconforming Term used to describe individuals who do not conform to traditional roles based on their biological sex. Though many gender nonconforming individuals are transgender, not all nonconforming people are.

Major Depressive Disorder (MDD) A mood disorder where individuals have persistent feelings of sadness and despair, often showing little or no interest in daily life or social relationships.

Major Depressive Episode (MDE) A period of two weeks or longer during which an individual experiences a number of symptoms of depression, including thoughts of suicide.

Statutory rape Any act of sexual intercourse with a juvenile under the age of consent (differs by state; may be 16, 17, or 18 years of age). Charges of statutory rape can be brought, even if sexual intercourse is consensual or both participants are juveniles and only one is under the age of consent.

Stolen Generation (Australia) Period between the 1800s and the 1970s when indigenous Aboriginal children in Australia were forcibly removed from their homes and placed in schools or missions with the goal of erasing their indigenous culture.

Superpredator Term and theory developed by political scientist John J. Dilulio, Jr., proposing that there was an increase in violent, chronic juvenile offenders since the 1980s, that has since been discredited by subsequent research. The term became synonymous with racial biases, as it was used primarily to describe Black male urban youth.

Transgender youth Juveniles to young adults who suffer from gender dysphoria, some of whom seek out gender reassignment therapies. SEE *Gender Dysphoria*

Waywardness laws A series of juvenile justice laws in the mid-1880s through into the early 20th century, based on predominant views on morality and primarily targeting girls and women, that resulted in females being incarcerated for noncriminal offenses, including sexual promiscuity, incorrigibility, disobeying parents or guardians, or gender nonconformity.

REFERENCES AND ADDITIONAL SUGGESTED READINGS

American Bar Association (2003). "Sexually violent predators: Sexual offenders." *Mental and Physical Disability Law Reporter.* Vol. 33, issue 1: 77–88.

Andelic, N., T. Jerstad, S. Sigurddardottir, A. K. Schanke, L. Sandvik, and C. Roe (2010). "Effects of acute substance use and pre-injury substance abuse on traumatic brain injury severity in adults admitted to a trauma centre." *Journal of Trauma Management Outcomes.* Vol. 4: 6.

Associated Press (2021). "Judge orders release of Wisconsin woman in Slender Man case." National Public Radio (NPR). Jul 1. Retrieved from https://www.npr.org/2021/07/01/1012330011/judge-orders-release-of-wisconsin-woman-in-slender-man-case.

Barbu, S., G. Cabanes, and G. Maner-Idrissi (2011). "Boys and girls on the playground: Sex differences in social development are not stable across early childhood." *PLos ONE.* Vol. 6, issue 1: e16407.

Bergsman, I. R. (1989). "The forgotten few: Juvenile female offenders." *Federal Probation.* Vol. 53, issue 1: 73–78.

Berlinger, L., and D. M. Elliot (2017). "Sexual abuse of children." In *The APSAC Handbook on Child Maltreatment,* 4th ed., ed. J. B. Klika and J. R. Conte. Thousand Oaks, CA: Sage Publications.

Bogert, C., and L. Hancock (2020). The media myth that demonized a generation of Black youth. The Marshall Project. Nov. 20. Retrieved from https://www.themarshallproject.org/2020/11/20/superpredator-the-media-myth-that-demonized-a-generation-of-black-youth.

Cattani, A., S. Bonifacio, M. Ferz, J. M. Iverson, E. Zocconi, and M. C. Caselli (2010). "Communicative and linguistic development in preterm children: A longitudinal study from 12 to 24 months." *International Journal of Language and Communication Disorders.* Vol. 45: 162–173.

Cauffman, E. (2008). "Understanding the female offender." *The Future of the Children, Juvenile Justice.* Vol. 18, issue 2 (Fall): 119–142.

Cauffman, E., and K. Monahan (2015). "Pathways to persistence: Female offending from 14–15." *Journal of Developmental and Life-Course Criminology.* Vol. 1, issue 3 (Sept.): 236–268.

Denov, M. S. (2004). "The long-term effects of child sexual abuse by female perpetrators: A qualitative study of male and female victims." *Journal of Interpersonal Violence.* Vol. 19: 1137–1156.

Ehrmann, S., N. Hyland, and C. Puzzanchera (2019). "Girls in the juvenile justice system." *Juvenile Justice Statistics: National Report Series Bulletin.* Office of Juvenile Justice and Delinquency Prevention (OJJDP), Office of Justice Programs, U.S. Department of Justice. Apr. Retrieved from https://ojjdp.ojp.gov/sites/g/files/xyckuh176/files/pubs/251486.pdf.

Feitel, B., N. Margetson, J. Chamas, and C. Lipman (1992). "Psychosocial background and behavioral and emotional disorders of homeless and runaway youth." *Hospital and Community Psychiatry.* Vol. 43: 155–159.

Garlock, P. D. (1979). "Wayward children and the law, 1820–1900: The genesis of the status offense jurisdiction of the juvenile court." *Georgia Law Review.* Vol. 13, issue 2: 341–447.

Ge, X., R. D. Conger, F. O. Lorenz, and R. I. Simons (1994). "Parents' stressful life events and adolescent depressed mood." *Journal of Health and Social Behavior.* Vol. 35: 28–44.

Goodwin, D. (2019). "Anything you can do, I can do shorter: An analysis of lenient sentencing for female sex offenders in the United States." *Gender and Social Justice.* Vol. 25, issue 2 (Winter): 433–460.

Green, E. L. (2016). "Lost girls: Young women face harsher punishment in Maryland's juvenile justice system." *Baltimore Sun.* Dec. 16. Retrieved from https://www.baltimoresun.com/news/investigations/bal-juvenile-justice-gender-gap-20161216-story.html.

Grisso, T. (2008). "Adolescent offenders with mental disorders." *The Future of the Children, Juvenile Justice*. Vol. 18, issue 2 (Fall): 143–164.

Hansen, L. L. (2005). "Girl 'crew' members doing gender, boy 'crew' members doing violence: An ethnographic and network analysis of Maria Hinojosa's New York gangs." *Western Criminology Review*. Vol. 6, issue 1: 134–144.

Hemminki, E., M. Merikukka, M. Gissler, K. Wahlbeck, J. Savolainen, T. Ristikari, and M. Aaltonen (2016). "Antidepressant use and violent crimes among young people: A longitudinal examination of the Finnish 1987 birth cohort." *Journal of Epidemiology and Community Health*. Vol. 71, issue 1: 12–18.

Hendriks, J., and C. C. Bijleveld (2004). "Juvenile sexual delinquents: contrasting child abusers with peer abusers." *Criminal Behavior and Mental Health*. Vol. 14: 238–250.

Holzer, K. J., S. Oh, C. P. Salas-Wright, M. G. Vaughn, and J. Landess (2017). "Gender differences in trends and correlates of major episodes among juvenile offenders in the United States." *Comprehensive Psychiatry*. Vol. 80: 72–80.

Human Rights Campaign (n.d.). Glossary of terms (LGBTQ+). Retrieved from https://www.hrc.org/resources/glossary-of-terms?utm_source=GS&utm_medium=AD&utm_campaign=BPI-HRC-Grant&utm_content=454854043833&utm_term=lgbt%20community&gclid=Cj0KCQjwspKUBhCvARIsAB2IYuvVJQHa1mDmfGypongY3GbTReOH6f7akB6mBCC5e-SIOUO9nhwddbmgaAoOJEALw_wcB.

Human Rights Watch (2013). Raised on the registry: The irreparable harm of placing children on sex offender registries. Retrieved from https://www.hrw.org/sites/default/files/reports/us0513_ForUpload_1.pdf.

Hunt, J., and A. C. Moodie-Mills (2012). The unfair criminalization of gay and transgender youth: An overview of the experiences of LGBT youth in the juvenile justice system. Center for American Progress. Jun 29. Retrieved from https://cdn.americanprogress.org/wp-content/uploads/issues/2012/06/pdf/juvenile_justice.pdf?_ga=2.85069977.1611758930.1652814129-1108310842.1652814128.

Interstate Commission for Juveniles (2021). *Juvenile Sex Offender Matrix*. Dec 3. Retrieved from https://www.juvenilecompact.org/resources/state-sex-offender-matrix.

Jantz, G. L. (2014). "Brain differences between the genders." *Psychology Today*. Feb 27. Retrieved from https://www.psychologytoday.com/us/blog/hope-relationships/201402/brain-differences-between-genders.

Johnson, L. D. (2018). "Juvenile sex offenders: Should they go to school with your children or should we create a pedophile academy." *University of Toledo Law Review*. Vol. 50, issue 39 (Oct.). Retrieved from https://advance-lexis-com.wne.idm.oclc.org/api/document?collection=analytical-materials&id=urn:contentItem:5X45-SCP1-JB2B-S3KW-00000-00&context=1516831.

Kimberly, L. L., K. M. Folkers, P. Friesen, D. Sultan, G. P. Quinn, A. Bateman-House, B. Parent, C. Konnoth, A. Janssen, L. D. Shah, R. Bluebond-Langner, and C. Salas-Humara (2018). "Ethical issues in gender-affirming care for youth." *Pediatrics*. Dec., Vol. 162, issue 6: e20181537.

Klein, S. (2017). "The new unconstitutionality of juvenile sex offender registration: Suspending the presumption of constitutionality for laws that burden juvenile offenders." *Michigan Law Review*. Vol. 115, issue 8: 1365–1391.

Manetsch, M., R. J. Nelson Aguiar, D. Hermann, C. van der Put, T. Grisso, and C. Boonmann (2021). "Mental health problems in girls who committed sexual offenses: Similarities and differences compared to girls with non-sex offenses and boys with sex offenses." *Frontiers in Psychology*. Dec 17. Retrieved from https://www.frontiersin.org/articles/10.3389/fpsyg.2021.721927/full#ref39.

Mathews, R., J. A. Hunter, and J. Vuz (1997). "Juvenile female sexual offender: Clinical characteristics and treatment issues." *Sexual Abuse: A Journal of Research and Treatment*. Vol. 9: 187–199.

Ment, L. R., B. Vohr, W. Allan, K. H. Katz, K. C. Schneider, and M. Westerveld (2003). "Change in cognitive function over time in very low-birth-weight children." *Journal of American Medical Association*. Vol. 286, issue 6: 705–711.

Minton, H. L. (2000). "Psychology and gender at the turn of the century." *American Psychologist*. Vol. 55, issue 6: 613–615.

Mullis, A. (2004). "Female juvenile offending: A review of characteristics and contexts." *Journal of Child and Family Studies*. Vol. 13, issue 2 (June): 205–218.

Myers, T. (2005). "Embodying delinquency: Boys' bodies, sexuality, and juvenile justice history in early-Twentieth-Century Quebec." *Journal of the History of Sexuality*. Vol. 14, issue 4: 383–414.

National Sexual Violence Research Center (2014). An overview of adolescent sexual development. Retrieved from https://www.nsvrc.org/sites/default/files/2014-01/saam_2014_overview-of-adolescent-sexual-development.pdf.

Ness, C. D. (2010). *Why Girls Fight: Female Youth Violence in the Inner City*. New York: New York University Press.

Office of Juvenile Justice and Delinquency Prevention (2018). "Specialized responses to girls in the juvenile justice system." *Literature Review*, Model Programs Guide. June. U.S. Department of Justice. Retrieved from https://www.flcourts.gov/content/download/402743/file/Girls-in-the-Juvenile-Justice-System.pdf.

Oliverio, R., K. Katelina, and Z. M. Weil (2020). "Sex, drugs, and TBI: The role of sex in substance abuse related to traumatic brain injury." *Frontiers in Neurology*. Vol. 11 (Oct. 19). Retrieved from https://www.frontiersin.org/article/10.3389/fneur.2020.546775.

Plummer, M., and A. Cossins (2018). "The cycle of abuse: When victims become offenders." *Trauma, Violence, and Abuse*. Vol. 19, issue 3: 286–304.

Potter, S. (2004). " 'Undesirable relations': Same-sex relationships and the meaning of sexual desire at the Women's Reformatory during the Progressive Age." *Feminist Studies*. Vol. 30, issue 2 (Summer): 394–415.

Ryan, E. P. (2016). "Juvenile sex offenders." *Child and Adolescent Psychiatric Clinics North America*. Vol. 25, issue 1 (Jan.): 81–87.

Ryan, H. (2022). *The Women's House of Detention: A Queer History of a Forgotten Prison*. New York: Bold Type Books.

Sax, L. (2017). *Why Gender Matters: What Parents and Teachers Need to Know About the Emerging Science of Sex Differences*, 2d ed. New York: Harmony Books.

Schulte, M. T., D. Ramo, and S. A. Brown (2009). "Gender difference in factors influencing alcohol use progression among adolescents." *Clinical Psychology Review*. Vol. 29, issue 6 (Aug.): 535–547.

Sickmund, M. (2009). "Highlights: Girls and boys in the juvenile justice system: Are there differences that warrant policy changes in the juvenile justice system?" National Juvenile Justice Network. Retrieved from https://www.njjn.org/uploads/digital-library/Girls_and_boys_in_the_JJ_system_The_Future_of_Children_.pdf.

Slotboom, A. M., J. Hendriks, J. Verbruggen (2011). "Contrasting adolescent female and male sexual aggression: A self-report study of prevalence and predictors of sexual aggression." *Journal of Sexual Aggression*. Vol. 17: 15–33.

Spaulding, E. R. (1921). "Emotional episodes among psychopathic delinquent women." *Journal of Nervous and Mental Disease*. Vol. 54, issue 4 (Oct.): 293–323.

Statista Research (2021). Moral stance towards gay or lesbian relations in the United States 2021. Aug 12. Retrieved from https://www.statista.com/statistics/225968/americans-moral-stance-towards-gay-or-lesbian-relations/.

Steffensmeier, D., J. S. Schwartz, H. Zhong, and J. Ackerman (2005). "An assessment of recent trends in girls' violence using diverse longitudinal sources: Is the gender gap closing?" *Criminology*. Vol. 43, issue 2: 355–406.

Steffensmeier, D., H. Zhong, J. Ackerman, J. Schwartz, and S. Agha (2006). "Gender gap trends for violent crimes, 1980 to 2003: A UCR-NCVS comparison." *Feminist Criminology*. Vol. 1: 72–98.

Stiffman, A. R. (1989). "Physical and sexual abuse in runaway youth." *Child Abuse and Neglect*. Vol. 13: 417–426.

Tiihonen, J., M., M. Lehti, M. Aaltonen, J. Kivoivuori, H. Kautiainen, L. J. Virta, F. Hoti, A. Tanskanen, and P. Korhonen (2015). "Psychotropic drugs and homicide: A prospective cohort study from Finland." *World Psychiatry*. Vol. 14, issue 2: 245–247.

Transformative Justice Law Project of Illinois (n.d.). Quick guide to the criminalization of transgender and gender non-conforming people. Retrieved from https://www.prisonlegalnews.org/media/publications/Guide%20to%20Criminalization%20of%20Trans%20%26%20Gender%20Non-Conforming%20People%20Transformative%20Justice%20Law%20Proj.%20of%20IL.pdf.

Tulviste, T., L. Toome, M. Männamaa, and H. Varendi (2020). "Language skills at corrected age 2; 0 are poorer in extremely and very preterm boys but not girls compared with their full-term peers." *Early Human Development*. Vol. 151: e105164.

Turner, A. (2017). "#FlashbackFriday—On this day in 1973, the APA removed homosexuality from the list of mental illnesses." Human Rights Campaign. Dec 15. Retrieved from https://www.hrc.org/news/flashbackfriday-today-in-1973-the-apa-removed-homosexuality-from-list-of-me.

Vandiver, D. M., and G. Kercher (2004). "Offender and victim characteristics of registered female sexual offenders in Texas: A proposed typology of female sexual offenders." *Sexual Abuse*. Vol. 16: 121–137.

Welsh, L. A., F. X. Archambault, M. D. Janus, and S. W. Brown (1995). *Running for Their Lives: Physical and Sexual Abuse of Runaway Adolescents*. New York: Garland.

Yang, A., and S. Dooley (2019). "Investigators in 'Slender Man' case discuss chilling interviews with 12-year-old attempted murderers." ABC News. Oct 23. Retrieved from https://abcnews.go.com/US/investigators-slender-man-case-discuss-chilling-interviews-12/story?id=66320806.

Zahn, M. A., R. Agnew, D. Fishbein, S. Miller, D. Winn, G. Dakoff, C. Kruttschnitt, P. Giordano, D. C. Gottfredson, A. A. Payne, B. C. Feld, and M. Chesney-Lind (2010). "Causes and correlates of girls' delinquency." In *Girls Study Group: Understanding and Responding to Girls' Delinquency*. Office of Juvenile Justice and Delinquency Prevention (OJJDP), Office of Justice Programs, U.S. Department of Justice. Apr. Retrieved from https://www.ojp.gov/pdffiles1/ojjdp/226358.pdf.

Zaliznyak, M., C. Bresee, and M. M. Garcia (2020). "Age at first experience of gender dysphoria among transgender adults: Seeking gender-affirming surgery." *Journal of the American Medical Association Network Open*. Vol. 3, issue 3 (March): e201236.

Zimring, F. E. (2011). *The City That Became Safe: New York's Lessons for Urban Crime and Its Control*. Oxford, UK: Oxford University Press.

Chapter **TEN**

Juvenile Delinquency in Schools[1]

There is only one way to eat an elephant: one bite at a time.

—Desmond Tutu, South African Anglican cleric and anti-apartheid activist

Chapter Objectives

- Emphasize the partnership(s) between parents, schools, and law enforcement in the prevention of juvenile delinquency: the "three-legged stool."
- Review the ways in which schools either contribute to or prevent juvenile delinquency.
- Introduce the means by which schools punish or remove deviant or delinquent students.
- Review of some evidence-based programs in schools that target juvenile delinquency.

Key Terms

Alternative school
Corporal punishment (in schools)
Detention
Expulsion
Peer groups
School resource officers (SROs)
School-to-prison pipeline
Suspension
Tracking
VARK model of learning styles

[1] An earlier version of this chapter was published as Chapter 1,"Baby Steps: Urban Violence, Gangs, and School Safety," in *Global Perspectives on Youth Behavior, Violence, and Weapons Use*, edited by S. Harding and M. Palasinki (UK: IGI Global, 2016).

INTRODUCTION

Whether trying to save one child or many, preventing juvenile delinquency can seem to be a problem so complex and overwhelming that it is impossible to resolve. This chapter discusses one approach: the three-legged stool—the partnership between parents/guardians, schools, and law enforcement. Taking incremental measures can sometimes be the best strategy, but unfortunately, as we will see, the three-legged stool is sometimes wobbly.

Parents or guardians who can afford to do so generally make every effort to move to neighborhoods with well-performing schools. There is a reason why realtors will emphasize the quality of schools in "better" neighborhoods. When it comes to home purchases, it can be one of the deciding factors about the neighborhood in which people prefer to buy a home. This choice is not available to families living in poverty, however, and even less so when a family is transient or unhoused.

Whether teaching in an inner-city school district, suburban school, or rural community, few newly minted teachers, fresh credentials in hand, are equipped for the realities of juvenile delinquency, much less the presence of gangs. Except in sociology, social justice, social work, or criminal justice courses, little attention is given to the challenges of teaching students whose daily reality includes negotiating gang territories, violence, family disruption at home, and poverty, although sometimes a student teacher will have been placed in a struggling school before graduating from a teaching program.

When schools fail to recognize the risks for delinquency, it results in a number of negative outcomes. Parents or guardians may be unaware of the risks, ignore them, or provide risks themselves, as in the example of addicted parents. Some children are born into gang life because an older sibling is involved or parental units are active members, as in the example of the Almighty Latin King and Queen Nation (ALKQN).[2] There is also the risk of incorrectly labeling a poor performing student as having the potential for being deviant or delinquent.

Beyond bullying, youth gangs, including those in schools, have gained attention from media and academic researchers (Esbensen et al., 2013). Since the 1990s, in California alone, billions of dollars have been spent on gang suppression on the streets and in schools (e.g., Governor's CalGRIP program in 2007) (Ramadas, 2008). However, few programs have proven to be successful, in spite of the vast amounts of financial resources that have been thrown at the problem. And as we note throughout this book, part of the problem is the failure to initiate evidence-based programs.

As we also highlight in this book, for those in the trenches of applied social science, preventing juveniles from delinquency or from joining gangs is the

[2] ALKQN is a family-oriented street gang, with most, if not all, family members becoming affiliated.

Achilles' heel of violence prevention policy in and out of schools. Even with the best intentions, families living in gang-infested communities are challenged to find solutions to limit their child's exposure to violence in their neighborhood and in the public schools themselves.

Key to finding solutions lies in the joint efforts of parents, schools, and law enforcement, many times a teetering three-legged stool with little stability if these three entities do not effectively, formally collaborate to bring about changes in communities. This chapter explores the macro (community-level) and micro (family-level) variables that contribute to the risk for delinquency that spill over into schools. Recommendations in this chapter include taking "baby steps" to educate parents, teachers, and administrators on the risks of delinquency, violence, and gang recruitment in schools, as well as looking at evidence-based programs to address it.

This chapter deviates from the format of other chapters by not including an "International Perspectives" section. This will allow us to spend more time examining some solutions being implemented in schools and communities in the United States. Since juvenile crimes, including serious violent felonies in American schools, continue to be an impediment to the education of large numbers of students, this chapter will keep its focus there.

This chapter introduces as a case study the valiant grassroots efforts of one community to combat gang violence and recruitment, particularly among school-age juveniles. Since 2011, the Holyoke Safe Neighborhood Initiative (formerly SHSNI) in western Massachusetts, has taken a "weed and seed" approach, adopted from the Massachusetts State Police C3 model, outlined later in the chapter. Through a grassroots campaign, HSNI has worked with the community, including Morgan Elementary School, located in a neighborhood that has historically been gang-plagued, to provide after-school and family programs that offer positive alternatives to gang life. The nearly all-volunteer organization does so in hopes of establishing a collaboration between parents, schools, and law enforcement, as well as social service agencies in the community.

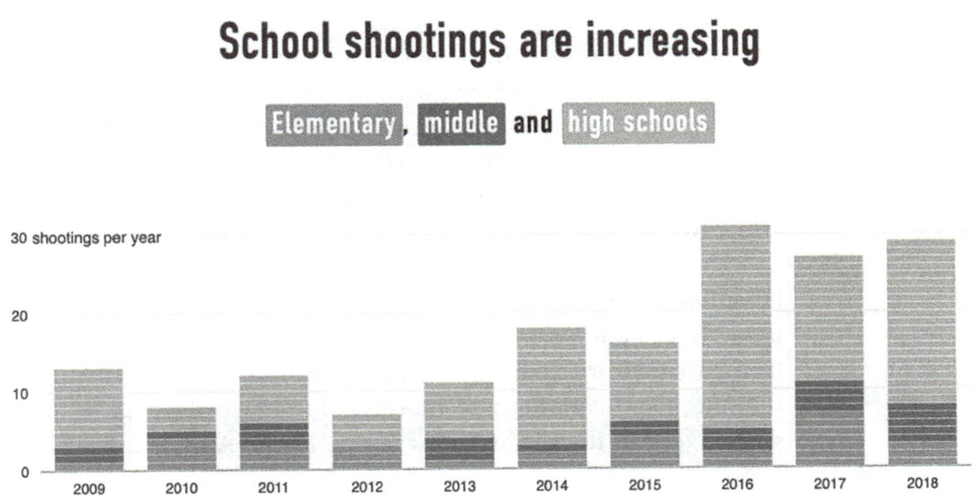

EXHIBIT 10.1 || School Shootings, 2009–2018

EARLY WARNING SIGNS

It is a misconception that delinquency begins in the rebellious teen years. As the U.S. Justice Department notes (n.d.), three types of delinquents are generally seen in schools, including elementary schools:

1) Children who have early onset of severe antisocial behavior
2) Children displaying sporadic or infrequent delinquency that coincides with the beginning of adolescence
3) Chronic juvenile offenders

The first and third types of delinquents can be diagnosed as early as the preschool years. Yet preschool and elementary school teachers are less likely to be trained in recognizing the early signs of serious delinquency and may simply and mistakenly label the child "difficult" or a "slow learner." Though it's true that we are less likely to see serious delinquency before middle school, we do have to consider that the poverty that puts children at risk for delinquency and dropping out in the future has effects as early as elementary school (ages 5 through 12) (O'Donnell et al., 1995).

The most obvious signs of potential delinquency for parental units, family members, and teachers to look for are using drugs or alcohol and having deviant, delinquent children as friends. Other obvious signs to look for, according to the American Psychological Association (2013), include:

- History of violent, aggressive behavior
- Frequent conflicts with authority
- History of cruelty to animals
- Lack of empathy for others
- Diagnosed with a serious mental illness

Less obvious warning signs include having been a victim of bullying both in and out of school, which we will discuss in more detail later in this chapter, and minor acts of vandalism or property damage (American Psychological Association, 2013). Even in the school setting, warning signs often may be passed off as "kids being kids," particularly for boys, when in actuality more serious problems are brewing.

There are a number of reasons for delinquency and violence in schools. Most juveniles are still learning self-control, even into the early adult years when, as we noted in Chapters 1 and 6, the frontal cortex finishes developing. Researchers are trying to answer the question of why juveniles might cross the line from simply thinking about harming someone else to following through with punching, kicking, stabbing, or in the extreme case, firing a gun (American Psychology Association,

2013). Some of the reasons that juveniles (and adults) give for acting on impulse or premeditation include (American Psychological Association, 2013):

1) **Expression:** Using violence to resolve or express feelings of anger.
2) **Manipulation:** Using violence as a way to control others.
3) **Retaliation:** Using violence against those who hurt them.
4) **Violence as a learned behavior:** Justifying the use of violence as "normal" and the way they have learned how to resolve conflict.

Any form of delinquency can have long-term effects on school behavior and performance. Some of the consequences include

- Poor school performance
- Low attachment to school and little school involvement
- Poor relationships with teachers
- Low educational and occupational goals
- Risk for school dropout
- School misbehavior

THE THREE-LEGGED STOOL

If you have ever seen a three-legged stool, it is not too difficult to imagine what would happen if suddenly an unwitting sitter had one or more of the legs collapse from under them. Without the support, they would tumble to the ground, in some cases resulting in serious injury. Similarly, there are three main stakeholders whose partnership is needed to keep juveniles out of trouble: parental units, schools, and law enforcement. If we think of the child or adolescent as the person sitting on the stool, we can see that they depend on the three stakeholders to keep them from failure. The disinterest or removal of one of the three partners can lead to the juvenile becoming another juvenile justice statistic—a child who fell through the cracks.

The challenge is that parental units, schools, and law enforcement often live in silos and infrequently come in contact with one another, unless there is a problem. By then it may be too late.

DELINQUENCY IN ELEMENTARY SCHOOLS

Early research on delinquency indicated that children who come from less affluent families face more difficulties in adjusting to early socialization in school.

We noted in Chapter 1 the importance of social class in preventing delinquency. In Cohen's theory of working-class families and status frustration (1955), he argued that parents from lower socioeconomic classes do not have the resources to prepare their children for the rigors of a middle-class school. By today's standards, this includes the ability, to send their children to preschool. Daycare can be equally beneficial, but not all daycare settings offer opportunities for enrichment, and many offer only babysitting services.

Preschool, elementary school, and high school curricula and structure are all premised on some common expectations of students:

- They should be quiet in class.
- They should conform to classroom norms.
- They should adapt well to routine.
- They should demonstrate obedience to teachers and staff.
- They should possess good social manners.
- They should focus their learning more on cognitive activities than on physical ones.

These can be tough expectations to meet, particularly in preschool and K–3 classes, based on findings about the developmental stages children go through when they are trying to establish autonomy while conforming to everyone's expectations (e.g., "the terrible twos"). If we also consider that students have different learning styles, something those of us in education are much more aware of in recent decades, it is difficult to create a cookie-cutter, one-size-fits-all model of education. Different learning styles are described in Exhibit 10.2.

A more recent version of learning style typology includes the reading/writing learning style—a more traditional approach, seen in the *VARK* model (Prithishkumar and Michael, 2014). It continues to be the case, especially in public schools, that alternative learning styles, when not recognized by teachers or parents/guardians, may lead to labeling students as "delinquent" or "problem children," when in reality they are simply exhibiting learning disorders or working within individual learning styles. Of course, we have to appreciate the challenge of teaching 30 or more students in a classroom if one cannot use a uniform teaching style that targets the majority rather than individual students' needs.

Learning and teaching styles aside, we need to also consider the fact that children who are in poor-quality elementary schools will be disadvantaged when they enter middle and high school, as they will not receive the same basic foundations for school success as students in better-funded schools. Unfortunately, most juvenile delinquency prevention programs offered in elementary schools primarily focus on substance abuse and do not address all the other issues younger students face, including poverty.

Blame for students doing poorly in school cannot only be placed on parents/guardians or their lower socio-economic status. Classroom mismanagement, inept teachers or severe punishment in schools, conflict between teachers and students, and

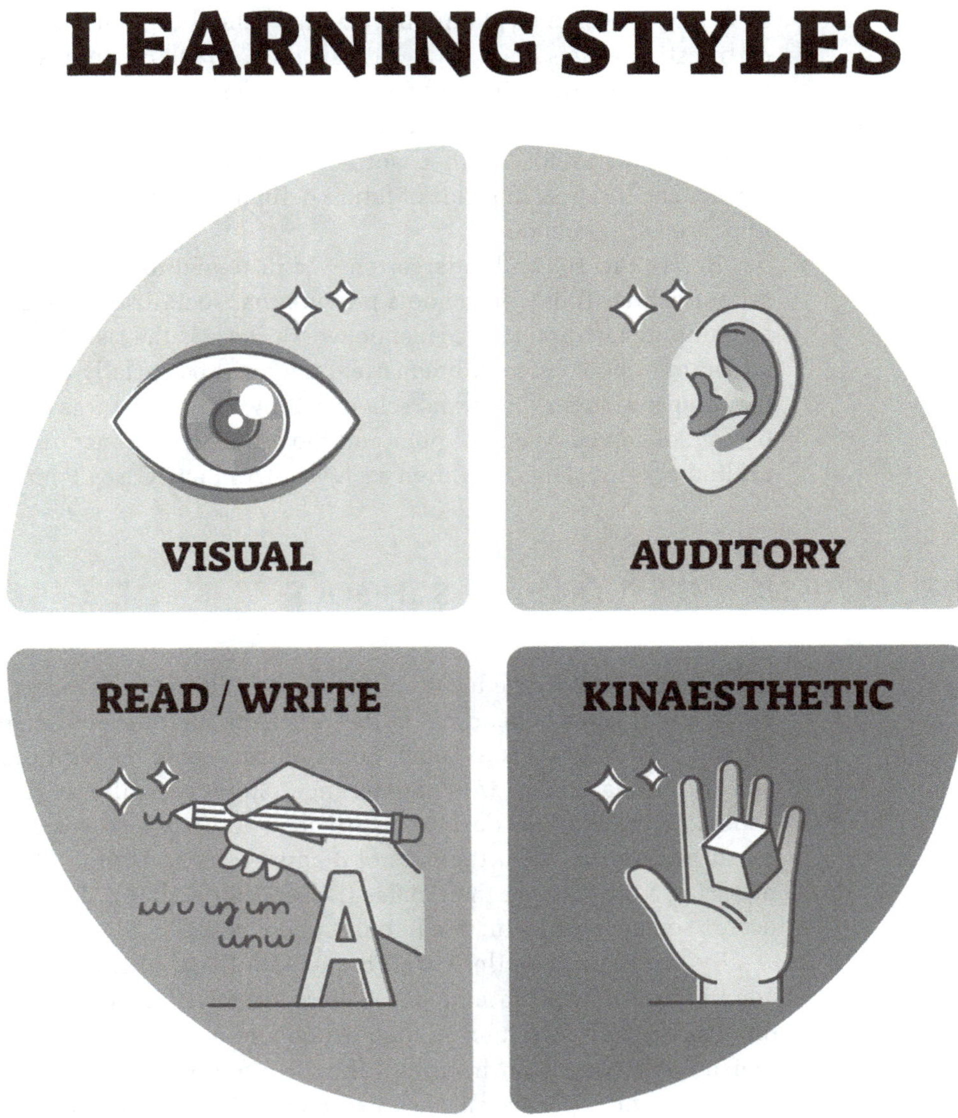

EXHIBIT 10.2 ‖ Learning Styles

poor teacher preparation all contribute to delinquency and particularly increase student aggression (Sanders et al., 2020; Atkins et al., 2017; Weyns et al., 2017; Bradshaw et al., 2009).

Given the teacher shortages that developed during the COVID-19 pandemic, there are concerns that when seasoned professionals leave teaching, those who replace them will be less well-equipped to handle delinquent behavior in the classroom. This holds true for substitute teachers as well. As an example, in New Mexico, the minimum age for a substitute teacher in K–8 classrooms is 18;

substitute teachers need only have a high school diploma or GED[3] and pass state certification exams (Teachingcertificate.com, 2022). Earlier research indicates that the atmosphere in an individual classroom has a more important effect on delinquency and aggression than do general school conditions (Sanders et al., 2020; Kellam et al., 1998). In other words, a bad or poorly trained elementary school teacher can increase the odds of future delinquency in their students, even more so in poor-quality schools.

Before the 1970s, kindergarten was designed to socialize the child to good school habits. Today preschools provide that socialization, leaving kindergarten for jumping feet-first into academic work. There is the risk that if a child does not attend preschool before kindergarten, they will be socially behind those who had that preparation for the formal school setting. Head Start was designed to close the preschool gap between the poor and the affluent; however, it reaches less than a million preschool-aged children each year (Annie E. Casey Foundation, 2021).

DELINQUENCY IN SECONDARY SCHOOLS

It is often said among educators that the middle-school years, generally seventh and eighth grades depending on the configuration of school district, are some of the most difficult ones to teach. Some of this has to do with the peculiarities of children transitioning into adolescence. Stereotypically, it also has to do with behaviors in juveniles during the preteen and early teen years, who, on average, reach puberty between the ages of 8 and 14 in the United States, with females maturing a bit younger than males (Duke Health, 2020). Thus, puberty generally occurs somewhere during the middle-school years.

By the time juveniles reach high-school age, unless they have effectively adapted to the expectations of teachers, they will be at risk for failure. This is one reason why freshmen in high school are at risk for poor grades and absenteeism. The transition from childhood to adolescence is fraught with social, hormonal, and cognitive changes, exacerbated by the transition from middle school to high school, and represents a period when juveniles are at greater risk for delinquency (Thoyibah et al., 2017).

More importantly, the freshman year in high school is described as the "make it or break it year," as the future of the student's grade point average (GPA) can rest on how well they do in their first year (Consortium on School Research, 2007). It is not unusual for students to fail a course in this year, sometimes at alarming rates, as in Chicago, where more than half of freshmen fail one course and about 40% miss more than a month of school because of skipping class (Consortium on School Research, 2007).

[3] The GED is the equivalent to a traditional high school diploma, most often pursued when a student has dropped out of school.

Though drug and alcohol experimentation can begin before high school, substance abuse can start in earnest during adolescence. Other mental disorders may only emerge after puberty, even though the warning signs may have been there from the beginning. For instance, bipolar disorders generally do not fully emerge until around the age of 25, but symptoms can begin to emerge in the teen years (National Alliance on Mental Illness, n.d.). The extreme mood swings of bipolar disorders can be mistakenly diagnosed as nothing more than hormonal changes. Any of these conditions and others, if gone undiagnosed and with no intervention, can result in poor school performance and/or a slippery slope toward delinquency during adolescence.

Peer Groups

We cannot underestimate the importance and influences of *peer groups* during the secondary school years. Delinquent and deviant decision making can be a result of, as Edwin Sutherland predicted, differential association, where criminal behavior is learned from one's peers. Adolescents on occasion will misbehave; in fact, it would be pretty abnormal for an adolescent not to step out of line from time to time while seeking autonomy. If juveniles hang out with others who are habitually deviant or delinquent, however, in all likelihood they will display the same behavior (e.g., smoking, drinking, truancy). Labeling Theory, discussed earlier in this textbook, suggests that hanging around with delinquent peers in high school results in an adolescent being labeled by nondelinquent students, as well as teachers, as being "troubled."

SCHOOL PERFORMANCE AND DELINQUENCY

Student Tracking

From a very early age, the educational system, including teachers and administrators, begins to track students. *Tracking* happens in earnest by middle school and high school, where students are sorted into groups on the basis of perceived abilities, IQ, or achievement levels (National Association of Secondary School Principals, 2006). This means that students will be given different and sometimes unequal curricula. For example, students who do not appear to show the potential for college may not be placed in the high-school classes they need, such as the sciences and foreign languages, that are prerequisites to four-year college admissions. Tracking is used not only in the United States, but also in other countries around the world. For example, in Germany tracking begins as early as fourth grade (Strello et al., 2021). Thankfully, in the United States, the truly motivated have a legitimate backdoor route to a four-year education by starting at community college, where the requirements for admission are not so strictly dictated as at most universities.

The challenge comes with late bloomers, whose intellectual awakening or motivation to do well in school comes later in life. Juveniles who have slow starts in school may be labeled deficient or lazy by teachers early on, making it more difficult to convince subsequent teachers of their potential.[4] Considering the examples of Bill Gates, founder of Microsoft, who dropped out of college, or Arnold Schwarzenegger, who dropped out of high school, but eventually earned his bachelor's degree and became governor of California (2003–2007), it is clear that not everyone who becomes successful completes a formal education[5] or completes it on the traditional timeline set by society. Unfortunately, Gates and Schwarzenegger are outliers in a culture that values formal credentials, as first described by Randall Collins in the 1970s (Collins, 1979).

It is understandable that schools would want to organize classes around students' abilities. However, the problem comes with education inequality, which causes biases, primarily against poor and minority students (Strello et al., 2021; Slavin, 1990). For example, because the extracurricular activities that help keep students engaged in school often require parents or guardians to pay fees for participation (including rental of school band instruments, cheerleading and sports uniforms, travel, and so on), poor students, regardless of race, will be disadvantaged.

Truancy

Truancy, or student absenteeism, whether it includes skipping classes or showing up late to school, has an economic impact on schools. There is a reason why school attendance is taken every day. States budget for schools on the basis of attendance. Secondary to the financial considerations, chronic truancy often contributes to dropout rates, subsequent defunding of schools, and, for good reason, poor school performance. It is crucial in courses that are cumulative, like those in STEM disciplines or foreign languages, that a student attend regularly, or they quickly fall behind.

Unfortunately, remote learning during the COVID-19 pandemic led to increased absenteeism. This was greater in poverty-stricken schools, where computers and Internet service were less available (Malkus, 2020). Early in the pandemic, the Pennsylvania School Districts identified the keys to keeping students engaged, even in the unusual circumstances of hybrid or online courses: increased communication with parents or guardians, and using data to identify and overcome barriers to virtual school attendance (Comley et al., 2020).

---

[4] As you may have found to be the case in your own education, teachers and professors working at the same school often talk to each other about their students' performance, which can result in a halo effect, for good or bad, when you advance from one grade to the next.

[5] This author's father dropped out of high school and managed to go on to become a successful mechanical engineer with patents to his name and award-winning designs. But not possessing a high school degree, much less a college degree in engineering, made the road to career success difficult for him, particularly from the 1960s onward, when college degrees became more commonplace.

Truancy, when it comes to the attention of juvenile authorities, is a *status offense*, as we noted in Chapter 1.[6] The only crime is that the juvenile is not attending school regularly, though it can be considered a serious offense with serious consequences. Though parents or guardians can and will be held accountable for their child's school attendance, parents working outside the home may not physically take the child to school, making it difficult to ensure they get there. Even when they do drop them off at school, they cannot ensure they stay there, in the case of open campuses.[7] Of course, it is much more difficult to sneak off campus today as compared to decades past, largely due to added security on the heels of the school shootings that have become more prevalent in recent decades.

BULLYING IN SCHOOLS

We have already covered *bullying* extensively in Chapter 3 on current youth crime trends. Our focus in this section is on bullying specifically in schools. Up until recently, bullying was largely ignored in schools and rarely disciplined beyond a trip to the principal's office or to school counseling. However, in the cyberage, children and juveniles who are being bullied at school are also likely to be bullied online, meaning that they receive little to no reprieve from their tormentors. Today bullying is considered to be a serious issue in schools, with over 10% of students globally reporting some form of bullying (e.g., physical, verbal, social, or cyber) at least two or three times a month (Li et al., 2020). Verbal bullying continues to be the most prevalent form of abuse seen in schools (Olweus, 2012).

For more seasoned veteran teachers, school policies may not include strategies to address the issues that can arise in the classroom that are a direct effect of the exposure their students have to violence. Bullying has gained greater attention in recent years, and addressing bullying behavior should include becoming more aware of intimidation in schools, including attempts at gang recruitment. In fact, for some individuals, joining gangs in or out of schools is believed to be a means of gaining protection from bullying (Forber-Pratt et al., 2014).

As indicted in the data (and in Exhibit 10.3), bullying is on the rise, including cyberbullying. As the graph depicts, it appears that there are more victims than bullies, meaning that the tormentors are targeting more than one person at a time.[8]

[6] We are revisiting the definitions of truancy, status offenses, and bullying in this chapter as a refresher to key vocabulary terms.

[7] Open campuses, very popular beginning in the 1970s, allowed older high school students to go off campus for lunch. However, this led to afternoon truancy. Since a rash of school shootings, including Columbine High School in Colorado, the majority of U.S. high school campuses, as well as elementary and middle schools, are now closed campuses.

[8] This author was regularly threatened with physical violence by a fellow middle-schooler, making for a very lonely (and scary time) in junior high school. I found out several years later (thanks to the magic of Facebook) that she was targeting a number of other students at the same time that she was victimizing me.

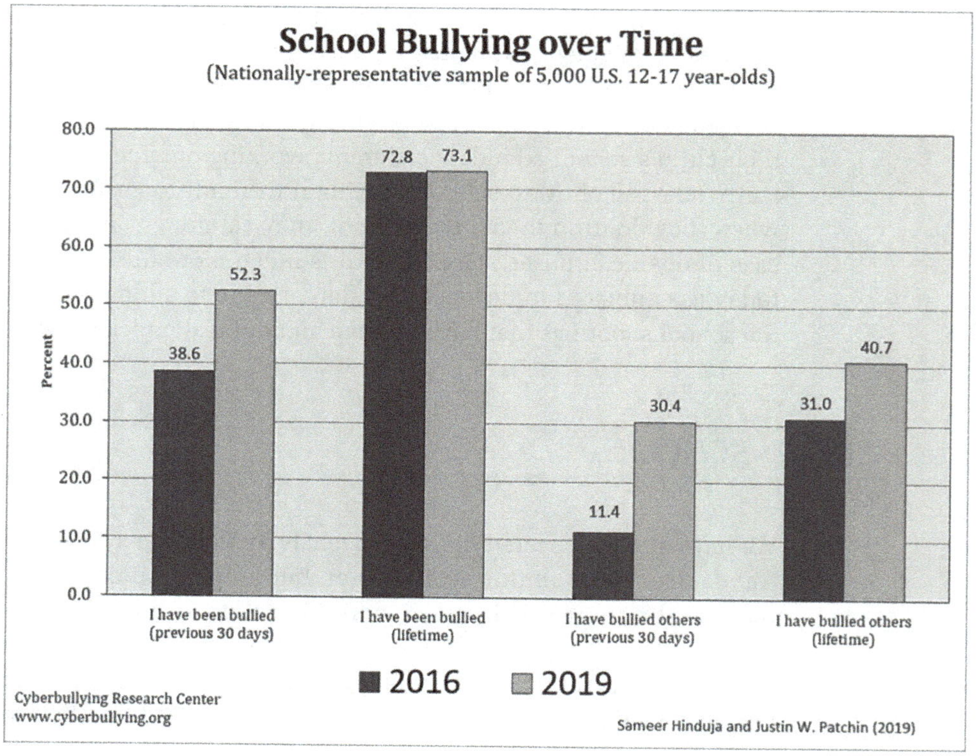

EXHIBIT 10.3 ‖ School Cyberbullying, 2016 and 2019

It is too easy to pass off coping with bullying or bullying behavior as being part of surviving childhood or, falsely, character building. However, research provides good indications that bullies are at greater risk for more serious offending, and victims are at greater risk for juvenile delinquency, particularly in cases of sustained and persistent bullying (Walters, 2020). Schools and parents and guardians should take bullying seriously, no matter how much the behavior was ignored in bygone years.

Exhibit 10.3 also indicates increased bullying in schools. It is important to note that we are only reviewing data up to 2019, as the COVID-19 pandemic began in earnest in 2020 in the United States and continued to change the dynamics of bullying, with schools forced to implement virtual learning. More recent, ongoing research on bullying no doubt will be forthcoming as the data come in.

EFFECTS OF URBAN VIOLENCE ON DELINQUENCY IN SCHOOLS

Urban violence is generally defined as "street crime," committed out in public, including assault and homicide. However, the variables contributing to urban violence spill over into public school systems and into homes. Likewise, domestic violence and problems in schools spill over into the streets. Whether discussion of urban violence includes that which occurs outside the public eye is a complex question. This is best explored using Moser and Winton's (2002; 2004) urban crime/violence classifications, focused on the intersection of economic and social variables (Table 10.1). Urban violence is not solely an "American Problem" nor is it restricted to the Black American community. It has increasingly become a global issue.

A number of factors, including structural and social explanations, have been argued as being the causes of urban violence. Poverty continues to be the foremost reason given for why cities continue to be centers of racial/ethnic tensions and violence. High unemployment rates, intergenerational poverty, and higher than average high-school dropout rates have also contributed to high numbers of urbanites living in poverty. Randall Collins (2009) contradicts economic explanations for violence, theorizing that violence is exceptional and goes against human nature, in spite of media depictions (films, television, and news shows) to the contrary. It is important to note that Collins's views are controversial and do not reflect the majority of research findings on the causes of urban violence.

The social construct of race has also been blamed for high rates of high school dropouts among minorities living in poverty. One explanation for perpetuation of Black poverty in the inner city has been U.S. immigration policies since the 1960s, which have allowed increasing numbers of Latinos/Latinas to compete with Blacks for low-skill jobs in agriculture, manufacturing, and construction (Shihadeh and Barranco, 2010). Urban violence among minority populations is seen as an indirect effect of this increased economic deprivation (Shihadeh and Ousey, 1998).

Additional explanations for poverty within urban Black populations include the disappearance of low-skilled, as well as white-collar, middle-class jobs from cities with increased investment in global transactions, or as Elsinger and Smith (2000) succinctly note, corporate policies of "export jobs or die." Another argument is that in our new global economy, jobs have been exported overseas to peripheral and semi-peripheral countries in order to exploit a cheaper labor force, as compared to the costlier, historically unionized workforce in the United States. Due to our current global economic crisis, even the most vibrant cities have suffered massive unemployment, whether they are active participants in the global economy or not, as exemplified by Detroit, Michigan.

Most urban violence is associated with gang activity, as well as related drug enterprises and prevalence of guns. Less well-known and misunderstood is the role of gangs as protective agents curbing urban violence. Adolescents in particular join gangs in response to violent crimes within their community (Sobel and Osoba, 2009), even though gangs are key contributors to urban violence, creating a distressing tautology. It is too simple to propose that gang activity per se is exclusively responsible for urban violence. Density of gangs within a small urban area appears to play a role (Robinson et al., 2009).

TABLE 10.1 Moser and Winton's (2002; 2004) Urban Crime/Violence Classifications, Focusing on the Intersection of Economic and Social Variables

Table 1: Roadmap of categories, types and manifestations of violence in urban areas		
Category of violence	**Types of violence by perpetrators and/or victims**	**Manifestations**
Political	• State and non-state violence	• Guerrilla conflict • Paramilitary conflict • Political assassinations • Armed conflict between political parties
Institutional	• Violence of state and other "informal" institutions • Including the private sector	• Extra-judicial killings by police • Physical or psychological abuse by health and education workers • State or community vigilante-directed social cleansing of gangs and street children • Lynching of suspected criminals by community members
Economic	• Organized crime • Business interests • Delinquents • Robbers	• Intimidation and violence as means of resolving economic disputes • Street theft, robbery and crime • Kidnapping • Armed robbery • Drug-trafficking • Car theft and other contraband activities • Small-arms dealing • Assaults including killing and rape in the course of economic crimes • Trafficking in prostitutes • Conflict over scarce resources
Economic/social	• Gangs • Street children (boys and girls) • Ethnic violence	• Territorial or identity-based "turf" violence; robbery, theft • Petty theft • Communal riots
Social	• Intimate partner violence inside the home • Sexual violence (including rape) in the public arena • Child abuse: boys and girls • Inter-generational conflict between parent and children • Gratuitous/routine daily violence	• Physical or psychological male–female abuse • Physical and sexual abuse, particularly prevalent in the case of stepfathers but also uncles • Physical and psychological abuse • Incivility in areas such as traffic, road rage, bar fights and street confrontations • Arguments that get out of control

SOURCE: Adapted from Moser, C and A Winton (2002), "Violence in the Central American region: towards an integrated framework for violence reduction", ODI Working Paper No 171, ODI, London; also Moser, C and C McIlwaine (2004), *Encounters with Violence in Latin America: Urban Poor Perceptions from Colombia and Guatemala*, Routledge, London; and Moser, C and D Rodgers (2004), "Change and violence in non-conflict situations", Scoping Background Paper for the DFID Rural-Urban Change Team, DFID, London.

Other explanations for urban violence are more anthropological than sociological or psychological and propose that the culture of marginalized inner-city groups, including young Black males, has led to violence in the streets. One of the best-known theorists of recent decades to address the issues surrounding urban violence is Elijah Anderson of the University of Pennsylvania. In his seminal works, *A Place on the Corner* (1978), *Code of the Streets: Decency, Violence, and the Moral Life of the*

Inner City (1999), and more recently, *The Cosmopolitan Canopy: Race and Civility in Everyday Life* (2012), Anderson argues that urban violence is a function of the culture that emerges out of the stresses of living in violent, impoverished communities. In this model, violence is perpetuated by cultural transmission. This supports the earlier theories of Edwin H. Sutherland (1947), who suggested that deviance and crime, in this case urban violence, are learned through intimate peers.

Yet other explanations for urban violence include social disorganization, where urban dwellers are viewed as being less tethered to their communities, particularly in more impoverished areas of cities where there are greater numbers of renters, fewer owner-occupied homes, and more government-subsidized housing. Breakdown of social controls, including community investment, results in individuals feeling free to commit violent acts (Robinson et al., 2009), and some of this inevitably occurs in schools. However, these explanations runs counter to theories of racial/ethnic identity and solidarity within urban communities.

Urban violence appears to be, on the most part, a function of the intersection of several factors, including poverty, population (and gang) density, and community disorganization, as well as social culture. Urban violence in general will continue to be the major challenge for law enforcement and other criminal justice professionals in the coming decades, if not centuries. Causes for urban violence have been exhaustively explored, but there have been no easy solutions. Unfortunately, urban violence spills over into schools, leaving challenges for teachers, students, parents, and law enforcement.

VIOLENCE IN SCHOOLS

In an alarming study conducted by the Centers for Disease Control Prevention (2011), 16.6% of high school students had carried a weapon at least once in the preceding 30 days, and 7.4% reported threats or injury with a weapon (American Psychological Association, 2013). Schools are becoming increasingly violently contested terrains, particularly in the inner city. And boys are not solely to blame for violence in schools. Increasingly girls, in particular those who are gang members, are also demonstrating violent tendencies (Hansen, 2005).

The crime statistics in U.S. schools are alarming, given the school-to-prison pipeline policies of recent decades and the prevalence of unreported crimes. The U.S. Bureau of Justice Statistics (BJS), in partnership with the Institute of Education Sciences, offer in their Indicators of School Crime and Safety Report the following school environment statistics (Roberts et al., 2013):

- 85% of public schools reported one or more crime incidents taking place, accounting for an estimated 1.9 million crimes in 2009–2010.
- 74% of public schools reported incidents of violent crime, with 16% reporting serious offenses in 2009–2010.

- 16% of public schools reported that gang activities took place in their schools in 2009–2010. This translates to nearly 16,000 schools nationwide, based on the number of public schools in the U.S. in 2009–2010 as reported by the National Center for Education.

Gangs in Schools

The middle-school years are the juncture at which gang membership may become exceptionally attractive. Encompassing grades six through eight or seven through nine in the United States, juveniles in middle school are generally between the age of 11 and 14, and as we noted, children in those years are in the early stages of puberty and on the cusp of adolescence and young adulthood. Add the attention given to media icons, some of whom glamorize gang lifestyles, schools are challenged to ban items that might be viewed as affiliated with real gangs. In comparison to the 19% of U.S. school-aged students who report that gangs exist in their schools (Roberts et al., 2013), the 2010 National Survey of American Attitudes on Substance Abuse XV revealed, "that 35% of middle school students reported that there were gangs in their schools or students who consider themselves to be part of a gang" (Estrada et al., 2013, p. 626).

Two key indicators of susceptibility to gang recruitment at any grade level, including elementary, are poor school performance and low attachment to learning. Large class sizes, fewer resources for schools in low-income communities, and violence spilling into schools from the surrounding community may make the attraction to gang membership an inevitable outcome in the absence of prevention and intervention measures.

As school administrators come and go, they may not be cognizant of the specific risks for gang recruitment within the walls of their institution. One reason to take a micro-macro approach to gang issues in schools is that many inner-city schools (and increasingly, suburban schools) are faced with highly organized gangs that represent an isolated urban underclass with strong, long-standing cohesive ties, making it difficult to separate the student from the neighborhood environment once they reach the steps of the school. Though the culture of violence within gangs varies, along with the racial/ethnic makeup, the end result is the same: if schools do not provide an alternative to gang life, aggressive recruitment into gangs or self-selection for membership becomes almost inevitable by middle school (Hansen, 2005).

Reports of serious, violent offending in schools are not new phenomena. In the 1980s, schools were progressively deteriorating, most notably in inner cities. As teaching salaries stagnated and instances of violence in schools increased, teacher morale deteriorated as well (Price, 2009). Within two decades following the 1980s, most public schools throughout the U.S. were living under the cloud of punitive discipline with zero-tolerance procedures and policies for a broad range of behavioral problems (Skiba and Peterson, 2000).

Zero-tolerance policies in schools may be an extension of the general movement toward militarism in the United States since 9/11. As police departments attempt to move away from the impression of being invading armies (e.g., to community policing), American culture, in general, is increasingly becoming more tolerant of strong punitive actions for social problems. The "war on drugs" has segued into a "war on violence" and, by extension, a "war on gangs." As Bacevich (2005, p. 36) proposes, using the social construct "war" allows for "'wartime' prerogatives by expanding the police powers of the state and circumscribing constitutional guarantees of due process."

According to the BJS report, juveniles between the ages of 12 and 18 are particularly vulnerable for violent offending and gang recruitment (Roberts et al., 2013). A strong argument for adoption of anti-gang recruitment strategies in elementary schools is that by the time students reach middle school, if they are at risk to join a gang, in absence of prevention or intervention, it can be too late to stop them from becoming a statistic.

Few if any anti-gang programs in schools are universally successful. Yet policy, as in most cases of tackling social problems, tends to take a one-size-fits-all stance. An example of a school-based program with mixed results is Gang Resistance Education and Training (G.R.E.A.T.), first introduced in the 1990s. Until academics began to independently evaluate the program, primarily the program developers conducted program evaluations that, on the surface, implied that significant changes had resulted from the program. However, a 2013 longitudinal study by Esbensen et al. found that students who participated in the G.R.E.A.T. program "expressed more positive attitudes to the police and [had] lower odds of gang membership . . . more use of refusal skills. . . . [But] the effect sizes are small" (p. 399) compared to the control group, which did not participate in the program.

In some cities, such as Chicago and Philadelphia, results from studies of the G.R.E.A.T. program were null (Esbensen et al., 2013), offering further evidence that school anti-gang programs have not historically been found to be transportable. Yet it is not uncommon for a school program to become the new shiny policy object that becomes universally implemented without thorough vetting to determine if it will work beyond the pilot study site. It should be noted that after the G.R.E.A.T. program reviewed the mixed results in different cities, the program was amended and currently experiences greater universal success, as compared to its earlier versions.

A more effective response is a grassroots preventative model like the one described in the case study in this chapter, South Holyoke Safe Neighborhoods Initiative. As challenging as it might be, a program that addresses potential discipline problems, including students living on the fringes of gang involvement, allows for diversion rather than punishment. One alternative to zero-tolerance policies is early response, where students are taught to solve interpersonal and intrapersonal problems with more socially acceptable, positive strategies than resorting to violence (Skiba and Peterson, 2000).

Whole-family approaches are also gaining momentum, where not only is the child "diagnosed" and "treated" for problems within the confines of the school, but issues in the home are addressed as well. Unfortunately, the alternative strategies offered here are labor intensive for school and community departments and agencies and may depend on grants to sustain. Plus, they require the continued commitment of parents, a particular issue with more transient populations. The other weakness in these programs is that many do not begin until middle school, when the problem may already be beyond repair for both students and their families.

One means by which schools have attempted to stem gang influence within them is to implement mandatory school uniform policies. This is not a new concept. Certainly these policies have always been in effect at many private and/or parochial schools, albeit not initially for the purposes of preventing gang activities. Uniforms have tentatively been found to have a positive effect on school behavior (Stanley, 1996). It is ironic, though, to observe school-aged children walking to school in polo-style shirts in the same colors as those co-opted by neighborhood gangs. Worse yet is when a school adopts a rival gang's colors, though little research has been done on whether this has a negative effect outside the school setting.

Beyond the esthetics of mandatory uniforms, the argument for institutionalizing the policy at the secondary-school level is that it improves academic performance, student safety, discipline, and morale, while reducing clothing costs for parents (Caruso, 1996). In comparative studies, uniforms themselves appear to be less a determining factor in delinquency rates than the culture of the institution itself (Tanioka and Glaser, 1991). However, it may possibly be reflexive in that the culture in some schools may be changed by mandatory uniform policies, just as clothing uniformity within the military deemphasizes individuality.

In discussions, elementary school staff and teachers report that uniforms do not quash students' urges for individuality (Hansen, 2011b). Students may collude to adopt new hairstyles, shoelace colors, or shoe brands, or even chose to wear untidy or unironed uniforms to demonstrate either individuality or group/gang affiliation (Hansen, 2011b). Of greater concern is when gang graffiti shows up on homework assignments and other handed-in schoolwork. Teachers will either jump to conclusions that the student is gang-affiliated, or will be oblivious of the warning signs of student interest in gangs, unless educators and school staff receive extensive training in recognizing these signs in the classroom or on school grounds (Hansen, 2011a, 2011b).

Of graver concern are the economic enterprises that come off the streets and into schools as a direct result of gang affiliation. Gang members are more likely to be involved in selling drugs than nongang juveniles (Hill et al., 2001). This is also true in comparison to other at-risk youth who are not gang members (Huff, 1998). Schools have little control over the drug activities, including distribution, that take place in the surrounding neighborhoods, but these directly affect the school-aged population as they walk or commute to and from school.

When students do attempt to be part of the labor force, either due to the need to supplement family income or to afford some of the luxuries that teens covet (e.g., smartphones), they may find that the only legitimate means of employment is at a minimum-wage job. As in the case of fast food employees, this may require working late hours that are not conducive to maintaining passing grades in school (Hansen, 2005; Hernandez, 1998). Again, this makes gangs appear to be the more attractive and lucrative alternative.

There have been a number of studies to indicate that gang members commit violent crimes at higher rates than non-gang members. What is becoming more apparent in recent research is that gang members also experience higher rates of violent victimization (Estrada et al., 2013; Katz et al., 2011), which itself creates another challenge in attempting to keep students from dropping out of school.

Beyond the extent to which violent victimization, gang related and otherwise, is a public health issue, it becomes an additional factor in poor school performance. Students cannot learn with the added fear for their personal safety. Contrary to perception, gangs do not have protective value (Peterson et al., 2004). Given the growing focus on bullying in schools, attention should be paid as well to gang recruitment on school grounds. Victimized students may believe that joining a gang is the only alternative to being bullied. However, this sets up a dangerous tautology. Strong evidence indicates that it is critical for schools to establish programs that dispel the myth that gangs provide safe havens (Peterson et al., 2004).

Finding Safer Schools

As witnessed in Moreno Valley, California, a bedroom community about 60 miles east of Los Angeles, families who moved to the city in the 1990s, believing the town to be "gang-free," found that gang membership and criminality are easily imported into new neighborhoods, particularly if convenient transportation is available, such as easy access to highways in Southern California. It didn't help that Moreno Valley is in close proximity to Riverside, with an Eastside neighborhood historically plagued by gang violence (Riverside Police Department, 2018). Unfortunately, these influences seeped into the Moreno Valley schools.

Students with Special Needs and Gangs

Students with special needs, including those with specific learning disabilities and children who have emotional challenges, are at greater risk for poor school performance, making them a population at risk for gang recruitment. Juveniles who struggle in school, falling behind their peers, including being held back a grade, and particularly those with undiagnosed learning disabilities, face uphill battles to graduate, are more likely to drop out of school, and ultimately struggle to attain gainful employment (Ravipati, 2017). This is also confirmed by a recent U.S. Bureau of Labor Statistics report that indicates that those who never

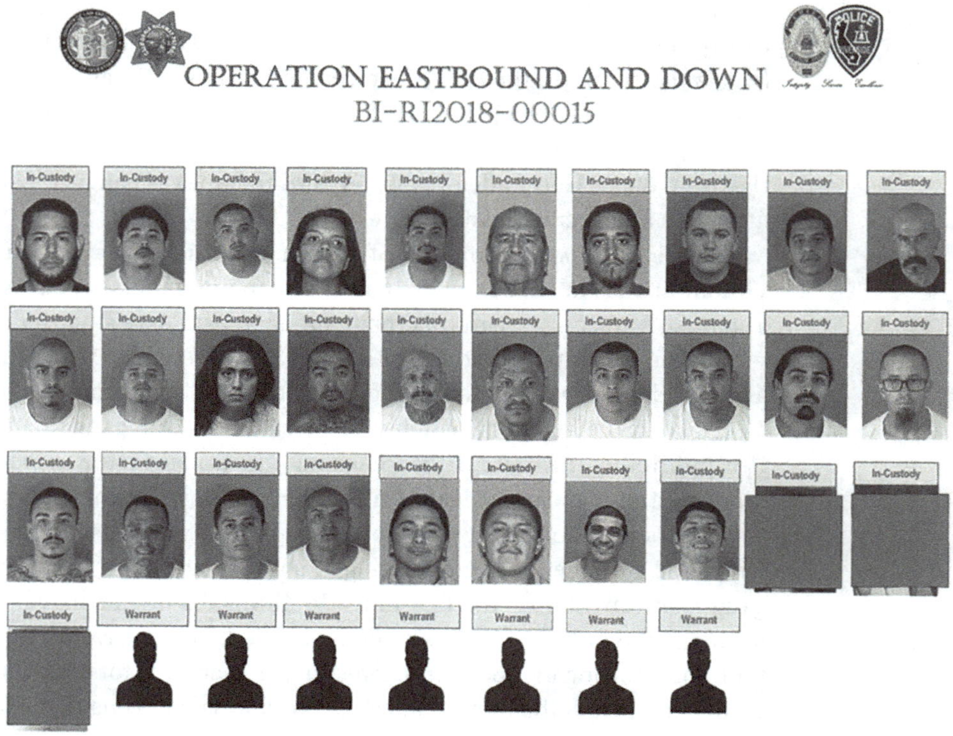

Arrest chart, Operation Eastbound and Down (gang suppression operation), Eastside, Riverside, California.

earn a high school diploma are less likely, on average, to be employed, compared to others with greater educational attainment (U.S. Bureau of Labor Statistics, 2022).

In a credentialed society, the four-year college degree will be (and is) increasingly viewed in the same vein as the high school diploma was 50 years ago (Collins, 1979). For juveniles who become gang-affiliated faced with little prospect of succeeding in school, much less any hope of attending university without intensive early intervention, there is concern that they will forever be underemployed in professions that may not tap into their true potential.

SCHOOL RESOURCE OFFICERS

In some schools, the delinquency problems are so great, as in the case of poor inner-city schools, that law enforcement, called *school resource officers* or *SROs*, will be part of the staff. In some cases, they dress less formally than regular police (similar to what officers doing bike patrol wear; e.g., polo shirts and khakis); in other cases, they are fully uniformed police officers. Whether they are dressed in formal uniforms or less formal polo shirts, placing law enforcement directly into schools changes the educational environment and may have an effect on both staff and students.

More urgently, funding for SROs has been driven by the rash of school shootings in recent decades, particularly after the 2012 mass shooting at Sandy Hook Elementary School in Newtown, CT, where 20 children and 6 teachers were killed (Becket, 2017; O'Murphy, 2013). However, in the United States, few private schools have SROs. Many SROs serve more than one school at a time, and only an estimated 20% of all K–12 schools have SROs (National Association of School Resource Officers, n.d.).

ZERO-TOLERANCE APPROACH TO DELINQUENCY IN SCHOOLS

Once upon a time, if a child or adolescent acted up at school, they were simply sent to the principal's office for discipline. This may have included a strong warning, detention, suspension, or expulsion, depending on how serious the behavioral problem was. Teachers and principals in the past were allowed to paddle or hit students who were misbehaving in class. However, *corporal punishment* has steadily declined since the 1970s, with few schools resorting to spanking or hitting, though school corporal punishment is still legal in some states (Keierleber, 2021; Gershoff and Font, 2016).

The consequences of juvenile arrests, whether they take place within or outside of school, are devastating. Even for minor offenses, the probability of enrolling in a four-year college is 16% lower than for adolescents who have never been arrested (Edwards, 2014). Moreover, 60% of colleges consider arrest records in their admissions processes (Edwards, 2014). Although not all arrests result in conviction, the stigma of an arrest remains.

More recently, there has been pushback against zero-tolerance policies. Like three-strikes laws in some states, these policies can seem in the abstract like good ideas. However, once they become a reality, a greater appreciation develops not only of the personal consequences to the offender, but of the practicalities and costs of putting the policies into practice. Over the past few decades, news accounts have included stories of public school students being suspended, expelled, or, worse, referred to juvenile authorities for possession of items like craft safety scissors or nail clippers, or for possession of everyday, over-the-counter drugs and other innocuous items (Black, 2016). In one extreme instance in Colorado Springs, Colorado, a six-year-old boy with a history of discipline problems was suspended from school for "sexual harassment" when he kissed a classmate's hands (Wallace, CNN, December 2013). These stories take attention away from the real issues of serious, violent offenses that warrant zero-tolerance policies.

Detention, Suspension, and Expulsion

Detention, suspension, and *expulsion* are not new forms of punishment in schools. Detention typically includes after-school punishment requiring the student to attend a mandatory study hall or perform some unpleasant on-campus task, for example, picking up trash on campus after school. Suspension requires the student to remain off-campus and out of school, presumably at home, for a period of time after serious rule-breaking, with school assignments to be completed outside of class. Expulsion is reserved for the most serious of offenses, in many cases those considered to be criminal, as well as infractions of school rules or policies, as in the examples of frequent truancy or violent confrontations on campus. Expulsion is not always permanent. However, because education is compulsory up to the age students are allowed to drop out (which varies from state to state), more than likely the offender who is expelled will be sent to an *alternative school.*

Alternative Schools

Because education is compulsory, when students are expelled from mainstream schools, continue to be disruptive, or are not succeeding in the traditional classroom setting, they will be placed in alternative schools instead. Alternative schools do not always have a negative connotation, as in the example of private Montessori schools. However, historically they have been used primarily to educate troubled students, since their inception in 19th century (Barrington, 2019).

In theory, placement of delinquents in alternative schools puts students in a setting with smaller classes, more intense counseling sessions, and programs focused on school success (Ingersoll and Leboeuf, 1997). The reality is that alternative schools present a number of drawbacks for juvenile delinquents, some with lifelong consequences. Not all alternative schools are created equal. Although not always based in evidence, earlier evaluations of alternative schools found that they did not produce positive results, with their failures blamed on weak program implementation (Cox, 1999; Raywid, 1983).

The issue with alternative schools designed for troubled students is that once children or adolescents are placed there, they are forced to interact only with other delinquent juveniles. A number of long-term social disadvantages of being placed in an alternative school for expelled or low-achieving students have been identified, though notably, early studies were fraught with methodological problems, including a lack of follow-up data on students (Cox, 1999; Cox, Davidson and Bynam, 1995; Duke and Muzio, 1978):

- Less-qualified teachers, or teachers who focus more on discipline than on education
- Fewer or lower-quality resources
- Focus on vocational skills, rather than critical thinking skills

Understanding that having an alternative school for juvenile delinquents listed as one's alma mater on a resume could be stigmatizing, alternative schools geared to housing more difficult students should represent a last resort. Evidence-based research from Coffee and Pestridge (2001) indicates that the schools most likely to succeed with juvenile deviants or delinquents have the following characteristics (OJJDP, 2001; Coffee and Pestridge, 2001, retrieved from https://ojjdp.ojp.gov/mpg/literature-review/alternative-schools.pdf):

- Strong leadership
- Lower student-to-staff ratio
- Carefully selected personnel
- Early identification of student risk factors and problem behaviors
- Intensive counseling/mentoring
- Prosocial skills training
- Strict behavior requirements
- Curriculum based on real-life learning
- Emphasis on parental [or guardian] involvement
- Districtwide support of the programs

There is some evidence that nonresidential alternative schools work and provide positive outcomes, but researchers tend to agree that there needs to be much more research conducted on the effectiveness of these schools to determine just what elements make them successful (Pronk et al., 2020).

SCHOOL DROPOUTS AND DELINQUENCY

The decision to drop out of school before completing a high school degree in most cases does not occur overnight. The process begins with gradual disenchantment and disengagement with school (Sweeten et al., 2009). Evidence of risk factors, including delinquency, is present long before dropping out occurs (Sweeten et al., 2009). Decades of research indicates that school dropouts are much more likely to end up committing juvenile and adult crimes (Anderson, 2014; Fagan and Pabon, 1990; Thornberry et al., 1985).

Less noticeable in school statistics is the number of high school students who do not earn their diploma in four years. An estimated one-third of high school students do not complete their education on time; for Black and Hispanic students, the figure is closer to one-half (Sweeten et al., 2009). Dropout rates alone do not fully reflect how education denied or delayed can have long-term effects, including on job prospects and college admissions, not to mention delinquency. The good news is that dropout rates have steadily decreased over the past few decades; however, Hispanic and Black students continue to be at greatest risk (Gramlich, 2017), as demonstrated in Exhibit 10.4.

SCHOOL-TO-PRISON PIPELINE

One side effect of zero-tolerance and harsh school discipline policies is that when juveniles are referred by schools to law enforcement, it sets in motion the child's move over time from simple deviance, to delinquency disciplined by schools, to referral to the juvenile justice system, to, in some cases, adult prison. This process is called the *school-to-prison pipeline*. In addition, there is good evidence that a great number of adults in prisons today started out as juveniles who experienced difficulties in school, in what is termed the "learning-disabilities-to-prison" pipeline (Mallet, 2014; 2016).

Special Education in Schools and the School-to-Prison Pipeline

By law, schools are required to provide special services with trained teachers and staff to students with disabilities. However, physical disabilities are much easier to detect than psychological problems or developmental challenges or delays. As an example, according to the Mayo Clinic (2022), attention-deficit hyperactivity disorder (ADHD), a condition that can result in poor school performance, low self-esteem, and unstable relationships, may not be detected until adulthood. If the disorder is undetected in childhood, individuals may not receive the type of specialized education they need. A child that might be labeled "difficult" by teachers and family may actually require special education. As we have noted in discussing individual risks for juvenile offending, the need for special education services is not necessarily associated with low intelligence; it often results when individuals require a different type of curriculum delivery than is experienced in mainstream education for children.

Even though racial segregation in schools was abolished with *Brown v. Board of Education of Topeka* (1954), it does not mean there is equality in special education. Schools in poorer, minority communities do not necessarily have adequate resources for juveniles with special needs. Lack of services and the rates of certain special education classifications (e.g., autism and intellectual disabilities) that would result in more services varies from community to community, with research findings indicating this is a function of both race and economic disadvantage (Howard et al., 2021). Bottom line, juveniles of color with disabilities are less likely to receive the special education that they need, either due to the inadequacies of programs in place or missing diagnoses.

There are a number of areas of concern for juvenile delinquents when they are candidates for special education services. The first is that if their education needs within school are mismanaged, they are at risk of becoming part of the school-to-prison pipeline. Researchers and practitioners advise that special education students should not be exposed to school resource officers (SROs), the main source of referrals from schools to juvenile authorities (Murphy, 2022). The

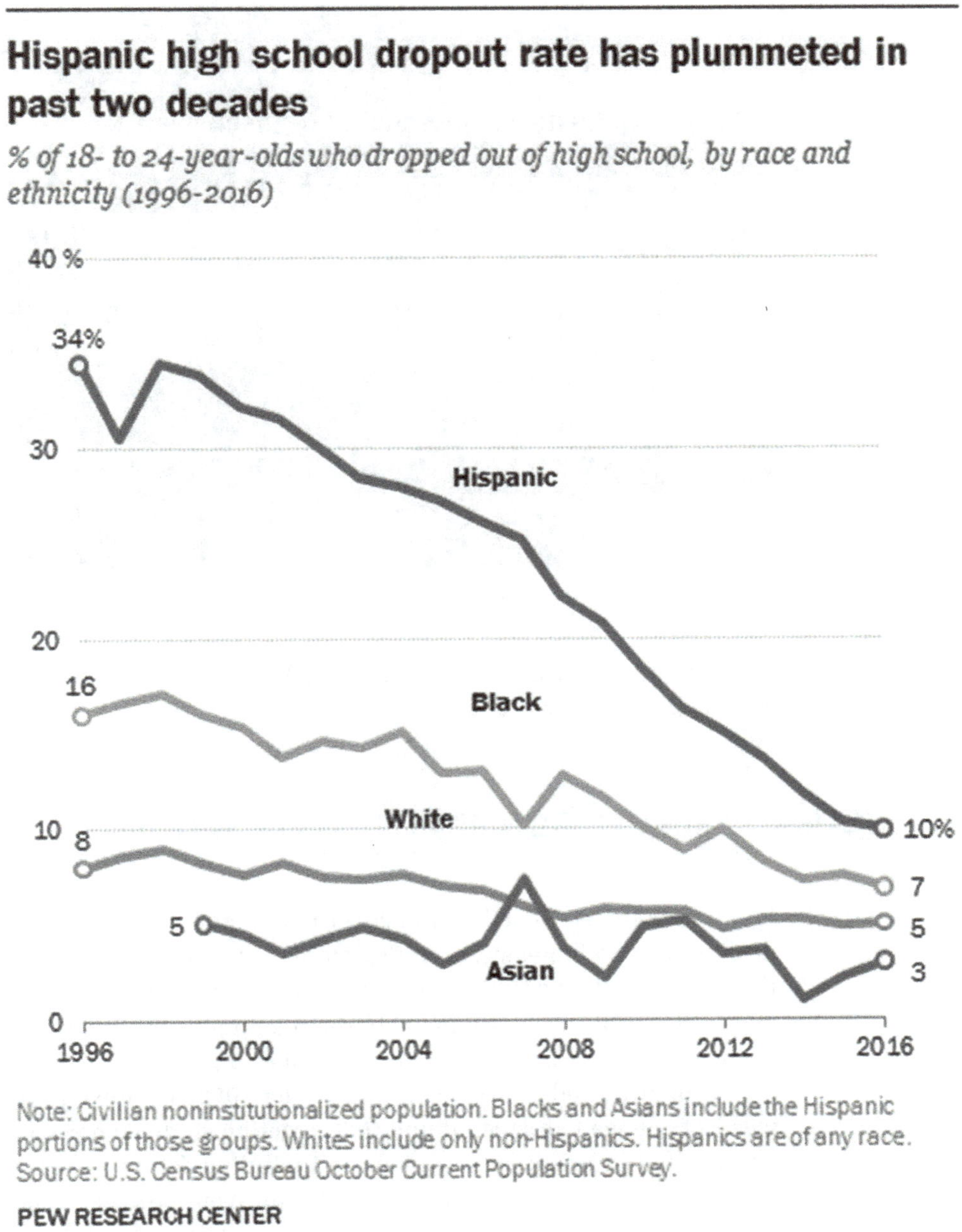

EXHIBIT 10.4 ‖ **Dropout Rates by Race, 1996–2016**

second concern is over whether their educational needs are being met while they are incarcerated. The final concern is how to reintegrate juvenile offenders who need special education into schools once they have been released from custody. Juvenile delinquents who receive specialized reentry support, including

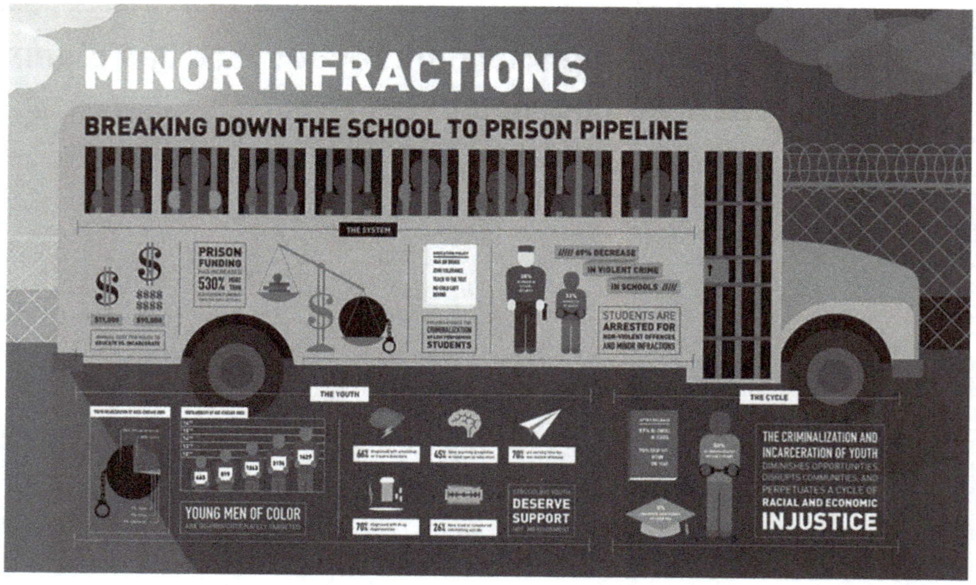

EXHIBIT 10.5 ‖ School-to-Prison Pipeline

special education if needed, are less likely to reoffend within 120 days post-release (Mather et al., 2021).

DELINQUENCY PREVENTION PROGRAMS IN SCHOOLS

Policy makers in education and government tend to take a back-end approach to dealing with delinquency, spending more money on juvenile and adult corrections than on prevention or public education, for that matter. However, there is good evidence that long-term, sustained efforts to help juveniles who are at risk for delinquency will result in more positive outcomes.

A longitudinal study beginning in the 1980s of preventative interventions with school-aged children found that targeting students between grades one and six resulted in much better behavior, including self-regulation and school performance (Hill et al., 2020). The study followed children who participated in the Raising Healthy Children intervention that included (1) training elementary school teachers on the methods of good classroom management and instruction, (2) teaching parents skills to help them promote their children's active classroom involvement, and (3) providing social and emotional skills training to students. A detailed list of the strategies of the Raising Healthy Children program can be seen in Table 10.2.

Increasingly, youth violence and delinquency is being viewed as a public health crisis, including by the Centers for Disease Control and Prevention. As we noted earlier in this chapter, recommendations continue to take a "three-legged stool" approach, with evidence-based programs that include community involvement. More importantly, researchers and the CDC recommend that evidence-based programs be tailored to individual schools and communities, instead of using one-size-fits-all approaches that often fail (Kingston et al., 2016).

Guidance Counseling in Schools

As early as the 1960s, educators saw the value in providing guidance counseling in both elementary and secondary schools. Guidance counseling, then as now, included identifying gifted children, as well with identifying students who were experiencing physical, social, or emotional difficulties that can contribute to delinquency, dropout rates, and unemployment (Sievers, 1963). Recently there are legislative efforts to remove school resource officers from school to stem the school-to-prison pipeline and replace them with more school counselors and social workers (e.g., introduction of the Counseling Not Criminalization in Schools Act, 2021, in the House of Representatives). As of this writing, it is too early to see if any real traction will be had on these types of legislative acts, at the federal or state level.

SUMMARY

The problem of delinquency, violence, and gangs in school is complex. Because of the violence and criminal activities associated with gangs, inner-city schools become contested terrains between school personnel, parents, law enforcement, and their neighborhoods. Add the pressure of schools to perform well in standardized testing, without necessarily having the resources to do so, and juveniles will continue to slip through the cracks and be at risk for delinquency and gang recruitment. It appears to be a losing battle, one that has been ongoing since the 1960s when deindustrialization created far fewer legitimate employment opportunities for parents and their offspring, particularly those with limited education.

For all the pessimism introduced here, there do appear to be solutions. Collaborative, multi-agency initiatives are beginning to find traction, as in the case of SHSNI. Prevention continues to be the greatest challenge, as there is little research on what variables help prevent some juveniles from becoming gang members, when others in the same environment succumb.

The first "baby step" in addressing the gang problems that spill into schools is to educate school administrators, staff, and faculty on the risks. This can be met with resistance (as this author has found) as the responsibilities of school personnel already constitute well beyond a 40-hour workweek, even in the imaginary, nonexistent freedom of summer vacations when a substantial amount of course preparation is done by teachers. Requiring additional in-service training in

TABLE 10.2 Strategies of the Raising Healthy Children program

Table 1. Differences in Children of Parents Who Were in Full Intervention in Grades 1 Through 6 Compared With Control Participants[a]

Characteristic	Mean (SD) Control	Mean (SD) Intervention	Standardized β (95% CI)[b]	P value	False discovery rate significance (P < .021)
Developmental functioning per Ages and Stages Questionnaire[c]					
Communication	49.2 (10.2)	54.0 (5.8)	0.56 (0.29-0.83)	.001	Yes
Gross motor	51.6 (8.6)	55.3 (6.3)	0.48 (0.17-0.79)	.002	Yes
Fine motor	44.4 (13.1)	49.6 (10.3)	0.45 (0.14-0.76)	.005	Yes
Problem solving	49.3 (11.8)	51.3 (7.3)	0.22 (−0.16 to 0.59)	.26	No
Personal social	52.3 (8.6)	53.0 (7.2)	0.08 (−0.27 to 0.43)	.64	No
Across all areas	49.2 (10.2)	52.5 (4.6)	0.49 (0.18-0.98)	.002	Yes
Teacher-rated child behavior[d]					
Oppositional defiance	0.11 (0.73)	−0.16 (.059)	−0.39 (−0.63 to −0.15)	.004	Yes
Conduct problems	0.06 (0.52)	−0.10 (0.52)	−0.31 (−0.58 to −0.04)	.03	No
Attention-deficit/hyperactivity disorder	0.14 (0.76)	−0.19 (0.65)	−0.46 (−0.76 to −0.20)	.003	Yes
Social problems	0.06 (0.51)	−0.01 (0.52)	−0.16 (−0.52 to 0.21)	.39	No
Anxiety	0.05 (0.63)	−0.04 (0.52)	−0.16 (−0.49 to 0.17)	.35	No
Affective problems	0.12 (0.60)	−0.08 (0.52)	−0.34 (−0.65 to −0.03)	.03	No
Externalizing problems[e]	0.25 (1.40)	−0.36 (1.23)	−0.41 (−0.67 to −0.14)	.002	Yes
Internalizing problems[e]	0.20 (1.28)	−0.12 (1.07)	−0.32 (−0.63 to −0.01)	.04	No
Teacher-rated skills and performance[f]					
Cognitive skills	3.47 (0.79)	3.77 (0.67)	0.39 (0.11-0.67)	.006	Yes
Academic skills	3.59 (0.89)	3.89 (0.71)	0.34 (0.09-0.60)	.009	Yes
Relative academic performance	3.03 (0.86)	3.22 (0.84)	0.21 (−0.06 to 0.48)	.12	No
Grades[g]	2.63 (1.07)	2.86 (0.98)	0.18 (−0.08 to 0.44)	.17	No
Emotional skills	3.67 (0.88)	4.10 (0.73)	0.49 (0.29-0.68)	.001	Yes
Child-reported risk behavior, No. (%)[h]					
Early sex (<17 y)	21 (40.4)	9 (32.1)	0.69 0.25-1.88)[f]	.46	No
Ever drank alcohol	26 (30.2)	10 (16.4)	0.47 (0.21-1.03)[f]	.06	No
Ever smoked cigarettes	18 (20.9)	7 (11.5)	0.58 (0.23-1.47)[f]	.25	No
Ever smoked marijuana	16 (23.9)	7 (17.1)	0.73 (0.31-1.71)[f]	.47	Yes
Ever tried any drug	32 (37.2)	10 (16.4)	0.27 (0.10-0.73)[f]	.01	No
Ever violent (fighting, hitting, beating, or robbing)	46 (52.9)	24 (40.0)	0.64 (0.31-1.35)[f]	.25	No
Ever committed nonviolent crime (theft or drug sales)	35 (40.2)	17 (27.9)	0.63 (0.23-1.74)[f]	.38	No

[a]All analyses controlling for maternal age at childbirth and cohort clustering. Significance is indicated in the rightmost column after applying Benjamini-Hochberg false discovery rate multiple comparisons adjustment.

[b]β For standardized outcome (standardized on the dependent variable only).

[c]Mean score across all ages available for each measure and across all 7 waves (N = 182); collected on children aged 1 to 5 years.

[d]Standardized within age; collected on participants aged 6 to 18 years.

[e]Externalizing problems include oppositional defiance, conduct problems, and attention-deficit/hyperactivity disorder; internalizing problems include social problems, anxiety, and affective problems.

[f]Mean score across all ages available for each measure and across all 7 waves (N = 182); collected on children aged 6 to 18 years.

[g]Mostly F (quantified as 0) to mostly A grades (quantified as 4).

[h]Cumulative across waves; collected in participants aged 6 to 18 years. All values in this section are reported as numbers (percentages) and odds ratios (95% CIs).

anything beyond classroom instruction can result in the message not being heard. Understanding gangs and general violent behavior should be part of every education program curriculum in universities, particularly for future educators and administrators who intend to be employed in urban school districts.

Either way, if juveniles are not receiving the direction and attention they need to succeed in school from home or the community, schools become the last line of defense in the prevention of juvenile delinquency. As one former gang member reported in his autobiography, school represented a safe haven from his abusive home life: "Back in school I was in heaven. . . . I was a model student, always on time, my homework neatly completed . . ." (Sanchez, 2000, p. 11). It is important to recognize that, for some, school can offer a means of escape from gang life and from a vicious cycle of poverty and delinquency (Hansen, 2005).

The answer does not lie in across-the-board zero-tolerance procedures and policies for a range of offenses. On the other hand, violence and felonious criminal behavior should never be tolerated in schools, as they are massively disruptive to the learning process. The key is to avoid throwing out the proverbial baby with the bathwater, where the marginally delinquent juvenile (e.g., cases such as the occasional truancy) should be given ample opportunity to stay in mainstream schooling. To segregate them into populations of more serious juvenile offenders in alternative schools or in the juvenile justice system only increases their risk of joining gangs by way of differential association and delinquent networks (as posited by Sutherland).

The real fear is that the three-legged stool, described in this chapter, is teetering. Unless school, parents, and law enforcement form a united front against gang recruitment and gangs in schools, without overt militarization, some communities will always face sending their children to schools that are essentially minefields of risk for gang recruitment. And as we noted, the COVID-19 pandemic may have exacerbated delinquent behavior due to increased truancy and the social adjustments of returning to face-to-face instruction.

CASE STUDY

Eating the Elephant One Bite at a Time: South Holyoke Safe Neighborhoods Initiative (SHSNI)[9] and Morgan Elementary School

Schools cannot be the first line of defense for gang prevention. School populations reflect the surrounding neighborhoods that feed into them. In South Holyoke in western Massachusetts, community stakeholders including social agencies, law enforcement, and the school district personnel are attempting to take matters in their own hands to reduce gang presence in their schools and neighborhood. The challenges are multifaceted, from higher rates of unemployment to greater numbers of young, single female-headed households, to a disproportionate number of children living in poverty. Add to that an elementary school that has been downgraded to "Level 5" for underperformance on standardized tests (see http://www.doe.mass.edu/apa/sss/turnaround/level5/schools/), and the outlook, on the surface, appears to be grim.

[9] SHSNI is now simply Holyoke Safe Neighborhoods Initiative (HSNI), as the program has expanded to serve the whole city.

For those unfamiliar with American pedagogy, in a controversial move to improve teaching and the quality of education, standardized testing mutated from "no child left behind" to increasing school failures across the country. Approximately 4% of public schools are in receivership in the United States, with the number growing every year (Center for Research on Education Outcomes, 2013). Standardized testing further stratifies education between communities with funding to bring about excellence in personnel and resources to better prepare students for the exams (e.g., communities with higher property values with the associated higher property taxes funding schools) and those without the funding, due to depressed home property values, fewer homeowners, and more transient populations. The latter is an apt description of the target area of South Holyoke around Morgan Elementary School.

South Holyoke, a mid-size city, has historically been a disadvantaged neighborhood with a disproportionate number of families living in poverty, high rates of teen pregnancy, and in more recent years, it has been a center of gang activity. Inspired by the Massachusetts State Police C3 Policing (MSPC3) approach adopted by neighboring Springfield, Massachusetts, a grassroots organization was formed in South Holyoke to customize the approach to the specific needs of the targeted neighborhood, which was experiencing the worst of the gang activity (shsni.org).

As described by the MSPC3 website (mspc3policing.com), C3 policing or Counter Criminal Continuum Policing incorporates a strategic program to extract criminal gangs and drug dealers from the community. While MSPC3 does not abandon traditional community policing, SHSNI in South Holyoke takes this one step further to a "weed-and-seed" philosophy of removing criminal elements, while simultaneously encouraging community members toward self-efficacy, through collaboration with social service agencies, law enforcement, and the public schools.

In 2012 and 2013, SHSNI conducted door-to-door surveys of residents to collect data on perceptions of public safety, crime, social service needs, and availability of after-school programs that target prevention of gang recruitment. While only 35% of households reported that their children were in after-school programs in 2012, this number increased to 63% by 2013 (Hansen and Morin, 2012; Hansen et al., 2013). The greatest interest was in sports programs, followed by arts and craft programs, both of which had become casualties of cash-strapped school districts since the 1970s.

Of value to the school community, as shown in the SHSNI survey reports, were statistics on perceptions of safety. Though domestic violence is admittedly underreported, as compared to agencies' perceptions of how big a problem it is within Holyoke (Hansen et al., 2013), the most pressing issue for residents was drug activity around the housing projects, followed by the gang presence around Morgan Elementary School (Hansen and Morin, 2012).

Parents are an integral part of SHSNI's strategy. By offering a "Family Fun Night" each month that encourages families to participate in a number of activities with subliminal and not so subliminal antiviolence messages, a no-judgment safe zone is established, where parents can contact needed social services and interact with school personnel and law enforcement. The initiative has used data from the 2012 and 2013 surveys to create programs tailored to specific community needs. By 2014, substantially more children were in after-school programs once SHSNI implemented the study recommendations.

An additional benefit of the "Family Fun Night" is that it works with community partners to provide much-needed school supplies. As schools are less able to provide the materials students need to succeed in school (pens, pencils, notebooks, backpacks, etc.), the initiative has a "Back to School" event every fall to provide children within this financially depressed neighborhood with school supplies. In addition to offering much-needed materials to students, these family-oriented events also serve meals that feel more communal than like charity meals.

The SHSNI program was so successful, it now has expanded to include the whole city of Holyoke, renamed Holyoke Safe Neighborhoods Initiative (HSNI). Currently, the initiative depends on using Holyoke school facilities for many of its programs. Ultimately, the initiative would like to establish a multiagency community center in the South Holyoke neighborhood that can provide after-school programs, as well as direct access to social services that take a whole-family approach to violence and gang prevention and intervention that reaches residents who would otherwise go underserved due to transportation constraints.

SOURCES

Hansen, L., and M. Morin (2012). Survey report, first wave, South Holyoke Safe Neighborhood Initiative. SHSNI. Fall.

Hansen, L., M. Simpson, and M. Morin (2013). Survey report, Residents and Agencies, South Holyoke Safe Neighborhood Initiative. SHSNI. Fall.

CHAPTER DISCUSSION QUESTIONS

1. Pretend you have an unlimited budget to create a delinquency prevention program in a school. What would it look like? Would you target one form of delinquency or have a number of programs? Or would you create a general delinquency prevention program? What problems might you encounter in designing such a program?
2. Think back to when you were in grade school, middle school, or high school. What were some of the characteristics of the children or adolescents who behaved in a delinquent way? Did other people shun them?
3. Once a child or adolescent is labeled a delinquent, either by fellow students or by teachers, how might they redeem their reputation?
4. What type of policy alternative to the zero-tolerance policies in today's schools might you design? What forms of delinquency would you address?
5. Who are the key personnel in schools or in the community who can help prevent delinquency in schools?

GLOSSARY

Alternative school Any school that is not a mainstream public school. They are not necessarily only reserved for juvenile delinquents or those struggling in traditional school; some are elite boarding schools.

Corporal punishment (in schools) Any type of physical punishment, including spanking.

Detention Mandatory after-school punishment spent either in a study hall or doing some type of on-campus service.

Expulsion The removal of a student for serious, and sometimes criminal, violation of school rules or policies.

Peer groups Friend networks that share the same world view, interests, and hobbies. Usually formed among people in close proximity, such as classmates who become friends or neighborhood cliques.

School resource officers (SROs) Police officers assigned to provide security on campuses.

School-to-prison pipeline The process by which students are harshly disciplined, including expulsion and juvenile detention, possibly leading to further delinquency, which may in turn lead to adult offending and incarceration.

Suspension School punishment for serious violation of school rules or policies that requires the student to remain off campus for a short period of time (e.g., one-week suspension), after which they can return to school.

Tracking Process and policies by which students are identified early on in school by their abilities, aptitudes, attitudes, and in some cases, social economic status, affecting which classes they are placed in. For example, if a student shows promise of attending college, they will be placed in a college-prep curriculum and take the prerequisite courses for college admission. Criticisms of tracking include that it fails to identify late bloomers.

VARK model A model for learning that identifies students by learning style—visual, audio (hearing), reading/writing, or kinetic (hands-on)—and designs curricula to suit those styles.

REFERENCES AND ADDITIONAL SUGGESTED READINGS

American Psychological Association (2013). "Warning signs of youth violence." Retrieved from https://www.apa.org/topics/physical-abuse-violence/youth-warning-signs.

Anderson, D. M. (2014). "In school and out of trouble? Minimum dropout age and juvenile delinquency." *Review of Economics and Statistics*. Vol. 96, Issue 2 (May): 318–331.

Annie E. Casey Foundation (2021). "Head Start enrollment by age group." Retrieved from https://datacenter.kidscount.org/data/tables/9786-head-start-enrollment-by-age-group?loc=1&loct=1#//any/false/any/any/any.

Atkins, M. S., E. Cappella, E. S. Shernoff, T. G. Mehta, and E. Gustafson (2017). "Schooling and children's mental health: Realigning resources to reduce disparities and advance public health." *Annual Review of Clinical Psychology*. Vol. 13: 123–147.

Bacevich, A. J. (2005). "The real World War IV." *Wilson Quarterly*. Vol. 29, issue 1: 36–61.

Barrington, K. (2019). "What are alternative schools and how do they impact college admissions?" *Public School Review*. Sep. 5. Retrieved from https://www.publicschoolreview.com/blog/what-are-alternative-schools-and-how-do-they-impact-college-admissions.

Beckett, L. (2017). "Remembering the 26: How families honor Sandy Hook victims five years later." *Guardian*. Dec 14. Retrieved from https://www.theguardian.com/us-news/2017/dec/13/newtown-sandy-hook-shooting-victims-five-years-later.

Black, D. W. (2016). *Ending Zero Tolerance: The Crisis of Absolute School Discipline*. New York: New York University Press.

Bradshaw, C. P., A. L. Sawyer, and L. M. O'Brennan (2009). "A social disorganization perspective on bullying-related attitudes and behaviors: The influence of school context." *American Journal of Community Psychology*. Vol. 3, issues 3–4: 204–220.

Brown, E. (2010)."Race, urban governance, and crime control: creating model cities." *Law and Society Review*. Vol. 44, issues 34: 769–804.

Caruso, P. (1996). "Individuality vs. conformity: The issue behind school uniforms." *National Association of Secondary School Principals (NASSP) Bulletin*, Sage Publications. Vol. 80: 83–88.

Center for Research on Education Outcomes (2013). Executive Summary. *National Charter School Study*. Stanford, CA: Stanford University. Available at http://credo.stanford.edu/documents/NCSS%202013%20Executive%20Summary.pdf. Cohen, A. (1955). *Delinquent Boys: The Culture of the Gangs*. New York, NY: Free Press.

Collins, R. (2009). *Violence: a Micro-Sociological Theory*. Princeton, NJ: Princeton University Press.

Collins, R. (1979). *The Credentialed Society: A Historical Sociology of Education and Stratification*. Waltham, MA: Academic Press.

Consortium on School Research (CCSR) (2007). "Freshman year: The make-it or break-it year." Retrieved from https://www2.ed.gov/programs/slcp/2011progdirmtg/9thgrmatters.pdf.

Comly, R., J. Fontana, and A. Shaw-Amoah (2020). *Strategies for Reducing Student Absenteeism in Philadelphia*. Philadelphia, PA: Research for Action.

Cox, S. (1999). "An assessment of an alternative education program for at-risk delinquent youth." *Journal of Research in Crime and Delinquency*. Vol. 36, issue 3: 323–336.

Cox, S., W. Davidson, and T. Bynam (1995). "A meta-analytic assessments of delinquency-related outcomes of alternative education programs." *Crime and Delinquency*. Vol. 41, issue 2: 19–34.

De La Rue, L., and D. L. Espelage (2014). "Family and abuse characteristics of gang-involved, pressured-to-join, and non-gang involved girls." *Psychology of Violence*. July: 253–265.

Del Barco, M. (2011). "L.A.'s homicide rate lowest in four decades." Morning Edition, *National Public Radio*. January 6.

Development Service Groups, Inc. (2001). Alternative schools: Literature review. Washington, DC: U.S. Justice Department, Office of Juvenile Justice and Delinquency Prevention (OJJDP).

Duke, D., and I. Muzio (1978). "How effective are alternative schools? A review of recent evaluations and reports." *Teachers College Record*. Vol. 79: 461–483.

Duke Health (2020). "When is puberty too early?" *Duke Health Blog*. Jul 7. Retrieved from https://www.dukehealth.org/blog/when-puberty-too-early.

Edwards, S. (2014). "How law and education policies hurt more than help." *Chicago Policy Review.* Mar 28. Retrieved from https://chicagopolicyreview.org/2014/03/28/consequences-of-juvenile-arrests-on-education-how-law-and-educational-policies-hurt-more-than-help/#:~:text=Specifically%2C%20the%20study%20revealed%20that,only%2016%20percent%20of%20arrestees.

Elsinger, P. S., and C. Smith (2000). "Globalization and metropolitan well-being in the U.S." *Social Science Quarterly.* June: 634–644.

Esbensen, F., D.W. Osgood, D. Peterson, T. Taylor, and D.C. Carson (2013). "Short- and long-term outcome results from a multisite evaluation of the G.R.E.A.T. Program." *Criminology and Public Policy.* Vol. 12, issue 3 (Aug.): 375–411.

Estrada, J. N., T. D. Gilbreath, R. A. Astor, and R. Benbenishty (2013). "Gang membership of California middle school students: Behaviors and attitudes as mediator of school violence." *Health Education Research.* Vol. 28, issue 4: 626–639.

Fagan, J., and E. Pabon (1990). "Contributions of delinquency and substance use to school dropout among inner-city youths." *Youths and Society.* Vol. 21: 306–354.

Forber-Pratt, A., S. R. Aragon, and D. L. Espelage (2014). "The influence of gang presence on victimization in one middle school environment." *Psychology of Violence.* Vol. 4, issue 1: 8–20.

Gebo, E., and C. J. Sullivan (2014). "A statewide comparison of gang and non-gang youth in public high schools." *Youth Violence and Criminal Justice.* Vol. 12, issue 3 (July): 191–208.

Gershoff, E. T., and S. A. Font (2016). "Corporal punishment in U.S. public schools: Prevalence, disparities in use, and status in state and federal policy." *Social Policy Report,* Society for Research in Child Development. Vol. 30, issue 1. ISSN: 1075-7031.

Gramlich, J. (2017). "Hispanic dropout rate hits new low and college enrollment at new high." Pew Research Center. Sept 29. Retrieved from https://www.pewresearch.org/fact-tank/2017/09/29/hispanic-dropout-rate-hits-new-low-college-enrollment-at-new-high/.

Grekul, J., and P. LaBoucane-Benson (2008). "Aboriginal gangs and their (dis)placement: Contextualizing recruitment, membership, and status." *Canadian Journal of Criminology and Criminal Justice.* 5 (Jan.): 59–82.

Grover, A. R., W. G. Jennings, and R. Tewksbury (2009). "Adolescent male and female gang members' experiences with violent victimization, dating violence, and sexual assault." *American Journal of Criminal Justice.* 34: 103–115.

Hansen, L. L. (2011a). "'Baby Steps': Educating educators on the risks of gang recruitment." Paper delivered at Annual Conference, American Society of Criminology. November, Chicago, Ill.

Hansen, L. L. (2011b). Recognizing the signs of gang recruitment. Workshop, Western New England College, June 11.

Hansen, L. L. (2005). "Girl 'crew' members doing gender, boy 'crew' members doing violence: An ethnographic and network analysis of Maria Hinojosa's New York gangs." *Western Criminology Review.* Vol. 6, issue 1: 134–144.

Hernandez, A. (1998). *Peace in the Streets: Breaking the Cycle of Gang Violence.* Washington, D.C.: Child Welfare League of America.

Higgins, G. E., G. F. Vito, and W. F. Walsh (2008). "Searches: an understudied area of racial profiling." *Journal of Ethnicity in Criminal Justice.* Vol. 6, issue 1: 23–39.

Hill, K. G., J. A. Bailey, and C. M. Steeger (2020). "Outcomes of childhood preventive interventions across two generations: A nonrandomized controlled trial." *Journal of the American Medical Association Pediatrics.* Vol. 174, issue 8: 764–771.

Hill, K. G., C. Lui, and J. D. Hawkins (2001). "Early precursors of gang membership: A study of Seattle youth." *Office of Juvenile Justice and Delinquency Prevention (OJJDP) Bulletin.* Dec: 1–5.

Howard, J., J. N. Copeland, E. J. Gifford, J. Lawson, Y. Bai, N. Heilbron, and G. Maslow (2021). "Brief report: Classifying rates of students with autism and intellectual disability in North Carolina: Roles of race and economic disadvantage." *Journal of Autism and Developmental Disorders.* Vol. 51, issue 1 (Jan.): 307–314.

Howell, J. C. (2015). *The history of Gangs in the United States: Their Origins and Transformations.* Lanham, Maryland: Lexington Books.

Huff, R. C. (1998). "Comparing the criminal behavior of youth gangs and at-risk youth." Research brief. Department of Justice. Washington, D.C., NCJ-172852.

Ingersoll, S., and D. LeBoeuf (1997). *Reaching Out to Youth Out of the Education Mainstream.* Office of Justice Programs, Office of Juvenile Justice and Delinquency Prevention (OJJDP). Washington, DC: U.S. Department of Justice.

Katz, M. B. (2007). "Why aren't U.S. cities burning?" *Dissent.* Vol. 54, issue 3: 23–29.

Katz, C. M., V. J. Webb, K. Fox, and J. N. Shaffer (2011). "Understanding the relationship between violent victimization and gang membership." *Journal of Criminal Justice.* Jan–Feb: 48–59.

Keierleber, M. (2021). "'It's barbaric': Some US children getting hit at school despite bans." *The Guardian.* May 19. Retrieved from https://www.theguardian.com/education/2021/may/19/us-children-corporal-punishment-schools.

Kellam, S. G., X. Ling, R. Merisca, C. H. Brown, and N. Ialongo (1998). "The effect of the level of aggression in the first grade classroom on the course and malleabilty of aggressive behavior into middle school." *Developmental Psychopathology,* Vol. 10, issue 2: 165–185.

Kingston, B., M. Bacallo, P. Smokowski, T. Sullivan, and K. Sutherland (2016). "Constructing 'packages' of evidence-based programs to prevent youth violence: Processes and illustrative examples from the CDC's Youth Violence Prevention Centers." *Journal of Primary Prevention.* Vol. 37 (April): 141–163.

Klein, M. W., and C. Maxson (2006). *Street Gang Patterns and Policies.* New York: Oxford University Press.

Klein, M. W., F. M. Weerman, and T. P. Thornberry. (2006). "Street gang violence in Europe." *European Journal of Criminology.* Vol. 3, issue 4: 413–437.

Lenzi, M., J. Sharkey, A. Vieno, A. Mayworm, D. Doughety, and K. Nylund-Gibson (2015). "Adolescent gang involvement: The role of individual, peer, and school factors in a multilevel perspective." *Aggressive Behavior.* Vol. 41, issue 4 (July–Aug.): 386–397.

Li, R., Q. Lian, Q. Su, L. Li, M. Xie, and J. Hu (2020). "Trends and sex disparities in school bullying victimization among U.S. youth, 2011–2019." *BMC Public Health.* Vol. 20: 1583.

Malkus, N. (2020). *Too Little, Too Late: A Hard Look at 2020 Remote Learning.* Washington, DC: American Enterprise Institute.

Mallet, C. A. (2016). *The School-to-Prison Pipeline: A Comprehensive Assessment.* New York: Springer.

Mallet, C. A. (2014). "The 'learning disabilities to juvenile detention' pipeline: A case study." *Children and Schools.* Vol. 36, issue 3: 147–155.

Mather, S. R., H. G. Clark, and J. M. Gau (2021). "A cross-comparison study of reentry intervention and support of engagement: Finding on youth with disabilities." *Behavioral Disorders.* Vol. 46, issue 3: 163–174.

Mayo Clinic (2022). Overview: Adult attention-deficit/hyperactivity disorder (ADHD). Retrieved from https://www.mayoclinic.org/diseases-conditions/adult-adhd/symptoms-causes/syc-20350878.

Merton, R. K. (1957). *Social Theory and Social Structure.* New York: Free Press.

Miller, J. (2000). "Getting into gangs." In *One of the Guys: Girls, Gangs, and Gender.* New York: Oxford University Press.

Moser, C. (2004). "Urban violence and insecurity: an introductory roadmap." *Environment and Urbanization.* Vol. 16, issue 3: 3–16.

Moser, C., and C. McIlwaine (2004). *Encounters with Violence in Latin America: Urban Poor Perceptions from Colombia and Guatemala*. London: Routledge.

Moser, C., and A. Winton (2002). "Violence in the Central American region: Towards an integrated framework for violence reduction." ODI Working Paper No. 171. *ODI*, London.

Murphy, S. L. (2022). "It starts and ends with the schools: Using strict IDEA enforcement to sunder the school-to-prison pipeline for special education students." *Ohio Northern University Law Review*. Vol. 48: 359.

National Alliance on Mental Illness (NAMI) (n.d.). "Bipolar disorder." Retrieved from https://www.nami.org/About-Mental-Illness/Mental-Health-Conditions/Bipolar-Disorder.

National Association of School Resource Officers (NASRO) (n.d.). Frequently asked questions: How many school resource officers are there in the United States? Retrieved from https://www.nasro.org/faq/#:~:text=Because%20fewer%20private%20school%20than,have%20more%20than%20one%20officer.

National Association of Secondary School Principals (NASSP) (2006). "Tracking and ability grouping in middle level and high schools." Retrieved from https://www.nassp.org/tracking-and-ability-grouping-in-middle-level-and-high-schools/.

O'Donnell, J., J. D. Hawkins, R. F. Catalano, R. D. Abbott, and L. E. Day (1995). "Preventing school failure, drug use, and delinquency among low-income children: Long-term intervention in elementary schools." *American Journal of Orthopsychiatry*. Vol. 65, issue 1: 87–100.

Office of Juvenile Justice and Delinquency Prevention (OJJDP) (2001). "Alternative schools." *Literature Review*, Model Programs Guide. U.S. Department of Justice. Retrieved from https://ojjdp.ojp.gov/model-programs-guide/literature-reviews/alternative_schools.pdf.

O'Murphy, A. (2013). Preface. *School Resource Officers: Analysis of Law Enforcement in Schools*, ed. A. O'Murphy. Law, Crime, and Law Enforcement. New York: NOVA.

Olweus, D. (2012). "Cyberbullying: An overrated phenomenon?" *European Journal of Developmental Psychology*. Vol. 9, issue 5: 520–538.

Peterson, D. (2012). "Girlfriends, gun-holders, and ghetto-rats? Moving beyond narrow views of girls in gangs." Ch. 5 in *Delinquent Girls: Contexts, Relationships, and Adaption*, ed. S. Miller, L. D. Leve, and P. K. Kerig. Switzerland: Springer International.

Peterson, D., T. J. Taylor, and F. Esbensen (2004). "Gang membership and violent victimization." *Justice Quarterly*. Vol. 21, issue 4 (Dec.): 793–815.

Price, P. (2009). "When is a police officer an officer of the law?: The status of police officers in schools." *Journal of Criminal Law and Criminology*. Vol. 99, issue 2 (Winter): 541–70.

Prithishkumar, I. J., and S. A. Michael (2014). "Understanding your student: Using the VARK model." *Education Forum*. Vol. 60, issue 2: 183–186.

Pronk, S., C. Kuiper, D. Smit, G. J. Stams, A.Popma, E. Mudler, and G. van den Berg (2020). "A meta-analysis on the outcomes of adolescents for school drop-out attending nonresidential alternative educational facilities." *Preventing School Failure*. Vol. 64, issue 2: 162–171.

Ramadas, S. (2008). "California youth and criminal law: 2007 juvenile justice reform and gang prevention initiatives." *Berkeley Journal of Criminal Law*. Vol. 13: 145–174.

Ravipati, S. (2017). "Report: Students with learning and attention issues three times more likely to drop out." Special Education, *The Journal*. May 17. Retrieved from https://thejournal.com/articles/2017/05/17/students-with-learning-and-attention-issues-three-times-more-likely-to-drop-out.aspx.

Raywid, M. A. (1983). "Schools of choice: Their current nature and prospects." *Phi Delta Kappan*. Vol. 94, issue 10: 684–688.

Riverside Police Department (2018). "Operation 'Eastbound and Down.'" Press release, City of Riverside, California. Oct 19. Retrieved from https://riversideca.gov/press/riverside-police-departments-operations-eastbound-down.

Roberts, S., J. Kemp, A. Rathburn, R. E. Morgan, T. D. Snyder (2013). *Indicators of School Crime and Safety: 2013.* Bureau of Justice Statistics (BJS) and Institute of Education Sciences, National Center for Education Statistics.

Robinson, P. L., W. J. Boscardin, S. M. George, S. Teklehaimanot, K. C. Heslin, and R. N. Bluthenthal (2009). "The effect of urban street gang densities on small area homicide incidences in a large metropolitan county, 1994–2002." *Journal of Urban Health: Bulletin of the New York Academy of Medicine.* Vol. 86, issue 4: 511–523.

Sanchez, R. (2000). *My Bloody Life: The Making of a Latin King.* Chicago: Chicago Review Press.

Sanders, M. T., K. L. Beirman, B. S. Heinrichs (2020). "Longitudinal associations linking elementary and middle school contexts with student aggression in early adolescence." *Journal of Abnormal Child Psychology.* Vol. 48: 1569–1580.

Shihadeh, E. S., and R. Barranco (2010). "Latino employment and black violence: The unintended consequences of U.S. immigration policy." *Social Forces.* Vol. 88, issue 3: 1393–1420.

Shihadeh, E. S., and G. C. Ousey (1998). "Industrial restructuring and violence: The link between entry-level jobs, economic deprivation, and Black and White homicide." *Social Forces.* Vol. 77, issue 1: 185–207.

Sievers, F. L. (1963). Forward. *Guidance for Children in Elementary Schools,* H. M. Smith and L. O. Eckerson. Washington, DC: U. S. Department of Health, Education, and Welfare.

Skiba, R. J., and R. L. Peterson (2000). "School discipline at a crossroads: From zero tolerance to early response." *Exceptional Children.* Vol. 66, issue 3 (Spring): 335–347.

Slavin, R. E. (1990). "Achievement effects of ability grouping in secondary schools: A best-evidence synthesis." *Review of Educational Research.* Vol. 80: 471–499.

Sobel, R. S., and B. J. Osoba (2009). "Youth gangs as pseudo-governments: implications for violent crime." *Southern Economic Journal.* Vol. 75, issue 4: 996–1019.

Stanley, S. M. (1996). "School uniforms and safety." *Education and Urban Society.* Vol. 28, issue 4: 424–35.

Strello, A., R. Striethold, I. Steinmann, and C. Siepmann (2021). "Early tracking and different types of inequalities in achievement: Difference-in-differences evidence from 20 years of large-scale assessments." *Educational Assessment, Evaluation, and Accountability.* Vol. 33: 139–167.

Sutherland, E. H. (1947). *Principles of Criminology.* Philadelphia: J. B. Lippincott.

Sweatt, L. C., G. Harding, L. Knight-Lynn, S. Rasheed, and P. Carter (2002). "Talking about the silent fear: Adolescent's experiences of violence in an urban high-rise community." *Adolescence.* Vol. 37, issue 145: 109–121.

Sweeten, G., S. D. Bushway, and R. Paternoster (2009). "Does dropping out of school mean dropping into delinquency?" *Criminology.* Vol. 47, issue 1: 47–91.

Tanioka, I., and D. Glasier (1991). "School uniforms, routine activities, and social control of delinquency in Japan." *Youth and Society.* Vol. 23, issue 1 (Sep.): 50–75.

Teachingcertificate.com (2022). "New Mexico substitute teaching license." Retrieved from https://www.teaching-certification.com/teaching/new-mexico-substitute-license.html.

Thornberry, T., M. Moor, and R. L. Christenson (1985). "The effect of dropping out of high school on subsequent criminal behavior." *Criminology.* Vol. 23: 3–18.

Thoyibah, Z., N. Intansari, and D. W. Sumarni (2017). "Correlation between family communication patterns and juvenile delinquency in junior high school." *Belitung Nursing Journal.* Vol. 3, issue 4: 297–306.

U.S. Department of Labor Statistics (2022). Education pays. U.S. Department of Labor. Sep 8. Retrieved from https://www.bls.gov/emp/chart-unemployment-earnings-education.htm.

Wallace, K. (2013). "6-year-old suspended for kissing girl, accused of sexual harassment." CNN. December 12. Available at http://www.cnn.com/2013/12/11/living/6-year-old-suspended-kissing-girl/.

Walters, G. D. (2021). "Trajectories of bullying victimization and perpetuation in Australian school children and their relationship to future delinquency and conduct problems." *Psychology of Violence*. Vol. 11, issue 1: 19–27.

Weyns, T., K. Verschueren, G. Leflot, P. Onghena, S. Wouters, and H. Colpin (2017). "The role of teacher behavior in children's relational aggression development: A five-wave longitudinal study." *Journal of School Psychology*. Vol. 64: 17–27.

Wiemann, C. M., C. A. Agurcia, A. B. Berenson, R. J. Volk, and V. L. Rickert (2000). "Pregnant adolescents: Experiences and behaviors associated with physical assault by an intimate partner." *Maternal and Child Health Journal*. Vol. 4, issue 2: 93–101.

Zamble, E., and E. Porporino (1988). *Coping Behavior and Adaptation in Prison Inmates*. New York: Springer-Verlag.

RECOMMENDED VIDEOS

The Marshall Project (2015). *American Kids and the School-to-Prison Pipelines*. Available at https://www.youtube.com/watch?v=04pcSyzwoTg.

Office of Juvenile Justice and Delinquency Prevention (2020). *Recognizing Gang Activity in Schools*. Available at https://ojjdp.ojp.gov/media/video/10566.

Office of Juvenile Justice and Delinquency Prevention (2021). *Alternatives to Traditional School Discipline*. National Institute of Justice Conference on School Safety. Available at https://nij.ojp.gov/taxonomy/term/6186.

VICE News (2014). *Last Chance High: Expelled from Every Other School*. Available at https://www.youtube.com/watch?v=n-B_kmAebbQ.

Chapter **ELEVEN**

The Juvenile Justice System

> *Society tells my students that people like them should aspire to prison the same way I understood I would go to college. They only listen to media that reinforces what they've been told all their lives: that they are worthless and that they will die or be incarcerated before they reach twenty-five.*
>
> —Thomm Quackenbush, novelist, former teacher of adjudicated minors in New York; in *Juvenile Justice: A Reference Handbook*, 2nd ed. (2016), ed. D. J. Shoemaker and T. W. Wold

Chapter Objectives

- Identify the parts of the U.S. Juvenile Justice System.
- Compare and contrast the adult system with the juvenile justice system.
- Review the protocol for arresting juveniles.
- Review court proceedings in juvenile cases.
- Identify the types of juvenile custody, including detention and correctional facilities.
- Review probation and other alternatives to incarceration for juveniles.
- Discuss why aftercare is critical to preventing further offending.

Key Terms

Age of criminal responsibility or majority
Alternative schools
Blended sentences
Case petitioning
Child Protective Services (CPS)
Citizen's arrest
Community-based corrections
Court-Appointed Special Advocates (CASA)
Detention hearing
Disposition hearing
Fitness hearing
General deterrence

Group homes
Incapacitation
Indian Child Welfare Act (1911)[1]
Individuals with Disabilities Education Act (IDEA)
Intake
Jurisdictional hearing
Juvenile boot camps
Juvenile detention
Juvenile parole
Juvenile probation
Mandated reporters
Miranda Rights
National Survey of Youth in Custody (NSYC)
Pretrial hearing
Probation
Reformatories
Restitution
Restorative Justice
Shaming and reintegration
Specific deterrence
Technical violation
Tribal justice
Tribal Law and Order Act (2010)
Wards of the Court
Wilderness programs
Wraparound programs

INTRODUCTION

Most of this book consists of exploration into why juveniles offend, what kind of offenses juveniles commit, and currently proposed solutions to preventing juvenile delinquency. In this chapter we turn our attention to the juvenile justice system itself. We will be examining how law enforcement generally deals with juveniles suspected of committing crimes, as well as how the juvenile court system functions and what happens to juveniles once they have been adjudicated.

Much will be familiar to you if you have taken other criminal justice courses. For example, if you have already taken a class in corrections, you will no doubt be familiar with the basics of *community-based corrections*, including probation and parole. We will be covering extensively legal language that, even if a term is familiar, represents the core vocabulary for the juvenile justice system. For example, coverage here of community-based corrections will focus on the involvement of parental units or guardians in the juvenile offender's treatment.

The vocabulary used in the juvenile justice system varies from state to state, even in academic research. "Youth," "juvenile," and "minor" are not defined in the same way in all 50 states (Hansen, 2023). The juvenile justice system, however, like the adult system, is based on the three pillars of criminal justice—law enforcement, courts, and corrections—though the processes of each may be decidedly different for juveniles.

[1] Though the label "Indian" is now believed to be a derogatory name and the preferred name used for indigenous people in North America is either Native American (U.S.) or First Nations (Canada), we use "Indian" wherever it is used in the legal acts, documents, and as part of the name of government agencies.

As in the adult criminal justice system, financial means can influence how a referred individual fares within the juvenile justice system. Parental units able to obtain adequate legal representation can help protect their children from serious consequences for relatively minor offenses, or even keep their children out of the juvenile justice system altogether (e.g., by sending them to private rehabilitation centers for drug offenses) (Hansen, 2023).

AGE OF CRIMINAL RESPONSIBILITY (MAJORITY)

Though juvenile justice is part of the larger criminal justice system in the United States, it is decidedly separate from the adult system, with a few exceptions. Those exceptions include times when juveniles are tried as adults for serious violent crimes. The age at which juveniles can be transferred to adult court jurisdiction is called the *age of criminal responsibility or majority* (Interstate Commission for Juveniles, 2022). Though most people define the end of childhood and adolescence as age 18, states disagree as to the age when someone no longer is considered a juvenile when suspected of serious criminal offending (Hansen, 2013).

In the United States,[2] the youngest age at which a minor can be tried in adult court and incarcerated is 12, set by Indiana and Washington state (Interstate Commission for Juveniles, 2022). In Rhode Island, there is currently no age limit for convictions calling for mandatory sentences of life in prisons (Interstate Commission for Juveniles, 2022). Juveniles there can also be transferred to adult court and subsequently to adult prison. If they commit additional crimes, including while in detention or on probation, they can be remanded to the adult state system after they reach the age limit enforced by the state in which the crimes were committed, along with the maximum age that probation or parole can be extended.

OVERVIEW OF THE JUVENILE JUSTICE SYSTEM

In many ways, the juvenile justice system, for all its faults, is much more streamlined than adult systems. There are more safeguards in place as well, acknowledging that people entering the juvenile justice system are minors at the time of arrest (although, as noted, with rare adult-system referrals for the most serious cases).

[2] See Yu (2014) for complete list of states and age ranges for age of criminal responsibility (majority).

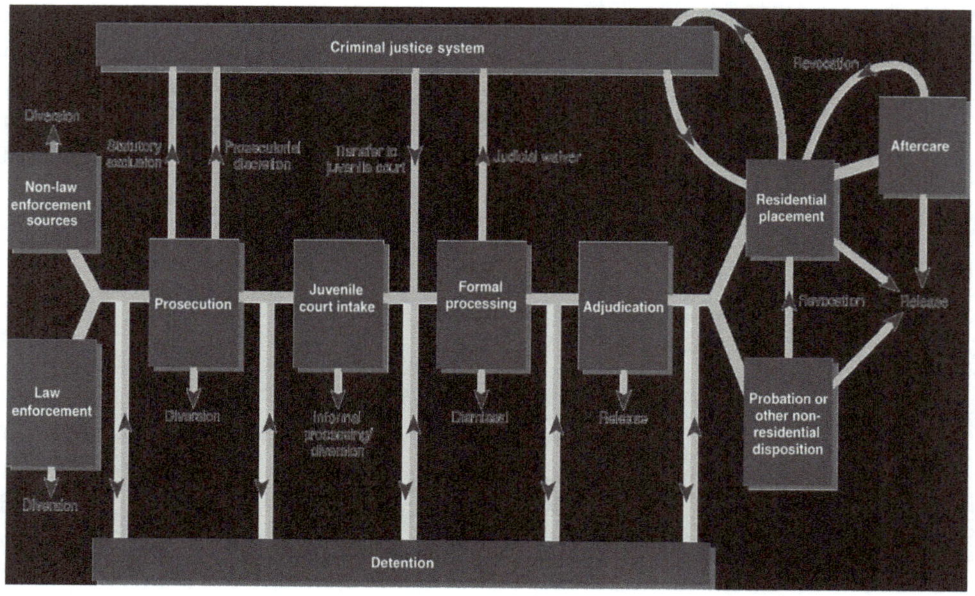

EXHIBIT 11.1 ‖ U.S. Juvenile Justice Structure and Processes

Case Processing

At any point, as we see in the flow chart in Exhibit 11.1, prosecutors in the juvenile justice system decide to either release or detain a suspected juvenile offender. The following list shows the stages in the process (Hansen, 2023, p. 280):

1. Arrest
2. Referral to court
3. Diversion
4. Secure detention
5. Judicial waiver to adult court
6. *Case petitioning*
7. Delinquency finding and adjudication
8. Probation
9. Residential placement

POLICE CONTACT

There are three primary places where police will most likely have contact with delinquent and nondelinquent youth. First is in schools with school resource officers (SROs). Second is on the street or elsewhere in public, including on public transportation. Third is when police are called to private residences. The types of law enforcement personnel who might encounter juveniles in the course of their work include sworn officers in towns and cities, in sheriff's and state police departments, and in special jurisdiction agencies, including on transit, in parks (e.g., state or national park police), or on university campuses (Office of Juvenile Justice and Delinquency Prevention, 2018b; Hyland et al., 2015).

Even though most college students are legally adults, a number of them, mostly freshmen, have not reached 18 when they begin their post-secondary education. According to college enrollment data, only 2.8% of college students are under 18 (Hanson, 2022). In this case, even though many are living away from home in dormitories, if they were to be charged with a criminal offense,[3] it would be through the juvenile courts. Even though town and city police can make arrests on college campuses within their jurisdictions, in some states, depending on the school, campus police cannot make arrests off campus property, nor arrest someone who committed a crime off campus, even if they are a college resident (Fayyad, 2020).

In each location, as with adult offenders, law enforcement may have to use their own best judgment along with their understanding of laws to determine how to approach a juvenile suspected of criminal offending or who is committing a crime. There are three cases by which juveniles are most likely to encounter police in the locations listed at the beginning of this section: (1) a crime is reported by another youth, (2) police discover the crime, or (3) an adult other than police personnel discover the crime (Office of Juvenile Justice and Delinquency Prevention, 2018b). Youth-initiated contact is voluntary, police-initiated contact is involuntary, and contact initiated by other non-law-enforcement adults can be voluntary or involuntary. For example, teachers and other school personnel, as *mandated reporters*, are required by the Federal Child Abuse Prevention and Treatment Act (CAPTA)[4] to report suspected child abuse or neglect to law enforcement and/or child welfare agencies (Children's Bureau, 2019). Probation and parole officers are likewise mandated reporters, by law (Children's Bureau, 2019). It is important to note that young adults ages 18 to 24, not juveniles, are the age group law enforcement is most likely to encounter and engage with (Office of Juvenile Justice and Delinquency Prevention, 2018b).

What distinguishes police from ordinary citizens, besides their authority to make arrests, is that they possess the authority to use force. However, with this authority, there is the responsibility to refrain from using it, unless absolutely necessary. Police should use force only if they believe their lives or those of others are in danger (Fyfe, 1982). This can be a subjective judgment call, hence the current controversies surrounding policing. It goes without saying that in dealing with juveniles, law enforcement must take additional precautions. The difficulty, in the case of confronting older juveniles, is that it can be a challenge to determine whether the individual in question is a minor.

[3] The Clery Act (1990) requires colleges and universities to publicly report crime statistics on and around their campuses.

[4] 42 U.S.C. §5106a(b)(2)(B)(i).

Though police are the ultimate authority in making arrests, conceivably private citizens and private security personnel who are not sworn law enforcement officers can make *citizen's arrests*, if they have witnessed a crime being committed, including those committed by juveniles. For example, if store security has caught a juvenile shoplifting, they have the authority to hold them until police arrive. Every state allows some form of citizen's arrest (*Economist*, 2021). The argument not to allow citizen's arrests is that it might encourage vigilantes to make arrests on the basis of hearsay[5] and questionable evidence. Technically, when citizens do make arrests, they are merely detaining a suspect until law enforcement arrives to make the actual arrest. Those who make citizen's arrests are required to satisfy the same litmus tests that sworn officers must adhere to with regard to having probable cause and reasonable grounds[6] for making an arrest (Bassiouni, 1977).

We should also note that juveniles' attitudes toward police will affect how they behave when they do encounter law enforcement, whether in school, in public, or elsewhere, and whether they will be cooperative when stopped. They can develop either positive or negative attitudes toward law enforcement at home, in schools, or from what they witness in their neighborhoods, and in some cases, may have deeply seated prejudices against police.

News and social media can also have an influence on juveniles' attitudes toward police. Though researchers disagree on whether variables like gender and socioeconomic status have an effect on these attitudes, they are in general agreement that race and ethnicity are key variables in understanding attitudes toward police. Not surprisingly, juveniles who have been arrested are more likely to have unfavorable opinions about police, as compared to those who have had no contact with law enforcement or were reporting victimization themselves (Brick et al., 2009). According to a recent Gallup poll, confidence in police is at an all-time low among American adults, at just 48% (Ortiz, 2020), which cannot help but affect the opinions of juveniles as well.

Juvenile Arrest Procedures

In most, if not all jurisdictions, when a juvenile is suspected of committing a serious or violent crime, it will result in an arrest. Of the types of encounters that juveniles have with law enforcement, as described previously in this chapter, the most common contact that police have with juveniles is on the street and involuntary (Office of Juvenile Justice and Delinquency Prevention, 2019). In addition to responding to serious juvenile offending, police are required to deal with juveniles who are truant and violating curfews (Bolden-Barrett, 2022). Police must also

[5] Hearsay is information that has been received secondhand: "I was told that. . . ." Hearsay evidence is often inadmissible in a court of law.

[6] "Probable cause and reasonable grounds" means that there is enough evidence to warrant an arrest, search, or seizure of property. This does not mean that this evidence is enough to secure a conviction in a court of law.

Arrest of a juvenile suspect, U.S. Marshals Service sting operation, Omaha, Nebraska.

respond to reported cases of missing children or those suspected of being abused (Bolden-Barrett, 2022).

In less serious juvenile criminal offending, many jurisdictions do not require that the juvenile be arrested in the stereotypical fashion seen in the media: handcuffed (or in the case of smaller children, restrained with zip ties) and placed in a police cruiser. In Los Angeles County, California, for example, an officer will issue a police citation,[7] with an order for the child and their parental units to appear in court (Kraut, 2020). Citations are the same as referrals to juvenile court.

A number of procedures must be followed during arrests of minors. The challenge is in determining if the person is indeed a juvenile if the individual has no form of identification, which is common, since minors may be not have drivers' licenses or carry school identification. As reported by National Public Radio (2012), even millions of adult Americans, including the elderly and the poor, have no form of government identification, for a variety of reasons; some may never have had a birth certificate, as in cases of home or unrecorded births, which were common into the 20th century, and in some cases of foreign born–minors. Without identification, the arresting officer must use judgment and what information they can gather to decide whether to take an individual to adult jail or to *juvenile detention*.

[7] A police citation is a written notice to appear in court or report to a police station for booking. This should not be confused with traffic citations, as these mostly consist of fines to be paid for a traffic infraction. Failure to respond to a citation can result in further criminal charges and fines.

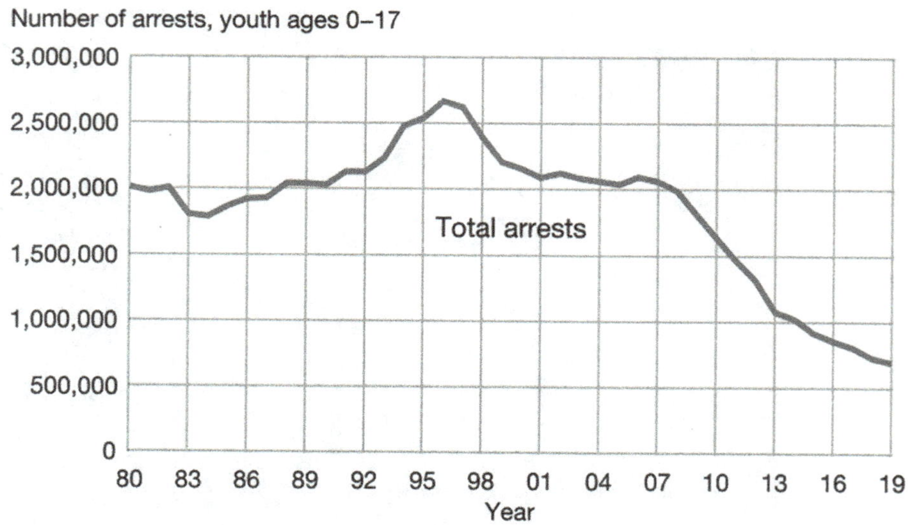

Data source: Analysis of arrest data from the Bureau of Justice Statistics and the National Center for Juvenile Justice.

EXHIBIT 11.2 ‖ Juvenile Arrest Records, 1980–2019

Once it has been confirmed that the individual being taken into custody is a minor, the following protocols must be followed (U.S. Department of Justice Archives, 2020; HG.org Legal Resources, n.d.):

- As in the case of arresting an adult, a juvenile who is being arrested for delinquency must be advised of their rights, pursuant to 18 U.S.C.A. §5033. The *Miranda Rights* include
  1. The right to remain silent and the right not to answer questions;
  2. Anything said can be used against you in court;
  3. The right to speak with an attorney prior to, and during police questioning;
  4. The right to a public defender if you cannot afford to hire a lawyer; and
  5. The right to cease police questioning at any time and request to have an attorney present.
- The U.S. Attorney's General [U.S. Attorney] must be notified in federal cases.
- The juvenile's parents, guardian, or other custodian must be immediately notified of their arrest, their rights, and the alleged offense.
- If the juvenile is a non-citizen, every effort must be made to notify their parents, guardian, or custodian as soon as possible. Their country's Consulate should be notified as well, pursuant to United States v. Doe, 862 F. 2d 776, 780 (9th Cir. 1988).
- The juvenile must be presented before a magistrate [judge] immediately. If not immediately available, the juvenile can only be held for a reasonable amount of time, typically 6 hours. Any delay results in any of the statements made by the juvenile being suppressed.

- Depending on the suspected offense, the U.S. Attorney in the case of suspected federal offenses can either refer the case to state authorities, or the juvenile can be transferred to adult authorities for criminal prosecution as an adult.

According to HG.org (n.d.), other marked differences between adult and juvenile arrests include:

- Juveniles are given special considerations apart from adult crimes based on their status as minors.
- Depending on the state, children may be questioned by police without parental units present.
- If a minor confesses to a crime during police questioning, a judge later may determine that the juvenile did not fully understand their constitutional rights at the time of arrest or interview, even if they had been read their Miranda Rights.
- If a juvenile is already under court supervision, as in the case of reoffending, it is critical that a criminal defense attorney be present before police interrogation.
- In adult cases, a suspect can be held for 24 to 72 hours, depending on jurisdiction, in order to give prosecutors time to decide what charges, if any, to pursue, and to schedule a pretrial *detention hearing*–again, depending on the jurisdiction. If the arrest has been made later in the day on a Friday, over the weekend, or over a long holiday weekend, and no judge is on call to hear cases in off hours, they can conceivably be held in custody longer than the 72 hour time limit.

Police officers have a variety of responsibilities when handling juvenile suspects after arrest. Once a juvenile is arrested, police officers are required to do the following:

> *Bring in or summon young offenders to the police department's juvenile division and question, fingerprint, book and, if necessary, detain them. At the time of arrest, officers decide whether to refer young offenders to juvenile court or to route these cases out of the justice system [into the child welfare system]. Police account for most referrals to juvenile court.* (Bolden-Barrett, 2022, retrieved from https://work.chron.com/police-officers-roles-juvenile-justice-system-24909.html)

All documentation of the juvenile's arrest, beyond police reports, is conducted during *intake*, including fingerprinting, once the youth has been taken to a police station. After the juvenile has been processed, the police officer makes a formal referral, if warranted, to juvenile court. Police referrals to juvenile courts make up approximately 82% of all juvenile cases; the rest are due to parents, victims, and school officials making referrals (Bolden-Barrett, 2022). When police officers are required to handle noncriminal status offenses of juveniles, there is generally no arrest, unless the status offense occurred while the juvenile was on probation or parole. If the offense is serious enough, the juvenile will be placed in detention. However, as in the example of the New York State juvenile system, in most jurisdictions in the United States, juveniles will be released to the custody of parental units or relatives, rather than being detained after arrest for minor offenses (NYCourts.gov, n.d.), which is common practice in police departments across the United States.

School Resource Officers (SROs)

Though we touched briefly on school resource officers (SROs) in our chapter on crime in schools and earlier in this chapter, some of the restrictions that SROs work under bear repeating. As we noted, SROs are part of police departments, even though they are located in public schools, and they are required, in some cases and depending on the suspected offense, to refrain from arresting students on school property. Unlike other sworn law enforcement, SROs in schools also serve as educators, school emergency managers, and informal counselors (Community Policing in Action Services, n.d.).

It is also important to note, however, that since the increased presence of SROs in schools, there has been a steady increase in the number of juveniles being referred to the juvenile justice system (Petteruti, 2011) in the so-called school-to-prison pipeline under zero-tolerance policies (see Chapter 10). As SROs are sworn law enforcement officers, they have the authority to make arrests at schools and on any other school district property.

In some states, such as Florida, SROs carry firearms on campus while on duty (Florida Legislature, 2021). We should also note, after a rash of mass shootings on campuses, controversy surrounds whether teachers should be armed or schools should be gun-free zones.

A Rand Corporation study (2020, retrieved from https://www.rand.org/research/gun-policy/analysis/laws-allowing-armed-staff-in-K12-schools.html#fn5) notes:

> *[S]everal states, including Colorado, Montana, and Ohio, allow armed teachers if the school district or charter school allows it. Other states, such as Indiana, allow individuals (including teachers) who have been specifically authorized by the school board to carry firearms on school property. Five states*[8] *allow any individual with a concealed-carry permit to carry a gun into a K-12 school, and Wyoming allows school employees with such permits to carry a gun on school grounds. Relatedly, some states allow any licensed concealed-carry permit holders who have been authorized by the school district or other relevant authority (as in Idaho) or enhanced permit holders performing their official duties (as in Mississippi) to carry weapons onto school property.*[9]

[8] Alaska, New Hampshire, Oregon, Rhode Island, and Utah.

[9] Rand Corporation, 2020; MontanaCode Ann. §45-8-361; Ohio Rev. Code §2923.122(B); Indiana Code Ann. §35-47-9-1(a); Alaska Stat. §§18.65.755, 11.61.210; New Hampshire Rev. Stat. Ann. §§193-D:1,193.13; Oregon Rev. Stat. §166.370; Rhode Island Gen. Laws §11-47-60; Utah Code Ann §76-10-505.5; Wyoming Stat. 21-3-132; Indiana Code Ann §18-3302D(g); Mississippi Code Ann. §97-37-17).

This does not necessarily mean that anyone other than sworn law enforcement officers, including teachers and school administrators, has the authority to make arrests or detain suspects. At least in the case of Colorado, no state-wide regulations prescribe training for school personnel who carry firearms on campus (Hernandez, 2018).

The fact that SROs have daily contact with students at school is why some schools adopt a modified and more casual uniform for SROs, typically khaki pants and polo shirts with the police logo, rather than more formal, traditional attire of police on the street. For example, the Columbia, Missouri police department changed their SRO uniforms to khaki pants and polo shirts, as the traditional police uniform is viewed as intimidating; the intent is to make SROs seem more approachable to high school students (Renkoski, 2016). In this way, a school looks less like an armed camp, which can further alienate juveniles from police officers.

Rights of Juveniles in Custody

Though it would seem that juveniles taken into custody under arrest would have very few legal rights, they surprisingly have a great number of constitutional rights in the United States, as do adults under suspicion of committing a crime (Hansen, 2023; Umpierre, 2014):

- **Free speech (First Amendment)**
  Speech is limited in juvenile detention centers and adult prisons if it interferes with the security of the facility. The classic example of prohibited speech is someone shouting "Fire!" in a crowded theater when there is no fire, which can result in injuries or even death as occupants frantically try to exit the building.
- **Equal protection under the law (Fifth Amendment)**
  In a number of areas, juveniles in custody are given equal protection under the law. These include nondiscriminatory treatment and compliance with Title VI of the Civil Rights Act of 1964 and Executive Order 13166, where staff are required to take steps to make sure that non-English-speaking detainees have access to interpreter and translation services. Materials written in their native language must be made available to juveniles in detention. Juveniles cannot be discriminated against on the basis of sex, race, ethnicity, or religion. This is, of course, what is legal. In reality, biases and prejudices are everywhere, whether acted on consciously or unconsciously.

  Staff are also required to treat LGBTQIA+[10] juveniles equally. This is particularly crucial, as juveniles in childhood or adolescence, and even young adults,

[10] There are a number of similar initialisms. LGBTQIA+ is the most inclusive and stands for lesbian, gay, bisexual, transsexual or transgender, questioning or queer, intersex, asexual, with + standing for any other non-heterosexual, non-cisgender status.

may still be figuring out their gender and/or sexual identity, and LGBTQIA+ youth are at great risk in and out of detention for psychological distress, bullying, assault, and suicide. It cannot be emphasized enough that staff needs to be specifically trained to help juveniles who identify with one or more of these categories.

- **Right to seek legal counsel (Sixth Amendment)**
  Similar to adults, juveniles being prosecuted in either the juvenile or adult systems have the right to have an attorney, and it is the responsibility of the facility staff to allow them access to meetings, including by phone. It is safe to assume that if parents or guardians are actively involved in the juvenile's defense, they may also be active in facilitating these meetings and phone calls.

Parental Legal Rights

We should note that once a child is taken into custody, the message sent consciously or unconsciously to both the parental units and society in general is that the parental units are unfit and unable to keep their children from committing crimes. In other words, they are viewed as failures as parental units (Hansen, 2023). On top of the social shame, parental units also lose control of a number of their legal rights in regards to the care and instruction of a child who is in custody. This includes medical and psychiatric care as well.

Generally, parents and others responsible for care of a child or children are not aware of their legal rights until their wards run afoul of the law. Even in sending a child to school, parental units lose some control over what their children are required to do and learn. The ultimate authority over children is the state (Hansen, 2023). The state has the right to intervene in what some might see as private family matters if it is considered to be in the best interest of the child. Some decisions made by the state and courts can result in dire consequences for parental units, in the event that their child is found to be delinquent (Hansen, 2023).

In the course of juvenile court proceedings, parental units have the right to relinquish any and all rights to making decisions about the care of their children. However, whether their child has had an encounter with the juvenile court system or parental units find themselves no longer in a position to care for a child or children, once their petition to relinquish responsibility has been approved by a judge, it is an uphill battle to reinstate those rights (Hansen, 2023). Whether the child is in custody or not, the courts can also remove parental rights in the following situations (Hansen, 2023; Miller-Perrin and Perrin, 2013):

- There has been intervention by *Child Protective Services* (CPS; e.g., multiple calls to the home).
- There are court-ordered services in place (e.g., therapy), but problems continue, including abuse and/or delinquency.

- The child has lived away from their parental units' home, in foster care, or with a relative for a number of months (the number differs from state to state).
- There is no optimism that conditions will improve in the home once a juvenile is released from custody or detention.
- It will become increasingly difficult to find placement, either in foster care or a permanent home, if the child continues to live with the parental units.

Though courts do make every attempt to find detention and corrections placement close to parental units' homes, this is not always possible, as in some jurisdictions there are few, if any, facilities. The parental units, through their attorney, can make a request as to where their child is placed after adjudication, but they do not have the right to demand that the child be housed in a facility close to their homes. This becomes problematic for visitation if the parental units have little or no access to a vehicle or public transportation.

Racial and Ethnic Disparities

Racial and ethnic disparities add complexities. It is not merely a question of individuals or, in this case, the juvenile justice system holding biases against youth of color. And the criminal justice system is not exclusive in having documented inequality of treatment, whether in discussions of suspects, the convicted, or victims. As Berk (2019) suggests, there are a number of junctures where biases can play out in the criminal justice system: in inequality of treatment, inequality of opportunities to reform, and inequalities in long term outcomes (aftercare).

Police and other criminal justice professionals, like every other human being, are subject to human frailties and are products of where and when they were raised, who raised them, and what life lessons they might have had along the way. Police are not infallible and can and do make mistakes in the course of their jobs, just like the rest of us. However, it is of grave concern when they have racial or ethnic prejudices. It can have an effect on their judgment when it comes to arrests of adult and juvenile suspects. In findings from the National Longitudinal Survey of Youth, Black youth were more likely to have been arrested, and even more worrisome, they were more likely to be arrested multiple times compared to white juveniles (Robles-Ramamurthy and Watson, 2019).

Perception of biases can also affect how citizens, including juveniles, perceive the police, as we noted earlier in this chapter. The Michael Brown police-involved shooting in 2014, where an unarmed 18-year-old teenager was shot and killed by a white police officer in Ferguson, Missouri, sparked a rash of protests there and in Baltimore, Maryland, Charlotte, North Carolina, and Baton Rouge, Louisiana, with at times violent demands for police reforms (Shjarback, 2019; Rosenfeld, 2015). The argument of reform activists, which is based on a number of academic studies, is that generally the use of force by some police against racial and ethnic minorities is based in racial stereotyping and implicit biases (Duke and Kahn, 2017).

There are a number of safeguards in federal and state legislation to combat racial discrimination in the criminal justice system. However, to date, critics, particularly those of the juvenile justice system, see little progress in achieving their aims (Robles-Ramamurthy and Watson, 2019). Black students are more likely to be subjected to zero-tolerance policies in schools that have SRO presence, making them also more likely to be arrested, expelled, or suspended at a young age (Robles-Ramamurthy and Watson, 2019).

JUVENILE COURT

The official purpose of juvenile court is not only to protect the public, but to preserve the rights and safety of the juvenile. Up until the 1960s, juveniles lacked a number of due process protections, including right to counsel. The Center on Juvenile and Criminal Justice states that the primary purpose of juvenile courts today is to provide opportunities for rehabilitation and supervision of delinquent youth, including while in custody, if parental units are found to be ill-equipped to provide those two essential elements needed to reform them (Center for Juvenile and Criminal Justice, 2022).

For practical purposes, we use the term "arrest" in this chapter when a suspected juvenile offender is taken into custody. However, there are some nuanced differences between the language used in the juvenile and adult systems after an arrest has been made. Though criminal complaints (or civil, for that matter) can be brought against both adults and juveniles, we tend to see it more often in the case of minors. A complaint can be filed far more quickly than an indictment, and as expediency is critical in juvenile cases, this is how criminal matters are likely to be handled. A criminal police complaint against a juvenile usually follows an arrest. However, parental units, school personnel, social workers, and aggrieved citizens may also file a complaint (Berk, 2019).

As in the case of all aspects of treatment and prevention programs (discussed in Chapter 13), increasingly there is a demand for data-driven evidence that sentencing through the juvenile court systems is equitable and appropriate for the offenses the juveniles have been adjudicated for (Martin, 2018). In other words, are courts serving the best interests of communities and juveniles and their families, based on systematic data analyses of outcomes? As we will see in Chapter 13, often once juveniles leave the court system, information may be lost, as agencies work within their own jurisdictions with little or no interaction. For example, the therapist for a juvenile in court-ordered treatment for substance abuse may have only superficial contact with the probation officer.

Legal Representation

Like adult suspects, if a juvenile, or more realistically, their parental unit, does not have the means to hire a defense attorney, a court-appointed public defender will be assigned. Unfortunately, public defenders are often overwhelmed with a number of cases and may only learn the particulars of the case and their client on the day of their first court appearance.

Unlike adult defendants, suspected juvenile offenders may not represent themselves in court. If they waive the right to an attorney, termed *waiver of counsel*, they are essentially waiving their right to a trial. It is not uncommon for juveniles to waive their Sixth Amendment right to an attorney, but doing so is considered an admission of guilt or is associated with a guilty plea (Woolard, 2019).

Proceedings

A few types of hearings are typical for juveniles who have been arrested or have a criminal complaint against them. The following are the types of hearings that juveniles may expect to attend with their attorneys (Kraut, 2020):

- The first is most likely to be the *detention hearing*, similar to an arraignment of an adult defendant.
- In more serious offenses charges, juveniles will attend a *fitness hearing* to determine if the matter should be referred to adult court.
- The *jurisdictional hearing*, also referred to as adjudication hearing, is a trial in which a representative for the district attorney's office has to make their case.
- If a judge has determined that a crime has indeed been committed by the minor, beyond reasonable doubt, as the case has been presented to him and on the basis of evidence against the minor, a *disposition hearing* will be held in order to determine the punishment for the juvenile.

The purposes of *pretrial hearings* are to establish what evidence will be permissible in court, as well as which charges will actually be pursued. The prosecution has the right to dismiss or reduce the counts against the juvenile. This requires that the district attorney's office turn over evidence to the defense attorney. The prosecution also can determine what records, if any, should be subpoenaed, including school records, which are ordinarily protected by the Family Educational Rights and Privacy Act (FERPA) (U.S. Department of Education, n.d.). The judge specifies the length of time in which evidence must be provided to the defense attorney. Possible sentencing outcomes are also discussed at this time if the child is found to be delinquent.

There are no juries in juvenile court proceedings. The evidence is heard by a judge, who makes a ruling in the case.

Pretrial Detention

If it is determined in a detention hearing that a juvenile should be held in custody before their actual trial begins due to the seriousness of the charges, they will be held in the equivalent of adult jail. This is only done in the most serious cases, though juveniles can be held in detention before their detention hearing. In minor offenses, typically juveniles are relinquished to the care of their parental units, who are ordered to bring the accused child to court on the specified dates.

Most will agree that everything possible should be done to avoid detention of suspected juvenile offenders. Detention should be used as a last resort and only in the most serious cases or when there is some concern as to whether the juvenile will show up in court, on the basis of the attitudes of the juvenile's parental units. In 75% of juvenile cases, detention is used to assure that the accused juvenile offender will attend court hearings (Walker and Herting, 2020). However, a number of studies indicate that juveniles who have had pretrial detention may be more likely to be found delinquent at trial, whether the evidence points in that direction or not. In addition, recidivism rates are 11%, with new felony offense(s) within a year of release from detention (Walker and Herting, 2020) with some evidence showing that the risk increases with the length of pretrial detention stay.

Similar to adult jails, pretrial detention centers have generally high security. This is more practical than anything else, as juveniles have been accused of committing serious crimes that might or might not have been violent. Detention centers, like jails, must be prepared to house the worst of the worst juvenile offenders, including those accused of murder. Of greatest concern is that juvenile detention centers have routinely been accused of abuses. According to Frazier and Bishop (1986, p. 1132), they have historically and notoriously represented "greater abuses of law and power than any other aspect of the juvenile justice system."

Juveniles Tried in the Adult Court System

One of the controversies in juvenile justice is about whether cases where juveniles who have committed serious, often violent crimes may be referred to the adult court system. As a direct result of the push for tougher laws and consequences for juvenile crime, 45 of 50 states have passed laws and amended legislation that lays the foundation for arguing for trying violent young offenders in adult court (Hansen, 2023; Austin et al., 2000).

Blended Sentences

In cases of serious, particularly violent, offending, or if the offender is older and approaching adulthood, judges have the discretion to adjudicate the juvenile to a *blended sentence*. A blended sentence means that the juvenile offender will initially be remanded to custody in a juvenile correctional facility and, when they reach adulthood, generally between ages 18 and 21, they may be transferred and serve the rest of their sentence in an adult facility.

Privacy Rights of Juveniles

Only a limited number of people can access the criminal records of minors. Among them are (Hansen, 2023, p. 280; Nolo, n.d.):

- Parents or legal guardians
- Defense attorneys
- Federal, state, or city attorneys (prosecutors)
- School officials
- Child protective services
- Academic or institutional researchers

Of the last group, since juveniles represent a special population in research, the research design, including surveys and interview questions, is rigorously scrutinized. A special population includes any research subjects who have less say in their participation in research, including prisoners, patients, and children. For those who are institutionalized, including juveniles in custody, researchers must follow ethical standards and Belmont Report principles, including (i) ensuring respect for all research subjects, (ii) guaranteeing that the research will benefit society, and (iii) allowing research subjects to withdraw at any time, for any reason (U.S. Department of Health and Human Services, 1979). These principles apply to medical, psychological, or social science research.

TRIBAL PROVISIONS; JUVENILE JUSTICE REFORM ACT (2018)

There is essentially another criminal justice system, including systems of juvenile justice, within the United States that recognizes and respects the unique cultures of Native Americans and Alaska Natives.[11] Based in the cultural practices in indigenous populations, *tribal justice* is incorporated into the requirements of state and federal laws. Other than Black youth, Native American and Alaskan Native youth face some of the highest and most disproportionate incarceration rates

[11] As in the case of Native American tribes in the lower 48 states, Alaska is made up of a number of indigenous groups, with distinct cultures, including Northwest Coast, Inupiaqs, Yupiks, Aleuts, and Athabascans (Alaska, State of, n.d.).

in the United States. The United States is not alone in these alarming numbers. According to Canada's Department of Justice (2021), indigenous youth make up only 8% of the juvenile population, but they represent 48% of admissions to youth custody, based on data from all provinces and territories except Nova Scotia, Québec, Alberta, and Yukon.

Within the U.S. Juvenile Justice and Delinquency Prevention Act (1974), which we will cover in Chapter 13 when we discuss preventative measures in depth, five provisions support Native American and Alaskan Native youth, including (Office of Juvenile Justice and Delinquency Prevention, 2019):

- Provision requiring that the Office of Juvenile Justice and Delinquency Prevention (OJJDP) consult with representatives of Native American and Alaskan tribes.
- Provision requiring that an annual report be produced, which includes a description of funding provided to tribes for juvenile delinquency and other prevention programs, under the *Tribal Law and Order Act* (2010).
- Provision requiring that states devise and implement regular three-year plans, which will include the input of experts in tribal law enforcement and juvenile justice in Native American and Alaskan Native communities.
- Provision that within one year of enactment of the Juvenile Justice and Delinquency Prevention Act (i.e., by 1975), research be conducted to identify the barriers that states and Native American populations face in providing services to juveniles who were in the state welfare system before being placed in the juvenile justice system.
- Provision that Native American tribes continue to have delinquency programs funded, with 11% of Title VI funding to go to Tribal Youth programs.

There are a number of other provisions for Native American and Alaskan Native youth when it comes to court proceedings. Under the *Indian Child Welfare Act* (ICWA, §1911(b)), a tribal court can request and accept transfer from a state court for child custody and other juvenile legal matters that affect tribal members (Native American Rights Fund, n.d.). However, despite the autonomy provided by tribal law, juvenile crimes committed on established tribal land (i.e., reservations) can fall under the jurisdiction of federal, state, or tribal justice systems (Office of Juvenile Justice and Delinquency Prevention, 2016; Dorgan et al., 2014; Adams et al., 2011). Jurisdiction depends on four factors: (1) location of crime, (2) type of crime, (3) whether the perpetrator is an adult or juvenile and/or a resident on tribal land, and (4) the status of the victim, again, whether or not they live on tribal land (OJJDP, 2016).

We should note that other complexities arise in Hawaii, where a number of indigenous people reside. There are no federally recognized tribes in Hawaii, but some members of recognized indigenous tribes from the lower 48 states and Alaska live there, so the 1911 Indian Child Welfare Act applies (U.S. Bureau of Justice

Tribal Court, Hualapai Tribe, Peach Springs, Arizona.

Assistance, n.d.). After a ten-year battle to pass the Native Hawaiian Reorganization Act ("Akaka Bill," named after Senator Daniel Akaka), the act finally passed in 2009 and was signed into law by then-President Obama (Toensing, 2018). The act establishes and authorizes a Native Hawaiian governing body, with the same basic rights and privileges as are provided in Native American and Alaskan Native tribal law, with some exceptions (Toensing, 2018).

One of the most important factors in trying indigenous youth in tribal courts, as well as in the calls to house them in juvenile facilities on Native land, is to avoid exposing them to yet more trauma. As Dorgan et al. (2014, p. 129) advises,

> *The impact of immaturity is a factor in every juvenile case. However, in those cases involving AI/AN* [Native American and Alaska Native] *youth, the effects of exposure to violence and trauma are more likely to be also present. . . . It is highly likely that the parents are in the cycle of intergenerational violence and trauma exposure and are limited in their understanding of how this impacts their child.*

Girls' Courts

Not all jurisdictions treat female and male juvenile offenders the same in the courts. In some jurisdictions, the juvenile court system recognizes different considerations for young females taken into custody. In 1992, authorized under the Juvenile Justice and Delinquency Prevention Act, gender-specific programming was mandated in the courts and corrections (Jones et al., 2020). Girls' courts in California, for example, knowing that females are more likely to be abused or exploited and to have family histories of trauma, or to be at risk for any of these, see to the gender-specific needs of female delinquents (California Courts, 2022). However, at this time, there are only a limited number of girls' courts in the United States, with California leading the trend with ten juvenile courts in the state offering more services when sentencing female juvenile offenders (California Courts, 2022; Jones et al., 2020). However, one criticism of girls' courts, common to juvenile delinquency programs in general, is that they have not been adequately evaluated to determine their effectiveness (Jones et al., 2020).

PURPOSES OF PUNISHMENT

There are a number of functions of punishment, both in the adult court system, as well as the juvenile system. A number of theorists in sociology, including Max Weber, suggest that the concept of crime itself is functional in society, so that there is a clear delineation between acceptable and unacceptable behavior. What is distinctly different is that even though the functions are the same for both systems, in the juvenile system, there is more focus on rehabilitation. In other words, like the ideal within a family, punishment of juvenile offenders is not so much to punish, per se, but to correct delinquent behavior. In reality, this is not always the case. As with adult offenders, juveniles' punishment may result in anger and resentment toward the criminal justice system, and often toward society in general, judging by juvenile recidivism rates.

Punishment also serves, in theory, to act as a deterrence to other would-be offenders. Punishment that targets crime in general is termed *general deterrence*. Punishment that targets a specific crime is called a *specific deterrence*. Examples include general sentencing guidelines for types of punishment appropriate for specific types of thievery. Having mandatory, involuntary residential drug treatment as part of sentencing in an adult or juvenile case can also be intended as a specific deterrence, as treatment centers generally offer as little freedom of movement as correctional facilities, no matter how much more pleasant their settings might be. And of course, drug treatment also fits the rehabilitation model as well.

JUVENILE CORRECTIONS

Juvenile corrections, like all government functions, including those throughout the criminal justice agencies, are bureaucratic structures. As described by Max Weber (1922), bureaucracy is the most efficient way to run organizations, and in this case, government offices. In adult corrections, the structure is described as quasi-military, modeled after the branches of U.S. armed forces and law enforcement, down to the ranks of correction officers (Hansen, 2023).

As bureaucracies, juvenile correctional facilities are required to have written rules, records, jurisdictional areas, clear job descriptions, and other characteristics identified by Weber (1922). And like in any bureaucracy (and adult corrections systems), the people who work in them have to meet the job requirements for positions at all levels, including detention centers and probation. For example, juvenile probation officers are often expected to have earned a bachelor's or master's degree in criminal justice or a related field (Hansen, 2023; University of Central Florida, 2022). The high rates of mental health issues in the juvenile offender population requires personnel with extensive training in juvenile counseling, social work, and psychology. Once employed, individuals should also pursue continuing education, including seminars, in-service education, and conferences.

It is more expensive to house a juvenile in a correctional facility or detention center, compared to adult corrections. Sanders (2021; Holman and Zeidenberg, 2006), and the Center on Budget and Policy Priorities in the United States, state that juvenile incarceration is currently both expensive and ineffective, with billions of dollars spent nationally and "young people who have been incarcerated. . . . [are] more likely to be arrested again, [facing] barriers in obtaining an education and stable employment." According to the Justice Policy Institute (2020), the most expensive facilities cost states, on average, over $200,000 per year to incarcerate one juvenile, a jump of 44% from 2014.

Types of Juvenile Facilities

The majority of juveniles in custody are being held in secure facilities that essentially look exactly like adult maximum security. This is for a number of reasons. Because many juveniles held in custody are violent offenders, they need to be held in secure facilities. Also, there are not nearly as many juveniles in custody as adults, making it impractical to have the many types of prisons (e.g., maximum security, medium security, etc.) seen in adult corrections.

The two primary types of centers that house juvenile offenders are detention centers and residential facilities. Simply put, detention is locked custody used after arrest and before trial, or in cases of probation, parole violations, or an adjudicated juvenile awaiting transfer to a more permanent corrections facility (Holman and Ziedenberg, 2006). In some jurisdictions, correctional facilities other than detention centers have the harsher name of *juvenile corrections*, while others use softer labels.

Depending on the jurisdiction, there are nine types of facilities within these two categories. Sawyer (2019) and the Prison Policy Initiative organization describe the types and their functions as follows:

The oldest juvenile facility in the United States, Glenn Mills School, Youth Detention Center for Delinquent Boys, Pennsylvania (founded in 1826).

- **Correctional Facilities**
  1. **Detention center:** Provides temporary care in a restricted environment, for juveniles who are awaiting court disposition, who have been adjudicated and waiting for disposition (sentencing), or who are waiting to be transferred to other facilities.
  2. **Long-term secure facility:** Provides strict confinement; includes training schools and *reformatories.*
  3. **Reception/diagnostic center:** Short-term facilities that are used to screen juvenile offenders in order to determine the best facility that they should ultimately be placed in.
- **Residential-style facilities**
  1. **Residential treatment center:** Provides individually planned treatment in a residential setting, including for mental health care and drug and/or alcohol abuse.
  2. **Group homes and halfway houses:** Long-term residential facilities that allow for contact with the outside community, including in order to attend school or holding a job.
  3. **Ranch/wilderness camp:** Long-term residential facilities for less serious juvenile offenders in outdoor settings, including ranches, farms, wilderness, or coastal locations.
  4. **Shelter:** Short-term facilities for status offenses, with an unrestricted environment where temporary residents can come and go into the community. Intended to house runaways and other unhoused juveniles.

5. **Boot camp:** A secure facility that is modeled after military basic training, with emphasis on physical activity and discipline. Confinement can be short-term, or longer than detention, but boot camps are intended to be long-term facilities.
6. **Other types of juvenile facilities:** *Alternative schools* (continuation schools) and independent living facilities.

Many facilities require personnel with specialized training. Research estimates indicate that as many as 70% of juveniles involved in the juvenile justice system suffer from some mental health issue, if not crisis (Jackson, 2022). Jackson (2022) suspects this has been exacerbated by the COVID-19 pandemic, during which facilities reduced their mental health services.

Not all facilities are equal, and they can vary from jurisdiction to jurisdiction. According to a number of sources, including Schwartzapeel (2022) and Mamone (2022), the Acadiana Center for Youth in St. Martinville, Louisiana, is one of the worst juvenile facilities. Described by the Office of Juvenile Justice, State of Louisiana (n.d., retrieved from https://ojj.la.gov/acadiana-center-for-youth/):

> *Opened in March 2019. . . . The campus includes nine buildings, including administration, housing units, gymnasium, a school with classrooms, and a vocational-technical area, a kitchen and dining hall and maintenance buildings. Included on the site will be a soccer field and outdoor basketball court.*

The Acadiana Center for Youth facility was originally intended to be a transitional treatment unit for violent juveniles. It has been described by one 15-year-old at the facility as round-the-clock solitary confinement with, in his case, no education provided, which violates state and federal law. He also did not receive the substance abuse counseling ordered by the court (Schwartzapeel, 2022; Mamone; 2022). While in long-term solitary confinement at the center, juveniles, some of whom already suffer from serious mental illness, are shackled with leg irons (Equal Justice Initiative, 2022). In response to reports of the conditions at the Acadiana Center for Youth, State Representative Royce Duplessis filed a bill to restrict use of solitary confinement of juveniles to no more than four hours at a time, and to require authorities to notify a juvenile's parental units and attorney; the bill also requires the facility to keep track of uses of solitary confinement in Louisiana youth detention and correctional centers (Equal Justice Initiative, 2022).

Louisiana is not alone in being investigated for questionable practices in juvenile facilities. In 2021 the U.S. Attorney's Office for Eastern District of Texas launched an investigation into the conditions in five juvenile secure facilities, including whether children in the facilities were adequately protected against physical and sexual abuse (U.S. Department of Justice, 2021). U.S. Assistant Attorney Kristen Clarke states that in addition to concerns about physical and sexual abuse, there were concerns over excessive use of chemical restraints (e.g., sedatives), excessive use of solitary confinement, and/or a general lack of adequate mental health services (Balderrama, 2021).

A number of attempted and successful escapes have been made from the Acadiana Center. The most recent attempt took place in June 2022, when a 17-year-old male escaped during transport to Bunkie General Hospital. His third attempted escape, he was arrested sixteen days later in Houston, Texas (Jones, 2022; Lacen and Roy, 2022). Two 19-year-olds had escaped Acadiana less than a month earlier (Little, 2022).

At the other end of the spectrum of juvenile custody facilities are those designed for short-term stays or long-term treatment. These are considered among the best facilities, though typically they do not house more serious offenders. The Fairbanks Youth Facility, in Fairbanks, Alaska, is designed to hold only 12 juveniles in short-term detention and an additional 15 in long-term treatment. In recent years it has been operating at approximately 65% capacity, while facilities elsewhere report overcrowded conditions (Division of Juvenile Justice, Alaska Department of Family and Community Services, n.d.). From the outside, the Fairbanks facility looks more like a public school than a correctional facility.

The COVID-19 pandemic had an effect on both juvenile arrests and detention. According to Lovett (2021), the average daily number of juveniles in each detention center was 44; "six months later as COVID-19 spread . . . that number was halved to an average of 22 youths." There was a slight increase as pandemic

A juvenile facility in Fairbanks, Alaska.

protocols and prevention measures were put into place, followed by a decrease in April 2021 to an average daily population of 30 detained juveniles; youth detention reached its highest levels in October 2021 (Lovett, 2021; Annie E. Casey Foundation, 2021). Detention centers reported early releases due to the pandemic so decreases in detention are not an indication of less juvenile offending (Lovett, 2021).

Private Juvenile Facilities

Not all juvenile detention and correctional centers are managed by state or federal government. Since the Juvenile Justice and Delinquency Prevention Act was passed in 1974, states have increasingly turned to private corporations specializing in corrections to house delinquent juveniles—by 1989, 40% of detained juveniles were being held in private facilities (Hansen, 2023; McDonald, 1992).

A number of controversies surround the use of for-profit facilities, the least of which is how few studies have compared private and public juvenile facilities other than for comparative cost savings per state (Hansen, 2023). One major concern is possible relationships between sentencing judges and private corporations. In a particularly offensive ethics breach, in the "kids for cash" scandal in Pennsylvania, two judges were paid bribes in return for harsher sentencing in juvenile cases, often sending delinquents to private juvenile facilities when it would not ordinarily be the usual sentencing based on the offenses (Hansen, 2023). An additional concern is that personnel in private facilities, whether intended for adults or juveniles, are not paid as well as in public facilities, where correctional officers are members of labor unions, nor are they as well-trained as state or federal employees (Hansen, 2023).

Juvenile Correctional Centers

Whenever possible, it is in the best interest of the child and their family to have them serve their sentence in the community. However, depending on the jurisdiction and the charges, there may be no alternative but to send the adjudicated juvenile offender to detention. This becomes a more expensive alternative, as the juvenile will require specialized rehabilitation (provided by the center, in most cases), and depending on the juvenile's age, compulsory education (Hansen, 2023). In 2020, the typical cost of housing a juvenile was between $100,000 and $500,000, depending on the location and types of services needed (Hansen, 2023; Justice Policy Institute, 2020). And while the number of juveniles held in custody has steadily decreased since the 1990s, the number of adults in prison has increased by 23% (Hansen, 2023; BJS, 2019), many of whom may have previously been on probation or other community-based programs within the juvenile justice system.

As a bureaucratic structure, the juvenile correctional centers, along with other forms of physical custody, are required to provide the following formal functions (Hansen, 2023; Clark, 2014):

- Maintain public safety
- Maintain the safety of children placed in detention centers
- Maintain humane and constitutional conditions of confinement
- Fulfill the requirements of the specific facility

Meeting Educational Needs of Juveniles in Detention

Because the population housed in juvenile detention are primarily minors, many are still young enough to qualify for compulsory schooling. Compulsory education laws vary from state to state. Juveniles who have been in detention are less likely to complete their high school education. In a study of post-released youth, the California Department of Education reported that one year after institutional release, 28% enrolled in school on the outside, 27% attended school but subsequently dropped out, and a disturbing 45% never returned to school (Youth Law Center, 2018). High-school dropouts have a more difficult time finding employment, experience poorer health, and have lower lifetime earning potential (Holman and Ziedenberg, 2006). Knowing that high school dropouts are more likely to become criminal offenders and end up in adult prison, keeping juveniles in school during custody and while on probation or parole is a priority.

COMMUNITY-BASED CORRECTIONS AND ALTERNATIVE SOLUTIONS FOR JUVENILE OFFENDERS

There are many benefits to allowing a juvenile offender to remain in the community, rather than face time in a correctional facility. The most obvious is that it allows for closer contact with parental units, if the child does not have out-of-home placement (e.g., foster care), and it allows them to stay in mainstream schools, whenever possible. Though not ideal, even community-based alternative schools for juveniles who cannot function in the regular school setting can be a better alternative than receiving education from behind bars.

There are a number of types of community-based corrections; the most commonly known for both adults and minors are probation and parole. Other types of programs include court-ordered community service and reporting centers. Greater opportunities for treatment exist in the community, though this can vary from jurisdiction to jurisdiction.

Juvenile Probation and Parole

As in the adult court system, a sentence of probation will either front-end any time spent in physical custody in a juvenile correctional facility, or it will coincide with incarceration after the juvenile has spent time behind bars. Juvenile probation, even more so than in adult corrections, is a form of forgiveness. Juveniles who have been placed on probation are not, however, given a pass on the behavior that landed them in the juvenile courts in the first place. The adjudication and arrests remain on their juvenile records, unlike a dismissal of charges.

Juveniles placed on probation have to follow the conditions of their release to the community, similar to those required of adult offenders on probation. Included in these conditions can be the following (Hansen, 2023, p. 285):

- Do not associate with known criminals, including gang members.
- Do not use nonprescription street drugs or illegally obtained prescription drugs or alcohol while on probation.
- Maintain a curfew, as set by the courts.
- Receive mandatory drug and/or alcohol testing.
- Submit DNA samples as required (e.g., California).
- Complete court-ordered community service hours if required.
- Maintain good school attendance and good behavior at school and at home.
- Attend frequent court dates during probation, as required, to provide updates on progress (Kraut, n.d.).

Many of the same conditions apply to juveniles who have spent time in detention centers and have been paroled (Hansen, 2023). Other conditions may apply as well, depending on jurisdiction and the recommendation of the juvenile probation or parole officer. Probation or parole can be revoked at any time for reoffending or for a *technical violation*. A technical violation means a condition of probation or parole has not been met, but it would ordinarily not be considered a crime per se. An example is failure to meet with a probation officers.

Parole, on the other hand, like in adult cases, comes after the juvenile has spent time in a correctional facility. Like probation, juveniles who have been paroled for good behavior as a condition of their adjudication or due to overcrowding in a facility are required to meet certain conditions to remain in the community. The challenge in both probation and parole is that juveniles often return to the same environments that put them at risk for offending. Doubly challenging is keeping juveniles away from known criminals, as a condition of probation or parole, if they have relatives or friends who have criminal records. An example of this would be a juvenile whose family members belong to an organized crime group, including street gangs.

Group Homes

Group homes are yet one more alternative to incarceration of youth in correctional facilities. However, there are some inconsistencies in the definitions of group homes. Though generally group homes are community-based, long-term facilities for juvenile offenders, they can be confused with residential treatment centers (Office of Juvenile Justice and Delinquency Prevention, 2008). Group homes typically house a limited number of residents, allowing for more individualized attention.

Group homes allow juveniles extensive contact with the community. This is similar to work-release programs for adult offenders and is less restrictive than treatment centers (Office of Juvenile Justice and Delinquency Prevention, 2008). However, often group homes also provide less intensive treatment of drug and/or alcohol abuse when warranted, however, there is even more focus on rehabilitation than can be found in a traditional juvenile corrections facility. One disadvantage of group homes is that conditions there may be better than what the juvenile experiences in their parental units' home or in foster care. If this is the case, the juvenile may reoffend in the hope of being placed back into a group home.

In this chapter we speak in generalities of the components of the juvenile justice system, as they affect all juveniles. Gender identification aside, there are some distinct differences that should be noted. As we have highlighted elsewhere in this book, young female offenders are more likely to have been abused. Historically, female juvenile offenders have been incarcerated largely due to supposed "immoral behavior" (Anderson et al., 2019; Chesney-Lind and Shelden, 2014). Today young females find themselves in the juvenile system for many of the same offenses that males (and other identifiable genders) do.

Due to the higher rates of victimization experienced by females, rehabilitation should be twofold, addressing both the mental health issues resulting from exploitation and the criminal behavior. Group homes that house female juvenile offenders are often better equipped than other out-of-home placements, and may include foster care to provide the often court-ordered types of mental health, trauma, and substance abuse services these female offenders need, while allowing them to continue to interact with the community (Anderson et al., 2019).

Restorative Justice Strategies

Restorative justice programs are intended to allow the juvenile offender to make amends to their victim, as well as allowing them to see firsthand the damage they have done. Restorative justice programs are not punitive per se, but rather a means by which the offender can repair the damage done to the victim and the community. Often the offender and victim are brought together in a formal meeting that is meant to be nonconfrontational and nonadversarial, encouraging communication and accountability on the part of the offender (Developmental

Service Groups, Inc., 2021) following five steps ("5 R's") to restorative justice (Capstick, n.d.):

- Attempt to restore a damaged **relationship**.
- Encourage **respect** between parties.
- The offender takes **responsibility** for the harm they have inflicted.
- **Repair** any damage or harm done to the victim.
- **Reintegration** of the offender back into the community.

Earlier we discussed the types of tribal justice processes within the juvenile court systems of the United States and Canada. Canada's Department of Justice (2021) reports that one of the best strategies in preventing further offending among indigenous youth is restorative justice strategies grounded in native culture. The difficulty is in maintaining the culture once they are released from custody. As one roundtable participant explained in the Canadian Department of Justice Canada report (2021),

> *You get out, you go back in the same house you were in before being locked-up, and everything is the same. You go right back into the situation that got you locked-up. If you were lucky enough to get cultural activities* [while in custody] *and they helped, those are gone again, if you go back to the reservation it doesn't have the resources you need.*

Juvenile female being publicly shamed.

Much the same can be said about youth in juvenile facilities in the United States. Unless whatever rehabilitation strategies worked during detention are continued after release, often no real long-term change can be achieved.

Shaming and Reintegration Strategies

Shaming and reintegration programs are similar to those in restorative justice. They require that the offender face their victim and the community, in the hope that it will humble them into understanding the damage they have done. What makes it different from restorative justice is the shaming component. There is evidence that shaming punishment is counterproductive for both adults and juvenile offenders, resulting in public stigma (Harden, 2012). Whereas the restorative justice model is nonconfrontational, in the shaming and reintegration model, the victim and the community are expected to be more vocal and public in condemning the delinquent's behavior. A startling trend is toward parents shaming their children on social media when they misbehave, with so-called tough love tactics (Gaston, 2017).

Unless done right, the approach carries risks. Juliet Hiznay, co-founder of the Coalition for Trauma Informed Schools in Virginia (Devoe, 2022), contends that punishment can often make things worse by causing further trauma, in this case, with shaming. As in the case of a parental unit who is unhappy with a child's behavior, reprimand and punishment should send the message, "I don't like what you did, but I still love you." In this way, the behavior is condemned, not the offender. This is important when dealing with minors, particularly those who have been subjected to psychological or emotional abuse at home. Otherwise it can be destructive to the juvenile identity and is, in itself, another form of abuse (Colorado Children's Hospital, 2022).

REENTRY

Release, whether from corrections or from a hospital for medical, psychological, or psychiatric treatment or drug rehabilitation, can be the most difficult time for anyone, whether an adult or a juvenile, the more so the longer they were institutionalized. *Reentry* refers to the process by which juveniles transition from juvenile placement back in to their community (Youth.gov, n.d.). As sociologist Erving Goffman (1963) proposed, the institutional identity can become the master status, making it difficult to shake the stigma of having been incarcerated and to have others in the community see the juvenile delinquent as anything but a delinquent.

Reentry, whether in preparation for release or immediately after release from an adult or juvenile facility, continues to be one of the weakest points in the criminal justice system. More recently, President Joe Biden declared April 2022 Second Chance Month, underscoring the need to provide more opportunities for rehabilitation and redemption and asking communities to refocus on the Second Chance Act (2008) and First Step Act (2018). As reported by the Office of Juvenile Justice and Delinquency Prevention (2022, retrieved from https://ojjdp.ojp.gov/newsletter/ojjdp-news-glance-marchapril-2022/top-story-reentry-programs-offer-resources-youth-after-residential-placement), several million dollars in government funding have been set aside in recent years to assist state governments and local communities in providing services to released juveniles, including "employment and education opportunities, housing assistance, treatment for substance use disorders, mental healthcare, family engagement and mentoring."

Aftercare for Juveniles and Their Families

The challenge for young people who have been adjudicated in a juvenile court and are on the cusp of adulthood is that, for the most part, if their own home is not conducive to continuing their rehabilitation progress, there might not be any other place for them to go after release. Unless a relative or family friend is willing to take on the responsibility of housing them, they may very well end up in the foster care system.

From the moment that a juvenile enters the juvenile justice system, plans should be put in place for their reentry. As the website Youth.gov[12] suggests, there are four junctures in a juvenile offender case where aftercare options should be actively discussed:

- **The entry phase:** The moment the youth enters residential placement.
- **The placement phase:** The time the youth is in the secure care facility.
- **The transitional phase:** The point of leaving the facility and reentering the community, immediately before and after the date of exit.
- **The community-based aftercare phase:** Usually the 120-day (or longer) period after a youth returns to the community.

The need is most acute for adequate programs in poorer, primarily minority communities. As we note frequently in this book, the problem generally is one of funding. Without the support within their neighborhoods that juveniles and parental units need, or without in-home visits by agencies, there is a chance that young Black males particularly will eventually end up in custody in the adult criminal justice system. Juveniles with a variety of disabilities are also overrepresented in the juvenile justice system and are generally less successful in avoiding reoffending after release from a juvenile facility (Miller et al., 2019). Both disadvantaged groups need more than social workers trained in general social problems: they need specialists trained in reentry issues (Miller et al., 2019). However, these

[12] A U.S. government website designed to support juvenile justice and delinquency prevention programs.

professionals are not necessarily available in all communities. As Hampton (2020) advises, the key to transitioning successfully back into a community is the presence of adequate services to help juveniles to do so.

Foster Care After Institutionalization

When parental units are unable to serve as guardians of their children coming out of juvenile facilities, or have been determined by the court to be unsuitable to do so, the court will either appoint a guardian from among family members or friends, or as a last resort, place the child in foster care. The difficulty is that foster care is intended to be temporary, in the hopes that an adoption takes place in the future. However, the children in foster care often have special needs, predominantly for mental health services. The juvenile who is older, or worse yet, coming out of a juvenile correctional facility, may be doubly unadoptable in society's view, making permanent placement difficult.

One program that benefits juveniles in general, but can also be a benefit for children coming out of custody, is *Court-Appointed Special Advocates* (CASA). CASA consists of volunteers who assist in finding the best and most appropriate foster or permanent placement for children who have been abused, neglected, or abandoned by, and subsequently removed from, their parental units. As we suspect that a good portion of children who have gone through the juvenile justice system have been abused–80% by CASA's estimates (Orozco, 2019)–many of the juveniles released from custody require placement into foster care or with family members other than their parental units. CASA also suggests that their BRIDGES program is uniquely positioned to help juvenile delinquents who were in foster care prior to their offense (Orozco, 2019; Court-Appointed Special Advocates, n.d.).

Recidivism

One of the most frustrating and perplexing problems in both the adult and the juvenile justice system is recidivism. If the purpose of punishment is to make the penalty for criminal offending so awful (deterrence model) that the offender will never commit another crime, adult incarceration and juvenile detention are not working.

One of the issues with the criminal justice system in the United States is that records and data are not consistently kept or collected uniformly across states. Some states, like Oregon, are leaders in their collection of comprehensive data on juvenile offenders (Yu, 2014). Others, as seen in Exhibit 11.3, virtually do not report recidivism data, the measure used to determine the success of the juvenile justice system (Yu, 2014; PEW Research Center, 2014). Using all state data available to us, the rearrest rates for juvenile offenders in the United States is 55% one year after release from juvenile detention, with 24% of those offenders

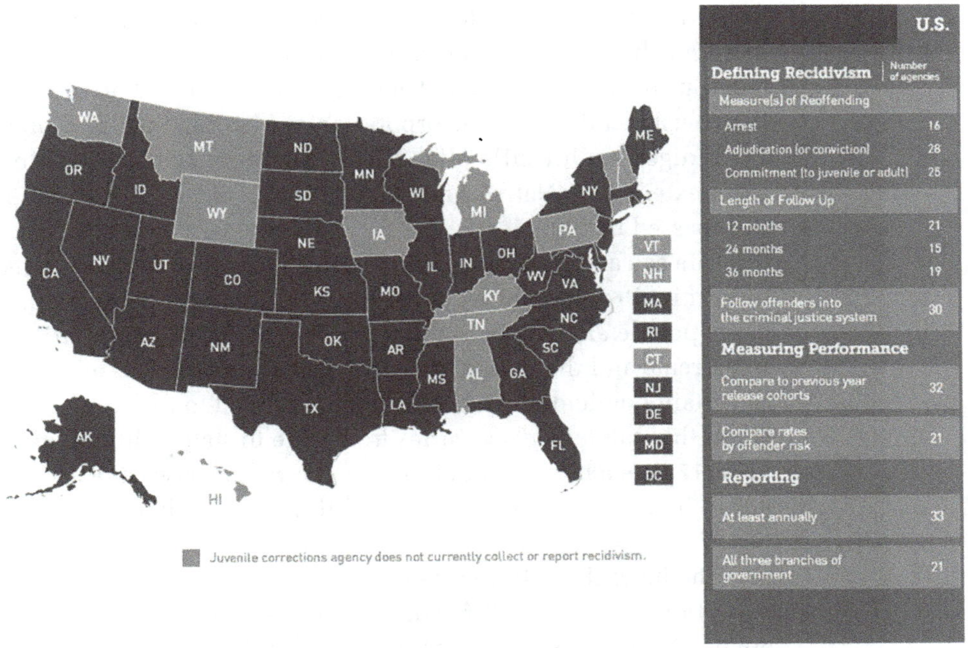

EXHIBIT 11.3 ‖ States Reporting Juvenile Recidivism Rates

ending up in detention again (Office of Juvenile Justice and Delinquency Prevention, 2020). In some states or jurisdictions that do collect recidivism data, rates of juvenile reoffending are reportedly as high as 75% three years after release (Seigel et al., 2014).

In recent years, the Office of Juvenile Justice and Delinquency Prevention launched a program to improve data collection methods across states. This included training and technical assistance, with a grant of one million dollars to PBS Learning Institute, Inc. (Braintree, Massachusetts) to increase the capacity of juvenile justice agencies to collect and analyze reentry data effectively and to enhance their ability to report the data (Office of Juvenile Justice and Delinquency Prevention, 2020; 2018a). Thus far, and in light of the COVID-19 pandemic beginning in 2020, data collection has been challenging.

SUMMARY

In this chapter we turned our attention to the legal considerations in juvenile offending. For all the complexities of the adult criminal justice system, there are distinct differences when it comes to the juvenile system. For one, despite the numbers of juveniles that are in custody, there is a greater emphasis on rehabilitation, including efforts to keep juvenile offenders in the community (community-based corrections) to serve any sentence that might be imposed. This can include probation and court-ordered social services interventions. As we note in this chapter, the U.S. has a second juvenile justice system, embedded within the tribal provisions of Native American and Alaskan Native communities, where tribal justice allows the incorporation of historical cultural practices in addressing indigenous juvenile offending. Only recently have some of the same provisions extended to Native Americans and Native Hawaiian people under the Akaka Bill, passed in 2009.

The age at which juveniles are held for their offenses is referred to as the age of criminal responsibility or majority. And as we note in this chapter, in most cases people are considered to be juveniles (or minors) until they reach age 18. In extreme and thankfully rare cases, when the charges are especially serious, as in certain homicides, a juvenile can be referred to the adult court system. The age when this can take place varies from state to state, with the most usual age being 16 or 17. In such cases, for all practical legal purposes, the juvenile is treated as an adult, including incarceration in adult prison, if they are found guilty in a court of law.

The juvenile justice system functions similarly to the adult system, with the exception of choosing different junctures in the process to interject diversion programs, if warranted. For example, if a juvenile is accused and found delinquent in a case of minor vandalism, they may be referred to a restorative justice program that allows them to make amends directly to the victim, whether in terms of monetary compensation or by volunteering with clean-up efforts. A minor accused of drug and/or substance use or abuse may be diverted to a drug rehabilitation program. The adult system in some jurisdictions has likewise incorporated similar diversion programs through drug courts.

Law enforcement must follow the same protocol in arresting a juvenile as they do for adults, including reading the suspect their Miranda Rights. Juveniles are afforded the same constitutional rights as adults, including free speech, equal protection under the law, and the right to seek legal counsel. However, juveniles have special rights that adults do not have because of their status as minors. If it is determined that the suspect is a juvenile, they will either be processed in a juvenile detention center or issued a citation to appear in court with their parental units. Unlike adult cases, the law requires that the parental units of the juvenile suspect be notified immediately of an arrest or citation. Parental units also have certain legal rights as well; however, the state has the ultimate authority over juvenile matters.

Most law enforcement contact with juveniles occurs on the streets, with the exception of school resource officers (SROs). One serious concern among social justice advocates and others is that there is a disproportionate number of minority adults and juveniles, particularly young Black males, represented in arrests and subsequent incarceration. SROs are more likely to be found in poor neighborhood schools where there are larger minority populations. The zero-tolerance policies in these schools are believed to contribute to the school-to-prison pipeline.

As Robles-Ramamurthy and Watson (2019) note, young Black males are not only more likely to be arrested compared to white males, but are also more likely to be arrested multiple times.

Within the juvenile court system, every effort is made to adhere to the constitutional right to a speedy trial, if applicable. When a juvenile is arrested and detained due to the seriousness of charges, they are required to be brought before a judge for the juvenile equivalent of an arraignment in adult court, where formal charges are brought against them in a reasonable amount of time, which may vary depending on the jurisdiction, as well as the time and day the arrest was made. There are a number of hearings that can be conducted, including detention hearings, jurisdictional hearings to determine if the juvenile should be tried as an adult, and the disposition hearing after a juvenile has been found to be delinquent.

The juvenile justice system, like the adult system, is run as a bureaucracy, with rules and a clear chain of command; it is organized around a quasi-military model. This is most evident in both policing and corrections. Juvenile corrections, at its worst, is essentially equivalent to adult corrections, with facilities looking almost identical. However, detention and correctional facilities for juveniles are required to house far fewer inmates compared to adult prisons (though juvenile facilities can also become overcrowded). The facilities that seem to have the best success are designed for short-term stays or serve as treatment centers. Juvenile facilities can be ran by a state or the federal government, but increasingly private for-profit centers are being used, though they raise a number of concerns–not the least of which is possible court corruption, leading unscrupulous judges to sentence juveniles to these centers in return for a bribe ("cash for kids" schemes).

Most juvenile offenders will be placed on probation, although some will spend a portion of their sentence in a juvenile facility; some older offenders, depending on the severity of their crime, will have a blended sentence, with the back-end of their sentence served in adult prison, though those cases are the exception. There are also the options for parole and residential placement in halfway houses after release from juvenile corrections. Other alternatives include boot camps and wilderness camps, though controversies have arisen about the harsh conditions in some of these.

Aftercare of formerly incarcerated juveniles is by far one of the most challenging parts of the juvenile justice system other than prevention. Without the appropriate social services in place for both the juvenile and parental units, there is greater risk for juveniles to reoffend. There are instances where a juvenile has to be placed in foster care after time spent in detention or a correctional facility, in which case they are very likely to be doubly traumatized. With the right preparation for life outside of a correctional facility planned from the time of the juvenile's first contact with the juvenile system, they will have a much greater chance to be genuinely rehabilitated. However, recidivism rates over time for both adult and juvenile offenders are grim, leaving little optimism that real aftercare planning is being applied in juvenile cases. Part of the problem is that social services are chronically overwhelmed with cases, and personnel working in juvenile justice suffer from high burnout rates, as will be discussed further in Chapter 13.

IN THE MEDIA

The Call for Juvenile Justice Reform

Yet another battle cry sounding throughout the pediatric medical community is the demand for reforms, not only throughout every stage in the criminal justice in general, but specifically in juvenile justice. Pediatricians are advocating that the mental and emotional well-being of juveniles held in detention centers should be a priority, as most of them have experienced one form of trauma or another not associated directly with their offending (Annie E. Casey Foundation, 2022). Arguing that 75% of juvenile offenders held in detention have not committed violent crimes and that their medical, mental health, and legal needs are not being met, the American Academy of Pediatrics (2021) argues that incarceration of juveniles only compounds their trauma.

As in the case of adult criminal justice, a number of efforts, some of them decades long, have been made to build a more just and efficient juvenile justice system. As Robert Sapolsky, a neuroendocrinology researcher at Stanford University, contends, "Juvenile justice is probably the area that's most ripe for reform, in the nice liberal sense of the word, simply because there's no getting around the fact that a teenage brain is not an adult brain" (Riggs, 2017, retrieved from

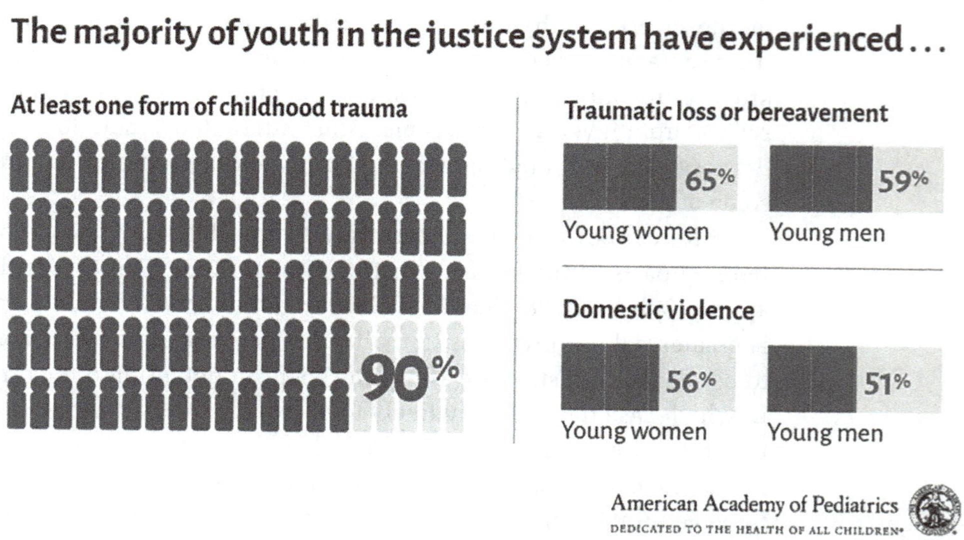

EXHIBIT 11.4 **Percent of Juveniles in the Justice System Who Have Experienced Childhood Trauma, Loss, and/or Domestic Violence**

https://reason.com/2017/09/15/why-people-do-awful-things-a-qa-with-rob/#:~:text=Sapolsky%3A%20Juvenile%20justice%20is%20probably,that%20in%20three%20different%20rulings).

On the basis of juvenile neurological makeup alone, opponents of the current juvenile justice system argue that we now know more about brain physiology and development, necessitating the need to reassess current policies in the punishment of juvenile offenders. Some juvenile justice system reformists question whether placing a juvenile in detention with other juvenile offenders doesn't just make them more hardened criminals. If the conditions and behaviors that led them to that point aren't corrected, juvenile justice becomes just one more pipeline into the adult corrections system (Hansen, 2023).

CRITICISMS OF THE CURRENT JUVENILE JUSTICE SYSTEM

The two main complaints of the criminal justice system are (1) the disproportionate numbers of minorities in jails and prisons, and (2) overcrowded conditions in correctional facilities. An additional concern is the lack of programs for prevention, intervention, or aftercare once juveniles are on the cusp or have already been swept into the juvenile justice system. Most importantly, as it applies to juvenile justice, in many people's estimations, including researchers', entirely too many children are sent to detention and correctional facilities.

Sending juveniles to detention or correctional facilities, whether designed for juveniles or adults, can lead to the following unwanted results (Hansen, 2023, p. 274):

- Individuals, including children, who commit crimes, are perceived as "bad" or "evil" people, in which case it may be difficult for them to find positive social role models and to hang out with the "right" crowd (a concern raised in Tannenbaum's *Labeling Theory*).[13]
- Juvenile detention increases any strain the child is already experiencing and may result in additional blocked educational and vocational opportunities (Merton's *Strain Theory*).[14]
- Self-labeling: "I must be bad; everyone says I am." This results in juveniles committing the very crimes and behaviors already expected from them, whether they had the propensity to reoffend or not (Merton's *Self-fulfilling Prophecy*).[15]
- By being in juvenile (or adult) detention, juveniles will learn from fellow juvenile delinquents more serious and creative ways to commit crimes (Aker's *Social Learning Theory*).[16]

---

[13] F. Tannenbaum, *Crime and the Community* (Boston: Ginn, 1938).

[14] R. Merton, "Social structure and anomie," *American Sociological Review* 38, issue 4 (1938): 319–361.

[15] R. Merton, "The self-fulfilling prophecy," *Antioch Review* 8, issue 2 (1948): 193–210.

[16] R. L. Akers, *Deviant Behavior: A Social Learning Approach*, 3d ed. (Belmont, CA: Wadsworth, 1985).

RECOMMENDATIONS

In a report to the Council of State Governments, Seigel et al. (2014) made recommendations, based on four principles, for improving the U.S. juvenile justice system. (See Table 11.1.)

The reality, as we will see in Chapter 13 on prevention measures, is that a number of places in the country are already using some, if not all, of the recommendations made by Seigel et al. (2014) to reduce offending and recidivism rates.

Taking a health-based approach to reform in the juvenile justice system, the American Academy of Pediatrics (2021) suggests the following advancements:

- Use incarceration of adolescents only as a last resort. Increase community-based diversion programs.
- Abandon practices in juvenile detention that are traumatizing, including solitary confinement.
- Promote and support policies and community action to reduce the risks for juvenile offending.
- Set the age of criminal responsibility at no younger than 12 in both state and federal laws.
- Abolish punitive and developmentally inappropriate sentencing, including life without the possibility for parole or trying juveniles as adults, except in extreme cases.
- Improve physical and psychological clinical care of juveniles held in detention.

SOURCES

Adams, W., J. Samuels, J. B. Willison, H. Dodd, M. Dank, B. Parthasarathy, K. Mallik-Kane, J. Kelly, S. Mendonca, and K. Kim (2011). *Tribal Youth in the Federal Justice System.* Washington, DC: Urban Institute.

American Academy of Pediatrics (2021). "Protect children, reform the juvenile justice system." Report. Nov 15. Retrieved from https://www.aap.org/en/advocacy/juvenile-justice/protect-children-reform-the-juvenile-justice-system/.

Annie E. Casey Foundation (2022). "Pediatric organization calls for juvenile justice reforms." April 19. Retrieved from https://www.aecf.org/blog/pediatric-organization-calls-for-juvenile-justice-reforms.

Hansen, L. P. (2023). *Introduction to Penology and Corrections.* Boston, MA: Aspen.

Riggs, M. (2017). "Why we fight and punish: A Q&A with Robert Sapolsky." Reason. Sep. 15. Retrieved from https://reason.com/2017/09/15/why-people-do-awful-things-a-qa-withrob/#:~:text=Sapolsky%3A%20Juvenile%20justice%20is%20probably,that%20in%20three%20different%20rulings.

Seigel, E., N. Walsh, J. Weber (2014). *Core Principles for Reducing Recidivism and Improving Other Outcomes for Youth in the Juvenile Justice System.* Lexington, KY: Justice Center, Council of State Governments. Retrieved from https://csgjusticecenter.org/wp-content/uploads/2020/01/Juvenile-Justice-White-Paper-with-Appendices-1-1.pdf.

TABLE 11.1 Policies and Practices That Reduce Recidivism and Improve Other Youth Outcome (Siegel et al., 2014)

***Principal 1:* Base supervision, service, and resource-allocation decisions on the results of validated risk and needs assessments.**
Recommendation A: Minimize juvenile justice system supervision and services for youth who are at a low risk of reoffending.
Recommendation B: Maximize the impact and value of system resources by prioritizing services for youth most likely to reoffend and by minimizing the use of confinement.
Recommendation C: Use validated assessments to identify the primary causes of a youth's delinquent behaviors and focus system interventions and resources on addressing these causes.
Recommendation D: Use specialized, validated screenings and assessments to identify youth with mental health and substance use treatment needs and match them to services, minimizing the use of juvenile justice.
***Principal 2:* Adopt and effectively implement programs demonstrated to reduce recidivism and improve other youth outcomes, and use data to evaluate system performance and direct system improvements.**
Recommendation A: Eliminate the use of programs and practices that do not reduce recidivism or improve other key youth outcomes.
Recommendation B: Support and fund services shown to reduce recidivism and improve other youth outcomes.
Recommendation C: Evaluate recidivism and other youth outcomes, and use this data to guide policy, practice, and resource allocation.
***Principal 3*: Employ a coordinated approach across service systems to address youths' needs.**
Recommendation A: Partner the juvenile justice system with the other key service systems in which youth are or should be involved in order to assess and effectively address their needs.
***Principal 4*: Tailor system policies, programs, and supervision to reflect the distinct developmental needs of adolescents.**
Recommendation A: Engage families and other supportive adults in major system decisions and processes.
Recommendation B: Employ a developmentally appropriate approach to system supervision by focusing resources on promoting positive behavior change and using a graduated response to violations.
Recommendation C: Hold youth accountable for their actions in ways that address the harm caused to victims and communities and that support positive change.
Recommendation D: Promote youths' respect for and compliance with the law by engaging them in system decisions and processes, and by addressing systemic bias and the disparate treatment of youth of color and other groups that are disproportionately represented in the juvenile justice system.

INTERNATIONAL PERSPECTIVES

Belgium: The World's Best Juvenile Justice System?

Belgium, part of the European Union, borders France to the west, Germany to the east, and Luxembourg in the southeast. Belgium today constitutes two distinct cultural communities, the French and the Flemish, and has three major languages: Dutch, French, and German. Belgium became independent of the Netherlands in 1830 and adopted the French penal system (Walgrave, 2002).

As in most emerging states, Belgium's transition to independence was not smooth. Almost immediately, the new nation was hit with economic problems caused by the decline of the textile industry, as well as by typhus and cholera epidemics (Walgrave, 2002). These problems in turn created new issues of juvenile crime. As a result, and similar to what happened in England, roving bands of vagrants, including children, begged on the streets to survive (Walgrave, 2002). By 1890, in efforts to reorganize the criminal justice system in Belgium, rather than send the vagrant children to prison, reformatory homes for juveniles were created (François, 2018; Christiaens, 1991).

In most cases, children brought before the courts were there for relatively minor crimes. Well into the early part of the 20th century, many of the criminal charges included vagrancy and, for girls in particular, prostitution (De Koster, 2018). During World War I, young girls who were arrested for prostitution would be sent to a convent by the Juvenile Court of Brussels, a not uncommon practice in a number of countries to reform "wayward girls" (François, 2008). It is of particular interest that an estimated 75% of girls between the ages of 14 and 18 brought before the court in Belgium were working class; many worked in factories or as servants, dressmakers, or at other wage-earning jobs (De Koster, 2018). Ordinarily, those who work are far less likely to commit crimes. However, in the context of late 19th century Europe, working-class women were often paid a barely living wage. Unless they were still living with family, they would be hard-pressed to support themselves on their legitimate income. After the economy resolved itself and the epidemics subsided, the wealthy class turned their attention to the care of the poor, for philanthropic and religious reasons, but also, more nefariously, to keep the poor under control by making them dependent on charity (Walgrave, 2002).

Today, in Belgium as in the United States, the legal system defines a juvenile as younger than 18. In a survey conducted by the Child Rights International Network (CRIN) of juvenile justice systems, Belgium's juvenile justice system was rated as number one in the world, followed by Portugal, Spain, Finland, and the Netherlands (Boyle, 2016; EUresidence Belgium, 2016). The accolades for the Belgian courts dealing with minors are not limited to criminal cases. Belgium is also reputed to have child-friendly family courts in divorce cases (EUresidence Belgium, 2016). The Belgian juvenile justice system is organized around looking to welfare solutions first in delinquency cases, as well as taking an educational (intervention) approach, rather than the use of punishment (Defence for Children International—Belgium, 2017).

Belgium, like other countries, has seen an increase in juvenile crime since 2020, after experiencing a steady decrease over the past few decades. Many of the offenders were sent to secure juvenile detention centers, with the greatest number being held in Antwerp and the smallest number in Limburg (Stetina, 2022). Construction of new facilities, particularly in De Grubbe, will double capacity (Stetina, 2022). More recently, the new Juvenile Delinquency Decree, even though it calls for expanded counseling services for juveniles and their families and friends, and even though the goal remains to keep juveniles out of detention centers, has been calling for more punitive options in juvenile cases and more protection for victims (Stetina, 2022). This could result in more juveniles being sent to detention and ultimately to correctional facilities in the future. Construction of new facilities suggests that there will be a future need to incarcerate more juveniles.

SOURCES

Boyles, R. (2016). "Belgium tops list of best juvenile justice systems." *Bulletin*. Feb 16. Retrieved from https://www.thebulletin.be/belgium-tops-list-worlds-best-juvenile-justice-systems.

Christiaens, J. (1991). "A history of Belgium's child protection act of 1912: The redefinition of the juvenile offender and his punishment." *European Journal of Crime, Criminal Law and Criminal Justice*. Vol. 7, issue 1: 5–21.

De Koster, M. (2018). "Girls' journeys to juvenile court, Antwerp, 1912–1933." Ch. 10 in *Youth and Justice in Western States, 1815–1950: From Punishment to Welfare*, ed. J. Trépanier and X. Rousseaux. Cham, CH: Palgrave/McMillian.

Defence for Children International—Belgium. (2017). "Country overview: Belgium." In *My Lawyer, My Rights*. National report, child Justice Projects. Retrieved from https://lachild.eu/wp-content/uploads/2016/05/CountryOverviewBelgium.pdf.

EUresidence Belgium (2016). "Belgium tops list of world's best juvenile justice systems." Feb 16. Retrieved from https://belgium.euresidence.me/residence-permit-eu/belgium-tops-list-of-worlds-best-juvenile-justice-systems/.

François, A. (2018). "Juvenile delinquency in wartime and peacetime: The activity of the Belgian juvenile courts, 1912–1950." Ch. 11 in *Youth and Justice in Western States, 1815–1950: From Punishment to Welfare*, ed. J. Trépanier and X. Rousseaux. Cham, CH: Palgrave/McMillian.

François, A. (2008). "From street walking to the convent: Young prostitutes judged by the Juvenile Court of Brussels during World War One." In *Untold War: New Perspectives in First World War Studies*, ed. H. Jones, C. Schmidt-Supprian, and J. O'Brien. Dublin, IR: Brill.

Stetina, A. (2022). "1,560 Belgian young offenders sent to community institutions in 2021." *Brussels Times*. July 8. Retrieved from https://www.brusselstimes.com/belgium/251339/1560-belgian-young-people-sent-to-community-institutions-in-2021.

Walgrave, L. (2002). "Juvenile justice in Belgium." In *Juvenile Justice Systems: International Perspectives*, ed. J. Winterdyk. Vancouver, B.C., CA: Canadian Scholars' Press.

CHAPTER DISCUSSION QUESTIONS

1. What are the reasons that juveniles may have either positive or negative attitudes toward law enforcement? What role, if any, does the media play in the formation of these attitudes?

2. Why are jurisdictions in the United States not uniform in their procedures for handling suspected juvenile offenders?
3. In what cases, in your opinion, should juveniles be referred to adult courts? At what age?
4. From this chapter and others in this book, why are juveniles who have been victimized at risk for delinquency?
5. What examples can you give for why juveniles should be placed on probation and not placed in juvenile corrections?
6. How could the foster care system be improved to help juveniles transition out of institutions and back into the community?

GLOSSARY

Age of criminal responsibility or majority The age at which an individual is considered to be an adult or can be referred to adult criminal court, if under the age of 18.

Alternative schools Also referred to as continuation schools, public schools that are intended for the education of juveniles who cannot function in mainstream schools, either due to behavior problems or delinquency.

Blended sentences In cases of serious juvenile offending, when the juvenile offender spends part of their sentence in a juvenile facility, then as they age out of the juvenile justice system, are transferred to adult corrections to finish the remainder of their sentence.

Case petitioning Document asking the court to assume jurisdiction over a juvenile, either due to delinquent behavior or status violations. Can also refer to the request to transfer a juvenile to adult court.

Child Protective Services (CPS) Known by other names, depending on the jurisdiction, this is the agency responsible for investigating child abuse allegations and making recommendations to the courts, depending on the findings. Agencies are also responsible for following up with interviews and investigations in cases where maltreatment has been documented.

Citizen's arrest An arrest, with limitations, made by anyone other than sworn law enforcement; limits to these arrests depend on the jurisdiction.

Community-based corrections Any form of sentenced punishment or treatment that takes place in the community, rather than in a correctional facility. Examples are probation and parole.

Court-Appointed Special Advocates (CASA) Volunteer organization that provides juveniles who have been abused or neglected advocacy before judges and courts.

Detention hearing Initial court hearing, similar to an adult arraignment, to determine if it is necessary to hold a suspected juvenile offender in pretrial custody. See juvenile *detention.*

Disposition hearing Hearing held after a juvenile has been found to be delinquent, in which the judge determines what is the most appropriate sentence in the case, depending on a number of factors, including the offense.

Fitness hearing Initial hearing to determine if the juvenile's case is appropriate for juvenile court or the case should be referred to the adult criminal justice system, depending on the severity of the charges.

General deterrence Crime prevention that targets a number of different crimes at once. Example: Police foot patrols.

Group homes Facilities for either adults or juveniles that allow the offender to remain in the community, while receiving the types of rehabilitation prescribed by social workers and the court.

Incapacitation In terms of corrections, removing a suspected or convicted offender from the community and placing them in a secure facility, including a jail or a prison.

Indian Child Welfare Act (1911)[17] Initial act to provide protections to Native American and Alaskan Native children, that was revised over time, including in 1978. Criticisms include the inability of all child welfare personnel to understand and apply the provisions in the act appropriately.

Individuals with Disabilities Education Act (IDEA) Legislation meant to guarantee all individuals with physical and neurological disabilities, including children, a free education that will meet their individual needs, with the goal of preparing them for independent adult life.

Intake The procedures followed for juveniles who are suspected of committing a crime or status offense, to determine whether a juvenile should be released or referred to juvenile court.

Jurisdictional hearing Hearing held in family court, with a follow-up determination in cases of abuse or neglect, as to whether a child should be removed from their home, if they haven't been as yet, and placed in the custody of the courts. Sometimes referred to as a dependency hearing.

Juvenile boot camps Quasi-military style camps that are highly controversial, intended to teach discipline, outdoor skills, and physical fitness.

---

[17] Though the label "Indian," is now believed to be a derogatory name and the preferred name used for indigenous people in North America is either Native American (U.S.) or First Nations (Canada), we use "Indian" wherever it is used in the legal acts and documents or in the names of government agencies.

Juvenile detention Comparable to adult jails, a correctional facility intended for temporary detention of a juvenile, generally before trial, if the seriousness of the charges warrants it. See *detention hearing.*

Juvenile parole Similar to adult parole, the release of a juvenile offender into the community to serve the remainder of their sentence, with a number of conditions.

Juvenile probation As with adult offenders on probation, a form of "forgiveness" where the juvenile offender serves their sentence within the community with a number of conditions for a period of time.

Mandated reporters Individuals who are required by law to report any suspected child maltreatment, including teachers, coaches, and health care workers.

Miranda Rights Suspects', including juveniles', rights upon arrest that are required by law to be read aloud to the suspect by an arresting officer.

National Survey of Youth in Custody (NSYC) A part of the U.S. Bureau of Justice Statistics (BJS), a rape and sexual assault prevention program mandated to be conducted by the Prison Rape Elimination Act of 2003. See Bureau of Justice Statistics, https://bjs.ojp.gov/data-collection/national-survey-youth-custody-nsyc#:~:text=The%20National%20Survey%20of%20Youth,PREA%3B%20P.L.%20108%2D79.

Pretrial hearing Hearing prior to a trial in juvenile court for the judge to rule on motions, including admissibility of evidence that the prosecutor or defense wish to present in court.

Reformatories A product of social movements and child-saver organizations beginning in the 19th century in the United States and elsewhere in the world; residential homes for delinquent youth intended to rehabilitate young offenders and to provide them with the structure lacking in their lives prior to offending, though many have reputations for harsh and cruel conditions.

Restitution Often court-ordered monetary or community service commitment to pay a crime victim or community for their losses.

Restorative Justice A means by which the offender and victim can meet face to face, ideally so that the offender can apologize and the victim has an opportunity to air their grievances and enlighten the offender about the damages caused by their crime. See *shaming and reintegration.*

Shaming and reintegration A form of restorative justice where the offender may be confronted by their victim and punishment includes public shaming. This should, in theory, be followed by forgiveness for the crime and reintegration back into the community.

Specific deterrence Crime-fighting prevention measures intended to target specific types of crime. Example: Metal bars on windows in a residential neighborhood.

Technical violation Any violation of a condition of probation or parole that, under ordinary circumstances, would not be considered to be a criminal act. Example: Failing to report a change of residence to a probation or parole officer.

Tribal justice A separate criminal and civil legal and court system conducted by Native American and Alaskan Native agencies. It is intended reduce incarceration and allow Native communities to use more traditional and culturally sensitive means to settle criminal and civil matters.

Tribal Law and Order Act (2010) Signed into law by President Barack Obama, intended to target crime in Native American and Alaskan Native communities by providing more law enforcement officers on Native lands (e.g., reservations). See U.S. Department of Justice, https://www.justice.gov/tribal/tribal-law-and-order-act.

Wards of the Court When a minor child (or in some cases, an adult) requires a court-named guardian to make decisions on their behalf, especially in cases where the child has been removed from home for neglect or abuse or there is no foster parent or suitable relative who can take on these responsibilities.

Wilderness programs Juvenile programs intended for nondelinquent, at-risk, and delinquent juveniles that take place in outdoor settings and are intended to build self-esteem, interpersonal skills, and discipline.

Wraparound programs When a number of programs, including anger management and drug or substance abuse rehabilitation, are built into a number of types of punishment to which a juvenile court might sentence a juvenile offender, including community corrections. Often includes parent education.

REFERENCES AND ADDITIONAL SUGGESTED READINGS

Alaska, State of (n.d.). Alaska Natives. Retrieved from https://alaska.gov/kids/learn/nativeculture.htm.

Anderson, V. R., B. M. Walerych, N. A. Campbell, A. R. Barnes, William S. Davidson, C. A. Campbell, E. Onifade, and J. L. Petersen (2019). "Gender-responsive intervention for female juvenile offenders: A quasi-experimental outcome evaluation." *Feminist Criminology*. Vol. 14, issue 1: 24–44.

Annie E. Casey Foundation (2021). "Youth detention use reaches highest level in 19 months." Dec 14. Retrieved from https://www.aecf.org/blog/youth-detention-use-reaches-highest-level-in-19-months.

Austin, J., K. D. Johnson, and M. Gregoriou (2000). *Juveniles in Adult Prisons and Jails*. NCJ 182503. Washington D.C.: Institute on Crime, Justice and Corrections at George Washington University and National Council on Crime and Delinquency.

Balderrama, V. (2021). "Justice Department to investigate five Texas juvenile correctional facilities." KRIS 6 News. Oct 14. Retrieved from https://www.kristv.com/news/texas-news/justice-department-to-investigate-five-texas-juvenile-correctional-facilities#:~:text=These%20are%20the%20Gainesville%20State,Evins%20Regional%20Juvenile%20State%20School.

Bassiouni, M. C. (1977). "Citizen's arrest—the law of arrest, search, and seizure for private citizens and private police." NCJ No. 44479. Office of Justice Programs, U.S. Department of Justice. Retrieved from https://www.ojp.gov/ncjrs/virtual-library/abstracts/citizens-arrest-law-arrest-search-and-seizure-private-citizens-and.

Berk, R. (2019). "Accuracy and fairness for juvenile justice risk assessment." *Journal of Empirical Legal Studies.* Vol. 16, issue 1: 175–194.

Bolden-Barrett, V. (2022). "Police officer's roles in the juvenile justice system." *CHRON* (Jun). Retrieved from https://work.chron.com/police-officers-roles-juvenile-justice-system-24909.html.

Brick, B. T., T. J. Taylor, and F. Esbensen (2009). "Juvenile attitudes towards the police: The importance of subcultural involvement and community ties." *Journal of Criminal Justice.* Vol. 37: 488–495.

Bureau of Justice Statistics (2019). "National Survey of Youth in Custody (NSYC)." Office of Justice Programs, U. S. Department of Justice. Retrieved from https://bjs.ojp.gov/data-collection/national-survey-youth-custody-nsyc.

California Courts (2022). "Girls' Courts/CSEC Courts Overview." Retrieved from https://www.courts.ca.gov/37353.htm.

Department of Justice Canada (2021). "Indigenous Youth Roundtables: Overrepresentation of indigenous youth in Canada's criminal justice system." Government of Canada. Jul 7. Retrieved from https://www.justice.gc.ca/eng/cj-jp/yj-jj/tools-outils/iyr-trja.html.

Capstick (n.d.) "The 5 R's of restorative justice." The Conflict Center. Retrieved from https://conflictcenter.org/the-5-rs-of-restorative-justice/.

Center for Juvenile and Criminal Justice (2022). "Juvenile justice history." Retrieved from https://www.cjcj.org/history-education/juvenile-justice-history.

Chesney-Lind, M., and R. G. Shelden (2014). *Girls, Delinquency, and Juvenile Justice*, 4th ed. Oxford, UK: Wiley-Blackwell.

Children's Bureau (2019). *Mandatory Reporters of Child Abuse and Neglect.* Children's Welfare Information Gateway. Washington, D.C.: ACYF/ACF/Department of Housing and Human Services.

Clark, P. (2014). "Types of facilities." Ch. 2 in *Desktop Guide to Quality Practice for Working with Youth in Confinement.* National Partnership for Juvenile Services and Office of Juvenile Justice and Delinquency Prevention (OJJDP). Retrieved from https://info.nicic.gov/dtg/node/4.

Colorado Children's Hospital (2022). "The shame game: Is public shaming effective?" Parent Resources. Retrieved from https://www.childrenscolorado.org/conditions-and-advice/parenting/parenting-articles/public-shaming/.

Community Policing in Action Services (COPS) (n.d.). Supporting safe schools. Office of Justice Programs, U.S. Department of Justice. Retrieved from https://cops.usdoj.gov/supportingsafeschools.

Court-Appointed Special Advocates (CASA) (n.d.). "BRIDGES Program." Retrieved from https://www.casadc.org/bridges.

Development Services Group, Inc. (2021). "Restorative justice for juveniles: Literature review." *Model Programs Guide.* Office of Justice Programs, U.S. Department of Justice, Office of Juvenile Justice and Delinquency Prevention. Retrieved from https://ojjdp.ojp.gov/model-programs-guide/literature-reviews/restorative-justice-for-juveniles.

Devoe, J. (2022). "Arlington implementing new program to divert youth from criminal justice system." *ARL Now* (News). Feb 22. Retrieved from https://www.arlnow.com/2022/02/22/arlington-implementing-new-program-to-divert-youth-from-criminal-justice-system/.

Division of Juvenile Justice (n.d.). Fairbanks Youth Facility. Alaska Department of Family and Community Services, State of Alaska. Retrieved from https://dfcs.alaska.gov/djj/Pages/Facilities/fyf.aspx.

Dorgan, B. L., J. Shenandoah, D. S. Bigfoot, E. Broderick, E. F. Brown, V. Davidson, A. Fineday, M. L. M. Fletcher, Jefferson Keel, R. Whitener, and M. J. B. Zimmerman (2014). *Attorney General's Advisory Committee on American Indian and Alaska Native Children Exposed to Violence: Ending Violence So Children Can Thrive.* Washington, D.C.: Office of Juvenile Justice and Delinquency Programs.

Duke, K. N., and K. B. Kahn (2017). "What social science research says about police violence against racial and ethnic minorities: Understanding the antecedents and consequences—An introduction." *Journal of Social Issues.* Vol. 73, issue 4: 690–700.

Equal Justice Initiative (2022). "Report details abusive conditions in Louisiana youth facility." Mar 17. Retrieved from https://eji.org/news/report-details-abusive-conditions-at-louisiana-youth-facility/.

Fayyad, A. (2020). "What happens when college cops patrol off campus?" *Boston Globe.* Dec 1. Retrieved from https://www.bostonglobe.com/2020/12/01/opinion/what-happens-when-college-cops-patrol-off-campus/.

Florida Legislature (2021). The 2021 Florida Statues: Title XLVIII, Ch. 1006, §1006.12. Retrieved from http://www.leg.state.fl.us/Statutes/index.cfm?App_mode=Display_Statute&URL=1000-1099/1006/Sections/1006.12.html.

Frazier, C. E., and D. M. Bishop (1986). "The pretrial detention of juveniles and its impact on case dispositions." *Journal of Criminal Law and Criminology.* Vol. 76, issue 4: 1132–1152.

Fyfe, J. J. (1982). Introduction. *Readings on Police Use of Deadly Force*, ed. J. J. Fyfe. Arlington, VA: Police Foundation.

Gaston, G. (2017). "Parent shaming on social media: Is it the right approach?" ABC 13. May 16. Retrieved from https://abc13.com/social-media-parents-shaming-parent/2001636/.

Goffman, E. (1963). *Stigma: Notes on the Management of Spoiled Identity.* New York: Simon and Schuster.

Hampton, M. D. (2020). "CSEY service provider perceptions of critical needs for effective care as youth transition from juvenile detention to the community." *Child Abuse and Neglect.* Vol. 100: e104084.

Hansen, L. P. (2023). *Introduction to Penology and Corrections.* Boston, MA: Aspen.

Hanson, M. (2022). "College enrollment demographic." Education Data Initiative. Apr 22. Retrieved from https://educationdata.org/college-enrollment-statistics#:~:text=The%20average%20age%20for%20students,college%20students%20are%20under%2018.

Harden, A. N. (2012). "Rethinking the shame: The intersection of shaming punishments and American Juvenile Justice." *Journal of Juvenile Law and Policy.* Vol. 16 (Winter): 93–153.

Hernandez, K. A. (2018). "At least 30 Colorado school districts allow teachers to carry guns, but no statewide training standards regulate them." *Denver Post.* Jul. 8. Retrieved from https://www.denverpost.com/2018/07/08/colorado-teacher-guns-schools-classroom/.

HG.org Legal Resources (n.d.). "The difference between juvenile and adult arrests." Retrieved from https://www.hg.org/legal-articles/the-difference-between-juvenile-and-adult-arrests-27689.

Holman, B., and J. Zeidenberg (2006). "The Dangers of Detention: The Impact of Incarcerating Youth in Detention and Other Secure Facilities." Report. Justice Policy Institute. Nov 28. Retrieved from https://justicepolicy.org/wp-content/uploads/2022/02/06-11_rep_dangersofdetention_jj.pdf.

Hyland, S., L. Langton, and E. Davis (2015). "Police Use of Nonfatal Force, 2002–2011." Washington, DC: U.S. Department of Justice, Office of Justice Programs, Bureau of Justice Statistics.

Interstate Commission for Juveniles (2022). "Age matrix." Jan 20. Retrieved from https://www.juvenilecompact.org/age-matrix.

Jackson, A. (2022). "The pandemic exacerbated mental health issues among incarcerated youth. How can we reverse the trend?" Urban Institute. Feb 21. Retrieved from https://www.urban.org/urban-wire/pandemic-exacerbated-mental-health-issues-among-incarcerated-youth-how-can-we-reverse-trend#:~:text=Research%20suggests%20as%20many%20as,exacerbate%20existing%20mental%20health%20problems.

Jones, A. (2022). "Juvenile escapes Acadiana Center for Youth custody during transport to hospital." KLFY News. Jun 13. Retrieved from https://www.klfy.com/louisiana/juvenile-escapes-acadiana-center-for-youth-custody-during-transport-to-hospital/.

Jones, A., D. Wallis, and A. Seibers (2020). "Gender-responsive practice and pregnant girls: A scoping review of America's girls courts." *Children and Youth Services Review*. Vol. 118 (Nov.): e105426.

Justice Policy Institute (JPI) (2020). *Sticker Shock 2020: The Cost of Youth Incarceration*. July. Retrieved from https://www.justicepolicy.org/uploads/justicepolicy/documents/Sticker_Shock_2020.pdf.

Kraut, M. D. (2020). "Juvenile court process." Child Crime Prevention and Safety Center. Retrieved from https://childsafety.losangelescriminallawyer.pro/juvenile-court-process.html.

Kraut, M. E. (n.d.). "Supervised juvenile probation." Child Crime Prevention and Safety Center. Retrieved from https://childsafety.losangelescriminallawyer.pro/supervised-juvenile-probation.html#:~:text=Possible%20terms%20and%20conditions%20of,driver's%20license%20restrictions%2C%20fines%20and.

Lacen, M. and C. Roy (2022). "Shreveport teen captured in Houston after third escape." KTAL News. Jun 29. Retrieved from https://www.arklatexhomepage.com/news/crime/shreveport-teen-captured-in-houston-after-third-escape/.

Lovett, K. G. (2021). "PBS Data Snapshot: Responding to the pandemic." PBS Special Issue Brief 3 (June): Fewer Youths in Custody. PBS Learning Institute, Inc.

Little, R. (2022). "2 teens at large, escaped Acadiana Center for Youth." KLFY News. May 31. Retrieved from https://www.klfy.com/local/st-martin-parish/2-juveniles-at-large-escaped-acadiana-center-for-youth/.

Martin, T. (2018). "Juvenile criminal defense: Not just kids' stuff." CISION PRWeb. July 7. Retrieved from https://www.prweb.com/releases/2018/04/prweb15450291.htm.

McDonald, D. C. (1992). "Private penal institutions." *Crime and Justice*. Vol 16: 361–419.

Miller, A. A., W. J. Therrien, and J. E. Romig (2019). "Reducing recidivism: Transition and reentry practices for detained and adjudicated youth with disabilities." *Education and Treatment of Children*. Vol. 42, issue 3: 409–438.

Miller-Perrin, C. L., and Perrin, R. D. (2013). *Child Maltreatment: An Introduction*, 3d ed. Los Angeles: SAGE Publications, Inc.

National Public Radio (NPR) (2012). "Why millions of American have no government ID." Transcript. Feb 1. Retrieved from https://www.npr.org/2012/02/01/146204308/why-millions-of-americans-have-no-government-id.

Native American Rights Fund (NARF) (n.d.). "Topic 8: Role of tribal courts." National Indian Law Library. Retrieved from https://narf.org/nill/documents/icwa/faq/role.html.

Nolo (n.d.). "Exceptions to confidentiality of juvenile court records." *Legal Encyclopedia*. Retrieved from https://www.nolo.com/legal-encyclopedia/exceptions-confidentiality-juvenile-criminal-records.html.

NYCourts.gov (n.d.) "Juvenile Delinquency." 7th Judicial District. Retrieved from https://ww2.nycourts.gov/courts/7jd/courts/family/case_types/juvenile_delinquency.shtml.

Office of Juvenile Justice, State of Louisiana (n.d.). Acadian a Center for Youth. Retrieved from https://ojj.la.gov/acadiana-center-for-youth/.

Office of Juvenile Justice and Delinquency Prevention (OJJDP) (2022). "Top story: Reentry programs offer resources to youth after residential placement." *OJJDP News @ a Glance*.

Department of Justice. Retrieved from https://ojjdp.ojp.gov/newsletter/ojjdp-news-glance-marchapril-2022/top-story-reentry-programs-offer-resources-youth-after-residential-placement.

Office of Juvenile Justice and Delinquency Prevention (OJJDP) (2020). "Research Central: Measuring what works in juvenile reentry." Office of Justice Programs, U.S. Department of Justice. Nov/Dec. Retrieved from https://ojjdp.ojp.gov/newsletter/ojjdp-news-glance-novemberdecember-2020/research-central-measuring-what-works-juvenile-reentry#:~:text=While%20national%20recidivism%20rates%20are,reconfinement%20rates%20averaged%2024%20percent.

Office of Juvenile Justice and Delinquency Prevention (OJJDP) (2019). "Juvenile Justice Reform Act tribal provisions fact sheet." NCJ no. 254703. Office of Justice Programs, U.S. Department of Justice. Jul. Retrieved from https://www.ojp.gov/publications/jjra-tribal-provisions-fact-sheet.pdf.

Office of Juvenile Justice and Delinquency Prevention (OJJDP) (2018a). "Improving juvenile reentry programs capacity for data collection, analysis, and reporting." Grant award, PBS Learning Institute, Inc. Office of Justice Programs, U.S. Department of Justice. Nov/Dec. Retrieved from https://ojjdp.ojp.gov/funding/awards/2018-cz-bx-k001.

Office of Juvenile Justice and Delinquency Prevention (OJJDP) (2018b). "Interactions between youth and law enforcement: Literature Review." *Model Programs Guide*. Office of Justice Programs, U.S. Department of Justice. Jan. Retrieved from https://ojjdp.ojp.gov/model-programs-guide/literature-reviews/interactions_between_youth_and_law_enforcement.pdf.

Office of Juvenile Justice and Delinquency Prevention (OJJDP) (2016). "Tribal youth in the juvenile justice system: Literature Review." *Model Programs Guide*. Office of Justice Programs, U.S. Department of Justice. Apr. Retrieved from https://ojjdp.ojp.gov/model-programs-guide/literature-reviews/tribal_youth_in_the_juvenile_justice_system.pdf.

Office of Juvenile Justice and Delinquency Prevention (OJJDP) (2008). "Group homes: Literature Review." *Model Programs Guide*. Office of Justice Programs, U.S. Department of Justice. Retrieved from https://ojjdp.ojp.gov/model-programs-guide/literature-reviews/group_homes.pdf.

Orozco, A. (2019). "Applying the CASA model on the juvenile justice system." Court-Appointed Special Advocates (CASA). Aug 7. Retrieved from https://www.casadc.org/post/applyingthecasamodeltothejuvenilejusticesystem#:~:text=Court%20Appointed%20Special%20Advocates%2C%20or,or%20family%20at%20a%20time.

Ortiz, A. (2020). "Confidence in police is at record low, Gallup survey finds." *New York Times*. Aug. 20. Retrieved from https://www.nytimes.com/2020/08/12/us/gallup-poll-police.html.

Petteruti, A. (2011). *Education Under Arrest: The Case Against Police in Schools*. Report. Washington, D.C.: Justice Policy Institute. Retrieved from https://justicepolicy.org/wp-content/uploads/2022/02/educationunderarrest_fullreport.pdf.

PEW Research Center (2014). "Measuring juvenile recidivism: Data visualization." May 21. Retrieved from https://www.pewtrusts.org/en/research-and-analysis/data-visualizations/2014/measuring-juvenile-recidivism.

Rand Corporation (2020). "The effects of laws allowing armed staff in K-12 schools." Apr 22. Retrieved from https://www.rand.org/research/gun-policy/analysis/laws-allowing-armed-staff-in-K12-schools.html#fn5.

Renkoski, K. (2016). "School resource officers look to be more approachable with new, 'soft' uniforms." *Columbia Missourian*. Mar 12. Retrieved from https://www.columbiamissourian.com/news/k12_education/school-resource-officers-look-to-be-more-approachable-with-new-soft-uniforms/article_7ad980f2-e7b4-11e5-9b13-1b33c1893169.html.

Robles-Ramamurthy, B., and C. Watson (2019). "Examining racial disparities in juvenile justice." *Journal of the American Academy of Psychiatry Law*. Vol. 47, issue 1: Online. Retrieved from https://web.archive.org/web/20200319134851id_/http://jaapl.org/content/jaapl/early/2019/02/13/JAAPL.003828-19.full.pdf.

Rosenfeld, R. (2015). "Ferguson and police use of deadly force." *Missouri Law Review*. Article 11. Vol. 80, issue 4 (Fall): 1–23. Retrieved from https://scholarship.law.missouri.edu/cgi/viewcontent.cgi?article=4167&context=mlr.

San Francisco Probation Department (n.d.). Definition of terms—juvenile probation and court processing. Retrieved from https://sfgov.org/juvprobation/definition-terms-%E2%80%93-juvenile-probation-and-court-processing#:~:text=and%20Court%20Processing-,Referral,case%20is%20to%20be%20handled.

Sanders, C. (2021). "State juvenile justice reforms can boost opportunity, particularly for communities of color." Center on Budget and Policy Priorities. Jul 27. Retrieved from https://www.cbpp.org/research/state-budget-and-tax/state-juvenile-justice-reforms-can-boost-opportunity-particularly-for.

Sawyer, W. (2019). "Youth confinement: The whole pie in 2019." Press release. Prison Policy Initiative. Dec 19. Retrieved from https://www.prisonpolicy.org/reports/youth2019.html.

Seigel, E., N. Walsh, J. Weber (2014). *Core Principles for Reducing Recidivism and Improving Other Outcomes for Youth in the Juvenile Justice System*. Lexington, KY: Justice Center, Council of State Governments. Retrieved from https://csgjusticecenter.org/wp-content/uploads/2020/01/Juvenile-Justice-White-Paper-with-Appendices-1-1.pdf.

Shjarback, J. A. (2019). "State-mandated transparency: A discussion and examination of deadly force data among law enforcement agencies in Texas." *Journal of Crime and Justice*. Vol. 42, issue 1: 3–17.

Simonton, S. (2014). "Report: Evidence shows community-based programs work better than incarceration." Retrieved from https://jjie.org/2014/06/25/report-evidence-shows-community-based-programs-work-better-than-incarceration/.

The Economist (2021). "How do America's citizen's arrest laws work?" Nov 22. Retrieved from https://www.economist.com/news/2021/11/22/how-do-americas-citizens-arrest-laws-work.

Toensing, G. C. (2018). "Akaka Bill gets Obama approval." *Indian Country Today*. Sep 12. Retrieved from https://indiancountrytoday.com/archive/akaka-bill-gets-obama-approval.

Umpierre, M. (2014). "Rights and responsibilities of youth, families and staff." Ch. 5 in *Desktop Guide to Quality Practice for Working with Youth in Confinement*. Washington, D.C.: National Partnership for Juvenile Services and Office of Juvenile Justice and Delinquency Prevention.

University of Central Florida (2022). "Juvenile probation officer: Salary, career outlook and requirements." UCF Online. Retrieved from https://www.ucf.edu/online/criminal-justice/news/juvenile-probation-office/.

U.S. Bureau of Justice Assistance (BJA) (n.d.). "Tribes: Hawaii. Walking on Common Ground." U.S. Department of Justice Programs, U.S. Department of Justice. Retrieved from http://walkingoncommonground.org/state.cfm?topic=20&fullstate=hawaii.

U.S. Department of Education (n.d.) Family Education Rights and Privacy Act (FERPA). Retrieved from https://www2.ed.gov/policy/gen/guid/fpco/ferpa/index.html.

U.S. Department of Health and Human Services (HHS) (1979). "The Belmont Report: Ethical Principles and Guides for the Protection of Human Subjects of Research." Apr 18. Washington, DC: Department of Health, Education, and Welfare.[18]

U.S. Department of Justice (2021). "Justice Department announces investigation into conditions at five juvenile facilities in Texas." Press Release, Office of Public Affairs. Oct 13. Retrieved from https://www.justice.gov/opa/pr/justice-department-announces-investigation-conditions-five-juvenile-facilities-texas.

U.S. Department of Justice Archives (2020). "Arresting Juveniles." *Criminal Justice Resource Manual*, CMR 118, U.S. Department of Justice. Jan 20. Retrieved from https://www.justice.gov/archives/jm/criminal-resource-manual-118-arresting-juveniles.

---

[18] The U.S. department name at the time of the Belmont Report.

Walker, S. W., and J. R. Herting (2020). "The impact of pretrial juvenile detention on 12-month recidivism: A matched comparison study." *Crime and Delinquency*. Vol. 66, issues 13–14: 1865–1887.

Weber, M. (1922). "Bureaucracy." Reprint (2013) in *Economy and Society*, Vol. 2, ed. G. Roth and C. Wittich. Oakland: University of California Press.

Woolard, J. (2019). Waiver of counsel in juvenile court. No. 253015. National Criminal Justice Reference Service. Jun. Retrieved from https://www.ojp.gov/pdffiles1/nij/grants/253015.pdf.

Youth Law Center (2018). Reenrollment of Juvenile Justice Youth. Nov. Retrieved from https://www.ylc.org/wp-content/uploads/2018/11/Reenrollment-of-Juvenile-Justice-Youth.pdf.

Youth.gov (n.d.). "Reentry." Retrieved from https://youth.gov/youth-topics/juvenile-justice/reentry.

Yu, E. (2014). "Juvenile recidivism measurement inconsistent across states." Juvenile Justice Information Exchange. Jun 13. Retrieved from https://jjie.org/2014/06/13/juvenile-recidivism-measurement-inconsistent-across-states/.

Chapter **TWELVE**

Challenges to Juvenile Delinquency Prevention

> *The chief problem in any community cursed with crime is not the punishment of the criminals, but the preventing of the young from being trained to [commit] crime.*
>
> —W. E. B. Du Bois, American sociologist and activist (1868–1963), in *The Souls of Black Folk* (1903)

Chapter Objectives

- Highlight the challenges to juvenile delinquency prevention in families and communities.
- Introduce the main challenges for people working in juvenile justice and social welfare programs that target delinquency.
- Emphasize the roadblocks to funding programs in delinquency prevention.

Key Terms

Additive bilingual programs
Compassion fatigue
Evidence-based programs
Food insecurity
Juvenile human trafficking (JHT)
Role overload
Rural culture

INTRODUCTION

As we have emphasized throughout this book, prevention is the weakest link, the Achilles' heel in addressing issues of juvenile delinquency in homes, schools, and communities. Chapter 10 described prevention as a "wobbly three-legged stool" that requires the cooperation, enthusiasm, and dedication of parents, schools, and local law enforcement. Prevention also necessitates the cooperation and willingness to reform of potential or actual juvenile delinquents as well. As former First Lady, Senator, and U.S. Secretary of State Hillary Clinton titled her 1996 book about raising responsible children and teenagers into adulthood, "it takes a village" of concerned community stakeholders. Unfortunately, given the many obstacles described in this chapter, there is much to be pessimistic about when it comes to delinquency prevention.

As daunting as prevention might be, numerous programs in the United States and elsewhere (covered in Chapter 13) have been created to help prevent delinquency. Less than 1% of those programs are *evidence-based*, however; many are implemented due to politics or as a copycat response to what is being done in other communities, regardless of any proof of efficacy. Evidence-based programs are grounded in data, preferably accumulated over time in longitudinal studies, that is then subjected to quantitative and qualitative analyses to see if they really work.

Structural and social problems interfere as well. As difficult to address as these are in the context of preventing juvenile delinquency, we pessimistically attempt to clarify them in the first half of this chapter. The roadblocks to prevention often seem insurmountable to scholars, human services workers, and law enforcement. However, as you will see in the last chapter of this book, cautious optimism is warranted due to a handful of programs that seem to work.

CHALLENGES TO JUVENILE DELINQUENCY PREVENTION

Many well-meaning people are working to find solutions to juvenile delinquency, but many challenges nonetheless remain. Our focus in this section is on some road blocks to effective juvenile delinquency prevention in the United States. We can only scratch the surface in the limited space available here, but we can address the most crucial current issues in prevention.

Funding

A primary cause of the failure of programs to suppress or prevent juvenile delinquency is funding. Without exception, states and the federal government spend more on adult and juvenile corrections than on education, even though it would make sense to shift to a front-end approach and fund prevention programs. In addition, federal and state programs are not consistently funded. Budgets largely depend on the prevailing political winds and the generosity of donors. Aftercare programs lack funding as well, as discussed in Chapter 13.

Poverty

Perhaps the second leading impediment to preventing juvenile delinquency is poverty. As discussed throughout this book, this is one of the most serious social issues in the United States today, with approximately one in five children living in poverty. It is a daunting task to tackle juvenile delinquency in the United States or anywhere if poverty is not also addressed. Poverty prevents parental units from affording after-school childcare, much less any unfunded extracurricular activities, which help to keep juveniles out of trouble. According to Dow (2021), the estimated per-student cost of extracurricular activities is around $150 for elementary students, $250 for middle-school students, and $350 for high-school students, per activity, per year, with athletics the costliest. For music programs, these figures do not include the cost of musical instruments.

Incarcerated Parents

Many children have at least one parent incarcerated. Bryant (2021) reports that more than five million children in the United States have had one incarcerated parent at some point in their childhoods. Maruschak et al. (2021) also report that, according to a 2016 survey of inmates in the United States, an estimated 47% of state prisoners and 58% of federal prisoners were parents to at least one minor child. A study of children with incarcerated parental units indicates that having a parent in prison results not only in physical and mental health issues, but in difficulties at school, behavioral problems, and illicit drug use (Chavez, 2017).

Food Insecurity

Hand in hand with poverty comes *food insecurity*. The U.S. Department of Agriculture (2022) defines food insecurity as limited or uncertain access to enough food on a consistent basis to sustain an active, healthy life. During the COVID-19 pandemic, rates of food insecurity increased, with higher levels of unemployment and supply-chain problems that led to higher prices and food items missing from grocery shelves (Ahn and Norwood, 2020). Thirty percent of those who actually contracted the virus and experienced symptoms[1] were food insecure as a result (Ahn and Norwood, 2020). Food insecurity and increases in gas and food prices have been further exacerbated due to record inflation starting in the first half of 2022, driven, among other reasons, by Russia's invasion of Ukraine and by pent-up post-pandemic consumer demand (Markovitz and Marchant, 2022).

[1] Some individuals who contract the COVID-19 virus are asymptomatic.

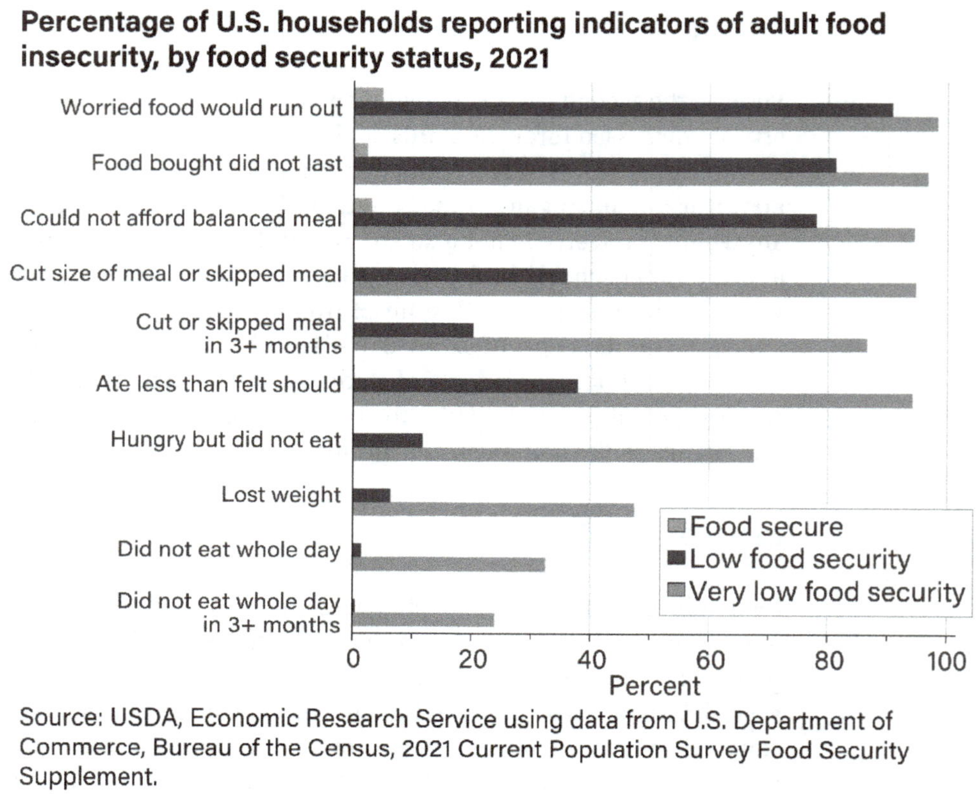

EXHIBIT 12.1 ‖ Food Insecurity in the United States, 2021

Food insecurity leads to hunger, and children growing up in these conditions are at increased risk for delinquency. As Semenza et al. (2020) found in their review of the Longitudinal Study of Adolescent to Adult Health, food insecurity in childhood often results in criminal offending in adolescence that is carried into adulthood; these effects can only be reduced with improved mental health services and employment opportunities.

Alcohol and Drugs

We have also established elsewhere in this book that a great deal of crime, in both the adult and the juvenile populations, is due to alcohol and/or drug use. Some of the crimes committed by adults affecting juveniles include use, procurement, and sale of alcohol or illegal drugs to minors. As we will note in Chapter 13, drug and alcohol abuses are increasingly being treated as public health crises rather than as crimes, and drug courts for juveniles and adults are coming into more frequent use.

Because of its ready availability, juveniles are more likely to use alcohol than any other drug. Studies have found that where strong alcohol policies are in place not only for juveniles but for adults, juvenile alcohol consumption declines

(Xuan et al., 2015). The policies that appear to be most successful control where alcohol can be sold and impose sales taxes, making purchase of alcoholic beverages more cost-prohibitive for the underage or binge drinker (Xuan et al., 2015; Xuan et al., 2013; Paschall, 2009; Chaloopka et al., 2002).

The availability of street drugs is not limited to large cities. As Paquette and Pollini (2018) warn, injection drug use outside of cities is increasingly becoming a public health problem, contributing to increases in HIV and other diseases attributed to the practice of sharing needles. Increasingly, illegal drugs, including sales of prescription opiates on the street, have become a problem even in rural communities. As examples, in 2010 in rural Nebraska and Missouri, opiate-related overdose deaths reached the level of deaths from motor vehicle accidents, numbers nearly unheard of a decade earlier (Dombrowski et al., 2016; Rudd et al., 2014). In fact, in many communities in the United States, including in rural towns and suburbia, drug overdoses have become a major cause of deaths not only of adults, but of juveniles as well (Faul et al., 2015). Rural communities are particularly vulnerable because they are underserved with resources to combat drug and alcohol problems and other public health care crises, including violence.

Lack of Supervision

In today's economy, even two-parent households can find it difficult to manage on one salary. As a result, according to the U.S. Bureau of Labor Statistics (2020), the number of dual-income households have increased exponentially since the 1960s with a rise in female labor participation. Today, in approximately 66% of households with at least one minor child, both parental units work (U.S. Bureau of Labor Statistics, 2020; PEW Research Center, 2017; Hodge and Lundeen, 2013).

The statistics only include biological or adoptive parents, leaving out other family configurations, including temporary guardianship. The first part of the COVID-19 pandemic led to some shifts in these numbers, with many people losing their jobs, temporarily or permanently, when their employers could not keep the doors open. By July 2020, 9.6 million U.S. workers were unable to work (U.S. Bureau of Labor Statistics, 2022b).

A good number of households are both single-income and single-parent. Often even with some child and/or spousal support for the single parent, the cost of childcare may remain too expensive for some families. Consequently, a good number of children go unsupervised after school, during the peak hours for acts of juvenile delinquency. Divorced single parents can also spoil their children due to feelings of guilt, overcompensating for the upheaval and absence of the noncustodial parent (Cui et al., 2019).

Parental Unit Disengagement

Studies from developmental psychology and schools, and other data, indicate that parents who are more involved in their children's lives, including during early

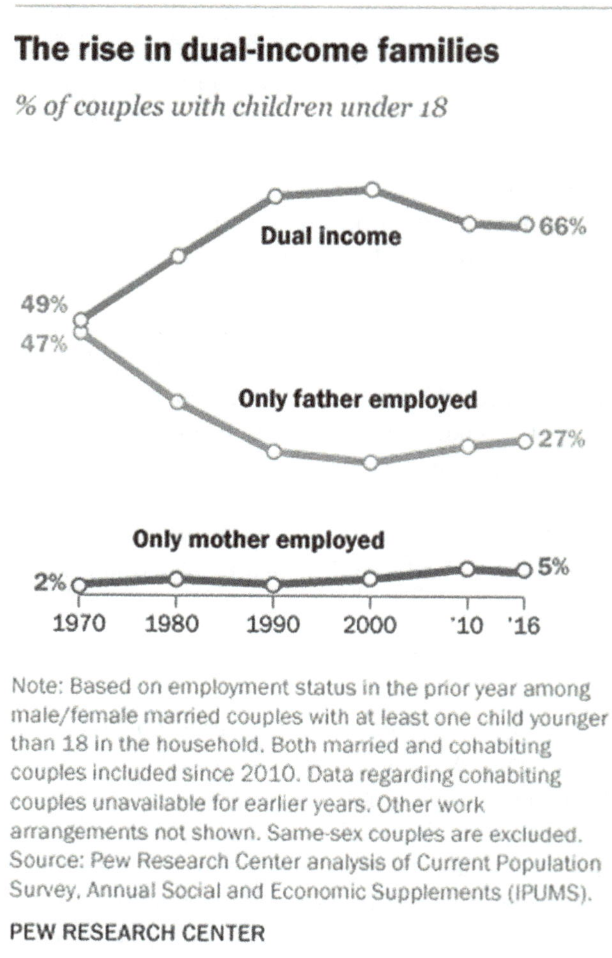

EXHIBIT 12.2 ‖ The Rise in Dual-Income Families

childhood, are more likely to be able to intervene before a delinquency problem occurs (Nokali et al., 2010). As we have already noted, however, child and adolescent delinquent behavior can be ignored or missed for a variety of reasons until it is too late and a misbehaving child has contact with school officials and/or law enforcement.

Study after study of school performance find that parental involvement is one key variable in predicting school success. Chen (2022) offers a summary of studies and reports on parental involvement in public schools, including the following points:

- Academic achievement increases when parents are involved in their children's education.
- Parental involvement leads to better classroom behavior.
- Parents should stay involved in their children's education from preschool through high school.

- Training helps parents of disadvantaged children get involved.
- Reading together at home greatly improves reading skills.

Some surveys have had mixed findings, however, with no significant association found between parental unit involvement and academic success (Okpala et al., 2001; Keith et al., 1986), and some studies even finding a negative effect (Sui-Chu and Willms, 1996; Milne et al., 1986), possibly due to "helicopter parenting"[2] as discussed earlier in this book. Chen (2022) also notes that studies indicate time constraints are often the greatest barriers to parental units' involvement in their child's education. This is particularly the case in dual-income families and single-parent households, as well as in households with a greater number of children.

It may be a challenge for families to follow any or all of the researchers' suggestions, even Chen's (2022) relatively brief list. One or both parental units in the household may hold down more than one job to make ends meet, leaving little time to directly care for children and adolescents. In other cases, in the United States and other countries, English may be the second language of one or both parental units and any extended family, in which case, depending on their proficiency in reading or writing English, they may not be able to effectively help children with school work, much less read to them, other than in their native language.[3] We should note, however, that bilingual homes can also culturally enrich children.

The "Spoiled Child"

In other cases, rather than being disengaged, parental units may be excessively involved in their children's lives. Not all juvenile delinquents live in economic deprivation, but they may suffer from lack of physical and emotional attention from their parental units, socioeconomic status aside. The so-called spoiled child may be without supervision, as well, with parental units using material goods and money to "prove" their love, without providing the guidance the child needs (Clinton, 1996). *Indulgent parenting* "is typically defined as high parental responsiveness and low parental demandingness" (Cui et al., 2019, p. 234; see also Maccoby and Martin, 1983; Baumrind, 1967).

We have all seen the whining, misbehaving child at the grocery store to whom one or the other parental unit gives in and purchases the demanded item, with

---

[2] A *helicopter parent* is best described as a parental unit that hovers over their children, micromanaging every aspect of their lives and, in some cases, contacting teachers excessively to check on their children's academic progress. This does not allow the child to develop healthy autonomy or self-efficacy.

[3] Not all bilingual school programs are equal. The most effective ones teach children growing up in households where English is the second language, providing the opportunity to learn reading and writing not only in English, but in their first language (in most cases in the United States, Spanish), in *additive bilingual programs* (Roberts, 1995), giving them a distinct advantage over students who grow up in monolingual households.

Child throwing a tantrum.

no correction of the inappropriate public behavior. The child comes to believe that every time they act up in public, they will be rewarded, making it difficult for the child to learn how to self-regulate their emotions (Cui et al., 2019).

Overindulgence of children's whims is a product of modernity, due to the many means of spoiling children, including electronic toys and devices. In today's context, this means parents may be generous with money and toys, and allowing children too much freedom in their behavior at home, in school, or in public (Cui et al., 2019; Kindlon, 2001).

A number of parental units have the means to spoil their children, but there are distinct differences between raising a child in privilege and overindulging a child. When young adults recount their childhood experiences, those raised by biological parents in a two-parent household report higher levels of parental indulgence than do those raised in single-parent households (Cui et al., 2019). It is a misconception that indulgent parents are more likely to raise juvenile delinquents, however. In fact, children raised in more traditional nuclear families are less likely to commit crimes. These children may seem to outsiders to be indulged, even spoiled, in terms of material goods and money, but the parents may in fact maintain a consistent set of household rules, including prohibition of underaged drinking, that guide the child away from delinquent behavior.

Another way overindulgent parents may help to create juvenile delinquents is by allowing or ignoring beer or wine consumption by their minor children, passing it off as relatively harmless in comparison to use of cannabis, street drugs, or hard liquor (Whitney and Foiland, 2015). Because beer drinking appears to be more problematic among adolescents, carrying over into young adulthood (and even more so for boys), researchers suggest that parents should reduce the exposure their adolescent boys have to beer (Whitney and Foiland, 2015).

Juvenile Recidivism

In preventing juvenile offending, the juvenile justice system and social services are tasked with finding ways to reduce further offending after a child or adolescent has been adjudicated. The unfortunate truth is that recidivism rates for both adults and juveniles who have spent time in jail, prison, or detention are grim. The numbers are even more discouraging for juveniles who have been in detention for long periods of time. Of greatest concern are findings that indicate that juvenile delinquents reoffend at greater rates than adults. Most juveniles involved in the juvenile justice system are placed on probation, and local systems have limited capacity to track juvenile recidivism, particularly of this larger population of juvenile offenders (National Reentry Resource Center, 2014).

In attempts to reduce recidivism rates, we see again the role that poverty plays. If juveniles, like adult offenders, are released back into the environment in which they originally offended, it is difficult to discourage them from reoffending. Poorer neighborhoods have fewer resources and less funding, and smaller communities compete with larger ones for grants to fund delinquency prevention measures, even if the small, poor communities have the greatest need.

Culture of Violence

The United States is not unique in the extreme levels of violence within its borders, but homicide rates in the United States have historically been higher than in any other developed nation (Gastil, 1971). The number of violent acts committed by adults and juveniles annually cannot be simply explained by the U.S. gun culture. In addition to military participation in two world wars and international police actions in Korea, Vietnam, and elsewhere, the United States has experienced violence of many other kinds, including armed conquest, enslavement and genocide of African and Native peoples, civil war, organized crime, assassination of politicians and civil rights activists, domestic and foreign terrorist attacks, and mass shootings. Most of the world's nations have also undergone or committed some or all of these calamities. Directly or indirectly, this history affects how juveniles view the world.

TABLE 12.1 Violent Crime in the United States, 2019 (Rates per 100,000 Inhabitants)

		Urban populations			
CRIME TYPE	**U.S., total**	**25,000–49,000**	**10,000–24,999**	**<10,000**	**Nonmetropolitan counties (rural)**
Violent crime	387	270.5	254.8	310.9	208.4
Murder and non-negligent manslaughter	5.0	3.3	3.0	3.0	3.8
Rape	44.0	38.4	38.5	48.3	41.1
Robbery	85.1	53.4	20.0	34.4	9.6
Aggravated assault	253.0	175.3	173.6	225.4	154.0

Source: Rural Health Information, 2021; Federal Bureau of Investigation, 2019, Crime in the United States, Table 16, available at https://ucr.fbi.gov/crime-in-the-u.s/2019/crime-in-the-u.s.-2019/topic-pages/tables/table-16.

Though the media seems to suggest otherwise, rural areas are not immune to violence. Frosch et al. (2022) contend that rural America is becoming increasingly violent. Whereas historically the worst crimes experienced in rural areas were property crimes, violent crime has increased in recent years in some locations around the country. For example, White County, Arkansas, had one homicide between 2018 and 2020; by December 2020, there had been 11, including an execution-style shooting of an 80-year-old retired schoolteacher (Frosch et al., 2022). Children in rural areas are exposed to abuse, sexual violence, neglect, assault, and homicide (Rural Health Information Hub, 2021).

One stumbling block in addressing these forms of violence in rural communities is that it is more likely that most everyone knows one another. The Pennsylvania Coalition Against Domestic Violence (2022) warns that *rural culture* means that police, social workers, and others who would ordinarily deal with domestic violence cases, more often than not, know both the offender and the victim and are reluctant to get involved.

It is also often difficult to reduce children's exposure to domestic violence, even if law enforcement has had to intervene in their household. By then, much of the damage has been done. And we do not know the true number of children exposed to domestic violence. Victims often fail to report it and neighbors or family members who are aware that it is occurring often do not want to interfere in what they see as a personal matter (Kidd and Chayet, 2010).

Gun violence in the United States is an ongoing concern and controversy. By May 2022, the *New England Journal of Medicine* reported that gun violence had surpassed motor vehicle accidents as the leading cause of death in the U.S. of children 17 and under. Researchers are at a loss to explain why, beyond the rash of school shootings in recent years (Price, 2022). The number of children who die in school shootings are only a small fraction of children who die in this country as a result of gun violence.

Evidence confirms the assumption that high rates of gun violence can be attributed to the high rates of gun ownership, as well as relatively easy accessibility to firearms (Abdalla, 2021). Sociologist Gregg Barak remarked in an interview on the *David Feldman Show* (2022) that even though the United States makes up 4% of the world's population, it represents 40% of private gun ownership, and he further warned that there are simply too many firearms out there to control illegal sales on the street. And unlike other countries that have successfully reduced gun violence, including Canada, Norway, and the United Kingdom, where aggressive laws restrict firearm purchases, the United States has not, to date, passed any robust federal laws to limit their availability (Abdalla, 2021).

School safety and violence at school, beyond gun violence, continue to be debated, with few good answers. According to Blad (2022, p. 19), "experts who study school safety caution that another round of task forces and best-practice reports won't make a difference if the resulting ideas sit on a shelf unheeded." It is not uncommon for researchers at universities and research organizations (e.g., PEW Research) to complete studies and suggest remedies, only to be ignored by policy makers. Schools officials ask what they can do to combat the violent influences in neighborhoods around them, but research indicates that characteristics of individual students, such as unresolved anger issues, rather than the nature of the surrounding neighborhood, may be more accurate predictors of violence at school (Hughes et al., 2022).

Child Maltreatment

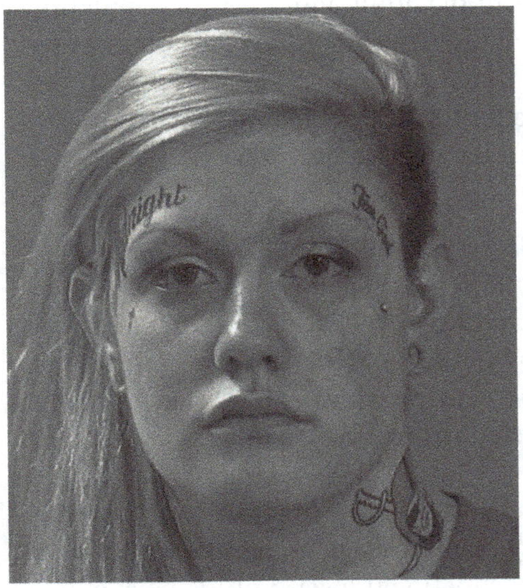

Shasta Groene, age 21, police mugshot, 2018.

Recently *People Magazine* (Aradillas, 2022) reported on Shasta Groene, a woman who at the age of eight was kidnapped and sexually abused, along with her nine-year-old brother, Dylan, by Joseph Duncan, a paroled convicted serial rapist and pedophile, after Duncan brutally murdered her mother, stepfather, and another brother. Dylan was killed by Duncan during the seven-week-long abduction, and Shasta was only rescued by police when a waitress recognized her at a restaurant (Aradillas, 2022). Groene, now an adult with children of her own, has stated that the ordeal and subsequent media attention after her rescue resulted in alcohol and drug abuse that led to addiction and time in juvenile detention for a drug-related crime by the time she was 12; by 21, she was accused of child endangerment for leaving methamphetamine out where her then one-year-old son could have ingested it (Aradillas, 2022; Lowe, 2018).

As in Groene's case, though her abuse was extreme, children and adolescents who have lived through abuse have a difficult time overcoming the trauma without intensive therapy or other interventions. Like Groene, they are at great risk of turning to drugs and/or alcohol to self-medicate. A number of studies, including those by McGrath et al. (2010), Morizot and Kazemian (2014), and others, indicate a connection between child abuse and neglect and juvenile delinquency. A study of child abuse and delinquency that consisted of primarily female participants (Ongah et al., 2021) found that emotional abuse showed an even greater impact on juvenile offending in late adolescence than did other forms of child maltreatment.

Juvenile Human Trafficking

Victimization can result in juvenile delinquency, as found in the previously described case of Shasta Groene. A number of juveniles who have encounters with juvenile authorities are actually victims of *juvenile human trafficking* (JHT) (Reid et al., 2019). One roadblock to readily identifying those at risk for JHT is that the victims, later charged as juvenile offenders in the case of the sex trade, come from diverse backgrounds, with little in common except, prior to abduction or seduction into child labor, having been victims of child maltreatment and/or given to risky behavior, including drug and alcohol use (Reid et al., 2019).

A misconception is that human trafficking of minors for sexploitation and servitude is limited to urban communities. Rural communities are less well-equipped to identify and deal with human trafficking as compared to urban areas, where professionals are better trained to spot it in the adult and juvenile populations, particularly among those who are swept into the criminal justice system as supposed offenders, as in the case of prostitution (Cole and Sprang, 2015). Even with this effort, countless numbers of juvenile human trafficking victims fall through the cracks of the juvenile justice and child welfare systems.

Burnout Among Juvenile Justice and Human Services Personnel

People who work in juvenile justice, including in probation and detention, and social service professionals are subject to high rates of job burnout. Considerable research has looked at emotional exhaustion and burnout as they relate to occupational stress. Many of you taking this course may experience this at some point in your own careers.

Compassion fatigue can set in on the job as social workers and others working in juvenile services face one seemingly insurmountable problem after another. Compassion fatigue is described as the occupational hazard of losing sympathy and empathy for social services clients over time (Voth Scharg et al., 2021), the category into which many juvenile delinquents fall. The emotional and mental exhaustion can result in self-isolation from coworkers, friends, and family (Philbin, 2022). It is a common phenomenon in the helping professions, including nursing, social work, and clinical psychology (Bouchoucha, n.d.), and it also affects those working in juvenile corrections.

Some of the things that contribute to compassion fatigue in juvenile justice professions, particularly for social workers, is a lack of organizational support, including adequate teamwork, training, and pay (Reyes-Quilodran et al., 2022). Social workers, like teachers, are notoriously underpaid in the United States, with the U.S. Bureau of Labor Statistics (2022a) reporting that the lower 10% of social workers earn less than $36,520 per year (2021 data), and child, family, and school social workers can earn even less. Also contributing to burnout among juvenile detention and probation officers is *role overload:* the demands of the job exceed the resources available to effectively accomplish them (Tang and Vanderbergh, 2021; Rhineberger-Dunn and Mack, 2020; Eatough et al., 2011).

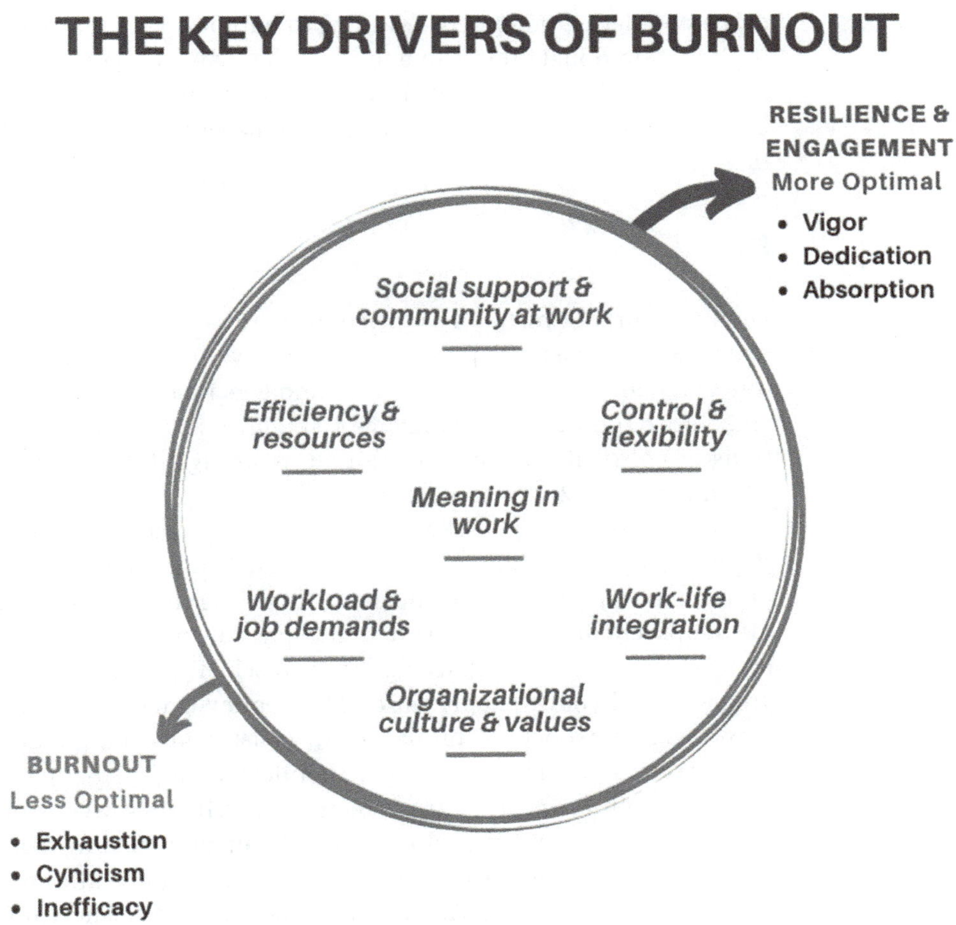

EXHIBIT 12.3 ‖ Sources of on the Job Burnout

The symptoms of burnout in social services employees include the following (Philbin, 2022):

- Inability to stay focused on the job.
- Loss of pride and/or accomplishment in work.
- Loss of patience with clients and co-workers.
- Habitual exhaustion on and off the job.
- Physical pain (e.g., headaches) and frequent illnesses.

People in the social services and juvenile justice are not the only ones subject to burnout. Volunteers, too, who help with juvenile delinquency prevention efforts, can become overwhelmed. A number of youth programs depend heavily on volunteers to run their programs, with scouting and athletic programs as key examples. Bakker et al. (2006), for example, found in a study of volunteer counselors that some had underestimated the demands of their service and the needs of the population they served, leading to burnout. Volunteers may be eager in the beginning to donate their time to what they view to be worthy causes, but over time they can become fatigued by their efforts as more is demanded of them or they find themselves and a handful of others to be among the few willing to contribute their time.

Politics

Few times in U.S. history has the country been as divided as it is today. Unfortunately, when it comes to juvenile delinquency prevention, we cannot discount the role that politics plays in the effort to find effective programs. In the United States and abroad, politicians vacillate between juvenile justice reform and demonstrations of political toughness exhibited in strong adult and juvenile crime laws (Goodman et al., 2017; Pitts, 1988).

The approach to juvenile crimes thus swings according to the needs of those in political power at any given time (Ward, 2018). Many of those who make the policy and law do not have educational or experiential backgrounds in developmental psychology or juvenile delinquency, so when policy is driven by politics, rather than by any real knowledge of the mechanics of juvenile criminal behavior, programs and young people suffer. Most policy makers will consult experts, but they are more likely to be influenced by constituents and political allies. And the experts themselves may be subject to political biases.

Philosophies in juvenile corrections vacillate between treating a juvenile delinquent as a troubled youth in need of help and labeling that youth as a criminal, which has been the approach most common in juvenile courts since the late 20th century (Feld, 2018). And as one former police academy director shared, with juvenile delinquency prevention, it is always a question of chasing the latest shiny object, while abandoning programs that have not been given a chance to succeed.

Racial politics is also a factor. According to Ward and Kupchik (2011), greater numbers of racial minorities are adjudicated to juvenile detention centers than white juvenile offenders. Ward and Kupchik (2011) suggest having more minority employees in the juvenile court system, including on probation staffs, as well as closely examining court workers' attitudes toward minority populations, regardless of their own minority status. More recently, national Black youth placement alone appears to be declining faster than white youth placement. The Sentencing Project (Rovner, 2021) place rates at 315 per 100,000, as compared to white youth placement at 72 per 100,000, compared to 2010 data, where approximately 700 per 100,000 Black youth were in placement and approximately 175 white youth per 100,000 were in placement in the same time period (OJJDP, 2022; Sickmund et al., 2021).

There is considerable pessimism as to whether institutional racism within the adult and juvenile systems can be adequately addressed, as criminal behavior continues to be seen as a character flaw in the individual, rather than as being due to ongoing issues of poverty, unemployment, and racial inequality (Feld, 2018). The same holds true for juvenile delinquency prevention programs that do not address the effect of these social problems on minority populations.

Environmental Threats

Increasingly, researchers are gaining a better understanding of how the physical environment in which children are raised can have a detrimental effect on their development. Specifically, exposure to toxic chemicals in the environment, including pesticides, herbicides, and other compounds used in landscaping and agriculture, can result in deficits in cognition and motor skills in children and contribute to aggressive behavior (Johansen, 2021). As the World Health Organization (Sripada, 2017, p. 1242) warned early in the 21st century, ongoing human-created environmental concerns include exposure to

EXHIBIT 12.4 || Children's Exposure to E-Waste in the Environment

air pollution, arsenic, asbestos, benzene, cadmium, dioxin and dioxin-like substances (such as polychlorinated biphenyls, or PCBs), inadequate or excess fluoride, lead, mercury, and highly hazardous pesticides. Many of these are neurotoxic.

Exposure to toxins in the environment is a worldwide problem. In the United States, research indicates that those with lower incomes, or who live or work in poorer communities, are exposed to more toxic pollution; structural racism reinforces this problem, putting minorities at greater risk (Huzur, 2021). And as Sripada (2017) notes, child-specific behaviors, like crawling, eating, and drinking without using hand-washing precautions, are likely to lead to ingestion of more toxic chemicals per pound of body weight than adults experience.

These problems are not easily resolved, particularly in heavily industrialized areas, and they may hinder the progress of any efforts to prevent delinquency in communities. An additional concern noted by the World Health Organization, described in Exhibit 12.4, is the amount of e-waste from electronics discarded into the environment.

SUMMARY

Much of what we discuss in this chapter is discouraging. Juveniles, parental units, and human services employees face many issues in attempting to combat juvenile delinquency. Among the most difficult challenges to overcome is poverty, and perhaps the second most dire is lack of funding for programs to prevent delinquency.

As we have examined in this chapter, juvenile delinquents are often victims. In some cases, juveniles outgrow delinquency as they approach young adulthood, but in others, delinquents offend well into adulthood. This risk is greater the longer they are held in juvenile detention after being found delinquent in juvenile court.

Poverty, conditions at home, and parenting skills do not explain all the risks for delinquency in the United States or elsewhere in the world. For all the positive outcomes of globalization, including cheaper goods, it has also resulted in illegal drug pipelines into the United States, contributing to addictions in both the adult and the juvenile populations. Illegal drugs can also be manufactured in the U.S., making them readily available.

Drug availability for juveniles is not limited to large cities. Increasingly, rural areas have witnessed an increase in the use of injectable drugs, including heroin, leading not only to addiction, but to transmission of communicable diseases through needle sharing. Likewise, alcohol is fairly easily available to individuals under 21 from indulgent or clueless parental units, or purchased by other adults. Though both young females and males are at risk of drug or underage alcohol use, males are at greater risk, particularly in the consumption of beer.

Some parenting styles contribute more to delinquency than others. Parental units who are neglectful or, at the other extreme, overindulgent and hovering, can raise children who turn to delinquency. Of greatest concern is when a child has been physically or emotionally abused–both risk factors for delinquency. Some abuses go undetected, hidden in families or by other family members, neighbors, and friends who may not wish to report it, believing that what happens within a household is private family business.

In the United States, an additional challenge to fighting juvenile delinquency is the legal and illegal availability of firearms. Firearms, a hotly debated topic centering on Second Amendment rights, have now surpassed motor vehicle accidents as the number one cause of death of children under 18. The availability of firearms in the United States is said to contribute to its culture of violence; however, the country also has a long history of violence, beginning before the ready availability of firearms. One additional contributing factor to the culture of violence is the presence of street gangs, not only in cities, but in suburban and rural areas as well, though rural areas are more likely to see white supremacy and armed militia groups.

We have highlighted the most obvious and troublesome challenges to combatting juvenile delinquency. It would take an entire book to fully outline all the factors that make juvenile delinquency prevention an uphill battle, both for parental units and professionals in the field. The next chapter will examine several programs, some of which are evidence-based, that show promise in the ongoing struggle to prevent delinquency and recidivism.

IN THE MEDIA

Mismanagement in Grant Programs

Not everyone involved in working with juveniles in trouble is there for the right reasons. As if difficulties getting program funding weren't enough, problems with fraud committed by some who run those programs is a recurring problem. Stealing grant funds is a white collar crime that often goes undetected until it is too late (Hansen, 2020). It is the responsibility of the people who receive grant awards to manage funds responsibly. The following types of grant fund mismanagement are federal violations (U.S. Department of Health and Human Services, n.d.):

- Embezzlement
- Theft or bribery concerning programs receiving federal funds
- False statements
- False claims
- Mail fraud and wire fraud

Federal grant programs are supposed to follow the rules and regulations set forth by the U.S. Department of Justice and Office of Justice Programs, and are subject to congressional oversight. In 2015, when some irregularities were found in the Office of Juvenile Justice and Delinquency Prevention (OJJDP), its practices were called into question. As stated in a news release from the office of Senator Chuck Grassley (2015, retrieved from https://www.grassley.senate.gov/news/news-releases/alleged-fraud-juvenile-justice-grant-program-fails-youths), the then-Chairman of the Senate Judiciary Committee:

> *These allegations that some states are receiving millions in taxpayer dollars despite failing to adequately serve at-risk minors are disturbing. Congress established important benchmarks for states applying for federal dollars to support their juvenile justice programs. Yet it appears that the federal Office of Juvenile Justice and Delinquency Prevention has turned a blind eye to these requirements, effectively rewarding states for failing to effectively protect children within their boundaries. The Department of Justice needs to explain its justification for this apparent disregard for legal requirements and its efforts to ensure the prudent use of tax dollars.*

Senator Grassley may very well have had political reasons for making such a statement, but the reality is that even the U.S. Government Accountability Office (2021), a nonpartisan office, admits that the Department of Justice's Inspector General found cases of possible fraud, waste, and abuses within programs funded by OJJDP. Before a grant is even awarded, the agency presenting the grant proposal is, in theory, supposed to undergo vigorous scrutiny for fraud risk. Yet there were inaccuracies and errors found in the risk scoring for 13% of the grants made between 2017 and 2019 (U.S. Government Accountability Office, 2021). This is yet another argument for evidence-based programs that include accurate records of expenses and outcomes.

SOURCES

Grassley, Chuck, Senate Office (2015). "Alleged fraud in Juvenile Justice Grant Program fails youth." News release. Jan 14. Retrieved from https://www.grassley.senate.gov/news/news-releases/alleged-fraud-juvenile-justice-grant-program-fails-youths.

U.S. Department of Health and Human Services (HHS) (n.d.). "Grant fraud and the responsibilities of award recipients." Retrieved from https://www.grants.gov/learn-grants/grant-fraud/grant-fraud-responsibilities.html.

U.S. Government Accountability Office (GAO) (2021). "Juvenile Justice Grants: The Office of Justice Programs could improve the quality of a key fraud control." GAO-21-302. Mar 31. Retrieved from https://www.gao.gov/products/gao-21-302.

INTERNATIONAL PERSPECTIVES

Russia

In the former Soviet Union, a closed society at the time, delinquency data were difficult to obtain. The "official" record coming out of the U.S.S.R. in the 1960s indicated that juvenile delinquency was in a state of constant decline, with no exception (Connor, 1970). Under Communist rule, following the principles of the 1918 Revolution, reformers took a progressive approach to juvenile justice, and juveniles under 18 were reported as suffering from social neglect rather than character flaws (Brinkhof, 2021).

Even after reforms and the dismantling of the U.S.S.R., it continues to be difficult to get accurate data. But we can surmise from the news of social ills, including an upended economy, that it is highly unlikely that juvenile delinquency is not a current problem in Russia. According to Statista (2022), 103,335 reported crimes were committed *against* juveniles in 2021, and as we see elsewhere in the world, much of that and other crime may very well have been committed by other juveniles.

In 2022, Russia invaded Ukraine, a former Soviet satellite country that became an independent nation in 1991. The invasion not only placed Russia and Ukraine in precarious economic positions, it sent ripples throughout a world already trying to recover from the COVID-19 pandemic. In addition to waging war, Russia has had a history of a number of social problems, and currently citizens report that inflation, corruption, poverty, economic crisis, and growing social inequality cause them the most worry (Statista Research, 2022).

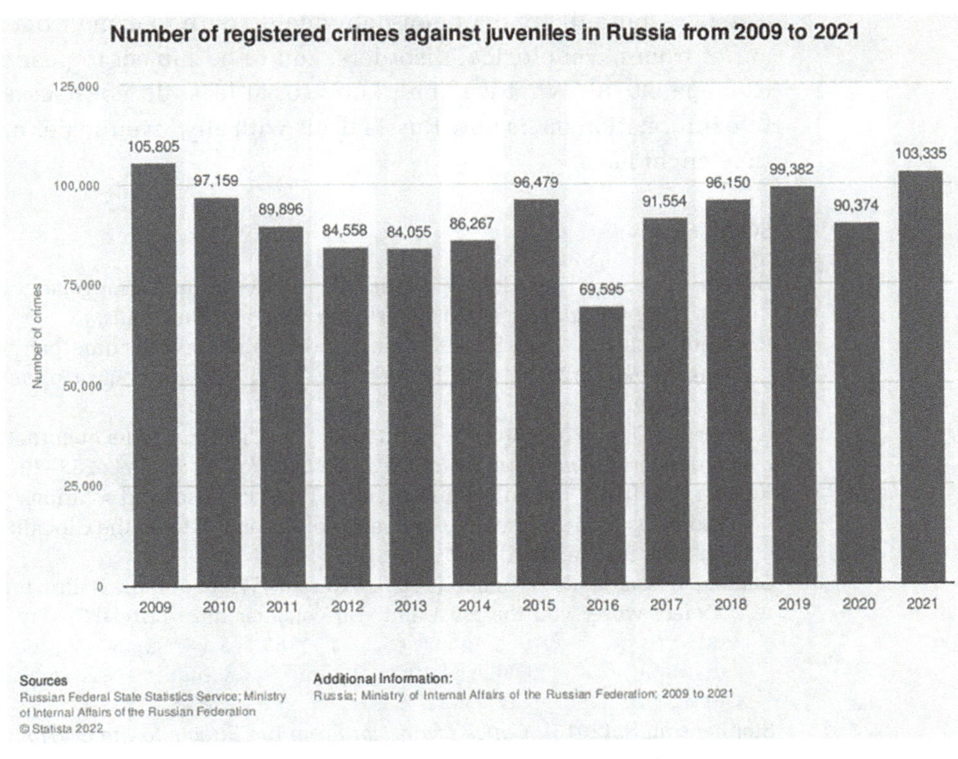

EXHIBIT 12.5 ‖ Number of Registered Crimes Against Juveniles in Russia, 2009–2021

More recently, prices of goods have increased by 60% in Russia, as a direct result of the war (Statista Research, 2022). Though we do not always get good crime data out of Russia, which remains a semi-closed society, we can surmise from what we know to be contributors to delinquency in the west, including those introduced in this book and chapter, Russia undoubtedly has its own juvenile crime problems. The cited causes for delinquency in Russia are familiar: poverty and social and psychological disorder (Belova and Gelpey, 2019).

Organized crime, including street gangs, along with a prolific black market, were a problem prior to political and economic reforms in the 1990s and continue to be. In the 1980s and 1990s, there was a massive movement of young men into racketeering in Russia (Stephenson, 2015). Runaway youth and unhoused children ended up in youth subcultures on the streets, some of which were part of organized crime, even if on the periphery:

> *Olesia left home as her parental family disintegrated under the pressure of poverty with her parents, formerly respectable and relatively well-off skilled blue-collar workers, trying to coerce her into selling herself. She escaped onto the streets and ultimately ended up in organized prostitution.* (Stephenson, 2015, p. 49)

What we do know about the characteristics of juvenile delinquents in Russia is that they have many of the same risk factors as youth in the United States. They are more likely than non-delinquent youth to come from poor families, to suffer from psychological disorders, and to be subject to peer group influences (Ranepa, 2018). What we don't know, or at least do not necessarily have accurate information on, is how Russia deals with any juvenile delinquency problems they might have.

SOURCES

Belova, A. A., and E. A. Gelpey (2019). "The sports volunteer movement in Modern Russia." In *Theory of Language and Translation*. Eng. and Rus. trans.

Brinkhof, T. (2021). "In the Soviet Union, murderers had an easier time than political dissenters." *Big Think*. Feb 21. Retrieved from https://bigthink.com/the-past/soviet-union-criminality-marxism-justice/.

Connor, W. D. (1970). "Juvenile delinquency in U.S.S.R.: Some quantitative and qualitative indicators." *American Sociological Review*. Vol. 35, issue 2: 283–297.

Ranepa, Y. (2018). "Juvenile delinquency in Russia: Causes and solutions." Conference paper, Problems of Management, Economy, Politics and Law in the Globalizing World. Rostov-on-Don, Russia. April 16–19.

Statista Research Department (2022). "Russia: Which of the following problems of our society worry you the most and you consider most critical?" May 19. Retrieved from https://www.statista.com/statistics/1034365/russia-regions-with-most-youth-crimes/#:~:text=Magadan%20Oblast%20and%20the%20Republic,as%20co%2Dperpetrators%20in%202021.

Stephenson, S. (2015). *Gangs of Russia: From the Streets to the Corridors of Power*. Ithaca, NY: Cornell University Press.

CHAPTER DISCUSSION QUESTIONS

1. Choose one of the challenges to juvenile delinquency prevention in this chapter and discuss some possible solutions.
2. Identify a challenge to juvenile delinquency prevention that is not included in this chapter.
3. What measures can be taken to make sure that workers in juvenile justice and social work professions are not at risk for burnout?
4. Besides the reasons stated in this chapter, why might parental units ignore their children's delinquent behaviors?
5. What can be done, if anything, to address the issues of children's exposure to violence, either in their homes or in their community?
6. What types of juvenile delinquency prevention programs did you have in your own schools, elementary through high school? In your opinion and from your observations, how effective were they?

GLOSSARY

Additive bilingual programs Programs in which a student's first language continues to be developed, including reading and writing, while they are learning a second language. Typically in bilingual programs in the United States, Spanish is the first language and English is the second.

Compassion fatigue Occupational hazard of working in human services professions, including the medical field, social work, and criminal justice system, as a response to the stresses of the job, including limited resources, and the population that employees work with. See *role overload.*

Evidence-based programs Programs that are implemented and regularly reviewed on the basis of data analysis indicating they may be effective in serving the intended population.

Food insecurity Conditions under which access to affordable, nutritious food adequate to nourish people and sustain a healthy life is limited or unreliable.

Juvenile human trafficking (JHT) Recruitment or forced abduction of juveniles with the intention of coercing them into forced labor, often in the illegal sex trades, including prostitution.

Role overload When a job is overwhelming because far too many responsibilities are placed on the employee and too few resources are provided to combat the inevitable fatigue associated with this overload. See *compassion fatigue.*

Rural culture Generally, the culture that emerges in remote areas, where there is less diversity within the population, as well as greater distances to travel for work opportunities or access to services or shopping.

REFERENCES AND ADDITIONAL SUGGESTED READINGS

Abdalla, S. M., K. M. Keyes, and S. Galea (2021). "A public health approach to tackling the role of culture in shaping the gun violence epidemic in the United States." *Public Health Reports*. Vol. 136, issue 1: 6–9.

Ahn, S. and F. B. Norwood (2020). "Measuring food insecurity during the COVID-19 pandemic of spring 2020." *Applied Economic Perspectives and Policy*. Vol. 43, issue 1: 162–168.

Aradillas, E. (2022). "Kidnapped at age 8 by a serial killer: She survived a monster." *People Magazine*. Jun 6. Vol. 97, issue 23: 60–65.

Bakker, A. B., K. I. Van der Zee, K. A. Lewig, and M. F. Dollard (2006). "The relationship between the big five personality factors and burnout: A study among volunteer counselors." *Journal of Social Psychology*. Vol. 146, issue 1: 31–50.

Baumrind, D. (1967). "Child care practices anteceding three patterns of preschool behavior." *Genetic Psychology Monographs*. Vol. 75: 43–48.

Blad, E. (2022). "A familiar fight about how to make schools safe." *Education Week*. Vol. 41, issue 34 (June): 19.

Bouchoucha, S. (n.d.). "What is compassion fatigue and how can it affect your career?" Deakin University. Retrieved from https://this.deakin.edu.au/career/what-is-compassion-fatigue-and-how-can-it-affect-your-career#:~:text=Compassion%20fatigue%20involves%20a%20gradual,at%20risk%20of%20compassion%20fatigue.

Bryant, E. (2021). "More than 5 million children have had an incarcerated parent." Vera Organization. May 7. Retrieved from https://www.vera.org/news/more-than-5-million-children-have-had-an-incarcerated-parent.

Chaloopka, F. J., M. Grossman, and H. Saffer (2002). "The effects of price on alcohol consumption and alcohol-related problems." *Alcohol Research and Health*. Vol. 26, issue 2: 22–34.

Chavez, J. (2017). "New UTSA study finds a link between incarcerated parents and their children's health." *UTSA Today*. University of Texas San Antonio. May 11. Retrieved from https://www.utsa.edu/today/2017/05/prisonstudy.html.

Chen, G. (2022). "Parental involvement is key to student success." *Public School Review*. May 20. Retrieved from https://www.publicschoolreview.com/blog/parental-involvement-is-key-to-student-success.

Clinton, H. (1996). *It Takes a Village and Other Lessons Children Teach Us*. New York: Simon and Schuster.

Cole, J., and G. Sprang (2015). "Sex trafficking of minors in metropolitan, micropolitan, and rural communities." *Child Abuse and Neglect*. Vol. 40 (Aug): 113–123.

Cui, M., J. A. Graber, A. Metz, C. A. Darling (2019). "Parental indulgence, self-regulation, and young adults' behavior and emotional problems." *Journal of Family Studies*. Vol. 25, issue 3: 233–249.

David Feldman Show (2022). "American Culture of Violence: Interview with Gregg Barak." Youtube.com. May 30. Retrieved from https://www.youtube.com/watch?v=nT7DpP88dqw.

Dombrowski, K., D. Crawford, B. Khan, and K. Tyler (2016). "Current rural drug use in the US Midwest." *Journal of Drug Abuse*. Vol. 2, issue 3: 22.

Dow, N. (2021). "5 tips to slash the cost of your kids' pricey extracurriculars." *Penny Hoarder*. Oct 1. Retrieved from https://www.thepennyhoarder.com/save-money/after-school-activities/#:~:text=Huntington%20Bank%20and%20Communities%20in,%24350%20for%20high%20school%20students.

Eatough E. M., Chang C.-H., Miloslavic S. A., Johnson R. E. (2011). "Relationships of role stressors with organizational citizenship behavior: a meta-analysis." *Journal of Applied Psychology*. Vol. 96: 619–632.

Faul, M., M. W. Dailey, D. E. Sugerman, S. M. Sasser, B. Levy, and L. J. Paulozzi (2015). "Disparity in naloxone administration by emergency medical service providers and the burden of drug overdose in US rural communities." *American Journal of Public Health*. Vol. 105 (Sup. 3): e26–e32.

Feld, B. C. (2018). *The Evolution of the Juvenile Court: Race, Politics, and the Criminalizing of Juvenile Justice*. New York: New York University Press.

Fostering Healthy Futures (FHF) (n.d.). "Programs." Regents University of Colorado. Retrieved from https://www.fosteringhealthyfutures.org/programs.

Frosch, D., K. Maher, and Z. Elinson (2022). "Rural America reels from violent crime. 'People lost their ever lovin' minds.'" *Wall Street Journal*. Jun 10. Retrieved from https://www.wsj.com/articles/violent-crime-rural-america-homicides-pandemic-increase-11654864251.

Gastil, B. (1971). "Homicide and a regional culture of violence." *American Sociological Review*. Jun, Vol. 36: 412–427.

Goodman, P., J. Page, and M. Phelps (2017). *Breaking the Pendulum: The Long Struggle Over Criminal Justice*. Oxford, UK: Oxford University Press.

Hodge, S. A., and A. Lundeen (2013). "America has become a nation of dual-income working couples." Tax Foundation. Nov 21. Retrieved from https://taxfoundation.org/america-has-become-nation-dual-income-working-couples/.

Hughes, L. A., E. V. Botchkovar, O. Antonaccio, and A. Timmer (2022). "Schools, subculture values, and the risk of youth violence: The influence of the code of the street among students in three U.S. cities." *Journal of Youth and Adolescence*. Vol. 51, issue 2 (Feb.): 244–260.

Huzar, T. (2021). "How and why are the poorest people most likely to have exposure to toxins?" *Medical News Today*. Aug 12. Retrieved from https://www.medicalnewstoday.com/articles/how-and-why-are-the-poorest-people-most-likely-to-have-exposure-to-toxins#:~:text=Research%20suggests%20that%20people%20with,Structural%20racism%20exacerbates%20these%20issues.&text=The%20degradation%20of%20the%20environment,direct%20effect%20on%20human%20health.

Johansen, B. E. (2021). "Environmental toxicology and mental health." In *Salem Press Encyclopedia of Health*. New York: Salem Press.

Keith, T. Z., T. M. Reimers, P. G. Fehrmann, S. M. Pottebaum, L. W. Aubey (1986). "Parental involvement, homework and TV times: Direct and indirect effects on high school achievement." *Journal of Educational Psychology*. Vol. 78: 373–380.

Kidd, R. F., and E. F. Chayet (2010). "Why do victims fail to report? The psychology of criminal victimization." *Journal of Social Issues*. Vol. 40, issue 1: 39–50.

Kindlon, D. (2001). *Too Much of a Good Thing*. New York: Hyperion.

Lowe, E. (2018). "Shasta Groene violates probation for endangering child." *Idaho Press*. Jun 25. Retrieved from https://www.idahopress.com/news/local/shasta-groene-violates-probation-for-endangering-child/article_7b583fdf-4a65-5e39-a982-f0d1a42a85d9.html.

Maccoby, E. E., and J. A. Martin (1983). "Socialization in the context of the family: Parent-child interaction." In *Handbook of Child Psychology*, Vol. 4, 4th ed., ed. P. H. Mussen and E. M. Hetheringon. New York: Wiley.

Markovitz, G., and N. Marchant (2022). "Why is inflation so high and will it stay that way? An economist explains." World Economic Forum. May 12. Retrieved from https://www.weforum.org/agenda/2022/05/inflation-rising-economist-explains/#:~:text=He%20gives%20three%20reasons%20for,and%20more%20goods%20through%202022.

Maruschak, L. M., J. Bronson, and M. Alper (2021). "Report: Parents in Prison and Their Minor Children: Survey of Prison Inmates." Bureau of Justice Statistics (BJS), U.S. Department of Justice Programs, U.S. Department of Justice. May. Retrieved from https://bjs.ojp.gov/library/publications/prents-prison-and-their-minor-children-survey-prison-inmates-2016.

McGrath, S. A., A. A. Nilsen, and K. R. Kerley (2010). "Sexual victimization in childhood and the propensity for juvenile delinquency and adult criminal behavior: A systematic review." *Aggression and Violent Behavior* Vol. 16: 485–492.

Milne, A. M., D. E. Myers, A. S. Rosenthal, and A. Ginsburg (1986). "Single parents, working mothers, and the educational achievement of school children." *Sociology of Education.* Vol. 59: 125–139.

National Reentry Resource Center (2014). "Measuring and using recidivism data to inform policy, practice and resource allocation." The Council of State Governments Justice Center. Jul. Retrieved from https://csgjusticecenter.org/wp-content/uploads/2020/02/Measuring-and-Using-Juvenile-Recidivism-Data-to-Inform-Policy-Practice-and-Resource-Allocation.pdf.

Nokali, N. E., H. J. Bachman, and E. Votruba-Drzal (2010). "Parent involvement and children's academic and social development in elementary school." *Child Development.* Vol. 81, issue 3 (May–June): 988–1005.

Office of Juvenile Justice and Delinquency Prevention (OJJDP) (n.d.) (or updated 2022?). Racial and ethnic disparity in juvenile justice processing. *Literature Review,* Models Program Guide. Office of Justice Programs, U.S. Department of Justice. Retrieved from https://ojjdp.ojp.gov/model-programs-guide/literature-reviews/racial-and-ethnic-disparity.

Okpala, C. O., A. O. Okpala, and F. E. Smith (2001). "Parental involvement, instructional expenditures, family socioeconomic attributes and student achievement." *Journal of Educational Research.* Vol. 95, issue 2: 110–115.

Ongah, Y., N. Soetikno, F. I. R. Dewi, and M. J. Batobara-Yap (2021). "The role of child maltreatment and tendency to juvenile delinquency in late adolescents." *Advances in Heath Science Research.* Vol. 41: 296–301.

Paquette, C. E., and R. A. Pollini (2018). "Injection drug use, HIV/HCVm and related services in nonurban areas of the United States." *Drug and Alcohol Dependence.* Vol. 188 (July): 239–250.

Paschall, M. J., J. W. Grube, and K. Kypri (2009). "Alcohol control policies and alcohol consumption by youth: A multi-national study." *Addiction.* Vol. 104, issue 11: 1849–1855.

Pennsylvania Coalition Against Domestic Violence (PCADV) (2022). Rural communities. Retrieved from https://www.pcadv.org/initiatives/underserved-populations/rural-communities/.

PEW Research Center (2017). The rise in dual-income families. Jun 15. Retrieved from https://www.pewresearch.org/ft_17-06-14_fathers_dual_income/.

Philbin, J. (2022). "Surviving social work burnout: Prevention strategies and advice." Student Training and Education in Public Service (Steps). May 11. Retrieved from https://www.publicservicedegrees.org/resources/surviving-burnout-social-work/.

Pitts, J. (1988). *Politics of Juvenile Crime.* Sage Contemporary Criminology Series. London, UK: Sage.

Price, J. T. (2022). "More children die from gun violence than car crashes. Are school shootings to blame?" *News@Northeastern.* Northeastern University. Jun 3. Retrieved from https://news.northeastern.edu/2022/06/03/children-gun-violence/.

Reid, J. A., M. T. Baglivio, A. R. Piquero, M. A. Greenwald, and N. Epps (2019). "No youth left behind to human trafficking: Exploring profiles of risk." *American Journal of Orthopsychiatry.* Vol. 89, issue 6: 704–715.

Reyes-Quilodran, C., M. C. Ruffolo, and S. Chang (2022). "Compassion fatigue among social workers in juvenile offender systems in Chile." *International Social Work.* May. P 1. https://doi.org/10.1177/00208728221088169

Rhineberger-Dunn, G. and K. Y. Mack (2020). "Predicting burnout among juvenile detention and juvenile probation officers." *Criminal Justice Policy Review.* Vol. 31, issue 3 (April): 335–355.

Roberts, C. A. (1995). "Bilingual education program models: A framework for understanding." *Bilingual Research Journal.* Vol. 10, issues 3–4: 369–378.

Rovner, J. (2021). "Black disparities in youth incarceration." Sentencing Project. Jul 15. Retrieved from https://www.sentencingproject.org/publications/black-disparities-youth-incarceration/#:~:text=The%20Black%20youth%20placement%20rate,rate%20of%2072%20per%20100%2C000.

Rudd, R. A., L. J. Paulozzi, M. J. Bauer, R. W. Burleson, R. E. Carlson et al. (2014). "Increases in heroin overdose deaths—28 states, 2010–2012." *Morbidity and Mortality Weekly Report*. Centers for Disease Control and Prevention (CDC). Vol. 63: 849–854.

Rural Health Information Hub (2021). "Violence and abuse in the rural America." Mar 26. Retrieved from https://www.ruralhealthinfo.org/topics/violence-and-abuse.

Semenza, D. C., A. M. Testa, D. B. Jackson, M. G. Vaughn, and N.C. Semenza (2020). "Criminal offending trajectories from adolescence through young adulthood and the risk of food insecurity: Evidence from the Add Health study." *Annals of Epidemiology*. Vol. 50: 20–26.e1.

Simons, R. L., C. A. Johnson, R. D. Conger, G. H. Elder (1998). "A test of latent trait versus life-course perspective on the stability of adolescent antisocial behavior." *Criminology*. Vol. 36: 217–244.

Sripada, K. (2017). "'Beginning with the smallest intake': Children's brain development and the role of neuroscience in global environmental health." *Neuron*. Vol. 95 (Sep.): 1242–1245.

Sui-Chu, E. H., and J. D. Willms (1996). "Effects of parental involvement on eighth-grade achievement." *Sociology of Education*. Vol. 69: 126–141.

Tang, W., and C. Vandenbergh (2021). "Role overload and work performance: The role of psychological strain and leader-member exchange." *Frontiers in Psychology*. May 21. Vol. 12:e691207. Retrieved from https://www.ncbi.nlm.nih.gov/pmc/articles/PMC8176030/#:~:text=Role%20overload%20is%20a%20specific,understood%20through%20the%20COR%20lens.

U.S. Bureau of Labor Statistics (BLS) (2022a). "Social Workers: Pay." *Occupational Outlook Handbook*. U.S. Department of Labor. Retrieved from https://www.bls.gov/ooh/community-and-social-service/social-workers.htm#tab-5.

U.S. Bureau of Labor Statistics (BLS) (2022b). "Supplemental data measuring the effects of the coronavirus (COVID-19) pandemic on the labor market." Labor Force Statistics from Current Population Survey. U.S. Department of Labor. May 12. Retrieved from https://www.bls.gov/cps/effects-of-the-coronavirus-covid-19-pandemic.htm.

U.S. Bureau of Labor Statistics (BLS) (2020). "Comparing characteristics and selected expenditures of dual- and single-income households with children." *Monthly Labor Review*. U.S. Department of Labor. Sep. Retrieved from https://www.bls.gov/opub/mlr/2020/article/comparing-characteristics-and-selected-expenditures-of-dual-and-single-income-households-with-children.htm#:~:text=As%20shown%20in%20the%20figure,have%20two%20or%20more%20children.

U.S. Department of Agriculture (USDA) (2022). Definitions of food insecurity. Apr 22. Retrieved from https://www.ers.usda.gov/topics/food-nutrition-assistance/food-security-in-the-u-s/definitions-of-food-security/#:~:text=Food%20insecurity%E2%80%94the%20condition%20assessed,may%20result%20from%20food%20insecurity.

Voth Shrag, R. J., L. G. Wood, and K. Wachter (2021). "Compassion fatigue among the intimate partner violence and sexual assault workforce: Enhancing organizational practice." *Violence Against Women*. Vol. 28, issue 1 (Jan.): 277–297.

Ward, G. K. (2018). "Review Symposium: Rethinking the Pendulum Model of criminal justice history—Contention and the pendulum pivot: Weighting equal justice." *Law and Social Inquiry*. Vol. 44, issue 3: 806–813.

Ward, G. K., and A. Kupchik (2011). "Racial politics of juvenile justice policy support." *Race and Justice*. Vol. 1, issue 2: 154–184.

Whitney, N., and J. M. Froiland (2015). "Parenting style, gender, beer drinking, and drinking problems of college students." *International Journal of Psychology: A Biopsychosocial Approach*. Vol. 16: 93—109.

Xuan, Z., J. G. Blanchette, T. F. Nelson, T. H. Nguyen, S. E. Hadland, et al. (2015). "Youth drinking in the United States: Relationships with alcohol policies and adult drinking." *Pediatrics*. Vol. 136, issue 1: 18–27.

Xuan, Z., T. F. Nelson, T. Heeren et al. (2013). "Tax policy, adult binge drinking, and youth alcohol consumption in the United States." *Alcoholism: Clinical and Experimental Res*earch. Vol. 37, issue 10: 1713–1719.

Chapter **THIRTEEN**

Programs and Strategies to Reduce and Prevent Juvenile Delinquency

The only effective way to reduce and prevent juvenile crime is to balance tough enforcement measures with targeted, effective and [sic] intervention initiatives.

—Janet Reno, U.S. Attorney General, 1993–2001

Chapter Objectives

- Introduce cautious optimism in the battle for juvenile delinquency prevention.
- Review evidence-based program practices.
- Identify programs that show promise to reduce delinquency and recidivism.
- Forecast the future of juvenile delinquency prevention.

Key Terms

Brady Law
Deinstitutionalization of juvenile offenders
Early developmental prevention
Gentrification
Grassroots organizations
Head Start Programs
Jail removal requirements
Juvenile awareness programs
Juvenile rehabilitation integrated treatment
Pilot program
Primary prevention
Revitalization
Secondary prevention
Tertiary prevention
Toothpaste effect
Waste management model (corrections)
Weed and Seed Program

INTRODUCTION

Juvenile and adult criminal offending concerns nearly every American, if not every citizen of the world. As juvenile crime can lead to adult offending and years, if not decades, of incarceration, delinquency prevention measures have long been an ongoing concern for child-saver movements and criminal justice systems. As Saminsky notes:

> *Every single person living in the United States today is affected by juvenile crime. It affects parents, neighbors, teachers, and families. It affects the victims of crime, the perpetrators, and the bystanders. While delinquency rates have been decreasing, rates are still too high. There have been numerous programs that have attempted to lower this rate. Some are greatly successful, while many others have minimal or no impact.* (Saminsky 2010, p. 1)

It is not all bad news when it comes to attempting to prevent juvenile delinquency, however. A number of well-meaning and committed individuals and agencies work tirelessly to find solutions. Some are paid to do so; others are volunteers who donate their time and expertise to promote juvenile well-being and thwart delinquency.

A number of noteworthy collaborations have taken place between local law enforcement agencies and community stakeholders. However, some communities steer clear of promising programs because their complexity requires extensive staff training or because they lack sufficient local support and administrative staff (Greenwood, 2013). It is a daunting task to get any new delinquency prevention program off the ground. It is always easier to use existing resources in a community, whether they are able to effect change or not.

The earliest formal delinquency prevention research in the United States came during the later years of the Great Depression and before American involvement in World War II. Conducted in 1939, the Cambridge-Somerville [Massachusetts] Youth Study (CSYS) is "recognized as the first delinquency prevention experiment" (Welsh et al., 2019, p. 441) and is the first controlled, longitudinal study in criminology (Welsh et al., 2019; Weisburd and Petrosino, 2004). The program involved identifying boys from disadvantaged families attending public school and labeled "difficult" or "pre-delinquent" (Welsh et al., 2019). The program consisted of intervention with mentoring, one of the oldest forms of delinquency prevention, aimed at character development through interaction with positive adult role models (Welsh et al., 2019). Not only is the study recognized as the first research design testing a juvenile delinquency prevention program, it provided data for the first evidence-based prevention program as well.

Much of what we saw before the mid- to late 20th century were strategies focused either on tougher laws or juvenile justice system reforms, with the exception of early childhood programs targeting poorer communities, including *Head Start Programs*. In 1961, President John F. Kennedy signed the Juvenile Delinquency and Youth Offenses Control Act, authorizing 10 million dollars annually for three years to develop and fund techniques and training for law enforcement, probation officers, and others who worked with juvenile delinquents (Juvenile Delinquency Act, 1961), mostly assisting at-risk youth indirectly.

The rift between those who wish to enact tougher laws, a deterrence model, and those who want to focus on rehabilitation demonstrates the great divide in the approaches to delinquency prevention, generally split down political party lines in the United States. As an example, in response to perceived increases in juvenile violent crimes in Connecticut in 2021, state Democrats argued that Connecticut ranks among the safest states and advocated workforce development, job training, and housing support to combat delinquency, while Republican leaders in Connecticut proposed these actions (Keating, 2021):

- Around-the-clock GPS (e.g., ankle bracelets) for juveniles arrested on serious charges.
- Hold juveniles longer in detention after arrest.
- Require next-day court appearances.
- Transfer serious juvenile cases to adult court.

Both approaches have been met with mixed results. In some cases tougher laws have not reduced juvenile offending, and some rehabilitation and prevention programs have likewise not affected the statistics. Results are limited, in part because only a small percentage of programs have regular, rigorous reviews of their effectiveness.

The 1974 Juvenile Justice and Delinquency Prevention Act identified four areas of focus for reforming the juvenile justice court system. These reforms are described as the Four Ds (Law Library, American Law and Legal Information, n.d.):

1) **Decriminalization**: Taking status offenses out of delinquency definitions and constraining court authority with these youth.
2) **Diversion:** Move lesser offenders, including status offenders, away from juvenile courts.
3) **Due process:** Provide due process for youth at all processing stages.
4) **Deinstitutionalization:** Remove status offenders and delinquents from institutions and expand community-based institutional alternative programs.

For states to receive federal funding, they were required to achieve and maintain these four foundations of the act, monitored by periodic review (Office of Juvenile Justice and Delinquency Prevention, n.d.a).

It is important when reviewing reports on delinquency prevention to look at them with a healthy dose of skepticism. Anyone who has taken a class in statistics will no doubt have been told that data and statistics can be skewed and interpreted to fulfill the political needs of the researcher or policy maker. Noted archeologist D. Clark Wernecke, writing about research reports, recently warned readers to watch for language such as "proves," "conclusively shows," "does not support," and "refutes the possibility." These are yellow, if not red flags, and good reason to be suspicious of the report's conclusions (Wernecke, 2022). Programs, like hypotheses, are only as good as current data supporting or refuting them and, more importantly, the consensus of researchers validating them.

THREE LEVELS OF CRIME PREVENTION

As in all crime prevention currently, there are three levels to juvenile delinquency prevention: *primary*, *secondary*, and *tertiary prevention*. According to the Texas Juvenile Probation Commission (1993), the functions of the three levels are identified as follows:

- Primary prevention focuses on preventing juveniles from offending in the first place.
- Secondary prevention focuses on intervention early in a juvenile offender's contact with the juvenile justice system.
- Tertiary prevention focuses on the rehabilitation of hardcore, serious juvenile offenders.

Most delinquency prevention programs target one or more risk factors for juvenile offending. This means sometimes customizing the programs to fit perceived risks within an individual or a community. For example, it would hardly make sense to target poverty in a more affluent neighborhood where there is a perceived increase in drug and/or alcohol use by minors.

Other programs are universally used, including mentoring programs and others that try to encourage juveniles to develop friendships with more prosocial peers. According to Small et al. (2005), the most cost-effective prevention programs include preschool education, home visitation, and social and emotional skills training at the elementary-school level. In Chapter 12, we noted that one constraint on prevention programming is funding. Even the most cost-effective programs may be cut if they prove to be ineffectual. And in some cases, programs proven to be effective in reducing delinquency may be terminated for a variety of reasons, including politics.

Some of the programs that we discuss in this chapter are designed to target both adults and juveniles, as in the example of gang suppression. For obvious reasons, we cannot review all juvenile delinquency programs in the United States and their effectiveness in this chapter, as that could be the subject of an entire book by itself, if not multiple volumes. However, this chapter provides a sample of programs at a variety of levels, from the individual to the federal, that have had varying degrees of success.

EXHIBIT 13.1 ‖ Community Stakeholders in Delinquency Prevention

It is important to note that none of the programs introduced here are "one-and-done" solutions. Juvenile delinquency prevention is an ongoing process and may require more than one approach. For example, if a student appears to be on the cusp of becoming a delinquent, or, of greater concern, has already become one, it is not solely the responsibility of the school to address the problem. It will take concerted and coordinated efforts of the school, parental units, and community agencies—the wobbly three-legged stool we referred to earlier in this book—to prevent or quash delinquency in the juvenile. All the possible stakeholders in the student's success can be seen in Exhibit 13.1.

EVIDENCE-BASED PROGRAMS

Some programs we present here are evidence-based. If you recall, evidence-based programs undergo rigorous study, often by academic researchers, to determine whether they accomplish what they set out to do. Other, if not most, programs are not evidence-based. There is also confusion over whether an agency targeting youth delinquency, including gang involvement, is implementing an evidence-based program or practice. "Programs" imply that they might possibly be short-lived, and are often dependent on grant funding that can be unpredictable, whereas practices can be based in agency and professional best practices policies that have more permanence. Practices and policies can inherently have built-in flexibility as compared to programs (Elliott et al., 2020). However, Elliott et al. (2020, p. 1305) caution, "currently no juvenile justice policies are evidence-based."

As Bishop (2012) noted, the 1980s saw a rise in juvenile crime and the erroneous conclusion drawn was that juvenile "superpredators" were responsible. (See also Dilulio, 1995.) As a result, a number of untried and ill-conceived programs sprouted up, along with more punitive measures passed by legislators (Bishop, 2012). It is important to note that evidence-based programs also come under criticism for being so "structured, preplanned, inflexible, and hard to individualize that they will be unable to match the potency and effectiveness of real-world clinical care by providers who are not constrained by protocols listed in manuals" (Weisz et al., 2006, p. 684).

Increasingly, policy makers and practitioners are coming to realize that even if a program for delinquency reduction sounds promising, they can't know it will work without running a more conservative, cost-effective *pilot program* to collect data on its effectiveness. It makes little financial sense, to some, to invest a considerable amount of time and money into an unproven program. In fact, many grant opportunities now require some evidence that a program will work before funding is awarded. One additional advantage of running a pilot program, beyond saving money, is that it helps identify and correct flaws before launching the full, wide-scale program.

Advocates of evidence-based programs argue that all programs, whether publicly or privately organized, funded, and managed, should proceed only after enough data are available that indicate they are worth the money and effort to implement. All programs, whether they already do so or not, should undergo regular review, preferably by outside evaluators, including researchers at policy institutions or universities. It is also critical to conduct internal and external financial audits to make sure that financial records are not only in order but that resources are going where they were intended to go.

HOME-BASED, PARENTAL UNIT STRATEGIES

At the most basic level, one of the best places to help combat juvenile delinquency is in the home, no matter how the family unit is structured. The best preventions of juvenile delinquency are early detection of the potential to offend and early intervention. *Early developmental prevention* approaches involve preventing the development of criminal potential in individuals, including targeting risk factors beginning in early childhood, and encouraging a protective, nurturing environment (e.g., family stability, school preparedness, etc.) (Walsh and Farrington, 2009).

There are a variety of ways to build positive individual characteristics in juveniles that can be nurtured to prevent delinquency (and, specifically, gang recruitment), beginning in the home. Some of these include building positive social skills and developing empathy, resilience, and self-control in the individual child (Lenzi et al., 2019). In the home, it is possible to do so from an early age, even before children enter preschool or kindergarten. However, this requires parental units who are aware, intuitively or by self-education or formal training, that these are some of the most important characteristics to nurture to prevent delinquency. Parental units should also maintain nonabusive, consistent discipline of their children, which often requires parent education courses.

Parent Education

We first learn how interpersonal relationships work from our families. Parental units can either contribute to the probability of delinquency and other negative behaviors in their children or effectively prevent them (Office of Juvenile Justice and Delinquency Prevention, 2010; Simons et al., 1998; Patterson et al., 1992). While for some good parenting comes naturally, either by instinct or by having had positive role models in their own childhoods, others may struggle in understanding the skills needed to be an effective caregiver. Better caregiving practices can be learned through parenting classes. One of the most important benefits of parent education is that it can help prevent child maltreatment.

We learn how to parent initially, and often primarily, from our own parental units. This is perhaps never so evident as in intergenerational philosophies of childrearing practices—and unfortunately, in some cases, intergenerational physical and/or emotional abuses. In juvenile offending, we often see a pattern of poor parenting habits, including poor supervision, abuse, and/or neglect, that gets transferred from one generation to the next. The most obvious form of parent education to stop this is directed at breaking patterns of intergenerational abuse.

There are a number of types of parent training. This reflects the diversity of communities, plus states' adopting programs on the basis of funding, politics, and local needs. Parent education can take place in a number of locations and is delivered by a variety of instructors. These can include teachers employed through social work agencies, religious organizations, and schools. Parent education can be court-ordered when a juvenile has been adjudicated or otherwise brought before the juvenile court. In some cases, the parent training takes place before a child's birth. In others, the training begins soon after birth, and yet others only begin when a problem has come to the attention of authorities, when children are older or during adolescence. Most commonly, parent education serves as an intervention measure. Like any other type of training, it might require a number of sessions or classes over time to address new, emerging problems or to reinforce previously learned parenting skills.

The National Academies of Sciences, Engineering, and Medicine (NASEM) identify the following effective types of parent training (Child Welfare Information Gateway, 2019):

- Focus on encouragement of positive behaviors, based on social learning theory.
- Teach parental units how to improve behavior in children with skills-based interventions (e.g., teaching home safety) and holistic family approaches, with attention given to parenting the at-risk child, but also other children in the household.
- Use training and consultation programs to teach parental units how to identify and understand their children's emotions and needs.

One concern is that fathers tend to be neglected in parenting classes, particularly in the prenatal stages. It is often assumed (falsely in many cases) that females are children's only caregivers. Lee et al. (2018) argued that the best evidence-based practices for prenatal parent education include training focused on how to encourage fathers to engage more with their children, co-parenting practices, the father's mental health, and ways fathers can be supportive of their partners, whether they are married, separated from, or cohabitating with the mother or guardian of their children.

The good news is that fathers have increasingly become more involved in their children's lives over the course of the last few decades (Bianchi et al., 2007). Much of this has had to do with an increase in women's participation in the labor force. More recently, Weissbourd et al. (2020) observed in their research that the COVID-19 pandemic protocols forcing people to stay home strengthened father-child

Father and daughter shopping. *Source:* Pexels, retrieved from https://www.pexels.com/.

relationships, with fathers reporting that they now feel much closer to their children and have discovered new shared interests and activities. This is presumably due to a number of factors. There were layoffs early in the pandemic, and many of those who did keep their jobs were ordered to work from home remotely; some have yet to return to an office outside the home. Children were likewise required to stay home during a large part of the pandemic, taking school instruction online.

It is too early to tell if this increase in both father-child and mother-child interactions will in turn contribute to a downturn in reported juvenile delinquency in the coming years. However, we understand from the Weissbourd et al. (2020) study that fathers reported the following positive outcomes from pandemic measures:

- Fathers felt closer to all family members because they had more opportunities to communicate and interact on a deeper level.
- Families spent more time discussing social and family issues deeply.
- Divorced fathers spent more time with their children during the pandemic.
- Children had opportunities to do or learn some things that they would not ordinarily have had the chance to do if they were in school.

Even though the pandemic did not bring about new parent education programs per se to prevent delinquency, and face-to-face classes had to be suspended, some of the documented positive changes in families as a result of stay-at-home orders, including those with divorced parental units, may in the long run contribute to positive outcomes.

PUBLIC HEALTH APPROACHES

Targeting juvenile delinquency by focusing on public health concerns, including the astronomical medical costs associated with violence, requires a two-pronged approach. In 2014, 501,581 youth and young adults, ages 10 to 24, were treated in emergency rooms for injuries caused in physical altercations (National Mentoring Partnership, 2021). The Centers for Disease Control and Prevention's 2019 Youth Risk Behavior Survey (National Mentoring Partnership, 2021) provided these findings supporting a public-health approach:

- Eight percent of high schoolers (grades 9 to 12) report being in a physical fight one or more times within a year.
- More than 7% report being either threatened or injured by a weapon on school property.
- Homicide is the third leading cause of death in minors and young adults ages 10 to 24 in the United States.
- Homicide is the leading cause of death for African American youth ages 10 to 24.

Like at other agencies and institutions that target delinquency prevention, public health personnel have to walk the fine line between advocacy and politics. As in the example of gun violence, public health advocates have to frame any discussion centered on gun violence, whether to policy makers or to the media, as being a public health issue, outside of political Second Amendment controversies surrounding the problem (Abdalla et al., 2021). Some argue that physicians have a moral obligation to actively engage in discussions of gun violence prevention, but a contradiction lies in part of the ethics and moral code of medicine, where the rights and preferences of patients have to be respected (Baghel and Singer, 2021).

Mental Health Approaches

It is common for mental health issues in children to go undiagnosed, or in some cases ignored, until a problem arises. Some of the behaviors associated with mental illness can be passed off as being part of a normal developmental stage of childhood, as in the examples of defiance in toddlers ("terrible twos") or in adolescence. For some time, the connection between mental health and delinquency went largely ignored and has only recently been a focus in juvenile law (Office of Juvenile Justice and Delinquency Prevention, 2017; Goldstein et al., 2005). And it is only more recently that we have achieved a better understanding of the relationship between substance abuse in children and adolescents and criminal offending.

When mental health issues come to the attention of juvenile courts, treatment may be one alternative to detention. One form of treatment for children who have to be removed from the home is Multidimensional Treatment Foster Care (MTFC). MTFC serves as an alternative to group homes, residential homes, or hospitalization for adolescents suffering from severe chronic emotional and behavioral disorders (Underwood and Washington, 2016). In studies of both boys and girls, MTFC treatment has been shown to significantly reduce delinquency, criminal referral rates, criminal activities, and time spent in detention (National Institute of Justice, 2011).

Beyond specific programs like MTFC treatment, the Office of Juvenile Justice and Delinquency Prevention (2017) recommends the following two steps to identify the mental health needs of juveniles in the juvenile justice system:

- **Screening** juveniles who have contact with the juvenile justice system who might require immediate care for a mental health crisis and identifying those having a higher likelihood of needing special attention. Two commonly used instruments are the Massachusetts Youth Screening Instrument and the Diagnostic Interview Schedule for Children. Also suggested is the Suicide Ideation Questionnaire, to determine if a juvenile in a facility should be monitored for suicide attempts.
- **Assessment** to gather more comprehensive and individualized profiles of juveniles. Mental health assessments should be conducted by mental health

professionals with specialized training in juvenile delinquency. Assessment instruments suggested include the Achenbach System of Empirically Based Assessment, which includes surveys and reports completed by the juveniles themselves, parental units, and/or teachers. (See also Vincent, 2012; Achenbach and Rescoria, 2001; Reynolds, 1988.) The sooner mental health needs are identified and addressed, the better and faster preventative measures can be put in place to avoid offending or recidivism in juveniles who have already been in either foster care or the juvenile justice system.

LAW ENFORCEMENT STRATEGIES

As noted elsewhere throughout this book, juvenile delinquency prevention necessitates a partnership between law enforcement and the communities they serve. Short (1990) described the ideal role of law enforcement as upholding the law within the confines of the values and norms of a community, but law enforcement personnel are also bound by their own experiences and views of human nature, so different police officers and departments may hold differing beliefs on the legal and social means by which to control the behavior of children.

Including law enforcement in any community efforts to prevent delinquency helps them to better understand the extent of the problem and to find more innovative ways to combat juvenile crime than merely incarcerating juvenile offenders ad nauseam. The following programs and strategies are a handful of local efforts that, with state and federal assistance, work to prevent juvenile delinquency by incorporating law enforcement participation.

Comprehensive Gang Model (Spergel Model of Gang Intervention and Suppression)

One of the key strategies for police in juvenile delinquency prevention is to target gangs and their criminal activities. Supported by the Office of Juvenile Justice and Delinquency Prevention (OJJDP), the *Comprehensive Gang Model*, similar to neighborhood initiatives, coordinates the efforts of criminal justice agencies, schools, social services, private agencies, and others in communities that serve the juvenile population (National Gang Center, 2017). The model requires the commitment of local, state, and federal law enforcement agencies to doing the following (Office of Juvenile Justice and Delinquency Prevention, 2017b, p. 2):

- A personal commitment by the law enforcement agency head to serve on a Steering Committee that drives the process.
- Potentially serving as the project's lead agency (providing fiscal management and administrative support).

- Providing data and analysis to support the initial local assessment and ongoing evaluation [evidence-based].
- Establishment of a multiagency gang task force.
- Committing personnel to participate in a multidisciplinary Intervention Team.
- Conducting prevention and education programs.
- Supporting community mobilization activities.

Community agencies may be operating in their own world, with little comprehension of other gang suppression efforts elsewhere in the community. There could be duplication of services, including competition for the same grants, and by not communicating with one another, gaps in prevention strategies may be missed. The Comprehensive Gang Model also requires that a research partner, usually a local university, be part of the team. After over 20 years of implementing the model, some reduction in more serious gang-related juvenile crimes has been recorded (Office of Juvenile Justice and Delinquency Prevention, 2017b).

"Weed and Seed" Program

The *Weed and Seed Program* (or Operation Weed and Seed) is, as the name implies, an effort by law enforcement and communities to weed out crime, specifically gang-related violence and drug-related offenses, while at the same time planting the seeds locally to encourage self-efficacy in cities' crime-ridden neighborhoods. The "seeding" component also is intended to bring in more social services as well, to combat risks leading to criminal activity (U.S. States Attorney's Office, 2018).

As these things go, the program was fairly successful, but it was later passed over or discontinued in favor of other programs. Solina (2021) describes the examples of Chinatown and Kalihi-Palama neighborhoods in Honolulu on the island of Oahu, Hawaii, where the Weed and Seed Program has been inactive for twenty years after it "fizzled out." Solina (2021) reports that once the program was dropped in these neighborhoods, crime returned, necessitating the program's recent revival in Honolulu.

One danger of a weed and seed program is the risk that crime will be squeezed out, only to move to other neighborhoods or cities (the *toothpaste effect*). For example, as police in Chicago pushed gangs out of the inner city, they simply moved to the western suburbs (Main, 2012). Crime did not really go away, it just relocated.

SCHOOL PROGRAMS TO PREVENT JUVENILE DELINQUENCY

Many of us have fond memories of participating in extracurricular activities when we were in elementary and high school. Extracurricular activities are not only fun for the most part, but they help promote teamwork and build friendships among people with the same interests. Extracurricular activities also help students when applying for college, both by supplementing their academic records and by offering scholarship opportunities. Prosocial friends made by participating in extracurricular activities provide a substantial protective factor in preventing drug use or other forms of delinquency (Walters, 2020).

Extracurricular activities that take place after school ends also help address the problem of children left alone in the afternoon, particularly those with two working parents or guardians. As most juvenile arrests occur between the afternoon hours of two and six (Gottfredson et al., 2004), after-school programs are one means to keep children safe and out of mischief.

Historically, schools have organized a number of after-school athletic and cultural activities (e.g., music, drama) for juveniles. Some are also part of the regular school curriculum. Some of these classes and programs have been discontinued in schools across America. For example, Pergola (2014) reported that music education and programs were cut from school budgets[1] and targeted for defunding for economic reasons, and that these types of programs are more likely to be discontinued in poorer communities.

For families trying to meet the costs of participation for their children, Dow (2021) makes the following suggestions for reducing the cost of extracurricular activities:

- Look for government or nonprofit programs. Note that these often have waiting lists.
- For community programs, ask if there are need-based discounts or discounted rates for returning participants or if more than one child in a family is signed up.
- To reduce other costs of extracurricular activities, carpool with other parental units, and buy secondhand equipment and attire.
- Create your own extracurriculars at home for your children, for example, by using free online music or cooking lessons or free library resources. The drawback to this is that it often requires supervision by an adult or older sibling.
- Learn to say no to your children's requests to enroll in yet another extracurricular activity; for older children, ask them to contribute to the extracurricular costs with babysitting or other part-time work.

Outside of school, until the past decade, community after-school programs received much public support to compensate for the diminishing number of job opportunities for teenagers, largely driven by the changing workforce; in economic recessions or crises, adults take jobs that teenagers have historically filled. It is interesting to note that the Gottfredson et al. (2004) study of Maryland students during the 1999–2000 school year found that after-school programs effectively reduce delinquency in older juveniles, but not in elementary school students.

[1] School budgets rely heavily on county and local real estate taxes for funding. During recessions, home prices and values typically drop, meaning real estate tax revenues do as well.

Whether we examine statistics in the United States or in other parts of the world, crime is often associated with lower levels of education. Minors who do not complete their high-school educations are at greater risk of offending, if the number of adult prisoners without a diploma or GED equivalent is any indication. According to Hobson (2021), with two-thirds of all jobs today requiring *more* than a high school education, the 37% of state prisoners without a diploma and the 86% of individuals in federal and state prisons without any education beyond high school are at a distinct disadvantage. A key crime preventing measure is thus to aggressively pursue programs, including extracurriculars, that keep juveniles in school.

COMMUNITY-BASED POLICIES AND PROGRAMS

There is much to be said about the advantages of running prevention and intervention programs at the community level. First, volunteers generally come from the local community and are stakeholders in the successful outcome of any program. Second, there is more opportunity to find donors of space, materials, and other resources within the immediate or surrounding community. For example, Tia Martinez came up with a community-based solution to food insecurity in her Staten Island, New York, neighborhood by organizing a team of young people to distribute food to hundreds of families twice a week, with resources coming from local restaurants (Morales, 2022). As Bettencourt (2022) notes, *grassroots organizations*, like the one Martinez organized, can be just as important as cash donations by working bottom-up and utilizing local volunteers to facilitate local change.

Voluntary Sector

For all the pessimism voiced in Chapter 12 about relying on volunteers,[2] studies indicate that *voluntary organizations* have success in reducing crime in neighborhoods, including juvenile delinquency. Examples of these include Red Cross, YMCA, YWCA,[3] Boys and Girls Clubs, and other nonprofit organizations. Key to their success is bringing in donation income and volunteer support (Wo, 2019). Wo proposes three theories as to why volunteer organizations can influence neighborhood crime rates over time:

[2] If you or someone you know would like to volunteer in a juvenile delinquency prevention program, see VolunteerMatch (https://www.volunteermatch.org/) to find opportunities in your community.

[3] YMCA stands for the Young Men's Christian Association; YWCA stands for the Young Women's Christian Association.

- Voluntary organizations that generate more income (e.g., fees, donations) have more success in communities with several voluntary organizations that do not bring in as much revenue, even collectively.
- The presence of voluntary organizations with more income inhibits most crime types.
- Need-based social services provide opportunities for social interaction between neighbors, contributing to more social ties, mutual trust, and cohesion–all protective factors against crime, including juvenile delinquency.
- Location is key. Voluntary organizations only provide crime-control benefits within a 0.5-mile radius surrounding the targeted neighborhoods.

Work-Based Strategies

As we noted in the last chapter, one challenge in juvenile delinquency prevention is addressing the problem of social service worker and volunteer burnout. One strategy to avoid this is for workplaces to build foundations for worker and volunteer resilience in the face of what seems like an endless uphill battle dealing with delinquent youth and their families.

Local businesses can also provide much-needed support by encouraging their employees to volunteer in the community. In some cases, they can be paid for their volunteer services, if the work is company-sponsored and conducted during company or agency time. For example, a number of individuals who participate in the Holyoke Safe Neighborhood Initiative (HSNI) in Massachusetts (described in the following section) are employed by social service agencies in the community and are paid to attend HSNI meetings or activities.

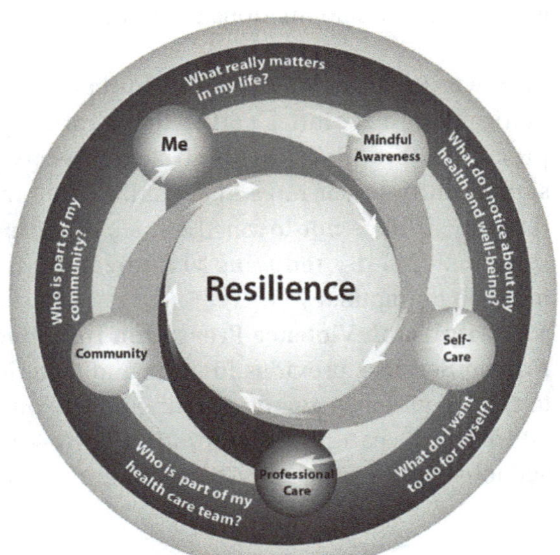

EXHIBIT 13.2 ‖ Circle of Resilience

Neighborhood Initiatives

Neighborhood initiatives often focus on beautification and safety. They are a two-prong approach, as communities with more greenspace and places for neighbors to comfortably gather tend to at least be perceived as safer. Taking the safe neighborhood initiatives in New York City as one example, the focus there is on positively transforming public spaces, in particular, public housing, working toward racial equality, providing access to resources, and encouraging community members' participation (Center for Court Innovation, n.d.).

Taking Wo's findings (2019), noted in the previous section, as an example, the focal block or neighborhood initially targeted for the Holyoke Neighborhood Initiative in Western Massachusetts, centered on Morgan Elementary School, is located in a low-income South Holyoke neighborhood. Many of the children attending Morgan Elementary School live in public housing. However, historically, few permanent voluntary resource offices are located in or around the Morgan Elementary School. The successful work done in South Holyoke led to expansion of the initiative to include the entire city of Holyoke.

Minority Community Programs

Even though juvenile delinquency overall has dropped, communities of color still experience higher rates of youth contact with law enforcement, and even though numbers are improving, Black, Native American, and ethnic minority youth continue to be sentenced at higher rates than white juveniles (Office of Juvenile Justice and Delinquency Prevention, 2022b). Here is a sampling of recent programs that have been initiated to address the challenges in the prevention of juvenile delinquency in specific populations of minority youth:

- **IMpower Program for American Indian Girls:**[4] This program on sexual assault victimization includes self-defense training. Current data indicate that the program is promising, with girls who received the intervention experiencing significantly lower rates of sexual assault and sexual harassment, but unfortunately, it does not lower the rates of dating violence (National Institute of Justice, 2021). By reducing victimization, the program also hopes to reduce juvenile delinquency.
- **Minority Youth Violence Prevention Initiative:** The Department of Health and Human Services provides funding and technical assistance to projects working to reduce violence among at-risk minority male juveniles and young men (ages 10 to 18). It features collaboration between law enforcement, public health agencies, and community-based mentors, as well as improving coordination

[4] This is the actual program name, even though the term "Indian" to refer to indigenous people is considered by many, including Native Americans, to be offensive.

between state and local agencies using evidence-based strategies (Henry and Watkins, 2020; Office of Minority Health, U.S. Department of Health and Human Services, 2014).

- **Opioid Affected Youth Initiative:** A program funded by Offices of Juvenile Justice and Delinquency Prevention in a number of communities, including tribal jurisdictions, to identify, respond to, and support children, youth, and families affected by the opioid epidemic. It includes coordinated efforts between law enforcement, juvenile courts, emergency responders, and medical and mental health services (Opioid Affected Youth Initiative, n.d.).

Some targeted programs for minorities focus on providing psychotherapy, including for depression and delinquent behavior. More recent studies indicate that the most efficient and successful forms of targeted therapies for minority youth and their families draw on cognitive behavior therapy, family therapy, or a combination of both (Pina et al., 2019).

Communities are not alone in creating programs to address delinquency among minority youth. For example, in 2014, President Barack Obama launched My Brother's Keeper (MBK) to serve young males of color and prevent delinquency. The initiative specifically targeted key life events that can predict a positive outcome later in life if the right interventions are in place at each of these junctures (Obama White House Archives, 2016a):

1. Entering school ready to learn.
2. Reading at grade level by third grade.
3. Graduating from high school ready for college and career.
4. Completing postsecondary education or training.
5. Successfully entering the workforce.
6. Reducing violence and providing a second chance to justice-involved youth.

In the first two years of the initiative, My Brother's Keeper was able to secure substantial corporate and nonprofit-sector sponsorship. As we emphasized in Chapter 12, funding is key to the success of any program, and corporate sponsorship is an effective way to secure it. By 2016, MBK programs had been started in nearly 250 communities and in all 50 states, receiving more than $600 million from the private sector and philanthropic organizations (Obama White House Archives, 2016b). The initiative also promoted equity for students of color who required special education or disabilities accommodations, as even under the Individuals with Disabilities Education Act,[5] racial and ethnic disparities remained.

After President Obama left office in 2017, the program became part of the Obama Foundation, rebranded as the My Brother's Keeper Alliance (Obama Foundation, n.d.). One small example of the successes of nonprofit alliances is a Detroit

[5] For more information, see Individuals with Disabilities Education Act (IDEA), U.S. Department of Education, at https://sites.ed.gov/idea/.

job fair organized by the My Brother's Keeper Alliance: 300 young men of color left the fair with offers for jobs in a number of industries, including retail, banking, and the energy sector (Chiles, 2017). The program continues to be evidence-based and continues to recognize that delinquency and adult offending is best prevented with "the collective work of community leaders, members, and public and private agencies pursuing the same goals for these young men [which] can lead to sustainable, place-based change" (Obama Foundation, 2022, retrieved from https://www.obama.org/mbka/eighth-anniversary/).

Vocational Education

The goals of the Obama initiative mention college but also, in fourth place, trade school. After a significant push over the past 50 years to encourage all young people to complete a two- or four-year college education, rising costs are convincing many that traditional college education is not the only route to career success. For example, while community and four-year college enrollments are down, Steinberg and Nadorny (2022) report that skilled-trade programs are booming and that since the pandemic began, millions of students in the United States have decided to go directly into the workforce rather than go to college immediately after high school.

As Melanie Anderson, director of government affairs for Opportunity Nation, a nonprofit supporting upward mobility through positive career choices, has stated (Woodruff-Santos, 2015, retrieved from https://opportunitynation.org/latest-news/media-highlights/telling-young-people-need-4-year-degree-disservice/):

> *We think that we've done a disservice by focusing on a four-year degree as the only pathway to success. . . . Young adults can look at two-year community colleges. They can look at trade schools and other options to make sure that they find a career.*

Even in academia, it is increasingly recognized that all juveniles, no matter their ethnic or racial background or socioeconomic status, should be given a number of career options, not only those requiring a college degree. This includes exploring the trades (e.g., carpentry, plumbing, construction, etc.) and offering skills training in high school. As we have seen in Merton's strain theory, blocked opportunities to societal goals–in this case, the unrealistic goal of a college education for everyone–may lead to delinquency or adult offending.

Mentoring Programs

For a number of decades, with the rise in divorce rates, programs similar to the My Brother's Keeper Alliance have offered support to juveniles by filling in gaps in family households, particularly if there is little extended family to do so. Mentor programs provide adolescents or adults who volunteer to serve as positive role models for at-risk juveniles. Some programs are intended to provide a same-sex adult role model, substituting for one missing within the family, as in the most common example of fathers missing after divorce or desertion. Others, like the example in the next paragraph, provide mentors who act as older, wiser siblings.

One of the oldest mentoring programs is Big Brothers Big Sisters of America. The Big Brothers organization started in 1904, when Ernest Coulter, a New York City court clerk, began to see more young males offending and in need of adult guidance (Big Brothers Big Sisters, 2022). At around the same time, Ladies of Charity (eventually becoming Catholic Big Sisters) were mentoring girls coming through the New York Children's Court. The two organizations eventually combined to serve both boys and girls. In 2019, the Office of Juvenile Justice and Delinquency Prevention awarded Big Brothers Big Sisters of America $83 million and 10,141 hours in technical support (Office of Juvenile Justice and Delinquency Prevention, n.d.b).

Mentoring programs are community-based and encourage matching mentors in the community with local at-risk youth. This allows the mentors more opportunity for continuity in their commitment to the youth. Local volunteers also have a more intimate view of the conditions under which the juvenile lives; some may have been raised in the same type of neighborhood. Mentors with the attitude "What can I do to help?" rather than "I've come here to fix things," are more effective, as often juveniles see volunteers and programs come and go, making them suspicious of volunteers' motives and commitment.

A well-established, large organization that takes in considerable charitable donations, both from individuals and corporations, Big Brothers Big Sisters of America, like most large charities, is required to document its efforts. The 2013 Big Brothers Big Sisters Youth Outcome Survey reported a number of positive changes within participants over the course of a year in their one-on-one mentoring program for middle-school juveniles, including improvements in self-esteem, academic performance, and attitudes towards risky behavior (Big Brothers Big Sisters, 2013).

Mentoring programs grounded in evidence-based approaches, like Big Brothers Big Sisters of America, have demonstrated the following positive outcomes (National Mentoring Partnership, 2019):

- Mentoring continues to be a staple in juvenile justice and violence prevention efforts.
- Mentoring has the potential to offer comprehensive support to juveniles at risk of committing violence, addressing many risk factors at once.
- Mentoring can be integrated with other programs for delinquency prevention.
- Mentoring can reduce aggressive behavior and other indicators of the potential for violence in juveniles.

Sports Programs

A number of youth sports groups are separate from those offered as school-based extracurricular activities. Often available to all juveniles, not just those at risk, sports-based interventions can be found worldwide, funded by governments and local municipalities (Spruit et al., 2018). Participating in sports teaches discipline, teamwork, anger management skills, and physical fitness habits that can last a lifetime, to name a few of the benefits of participation. Sports-based interventions for juvenile delinquents and delinquency prevention originates in social bonding theory, where the assumption is that youth who become friends with team members, and are exposed to positive mentoring by coaches, will be less tempted to commit crimes (Spruit et al., 2018; Hirschi, 1969). The Spruit et al. (2018) study of at-risk youth participating in sports-based interventions found that negative behaviors were reduced and a number of positive attitudes increased over time.

One drawback of a sports-based intervention program is that they often are not inclusive and do not always accommodate children with special needs. A few organizations do provide programs for special needs children of varying physical and cognitive abilities, most notably Special Olympics and Paralympics (Mauro, 2022). Although these are not specifically designed to target at-risk youth or to intervene with children already termed delinquent, they can provide the same benefits as other sports-based programs that do target at-risk youth.

Faith-Based Programs

Faith-based programs are developed by churches, mosques, synagogues, and other religious entities. These were the source of many child-saver organizations in the late 19th century. Religion is perhaps the oldest form of social control. In fact, according to sociologists, social control is one of the main purposes and functions of religious instruction.

A number of studies have found religious teachings and the fear of God to have a positive effect in reducing juveniles' delinquent behavior (Panezai et al., 2019; Malik and Shirazi, 2010). The fear of displeasing a superior being and the consequences for doing so is an age-old means of keeping social order, and juveniles introduced to religious programming may also be concerned about their own spiritual fates. Faith-based programs, if under the umbrella of federal or state governments, however, may be criticized as violating the constitutional doctrine of separation of church (religion) and state.

Though around for centuries, faith-based solutions to crime and other social problems in the late 20th century brought about renewed interest in turning to religious groups for support in fighting juvenile delinquency. This was encouraged by then-President George W. Bush, allegedly as a cost-saving measure for the federal government. Bush created the White House Office of Faith-Based and Community Initiatives in 1999 to provide support to efforts by local religious organizations to combat poverty (White House Archives, n.d.). Ironically, and controversially at the time, the Bush initiative required the diversion of 8 billion dollars in federal funding and became one of the defining features of the Bush administration (Steinfels, 2009), with opponents arguing that it violated the separation of church and state outlined in the First Amendment of the U.S. Constitution. As previously noted, politics can play a substantial role in creating, or in some cases, destroying efforts to fight juvenile delinquency.

After it fell out of favor for a period of time, President Joseph Biden signed an executive order to reinstate the White House Office of Faith-Based and Community Initiatives in 2021. President Biden recognized that faith-based community programs were needed in light of the global pandemic and an unpredictable economy that caused many to lose their jobs (White House Briefing Room, 2021). As we have seen, such economic factors can contribute to delinquency. Hockensmith (2003) contends that some of the advantages of faith-based programs for juveniles are that they are generally conducted in small groups, and that the volunteer staff are highly motivated to help.

Urban Renewal Programs

Programs that tackle the esthetics of rundown neighborhoods directly and indirectly show promise in reducing juvenile crime. Urban renewal or *revitalization*, loosely based in broken windows theory,[6] seeks to improve housing and eliminate dilapidation in neighborhoods. These efforts are found to reduce vandalism, a common crime committed by juveniles.

Beginning in the 1950s with expanding highway systems, the more affluent, including the middle class, began to migrate to newly emerging, post-WWII suburbs, eventually leading to suburban sprawl. Suburbs offered new schools, green spaces, and more elbow room to young families in the form of single-family dwellings. Families were not the only ones migrating to the suburbs. Businesses moved as well to serve the growing suburban population, creating more job opportunities in suburbs but reducing those in cities, particularly in manufacturing. Central cities went into decline, with the disadvantaged, primarily the poor and less educated, left behind, resulting in less taxable income, reduced retail buying power, and plummeting property values. Large cities like Chicago and New York were financially devastated (Freeman and Braconi, 2004; Meiszkowski and Mills, 1993). As a result, inner cities began to decay. Both cities and businesses abandoned projects ("disinvested") in poorer neighborhoods, resulting in little new development or maintenance of existing buildings (National Low-Income Housing Coalition, 2019).

A study conducted by Wo (2016) found that in the nine cities examined, it wasn't the civic or social organizations that were working to reduce crime; it was the so-called third places—coffee shops, cafés, and similar sites—that brought neighbors together to create change. Not only were neighbors out and more visible at these sites, which helps to reduce crime, but by networking they began to watch out for one another and for each other's property. The presence of these sites indicated

[6] In broken windows theory, buildings and cars that appear to be neglected or abandoned invite vandalism. As noted elsewhere in the book, however, the theory has been dismissed by critics as being too simplistic.

that business owners were not afraid to set up shop, diminishing the fear of being victimized or vandalized, which is common in poor, neglected neighborhoods.

The downside with urban renewal programs is *gentrification*. Revitalization and gentrification differ substantially. Whereas neighborhood revitalization fights social injustice, inequality, and racism, gentrification displaces communities of color (Stevens, 2021; National Low-Income Housing Coalition, 2019). It can also mean replacing industrial and warehouse spaces, and subsequently jobs, with additional housing, restaurants, and upscale stores. This has occurred in a number of city neighborhoods over the past 50 years, including Harlem in New York City, some north Philadelphia neighborhoods, and areas of Boston, Massachusetts.

A byproduct of gentrification, often intended by real estate developers and investors, is a sharp rise in real estate prices, including rent. Poor communities of color are priced out of the market and unable to continue to live in their old neighborhoods. Anti-gentrification activists contend that, unlike revitalization to improve the lives of low income, minority communities, gentrification is solely profit-driven (National Low Income Housing Coalition, 2019).

As we have seen since the most recent real estate bubble began, even rental property in major cities, where often many of the best job opportunities are, have become out of reach for most, except for the very affluent. As an example, the average rent for a one-bedroom apartment in New York City in 2022 was approximately $3,260 per month in 2022 (Esajian, 2022). We should acknowledge, though, that since the COVID-19 pandemic, a number of jobs have shifted to remote work, with many remaining online after the worst of the health crisis passed. This means that workers no longer are required to live close to where they work and can move to more affordable communities, if they can continue to work remotely.

In many ways, the mass exodus to the suburbs that began in the post-WWII decades has reversed itself, with younger people, many employed in the

Moreno Valley, California, 2021.

well-paying tech industry, wanting to live in cities that offer more nightlife and culture. Again, the problem then becomes one where lower- and even most middle-class families are unable to afford living in cities, where the job opportunities are. Forced to move to the suburbs themselves, they either face long commutes to work or must accept lower-paying jobs locally (Freeman and Braconi, 2004).

Adult and juvenile crime can be exported from the cities into the suburbs, as in the example of Moreno Valley, California. Beginning in the 1980s, Moreno Valley was becoming a promising community of affordable new homes in neatly laid out subdivisions. Within a decade, however, it was plagued with gang activity, much of it transplanted primarily from Los Angeles and the neighboring city of Riverside. Families dreaming of home ownership, some for the first time, often came from poorer communities to realize this dream. Unfortunately, in some cases, their children were already gang-affiliated. By 2010, the city had received a $500,000 federal grant to help "prevent and combat juvenile delinquency, substance abuse, and violence in relation to gang-activity in areas near Rancho Verde High School" (Bureau of Justice Assistance, 2010, retrieved from https://bja.ojp.gov/funding/awards/2010-dd-bx-0445), including increasing law enforcement presence, as response times of police around the school were inadequate.

Programs for Out-of-Home Children

Juveniles who have been removed from their homes and placed in foster care because of mistreatment or neglect by their parental units, as we have noted earlier in this book, are at greater risk for delinquency. However, results of programs addressing the prevention needs of foster children have been mixed.

For example, the Fostering Healthy Futures (FHF) program in Denver, Colorado, had a modest impact over time on children in a longitudinal experimental study of the program's effectiveness. Long-term benefits were not actualized until the participants were teenagers (Taussig et al., 2021). The FHF provides two programs, one for preteens and the other for teens, and requires participation for nine months in weekly skills groups with a cognitive-behavioral curriculum, plus one-on-one, community-based mentoring (Taussig et al., 2021; Fostering Healthy Futures, Denver, n.d.). The cognitive behavioral curriculum consists of "units addressing emotion recognition, perspective talking, problem solving, anger management, cultural identity, change and loss, healthy relationships, peer pressure, abuse prevention, and future orientation" (Taussig et al., 2021, p. 1122). This limited approach raises questions about how much intervention is needed to help foster children who have already been abused, displaced, and abandoned, even in some cases, seen as presumably beyond repair.

Juvenile Rehabilitation Programs

As we have noted elsewhere, approaches to juvenile justice are more likely to take the form of rehabilitation after juveniles have encountered the system, in contrast to the seeming throw-away model of some adult sentencing, referred to as the *waste management model* of corrections (Hansen, 2023). Instead, in most instances and with the exception of juvenile cases that get referred to adult courts, the goal of juvenile corrections is to correct the behavior or conditions that contributed to the delinquency in the first place. As we noted, "child saver" strategies have been around since the end of 19th century and were partially the basis for the push to institute a separate juvenile justice system (Moon et al., 2000). Like rehabilitation programs in adult corrections, the hope is to reduce recidivism rates.

A juvenile rehabilitation program in Washington state has taken a new prevention approach. Beginning in 2019, juvenile rehabilitation has targeted the highest-risk juveniles adjudicated in the state's juvenile court or convicted in adult court (Fox and Veele, 2020). The integrated program takes a holistic approach that includes addressing family issues that may have landed the juvenile or young adult in the criminal justice system in the first place. According to a legislative report published by the Washington State Department of Children, Youth and Families (Fox and Veele, 2020), the program is intended to accomplish the following goals:

- Utilize evidence-based strategies.
- Motivate and encourage the engagement of the delinquent and the family.
- Establish common language and vocabulary[7] throughout all phases of juvenile justice contact.
- Include a uniform and consistent set of cognitive-behavioral skills.
- Maintain positive changes over time.
- Provide consistent and ongoing clinical treatment to ensure that interventions continue and adhere to the *rehabilitation integrated* treatment plan.

FEDERAL AND STATE PROGRAMS

Most of what we see in programs to prevent juvenile delinquency operates at the local public or private level. However, federal and state governments also provide grant opportunities to cities and local communities. Another role of the federal government and states is to monitor the progress of juvenile delinquency prevention programs, though states are responsible for administrating and managing juvenile justice within their borders (Hanson and Finklea, 2022). Much of what federal government agencies do, including those within the U.S. Department of Justice, is set policy or provide grants or loans for prevention.

Examples of types of funding available include federal grant programs provided to selected applicants to combat tribal youth delinquency, to provide first-time offender interventions, to promote youth gang prevention efforts, or to enhance

[7] One issue found in coordinating agencies and services is that they do not always work with the same vocabulary or definitions. We see this to be true in emergency management as well.

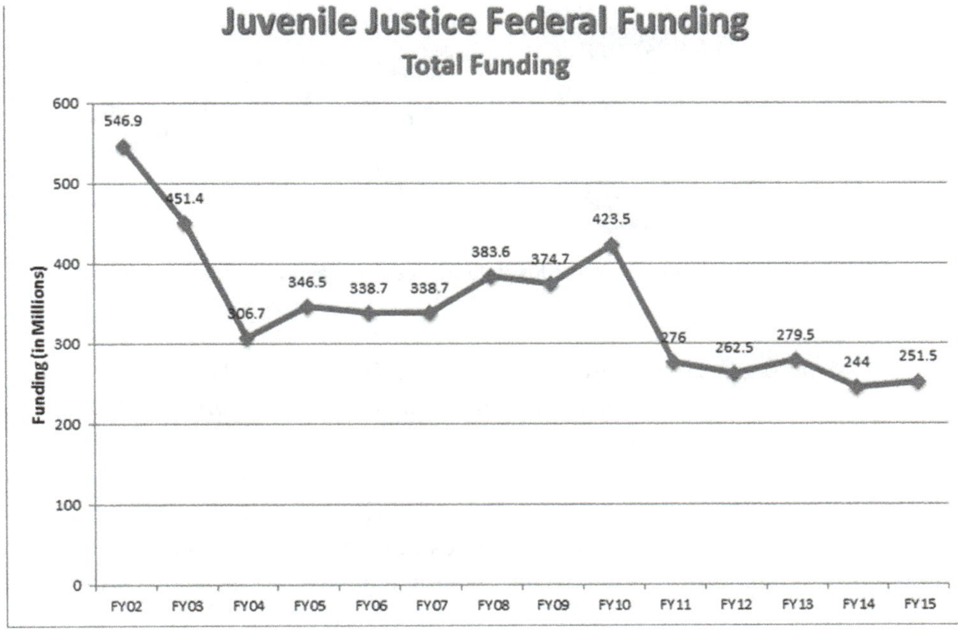

EXHIBIT 13.3 ‖ **Juvenile Justice Federal Funding (in Millions)**

positive offender re-entry (Federal Grants Wire, 2022). Over the past decade, federal funding of juvenile delinquency prevention decreased substantially, but within the past couple of years it has increased modestly, most notably between 2020 and 2022 during the COVID-19 pandemic (Hanson and Finklea, 2022).

Juvenile delinquency programs at the federal and state levels can also be embedded in other programs. For example, in New Mexico, the Children, Youth, and Families Department (CYFD) also includes a department of Juvenile Justice Services (JJS) that supports initiatives, including the following (New Mexico Children, Youth and Families Department, 2022):

- Monitoring and addressing racial and ethnic disparities within the juvenile justice system, assuring equal treatment for all New Mexico juveniles in custody.
- Enhancing/maintaining adequate review of state detention centers to assure they follow both state and federal requirements.

Office of Juvenile Justice and Delinquency Prevention

One of the most positive and forward-thinking advances in the United States in the prevention of juvenile delinquency, whether politically motivated or not, was the creation of the Office of Juvenile Justice and Delinquency Prevention (OJJDP) as part of the Juvenile Justice and Delinquency Prevention Act (1974).[8] The act is

[8] JDDP, Pub. L. No.93-415, 42 U.S.C. §5601 et seq.

United States Office of Juvenile Justice and Delinquency Prevention.

regularly reviewed and updated (most recently in 2018) to respond to the most recent developments in juvenile delinquency (Office of Juvenile Justice and Delinquency Prevention, n.d.a).

As we noted at the beginning of this chapter, the OJJDP, as an arm of the Department of Justice, supports local and state efforts to reduce juvenile crime. A timeline of some of the milestones in the Juvenile Justice and Delinquency Act include the following (Office of Juvenile Justice and Delinquency Prevention, n.d.c) :

- Act is signed into law (1974)
- Increased and expanded *deinstitutionalization of juvenile offenders* (1977)
- Emphasized prevention and treatment (1977)
- Established rules for movement of juveniles between facilities (*jail removal requirements*) (1980)
- Required that the disproportionate number of minority youth be addressed (1988)
- Established new programs to address gender bias (1992)
- Emphasized prevention and treatment, family strengthening, graduated sanctions, and risk-need assessments (1992)
- Created a new section of the OJJDP, authorizing research training, technical assistance, and information sharing (2002)
- Substantially amended the JJDA, adding the Juvenile Justice Reform Act (2018)

The latest milestone, the Juvenile Justice Reform Act, reinforced four protections for juveniles in custody (Annie E. Casey Foundation, 2018):

- Prohibits putting juveniles in custody for age-related status offenses, including truancy, running away, or violating curfew.
- Limits the types of crimes and ages where juveniles are allowed to be incarcerated or detained in adult facilities.
- Keeps juvenile offenders away from incarcerated adults, with few exceptions.
- Requires states to identify and address racial and ethnic disparities in arrests and sentencing in the juvenile justice system.

The Office of Juvenile Justice and Delinquency Prevention at the federal level also makes suggestions for new programs. Based on review of current research into what seem to be the most effective programs for early prevention and intervention, the OJJDP has made the following recommendations (Youth.gov, n.d.):

- Classroom and behavior management programs
- Multi-component classroom-based programs
- Social competence promotion curriculums
- Conflict resolution and violence prevention curriculums
- Bullying prevention programs
- After-school recreation programs
- Mentoring programs
- School organization programs
- Comprehensive community interventions

Most of the suggestions made by OJJDP for successful programs fall within the jurisdiction of schools, which are managed under states' departments of education, as well as by local school districts. Because of standardized testing and the pressures placed on schools that earn sometimes discouraging scores, it is questionable how many OJJDP suggestions will make their way into curricula and programs. This uncertainty is worsened by the online instruction necessitated during the COVID-19 pandemic (DeMatthews, 2021).

Not all government initiatives focus on creating community programs. Federal and state government initiatives have historically spent more time and money on anti-violence prosecution campaigns such as President Bill Clinton's four-pronged approach (Office of Justice Programs, 1998; Clinton White House Archive, 1998):

- The first component was to fight youth and gang violence and proposed tougher anti-gang prosecution initiatives and tougher penalties for violent juvenile crimes, including adult court trials.
- The second component was intended to keep juveniles gun- and drug-free, including by expanding the *Brady Law*.
- The third component required tougher measures targeting juvenile drunk and drug-influenced driving, and included anti-truancy strategies and keeping schools open later and on weekends.
- The fourth component included funding to hire more prosecutors and ATF agents, after-school programs, and youth anti-drug media campaigns, among a number of other funding initiatives.

Grant programs are one of the most important functions of the federal government and the OJJDP. These are sometimes awarded to the wrong person or group or abused by recipients. But every year, the OJJDP grants millions of dollars to groups and communities, many of them managing worthwhile causes and evidence-based programs that are working to reduce juvenile delinquency. In fiscal 2021 alone, the OJJDP awarded nearly $344 million in support to prevention efforts, including $43.1 million to programs helping child abuse victims (Office of Juvenile Justice and Delinquency Prevention, 2022a).

PREVENTION OUTLOOK

It is important to look at the future juvenile delinquency outlook from a variety of viewpoints. There are a number of contributing factors, including the economy. It is critical to continue to look at rates of juvenile offending, not merely the number of offenses. There also has to be some consideration that the United States is not uniform in its types of juvenile offending. Not only are there regional differences, but within states there are distinctly different types of communities. Even more sparsely populated states, like Alaska or Montana, have distinct differences between their rural and urban juvenile populations.

It may be an illusion that the number of juvenile offenses is declining in the United States, or the apparent decline may be due to the steadily decreasing birthrate over the last few decades. Basically, accounting for lag time, 10 to 18 years after a substantial drop in the birthrate, we would expect a drop in juvenile delinquency. But new factors arise, based on new opportunities to offend that emerge with new technology and changes in the economy. Because of the time it takes to fund and implement prevention programs, an unforeseen threat can arise that, as we witnessed during the opioid crisis, affects juveniles and adults alike.

Decisions have been made at the state and federal levels that are expected to have adverse effects on delinquency rates. With the Supreme Court of the United States overturning *Roe v. Wade*[9] in 2022, leaving abortion laws to states to decide, states that ban abortion may very well see a rise in teen pregnancies. This in turn may have the sadly expected result of higher child poverty rates.

Pregnancy does not only affect families financially. Unintended (and intended) pregnancy can create additional financial burden to taxpayers' states, as teen and single mothers, or any family living in poverty for that matter, are more likely to require assistance from welfare programs (National Conference of State Legislatures, 2018). Teen mothers are not the only ones at risk for living in poverty, as indicated in a University of California San Francisco longitudinal study ("The Turnaway Study"), where women were restricted from having an abortion due to gestational age of the fetus; some of these women had not received adequate pre-natal care (Greene Foster, 2021). Child poverty is one of the risk factors for delinquency, along with drug use and poor parenting by adolescent parents (Leve et al., 2013), if past history and research are indicators.

With abortion criminalized in some states, though it is still too early to know exactly how this will be treated in juvenile court, it may also result in additional younger female offending. Optimistically, any resulting rise in teen pregnancies may be met with additional delinquency prevention programs to counteract it, including those introduced by the U.S. Department of Health and Human Services and the U.S. Department of Education.

---

[9] *Roe v. Wade* (410 U.S. 113, 1973) was a Supreme Court decision that protected women's reproductive rights, including choosing whether to terminate a pregnancy.

The good news is that states and local jurisdictions continue to make efforts to reduce juvenile delinquency, as Kazemian (2021, p. 2) notes: "[M]any state and local jurisdictions have developed promising initiatives and interventions that draw on principles of the desistance paradigm." However, as Kazemian also warns, few programs are rigorously evaluated, meaning more efforts are needed to implement evidence-based, rather than untried, programs. This reinforces the need for systematic coordination and partnerships between parental units, agencies, law enforcement, schools, social workers, researchers, and policy makers.

The future of juvenile delinquency prevention will continue to be narrowly focused. The two ongoing places of most concern are the escalation of offending by some juveniles and the duration of their criminal careers, often carried over into adulthood in the case of serious, repeat offenders (Kazemian, 2021). Though it is too early to tell, the push for reform within the entire criminal justice program may very well have an impact on the juvenile justice system in the future if it comes to fruition.

SUMMARY

As we saw from Chapter 12 and discussions of roadblocks to delinquency prevention, if not crime prevention in general, it can be an uphill battle for all stakeholders. Much of what we see in prevention efforts can be held up due to fiscal restraints and the current political climate. Strategies have vacillated between getting tough on juvenile crime and rehabilitation efforts, depending on which way the political winds are blowing at the time and public sentiment. This chapter offers some optimism and hope now and into the future, particularly for those of you who intend to enter the human service sector and work with at-risk youth.

Prevention measures are not new. The child saver movements in the late 19th century ushered in a new era of delinquency prevention and were precursors to today's efforts to prevent delinquency. Delinquency prevention research began in earnest in the 1930s, beginning with the Cambridge-Somerville Youth Study (CSYS) in Massachusetts. Since then there have been numerous efforts to not only gather data about juvenile delinquency, but to implement evidence-based programs for greater success in prevention, though admittedly, those programs are still very much in the minority.

A number of programs show promise, but others have been abandoned, due to lack of funding, political disinterest, or lack of efficacy. Others continue, as described in our "In the Media" section, even though there is no empirical evidence that they work. Some of the more typical programs include parent education, mentoring, a sports-based structure, or the view that delinquency is a public health crisis.

The U.S. federal government established a number of measures beginning in the 1970s to effectively enhance efforts to prevent delinquency. The 1974 Juvenile

Justice and Delinquency Prevention Act identified four areas of focus for reforming the then-juvenile justice court system, or as they are known, the Four Ds: Decriminalization, diversion, due process, and deinstitutionalization. An additional measure was the creation of the Office of Juvenile Justice and Delinquency (OJJDP) in 1993. The OJJDP offers a number of grants in the millions of dollars each year that go to programs and communities that combat juvenile delinquency, including those fighting drugs, gangs, and child abuse, three of the biggest contributors to juvenile delinquency besides poverty.

As we noted at the end of this chapter, we cannot predict with any real accuracy what direction juvenile delinquency rates will take, nor what new programs may be on the horizon. However, we can predict the possibility that new delinquency opportunities will arise, as we saw in earlier discussions of cybercrimes. It will be the continued job and concern of human service agencies, in conjunction with local, state, and federal law enforcement and parental units and schools, to make any and all efforts to help prevent juvenile delinquency. As Saminsky (2010) advises, existing prevention programs are only the beginning—both researchers and practitioners alike must continue to create new programs that will reduce or end emerging and far-reaching problems of juvenile delinquency.

IN THE MEDIA

Debunking Juvenile Awareness Programs

First established in the 1970s, the Scared Straight program and similar shock programs, including boot camps with similar structures, are still alive and well, advertised to communities and parental units alike. After the popularity of the Academy Award–winning documentary, *Scared Straight!* (Golden West Television, 1978) and similar films and television shows, like the A & E series *Beyond Scared Straight* (2011–2015), the program has been widely adopted, despite little proof that it really works (VanLandingham, 2015).

We have purposely left out discussion of programs like Scared Straight in this book. *Juvenile awareness programs* have come under fire, as they have been proven to be not only ineffectual, but harmful. These programs are intended to frighten at-risk children and adolescents into law-abiding behavior, through firsthand exposure to prisons and talking with incarcerated prisoners (Petrosino et al., 2013).

Though juvenile awareness programs are relatively inexpensive, they can be costly in the long run. In the case of Washington state, due to future criminal behavior, as compared with control groups of nonparticipants, for every dollar invested in individuals participating in the Scared Straight program, there was a loss of $200 (VanLandingham, 2015). CrimeSolutions, funded by the National Institute of Justice and the OJJDP, is tasked with evaluating the effectiveness of juvenile delinquency prevention programs (OJJDP, 2022c). In their review of juvenile awareness programs, they found the following (OJJDP, 2022c, retrieved from https://nij.ojp.gov/topics/articles/five-things-about-juvenile-delinquency-intervention-and-treatment):

> *Juvenile awareness programs—like Scared Straight—involve organized visits to adult prison facilities for adjudicated youth and youth at risk of adjudication. Based on the review and rating by CrimeSolutions . . . youth participating in these types of programs were more likely to commit offenses in the future than adjudicated youth and youth at risk of adjudication who did not. Consequently, recidivism rates were, on average, higher for participants compared to juveniles who went through regular case processing.*
>
> *The results suggest that not only are juvenile awareness programs ineffective at deterring youth from committing crimes, but youth exposed to them are more likely to commit offenses in the future.*

And yet, these types of programs continue to be popular, even after repeated, rigorous peer-reviewed research has indicated that they are ineffective. For example, in 2003, then Illinois Governor Blagojevich[10] attempted to resurrect something similar to Scared Straight in a program called Choices in the Chicago Public Schools, where at-risk youth were expected to be given tours of state prisons (Petrosino et al., 2004), even though similar programs had been debunked in a number of studies prior to the development of Choices (Petrosino et al., 2004). More alarming, as Petrosino et al. (2013, retrieved from https://onlinelibrary.wiley.com/doi/pdf/10.4073/csr.2004.2) discovered in their review of a number of studies on juvenile awareness programs, "We concluded that programs such as 'Scared Straight' increase delinquency relative to doing nothing at all to similar youth. Given these results, we cannot recommend this program as a crime prevention strategy."

SOURCES

Office of Juvenile Justice and Delinquency Prevention (OJJDP) (2022c). "Five things about juvenile delinquency intervention and treatment." "Five Things" Series, National Institute of Justice. Mar 22. Retrieved from https://nij.ojp.gov/topics/articles/five-things-about-juvenile-delinquency-intervention-and-treatment.

Petrosino, A., C. Turpin-Petrosino, and J. Buehler (2004). "Juvenile Awareness Programs for Preventing Juvenile Delinquency." *Campbell Systematic Reviews.* Vol. 2. Retrieved from https://onlinelibrary.wiley.com/doi/pdf/10.4073/csr.2004.2.

Petrosino, A., C. Turpin-Petrosino, M.E. Hollis-Peel, and J. G. Lavenberg (2013). "'Scared Straight' and other juvenile awareness programs for preventing juvenile delinquency." *Cochrane Database of Systematic Reviews.* Vol. 2, issue 4 (Apr 30): CD002796. Retrieved from https://www.cochranelibrary.com/cdsr/doi/10.1002/14651858.CD002796.pub2/full.

VanLandingham, G. (2015). "Evidence trumps anecdote for 'Scared Straight' programs." PEW Research Center. Oct 14. Retrieved from https://www.pewtrusts.org/en/research-and-analysis/blogs/stateline/2015/10/14/evidence-trumps-anecdote-for-scared-straight-programs.

[10] Ironically, Governor Blagojevich was sentenced to a 14-year sentence in federal prison for a corruption conviction (Hansen, 2020). In 2020, then President Trump commuted his sentence by executive order, ending his sentence after eight years of incarceration (Hansen, 2020).

INTERNATIONAL PERSPECTIVES

Juvenile Delinquency Prevention Programs in Thailand

If the movie *Broken Palace* (1999) is any indication of conditions in Thai prisons, much less in juvenile facilities, one would think that alone would curb juvenile delinquency there. However, juvenile crime continues, as in the United States, to be an ongoing public concern in Thailand. The primary forms of delinquency in Thailand include truancy and drug use, attributed to peer influence and lack of prosocial daily activities, assumably after school ends for the day (Panezai et al., 2019). Property theft and vandalism are likewise problems (Sukpanich, 2012).

What is interesting to observe in comparing Thailand and the U.S. is the surprising similarity of the juvenile justice system processes, despite cultural differences. In Thailand, juveniles are not arrested except for serious crimes; probation officers investigate juvenile cases with the Risk and Needs Assessment Instrument (RNI) to determine risks for reoffending and to assist in determining the juvenile's need for treatment and/or interventions (Surarittthidham, 2020).

However, juvenile facilities in Thailand are not as secure as those in the United States. In 2000, escapes occurred from two separate facilities. One facility reported that 400 boys had broken out, and another 600 boys had escaped from a Bangkok remand home (detention center) (*Orlando Sentinel*, 2000). According to the Thailand Justice Ministry's Juvenile Observation and Protection Department, between

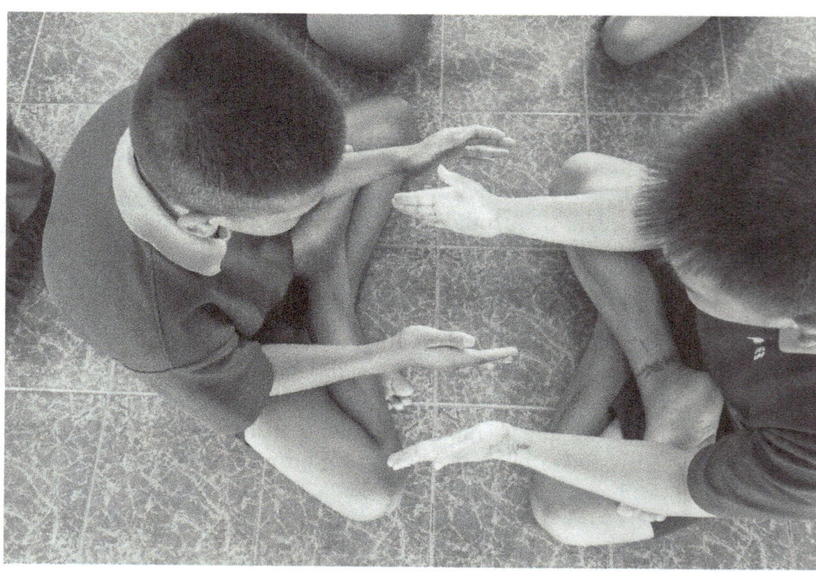

Juveniles Playing in Juvenile Detention Center, Department of Corrections, Nakhonsawan, Thailand (2017)

1997 and 2007, the period during which the remand center escapes took place, juvenile crime had increased by 41.3% (Sukpanich, 2012).

As in the United States, Thailand uses a number of strategies to combat juvenile delinquency. Religion appears to be one answer. A 2007 study (Thai Family Matters Project) had the significant finding that intergenerational diffusion of family religious beliefs and rituals (in Thailand, Buddhism) reduces both minor and serious juvenile offending (Chamratrithirong et al., 2013). Even if the juvenile does not practice the family religion, the Thai Family Matters Project indicated that observing parental units' spirituality without actually practicing the religious rituals themselves reduces problem behavior (Rhucharoenpompanich et al., 2013). However, we might argue that families practicing a religion may monitor their child's behavior more in the process of transmitting that religion to them.

Like elsewhere in the world, Thailand was in lockdown during the COVID-19 pandemic, including its school-aged children. The containment efforts had a latent effect in that following an initial sharp reduction of juvenile crimes, the rates of digital crimes committed by juveniles rose (Justice with Children, 2021).

There were also consequential increases in violence against juveniles held in detention centers, both committed by staff and by other children, as a result of the stresses of prolonged COVID-19 control measures (Justice with Children, 2021). In addition to these problems, rehabilitation programs within juvenile detention centers temporarily ceased under pandemic protocols. Efforts to provide education, career skills, and reintegration programs were suspended, as outsiders, including social welfare employees, were not allowed to enter the facilities (Justice with Children, 2021).

SOURCES

Chamratrithirong, A., B. A. Miller, H. F. Byrnes, O. Rhucharoenpompanich, P. K. Cupp, M. J. Rosati, W. Fongkaew, K. A. Atwood, and M. Todd (2013). "Intergenerational transmission of religious beliefs and practices and the reduction of adolescent delinquency in urban Thailand." *Journal of Adolescence*. Vol. 36, No. 1: 79–89.

Justice with Children (2021). "Preparatory Meeting Report Thailand." 2021 World Congress on Justice with Children. May 12–14. Retrieved from https://justicewithchildren.org/wp-content/uploads/2021/11/Thailand-Preparatory-Meeting-Report-for-WCJWC-.pdf.

Orlando Sentinel (2000). "Thai juvenile offenders state 2nd big breakout." *News*. Mar 18. Retrieved from https://www.orlandosentinel.com/news/os-xpm-2000-03-19-0003200281-story.html.

Panezai, S., H. Panezai, A. A. Wassan, and S. E. Saqib (2019). "Exploring juveniles' delinquent behavior and associated factors: A cross-country comparison of Pakistan and Thailand." *Journal of Geography and Social Sciences*. Vol. 1, issue 1: 57–71.

Sukpanich, T. (2012). "Rising youth crime levels confound justice system." *Bangkok Post*. Jan 22. Retrieved from https://www.bangkokpost.com/thailand/special-reports/276249/rising-youth-crime-levels-confound-justice-system.

Suraritthidham, C. (2020). "Juvenile crime in Thailand." Conference paper, 174th International Senior Seminar. United Nations Asia and Far East Institute for the Prevention Offenders (UNAFEI). Feb. Retrieved from https://www.unafei.or.jp/publications/pdf/RS_No111/No111_15_IP_Suraritthidham.pdf.

CHAPTER DISCUSSION QUESTIONS

1. Reflecting on the challenges to delinquency prevention listed in Chapter 12, choose one program introduced in this chapter and discuss its merits and flaws.
2. Why are evidence-based programs important in delinquency prevention, much more in any crime prevention program? What are the drawbacks of evidence-based programs?
3. This can be a group project: Assume that you have an endless revenue stream of funding to run a juvenile delinquency program. Design a program that you believe would address some of the issues presented in Chapter 12. Who would be your target population for the program?
4. Knowing that there are differing views on how tough we should be on juvenile offenders sent to detention centers, what essential services should be available to them?
5. What extracurricular school activities, if any, might inadvertently promote delinquency, not prevent it?
6. We know that foster children are at greater risk of becoming delinquent. What additional measures, not provided to them today, can be taken to help prevent delinquency?
7. Why is juvenile delinquency, particularly violent offending, viewed by some as a public health crisis? What public health programs might alleviate the problem of juvenile violent offending?
8. Why are juvenile awareness programs like Scared Straight still popular, even though they continue to be shown to be ineffectual, or even harmful?

GLOSSARY

Brady Law The Brady Handgun Violence Prevention Act (1993), amending the Gun Control Act (1968). Permanent provisions of the Brady Law apply to all firearms. See the Bureau of Alcohol, Tobacco, Firearms and Explosives website at https://www.atf.gov/rules-and-regulations/brady-law.

Deinstitutionalization of juvenile offenders Part of the Juvenile Justice and Delinquency Prevention Act (1974) calling for more community-based solutions and reducing the number of juveniles held in detention.

Early developmental prevention Crime prevention measures introduced in early childhood, including identifying negative behaviors, and introducing interventions, such as promotion of early childhood education for all preschoolers. Includes prenatal, infancy, early childhood, and adolescent programs for parental units and their children.

Gentrification The process by which poor neighborhoods are taken over by real estate developers who renovate and sell properties to wealthier people and crowd out the original inhabitants of these neighborhoods, who can no longer afford to live there. Examples: Oakland, California, Harlem in New York City, and Boston, Massachusetts. See *revitalization*.

Grassroots organizations Social movements that are locally based and focus on economic and political problems. Organizers mobilize at a local level, using collective action that can become larger regional, national, and international movements. Example: the American Civil Rights Movement in the 1960s.

Head Start Programs Federally funded programs beginning in 1965 that provide and promote school readiness for infants, toddlers, and preschool children, with services delivered at centers, child care settings, and in the child's own home. See Office of Head Start at https://www.acf.hhs.gov/ohs/about/head-start.

Jail removal requirements Part of the Juvenile Justice Reform Act (H.R. 6964, 2018), requiring that, pretrial, states remove juveniles being charged as adults from adult jails.

Juvenile awareness programs Programs intended to expose at-risk children who have yet to be convicted to the unpleasantness of prisons to deter them from offending or reoffending. Includes the use of scare tactics, including inmates talking with the program participants about prison life.

Juvenile rehabilitation integrated treatment Evidence- and research-based programs for juveniles in residential care who have been removed from their families and community, focused on skill building, including behaviorial treatment and vocational training.

Pilot program Smaller, cost-effective study conducted to test whether a program, in this case one targeting juvenile delinquency, accomplishes the designers' goals. This is a means by which to improve the nature and use of the intervention, as well as to find and correct flaws in training of personnel participating in program delivery.

Primary prevention Improving individuals' lives before they offend or become part of the at-risk population.

Revitalization Organized state or federally funded programs intended to improve the physical appearance of rundown, poor neighborhoods, in hopes of generating more civic pride, as well as encouraging more citizen interaction (e.g., meeting at local coffee shops). See *gentrification*.

Secondary prevention Providing interventions for those who are identified to be at risk of offending.

Tertiary prevention Preventative programs to keep criminal offenders from reoffending.

Toothpaste effect **(of crime)** The risk that a concerted effort to reduce crime in one neighborhood or community will simply push crime into other neighborhoods. See *Weed and Seed Programs*.

Waste management model (corrections) Philosophy in punishment that requires offenders who are sentenced to prison to be locked away, in most cases in jails or prisons, far from public view.

Weed and Seed Program Law enforcement programs, in coordination with human service organizations, to reduce crime in high crime neighborhoods and disseminate programs to prevent and reduce it. See *Toothpaste effect*.

REFERENCES AND ADDITIONAL SUGGESTED READINGS

Abdalla, S. M., K. M. Keyes, and S. Galea (2021). "A public health approach to tackling the role of culture in shaping the gun violence epidemic in the United States." *Public Health Reports*. Vol. 136, issue 1: 6–9.

Achenbach, T. M., and L. A. Rescorla (2001). *Manual for the ASEBA School-Age Forms and Profiles*. Burlington: University of Vermont, Research Center for Children, Youth and Families.

Annie E. Casey Foundation (2018). "Juvenile Justice Reform Act of 2018 affirms protections for young people." Dec 22. Retrieved from https://www.aecf.org/blog/juvenile-justice-reform-act-of-2018-affirms-protections-for-young-people.

Baghel, G., and E. A. Singer (2021), "Should physicians address firearm violence? A clinical response to a public health crisis." *Journal of Hospital Ethics*. Vol. 7, issue 3: 112–118.

Bettencourt, A. (2022). "Grassroots organizations are just as important as seed money for innovation." United Nations Refugee Agency. Retrieved from https://www.unhcr.org/innovation/grassroots-organizations-are-just-as-important-as-seed-money-for-innovation/.

Bianchi, S. M., J. P. Robinson, and M. A. Milkie (2007). *Changing Rhythms of the American Family Life*. New York: Russell Sage Foundation.

Big Brothers Big Sisters of America (2022). "History that spans more than a century." Retrieved from https://www.bbbs.org/history/.

Big Brothers Big Sisters of America (2013). "New Big Brothers Big Sisters Youth Outcomes Survey Report suggests mentoring has positive effects on the whole child." Apr 24. Retrieved from https://www.bbbs.org/news-item/2013/04/new-big-brothers-big-sisters-youth-outcomes-survey-report-suggests-mentoring-has-positive-effects-on-the-whole-child/.

Bishop, D. M. (2012). "Evidence-based practice and juvenile justice." *Criminal Justice and Public Policy*. Vol. 11, issue 3: 483–492.

Bureau of Justice Assistance (BJA) (2010). City of Moreno Valley Gang Prevention Program. Office of Justice Programs, U.S. Department of Justice. Retrieved from https://bja.ojp.gov/funding/awards/2010-dd-bx-0445.

Center for Court Innovation (n.d.). Building a model for the future by reimagining public safety at 17 New York housing sites across five boroughs. Retrieved from https://www.courtinnovation.org/programs/neighborhood-safety-initiatives.

Child Welfare Information Gateway (2019). Issue Brief: Parent education to strengthen families and prevent child maltreatment. Children's Bureau, ACYF, ACF, Department of Housing and Health Services. Feb. Retrieved from https://www.childwelfare.gov/pubpdfs/parented.pdf.

Clinton White House Archive (1998). President Clinton: Safe, Strong Schools for America's Children. Press release, The White House at Work. Apr 13. Retrieved from https://clintonwhitehouse3.archives.gov/WH/Work/041398.html.

DeMatthews, D. (2021). "Standardized testing amid pandemic does kids more harm than good." *Texas Perspectives*. University of Texas at Austin. Mar 15. Retrieved from https://news.utexas.edu/2021/03/15/standardized-testing-amid-pandemic-does-kids-more-harm-than-good/#:~:text=Negative%20consequences%20include%20the%20loss,what%20test%20scores%20actually%20mean.

Dilulio, J. (1995). "The coming of the super-predators." *Weekly Standard*. Vol. 1 (Nov. 19): 23–29.

Dow (2021).

Elliott, D. S., P. R. Buckley, D. C. Gottfredson, J. D. Hawkins, and P. H. Tolan (2020). "Evidence-based juvenile justice programs and practices: A critical review." *Criminology and Public Policy*. Vol. 19, issue 4: 1305–1328.

Esajian, J. D. (2022). "US cities with the highest rent." Fortune Builders, Inc. Retrieved from https://www.fortunebuilders.com/top-10-u-s-cities-with-the-highest-rents/#:~:text=in%20the%20country.-,New%20York%2C%20NY,prices%20are%20likely%20to%20follow.

Federal Grants Wire (2022). Juvenile delinquency prevention programs: Federal grants. Government Grants and Loans Index. Retrieved from https://www.federalgrantswire.com/juvenile-delinquency-prevention-programs-federal-grants.html#.Yq9z9uzMLt0.

Fostering Healthy Futures (FHF) (n.d). "Programs." Regents University of Colorado. Retrieved from https://www.fosteringhealthyfutures.org/programs.

Fox, A., and S. Veele (2020). Legislative Report: Juvenile Rehabilitation Treatment Model. Washington State Department of Children, Youth and Families. May. Retrieved from https://files.eric.ed.gov/fulltext/ED606144.pdf.

Freeman, L., and F. Braconi (2004). "Gentrification and displacement." *Journal of American Planning Association*. Vol. 70, issue 1 (Winter): 39–52.

Goldstein, N. E., O. Olubadewo, R. E. Redding, and F. Lexcen (2005). "Mental health disorders: The neglected risk factor in juvenile delinquency." In *Juvenile Delinquency: Prevention Assessment and Intervention*, ed. K. Heilbrun, N. E. Goldstein, and R. E. Redding. Oxford, UK: Oxford University Press.

Gottfredson, D. C., S. A. Gertenblith, D. A. Soulé, S. C. Womer, and S. Lu (2004). "Do after school programs reduce delinquency?" *Prevention Science*. Vol. 5, issue 4: 253–266.

Greene Foster, D. (2021). *The Turnaway Study: Ten Years, A Thousand Women, and the Consequences of Having—or Being Denied—an Abortion*. New York, NY: Simon and Schuster.

Greenwood, P. (2013). *Evidence-based Practice in Juvenile Justice: Progress, Challenges, and Opportunities*. New York: Springer Science and Business Media.

Hansen, L. P. (2023). *Introduction to Corrections and Penology*. Springfield, MO: Aspen.

Hansen, L. P. (2020). *White Collar and Corporate Crime: A Case Study Approach*. Philadelphia, PA: Aspen Publishing

Hanson, E. J., and K. Finklea (2022). Juvenile Justice Funding Trends. Congressional Research Service. Mar 31. Retrieved from https://sgp.fas.org/crs/misc/R44879.pdf.

Henry, M., and M. Watkins (2020). *Preventing Minority Youth Violence: Lessons from Law Enforcement—Public Health Collaborations*. New York: Center for Court Innovation.

Hirschi, T. (1969). *Causes of Delinquency*. Berkeley, CA: University of California Press.

Hobson, K. (2021). "Higher education is proven to help people in prison. New Pell grants aim to boost enrollment." *PBS News Hour*. Aug 25. Retrieved from https://www.pbs.org/newshour/nation/higher-education-is-proven-to-help-people-in-prison-new-pell-grants-aim-to-boost-enrollment#:~:text=About%2037%20percent%20of%20people,incarcerated%20lack%20post%2Dsecondary%20education.

Hockensmith, C. (2003). "Improving juvenile delinquency through faith-based services." NCJ No. 202186. Office of Justice Programs, U.S. Department of Justice. Retrieved from https://www.ojp.gov/ncjrs/virtual-library/abstracts/improving-juvenile-delinquency-through-faith-based-services.

Juvenile Delinquency Act (1961). *CQ Almanac 1961*. 17th ed. Washington, DC: Congressional Quarterly. Pp 204-206.

Kazemian, L. (2021). *Pathways to Desistance from Crime among Juveniles and Adults: Applications to Criminal Justice Policy and Practice.* National Institute of Justice. Nov. Washington, D.C.: Office of Justice Programs, U.S. Department of Justice.

Keating, C. (2021). "Connecticut Republicans want to get tough on juvenile crime. Here's a look at their plan—and what Democrats think." *Hartford Courant.* Oct 13. Retrieved from https://www.courant.com/politics/hc-pol-news-connecticut-republicans-crime-strategy-20211013-s4yfehe5xrhdvjocnp3f5einh4-story.html.

Law Library, American Law and Legal Information (n.d.). "Juvenile status offenders." Retrieved from https://law.jrank.org/pages/1539/Juvenile-Status-Offenders-Constraints-on-judicial-powers.html

Lee, J. Y., H. A. Knauer, S. J. Lee, M. P. MacEachern, C. F. Garfield (2018). "Father-inclusive perinatal parent education programs: A systematic review." *Pediatrics.* American Academy of Pediatrics. Vol. 142, issue 1 (July): e1–18.

Lenzi, M., J. D. Sharkey, A. Wroblewski, M. J. Furlong, and M. Santinello (2019). "Protecting youth from gang membership: Individual and school-level emotional competence." *Journal of Community Psychology.* Vol. 47, No. 3 (April): 563–578.

Leve, L. D., D. C. R. Kerr, and G. T. Harold (2013). "Young adult outcomes associated with teen pregnancy among high-risk girls in an RCT of multidimensional treatment foster care." *Journal of Child and Adolescent Substance Abuse.* Vol. 22, issue 5 (Sep. 1): 421–434. Main (2012).

Malik, M. A., and R. A. Shirazi (2010). "An analytical review of juvenile delinquents in jails of Sindh Province: Some problems and suggestions to overcome." *Industrial Journal of Management and Social Sciences.* Vol. 4, No. 1: 43–54.

Mauro, T. (2022). "Sports programs for kids with disabilities: Organizations for inclusive sports." *Very Well Family.* Jun 1. Retrieved from https://www.verywellfamily.com/special-needs-sports-programs-3106922.

Meiszkowski, P., and E. Mills (1993). "The causes of metropolitan suburbanization." *Journal of Economic Perspectives.* Vol. 7: 135–147.

Moon, M. M., J. L. Sundt, F. T. Cullen, and J. P Wright (2000). "Is child saving dead? Public support for juvenile rehabilitation." *Crime and Delinquency.* Vol. 46, issue 1 (Jan.): 38–60.

Morales, M. (2022). "Staten Island mom continues efforts to feed her neighborhood." PIX II News, New York. Mar 17. Retrieved from https://pix11.com/news/local-news/staten-island/staten-island-mom-continues-efforts-to-feed-her-neighborhood/.

Morizot, J., and L. Kazemian (2014). *The Development of Criminal and Antisocial Behavior: Research and Practical Applications.* New York: Springer.

National Conference of State Legislatures (2018). "Teen pregnancy prevention." Report. Oct 11. Retrieved from https://www.ncsl.org/health/teen-pregnancy-prevention#:~:text=Teen%20pregnancy%20is%20strongly%20linked,year%20of%20a%20child's%20birth.

National Gang Center (NGC) (2017). "A Law Enforcement Official's Guide to the OJJDP Comprehensive Gang Model." Washington, DC: Office of Justice Programs, U.S. Department of Justice. Retrieved from https://nationalgangcenter.ojp.gov/sites/g/files/xyckuh331/files/media/document/le-officials-guide-to-ojjdp-comprehensive-gang-model.pdf.

National Institute of Justice (NIJ) (2011). "Program profile: Multidimensional Treatment Foster Care—Adolescents." Office of Justice Programs, U.S. Department of Justice. Jun 10. Retrieved from https://crimesolutions.ojp.gov/ratedprograms/141.

National Low-Income Housing Coalition (NLIHC) (2019). "Gentrification and revitalization: What's the difference?" Apr 5. Retrieved from https://nlihc.org/resource/gentrification-and-neighborhood-revitalization-whats-difference.

National Mental Health Association (NMHA) (2004). *Mental Health Treatment for Youth in the Juvenile Justice System: A Compendium of Promising Practices.* Chicago, IL: MacArthur Foundation.

National Mentoring Partnership (2021). "Report: Mentoring and Youth Violence Prevention." *Mentor.* Retrieved from https://files.eric.ed.gov/fulltext/ED614513.pdf.

New Mexico Children, Youth and Families Department (NMCYFD) (2022). JJS special programs. Retrieved from https://cyfd.org/jjs-special-programs.

Obama Foundation (n.d.). "We are our brother's keepers." Retrieved from https://www.obama.org/mbka/.

Obama Foundation (2022). "A movement inspired by Trayvon Martin unleashes the power of communities to work together to solve problems for boys and young men of color." Retrieved from https://www.obama.org/mbka/eighth-anniversary/.

Obama White House Archives (2016a). "Fact sheet: My Brother's Keeper—Two years of expanding opportunity and creating pathways for success." Press release. Apr 22. Retrieved from https://obamawhitehouse.archives.gov/the-press-office/2016/04/22/fact sheet-my-brothers-keeper-%E2%80%93-two-years-expanding-opportunity-creating.

Obama White House Archives (2016b). "My Brother's Keeper 2016 Progress Report: Two Years of Expanding Opportunity and Creating Pathways to Success." Retrieved from https://obamawhitehouse.archives.gov/sites/whitehouse.gov/files/images/MBK-2016-Progress-Report.pdf.

Office of Justice Programs (1998). "President's anti-gang and youth violence strategy." NCJ No. 193818. U.S. Department of Justice. Retrieved from https://www.ojp.gov/ncjrs/virtual-library/abstracts/presidents-anti-gang-and-youth-violence-strategy.

Office of Juvenile Justice and Delinquency Prevention (OJJDP) (n.d.a). "About the Office." Office of Justice Programs, U.S. Department of Justice. Retrieved from https://ojjdp.ojp.gov/about#:~:text=%C2%A7%205601%20et%20seq.),has%20had%20on%20juvenile%20justice.

Office of Juvenile Justice and Delinquency Prevention (OJJDP) (n.d.b). "Enhancing law enforcement efforts and engagement with youth." Office of Justice Programs, U. S. Department of Justice. Retrieved from https://ojjdp.ojp.gov/programs/enhancing-law-enforcement-efforts-and-engagement-youth.

Office of Juvenile Justice and Delinquency Prevention (OJJDP) (n.d.c). "Legislation." Office of Justice Programs, U.S. Department of Justice. Retrieved from https://ojjdp.ojp.gov/about/legislation.

Office of Juvenile Justice and Delinquency Prevention (OJJDP) (n.d.d). "State compliance with JJDP Act core requirements." Office of Justice Programs, U. S. Department of Justice. Retrieved from https://ojjdp.ojp.gov/states/state-compliance-jjdp-act-core-requirements.

Office of Juvenile Justice and Delinquency Prevention (OJJDP) (2022a). "Funding." Office of Justice Programs, U.S. Department of Justice. Retrieved from https://ojjdp.ojp.gov/funding#:~:text=In%20fiscal%20year%20(FY)%202021,youth%20and%20to%20deter%20delinquency.

Office of Juvenile Justice and Delinquency Prevention (OJJDP) (2022b). "Racial and ethnic disparity in juvenile justice processing." *Model Programs Guide,* U.S. Department of Justice. Mar. Retrieved from https://ojjdp.ojp.gov/model-programs-guide/literature-reviews/racial-and-ethnic-disparity.

Office of Juvenile Justice and Delinquency Prevention (OJJDP) (2017). "Intersection between mental health and juvenile justice system: Literature Review." *Model Programs Guide.* Office of Justice Programs, U.S. Department of Justice. Jul. Retrieved from https://ojjdp.ojp.gov/model-programs-guide/literature-reviews/intsection_between_mental_health_and_the_juvenile_justice_system.pdf.

Office of Juvenile Justice and Delinquency Prevention (OJJDP) (2010). "Parent training." Literature Review, Model Programs Guide. Office of Justice Programs, U.S. Department of

Justice. Retrieved from https://ojjdp.ojp.gov/model-programs-guide/literature-reviews/parent_training.pdf.

Office of Juvenile Justice and Delinquency Prevention (OJJDP) (2005). The National Hispanic Juvenile Delinquency Program of the Self-Reliance Foundation. Funding Award, 2005. Department of Justice Programs, U.S. Department of Justice. Retrieved from https://ojjdp.ojp.gov/funding/awards/2005-jl-fx-0141.

Opioid Affected Youth Initiative (OAYI) (n.d). "Our initiative." Office of Juvenile Justice and Delinquency Prevention (OJJDP), U.S. Department of Justice. Retrieved from https://www.opioidaffectedyouth.org/.

Patterson, G. R., J. B. Reid, and T. J. Dishion (1992). *Antisocial Boys: A Social Interactional Approach*, Vol. 4. Eugene, OR: Castalia.

Pergola, J. (2014). "Music education in crisis." *School Band and Orchestra Magazine*. National Education Music Company. Retrieved from https://www.nemc.com/resources/articles/music-education-in-crisis.

Pina, A. A., A. J. Polo, and S. J. Huey (2019). "Evidence-based psychosocial interventions for ethnic minority youth: The 10-year update." *Journal of Clinical Child and Adolescent Psychology*. Vol. 48, No. 2: 179–202.

Reynolds, W. M. (1988). *Suicidal Ideation Questionnaire Professional Manual*. Odessa, FL: Psychological Assessment Resources.

Saminksy, A. (2010). "Preventing juvenile delinquency: Early interventions and comprehensiveness as critical factors." *Inquiries Journal*. Vol. 2, issue 1. Retrieved from http://www.inquiriesjournal.com/articles/165/preventing-juvenile-delinquency-early-intervention-and-comprehensiveness-as-critical-factors.

Short, J. F. (1990). "Delinquency and Society." NCJ No. 129399. Office of Justice Programs, U.S. Department of Justice. Retrieved from https://www.ojp.gov/ncjrs/virtual-library/abstracts/delinquency-and-society.

Simons, R. L., C. A. Johnson, R. D. Conger, G. H. Elder (1998). "A test of latent trait versus life course perspective on the stability of adolescent antisocial behavior." *Criminology*. Vol. 36: 217–244.

Small, S. A., A. J. Reynolds, C. O'Connor, S. M. Cooney (2005). "What works, Wisconsin: What science tells us about cost-effective programs for juvenile delinquency prevention." Report, Wisconsin Governor's Juvenile Justice Commissions and the Wisconsin Office of Justice Assistance. University of Wisconsin-Madison. Jun. Retrieved from https://fyi.extension.wisc.edu/criminaljusticeandprevention/files/2012/04/whatworkswisconsin.pdf.

Solina, S. (2021). "After 2 decades away, Weed and Seed program is back to target crime in Chinatown." *Hawaii News Now*. Sep 8. Retrieved from https://www.hawaiinewsnow.com/2021/09/09/after-2-decades-away-weed-seed-program-is-back-target-crime-chinatown/.

Spruit, A., P. Hoffenaar, C. van der Put, E. van Vugt, and G. J. Stams (2018). "The effect of a sports-based intervention to prevent juvenile delinquency in at-risk adolescents." *Children and Youth Services Review*. Vol. 94: 689–698.

Steinberg, A., and E. Nadworny (2022). "Community college enrollment is down, but skilled-trades programs are booming." *National Public Radio (NPR)*. Mar 28. Retrieved from https://www.npr.org/2022/03/28/1086454046/2-year-skilled-trades-programs-booming#:~:text=Two%2Dyear%20construction%20trades%20programs%20see%20spike%20in%20enrollment%20%3A%20NPR&text=Two%2Dyear%20construction%20trades%20programs%20see%20spike%20in%20enrollment%20Enrollment,in%20construction%20trades%20are%20booming.

Steinfels, P. (2009). "Despite a decade of controversy, the 'Faith-Based Initiative' endures." *The New York Times.* Jul 31. Retrieved from https://www.nytimes.com/2009/08/01/us/01beliefs.html.

Stevens, S. (2021). "The difference between gentrification and revitalization." *North Texas Daily.* May 4. Retrieved from https://www.ntdaily.com/the-difference-between-gentrification-and-revitalization/#:~:text=Revitalization%20is%20a%20positive%20approach,to%20important%20opportunities%20and%20resources.

Taussig, H. N., J. Dmitrieva, E. F. Garrido, J. L. Cooley, and E. Crites (2021). "Fostering Health Futures prevention intervention for children in foster care: Long-term delinquency outcomes from a randomized controlled trial." *Prevention Science.* Vol. 22: 1120–1133.

Texas Juvenile Probation Commission (1993). "Juvenile delinquency prevention in Texas." NCJ No. 142222. Office of Justice Programs, U.S. Department of Justice. Retrieved from https://www.ojp.gov/ncjrs/virtual-library/abstracts/juvenile-delinquency-prevention-texas#:~:text=Primary%20prevention%20is%20concerned%20with,in%20the%20juvenile%20justice%20system.

Underwood, L. A., and A. Washington (2016). "Mental illness and juvenile offenders." *International Journal of Environmental Research and Public Health.* Vol. 13, issue 2 (Feb.): 228.

U.S. Attorney's Office (2018). "Weed and seed." Northern District of California, United States Department of Justice. Oct. 5. Retrieved from https://www.justice.gov/usao-ndca/weed-and-seed#:~:text=Weed%20and%20Seed%20is%20a,crime%20neighborhoods%20throughout%20the%20country.

U.S. Department of Health and Human Services (HHS) (2014). "Office of Minority Health Minority Youth Violence Prevention Program: Grantee project summaries." Retrieved from https://minorityhealth.hhs.gov/omh/content.aspx?ID=10175.

Vincent, G. M. (2012). *Screening and Assessment in Juvenile Justice Systems: Identifying Mental Health Needs and Risk of Reoffending.* Washington, DC: Technical Assistance Partnership for Child and Family Mental Health.

Walsh, B. C., and D. P. Farrington (2009). "Early developmental prevention of delinquency and later offending: Prospects and challenges." *International Journal of Developmental Science.* Vol. 3, issue 3: 247–259.

Walters, G. D. (2020). "Prosocial peers as risk, protective, and promotive factors for the prevention of delinquency and drug use." *Journal of Youth and Adolescence.* Vol. 49 (March): 618–630.

Weisburd, D., and A. Petrosino (2004). "Experiments, criminology." In *Encyclopedia of Social Measurement*, ed. K. Kempf-Leonard. San Diego, CA: Elsevier.

Weissbourd, R., M. Batanova, J. McIntyre, and E. Torres (2020). "How the pandemic is strengthening fathers' relationships with their children." Making Caring Common Project, Graduate School of Education, Harvard University. Jun. Retrieved from https://static1.squarespace.com/static/5b7c56e255b02c683659fe43/t/5eeceba88f50eb19810153d4/1592585165850/Report+How+the+Pandemic+is+Strengthening+Fathers+Relationships+with+Their+Children+FINAL.pdf.

Weisz, J. R., A. Jensen-Doss, and K. M. Hawley (2006). "Evidence-based youth psychotherapies versus usual clinical care." *American Psychologist.* Vol. 61, issue 7 (Oct.): 671–689.

Welsh, B. C., N. E. Dill, and S. N. Zane (2019). "The first delinquency prevention experiment: A socio-historical review of the origins of the Cambridge-Somerville Youth Study research design." *Journal of Experimental Criminology.* Vol. 15: 441–451.

Wernecke, D. C. (2022). "An Idiot's Guide to the American Upper Paleolithic." Lecture. Archeological Conservancy. Santa Fe, NM. Jun 22.

White House Archives (n.d.). "White House Faith-Based and Community Initiative." Retrieved from https://georgewbush-whitehouse.archives.gov/government/fbci/president-initiative.html#:~:text=The%20Initiative%20in%20Action,FBCOs%20in%20providing%20social%20services.

White House Briefing Room (2021). "FACT SHEET: President Biden Reestablishes the White House Office of Faith-Based and Neighborhood Partnerships." Statements and Releases. Feb 14. Retrieved from https://www.whitehouse.gov/briefing-room/statements-releases/2021/02/14/fact-sheet-president-biden-reestablishes-the-white-house-office-of-faith-based-and-neighborhood-partnerships/.

Wo, J. C. (2019). "Revisiting the crime control benefit of voluntary organizations: Organizational presence, organizational capacity, and crime rates in Los Angeles neighborhoods." *Crime and Delinquency.* Vol. 65, issue 7: 916–940.

Wo, J. C. (2016). "Community context of crime: A longitudinal examination of the effects of local institutions on neighborhood crime." *Crime and Delinquency.* Vol. 62, issue 1: 1286–1312.

Woodruff-Santos, M. (2015). "Telling young people they need a 4-year degree is a 'disservice.'" Opportunity Nation: The Forum for Youth Investment. Jun 17. Retrieved from https://opportunitynation.org/latest-news/media-highlights/telling-young-people-need-4-year-degree-disservice/.

GLOSSARY

A

Aborigines (Australia) Indigenous people of Australia and surrounding islands.

Additive bilingual programs Programs in which a student's first language continues to be developed, including through reading and writing, as the student learns a second language. In the United States, the first language is most often Spanish and the second language English, in cases where individuals are bilingual.

Age of criminal responsibility or majority For those under 18, the age at which they can be considered an adult or be referred to adult criminal court.

Alternative school A non-mainstream school. Not only reserved for juvenile delinquents or those struggling in traditional schools (e.g., elite boarding schools), but generally indicates a public school in the context of juveniles who cannot function in mainstream schools due either to behavior problems or delinquency. Also termed *continuation schools.*

Anomie Lack, in an individual or group, of common mores or ethical standards, leading to deterioration or disappearance of social norms.

Arson Deliberate and malicious fire-setting, with the intent to destroy property or defraud an insurance company.

Attachment theory Theory focused on the development of long-term relationships, including with parental units, friends, and romantic partners, based on trust that these will be safe and secure relationships.

Autism spectrum disorder (ASD) A broad range of developmental disorders characterized by difficulty with social functions and interactions (such as communication and learning), repetitive behaviors, and possibly associated delays in childhood development. First signs can be detected as early as infancy. See *Neurodivergent.*

B

Bipolar disorder A medical condition typically characterized by alternating states of elation and depression, though it may take other forms.

Blended sentence Sentences in cases of serious juvenile offending in which the first part is spent in a juvenile facility and, when the offender ages out of the juvenile system, the remainder is spent in adult corrections.

Bounded rationality Theory put forward by Herbert A. Simon that decisions are made on the basis of imperfect or missing information. Individuals know this to be the case and run with "good enough" decisions, particularly when pressed for time.

Brady Law The Brady Handgun Violence Prevention Act (1993), amending the Gun Control Act (1968). Permanent provisions of the Brady Law apply to all firearms.

Breach of peace When one or more individuals in a public space or at a private home behave in ways disturbing to those around them. Examples: Use of obscene or abusive language in a public space; playing loud music late at night; obstructing vehicular or pedestrian traffic. Also termed *disturbing the peace* or *violating public peace or order.* See *Disorderly conduct.*

Burglary Illegal entry into a public or private building, with the intention of committing a crime (e.g., theft or vandalism).

C

Case petitioning Document asking the court to assume jurisdiction over a juvenile, either due to delinquent behavior or status violations. Can also refer to requests to transfer a juvenile to adult court.

Child maltreatment Any treatment of a child that results in physical suffering or psychological harm.

Child Protective Services (CPS) An agency, known by various names depending on the jurisdiction, responsible for investigating child abuse allegations and making recommendations to the courts depending on the findings. Agencies are also responsible for follow-up interviews and investigations in cases where maltreatment has been documented.

Childhood Separation Anxiety Disorder (CSAD) Mental health issue in which infants and children develop pathological attachment to certain family members and fear of separation from them, beyond what is appropriate for their developmental stage.

Citizen's arrest An arrest made by anyone other than a sworn law enforcement officer. These arrests are subject to limitations set by jurisdiction.

Cognitive theories Theories focused on the mechanics and patterns of individuals' thought processes, including creative processes.

Commercialized vice As defined by the FBI, "the unlawful promotion of or participation in sexual activities for profit, including attempts"; includes prostitution.

Community-based corrections Any form of sentenced punishment or treatment that takes place in the community rather than in a correctional facility. Examples are probation and parole.

Compassion fatigue Occupational hazard of working in human services professions, including the medical field, social work, and the criminal justice system, as a response to the stresses of the job, including limited resources and the type of population worked with. See *Role overload*.

Computer hacking Unauthorized use of or entry into computer systems or private networks, often with the intention of stealing information, including personal financial records.

Congregate care Licensed residential group home for juveniles.

Co-offend Commission of a crime by two or more individuals working together.

Corporal punishment Any physical punishment, including spanking, withholding food or water, or confinement in an uncomfortable position or place.

Court-Appointed Special Advocates (CASA) Volunteer organization that provides advocacy to abused or neglected juveniles before judges and courts.

Criminal trespassing Knowingly, and without the owner or operator's permission, entering, staying on, and/or refusing to leave private property.

Curfew Requirement to remain off the streets and out of public places during a designated period (e.g., 11 p.m. to 6 a.m). Exceptions are made for juveniles whose employment requires being out during curfew hours.

Cyberbullying Use of electronic means, including text messaging, social media, and emails, to intimidate, threaten, harass, or embarrass an intended target.

D

Dark Web Subset of the World Wide Web intended to provide users with extra encryption and secrecy, often used to commit cybercrimes.

Date rape Unconsented intercourse in the context of a dating relationship. See *Dating abuse, Dating violence.*

Dating abuse Similar to *intimate partner violence* (IPV), with one or both parties in a dating relationship physically, emotionally, or psychologically abusing the other. See *Date rape, Dating violence.*

Dating violence Any form of violence that takes place within the context of a dating relationship. See *Dating abuse, Date rape.*

Dating violent offender (DVO) A juvenile or adult who commits date rape, violent dating abuse, or any other form of violent crime against a romantic interest or partner. See *Date rape, Dating abuse, Dating violence.*

Deinstitutionalization of juvenile offenders The move to community-based solutions and reducing numbers of juveniles held in detention, specifically as called for in the Juvenile Justice and Delinquency Prevention Act (1974).

Detention Synonymous with adult jail or prison; refers to the incarceration of a juvenile offender.

Detention hearing Initial court hearing, similar to an adult arraignment, to determine if it is necessary to hold a suspected juvenile offender in pretrial custody. See *Juvenile detention.*

Developmental disorders Disabilities related to slowed or abnormal development in children and adults, including physical, learning, language, or behavior deficiencies.

Deviance Behaviors and cultures that run counter to mainstream society. ***Note:*** All crime is deviance, but not all deviance is crime.

Differential association Theory developed by Edwin Sutherland that individuals become deviant or criminal from associating with deviant or criminal individuals or groups.

Differential opportunity theory Cloward and Ohlin's theory that both individual and environmental factors contribute to creating or limiting opportunities to commit crime.

Digital piracy Illegally downloading from the Internet, or from dedicated websites, content that otherwise requires purchase, including movies, games, and music.

Disorderly conduct Similar to breach of the peace violations, behavior by an individual that is intended to cause public alarm or create a public nuisance, including fighting or threatening violent behavior. Examples: public drunkenness, rioting, or demonstrating after law enforcement asks participants not to do so. See *Breach of peace.*

Disposition hearing Hearing, held after a juvenile has been found to be delinquent, in which the judge determines the most appropriate sentence for the case, depending on a number of factors, including the offense.

Disturbing the peace See *Breach of peace; Disorderly conduct.*

Dysthymia A persistent mental health disorder stemming from depression, where individuals lose interest in daily activities, lack motivation, and chronically experience feelings of hopelessness.

E

Early developmental prevention Crime prevention measures introduced in early childhood, including identifying negative behaviors, introducing interventions, and providing early childhood education for all preschoolers. Includes prenatal, infancy, early childhood, and adolescent programs for parental units and their children.

Electronic dating aggression Targeting a romantic interest or partner with abusive and/or threatening content in emails, text messages, or direct messaging on social media.

Embezzlement Theft of cash, accounts, or material goods from an employer.

Emotional intelligence In contrast to *intelligence quotient (IQ)*, emotional intelligence measures the ability to put into practice the skills of self-awareness, perception, and regulation of emotions.

Emotional security theory Developmental theory proposing that the quality of relationships in a family will be either supported or undermined by how children are treated by parents and other household members.

Ethnic competition theory The fear that a particular racial, ethnic, or religious minority will grow in numbers and compete for resources, including jobs.

Evidence-based programs Prevention or treatment programs designed around studies and data analysis providing evidence of their effectiveness.

Expulsion Removal of a student for serious, sometimes criminal, violation of school rules or policies.

Extended family Family members outside the nuclear family, including grandparents, aunts, uncles, cousins, etc.

F

Family (legal definition) Individuals related by blood, legal adoption, or marriage.

Family cohesion The quality in a family of possessing a unifying emotional bond and functioning together in all aspects of family life, including communication, values, roles, and expectations.

Family stability The extent to which a family exhibits consistency in its structure, activities, and routines.

Felony Charges and convictions reserved for serious crimes, the exact description of which differs depending on the state. More likely to result in detention, jail, or prison than a misdemeanor offense.

Fight or flight response The biological and psychological imperative that individuals experience when faced with perceived dangerous or stressful situations, resulting in the instinct to stay and fight or to run.

Fitness hearing Initial hearing to determine if, based on the severity of the charges, a juvenile's case should be referred to the juvenile court or to the adult criminal justice system.

Food insecurity Conditions under which affordable or nutritious food adequate to nourish people and sustain a healthy life is limited or unreliable.

Foster care Temporary or permanent placement with foster parents; may remain in effect until the juvenile turns 18.

Free-range Parenting philosophy and style that allows children and adolescents freedom of movement in physical space. Example: Allowing children to play at a park close to home without adult supervision. See *Spatial autonomy.*

G

Gang enhancement laws Laws intended to bring stiffer penalties and longer jail or prison sentences for crimes suspected of being gang-related.

Gaslighting Form of psychological abuse where an abuser leads victims to believe they are at fault for their own abuse or mistreatment, or that they are mentally unstable.

Gender In sociological terms, the roles and identities individuals are expected to fulfill based on their biological sex (genitalia). ***Note:*** *Gender* and *sex* are often confused. *Sex* refers to biological markers identified at birth and to secondary sex characteristics emerging in puberty.

Gender dysphoria The disconnect between one's biological sex and the strong desire to be another gender, often resulting in considerable psychological stress. Gender dysphoria can be experienced as early as age 2 or 3 or more acutely between ages 4 and 6.

Gender non-conforming Term used to describe individuals who do not conform to traditional roles based on their biological sex. According to the Human Rights Campaign, many but not all gender non-conforming individuals are transgender.

General deterrence Crime prevention targeting multiple crimes at once. Example: Police foot patrols.

Gentrification The process by which poor neighborhoods are taken over by real estate developers who renovate and sell properties at higher prices than the original inhabitants of the neighborhoods cannot afford. Examples: Oakland, California; Harlem in New York City; and Boston, Massachusetts. See *Revitalization.*

Ghost guns Homemade rather than manufactured guns, including those made with a 3D printer.

Grassroots organizations Locally-based social movements focused on economic and political problems. Local organizers may use collective action, joining with regional, national, and international movements. Example: the American civil rights movement in the 1960s.

Group homes Community-based facilities for adults or juveniles where residents can receive the types of rehabilitation prescribed by social workers and the court.

H

Hate groups Groups of individuals, often organized through social media, that advocate hatred or violence against others based on race, ethnicity, religion, gender, or sexual orientation. See *Hate or bias crimes.*

Hate or bias crimes Any crime, including assault, vandalism, and threatening language, motivated by deep-seated prejudices based on race, ethnicity, religion, gender, or sexual orientation. See *Hate groups.*

Head Start Programs Federally funded programs, beginning in 1965, that provide resources and promote school readiness for infants, toddlers, and preschool children; services are delivered at centers, in child care settings, and in the child's own home.

Helicoptering Parenting style in which parental units compulsively and consistently monitor their children's every move, chaperoning them, closely supervising homework assignments, and attending school activities. In some cases, "helicopter parents" excessive contact their children's teachers and school administrators, interfering with normal pedagogical approaches to teaching and classroom management.

Hypomania A mild form of *hypermania* that can include abnormally high levels of excitement, happiness, and energy during a short period of time, marked by sleep deprivation, talkativeness, and inflated sense of self-worth. See *Mania.*

I

Incapacitation In corrections, a suspected or convicted offender's removal from the community to a secure facility, including jails and prisons.

Incorrigible child Term used in the late 19th century to describe a misbehaving child who does not follow rules and is often unmanageable.

Indian Child Welfare Act (1911) Act providing protections to Native American and Alaskan Native children (revised over time, including in 1978). Criticisms include inability of child welfare personnel to understand and appropriately apply its provisions to the indigenous population.

Individuals with Disabilities Education Act (IDEA) Legislation meant to guarantee individuals with physical and neurological disabilities, including children, a free education that meets their individual needs and will prepare them for an independent adult life.

Informal and formal sanctions Forms of punishment society hands out to accused deviants or offenders. Informal sanctions include shunning; formal sanctions are used to punish those convicted of a crime.

Informal housing Any flimsy, makeshift, unregulated structure built without regard to zoning laws or public safety for use as housing by unhoused or impoverished people.

Intake Procedures followed for juveniles suspected of committing a crime or status offense to determine whether the juvenile should be released or referred to juvenile court.

Intellectual property Any creative work, including publication, design, symbols, names, and images, that are the sole property of the creator and/or the company or organization they are affiliated with.

Interaction ritual chains A theory, proposed by Randall Collins, that constant negative interaction with others results in emotional exhaustion, while positive interaction reinforces and encourages continued, healthier relationships.

Interactional theory A theory, similar to Sutherland's differential association theory, proposing that exposure to delinquent peers can result in delinquent behavior, while parental units and home life play an important role in preventing delinquency.

Internet gaming disorder Addiction, recognized by the World Health Organization, in which an individual's life is disrupted by excessive time spent playing games on the Internet; marked by symptoms of withdrawal when the individual is unable or not allowed to play.

Interpersonal violence Abuse, aggression, and/or violence that occurs among two or more people, often in a close relationship. See *Intimate partner violence (IPV)*.

Intimate partner violence (IPV) Abuse, aggression, and/or violence between romantic partners. See *Interpersonal violence*.

J

Jail removal requirements As part of the Juvenile Justice Reform Act (H.R. 6964, 2018), requirement that, pretrial, states remove from adult jails juveniles being charged as adults.

Joyride Recklessly driving a motor vehicle for pleasure without the owner's permission or by theft.

Jurisdictional hearing A hearing held in family court to make a follow-up determination on whether an abused or neglected child should be removed from their home and placed in the custody of the court. Sometimes referred to as a *dependency hearing*.

Juvenile awareness programs Programs intended to expose at-risk but not convicted children to the unpleasantness of prisons (including inmates describing prison life), to deter them from offending or reoffending. Use of scare tactics.

Juvenile boot camps Highly controversial, quasi-military style camps intended to teach participants discipline, outdoor skills, and physical fitness.

Juvenile delinquency Term used for juveniles viewed as deviant or for criminals. Legal term for juveniles found delinquent in juvenile court for an offense committed before the juvenile's 18th birthday.

Juvenile detention Comparable to adult jails, a correctional facility intended for temporary detention of a juvenile, generally pretrial, if the seriousness of the charges warrant it. Quality of juvenile detention to meet the needs of minors varies from jurisdiction to jurisdiction. See *Detention hearing*.

Juvenile human trafficking (JHT) Recruiting or forced abduction of juveniles with the intention of coercing them into forced labor, often in the illegal sex trades, including prostitution.

Juvenile justice Courts and agencies that are part of the larger criminal justice system and handle the cases of juveniles under age 18.

Juvenile parole Similar to adult parole, release of a juvenile offender (subject to conditions) into the community to serve the remainder of a sentence.

Juvenile probation As with adult offenders on probation, a form of forgiveness where the juvenile offender serves the sentence in the community with specific conditions imposed for a period of time.

Juvenile rehabilitation integrated treatment Evidence- and research-based programs provided in residential care to juveniles who have been removed from their families and community. Rehabilitation focuses on building skills using behavior treatment (cognitive-behavioral therapy) and vocational training.

K

Kleptomania A recognized mental health disorder in which an individual has a chronic compulsion to steal from others, including by shoplifting.

L

Larceny General term used to describe theft of personal property.

Life-course theories A multidisciplinary approach to studying human development, based in life stages (e.g., infancy, early childhood, etc).

Limbic system The part of the brain responsible for behavior and emotional responses. The three main parts of the limbic system are the amygdala, cingulate gyrus, and hippocampus.

Loitering Remaining in a public place (e.g., a park or business), seemingly without purpose for a prolonged amount of time. Not illegal per se, unless prohibition of loitering is posted in the area.

M

Major depressive disorder (MDD) A mood disorder in which individuals have persistent feelings of sadness and despair, often showing little or no interest in daily life or social relationships.

Major depressive episode (MDE) A period of two weeks or longer in which an individual experiences symptoms of depression, including thoughts of suicide.

Mandated reporters Individuals, including teachers, coaches, health care workers, required by law to report any suspected child maltreatment.

Mania Common symptom in bipolar disorder, experienced to varying degrees, that includes exaggerated excitement or euphoria and episodes of delusion and hyperactivity. See *Hypomania.*

Megan's Law Federal law (a 1996 amendment to the Violent Crime Control and Law Enforcement Act of 1994), named after Megan Kanka, who was raped and murdered by a neighbor; requires sex offenders in a community to register to alert the public to their presence.

Miranda Rights Rights of suspects, including juveniles, upon arrest, a statement of which is required by law to be read to the suspect by an arresting officer.

Misdemeanor A punishable offense, varying by state depending on the type of crime, resulting on average in less than a year in jail. Misdemeanors for both juveniles and adults, if convicted or adjudicated, are most likely to result in fines, probation, community service, and/or referral to alcohol or substance abuse treatment.

Moral panic A period of widespread, often irrational fear during which large numbers of people demand that a solution be found to prevent or stop the perceived threat, which may or may not be criminal in nature. See *Social construct.*

N

National Survey of Youth in Custody (NSYC) A part of the U.S. Bureau of Justice Statistics (BJS) rape and sexual assault prevention program mandated under the Prison Rape Elimination Act of 2003.

Neurodivergent An individual with unique cognitive processes leading them to perceive the world or to behave differently from the mainstream.

Neurotransmitters Chemical substances released in the brain from the nervous system that transmit messages between neurons and from neurons to muscles.

Nuclear family Immediate family, typically including two adults and children.

P

Panhandling Begging for money or food in public, including on public transportation and streets.

Peer groups Friend networks sharing the same world view, interests, and hobbies. Usually formed among people living in close proximity, e.g., classmates who become friends, or neighborhood cliques.

Physiological psychology Branch of psychology that focuses on brain anatomy, including the relationship between physiology and behavior.

Pilot program Small, cost-effective studies conducted to test whether a program (here, targeting juvenile delinquency) accomplishes the designers' goals. Helps improve interventions, their use, and the training of personnel who will deliver the program.

Prefrontal cortex The part of the brain that is key in self-regulation, self-control, and conflict resolution; not fully developed in humans until about age 25.

Pretrial hearing A hearing prior to trial in juvenile court at which the judge rules on motions, including admissibility of the evidence the prosecutor or defense wish to present in court.

Primary prevention Improving an individual's life before they offend or become part of the at-risk population.

Pseudo family Individuals unrelated by blood, legal adoption, or marriage who form a cohesive unit performing all the functions of a nuclear family, including cohabitating and sharing expenses.

Psychopathology A mental or behavioral disorder likely to require medical and/or psychiatric intervention to control or resolve.

R

Recidivism Reoffending after being released from custody or during or after probation or parole.

Reformatory A product of 19th-century social movements and child saver organizations intended to rehabilitate and provide delinquent youth with the homes and structure they had previously lacked; many have reputations for harsh and cruel conditions.

Relative poverty An individual's feeling of being poor relative to the incomes and possessions of their neighbors.

Restitution Often court-ordered, an offender's monetary or community service commitment to repay a crime victim or community for their losses.

Restorative Justice A means by which offenders and victims meet face to face, ideally allowing the offender to apologize and the victim to air their grievances and enlighten the offender about the damage resulting from the crime. See *Shaming and reintegration.*

Revitalization Organized state or federally funded programs intended to improve the physical appearance of rundown, poor neighborhoods, in hopes of increasing civic pride and encouraging more citizen interaction (e.g., meetings at local coffee shops). See *Gentrification*.

Robbery Unlawful removal of property from a person or place by force or threat of force. Armed robbery involves a weapon, usually a gun.

Role overload When a job that overwhelms employees due to its many responsibilities and limited resources for combatting the resulting mental and physical fatigue. See *Compassion fatigue*.

Rural culture Generally, the culture in remote areas, where populations are less diverse and travel distances for work opportunities and access to services or shopping are greater.

S

School detention Mandatory after-school punishment spent either in a study hall or doing some type of on-campus service.

School resource officer (SRO) Police officer assigned to provide security on a school campus.

School-to-prison pipeline The process by which students who are overly harshly disciplined (e.g., expulsion or juvenile detention) may be led to further delinquency, adult offending, and incarceration.

Secondary prevention Interventions for those identified as being at risk of offending.

Section 8 housing Federally funded voucher program that assists very low-income families, the elderly, and the disabled with rent, typically paying between 30% and 40%, though in some cases, 100% of the qualified individual's rent.

Sexting Sending sexually explicit messages or photos using text messaging.

Sexual violence Any form of violent act against others that involves sexual abuse, including sexual assault and rape.

Shaming and reintegration A form of restorative justice in which offenders may be confronted by victims and punishment. Includes public shaming, followed, in theory, by forgiveness and reintegration into the community.

Shoplifting Removal of merchandise from a store without paying for it.

Sibling abuse Physical, emotional, and/or psychological abuse of a sibling, most often committed by an older sibling against a younger one. Includes sibling incest and molestation.

Slumlord Slang term describing an absentee owner of rental property who pays little or no attention to the property's condition or tenants' concerns.

Social anxiety disorder (SAD) A common disorder in which individuals experience anxiety in, or when anticipating, social interactions; untreated individuals will do anything to avoid social situations (avoidance behavior).

Social bond (and control) theory Travis Hirschi's 1969 theory that humans are naturally prone to delinquency but that social bonds to family, community, school, etc., and acceptance of societal norms, values, and culture all prevent them from committing crimes.

Social construct A rational or irrational idea created by society, often with little basis in fact. Example: The social construct of race has no basis in biological science. See *Moral panic.*

Social disorganization theory Theory describing conditions in neighborhoods, communities, towns, cities, and rural areas where there is little civic trust or unity and no effective social control for crime, including juvenile delinquency.

Spatial autonomy The freedom of individuals, in this case children, to exercise control over where they go and with whom they interact.

Specific deterrence Crime-fighting prevention measures intended to target specific types of crime. Example: Metal bars on windows in a residential neighborhood.

Status offenses Noncriminal offenses committed by juveniles, such as violating curfews or truancy. See *Truancy.*

Statutory rape Any act of sexual intercourse with a juvenile under the age of consent (varies from 16 to 18). Charges of statutory rape can be brought even if sexual intercourse is consensual, or if both are juveniles and one is under the age of consent.

Stigma The difficult-to-change condition in which an individual experiences negative behavior or receives a stereotype or other label from a community due to a previous offense. Use of the term was popularized by sociologist Erving Goffman.

Stolen Generation (Australia) The period during the 19th to late 20th centuries when Aborigine children in Australia were forcibly removed from their homes and placed in schools or missions, with the goal of erasing their indigenous cultures. Many distinct indigenous groups live in and around Australia, each with a different language, culture, and rituals.

Strain theory Robert Merton's theory that individuals who cannot meet society's goals and expectations (e.g., education, good job), and/or society's means for reaching those goals, will find deviant or criminal ways to do so, or will reject them altogether, becoming retreatists or rebels.

Superpredator A theory, developed by political scientist John J. Dilulio, Jr., that the number of violent, chronic juvenile offenders has increased beginning in the 1980s. Subsequent research has discredited the theory. Used primarily to describe Black male urban youth, the term has become synonymous with racial bias.

Suspension School punishment for serious violation of school rules or policies that requires the student to remain off campus for a short period of time (e.g., one week), after which they can return to school.

T

Technical violation Any violation of a condition of probation or parole that, under ordinary circumstances, would not be considered a criminal act. Example: Failing to report a change of residence to a probation or parole officer.

Tertiary prevention Preventative programs to keep criminal offenders from reoffending.

Theft General term used for the crime of stealing.

Toothpaste effect (of crime) The risk that a concerted effort to reduce crime in one community or neighborhood will simply push it into another. See *Weed and Seed Program.*

Tracking Process and policies by which schools place students in classes according to their abilities, aptitudes, attitudes, and in some cases, socioeconomic status. For example, a student showing promise for attending college will be placed in the college-prep curriculum, taking the prerequisite courses for college admission. Criticisms include those that tracking fails to identify late bloomers.

Transgender youth Juveniles to young adults experiencing gender dysphoria, some of whom seek out gender reassignment therapies, including surgery and hormone therapies. See *Gender dysphoria.*

Tribal justice A separate criminal and civil legal and court system conducted by Native American and Alaskan Native agencies, intended to reduce incarceration and allow Native communities to use traditional and culturally sensitive means to settle criminal and civil matters.

Tribal Law and Order Act (2010) Signed into law by President Barack Obama, intended to target crime in Native American and Alaskan Native communities by providing more law enforcement officers on Native lands (e.g., reservations).

Truancy Failure of a juvenile to attend school under compulsory education laws. See *Status offenses.*

U

Urban violence Violence witnessed in larger cities, including gang activities, assaults, and gun violence.

V

VARK model of learning styles A learning model that identifies students as visual, audio (hearing), reading/writing, or kinetic (hands on) learners, and designs curricula to maximize the benefits to the student of those styles.

Verbal violence Any form of verbal abuse, including insults, name-calling, and yelling, that can result in psychological and emotional health issues, particularly if the abuse is consistent and ongoing.

W

Wards of the Court Condition of a minor child (or in some cases, an adult) required to have a court-named guardian who makes decisions on their behalf when the child has been removed from their home for neglect or abuse and no foster parent or suitable relative can take on the responsibility.

Waste management model (corrections) Philosophy in punishment that requires locking away offenders, in most cases in jails and prisons far from public view.

Waywardness laws A series of morality-based juvenile justice laws from the mid-1880s through the early 20th century that primarily targeted girls and women, resulting in incarceration for noncriminal offenses such as sexual promiscuity, incorrigibility, disobedience to a parent or guardian, and gender non-conformity.

Weed and Seed Program Law enforcement programs, in coordination with human service organizations, to reduce crime in high-crime neighborhoods and introduce programs to prevent and reduce crime. See *Toothpaste effect*.

White collar crimes A broad range of crimes committed by employees, such as embezzlement and fraud (including falsely reporting work hours and overtime). White collar crimes can be committed against employers or customers or clients.

White supremacy gangs Any organized hate group that advocates extreme prejudice, and often violence, against anyone perceived to be a racial or ethnic minority and/or non-Christian. As in the case of the Aryan Brotherhood, often found in prisons, some white supremacy groups in the United States and around the world are described as neo-Nazi organizations. See *Hate groups* and *Hate or bias crimes*.

Wilderness programs Juvenile programs in outdoor settings intended for non-delinquent, at-risk, and delinquent juveniles to build self-esteem, interpersonal skills, and discipline.

Wraparound programs Programs, including anger management and substance abuse rehabilitation, built into punishments (including community corrections) to which a juvenile court might sentence an offender. Often includes parent education.

TABLE OF REFERENCES

A

Abdalla, S. M., K. M. Keyes, and S. Galea (2021). "A public health approach to tackling the role of culture in shaping the gun violence epidemic in the United States." *Public Health Reports*. Vol. 136, issue 1: 6–9.

Abdullah, A. Z. (2021). "IN FOCUS: Breaking the cycle of addiction passing from parent to child." Channel NewsAsia. Jan. 13. Retrieved from https://www.channelnewsasia.com/singapore/in-focus-singapore-inter-generational-drug-abuse-636611.

Achenbach, T. M., and L. A. Rescorla (2001). *Manual for the ASEBA School-Age Forms and Profiles*. Burlington: University of Vermont, Research Center for Children, Youth and Families.

Action Against Abuse (n.d.). Global child abuse statistics. https://actionagainstabuse.wordpress.com/child-abuse-need-to-know/global-child-abuse-statistics/.

Adams, W., J. Samuels, J. B. Willison, H. Dodd, M. Dank, B. Parthasarathy, K. Mallik-Kane, J. Kelly, S. Mendonca, and K. Kim (2011). *Tribal Youth in the Federal Justice System*. Washington, DC: Urban Institute.

Addiction Center (2022). Drug and alcohol slang: General drug slang. Retrieved from https://www.addictioncenter.com/drugs/drug-alcohol-slang/.

Agnew, R. (1985). "A revised strain theory of delinquency." *Social Forces*. Vol. 64, issue 1: 151–167.

Agnew, R. (2012). "Reflection on 'A revised strain theory of delinquency.'" *Social Forces*. Vol. 91, issue 1: 33–38.

Agnew, R. S. (2012). "Strain theory and violent behavior." In *The Cambridge Handbook of Violent Behavior and Aggression*, ed. D. J. Flannery, A. T. Vazsonyi, and I. D. Waldman. Cambridge, UK: Cambridge University Press.

Ahmed, S. P., A. Bittencourt-Hewitt, and C. L. Sebastian (2015). "Neurocognitive bases of emotion regulation development in adolescence." *Developmental Cognitive Neuroscience*. Vol. 15 (Oct.): 11–25.

Ahn, S. and F. B. Norwood (2020). "Measuring food insecurity during the COVID-19 pandemic of spring 2020." *Applied Economic Perspectives and Policy*. Vol. 43, issue 1: 162–168.

Akerlof, G. A., and J. L. Yellen (1996). Report: An analysis of out-of-wedlock births in the United States. The Brookings Institute. Aug. 1. Retrieved from https://www.brookings.edu/research/an-analysis-of-out-of-wedlock-births-in-the-united-states/.

Alaska, State of (n.d.). Alaska Natives. Retrieved from https://alaska.gov/kids/learn/nativeculture.htm.

Allam, L., and L. Murphy-Oates (2021). "Australia's anguish: the indigenous kids trapped behind bars." *Guardian*. Jan. 17. Retrieved from https://www.theguardian.com/australia-news/2021/jan/18/australias-anguish-the-indigenous-kids-trapped-behind-bars.

Alonso-Tapia, J., D. M. Abello, and E. Panadero (2020). "Regulating emotions and learning motivation in higher education students." *International Journal of Emotional Education*. Vol. 12, issue 2: 73-89.

Alton, L. (2017). "Phone calls, texts, or email. Here is how millennials prefer to communicate." *Forbes*. May 11. Retrieved from https://www.forbes.com/sites/larryalton/2017/05/11/how-do-millennials-prefer-to-communicate/?sh=5e150a036d6f.

Amador, X., and A. Johanson (2000). *I Am Not Sick: I Don't Need Help!* Tallinn, EE: ViDA Press.

American Academy of Child and Adolescent Psychiatry (AACAP) (2014). "Stealing in children and adolescents." Dec., No 12. Retrieved from https://www.aacap.org/AACAP/Families_and_Youth/Facts_for_Families/FFF-Guide/Children-Who-Steal-012.aspx.

American Academy of Child and Adolescent Psychiatry (AACAP) (2019). Marijuana and teens. Oct., issue 106. Retrieved from https://www.aacap.org/AACAP/Families_and_Youth/Facts_for_Families/FFF-Guide/Marijuana-and-Teens-106.aspx.

American Academy of Pediatrics (AAP) (2012). "Firearm-related injuries affecting the pediatric population." Council on Injury, Violence, and Poison Executive Committee. *Pediatrics*. Vol. 130, issue 5: e1416–e1423.

American Academy of Pediatrics (AAP) (2021). "Protect children, reform the juvenile justice system." Report. Nov. 15. Retrieved from https://www.aap.org/en/advocacy/juvenile-justice/protect-children-reform-the-juvenile-justice-system/.

American Bar Association (2003). "Sexually violent predators: Sexual offenders." *Mental and Physical Disability Law Reporter*. Vol. 33, issue 1: 77–88.

The American Century (n.d.). Television: The ideal American family. Retrieved from https://americancentury.omeka.wlu.edu/exhibits/show/reinforcement-of-gender-roles-/television--the-ideal-american.

American Civil Liberties Union (ACLU) (2022). "Picking up the pieces: A Minneapolis case study." Retrieved from https://www.aclu.org/issues/racial-justice/race-and-criminal-justice/picking-pieces.

American Psychiatric Association (2013). *Diagnostic and Statistical Manual of Mental Disorders*, 5th ed. Arlington, VA: American Psychiatric Publishing.

American Psychological Association (2013). "Warning signs of youth violence." Retrieved from https://www.apa.org/topics/physical-abuse-violence/youth-warning-signs.

Andelic, N., T. Jerstad, S. Sigurddardottir, A. K. Schanke, L. Sandvik, and C. Roe (2010). "Effects of acute substance use and pre-injury substance abuse on traumatic brain injury severity in adults admitted to a trauma centre." *Journal of Trauma Management Outcomes*. Vol. 4: 6.

Anderson, D. M. (2014). "In school and out of trouble? Minimum dropout age and juvenile delinquency." *Review of Economics and Statistic*. Vol. 96, issue 2 (May): 318–331.

Anderson, E. (1999). *The Code of the Streets: Decency, Violence, and the Moral Life of the Inner City*. New York: W.W. Norton.

Anderson, E. R., and D. A. Hope (2008). "A review of the tripartite model for understanding the link between anxiety and depression." *Clinical Psychology Review*. Vol. 28: 275-287.

Anderson, S. H., L. S. Richmond-Rakerd, T. E. Moffitt, and A. Caspi (2021). *Psychology and Cognitive Sciences*. Vol. 113, issue 31 (July 26): e2103896118. Retrieved from https://www.pnas.org/doi/pdf/10.1073/pnas.2103896118.

Anderson, V. R., B. M. Walerych, N. A. Campbell, A. R. Barnes, William S. Davidson, C. A. Campbell, E. Onifade, and J. L. Petersen (2019). "Gender-responsive intervention for female juvenile offenders: A quasi-experimental outcome evaluation." *Feminist Criminology*. Vol. 14, issue 1: 24–44.

Annie E. Casey Foundation (2018). "Juvenile Justice Reform Act of 2018 affirms protections for young people." Dec. 22. Retrieved from https://www.aecf.org/blog/juvenile-justice-reform-act-of-2018-affirms-protections-for-young-people.

Annie E. Casey Foundation (2021). "Head Start enrollment by age group." Retrieved from https://datacenter.kidscount.org/data/tables/9786-head-start-enrollment-by-age-group?loc=1&loct=1#//any/false/any/any/any.

Annie E. Casey Foundation (2021). "Youth detention use reaches highest level in 19 months." Dec. 14. Retrieved from https://www.aecf.org/blog/youth-detention-use-reaches-highest-level-in-19-months.

Annie E. Casey Foundation (2022). "Pediatric organization calls for juvenile justice reforms." Apr. 19. Retrieved from https://www.aecf.org/blog/pediatric-organization-calls-for-juvenile-justice-reforms.

APM Reports (2019). Students on the move: The children in the fields. Aug. 14. Retrieved from https://www.apmreports.org/episode/2019/08/14/the-children-in-the-fields#:~:text=Under%20federal%20law%2C%20children%20of,relatives%20during%20short%2D-term%20harvests.

Aradillas, E. (2022). "Kidnapped at age 8 by a serial killer: She survived a monster." *People Magazine*. Vol. 97, issue 23 (June 6): 60–65.

Arain, M., M. Haque, L. Johal, P. Mathur, W. Nel, A. Rais, R. Sandhu, and S. Sharma (2013). "Maturation of the adolescent brain." *Neuropsychiatric Disorder Treatment*. Vol. 9: 449–461.

Arnett, J. (1991). "Heavy metal music and reckless behavior among adolescents." *Journal of Youth and Adolescence*. Vol. 10, issue 6 (Dec.): 573–592.

Arthur, P. J., and R. Waugh (2009). Symposium Issue: Status offenders and the Juvenile Justice and Delinquency Prevention Act: the exception that swallowed the rule. National Conference on Homeless Youth and the Law. *Seattle Journal of Social Justice.* Spring/Sum. Vol. 555. Retrieved from https://advance-lexis-com.wne.idm.oclc.org/api/document?collection=analytical-materials&id=urn:contentItem:4X48-R680-0198-G00K-00000-00&context=1516831.

Arthur, R. (2010). "Protecting the best interests of the child: A comparative analysis of the youth justice systems in Ireland, England and Scotland." *International Journal of Children's Rights.* Vol. 18: 217–231.

Ashtiani, M. (2021). "The racially disparate effects of drug arrest on high school dropout." *Socius.* Vol. 7 (July). https://doi.org/10.1177/23780231211027097.

Associated Press (2021). "Judge orders release of Wisconsin woman in Slender Man case." National Public Radio (NPR). July 1. Retrieved from https://www.npr.org/2021/07/01/1012330011/judge-orders-release-of-wisconsin-woman-in-slender-man-case.

Associated Press News (2022). "Court: '3 strikes' life sentences can count juvenile crimes." Associated Press. Feb. 7. Retrieved from https://apnews.com/hub/juvenile-crime.

Atkins, M. S., E. Cappella, E. S. Shernoff, T. G. Mehta, and E. Gustafson (2017). "Schooling and children's mental health: Realigning resources to reduce disparities and advance public health." *Annual Review of Clinical Psychology.* Vol. 13: 123–147.

Attayuki, C. (1977). "Juvenile justice system in Thailand and the United States—A limited comparison." *NCJ.* No. 72118, National Criminal Justice Reference Service. Washington, DC: U.S. Department of Justice, Office of Justice Programs.

Austin, J., K. D. Johnson, and M. Gregoriou (2000). *Juveniles in Adult Prisons and Jails.* NCJ 182503. Washington D.C.: Institute on Crime, Justice and Corrections at George Washington University and National Council on Crime and Delinquency.

Australian Institute of Aboriginal and Torres Strait Islanders Studies (n.d.). "The Stolen Generations." Government of Australia. Retrieved from https://aiatsis.gov.au/explore/stolen-generations.

B

Bacevich, A. J. (2005). "The real World War IV." *Wilson Quarterly.* Vol. 29, issue 1: 36–61.

Baghel, G., and E. A. Singer (2021). "Should physicians address firearm violence? A clinical response to a public health crisis." *Journal of Hospital Ethics.* Vol. 7, issue 3: 112–118.

Baglivio, M. T., K. T. Wolff, J. A. Reid, S. L. Jackson, and A. R. Piquero (2022). "Did juvenile domestic offending change during COVID-19?" *Youth Violence and Juvenile Justice.* Vol. 20, issue 1 (Jan.): 63–79.

Bailey, J., A. Rouchard, C. Garcia, C. Roehrig, and J-P. Ferley (2015). "Alcohol use in young adolescents. A survey in French secondary schools." *Archives of Pediatric and Adolescent Medicine.* Vol. 22, issue 5: 510–517.

Bakker, A. B., K. I. Van der Zee, K. A. Lewig, and M. F. Dollard (2006). "The relationship between the big five personality factors and burnout: A study among volunteer counselors." *Journal of Social Psychology.* Vol. 146, issue 1: 31–50.

Balderrama, V. (2021). "Justice Department to investigate five Texas juvenile correctional facilities." KRIS 6 News. Oct. 14. Retrieved from https://www.kristv.com/news/texas-news/justice-department-to-investigate-five-texas-juvenile-correctional-facilities#:~:text=These%20are%20the%20Gainesville%20State,Evins%20Regional%20Juvenile%20State%20School.

Barbu, S., G. Cabanes, and G. Maner-Idrissi (2011). "Boys and girls on the playground: Sex differences in social development are not stable across early childhood." *Plos ONE.* Vol. 6, issue 1: e16407.

Barcellos, C., and A. Zaluar (2014). "Homicides and territorial struggles in Rio de Janeiro favelas." *Revista de Sáude Pública.* Vol. 48, issue 1 (Feb.): 94–102.

Barr, S. C., R. Hanson, A. M. Begle, D. G. Kilpatrick, B. Saunders, H. Resnick, and A. Amstadter (2012). "Examining the moderating role of family cohesion on the relationship between witnessed community violence and delinquency in a national sample of adolescents." *Journal of Interpersonal Violence.* Vol. 27, issue 2 (Jan.): 239–262.

Barrington, K. (2019). "What are alternative schools and how do they impact college admissions?" *Public School Review.* Sept. 5. Retrieved from https://www.publicschoolreview.com/blog/what-are-alternative-schools-and-how-do-they-impact-college-admissions.

Bassiouni, M. C. (1977). "Citizen's arrest—the law of arrest, search, and seizure for private citizens and private police." NCJ No. 44479. Office of Justice Programs, U.S. Department of Justice. Retrieved from https://www.ojp.gov/ncjrs/virtual-library/abstracts/citizens-arrest-law-arrest-search-and-seizure-private-citizens-and.

Bastug, S. (2002). "Household and family in contemporary Turkey: An historical perspective." In *Autonomy and Dependence in the Family: Turkey and Sweden in Critical Perspective*, ed. R. Lijestrom and E. Ozdalga. London, UK: Swedish Research Institute in Istanbul.

Battaglia, M. (2015). "Separation anxiety: At the neurobiologial crossroads of adaptation and illness." *Dialogues in Clinical Neuroscience.* Vol. 17, issue 3 (Sept.): 277–285.

Baumrind, D. (1967). "Child care practices anteceding three patterns of preschool behavior." *Genetic Psychology Monographs.* Vol. 75: 43–48.

Beard, J. (2022). *Youth Custody: Research Brief.* London, ENG: House of Commons Library.

Becker, H. (1953). "Becoming a marihuana user." *American Journal of Sociology.* Vol. 59, issue 3: 235–242.

Beckett, L. (2017). "Remembering the 26: How families honor Sandy Hook victims five years later." *Guardian.* Dec. 14. Retrieved from https://www.theguardian.com/us-news/2017/dec/13/newtown-sandy-hook-shooting-victims-five-years-later.

Bell, T. M., C. Robbins, and A. Gosain (2021). "The influence of the COVID-19 pandemic on pediatric firearm injuries." *Pediatrics.* Vol. 148, issue 1 (July): e2020049746.

Bellis, M. A., J. Downing, and J. R. Ashton (2006). "Adults at 12? Trends in puberty and their public health consequences." *Journal of Epidemiological Community Health.* Vol. 60, issue 11 (Nov.): 910–911.

Belova, A. A., and E. A. Gelpey (2019). "The sports volunteer movement in Modern Russia." In *Theory of Language and Translation.* Eng. and Rus. trans.

Bender, A. K., E. Koegler, S. D. Johnson, V. Murugan, and R. Wamser-Nanney (2020). "Guns and intimate partner violence among adolescents: A scoping review." *Journal of Family Violence.* Retrieved from https://www.researchgate.net/profile/Vithya-Murugan/publication/343653440_Guns_and_Intimate_Partner_Violence_among_Adolescents_a_Scoping_Review/links/605d2352a6fdccbfea084b6d/Guns-and-Intimate-Partner-Violence-among-Adolescents-a-Scoping-Review.pdf.

Benman, K. (2021). "Another teen suicide blamed on internet blackmail." 7 News. Apr. 12. Retrieved from https://www.wwnytv.com/2021/04/12/another-teen-suicide-blamed-internet-blackmail/.

Bergsman, I. R. (1989). "The forgotten few: Juvenile female offenders." *Federal Probation.* Vol. 53, issue 1: 73–78.

Berk, R. (2019). "Accuracy and fairness for juvenile justice risk assessment." *Journal of Empirical Legal Studies.* Vol. 16, issue 1: 175–194.

Berlinger, L., and D. M. Elliot (2017). "Sexual abuse of children." In *The APSAC Handbook on Child Maltreatment*, 4th ed., ed. J. B. Klika and J. R. Conte. Thousand Oaks, CA: Sage Publications.

Berman, M. R., and M. S. Boguski (2020). "Understanding Kanye West's bipolar disorder: From a presidential bid to Satanic vaccines, could this represent a full-blown manic episode?" *Med Page Today.* July 15. Retrieved from https://www.medpagetoday.com/popmedicine/celebritydiagnosis/87581.

Berryessa, C. M., and J. Reeves (2020). "The perceptions of juvenile judges regarding adolescent development in evaluating juvenile competency." *Journal of Criminal Law and Criminology.* Vol. 110, issue 3: 551–592.

Bettencourt, A. (2022). "Grassroots organizations are just as important as seed money for innovation." United Nations Refugee Agency. Retrieved from https://www.unhcr.org/innovation/grassroots-organizations-are-just-as-important-as-seed-money-for-innovation/.

Beyer, J. L., M. Kuchibhatla, C. Looney, E. Engstrom, F. Cassidy, and K. R. R. Krishnan (2003). "Social support in elderly patients with bipolar disorder." *Bipolar Disorder.* Vol. 5: 22–27.

Bianchi, S. M., J. P. Robinson, and M. A. Milkie (2007). *Changing Rhythms of the American Family Life.* New York: Russell Sage Foundation.

Big Brothers Big Sisters of America (2013). "New Big Brothers Big Sisters Youth Outcomes Survey Report suggests mentoring has positive effects on the whole child." Apr. 24. Retrieved from https://www.bbbs.org/news-item/2013/04/new-big-brothers-big-sisters-youth-outcomes-survey-report-suggests-mentoring-has-positive-effects-on-the-whole-child/.

Big Brothers Big Sisters of America (2022). "History that spans more than a century." Retrieved from https://www.bbbs.org/history/.

Bingel, J. (2022). "3 female juveniles lead deputies on chase in stolen car, Portage County sheriff says." 19 News. Feb. 24. Retrieved from https://www.cleveland19.com/2022/02/24/3-female-juveniles-lead-deputies-chase-stolen-car-portage-county-sheriff-says/.

Bishop, D. M. (2012). "Evidence-based practice and juvenile justice." *Criminal Justice and Public Policy.* Vol. 11, issue 3: 483–492.

Black, D. W. (2016). *Ending Zero Tolerance: The Crisis of Absolute School Discipline.* New York: New York University Press.

Blad, E. (2022). "A familiar fight about how to make schools safe." *Education Week.* Vol. 41, issue 34 (June): 19.

Blazak, R. (2001). "White boys to terrorist men: Target recruitment of Nazi Skinheads." *American Behavioral Scientist.* Vol. 44, issue 6: 982–1000.

Bloch, H. A., and A. Niederhoffer (1958). *The Gang.* New York: Philosophical Library.

Boccio, C. M., and K. M. Beaver (2019). "The influence of family structure on delinquent behavior." *Youth Violence and Juvenile Justice.* Vol. 17, issue 1: 88–106.

Bock, E. M., and D. Hosser (2014). "Empathy as a predictor of recidivism among young adult offenders." *Psychology, Crime, and Law.* Vol. 20, issue 2: 101–115.

Bogert, C., and L. Hancock (2020). The media myth that demonized a generation of Black youth. The Marshall Project. Nov. 20. Retrieved from https://www.themarshallproject.org/2020/11/20/superpredator-the-media-myth-that-demonized-a-generation-of-black-youth.

Bolden-Barrett, V. (2022). "Police officer's roles in the juvenile justice system." *CHRON.* June. Retrieved from https://work.chron.com/police-officers-roles-juvenile-justice-system-24909.html.

Bond, M. (2015). Criminology: Social disorganization theory explained. LinkedIn. Mar. 1. Retrieved from https://www.linkedin.com/pulse/criminology-social-disorganization-theory-explained-mark-bond/.

Bonnie, R. J., R. L. Johnson, B. M. Chemers, and J. A. Schuck, eds. (2013). *Reforming Juvenile Justice: A Developmental Approach.* Washington, D.C.: National Academies Press. Ch. 2.

Bouchoucha, S. (n.d.). "What is compassion fatigue and how can it affect your career?" Deakin University. Retrieved from https://this.deakin.edu.au/career/what-is-compassion-fatigue-and-how-can-it-affect-your-career#:~:text=Compassion%20fatigue%20involves%20a%20gradual,at%20risk%20of%20compassion%20fatigue.

Bovsun, M. (2017). "Teenage girls brutally murder 85-year-old woman 'just for fun' in 1983." *Daily New.* Aug. 20. Retrieved from https://www.nydailynews.com/news/crime/teen-girls-brutally-murder-woman-85-fun-1983-article-1.3426680.

Bowlby, J. (1969). "Attachment and loss." In *Attachment,* vol 1. New York: Basic Books.

Boyles, R. (2016). "Belgium tops list of best juvenile justice systems." *Bulletin.* Feb. 16. Retrieved from https://www.thebulletin.be/belgium-tops-list-worlds-best-juvenile-justice-systems.

Bracha, H. S. (2004). "Freeze, flight, fight, fright, faint: Adaptationist perspectives on Acute Stress Response Spectrum." *CNS Spectrums.* Vol. 9, issue 9: 679–685.

Bradley, K. (2008). "Welfare: Juvenile delinquency and the evolution of British juvenile courts c. 1900–1950." History in Focus. Oct. Retrieved from https://archives.history.ac.uk/history-in-focus/welfare/articles/bradleyk.html.

Bradshaw, C. P., A. L. Sawyer, and L. M. O'Brennan (2009). "A social disorganization perspective on bullying-related attitudes and behaviors: The influence of school context." *American Journal of Community Psychology.* Vol. 3, issues 3–4: 204–220.

Bretherton, I. (1992). "The origins of Attachment Theory: John Bowlby and Mary Ainsworth." *Developmental Psychology.* Vol. 28, issue 5: 759–775.

Brick, B. T., T. J. Taylor, and F. Esbensen (2009). "Juvenile attitudes towards the police: The importance of subcultural involvement and community ties." *Journal of Criminal Justice.* Vol. 37: 488–495.

Brinkhof, T. (2021). "In the Soviet Union, murderers had an easier time than political dissenters." *Big Think.* Feb. 21. Retrieved from https://bigthink.com/the-past/soviet-union-criminality-marxism-justice/.

British Broadcasting Company (BBC) (2021). London teen homicides: How killing broke 2008 record. Dec. 31. Retrieved from https://www.bbc.com/news/uk-england-london-59239893.

Broden, S. (2021). "A timeline of Rutherford County's history of illegally arresting and jailing minors." *Daily News Journal.* Oct. 26. Retrieved from https://www.dnj.com/story/news/2021/10/26/timeline-rutherford-county-illegal-arrests-and-incarcerations-children/6124000001/.

Brooks, K. (2018). *Small Animals: Parenthood in the Age of Fear.* New York: Flatiron Books.

Broussard, K. (2022). Arlington mall announces curfew for minors after brawl leads to arrests. *KERA News.* Apr. 21. Retrieved from https://www.keranews.org/business-economy/2022-04-21/arlington-mall-announces-curfew-program-for-minors-after-brawl-ends-in-arrests.

Brown, E. (2010). "Race, urban governance, and crime control: creating model cities." *Law and Society Review.* Vol. 44, issues 34: 769–804.

Brown, M. (2022). "Is TikTok safe for kids?" *Parents.* Jan. 28. Retrieved from https://www.parents.com/kids/safety/internet/is-tiktok-safe-for-kids/.

Brown, T. A. (2022). "Bar admission question is illegal and harms diversity." *Bloomberg Law.* Feb. 16. Retrieved from https://news.bloomberglaw.com/us-law-week/bar-admission-question-is-illegal-and-harms-diversity.

Bryant, E. (2021). "More than 5 million children have had an incarcerated parent." Vera Organization. May 7. Retrieved from https://www.vera.org/news/more-than-5-million-children-have-had-an-incarcerated-parent.

Buchhandler-Raphael, M. (2020). "Loss of self-control, dual-process theories and provocation." *Fordham Law Review.* Vol. 88, issue 5: 1815–1874.

Bunders, D. J., and F. M. Weerman (2020). "Social media and delinquency: Exploring the relation between online and offline interaction with friends and online and offline delinquency." *Kriminologie-Das.* Vol. 2, issue 2. Retrieved from https://www.kriminologie.de/index.php/krimoj/article/view/52/61.

Burdick-Will, J., M. L. Stein, and J. Grigg (2019). "Danger on the way to school: Exposure to violent crime, public transportation, and absenteeism." *Sociological Science.* Vol. 6: 118–142.

Bureau of Consular Affairs (2022). Brazil travel advisory. U.S. Department of State. Apr. 18. Retrieved from https://travel.state.gov/content/travel/en/traveladvisories/traveladvisories/brazil-travel-advisory.html.

Bureau of Justice Assistance (BJA) (2010). City of Moreno Valley Gang Prevention Program. Office of Justice Programs, U.S. Department of Justice. Retrieved from https://bja.ojp.gov/funding/awards/2010-dd-bx-0445.

Bureau of Justice Statistics (2019). "National Survey of Youth in Custody (NSYC)." Office of Justice Programs, U.S. Department of Justice. Retrieved from https://bjs.ojp.gov/data-collection/national-survey-youth-custody-nsyc.

Bursik, R. J. (1988). "Social disorganization and theories of crime and delinquency: Problems and prospects." *Criminology.* Vol. 26, issue 4: 519–551.

Butcher, I., K. Berry, and G. Haddock (2020). "Understanding individuals' subjective experience of negative symptoms of schizophrenia: A qualitative study." *British Journal of Clinical Psychology.* Vol. 59: 319–334.

Butts, J., and J. Travis (2002). *The Rise and Fall of American Youth Violence: 1980 to 2000.* Research report. Washington, D.C.: The Urban Institute.

Butts, J. A. (2019). "Older adults responsible for total growth in drug arrests." Research and Evaluation Center, John Jay College of Criminal Justice. Nov. 11. Retrieved from https://johnjayrec.nyc/2019/11/11/databits201902/.

C

Cahan, E. D. (1989). *Past caring: A history of U.S. preschool and education for the poor, 1820–1965.* National Center for Children in Poverty, Mailman School of Public Health. New York City, NY: Columbia University.

Cairns, R. B., and B. D. Cairns (1992). "The sociogenesis of aggressive and antisocial behaviors." *Frameworks and Forecasts: Advances in Criminological Theory.* Vol. 3: 157–191.

Cairns, R. B., and B. D. Cairns (1994). *Lifelines and Risks: Pathways of Youth in Our Time.* New York: Cambridge University Press.

California Courts (2022). "Girls' Courts/CSEC Courts Overview." Retrieved from https://www.courts.ca.gov/37353.htm.

Camacho, J., and W. Brown (2018). "The evolution of the tattoo in defiance of the immutable definition of deviance: current perceptions by law enforcement of tattooed arrestees." *Deviant Behavior.* Vol. 39, issue 8: 1023–1041.

Candido de Andrade, R., F. Assumpção, I. A. Teixeira, and V. Aparecida da Silva Fonseca (2011). "*Prevalencia de transtornos psiquiatrico em jovens infratores na cidade do Rio de Janeiro, Brasil: Estudo de genero e relacao com a gravidade do delito* [Prevalence of psychiatric disorders in young offenders in the city of Rio de Janeiro (RJ, Brazil): Study of gender and relationship with the severity of the offense]." *Ciência and Saúde Coletiva.* Vol. 16, issue 4: e1678–4561.

Cantillon, D., W. S. Davidson II, and J. H. Schweitzer (2003). "Measuring community social organization: Sense of community as a mediator in social disorganization theory." *Journal of Criminal Justice.* Vol. 31, issue 4 (July-Aug.): 321–339.

Capacity Building Center for States (2020). *Congregate Care in the Age of Family First: Overview.* Washington, DC: Children's Bureau, Administration for Children and Families, U.S. Department of Health and Human Services.

Capstick (n.d.). "The 5 R's of restorative justice." The Conflict Center. Retrieved from https://conflictcenter.org/the-5-rs-of-restorative-justice/.

Caron, S. L., and E. G. Moskey (2002). "Changes over time in teenage sexual relationships: Comparing the high school class of 1950, 1975, and 2000." *Adolescence.* Vol. 37, issue 147: 515–526.

Caruso, P. (1996). "Individuality vs. conformity: The issue behind school uniforms." *National Association of Secondary School Principals (NASSP) Bulletin.* Sage Publications. Vol. 80: 83–88.

Cassidy, P., and T. Turner (2021). "The fight continues to end child marriage in the U.S." UNICEF USA. Aug. 25. Retrieved from https://www.unicefusa.org/stories/fight-continues-end-child-marriage-us/38893#:~:text=International%20conversations%20about%20child%20marriage,married%20before%20their%2018th%20birthday.

Cattani, A., S. Bonifacio, M. Ferz, J. M. Iverson, E. Zocconi, and M. C. Caselli (2010). "Communicative and linguistic development in preterm children: A longitudinal study from 12 to 24 months." *International Journal of Language and Communication Disorders.* Vol. 45: 162–173.

Cauffman, E. (2008). "Understanding the female offender." *The Future of the Children, Juvenile Justice.* Vol. 18, issue 2 (Fall): 119–142.

Cauffman, E., and K. Monahan (2015). "Pathways to persistence: Female offending from 14–15." *Journal of Developmental and Life-Course Criminology.* Vol. 1, issue 3 (Sept.): 236–268.

CBS3 Staff (2019). "Police: Woman arrested for stealing baby formula from Target, man still on the loose after tossing baby at security." CBS3 Philadelphia. Dec. 18. Retrieved from https://philadelphia.cbslocal.com/2019/12/18/police-woman-arrested-for-stealing-baby-formula-from-target-man-still-on-loose-after-tossing-baby-at-security/.

Celona, L., and D. Balsamini (2022). NYC recorded 485 murders in 2021. New York Post. Jan. 1. Retrieved from https://nypost.com/2022/01/01/nyc-recorded-485-murders-in-2021/.

Center for Court Innovation (n.d.). Building a model for the future by reimagining public safety at 17 New York housing sites across five boroughs. Retrieved from https://www.courtinnovation.org/programs/neighborhood-safety-initiatives.

Center for Research on Education Outcomes (2013). Executive Summary. *National Charter School Study.* Stanford, CA: Stanford University. Available at http://credo.stanford.edu/documents/NCSS%202013%20Executive%20Summary.pdf.

Center on Juvenile and Criminal Justice (CJCJ) (2022). "Juvenile justice history." Retrieved from https://www.cjcj.org/history-education/juvenile-justice-history.

Centers for Disease Control and Prevention (CDC) (2020). Youth and tobacco use. Dec. 16. Retrieved from https://www.cdc.gov/tobacco/data_statistics/fact_sheets/youth_data/tobacco_use/index.htm.

Centers for Disease Control and Prevention (CDC) (2021). Economic trends in tobacco. May 25. Retrieved from https://www.cdc.gov/tobacco/data_statistics/fact_sheets/economics/econ_ facts/index.htm#::text=Smoking%2Drelated%20illness%20in%20the,%24300%20billion%20each%20year%2C%20including%3A&text=More%20than%20%24225%20billion%20for,due%20to%20secondhand%20smoke%20exposure.

Centers for Disease Control and Prevention (CDC) (2022). "Fast facts: What is sexual violence?" June 22. Retrieved from https://www.cdc.gov/violenceprevention/sexualviolence/fast-fact.html.

Centers for Disease Control and Prevention (CDC) (2022). Violence prevention: Risk and protective factors. Apr. 6. Retrieved from https://www.cdc.gov/violenceprevention/childabuseandneglect/riskprotectivefactors.html.

Chaloopka, F. J., M. Grossman, and H. Saffer (2002). "The effects of price on alcohol consumption and alcohol-related problems." *Alcohol Research and Health.* Vol. 26, issue 2: 22–34.

Chamratrithirong, A., B. A. Miller, H. F. Byrnes, O. Rhucharoenpompanich, P. K. Cupp, M. J. Rosati, W. Fongkaew, K. A. Atwood, and M. Todd (2013). "Intergenerational transmission of religious beliefs and practices and the reduction of adolescent delinquency in urban Thailand." *Journal of Adolescence.* Vol. 36, No. 1: 79–89.

Chavez, J. (2017). "New UTSA study finds a link between incarcerated parents and their children's health." *UTSA Today.* University of Texas San Antonio. May 11. Retrieved from https://www.utsa.edu/today/2017/05/prisonstudy.html.

Chegwidden, M. B., and B. J. Flaherty (1977). "Aboriginal versus non-Aboriginal alcoholics in an alcohol withdrawal unit." *Medical Journal of Australia.* Vol. 1, issue 19: 699–703.

Chen, G. (2022). "Parental involvement is key to student success." *Public School Review.* May 20. Retrieved from https://www.publicschoolreview.com/blog/parental-involvement-is-key-to-student-success.

Cheng, T. (2004). "Impact of family stability on children's delinquency: An implication for family preservation." *Journal of Family Social Work.* Vol. 8, issue 1: 47–60.

Cherry, K. (2019). "What is attachment?: The importance of early emotional bonds." *Very Well Mind.* July 17. Retrieved from https://www.verywellmind.com/what-is-attachment-theory-2795337.

Chesney-Lind, M., and R. G. Shelden (2014). *Girls, Delinquency, and Juvenile Justice*, 4th ed. Oxford, UK: Wiley-Blackwell.

Children's Bureau (2019). *Mandatory Reporters of Child Abuse and Neglect.* Children's Welfare Information Gateway. Washington, D.C.: ACYF/ACF/Department of Housing and Human Services.

Childs, M. J. (1992). Labour's Apprentices: Working-Class Lads in Late Victorian and Edwardian England. Montreal, Canada: McGill-Queen's University Press.

Child Welfare Information Gateway (2019). Issue Brief: Parent education to strengthen families and prevent child maltreatment. Children's Bureau, ACYF, ACF, Department of Housing and Health Services. Feb. Retrieved from https://www.childwelfare.gov/pubpdfs/parented.pdf.

Chin, Y., and K. Patten (2021). "Shifting focus from impairment to inclusion: Expanding occupational therapy for neurodivergent students to address school environments." *American Journal of Occupational Therapy.* Vol. 75, issue 3 (May/June): 1–7.

Chopin, J., and E. Beauregard (2020). "Juvenile sexual murderers: Examination and classification of the crime-commission process." *Journal of Forensic Sciences.* Vol. 65, issue 5: 1627–1637.

Chopin, J., and E. Beauregard (2023). "The unusual case of sexual homicide against males: Comparisons and classifications." *International Journal of Offender Therapy and Comparative Criminology.* Vol. 67, issue 5 (Apr.): 499–523.

Chou, L., C. Ho, C. Chen, and W. J. Chen (2006). "Truancy and illicit drug use among adolescents surveyed via street outreach." *Addictive Behaviors.* Vol. 31: 149–154.

Christensen, J. (2022). "Middle-school fall prey to fatal fentanyl overdoses." CNN. Feb. 18. Retrieved from https://www.cnn.com/2022/02/18/health/fentanyl-fatal-overdoses-middle-schoolers/index.html.

Christiaens, J. (1991). "A history of Belgium's child protection act of 1912: The redefinition of the juvenile offender and his punishment." *European Journal of Crime, Criminal Law and Criminal Justice.* Vol. 7, issue 1: 5–21.

Chuck, E., A. Johnson, and C. Siemasko (2018). "17 killed in mass shooting at high school in Parkland, Florida." NBC News. Feb. 15. Retrieved from https://www.nbcnews.com/news/us-news/police-respond-shooting-parkland-florida-high-school-n848101.

Chui, W. H., and H. C. Chan (2016). "The gendered analysis of self-control on theft and violent delinquency: An examination of Hong Kong adolescent population." *Crime and Delinquency.* Vol. 62, issue 12: 1648–1677.

Cioban, S., A. R. Lazar, C. Bacter, and A. Hatos (2021). "Adolescent Deviance and Cyberdeviance. A systematic literature review." *Frontiers in Psychology.* Oct. 12. Retrieved from https://www.frontiersin.org/articles/10.3389/fpsyg.2021.748006/full.

City of Portland Crime Prevention Program (2017). Car theft prevention. Office of Neighborhood Involvement Crime Prevention Program. Summer. Retrieved from https://www.portlandoregon.gov/civic/article/673532.

Clark, N. (2015). Education in Kenya. World Education News and Reviews. June 2. Retrieved from https://wenr.wes.org/2015/06/education-kenya#:~:text=In%202003%2C%20the%20government%20of,for%20secondary%20education%20in%202008.

Clark, P. (2014). "Types of facilities." In *Desktop Guide to Quality Practice for Working with Youth in Confinement.* National Partnership for Juvenile Services and Office of Juvenile Justice and Delinquency Prevention (OJJDP). Retrieved from https://info.nicic.gov/dtg/node/4.

Clark, R. D., and G. Shields (1996). "Family and delinquency: The interaction between cohesion and adaptability." *Journal of Crime and Justice.* Vol. 19, Iss. 2: 67–82.

Clarke, N. (2021). "London youth crime have fallen over the last five years." *SW Londoner.* Mar. 17. Retrieved from https://www.swlondoner.co.uk/news/17032021-london-youth-crime-figures-have-fallen-over-the-last-five-years.

Classen, T. (2007). *Icepick: Icelandic Street Art.* Corte Madera, CA: Gingko Press, Inc.

Claus, R. E., S. Vidal, and M. Harmon (2017). "Racial and ethnic disparities in handling juvenile arrests." Research report, U.S. Department of Justice. Document No 250804. Washington, DC: Office of Justice Programs' National Criminal Justice Reference Service.

Clinard, M. B., and A. L. Wade (1958). "Toward the delineation of vandalism as a sub-type in juvenile delinquency." *Journal of Criminal Law, Criminology, and Police Science.* Vol. 48, issue 5: 493–499.

Clinton, H. (1996). *It Takes a Village and Other Lessons Children Teach Us.* New York: Simon and Schuster.

Clinton White House Archive (1998). President Clinton: Safe, Strong Schools for America's Children. Press release, The White House at Work. Apr. 13. Retrieved from https://clintonwhitehouse3.archives.gov/WH/Work/041398.html.

Cloward, R. A., and L. E. Ohlin (1960). *Delinquency and Opportunity: A Theory of Delinquent Gangs.* New York: Free Press.

Cohen, A. (1955). *Delinquent Boys: The Culture of the Gangs.* New York, NY: Free Press.

Cohen, A. (2017). "Youth gangs, violence, and local culture in Chiang Mai, Northern Thailand." *Journal of Contemporary Ethnography.* Vol. 47, issue 4: 484–507.

Cohen, A. K., and J. F. Short (1958). "Research in delinquent subcultures." *Journal of Social Issues.* Vol. 14, issue 3 (Aug.): 20–37.

Cohen, L. E., and M. Felson (1979). Social change and crime: A routine activity approach. *American Sociological Review.* Aug., Vol. 44, issue 4: 588–608.

Cole, J., and G. Sprang (2015). "Sex trafficking of minors in metropolitan, micropolitan, and rural communities." *Child Abuse and Neglect.* Vol. 40 (Aug.): 113–123.

Cole, P. M., S. E. Martin, and T. A. Dennis (2004). "Emotion regulation as a scientific construct: Methodological challenges and directions for child development research." *Child Development.* Vol. 75: 317–333.

Coleman, A. R. (2020). "Expunging juvenile records: Misconceptions, collateral consequences, and emerging practices." *Juvenile Justice Bulletin,* Office of Juvenile Justice and Delinquency Prevention (OJJDP). Dec. Retrieved from https://ojjdp.ojp.gov/publications/expunging-juvenile-records.pdf.

Collier, N. L., and D. P. Mears (2022). "Delinquent by the dozen: Youth from larger families engage in more delinquency—Fact or myth?" *Crime and Delinquency.* Apr. 25. Sage Journals. https://doi.org/10.1177/00111287221088036.

Collins, R. (1979). *The Credentialed Society: A Historical Sociology of Education and Stratification.* Waltham, MA: Academic Press.

Collins, R. (2005). *Interaction Ritual Chains.* Princeton Studies in Cultural Sociology. Princeton, NJ: Princeton University Press.

Collins, R. (2009). *Violence: a Micro-Sociological Theory.* Princeton, NJ: Princeton University Press.

Colorado Children's Hospital (2022). "The shame game: Is public shaming effective?" Parent Resources. Retrieved from https://www.childrenscolorado.org/conditions-and-advice/parenting/parenting-articles/public-shaming/.

Coltrain, N. (2022). "A kid playing alone doesn't mean they're neglected, new Colorado law states." *News-Tribune.* Mar. 31. Retrieved from https://www.brushnewstribune.com/2022/03/31/colorado-reasonable-independence-for-children-neglect/.

Colvin, M., and J. Pauly (1983). "A critique of criminology: Toward an integrated Structural-Marxist Theory on delinquency production." *American Journal of Sociology.* Vol. 89, issue 3: 513–551.

Comly, R., J. Fontana, and A. Shaw-Amoah (2020). *Strategies for Reducing Student Absenteeism in Philadelphia.* Philadelphia, PA: Research for Action.

Commonwealth of Massachusetts (2022). Finding and removing lead. Retrieved from https://www.mass.gov/finding-and-removing-lead.

Community Policing in Action Services (COPS) (n.d.). Supporting safe schools. Office of Justice Programs, U.S. Department of Justice. Retrieved from https://cops.usdoj.gov/supportingsafeschools.

Connor, W. D. (1970). "Juvenile delinquency in U.S.S.R.: Some quantitative and qualitative indicators." *American Sociological Review.* Vol. 35, issue 2: 283–297.

Consortium on School Research (CCSR) (2007). "Freshman year: The make-it or break-it year." Retrieved from https://www2.ed.gov/programs/slcp/2011progdirmtg/9thgrmatters.pdf.

Conway, K. P., and J. McCord (2002). "A longitudinal explanation of the relationship between co-offending with violent accomplices and violent crime." *Aggressive Behavior.* Vol. 28: 97–108.

Cook, L. (2021). NYC shootings involving children, teens skyrocket at an alarming rate, NYPD data shows. PIX 11. Oct. 12. Retrieved from https://pix11.com/news/local-news/nyc-shootings-involving-children-teens-skyrocket-at-alarming-rate-nypd-data-shows/.

Cooley, C. H. (1902). *Human Nature and the Social Order.* New York: Scribner's.

Corley, C. (2021). "Michigan shooting suspect among thousands of U.S. minors charged as adults yearly." *All Things Considered*, National Public Radio. Dec. 4. Retrieved from https://www.npr.org/2021/12/03/1061333484/michigan-school-shooter-is-1-of-thousands-of-u-s-juveniles-charged-as-adults-in-.

Costa, M., T. Barré, M. Coste, I. Yaya, C. Berenger, M. Tanti, C. Cutarella, M. Mora, P. Poloméni, M. Maynard, D. Teuma, M. Bazin, G. Maradan, P. Rou, and P. M. Carrieri (2020). "Screening and care for alcohol use disorder in France: Expectations, barriers and levers using a mixed-methods approach." *BMC Public Health.* Vol. 20, issue 358. Retrieved from https://bmcpublichealth.biomedcentral.com/articles/10.1186/s12889-020-08495-x#citeas.

Court-Appointed Special Advocates (CASA) (n.d.). "BRIDGES Program." Retrieved from https://www.casadc.org/bridges.

Cox, S. (1999). "An assessment of an alternative education program for at-risk delinquent youth." *Journal of Research in Crime and Delinquency.* Vol. 36, issue 3: 323–336.

Cox, S., W. Davidson, and T. Bynam (1995). "A meta-analytic assessment of delinquency-related outcomes of alternative education programs." *Crime and Delinquency.* Vol. 41, issue 2: 219–234.

Coyne, C. A., N. M. G. Fontaine, N. Långström, P. Lichtenstein, and B. M. D'Onofrio (2013). "Teenage childbirth and young adult criminal convictions: A quasi-experimental study of criminal outcomes for teenage mothers." *Journal of Criminal Justice.* Vol. 41, issue 5 (Sept.-Oct.): 318–323.

Crane, J. (1991). "The epidemic theory of ghettos and neighborhood effects on dropping out and teenage childbearing." *American Journal of Sociology.* Vol. 96, issue 5 (Mar.): 1226–1259.

Creamer, J., and A. Mohanty (2018). U.S. poverty rate drops to 11.8% in 2018. United States Census Bureau. Sept. 10. Retrieved from https://www.census.gov/library/stories/2019/09/poverty-rate-for-people-in-female-householder-families-lowest-on-record.html.

Crime and Justice News (2018). " 'Generational curse': Fathers in prison with their sons." *The Crime Report.* Jan. 25. Retrieved from https://thecrimereport.org/2018/01/25/generational-curse-fathers-in-prison-with-their-sons/.

Cui, M., J. A. Graber, A. Metz, C. A. Darling (2019). "Parental indulgence, self-regulation, and young adults' behavior and emotional problems." *Journal of Family Studies.* Vol. 25, issue 3: 233–249.

Cummings, E. M., and P. T. Davies (2010). *Marital Conflict and Children: An Emotional Security Perspective.* New York, NY: Guilford Press.

D

Dailey, L. F., S. W. Townsend, M. W. Dysken, and M. A. Kuskowski (2005). "Recidivism in medication-noncompliant serious juvenile offenders with bipolar disorder." *Journal of Clinical Psychiatry.* Vol. 66, issue 4 (Apr.): 477–484.

Daily Record Staff (2015). Law Digest—Maryland Court of Appeals. Regional Business News, *Daily Record.* Oct. 8. Retrieved from https://discovery-ebsco-com.wne.idm.oclc.org/c/lhmm22/viewer/html/YndoLUw1NDkxODI1NURSTUQ=.

Daoud, E., and K. Steadman (2022). "Parents warned of potentially deadly TikTok 'blackout challenge.'" 7 News. Mar. 21. Retrieved from https://7news.com.au/technology/tiktok/parents-warned-of-potentially-deadly-tiktok-blackout-challenge-c-6143424.

David Feldman Show (2022). "American Culture of Violence: Interview with Gregg Barak." Youtube.com. May 30. Retrieved from https://www.youtube.com/watch?v=nT7DpP88dqw.

Davis, C. A. (2011). *Children Who Kill: Profiles of Teen and Pre-teen Killers.* London, UK: Allison and Busby.

Deavers, K. L., and R. A. Hoppe (1992). "Overview of the rural poor in the 1980s." In *Rural Poverty in America,* ed. C. M. Duncan. New York: Auburn House.

Dedel, K. (2006). "The Problem with Juvenile Runaways." In *Juvenile Runaways,* Guide No. 37. ASU Center for Problem Oriented Policing. Retrieved from https://popcenter.asu.edu/content/juvenile-runaways-0#::text=Juveniles%20run%20away%20from%20home,foster%20care%20or%20group%20homes.&text=%C2%A7%20The%20term%20%22runaway%22%20typically,by%20a%20parent%20or%20guardian.

Deegan, S. J. (2021). "The meaning of murder: Family members in the lives of juvenile homicide offenders." *British Journal of Criminology.* Vol. 61: 85–103.

Defence for Children International—Belgium. (2017). "Country overview: Belgium." In *My Lawyer, My Rights.* National report, Child Justice Projects. Retrieved from https://lachild.eu/wp-content/uploads/2016/05/CountryOverviewBelgium.pdf.

DeJames, J. (1980). Issues in rural juvenile justice. Office of Justice Programs, U.S. Department of Justice. Retrieved from https://www.ojp.gov/ncjrs/virtual-library/abstracts/issues-rural-juvenile-justice-juvenile-justice-rural-america-p-4-15#:~:text=Rural%20areas%20lack%20social%20service,the%20rural%20juvenile%20delinquency%20problem.

De Koster, M. (2018). "Girls' journeys to juvenile court, Antwerp, 1912–1933." In *Youth and Justice in Western States, 1815–1950: From Punishment to Welfare,* ed. J. Trépanier and X. Rousseaux. Cham, CH: Palgrave/McMillian.

De La Rue, L., and D. L. Espelage (2014). "Family and abuse characteristics of gang-involved, pressured-to-join, and non-gang involved girls." *Psychology of Violence.* July: 253–265.

Del Barco, M. (2011). "L.A.'s homicide rate lowest in four decades." *Morning Edition,* National Public Radio. Jan. 6.

De León, A. (1983). *They Called Them Greasers: Anglos Attitudes toward Mexicans in Texas, 1821–1900.* Austin, TX: University of Texas Press.

DeLisi, M., M. G. Vaughn, D. A. Gentile, C. A. Anderson, and J. J. Shook (2012). "Violent video games, delinquency, and youth violence: New evidence." *Youth Violence and Juvenile Justice.* Oct. Retrieved from http://www.sabineduflo.fr/wp-content/uploads/2016/12/jeux-video-violents-et-dc3a9linquance.pdf.

DeMatthews, D. (2021). "Standardized testing amid pandemic does kids more harm than good." *Texas Perspectives.* University of Texas at Austin. Mar. 15. Retrieved from https://news.utexas.edu/2021/03/15/standardized-testing-amid-pandemic-does-kids-more-harm-than-good/#:~:-text=Negative%20consequences%20include%20the%20loss,what%20test%20scores%20actually%20mean.

Denov, M. S. (2004). "The long-term effects of child sexual abuse by female perpetrators: A qualitative study of male and female victims." *Journal of Interpersonal Violence.* Vol. 19: 1137–1156.

Department of Justice Canada (2021). "Indigenous Youth Roundtables: Overrepresentation of indigenous youth in Canada's criminal justice system." Government of Canada. July 7. Retrieved from https://www.justice.gc.ca/eng/cj-jp/yj-jj/tools-outils/iyr-trja.html.

Development Services Group, Inc. (2001). Alternative schools: Literature review. Washington, DC: U.S. Justice Department, Office of Juvenile Justice and Delinquency Prevention (OJJDP).

Development Services Group, Inc. (2021). "Restorative justice for juveniles: Literature review." *Model Programs Guide*. Office of Justice Programs, U.S. Department of Justice, Office of Juvenile Justice and Delinquency Prevention. Retrieved from https://ojjdp.ojp.gov/model-programs-guide/literature-reviews/restorative-justice-for-juveniles.

Devoe, J. (2022). "Arlington implementing new program to divert youth from criminal justice system." *ARL Now* (News). Feb. 22. Retrieved from https://www.arlnow.com/2022/02/22/arlington-implementing-new-program-to-divert-youth-from-criminal-justice-system/.

Dickens, C. (1838; 1992). *Oliver Twist*. Ware, England: Wordsworth Editions.

Dilulio, J. (1995). "The coming of the super-predators." *Weekly Standard*. Vol. 1 (Nov. 19): 23–29.

Disner, S. G., C. G. Beevers, E. A. P. Haigh, and A. T. Beck (2011). "Neural mechanisms of the cognitive model of depression." *Nature Reviews Neuroscience*. Vol. 12, issue 8: 467-477.

Ditch the Label (2019). *The Annual Bullying Survey: Annual Benchmark of Bullying in the UK*. London, UK: Ditch the Label.

Division of Juvenile Justice (n.d.). Fairbanks Youth Facility. Alaska Department of Family and Community Services, State of Alaska. Retrieved from https://dfcs.alaska.gov/djj/Pages/Facilities/fyf.aspx.

Dixon, A., and G. Farrell (2020). "Age-period-cohort effects in half century of motor vehicle theft in the United States." *Crime Science*. Vol. 9, issue 7 (Oct. 1). Open access. Retrieved from https://crimesciencejournal.biomedcentral.com/articles/10.1186/s40163-020-00126-5#citeas.

Dodaj, A., K. Sesar, and S. Jerinic (2020). "A prospective study of high-school adolescent sexting behavior and psychological distress." *Journal of Psychology*. Vol. 154: 111–128.

Dombrowski, K., D. Crawford, B. Khan, and K. Tyler (2016). "Current rural drug use in the US Midwest." *Journal of Drug Abuse*. Vol. 2, issue 3: 22.

Dorgan, B. L., J. Shenandoah, D. S. Bigfoot, E. Broderick, E. F. Brown, V. Davidson, A. Fineday, M. L. M. Fletcher, Jefferson Keel, R. Whitener, and M. J. B. Zimmerman (2014). *Attorney General's Advisory Committee on American Indian and Alaska Native Children Exposed to Violence: Ending Violence So Children Can Thrive*. Washington, D.C.: Office of Juvenile Justice and Delinquency Programs.

Dow, N. (2021). "5 tips to slash the cost of your kids' pricey extracurriculars." *Penny Hoarder*. Oct. 1. Retrieved from https://www.thepennyhoarder.com/save-money/after-school-activities/#:~:text=Huntington%20Bank%20and%20Communities%20in,%24350%20for%20high%20school%20students.

Duffin, E. D. (2021). Graph: U.S. teens (16–19) who are enrolled in school and working. Statista. Retrieved from https://www.statista.com/statistics/477668/percentage-of-youth-who-are-enrolled-in-school-and-working-in-the-us/.

Duffy, M. P. (2004). Introduction. In *Teen Gangs: A Global View*, ed. M. P. Duffy and E. Gillig. Westport, CT: Greenwood.

Duke, D., and I. Muzio (1978). "How effective are alternative schools? A review of recent evaluations and reports." *Teachers College Record*. Vol. 79: 461–483.

Duke, K. N., and K. B. Kahn (2017). "What social science research says about police violence against racial and ethnic minorities: Understanding the antecedents and consequences—An introduction." *Journal of Social Issues*. Vol. 73, issue 4: 690–700.

Duke Health (2020). "When is puberty too early?" *Duke Health Blog*. July 7. Retrieved from https://www.dukehealth.org/blog/when-puberty-too-early.

Durkheim, E. (1895). *Rules of Sociological Method*, 2d ed. Reprint 1982. Ed. S. Lukes, trans. W. D. Halls. New York: Free Press.

E

Eatough, E. M., Chang C.-H., Miloslavic S. A., Johnson R. E. (2011). "Relationships of role stressors with organizational citizenship behavior: a meta-analysis." *Journal of Applied Psychology*. Vol. 96: 619–632.

The Economist (2021). "How do America's citizen's arrest laws work?" Nov. 22. Retrieved from https://www.economist.com/news/2021/11/22/how-do-americas-citizens-arrest-laws-work.

Edwards, J. (2019). "Helicopter parenting: Control vs. support makes all the difference." *News*. University Communications, Brigham Young University. June 17. Retrieved from https://news.byu.edu/news/helicopter-parenting-control-vs-support-makes-all-difference#:~:text=Further%2C%20the%20researchers%20found%20that,delinquent%20behavior%20and%2For%20depression.

Edwards, S. (2014). "How law and education policies hurt more than help." *Chicago Policy Review*. Mar. 28. Retrieved from https://chicagopolicyreview.org/2014/03/28/consequences-of-juvenile-arrests-on-education-how-law-and-educational-policies-hurt-more-than-help/#:~:-text=Specifically%2C%20the%20study%20revealed%20that,only%2016%20percent%20of%20arrestees.

Ehrenreich, J. T., L. C. Santucci, and C. L. Weiner (2008). "Separation anxiety disorder in youth: Phenomenology, assessment, and treatment." *Psicología Conductual*. Vol. 16, issue 3 (Jan. 1): 369–412.

Ehrmann, S., N. Hyland, and C. Puzzanchera (2019). "Girls in the juvenile justice system." *Juvenile Justice Statistics: National Report Series Bulletin*. Office of Juvenile Justice and Delinquency Prevention (OJJDP), Office of Justice Programs, U.S. Department of Justice. Apr. Retrieved from https://ojjdp.ojp.gov/sites/g/files/xyckuh176/files/pubs/251486.pdf.

Elkins, F. (2019). "Animal cruelty: A serious crime leading to horrific outcomes." U.S. Department of Justice. *Dispatch*. Vol. 12, issue 3 (Apr.). Retrieved from https://cops.usdoj.gov/html/dispatch/04-019/animal_cruelty.html.

Elliott, D. S., P. R. Buckley, D. C. Gottfredson, J. D. Hawkins, and P. H. Tolan (2020). "Evidence-based juvenile justice programs and practices: A critical review." *Criminology and Public Policy*. Vol. 19, issue 4: 1305–1328.

Elliott, M. R., S. M. Reilly, J. Drummond, and N. Letourneau (2002). "The effect of different soothing interventions on infant crying and parent-infant interaction." *Infant Mental Health Journal*. Vol. 23, issue 3 (May/June): 310–328.

Elsinger, P. S., and C. Smith (2000). "Globalization and metropolitan well-being in the U.S." *Social Science Quarterly*. June: 634–644.

Emotional Intelligence Network (n.d.). Plutnik's wheel of emotions: Exploring the emotion wheel. 6 Seconds Organization. Retrieved from https://www.6seconds.org/2020/08/11/plutchik-wheel-emotions/.

Equal Justice Initiative (2022). "Report details abusive conditions in Louisiana youth facility." Mar. 17. Retrieved from https://eji.org/news/report-details-abusive-conditions-at-louisiana-youth-facility/.

Eron, L. D. (1983). "The consistency of aggressive behavior across time and situations." Paper delivered at *Consistency of Aggression and Its Correlates Over 20 Years*, Annual Meeting, American Psychological Association, Anaheim, CA.

Eron, L. D., L. O. Walder, L. R. Hussmann, M. M. Lefkowitz (1974). "The convergence of laboratory and field studies of the development of aggression." In *Determinants and Origins of Aggressive Behavior*, ed. J. deWitt and W. W. Hartup. Foxboro, MA: Moulton Publishing.

Esajian, J. D. (2022). "US cities with the highest rent." Fortune Builders, Inc. Retrieved from https://www.fortunebuilders.com/top-10-u-s-cities-with-the-highest-rents/#:~:text=in%20the%20country.-,New%20York%2C%20NY,prices%20are%20likely%20to%20follow.

Esbensen, F., D. W. Osgood, D. Peterson, T. Taylor, and D. C. Carson (2013). "Short- and long-term outcome results from a multisite evaluation of the G.R.E.A.T. Program." *Criminology and Public Policy*. Vol. 12, issue 3 (Aug.): 375–411.

Esser, M. B., H. Clayton, Z. Demissie, D. Kanny, and R. D. Brewer (2017). "Current and binge drinking among high school students—United States, 1991–2015." Centers for Disease Control and Prevention (CDC). *Morbidity and Mortality Weekly Report*, Vol. 66, issue 18 (May 12): 474–478.

Estrada, J. N., T. D. Gilbreath, R. A. Astor, and R. Benbenishty (2013). "Gang membership of California middle school students: Behaviors and attitudes as mediator of school violence." *Health Education Research*. Vol. 28, issue 4: 626–639.

EUresidence Belgium (2016). "Belgium tops list of world's best juvenile justice systems." Feb. 16. Retrieved from https://belgium.euresidence.me/residence-permit-eu/belgium-tops-list-of-worlds-best-juvenile-justice-systems/.

Evans, B. (2013). "How autism became autism: The radical transformation of a central concept of child development." *History of Human Sciences*. Vol. 26, issue 3 (July): 3–31.

F

Fagan, J., and E. Pabon (1990). "Contributions of delinquency and substance use to school dropout among inner-city youths." *Youths and Society.* Vol. 21: 306–354.

Family Vacation Design (n.d.). "10 things that will get you banned from Walt Disney World." Retrieved from https://familyvacationdesign.com/10-things-that-will-get-you-banned-from-walt-disney-world/#:~:text=Shoplifting,-The%20shops%20in&text=In%20addition%20to%20uniformed%20security,blend%20in%20with%20the%20crowd.&text=Besides%20being%20one%20of%20the,value%20of%20the%20stolen%20goods.

Farrington, D. P. (1978). "The family background of aggressive youths." In *Aggressive and Antisocial Behaviour in Childhood and Adolescence*, ed. L. Hersove, M. Berger, and D. Shaffer. Oxford, UK: Pergamon., 162

Farrington, D. P. (1986). "Age and crime." *Criminal Justice.* Vol. 1: 189–250.

Farrington, D. P. (2011). "Families and crime." In *Crime and Public Policy*, ed. J. Q. Wilson and J. Petersilia. London, UK: Oxford University Press.

Farrington, D. P., H. Gaffney, and M. M. Ttofi (2017). "Systematic reviews of explanatory risk factors for violence, offending, and delinquency." *Aggression and Violent Behavior.* Vol. 33: 24–36.

Faul, M., M. W. Dailey, D. E. Sugerman, S. M. Sasser, B. Levy, and L. J. Paulozzi (2015). "Disparity in naloxone administration by emergency medical service providers and the burden of drug overdose in US rural communities." *American Journal of Public Health.* Vol. 105 (Sup. 3): e26–e32.

Fayyad, A. (2020). "What happens when college cops patrol off campus?" *Boston Globe.* Dec. 1. Retrieved from https://www.bostonglobe.com/2020/12/01/opinion/what-happens-when-college-cops-patrol-off-campus/.

Federal Bureau of Investigation (FBI) (1999). *Columbine High School* (monograph). Washington, DC: General Accounting Offices (GAO) Publications.

Federal Bureau of Investigation (FBI) (1999). *Freedom of Information and Privacy Acts: Columbine High School.* Washington, DC: General Accounting Offices (GAO) Publications. Pt. 1.

Federal Bureau of Investigation (FBI) (2011). *National Gang Threat Assessment: Emerging Trends.* Washington, DC: General Accounting Offices (GAO) Publications.

Federal Bureau of Investigation (FBI) (n.d.). Motor vehicle theft. U.S. Department of Justice. Retrieved from https://ucr.fbi.gov/crime-in-the-u.s/2010/crime-in-the-u.s.-2010/property-crime/mvtheftmain.

Federal Grants Wire (2022). Juvenile delinquency prevention programs: Federal grants. Government Grants and Loans Index. Retrieved from https://www.federalgrantswire.com/juvenile-delinquency-prevention-programs-federal-grants.html#.Yq9z9uzMLt0.

Feitel, B., N. Margetson, J. Chamas, and C. Lipman (1992). "Psychosocial background and behavioral and emotional disorders of homeless and runaway youth." *Hospital and Community Psychiatry.* Vol. 43: 155–159.

Feld, B. C. (2018). *The Evolution of the Juvenile Court: Race, Politics, and the Criminalizing of Juvenile Justice.* New York: New York University Press.

Femme Killers: Shirley Wolf and Cindy Collier Murder Anna Brackett (2020). Video, Youtube.com. July 11. Retrieved from https://www.youtube.com/watch?v=usWPzaLC5k8.

Feriante, J., and B. Bernstein (2021). "Separation anxiety." The National Center for Biotechnology Information, National Library of Medicine, National Institute of Health. July 26. Retrieved from https://www.ncbi.nlm.nih.gov/books/NBK560793/.

Fertig, M., J. Kirby, and W. Eisner (2017). *Take That, Adolf!: The Fighting Comic Books of the Second World War.* Seattle, WA: Fantagraphics.

Feurer, C., K. M. James, C. E. Foster, and B. E. Gibb (2020). "Sustained attention and individual differences in adolescents' mood and physiological reactivity to stress." *Journal of Abnormal Child Psychology.* Vol. 48: 1325–1336.

Finkelhor, D., S. L. Hamby, D. Moore, and M. A. Straus (1997). "Sexually abused children in a national survey of parents: Methodological issues." *Child Abuse and Neglect.* Vol. 21, issue 1: 1–9.

Finkelstein, B. (2000). A crucible of contradictions: Historical roots of violence against children in the United States. History of Education Quarterly. Vol. 40, issue 1: 1–21.

Fischer, D. G. (1984). "Family size and delinquency." *Perceptual and Motor Skills*. Vol. 58, issue 2: 527–534.

Flores, R., and S. Weisfeld (2020). "Body camera videos show 6-year-old sobbing and pleading during arrest." CNN. Feb. 26. Retrieved from https://www.cnn.com/2020/02/26/us/body-camera-video-6-year-old-arrested/index.html.

Florida Legislature (2021). The 2021 Florida Statutes: Title XLVIII, Ch. 1006, § 1006.12. Retrieved from http://www.leg.state.fl.us/Statutes/index.cfm?App_mode=Display_Statute&URL=1000-1099/1006/Sections/1006.12.html.

Florida Statutes (2021). Weapons and firearms. Title XLVI, Ch 790. Tallahassee, FL: Florida Legislature.

Flynn, C., N. Van Dyke, and K. Gelb (2017). "Intergenerational offending: The case for exploring resistance." *Probation Journal*. Vol. 64, issue 2: 146–154.

Font, S. A., and H. Woo Kim (2021). "Sibling separation and placement instability for children in foster care." *Child Maltreatment*. Apr. Retrieved from https://pubmed.ncbi.nlm.nih.gov/33910412/.

Forber-Pratt, A., S. R. Aragon, and D. L. Espelage (2014). "The influence of gang presence on victimization in one middle school environment." *Psychology of Violence*. Vol. 4, issue 1: 8–20.

Forster, L. M., M. Tannhauser, and H. M. Barros (1996). "Drug use among street children in southern Brazil." *Drug and Alcohol Dependence*. Vol. 43: 57–62.

Fostering Healthy Futures (FHF) (n.d.). "Programs." Regents University of Colorado. Retrieved from https://www.fosteringhealthyfutures.org/programs.

Fox, A., and S. Veele (2020). Legislative Report: Juvenile Rehabilitation Treatment Model. Washington State Department of Children, Youth and Families. May. Retrieved from https://files.eric.ed.gov/fulltext/ED606144.pdf.

Frailberg, S., E. Adelson, and V. Shapiro (1975). "Ghosts in the nursery: A psychoanalytic approach to the problems of impaired infant-mother relationships." *Journal of American Academy of Child Psychiatry*. Vol. 14, issue 3: 387–421.

France, A. (2021) London "on track" for worst year of teenage killings, police say. *Evening Standard*. June 17. Retrieved from https://www.standard.co.uk/news/crime/london-teen-killings-track-worst-year-b941083.html.

François, A. (2008). "From street walking to the convent: Young prostitutes judged by the Juvenile Court of Brussels during World War One." In *Untold War: New Perspectives in First World War Studies*, ed. H. Jones, C. Schmidt-Supprian, and J. O'Brien. Dublin, IR: Brill.

François, A. (2018). "Juvenile delinquency in wartime and peacetime: The activity of the Belgian juvenile courts, 1912–1950." In *Youth and Justice in Western States, 1815–1950: From Punishment to Welfare*, ed. J. Trépanier and X. Rousseaux. Cham, CH: Palgrave/McMillian.

Frazier, C. E., and D. M. Bishop (1986). "The pretrial detention of juveniles and its impact on case dispositions." *Journal of Criminal Law and Criminology*. Vol. 76, issue 4: 1132–1152.

Fréchette, S., M. Zoratti, and E. Romano (2015). "What is the link between corporal punishment and child physical abuse?" *Journal of Family Violence*. Vol. 30, issue 2: 135–148.

Free, M. D. (1991). "Clarifying the relationship between the broken home and juvenile delinquency: A critique of the current literature." *Deviant Behavior*. Vol. 12, issue 2: 109–167.

Freeman, A. J., E. A. Youngstrom, E. Michalak, R. Siegel, O. I. Meyers, and R. L. Findling (2009). "Quality of life in pediatric bipolar disorder." *Pediatrics*. Vol. 123, issue 3: e446–e452.

Freeman, L., and F. Braconi (2004). "Gentrification and displacement." *Journal of American Planning Association*. Vol. 70, issue 1 (Winter): 39–52.

Friese, B., J. W. Grube, R. S. Moore, and V. K. Jennings (2012). "Parents' rules about underage drinking: A qualitative study of why parents let teens drink." *Journal of Drug Education*. Vol. 42, issue 4 (July): 379–391.

Frontline (n.d.). "Juvenile Justice: The reasons for treating juveniles differently." Public Broadcasting Service (PBS), New Mexico. Retrieved from https://www.pbs.org/wgbh/pages/frontline/shows/juvenile/bench/different.html.

Frosch, D., K. Maher, and Z. Elinson (2022). "Rural America reels from violent crime. 'People lost their ever lovin' minds.'" *Wall Street Journal*. June 10. Retrieved from https://www.wsj.com/articles/violent-crime-rural-america-homicides-pandemic-increase-11654864251.

Fyfe, J. J. (1982). Introduction. *Readings on Police Use of Deadly Force*, ed. J. J. Fyfe. Arlington, VA: Police Foundation.

G

Gallardo, M. (2021). "11-year-old boy arrested, considered a 'prolific carjacker.'" ABC 7. Nov. 29. Retrieved from https://abc7.com/11-year-old-boy-arrested-for-carjacking-grand-theft-auto-chicago-crime/11282410/.

García-Baamonde, M. E., M. Blázquez-Alonso, J. M. Moreno-Manso, E. Guerrero-Barona, and M. Guerrero-Molina (2022). "Youth serial killers: Psychological and criminological profiles." *International Journal of Environmental Research and Public Health*. Vol. 19. Retrieved from https://www.mdpi.com/1660-4601/19/9/5359.

Garcia-Gomez, A. (2017). "Teen girls and sexual agency: exploring the intrapersonal and intergroup dimensions of sexting." *Media, Culture, and Society.* Vol. 39: 391–407.

Garlock, P. D. (1979). "Wayward children and the law, 1820–1900: The genesis of the status offense jurisdiction of the juvenile court." *Georgia Law Review.* Vol. 13, issue 2: 341–447.

Gastil, B. (1971). "Homicide and a regional culture of violence." *American Sociological Review.* Jun, Vol. 36: 412–427.

Gaston, G. (2017). "Parent shaming on social media: Is it the right approach?" ABC 13. May 16. Retrieved from https://abc13.com/social-media-parents-shaming-parent/2001636/.

Ge, X., R. D. Conger, F. O. Lorenz, and R. I. Simons (1994). "Parents' stressful life events and adolescent depressed mood." *Journal of Health and Social Behavior.* Vol. 35: 28–44.

Gebo, E., and C. J. Sullivan (2014). "A statewide comparison of gang and non-gang youth in public high schools." *Youth Violence and Criminal Justice.* Vol. 12, issue 3 (July): 191–208.

Geer, P. (2008). "Justice served? The high cost of juvenile sex offender registry." *Developments in Mental Health Law.* Vol. 27, issue 2 (July): 33–52.

Gershoff, E. T., and S. A. Font (2016). "Corporal punishment in U.S. public schools: Prevalence, disparities in use, and status in state and federal policy." *Social Policy Report*, Society for Research in Child Development. Vol. 30, issue 1. ISSN: 1075-7031. Available at https://www.ncbi.nlm.nih.gov/pmc/articles/PMC5766273/.

Gershoff, E. T., and S. J. Lee, eds. (2019). *Ending the Physical Punishment of Children: A Guide for Clinicians and Practitioners.* Washington, D.C.: American Psychological Press.

Gibbens, T. C. N. (1961). *Trends in Juvenile Delinquency.* Report. Geneva, Switzerland: World Health Organization.

Gibson, J. M., J. M. MacDonald, M. Fisher, and P. J. Cook (2022). "Early life lead exposure from private well water increases juvenile delinquency risk among US teens." *Proceedings of the National Academy of Sciences of the United States* (PNAS). Jan. 31. Retrieved from https://www.pnas.org/doi/10.1073/pnas.2110694119.

Gilbert, R., A. Kemp, J. Thoburn, P. Sidebotham, L. Radford, D. Glaser, and H. L. MacMillan (2009). "Recognising and responding to child maltreatment." *The Lancet.* Vol. 373 (Jan. 10): 167–180.

Gilmore, M. (1994). *Shot in the Heart: One Family's History in Murder.* New York: Viking Press.

Godinet, M. T., and R. Stotzer (2017). "Juvenile perpetrators of race/ethnicity-based bias crimes." *Journal of Ethnicity in Criminal Justice.* Vol. 15, issue 1: 21–35.

Goffman, E. (1963). *Stigma: Notes on the Management of Spoiled Identity.* New York, NY: Simon and Schuster.

Goldstein, N. E., O. Olubadewo, R. E. Redding, and F. Lexcen (2005). "Mental health disorders: The neglected risk factor in juvenile delinquency." In *Juvenile Delinquency: Prevention Assessment and Intervention*, ed. K. Heilbrun, N. E. Goldstein, and R. E. Redding. Oxford, UK: Oxford University Press.

Goldstick, J. E., R. M. Cunningham, and P. M. Carter (2022). "Current causes of death in children and adolescents in the United States." *New England Journal of Medicine.* Vol. 386 (May): 1955–1956.

Goode, E., and N. Ben-Yehuda (1994). *Moral Panics: The Social Construction of Deviance.* Cambridge, MA: Blackwell.

Goodman, P., J. Page, and M. Phelps (2017). *Breaking the Pendulum: The Long Struggle Over Criminal Justice.* Oxford, UK: Oxford University Press.

Goodwin, D. (2019). "Anything you can do, I can do shorter: An analysis of lenient sentencing for female sex offenders in the United States." *Gender and Social Justice.* Vol. 25, issue 2 (Winter): 433–460.

Gottfredson, D. C., S. A. Gertenblith, D. A. Soulé, S. C. Womer, and S. Lu (2004). "Do after school programs reduce delinquency?" *Prevention Science*. Vol. 5, issue 4: 253–266.

Gottfredson, M. R., and T. Hirschi (1990). *A General Theory of Crime*. Stanford, CA: Stanford University Press.

Graff, N. (2019). Key findings on marriage and cohabitation in the U.S. Pew Research Center. Nov. 6. Retrieved from https://www.pewresearch.org/fact-tank/2019/11/06/key-findings-on-marriage-and-cohabitation-in-the-u-s/.

Graffiti Solutions (2021). "How much should I charge?" Retrieved from https://www.graffitisolutions.com/faq/how-much-should-i-charge.

Gramlich, J. (2017). "Hispanic dropout rate hits new low and college enrollment at new high." Pew Research Center. Sept. 29. Retrieved from https://www.pewresearch.org/fact-tank/2017/09/29/hispanic-dropout-rate-hits-new-low-college-enrollment-at-new-high/.

Grassley, Chuck, Senate Office (2015). "Alleged fraud in Juvenile Justice Grant Program fails youth." News release. Jan. 14. Retrieved from https://www.grassley.senate.gov/news / news-releases/alleged-fraud-juvenile-justice-grant-program-fails-youths.

Grasso, D. J., C. Doyle, and R. Koon (2019). "Two rapid screens for detecting probable Post-Traumatic Stress Disorder and interpersonal violence exposure: Predictable utility in a juvenile justice sample." *Child Maltreatment*. Vol. 24, issue 1: 113–120.

Gray, J. A. (1988). *The Psychology of Fear and Stress*, 2d ed. Cambridge, UK: Cambridge University Press.

Green, E. L. (2016). "Lost girls: Young women face harsher punishment in Maryland's juvenile justice system." *Baltimore Sun*. Dec. 16. Retrieved from https://www.baltimoresun.com/news/investigations/bal-juvenile-justice-gender-gap-20161216-story.html.

Greenberg, D. F. (2011). Delinquency and the age structure of society. In *Radical and Marxist Theories of Crime*, P. B. Stretesky and M. J. Lynch. Philadelphia, PA: Routledge Publishers. Pp. 189–223.

Greenblatt, A. (2013). "When it comes to guns, how young is too young?" New England Public Radio (NEPR). May 2. Retrieved from https://www.npr.org/2013/05/02/180607299/when-it-comes-to-guns-how-young-is-too-young.

Greene Foster, D. (2021). *The Turnaway Study: Ten Years, A Thousand Women, and the Consequences of Having—or Being Denied—an Abortion*. New York, NY: Simon and Schuster.

Greenwood, P. (2013). *Evidence-based Practice in Juvenile Justice: Progress, Challenges, and Opportunities*. New York: Springer Science and Business Media.

Grekul, J., and P. LaBoucane-Benson (2008). "Aboriginal gangs and their (dis)placement: Contextualizing recruitment, membership, and status." *Canadian Journal of Criminology and Criminal Justice*. 5 (Jan.): 59–82.

Griffin, J. (2017). "Is brutal treatment of young offenders fuelling crime rates in Brazil?" *Guardian*. Mar.. Retrieved from https://www.theguardian.com/global-development/2017/mar/03/brazil-crime-rates-brutal-treatment-young-offenders.

Grisso, T. (2008). "Adolescent offenders with mental disorders." *The Future of the Children, Juvenile Justice*. Vol. 18, issue 2 (Fall): 143–164.

Grover, A. R., W. G. Jennings, and R. Tewksbury (2009). "Adolescent male and female gang members' experiences with violent victimization, dating violence, and sexual assault." *American Journal of Criminal Justice*. Vol. 34: 103–115.

Guo, S. (2016). "A meta-analysis of the predictors of cyberbullying perpetration ad victimization." *Psychology in the Schools*. Vol. 53, No. 4: 432–453.

Guo, S. (2021). "Moderate effects of delinquent peer association, social control, and negative emotion on cyberbullying and delinquency." *School Psychology*. Vol. 36, issue 6: 445–454.

H

Hahn, C. K., A. M. Hahn, R. M. Simons, and S. J. Caraway (2021). "Women's perceived likelihood to engage in sexual risk taking: Posttraumatic stress symptoms and poor behavioral regulation." *Journal of Interpersonal Violence*. Vol. 36: 11–12.

Hahn, L. (2012). "Juvenile justice and piracy: Prosecutions of juvenile pirates in the United States." *George Mason Law Review*. Vol. 20, issue 1 (2012–2013): 241–274.

Hamilton, A. (1929). *Industrial Poisons in the United States*. New York: Macmillan.

Hammer, H., D. Finkelhor, and A. J. Sedlak (2002). *National Incidence Studies of Missing, Abducted, Runaway, and Throwaway Children: Runaway/Throwaway Children: National Estimates and Characteristics.* Office of Juvenile Justice and Delinquency Prevention (OJJDP). Oct. Washington, D.C.: U.S. Department of Justice.

Hampton, M. D. (2020). "CSEY service provider perceptions of critical needs for effective care as youth transition from juvenile detention to the community." *Child Abuse and Neglect.* Vol. 100: e104084.

Hansen, L. L. (2005). "Girl 'Crew' Members Doing Gender, Boy 'Crew' Members Doing Violence: An Ethnographic and Network Analysis of Maria Hinojosa's New York Gangs." *Western Criminology Review.* Vol. 6, issue 1: 134–144. Retrieved from http://www.westerncriminology.org/documents/WCR/v06n1/article_pdfs/hansen.pdf.

Hansen, L. L. (2011). " 'Baby Steps': Educating educators on the risks of gang recruitment." Paper delivered at Annual Conference, American Society of Criminology. Nov., Chicago, IL.

Hansen, L. L. (2011). Recognizing the signs of gang recruitment. Workshop, Western New England College, June 11.

Hansen, L. L. (2013). *Survey Report, First Wave: South Holyoke Safe Neighborhood Initiative, Fall 2012.* Holyoke, MA: Holyoke Safe Neighborhood Initiative.

Hansen, L. L. (2014). *Survey Report, Residents and Agencies—2012–2013, South Holyoke Safe Neighborhood Initiative, Fall 2012.* Holyoke, MA: Holyoke Safe Neighborhood Initiative.

Hansen, L. L., and M. E. Freitag. (2016). " 'Come on now, I want to see blood!': Choreographed violence in gang initiation rites." In *Global Perspectives on Youth Behavior, Violence, and Weapons Use*, ed. S. Harding and M. Palasinki. UK: IGI Global.

Hansen, L. L., and M. Morin (2012). Survey report, first wave, South Holyoke Safe Neighborhood Initiative. SHSNI. Fall.

Hansen, L. L., M. Simpson, and M. Morin (2013). Survey report, Residents and Agencies, South Holyoke Safe Neighborhood Initiative. SHSNI. Fall.

Hansen, L. P. (2020). *White Collar and Corporate Crime: A Case Study Approach.* Philadelphia, PA: Aspen Publishing

Hansen, L. P. (2023). *Introduction to Penology and Corrections.* Springfield, MO: Aspen Publishing.

Hanson, E. J., and K. Finklea (2022). Juvenile Justice Funding Trends. Congressional Research Service. Mar. 31. Retrieved from https://sgp.fas.org/crs/misc/R44879.pdf.

Hanson, M. (2022). "College enrollment demographic." Education Data Initiative. Apr. 22. Retrieved from https://educationdata.org/college-enrollment-statistics#:~:text=The%20average%20age%20for%20students,college%20students%20are%20under%2018.

Hao, L. X., and G. H. Xie (2002). "The complexity and endogeneity of family structure in explaining children's misbehavior." *Social Science Research.* Vol. 31, issue 1: 1–28.

Harcourt, B. E., and J. Ludwig (2005). "Broken windows: New evidence from New York City and a five-city social experiment." Public Law and Legal Theory Working Paper No. 93. *University of Chicago Law Review.* Vol. 73. The Law School, University of Chicago. Retrieved from http://www.law.uchicago.edu/academics/publiclaw/index.html.

Harden, A. N. (2012). "Rethinking the shame: The intersection of shaming punishments and American Juvenile Justice." *Journal of Juvenile Law and Policy.* Vol. 16 (Winter): 93–153.

Harry, B. (2021). "Juveniles in Morgan County vandalism case found in stolen SUV in Prattville." ABC WAAY 31. Dec. 1. Retrieved from https://www.waaytv.com/news/juveniles-in-morgan-county-church-vandalism-case-found-in-stolen-suv-in-prattville/article_d55bebce-7d76-5bae-a149-3b56db8e1b77.html.

Hart, S. N., M. R. Brassard, N. J. Binggeli, and H. A. Davidson (2002). "Psychological maltreatment." In *The APSAC Handbook on Child Maltreatment*, ed. J. E. B. Myers, L. Berliner, J. Briere, C. T. Hendrix, C. Jenny, and T. A. Reid. Thousand Oaks, CA: Sage Publications, Inc.

Hartinger-Saunders, R. M. (2008). "The history of defining youth: Current implications for identifying and treating delinquent youth." *New York Sociologist.* Vol. 3: 87–106.

Hartshorn, K. J. S., L. B. Whitbeck, and P. Prentice (2015). "Substance use disorder, comorbidity, and arrest among indigenous adolescents." *Crime and Delinquency.* Vol. 61, issue 10: 1311–1332.

Havighhurst, R. J., P. H. Bowman, G. P. Liddle, C. V. Matthews, and J. V. Pierce (1962). *Growing Up in River City.* New York: Wiley.

Hawes, A. (2014). Housing policies contributing to juvenile delinquency. Lexington Fair Housing. Dec. 29. Retrieved from https://lexingtonfairhousing.com/wp/wp-content/uploads/2015/03/Housing-Policies-Contributing-to-Juvenile-Delinquency.pdf.

Hawk, J. (2021). "New trial for Petric? Anti-video game activist wants second chance for Brighton man who shot his parents." *Chronicle.* Nov. 13. Retrieved from https://chroniclet.com/news/281679/new-trial-for-petric-anti-video-game-activist-wants-second-chance-for-brighton-man-who-shot-parents/.

Hawke, A. (n.d.). "Chances of going pro: What is the likelihood of your child making it to the big leagues?" *League Side.* Retrieved from https://leagueside.com/chances-of-going-pro/#:~:text=Take%20football%20for%20instance%2C%20only,will%20make%20it%20to%20NFL.

Hayward, R. A., and L. Honegger (2014). "Gender differences in juvenile gang members: An exploratory study." *Journal of Evidence-Based Social Work.* Vol. 11: 373–382.

He, E., Y. Hongtao, and X. Zhou (2022). "The influence of modernity on juvenile delinquency." *Advances in Social Science, Education and Humanities Research.* Vol. 664: 270–274.

Healthline Newsletter (n.d.). "CBD vs. THC: What's the difference?" Retrieved from https://www.healthline.com/health/cbd-vs-thc#medical-benefits.

Healy, J. (2021). "Behind the charges faced by the parents of the Michigan shooting suspect." *New York Times.* Dec. 4. Retrieved from https://www.nytimes.com/2021/12/03/us/crumbley-parents-charged-michigan-shooting.html.

Hedden, S. L., J. Kennet, R. Lipari, G. Medley, P. Tice, E. A. P. Coppello, and L. A. Kroutil (2015). *Behavioral Health Trends in the United States: Results from the 2014 National Survey on Drug Use and Health.* Washington, D.C.: Substance Abuse and Mental Health Services Administration.

Heide, K. M. (2020). "Juvenile homicide offenders look back 35 years later: Reasons they were involved in murder." *International Journal of Environmental Research and Public Health.* Vol. 17, issue 11 (June): 3932.

Heitgerd, J. L., and R. J. Bursik (1987). "Extracommunity dynamics and the ecology of delinquency." *American Journal of Sociology.* Vol. 92, issue 4 (Jan.): 775–787.

Helgott, J. (2020). *Copycat Crime: How Media, Technology and Digital Culture Inspire Criminal Behavior and Violence.* Westport, CT: Praeger.

Hemez, P. (2020). Distributions of age at first marriage, 1960–2018. Family Profile. No. 9. National Center for Family and Marriage, Bowling Green University. Retrieved from https://www.bgsu.edu/ncfmr/resources/data/family-profiles/hemez-distribution-age-first-marriage-fp-20-09.html#:~:text=In%201960%2C%20men's%20median%20age,FP%2D19%2D06).

Hemez, P., and C. Washington (2021). Percentage and number of children living with two parents has dropped since 1968. United States Census Bureau. Apr. 12. Retrieved from https://www.census.gov/library/stories/2021/04/number-of-children-living-only-with-their-mothers-has-doubled-in-past-50-years.html.

Hemminki, E., M. Merikukka, M. Gissler, K. Wahlbeck, J. Savolainen, T. Ristikari, and M. Aaltonen (2016). "Antidepressant use and violent crimes among young people: A longitudinal examination of the Finnish 1987 birth cohort." *Journal of Epidemiology and Community Health.* Vol. 71, issue 1: 12–18.

Hendriks, J., and C. C. Bijleveld (2004). "Juvenile sexual delinquents: contrasting child abusers with peer abusers." *Criminal Behavior and Mental Health.* Vol. 14: 238–250.

Henry, M., and M. Watkins (2020). *Preventing Minority Youth Violence: Lessons from Law Enforcement—Public Health Collaborations.* New York: Center for Court Innovation.

Hermawati, T., R. Setyaningsih, and R. P. Nugraha (2021). "Teen motivation to create fake identity account on Instagram social media." *International Journal of Multicultural and Multireligious Understanding.* Vol. 8, issue 4: 87–98.

Hernandez, A. (1998). *Peace in the Streets: Breaking the Cycle of Gang Violence.* Washington, D.C.: Child Welfare League of America.

Hernandez, K. A. (2018). "At least 30 Colorado school districts allow teachers to carry guns, but no statewide training standards regulate them." *Denver Post.* July 8. Retrieved from https://www.denverpost.com/2018/07/08/colorado-teacher-guns-schools-classroom/.

Herniter, M. (2020). "Location, location, location: An analysis of arson risk factors in Pennsylvania cities." *TCNJ Journal of Student Scholarship.* Vol. 22: 1–5.

Herrnstein, R., and C. Murray (1994). *The Bell Curve: Intelligence and Class Structure in American Life.* New York: Free Press.

Herrnstein, R., and C. Murray (2009). "The link between cognitive ability and criminal behavior." In *Key Readings in Criminology*, ed. T. Newburn. Portland, OR: Willan Publishing.

HG Legal Resources (n.d.). "Juvenile criminal conduct—At what age are they not liable?" Retrieved from https://www.hg.org/legal-articles/juvenile-criminal-conduct-at-what-age-are-they-not-liable-49366.

HG Legal Resources (n.d.). "Laws regarding carrying knives." Retrieved from https://www.hg.org/legal-articles/laws-regarding-carrying-knives-31129.

HG Legal Resources (n.d.). "The difference between juvenile and adult arrests." Retrieved from https://www.hg.org/legal-articles/the-difference-between-juvenile-and-adult-arrests-27689.

Hickle, K. E., and D. E. Roe-Sepowitz (2010). "Female juvenile arsonists: An exploratory look at characteristics and solo and group arson offences." *Legal and Criminological Psychology*, British Psychological Society. Vol. 15, issue 2: 385–399.

Higgins, G. E., S. E. Scott, and C. D. Marcum (2008). "Digital piracy: An examination of three measurements of self-control." *Deviant Behavior.* July: 440–460.

Higgins, G. E., G. F. Vito, and W. F. Walsh (2008). "Searches: an understudied area of racial profiling." *Journal of Ethnicity in Criminal Justice.* Vol. 6, issue 1: 23–39.

Hill, K. G., C. Lui, and J. D. Hawkins (2001). "Early precursors of gang membership: A study of Seattle youth." *Office of Juvenile Justice and Delinquency Prevention (OJJDP) Bulletin.* Dec.: 1–5.

Hill, K. G., J. A. Bailey, and C. M. Steeger (2020). "Outcomes of childhood preventive interventions across two generations: A nonrandomized controlled trial." *Journal of the American Medical Association Pediatrics.* Vol. 174, issue 8: 764–771.

Hinduja, S., and Patchin, J. W. (2010). "Bullying, cyberbullying, and suicide." *Archives of Suicide Research.* Vol. 14: 206–221.

Hinton, S. E. (1967; 2006). *The Outsiders.* New York City, NY: Viking Press.

Hirschi, T. (1969). *Causes of Delinquency.* Berkeley: University of California Press.

Ho, L., Y. Lin, and C. Huang (2012). "Influences of Online Lifestyle on Juvenile Cybercrime Behaviors in Taiwan." 2012 International Workshop on Information and Electronics Engineering (IWIEE). *Procedia Engineering.* Vol. 29: 2545–2550.

Hobson, K. (2021). "Higher education is proven to help people in prison. New Pell grants aim to boost enrollment." *PBS News Hour.* Aug. 25. Retrieved from https://www.pbs.org/newshour/nation/higher-education-is-proven-to-help-people-in-prison-new-pell-grants-aim-to-boost-enrollment#:~:text=About%2037%20percent%20of%20people,incarcerated %20lack%20post%2Dsecondary%20education.

Hockensmith, C. (2003). "Improving juvenile delinquency through faith-based services." NCJ No. 202186. Office of Justice Programs, U.S. Department of Justice. Retrieved from https://www.ojp.gov/ncjrs/virtual-library/abstracts/improving-juvenile-delinquency-through-faith-based-services.

Hodge, S. A., and A. Lundeen (2013). "America has become a nation of dual-income working couples." Tax Foundation. Nov. 21. Retrieved from https://taxfoundation.org/america-has-become-nation-dual-income-working-couples/.

Hodgkinson, S., L. Godoy, L. S. Beers, and A. Lewin (2017). "Improving mental health access for low-income children and families in primary care setting." *Pediatrics.* Vol. 139, issue 1 (Jan.): e20151175.

Hoeben, E. M., R. C. Meldrum, and J. T. Young (2016). "The role of peer delinquency and unstructured socializing in explaining delinquency and substance use: A state-of-the-art review." *Journal of Criminal Justice.* Vol. 47: 108–122.

Hoeboer, C., C. de Roosm, G. E. van Son, P. Spinhoven, and B. Elzinga (2021). "The effect of parental abuse on the severity of PTSD in children and adolescents." *Child Abuse and Neglect.* Vol. 111: e104775.

Hoeve, M., J. S. Dubas, V. I. Eichelsheim, P. H. van der Laan, W. Smeenk, and J. R. M. Gerris (2009). "The relationship between parenting and delinquency: A meta-analysis." *Journal of Abnormal Child Psychology.* Vol. 37, issue 6 (Aug.): 749–775.

Holla, K. (2020). "Sexting types and motives detected among Slovak adolescents." *European Journal of Mental Health.* Vol. 15, issue 2: 75–92.

Holman, B., and J. Zeidenberg (2006). "The Dangers of Detention: The Impact of Incarcerating Youth in Detention and Other Secure Facilities." Report. Justice Policy Institute. Nov. 28. Retrieved from https://justicepolicy.org/wp-content/uploads/2022/02/06-11_rep_dangersofdetention_jj.pdf.

Holt, D. J., D. Ongur, C. I. Wright, B. Dickerson, and S. L. Rauch (2008). "Neuroanatomical systems relevant to neuropsychiatric disorders." In *Massachusetts General Hospital Comprehensive Clinical Psychiatry*, ed. T. Stern, M. Fava, T. Wilens, and J. Rosenbaum. Amsterdam, NL: Elsevier.

Holt, T. J., A. M. Bossler, and D. C. May (2012). "Low self-control, deviant peer associations, and juvenile cyberdeviance." *American Journal of Criminal Justice.* Vol. 37: 378–395.

Holzer, K. J., S. Oh, C. P. Salas-Wright, M. G. Vaughn, and J. Landess (2017). "Gender differences in trends and correlates of major episodes among juvenile offenders in the United States." *Comprehensive Psychiatry.* Vol. 80: 72–80.

Home Box Office (HBO) Documentaries (2010). *Homeless: The Motel Kids of Orange County.* July 26 (release date).

Hong, H., Y. Han, and D. H. Lee (2020). "Unselfish motives and deviance: An empirical examination of social concern theory among South Korean adolescents." *Deviant Behavior.* Vol. 41, issue 6: 705–717.

Howard, J., J. N. Copeland, E. J. Gifford, J. Lawson, Y. Bai, N. Heilbron, and G. Maslow (2021). "Brief report: Classifying rates of students with autism and intellectual disability in North Carolina: Roles of race and economic disadvantage." *Journal of Autism and Developmental Disorders.* Vol. 51, issue 1 (Jan.): 307–314.

Howell, J. (2022). "8 juveniles arrested after various carjackings, motor vehicle thefts over two day span." ABC. Feb. 23. Retrieved from https://www.hoiabc.com/2022/02/23/8-juveniles-arrested-after-various-carjacking-motor-vehicle-thefts-over-two-day-span/.

Howell, J. C. (1997). Youth gangs. Office of Juvenile Justice and Delinquency Prevention Fact Sheet. Office of Juvenile Justice and Delinquency Prevention (OJJDP), Office of Justice Programs, U.S. Department of Justice. FS-72.

Howell, J. C. (2015). *The History of Gangs in the United States: Their Origins and Transformations.* Lanham, Maryland: Lexington Books.

Hsu, C. (2010). *Humanitarian Criminology: Theory of Control and Restorative Justice.* Taipei, Taiwan: San Ming Book Inc., Ltd.

Hswen, Y. (2022). "Online hate: The new virus." *American Journal of Public Health.* Vol. 112, issue 4 (Apr.): 545–547.

Huang, J. (2007). "Labor force participation and juvenile delinquency in Taiwan: A time series analysis." *Journal of Family Economic Issues.* Vol. 28: 137–150.

Huff, R. C. (1998). "Comparing the criminal behavior of youth gangs and at-risk youth." Research brief. Department of Justice. Washington, D.C., NCJ-172852.

Hughes, L. A., E. V. Botchkovar, O. Antonaccio, and A. Timmer (2022). "Schools, subculture values, and the risk of youth violence: The influence of the code of the street among students in three U.S. cities." *Journal of Youth and Adolescence.* Vol. 51, issue 2 (Feb.): 244–260.

Huijsmans, T., V. I. Eichelsheim, F. Weerman, S. J. T. Branje, and W. Meeus (2018). "The role of siblings in adolescent delinquency next to parents, school and peers: Do gender and age matter?" Vol. 5: 220–242. Retrieved from https://link.springer.com/article/10.1007/s40865-018-0094-9.

Human Rights Campaign (n.d.). Glossary of terms (LGBTQ+). Retrieved from https://www.hrc.org/resources/glossary-of-terms?utm_source=GS&utm_medium=AD&utm_campaign=BPI-HRC-Grant&utm_content=454854043833&utm_term=lgbt%20community&gclid=Cj0KCQjwspKUBhCvARIsAB2IYuvVJQHa1mDmfGypongY3GbTReOH6f7akB6mBCC5e-SIOUO9nhwddbmgaAoOJEALw_wcB.

Human Rights Watch (2013). Raised on the registry: The irreparable harm of placing children on sex offender registries. Retrieved from https://www.hrw.org/sites/default/files/reports/us0513_ForUpload_1.pdf.

Hunt, J., and A. C. Moodie-Mills (2012). The unfair criminalization of gay and transgender youth: An overview of the experiences of LGBT youth in the juvenile justice system. Center for American Progress. June 29. Retrieved from https://cdn.americanprogress.org/wp-content/uploads/issues/2012/06/pdf/juvenile_justice.pdf?_ga=2.85069977.1611758930.1652814129-1108310842.1652814128.

Hussong, A. M., D. J. Jones, G. L. Stein, D. H. Baucom, and S. Boeding (2011). "An internalizing pathway to alcohol use and disorder." *Psychology of Addictive Behaviors*. Vol. 25, issue 3: 390–404.

Hutchinson, A. J., P. O'Leary, J. Squire, and K. Hope (2014). "Child protection in Islamic Contexts: Identifying appropriate mechanisms and processes using a roundtable methodology." *Child Abuse Review*. Vol. 24, issue 6: 395–408.

Huzar, T. (2021). "How and why are the poorest people most likely to have exposure to toxins?" *Medical News Today*. Aug. 12. Retrieved from https://www.medicalnewstoday.com/articles/how-and-why-are-the-poorest-people-most-likely-to-have-exposure-to-toxins#::text=Research%20suggests%20that%20people%20with,Structural%20racism%20exacerbates%20these%20issues.&text=The%20degradation%20of%20the%20environment,direct%20effect%20on%20human%20health.

Hyland, S., L. Langton, and E. Davis (2015). "Police Use of Nonfatal Force, 2002–2011." Washington, DC: U.S. Department of Justice, Office of Justice Programs, Bureau of Justice Statistics.

I

IDENTIV (2021). "What are RFID tags and how are they used?" Feb. 12. Retrieved from https://www.identiv.com/community/2021/02/12/what-are-rfid-tags-and-how-are-they-used/.

Igielnik, R. (2017). "Rural and urban gun owners have different experience, views on gun policy." PEW Research Center. July 10. Retrieved from https://www.pewresearch.org/fact-tank/2017/07/10/rural-and-urban-gun-owners-have-different-experiences-views-on-gun-policy/.

Independent (2016). "Dangerous neighborhoods." Nov. 15. Retrieved from https://www.independent.co.uk/travel/news-and-advice/world-s-most-dangerous-cities-countries-neighbourhoods-mexico-colombia-brazil-naples-johannesburg-a7418186.html.

Ingersoll, S., and D. LeBoeuf (1997). *Reaching Out to Youth Out of the Education Mainstream*. Office of Justice Programs, Office of Juvenile Justice and Delinquency Prevention (OJJDP). Washington, DC: U.S. Department of Justice.

Ingram, T. (2021). "Juveniles linked to recent Morgan County church vandalism, arrested after chase in stolen vehicle in Prattville." CBS 42. Nov. 10. Retrieved from https://www.cbs42.com/news/crime/juveniles-linked-to-recent-morgan-county-church-vandalism-arrested-after-chase-in-stolen-vehicle-in-central-alabama/.

International Center for Research on Women (2006). "Child marriage and domestic violence." Retrieved from https://www.icrw.org/files/images/Child-Marriage-Fact-Sheet-Domestic-Violence.pdf.

Interstate Commission for Juveniles (2021). *Juvenile Sex Offender Matrix*. Dec. 3. Retrieved from https://www.juvenilecompact.org/resources/state-sex-offender-matrix.

Interstate Commission for Juveniles (2022). "Age matrix." Jan. 20. Retrieved from https://www.juvenilecompact.org/age-matrix.

Ismail, L. (2021). Pastor preaches systematic change following revelations in scathing Rutherford Co. report. News Channel 5, Nashville, TN. Oct. 21. Retrieved from https://www.newschannel5.com/news/pastor-calls-for-systemic-change-following-revelations-in-scathing-rutherford-co-report.

J

Jackson, A. (2022). "The pandemic exacerbated mental health issues among incarcerated youth. How can we reverse the trend?" Urban Institute. Feb. 21. Retrieved from https://www.urban.org/urban-wire/pandemic-exacerbated-mental-health-issues-among-incarcerated-youth-how-can-we-reverse-trend#:~:text=Research%20suggests%20as%20many%20as,exacerbate%20existing%20mental%20health%20problems.

Jantz, G. L. (2014). "Brain differences between the genders." *Psychology Today*. Feb. 27. Retrieved from https://www.psychologytoday.com/us/blog/hope-relationships/201402/brain-differences-between-genders.

Jeanis, M. N., B. H. Fox, and C. Muniz (2019). "Revitalizing profiles of runaways: A latent class analysis of delinquent runaway youth." *Child and Adolescent Social Work Journal*. Vol. 36, issue 2 (Apr.): 171–187.

Jeanne, G., D. Purper-Ouakil, H. Rigole, and N. Franc (2017). "New patterns of substance use and abuse among adolescents: A knowledge synthesis." *Encephale.* Vol. 43, issue 4 (Aug.): 346–353.

Jensen, L. (2017). "Bad neighborhood." *Thought Catalog.* July 13. Retrieved from https://thought-catalog.com/lorenzo-jensen-iii/2017/07/25-signs-that-youre-in-a-bad-neighborhood/.

Joe, K. A., and M. Chesney-Lind (1995). " 'Just every mother's angel': An analysis of gender and ethnic variations in youth gang membership." *Gender and Society.* Vol. 9, issue 4: 408–431.

Johansen, B. E. (2021). "Environmental toxicology and mental health." In *Salem Press Encyclopedia of Health.* New York: Salem Press.

Johnson, L. D. (2018). "Juvenile sex offenders: Should they go to school with your children or should we create a pedophile academy?" *University of Toledo Law Review.* Vol. 50: 39–66.

Johnson, S. (2021). "Suicide still treated as a crime in at least 20 countries, report finds." *The Guardian.* Sept. 9. Retrieved from https://www.theguardian.com/global-development/2021/sep/09/suicide-still-treated-as-a-in-at-least-20-countries-report-finds.

Jones, A. (2022). "Juvenile escapes Acadiana Center for Youth custody during transport to hospital." KLFY News. June 13. Retrieved from https://www.klfy.com/louisiana/juvenile-escapes-acadiana-center-for-youth-custody-during-transport-to-hospital/.

Jones, A., D. Wallis, and A. Seibers (2020). "Gender-responsive practice and pregnant girls: A scoping review of America's girls courts." *Children and Youth Services Review.* Vol. 118 (Nov.): e105426.

Jones, R. M., M. Van den Bree, M. Ferriter, and P J. Taylor (2010). "Childhood risk factors for offending before first psychiatric admission for people with schizophrenia: A case-control study of high security hospital admissions." *Behavioral Science and the Law.* Vol. 28: 351–365.

Jorgensen, C. C. (1973). "IQ tests and their educational supporters." *Journal of Social Issues.* Vol. 29, issue 1 (Mar.): 33–40.

Jovanovic, D., M. Novakovic, A. Salamadic, N. Petrovic, and S. Maric (2012). "Analysis of the relationship between intelligence and criminal behavior." *Journal of Health Sciences.* Vol. 2, issue 3: 224–231.

Judge, C. (2015). "Thrown away for being gay: The abandonment of LGBT youth and their lack of legal recourse." *Indian Journal of Law and Social Equality.* Vol. 3, issue 2, Article 5 (Spring): 260–280.

Justice Policy Institute (JPI) (2020). *Sticker Shock 2020: The Cost of Youth Incarceration.* July. Retrieved from https://www.justicepolicy.org/uploads/justicepolicy/documents/Sticker_Shock_2020.pdf.

Justice with Children (2021). "Preparatory Meeting Report Thailand." 2021 World Congress on Justice with Children. May 12–14. Retrieved from https://justicewithchildren.org/wp-content/uploads/2021/11/Thailand-Preparatory-Meeting-Report-for-WCJWC-.pdf.

Juvenile Delinquency Act (1961). *CQ Almanac 1961.* 17th ed. Washington, DC: Congressional Quarterly. Pp 204-206.

Juvenile Justice Information Exchange (2022). Youth gun violence section. Resource Hub. Retrieved from https://jjie.org/hub/youth-gun-violence/.

K

Kaestle, C. F. (1978). "Social change, discipline, and the common school in early nineteenth-century." *Journal of Interdisciplinary History.* Summer. Vol. 9, issue 1: 1–17.

Kahn, L., S. A. Kinchen, B. I. Williams, J. G. Ross, R. Lowry, C. V. Hill, J. A. Grunbaum, P. S. Blumson, J. O. Collins, and L. J. Kolbe (1998). "Youth risk behavior surveillance—United States, 1997." *Morbidity and Mortality Weekly Report CDC Surveillance Summaries.* Vol. 47, issue 3: 1–89.

Kahn, R. E., E. Ermer, P. Salovey, and K. A. Kiehl (2016). "Emotional intelligence and callous-unemotional traits in incarcerated adolescents." *Child Psychiatry and Human Development.* Vol. 47: 903–918.

Karaian, L. (2012). "Lolita speaks: 'Sexting,' teenage girls and the law." *Crime, Media, Culture.* Vol. 8: 57–73.

Katz, C. M., V. J. Webb, K. Fox, and J. N. Shaffer (2011). "Understanding the relationship between violent victimization and gang membership." *Journal of Criminal Justice.* (Jan.–Feb.): 48–59.

Katz, L. F., and S. M. Low (2004). "Marital violence, co-parenting, and family-level processes to children's adjustment." *Journal of Family Psychology.* Vol. 18, issue 2 (June): 372–382.

Katz, M. B. (2007). "Why aren't U.S. cities burning?" *Dissent.* Vol. 54, issue 3: 23–29.

Katz, R. C., and J. Marquette (1996). "Psychosocial characteristics of young violent offenders: A comparative study." Criminal Behaviour and Mental Health. Vol. 6, issue 4: 339–348.

Kaur, A., S. Z. Kailash, K. Sureshkumar, C. Sivabackiya, and N. Rumaisa (2022). "Gender differences in emotional regulation capacity among the general population." *IAIM.* Vol. 9, issue 1: 22–28.

Kazemian, L. (2021). *Pathways to Desistance from Crime among Juveniles and Adults: Applications to Criminal Justice Policy and Practice.* National Institute of Justice. Nov. Washington, D.C.: Office of Justice Programs, U.S. Department of Justice.

Keating, C. (2021). "Connecticut Republicans want to get tough on juvenile crime. Here's a look at their plan—and what Democrats think." *Hartford Courant.* Oct. 13. Retrieved from https://www.courant.com/politics/hc-pol-news-connecticut-republicans-crime-strategy-20211013-s4yfehe5xrhdvjocnp3f5einh4-story.html.

Keierleber, M. (2021). " 'It's barbaric': Some US children getting hit at school despite bans." *The Guardian.* May 19. Retrieved from https://www.theguardian.com/education/2021/may/19/us-children-corporal-punishment-schools.

Keith, T. Z., T. M. Reimers, P. G. Fehrmann, S. M. Pottebaum, L. W. Aubey (1986). "Parental involvement, homework and TV times: Direct and indirect effects on high school achievement." *Journal of Educational Psychology.* Vol. 78: 373–380.

Kellam, S. G., X. Ling, R. Merisca, C. H. Brown, and N. Ialongo (1998). "The effect of the level of aggression in the first grade classroom on the course and malleabilty of aggressive behavior into middle school." *Developmental Psychopathology*, Vol. 10, issue 2: 165–185.

Kellogg, N. D. (2009). *Clinical Report—The Evaluation of Sexual Behaviors in Children.* Itasca, ILL: American Academy of Pediatrics.

Kena, G. and A. Thompson (2021). Hate crime victimization, 2005–2019. NCJ 300954. Bureau of Justice Statistics, U.S. Department of Justice. Sept. Retrieved from https://bjs.ojp.gov/sites/g/files/xyckuh236/files/media/document/hcv0519_1.pdf.

Kerig, P. K. (2019). "Linking childhood trauma exposure to adolescent justice involvement: The concept of posttraumatic risk-taking." *Clinical Psychology Science and Practice.* Jan.: e12280. Retrieved from https://www.researchgate.net/profile/Patricia-Kerig/publication/331586409_Linking_Childhood_Trauma_Exposure_to_Adolescent_Justice_Involvement_The_Concept_of_Posttraumatic_Risk-Seeking/links/60e4e8ac299b-f1b0319bbebc/Linking-Childhood-Trauma-Exposure-to-Adolescent-Justice-Involvement-The-Concept-of-Posttraumatic-Risk-Seeking.pdf.

Kessler, D. A., P. S. Barnett, A. Witt, M. R. Zeller, J. R. Mande, and W. B. Schultz (1997). "The legal and scientific basis for FDA's assertion of jurisdiction over cigarettes and smokeless tobacco." *Journal of the American Medical Association* (JAMA). Vol. 277, issue 5 (Feb.): 405–409.

Khoo, A. (2020). "The emotional brain." *Young Scientist Journal.* July 22. Retrieved from https://ysjournal.com/the-emotional-brain/.

Kidd, R. F., and E. F. Chayet (2010). "Why do victims fail to report? The psychology of criminal victimization." *Journal of Social Issues.* Vol. 40, issue 1: 39–50.

Kight, S. W., and M. Sykes (2018). "The deadliest city. Behind Chicago's segregated shooting sprees." *AXIOS.* Aug. 14. Retrieved from https://www.axios.com/2018/08/14/chicago-gun-violence-murder-rate-statistics.

Kimberly, L. L., K. M. Folkers, P. Friesen, D. Sultan, G. P. Quinn, A. Bateman-House, B. Parent, C. Konnoth, A. Janssen, L. D. Shah, R. Bluebond-Langner, and C. Salas-Humara (2018). "Ethical issues in gender-affirming care for youth." *Pediatrics.* Vol. 162, issue 6 (Dec.): e20181537.

Kindlon, D. (2001). *Too Much of a Good Thing.* New York: Hyperion.

Kingston, B., M. Bacallo, P. Smokowski, T. Sullivan, and K. Sutherland (2016). "Constructing 'packages' of evidence-based programs to prevent youth violence: Processes and illustrative examples from the CDC's Youth Violence Prevention Centers." *Journal of Primary Prevention.* Vol. 37 (Apr.): 141–163.

Kish, S. W. (2018). Hold the rod and spare the child. University of Utah Health. Dec. 17. Retrieved from https://uofuhealth.utah.edu/newsroom/news/2018/12/dd-laskey-spanking.php.

Klein, M. W., and C. Maxson (2006). *Street Gang Patterns and Policies*. New York: Oxford University Press.

Klein, M. W., F. M. Weerman, and T. P. Thornberry. (2006). "Street gang violence in Europe." *European Journal of Criminology*. Vol. 3, issue 4: 413–437.

Klein, S. (2017). "The new unconstitutionality of juvenile sex offender registration: Suspending the presumption of constitutionality for laws that burden juvenile offenders." *Michigan Law Review*. Vol. 115, issue 8: 1365–1391.

Korff, J. (2020). "Aboriginal students in higher studies at University." *Creative Spirits*. May 16. Retrieved from https://www.creativespirits.info/aboriginalculture/education/aboriginal-students-in-higher-studies-at-university.

Korff, J. (2022). "A guide to Australia's Stolen Generations." *Creative Spirits*. May 3. Retrieved from https://www.creativespirits.info/aboriginalculture/politics/stolen-generations/a-guide-to-australias-stolen-generations.

Kraut, M. E. (2020). "Juvenile court process." Child Crime Prevention and Safety Center. Retrieved from https://childsafety.losangelescriminallawyer.pro/juvenile-court-process.html.

Kraut, M. E. (n.d.). "Supervised juvenile probation." Child Crime Prevention and Safety Center. Retrieved from https://childsafety.losangelescriminallawyer.pro/supervised-juvenile-probation.html#:~:text=Possible%20terms%20and%20conditions%20of,driver's%20license%20restrictions%2C%20fines%20and.

Krishnamoorthi, M. (2019). "The dilemma of disempowerment: How generational trauma impacts alcohol abuse rates in the Australian Aboriginal community." *Humanities and Social Sciences*. Vol. 18 (Spring): 15–20.

Kroese, J., W. Bernasco, A. C. Liefbroer, and J. Rouwendal (2021). "Single-parent families and adolescent crime: Unpacking the role of parental separation, parental decease, and being born to a single-parent family." *Journal of Developmental and Life-course Criminology*. Vol. 7: 596–622.

L

Labree, W., H. Nijman, H. van Marle, and E. Rassin (2010). "Background and characteristics of arsonists." *International Journal of Law and Psychiatry*. Vol. 33: 149–153.

Lacen, M. and C. Roy (2022). "Shreveport teen captured in Houston after third escape." KTAL News. June 29. Retrieved from https://www.arklatexhomepage.com/news/crime/shreveport-teen-captured-in-houston-after-third-escape/.

Laderer, A. (2021). "How to spot gaslighting: 6 things gaslighters say to manipulate you." *Insider*. July 23. Retrieved from https://www.insider.com/gaslighting-examples.

Lai, Y. (2019). "Determinants of importation and deprivation on committed juvenile offenders' violent misconduct: A Taiwanese perspective." *International Journal of Offender Therapy and Comparative Criminology*. Vol. 63, issue 8: 1242–1264.

Laird, L. (2016). "Miranda for youngsters: Police routinely read juveniles their rights, but do kids really understand them?" *American Bar Association Journal*. Vol. 102, issue 6: 16–18.

Lansford, J. E., S. Miller-Johnson, L. J. Berlin, K. A. Dodge, J. E. Bates, and G. S. Pettit (2007). "Physical abuse and later violent delinquency: A prospective longitudinal study." *Child Maltreatment*. Vol. 12, issue 3: 233–245.

Lansford, J. E., S. Zietz, M. H. Bornstein, K. Deater-Deckard, L. Di Giunta, K. A. Dodge, S. Gurdal, Q. Liu, Q. Long, P. S. Malone, P. Oburu, C. Pastorelli, A. T. Skinner, E. Sorbring, L. Steinberg, S. Tapanya, L. M. Uribe Tirado, S. Yotanyamaneewong, L. P. Alampay, S. N. Al-Hassan, D. Bacchini, and L. Chang (2020). Opportunities and peer support for aggression and delinquency during adolescence in nine countries. *New Direction for Child and Adolescent Development*, MEDLINE. Sept. 23. Retrieved from https://pubmed-ncbi-nlm-nih-gov.wne.idm.oclc.org/32964604/.

Lantz, B. (2020). "Co-offending group composition and violence: The impact of sex, age, and group size on co-offending violence." *Crime and Delinquency*. Vol. 66, issue 1: 93–122.

Larivée, S., and F. Gagné (2007). "Les biais culturel de tests de QI: La nature du problem (The cultural biases of IQ tests: The nature of the problem)." *Canadian Psychology*. Vol. 48, issue 4: 221–239.

Lassiter, M. D. (2015). "Impossible criminals: The suburban imperatives of America's War on Drugs." *Journal of American History*. Vol. 102, issue 1 (June): 126–140.

Laursen, M. F., R. W. Licht, C. U. Correll, T. Kallehauge, A. Christensen, M. Rodrigo-Domingo, and R. E. Nielsen (2020). "Diagnostic stability in children and adolescents with bipolar disorder, a nationwide register-based study." *International Journal of Bipolar Disorders*. Vol. 8, issue 14. Retrieved from https://journalbipolardisorders.springeropen.com/articles/10.1186/s40345-020-0179-3#citeas.

Law Library, American Law and Legal Information (n.d.). "Juvenile status offenders." Retrieved from https://law.jrank.org/pages/1539/Juvenile-Status-Offenders-Constraints-on-judicial-powers.html.

Lee, B., S. Y. Paek, and R. Fenoff (2018). "Factors associated with digital piracy among early adolescents." *Children and Youth Services Review*. Vol. 86 (Feb.): 287–295.

Lee, B. H. (2018). "Explaining cyber deviance among school-aged youth." *Child Indictors. Research*. Vol. 11: 563–584.

Lee, C. (2005). "Youth in Trouble—Where Can They Call Home?" M. Hill, trans. *Taiwan Panorama*. May. Retrieved from https://www.taiwan-panorama.com/Articles/Details?Guid=-c9a5a95d-2b0e-4d99-b913-ce58ab7dc1b4&langId=3&CatId=11.

Lee, J. Y., H. A. Knauer, S. J. Lee, M. P. MacEachern, C. F. Garfield (2018). "Father-inclusive perinatal parent education programs: A systematic review." *Pediatrics*. American Academy of Pediatrics. Vol. 142, issue 1 (July): e1–18.

Lee, T. (2022). "We gotta talk about Kanye West: What Kanye West can teach us about bipolar disorder and Black mental health." Podcast. *Into America*, MSNBC. Mar. 25. Retrieved from https://www.msnbc.com/podcast/into-america/transcript-we-gotta-talk-about-kanye-west-n1293165.

Legal Information Institute (2021). "Disturbing the peace." Wex Definitions Team, Cornell Law School. July. Retrieved from https://www.law.cornell.edu/wex/disturbing_the_peace.

Legal Information Institute (n.d.). Arson. Cornell Law School. Retrieved from https://www.law.cornell.edu/wex/arson.

Legal Information Institute (n.d.). Suicide. Cornell Law School. Retrieved from https://www.law.cornell.edu/wex/suicide.

Leiber, M. J., and R. Fix (2019). "Reflections on the impact of race and ethnicity on juvenile court outcomes and efforts to enact change." *American Journal of Criminal Justice*. Vol. 44: 581–608.

Lenthang, M. (2021). "5-year old boy allegedly detained, handcuffed and threatened by police." NBC News. Mar. 27. Retrieved from https://abcnews.go.com/US/year-boy-allegedly-detained-handcuffed-threatened-maryland-police/story?id=76721492.

Lenthang, M. (2022). "Student 16 overdoses on suspected fentanyl-laced marijuana at Connecticut high school, police say." NBC News. Feb. 8. Retrieved from https://www.nbcnews.com/news/us-news/16-year-old-student-overdoses-fentanyl-laced-marijuana-connecticut-hig-rcna15302.

Lenzi, M., J. Sharkey, A. Vieno, A. Mayworm, D. Doughety, and K. Nylund-Gibson (2015). "Adolescent gang involvement: The role of individual, peer, and school factors in a multilevel perspective." *Aggressive Behavior*. Vol. 41, issue 4 (July–Aug.): 386–397.

Lenzi, M., J. D. Sharkey, A. Wroblewski, M. J. Furlong, and M. Santinello (2019). "Protecting youth from gang membership: Individual and school-level emotional competence." *Journal of Community Psychology*. Vol. 47, No. 3 (Apr.): 563–578.

Lerman, R. I. (2000). Are teens in low-income and welfare families working too much? Urban Institute. Nov. Series B, No. B-25. Retrieved from https://www.urban.org/sites/default/files/publication/62291/309708-Are-Teens-in-Low-Income-and-Welfare-Families-Working-Too-Much-.PDF.

Leve, L. D., D. C. R. Kerr, and G. T. Harold (2013). "Young adult outcomes associated with teen pregnancy among high-risk girls in an RCT of multidimensional treatment foster care." *Journal of Child and Adolescent Substance Abuse*. Vol. 22, issue 5 (Sept. 1): 421–434. Main (2012).

Levin, E. M., and C. Kozak (1979). "Drug and alcohol use, delinquency among upper middle class pre- and post-adolescents." *Journal of Youth Adolescence*. Vol. 8, issue 1 (Mar.): 91–101.

Levinson, E., I. Chapman, A. Ross, and S. Prokupecz (2022). "Uvalde school shooting suspect was a loner who bought two assault rifles for his 18th birthday." CNN. May 26. Retrieved from https://www.cnn.com/2022/05/25/us/uvalde-texas-school-shooting-salvador-ramos/index.html.

Lewis, M. D., and J. Steiben (2004). "Emotional regulation in the brain: Conceptual issues and directions for developmental research." *Child Development*. Vol. 75, issue 2 (Mar./Apr.): 371–376.

Li, D. K. (2019). "Massachusetts high court upholds Carter's convictions for texts encouraging boyfriend's suicide." NBC News. Feb. 7. Retrieved from https://www.nbcnews.com/news/us-news/massachusetts-high-court-upholds-michelle-carter-s-conviction-texts-encouraging-n968291.

Li, Q., F. Wang, and J. Ye (2021). "Impact of psychological abuse on children and social skill development." *Aggression and Violent Behavior*. Sept. 25: e101667.

Li, R., Q. Lian, Q. Su, L. Li, M. Xie, and J. Hu (2020). "Trends and sex disparities in school bullying victimization among U.S. youth, 2011–2019." *BMC Public Health*. Vol. 20: 1583.

Little, R. (2022). "2 teens at large, escaped Acadiana Center for Youth." KLFY News. May 31. Retrieved from https://www.klfy.com/local/st-martin-parish/2-juveniles-at-large-escaped-acadiana-center-for-youth/.

Little, S., and A. Rice (2021). "Considering autonomous exploration in healthy environments: Reflections from an urban wildscape." *International Journal of Environmental Research and Public Health*. Vol. 18: e11867.

Liu, J., and A. Bharadwaj (2020). "Drug abuse and the Internet: Evidence from Craigslist." *Management Science*. Vol. 66, issue 5 (May): 1783–2290.

Liu, L., M. du Toit, and G. Weidermann (2021). "Infants are sensitive to cultural differences in emotions at 11 months." *Plos ONE*. Vol. 16, issue 9: 1–15.

Liu, S. (2015). "Is the shape of the age-crime curve invariant by sex? Evidence from a national sample with flexible non-parametric modeling." *Journal of Quantitative Criminology*. Vol. 31: 93–123.

Livingston, G. (2019). "The way U.S. teens spend their time is changing but differences between boys and girls persist." Pew Research Center. Jan. 20. Retrieved from https://www.pewresearch.org/fact-tank/2019/02/20/the-way-u-s-teens-spend-their-time-is-changing-but-differences-between-boys-and-girls-persist/.

Loeber, R., and T. Dishion (1983). "Early predictors of male delinquency." *Psychological Bulletin*. Vol. 94, issue 1: 68–99.

Loeber, R., and D. Hay (1997). "Key issues in the development of aggression and violence in childhood to early adulthood." *Annual Review of Psychology*. Vol. 48: 371–410.

López-Cepero, H. E. Fabelo, L. Rodríguez-Franco, and F. J. Rodríguez-Díaz (2016). "The Dating Violence Questionnaire: Validation of the Cuestionario de Violencia de Novios using a college sample from the United States." *Violence and Victims*. Vol. 31, issue 3: 438–456.

Lovett, K. G. (2021). "PBS Data Snapshot: Responding to the pandemic." PBS Special Issue Brief 3 (June): Fewer Youths in Custody. PBS Learning Institute, Inc.

Lowe, E. (2018). "Shasta Groene violates probation for endangering child." *Idaho Press*. June 25. Retrieved from https://www.idahopress.com/news/local/shasta-groene-violates-probation-for-endangering-child/article_7b583fdf-4a65-5e39-a982-f0d1a42a85d9.html.

Lurtz, M. R., and A. Komarow (2021). "Inclusive financial well-being empowerment model for serving independent, neurodivergent individuals." *Journal of Financial Planning*. Vol. 34, issue 11 (Nov.): 70–81.

Lynam, D., T. Moffitt, and M. Stouthamer-Loeber (1993). "Explaining the relationship between IQ and delinquency: Class, motivation, school failure, or self-control." *Journal of Abnormal Psychology*. Vol. 102, issue 2: 187–196.

Lynch, J. P. (2002). "Trends in juvenile violent offending: An analysis of victim survey data." *Juvenile Justice Bulletin*, OJJDP. NCJ 191052. Oct. Retrieved from https://www.ojp.gov/pdffiles1/ojjdp/191052.pdf.

M

Maccoby, E. E., and J. A. Martin (1983). "Socialization in the context of the family: Parent-child interaction." In *Handbook of Child Psychology*, Vol. 4, 4th ed., ed. P. H. Mussen and E. M. Hetheringon. New York: Wiley.

MacKay, P. (1989). "Cloward and Ohlin's theory of delinquent subcultures—revisited." *Police Journal: Theory, Practices, and Principles*. Vol. 62, issue 4 (Oct.): 290–296.

MacPherson, H. A., A. Y. Kudinova, E. Schettini, G. A. Jenkins, A. C. Gilbert, S. A. Thomas, and K. L. Kim (2022). "Relationship between cognitive reflexibility and subsequent course of mood symptoms and suicidal ideation in young adults with childhood-onset bipolar disorder." *European Child and Adolescent Psychiatry.* Vol. 31, issue 2: 299–312.

Maginnis, R. L. (1997). "Single-Parent Families Cause Juvenile Crime." In *Juvenile Crime: Opposing Viewpoints*, ed. A. E. Sadler and S. Barbour. San Diego, CA: Greenhaven.

Maitland, K. (2016). *Wicked Children: Murderous Tales from History.* Auckland, NZ: Review Publishing Co., Ltd.

Mak, A. S. (1994). "Parental neglect and overprotection as risks in delinquency." *Australian Journal of Psychology.* Vol. 46, issue 2: 107–111.

Malik, M. A., and R. A. Shirazi (2010). "An analytical review of juvenile delinquents in jails of Sindh Province: Some problems and suggestions to overcome." *Industrial Journal of Management and Social Sciences.* Vol. 4, No. 1: 43–54.

Malkus, N. (2020). *Too Little, Too Late: A Hard Look at 2020 Remote Learning.* Washington, DC: American Enterprise Institute.

Mallet, C. A. (2014). "The 'learning disabilities to juvenile detention' pipeline: A case study." *Children and Schools.* Vol. 36, issue 3: 147–155.

Mallet, C. A. (2016). *The School-to-Prison Pipeline: A Comprehensive Assessment.* New York: Springer.

Mallet, C. A., P. A. Stoddard Dare, and M. M. Seck (2009). Predicting juvenile delinquency: The nexus of child maltreatment, depression, and bipolar disorder. *Social Work Faculty Publications.* School of Social Work, Cleveland State University. Retrieved from https://engagedscholarship.csuohio.edu/cgi/viewcontent.cgi?article1006&contextclsowo_facpub.

Manetsch, M., R. J. Nelson Aguiar, D. Hermann, C. van der Put, T. Grisso, and C. Boonmann (2021). "Mental health problems in girls who committed sexual offenses: Similarities and differences compared to girls with non-sex offenses and boys with sex offenses." *Frontiers in Psychology.* Dec. 17. Retrieved from https://www.frontiersin.org/articles/10.3389/fpsyg.2021.721927/full#ref39.

Marco, D. (2011). "The Dopamine Hypothesis of drug addiction and its potential therapeutic value." *Frontiers in Psychiatry.* Vol. 2: 64.

Marcum, C. D., G. E. Higgins, M. L. Ricketts, and E. Scott (2014). "Hacking in high school: Cybercrime perpetration by juveniles." *Deviant Behavior.* Vol. 35, issue 7: 581–591.

Marcus, R. (2022). "Why do we let children buy firearms?" Opinion. *Washington Post.* May 27. Retrieved from https://www.washingtonpost.com/opinions/2022/05/27/why-kids-can-buy-guns/.

Marcus, S. (1991). "Homelessness and Dickens." *Social Research.* Spring. Vol. 58, issue 1: 93–106.

Markovitz, G., and N. Marchant (2022). "Why is inflation so high and will it stay that way? An economist explains." World Economic Forum. May 12. Retrieved from https://www.weforum.org/agenda/2022/05/inflation-rising-economist-explains/#:~:text=He%20gives%20three%20reasons%20for,and%20more%20goods%20through%202022.

Markowicz, K. (2015). "America's girls have a violence problem." *New York Post.* Sept. 7. Retrieved from https://nypost.com/2015/09/07/americas-young-girls-have-a-violence-problem/.

Markowitz, G., and D. Rosner (2013). *Lead Wars: The Politics of Science and the Fate of America's Children.* Berkeley: University of California Press.

Martin, T. (2018). "Juvenile criminal defense: Not just kids' stuff." CISION PRWeb. July 7. Retrieved from https://www.prweb.com/releases/2018/04/prweb15450291.htm.

Martinez, E. (2009). "Game over for teen who killed mother over video game." CBS News. June 17. Retrieved from https://www.cbsnews.com/news/game-over-for-teen-who-killed-mother-over-video-game/.

Martinez, G., J. Abma, and C. Copen (2010). Educating teenagers about sex in the United States. National Center for Health Statistics Data Brief. Center for Disease Control and Prevention (CDC), U.S. Department of Health and Human Services. No. 44 (Sept.). Retrieved from https://www.cdc.gov/nchs/data/databriefs/db44.pdf.

Martschenko, D. (2018). "The IQ test wars: Why screening for intelligence is still so controversial." *The Conversation.* Feb. 1. Retrieved from https://theconversation.com/the-iq-test-wars-why-screening-for-intelligence-is-still-so-controversial-81428.

Maruschak, L. M., J. Bronson, and M. Alper (2021). "Report: Parents in Prison and Their Minor Children: Survey of Prison Inmates." Bureau of Justice Statistics (BJS), U.S. Department of

Justice Programs, U.S. Department of Justice. May. Retrieved from https://bjs.ojp.gov/library/publications/prents-prison-and-their-minor-children-survey-prison-inmates-2016.

Matheny, J. D. H. (1998). "Strategies for assessment and early treatment with sexually addicted families." *Sexual Addiction and Compulsivity.* Vol. 5: 27–48.

Mather, S. R., H. G. Clark, and J. M. Gau (2021). "A cross-comparison study of reentry intervention and support of engagement: Finding on youth with disabilities." *Behavioral Disorders.* Vol. 46, issue 3: 163–174.

Matherne, M. M., and A. Thomas (2001). "Family environment as a predictor of adolescent delinquency." *Adolescence.* Vol. 36, issue 144 (Winter): 655–664.

Mathews, R., J. A. Hunter, and J. Vuz (1997). "Juvenile female sexual offender: Clinical characteristics and treatment issues." *Sexual Abuse: A Journal of Research and Treatment.* Vol. 9: 187–199.

Mauro, T. (2022). "Sports programs for kids with disabilities: Organizations for inclusive sports." *Very Well Family.* June 1. Retrieved from https://www.verywellfamily.com/special-needs-sports-programs-3106922.

Mayo Clinic (2022). Overview: Adult attention-deficit/hyperactivity disorder (ADHD). Retrieved from https://www.mayoclinic.org/diseases-conditions/adult-adhd/symptoms-causes/syc-20350878.

Mayo Clinic Staff (n.d.). Bipolar disorder: Overview. Retrieved from https://www.mayoclinic.org/diseases-conditions/bipolar-disorder/symptoms-causes/syc-20355955#:~:text=Although%20bipolar%20disorder%20can%20occur,symptoms%20may%20vary%20over%20time.

Mayo Clinic Staff (n.d.). Schizoaffective disorder: Overview. Retrieved from https://www.mayoclinic.org/diseases-conditions/schizoaffective-disorder/symptoms-causes/syc-20354504#:~:text=Schizoaffective%20disorder%20is%20a%20mental,such%20s%20depression%20or%20mania., 7

McClendon, J. (2022). "He threatened to post NY teen's naked photos online. Her suicide leads to arrests in Pakistan." *Advance Local Media.* Mar. 28. Retrieved from https://www.syracuse.com/crime/2022/03/he-threatened-to-post-ny-teens-naked-photos-online-her-suicide-leads-to-arrests-in-pakistan.html.

McCormick, L. (2014). "NOTE: The Internet and social media sites: A shift in privacy norms resulting in the exploitation and abuse of adolescents and teens in dating relationships." *Albany Government Law Review.* Vol. 7: 591.

McDonald, D. C. (1992). "Private penal institutions." *Crime and Justice.* Vol. 16: 361–419.

McGee, T. R., and D. P. Farrington (2019). "Developmental and life-course explanations of offending." *Psychology, Crime and Law.* Vol. 25, issue 6: 609–625.

McGrath, S. A., A. A. Nilsen, and K. R. Kerley (2010). "Sexual victimization in childhood and the propensity for juvenile delinquency and adult criminal behavior: A systematic review." *Aggression and Violent Behavior.* Vol. 16: 485–492.

McKee, E., and L. Rapp (2014). "The current status of evidence-based practice in juvenile justice." *Journal of Evidence-Based Social Work.* Vol. 11, issue 4: 308–317.

McMillan, D. W., and D. M. Chavis (1986). "Sense of community: A definition and theory." *Journal of Community Psychology.* Vol. 14 (Jan.): 6–23.

McNamara, R. H., and C. Coward Bucher (2012). *Problem Children: Special Populations in Delinquency.* Durham, NC: Carolina Academic Press.

McQuilling, M., and *Sun Times* (2022). Robert Taylor Homes. Apr. 14. Retrieved from https://halbaronproject.web.illinois.edu/items/show/44.

Meiszkowski, P., and E. Mills (1993). "The causes of metropolitan suburbanization." *Journal of Economic Perspectives.* Vol. 7: 135–147.

Ment, L. R., B. Vohr, W. Allan, K. H. Katz, K. C. Schneider, and M. Westerveld (2003). "Change in cognitive function over time in very low-birth-weight children." *Journal of American Medical Association.* Vol. 286, issue 6: 705–711.

Merriam, J. (1998). *Little Girl Lost.* Bemidji, MN: Pinnacle Publishing, LLC.

Merriam, J. (n.d.). "Little Girl Lost: A True Story of Shattered Innocence and Murder." Website. Retrieved from https://www.joanmerriam.com/little-girl-lost-1.

Merrin, G. J., J. P. Davis, D. Berry, and D. L. Espelage (2018). "Developmental changes in violent behaviors from early to late adolescence: Associations with parental monitoring and peer deviance." *Psychology of Violence.* Vol. 9, issue 2: 196–208.

Merton, R. K. (1938). "Social structure and anomie." *American Sociological Review.* Vol. 3, issue 5: 37–45.

Merton, R. K. (1957). *Social Theory and Social Structure.* New York: Free Press.

Merton, R. K. (1967). "Social Structure and Anomie." In *Theories of Deviance*, 4th ed., ed. S. H. Traub and C. B. Little. Itaska, IL: F. E. Peacock.

Metropolitan Police, City of London (2021). Statement from Commander Alex Murray regarding teenage homicides. Press release. Dec. 31.

Metropolitan Police Homicide Report and Guardian Research (2021). Graph: In 2021 there were 30 teenage homicides in London, exceeding the 2008 peak. *The Guardian.* Dec. 31. Retrieved from https://www.theguardian.com/uk-news/2021/dec/31/knife-rises-in-london-with-30-teen-homicides-in-2021.

Miller, A. A., W. J. Therrien, and J. E. Romig (2019). "Reducing recidivism: Transition and reentry practices for detained and adjudicated youth with disabilities." *Education and Treatment of Children.* Vol. 42, issue 3: 409–438.

Miller, J. (2000). "Getting into gangs." In *One of the Guys: Girls, Gangs, and Gender.* New York: Oxford University Press.

Miller-Perrin, C. L., and R. D. Perrin (2012). *Child Maltreatment: An Introduction.* Los Angeles, CA: SAGE Publications, Inc.

Milne, A. M., D. E. Myers, A. S. Rosenthal, and A. Ginsburg (1986). "Single parents, working mothers, and the educational achievement of school children." *Sociology of Education.* Vol. 59: 125–139.

Ministry of External Affairs, India (n.d.). "Child protection laws in different countries." Consular, Passport, and Visa Division, Government of India. Retrieved from https://www.mea.gov.in/child-protection-laws-in-different-ccountries.htm.

Minor, A. D. (2016). "ESSAY: Sexting prosecutions: Teenagers and child pornography laws." *Howard Law Journal.* Vol. 60: 309.

Minton, H. L. (2000). "Psychology and gender at the turn of the century." *American Psychologist.* Vol. 55, issue 6: 613–615.

Miranda Rights (n.d.). Miranda Rights. Retrieved from http://www.mirandarights.org/index.html.

Modica, A. (2009). "Robert R. Taylor Homes, Chicago, Illinois (1959–2005)." *Black Past.* Dec. 19. Retrieved from https://www.blackpast.org/african-american-history/robert-taylor-homes-chicago-illinois-1959-2005/.

Modrowski, C. A., and P. K. Kerig (2019). "Investigating the association between posttraumatic risky behavior and offending in adolescents involved in the juvenile system." *Journal of Youth and Adolescence.* Vol. 48: 1952–1966.

Moffitt, T. E. (2006). "Life-course persistent versus adolescence-limited antisocial behavior." In *Developmental Psychopathology: Risk, Disorder, and Adaptation*, vol. 3, 2d ed., eds. D. Cicchetti and D. J. Cohen. New York: Wiley.

Moon, M. M., J. L. Sundt, F. T. Cullen, and J. P. Wright (2000). "Is child saving dead? Public support for juvenile rehabilitation." *Crime and Delinquency.* Vol. 46, issue 1 (Jan.): 38–60.

Morales, M. (2022). "Staten Island mom continues efforts to feed her neighborhood." PIX II News, New York. Mar. 17. Retrieved from https://pix11.com/news/local-news/staten-island/staten-island-mom-continues-efforts-to-feed-her-neighborhood/.

Morin, A. (2021). "The free-range style of parenting." *Very Well Family.* Sept. 26. Retrieved from https://www.verywellfamily.com/what-is-free-range-parenting-1095057.

Morizot, J., and L. Kazemian (2014). *The Development of Criminal and Antisocial Behavior: Research and Practical Applications.* New York: Springer.

Morrill, M. (2014). "Sibling sexual abuse: An exploratory study of long-term consequences for self-esteem and counseling considerations." *Journal of Family Violence.* Vol. 29: 205–213.

Morris, F. (2018). "Methamphetamine roils rural towns again across the U.S." *All Things Considered*, New England Public Media, NPR. Oct. 25. Retrieved from https://www.npr.org/sections/health-shots/2018/10/25/656192849/methamphetamine-roils-rural-towns-again-across-the-u-s.

Morris, G., K. Walder, S. L. McGee, O. M. Dean, S. J. Tye, M. Maes, and M. Berk (2017). "A model of the mitochondrial basis of bipolar disorder." *Neuroscience and Biobehavioral Research.* Vol. 74 (Mar.), Pt. A: 1–20.

Morse, A. (2021). U.S. births declined during the pandemic. U.S. Census Bureau. Sept. 21. Retrieved from https://www.census.gov/library/stories/2021/09/united-states-births-declined-during-the-pandemic.html#:~:text=The%20number%20of%20U.S.%20births%20has%20been%20declining%20every%20year,on%20average%200.96%25%20a%20year.

Moser, C. (2004). "Urban violence and insecurity: an introductory roadmap." *Environment and Urbanization*. Vol. 16, issue 3: 3–16.

Moser, C., and C. McIlwaine (2004). *Encounters with Violence in Latin America: Urban Poor Perceptions from Colombia and Guatemala*. London: Routledge.

Moser, C., and A. Winton (2002). "Violence in the Central American region: Towards an integrated framework for violence reduction." ODI Working Paper No. 171. *ODI*, London.

Mostafapoor, M., and S. M. Hoseini (2017). " 'Neurocriminology,' a new approach to the analysis of juvenile violent crime (with emphasis on age-crime curve)." *Faṣlnāmah-i Pizhūhish-i Huqūq-i Kiyfarī*. Vol. 5, issue 19: 127–196. Trans. from Farsi.

Moylan, C. A., T. I. Herrenkohl, C. Sousa, E. A. Tajima, R. C. Herrenkohl, and M. J. Russo (2009). "The effects of child abuse and exposure to domestic violence on adolescent internalizing and externalizing behavior problems." *Journal of Family Violence*. Vol. 25: 53–63.

Moynihan, D. P. (1998). "Is crime always functional?" In *Taking Sides: Clashing Views on Controversial Issues in Crime and Criminology*, 5th ed., ed. R. C. Monk. New York: McGraw Hill Education.

Muller, C., R. J. Sampson, and A. S. Winter (2018). "Environmental inequality: The social causes and consequences of lead exposure." *Annual Review of Sociology*. Vol. 44, issue 1: 263–282.

Mullis, A. (2004). "Female juvenile offending: A review of characteristics and contexts." *Journal of Child and Family Studies*. Vol. 13, issue 2 (June): 205–218.

Multisystemic Therapy (MST) Services (2021). Racial disparities among juvenile facilities. Apr. 28. Retrieved from https://info.mstservices.com/blog/racial-disparities-in-juvenile-facilities#:~:text=The%20Prison%20Policy%20Initiative%20shared,in%20detention%20centers%20are%20Black.

Mulvahill, E. (2019). Ways to encourage good behavior without junky prizes or sugary treats: Classroom Ideas. *We are Teachers*. Jan. 16. Retrieved from https://www.weareteachers.com/ways-to-encourage-good-behavior/.

Murphy, S. L. (2022). "It starts and ends with the schools: Using strict IDEA enforcement to sunder the school-to-prison pipeline for special education students." *Ohio Northern University Law Review*. Vol. 48: 359.

Murphy-Oates, L. (2022). "Revisited: How Isaiah survived Australia's juvenile justice system." Produced by E. Leabeater, M. Herbert, and J. Koning; executive production by M. Martignonim, G. Jackson, and L. Murphy-Oates. Podcast, *Guardian*. Jan. 3. Retrieved from https://www.theguardian.com/australia-news/audio/2022/jan/04/revisited-how-isaiah-survived-australias-juvenile-justice-system.

Murrie, D. C. (2012). "Placing sexual behavior problems in context: What is 'normal' sexual behavior among juveniles?" In *Juvenile Offenders: A Guide to Evaluation and Treatment for Mental Health Professionals*, ed. E. P. Ryan, J. A. Hunter, and D. C. Murrie. Oxford, UK: Oxford University Press.

My Crime Library (n.d.). Cindy Collier and Shirley Wolf teen killers. Retrieved from https://mycrimelibrary.com/cindy-collier-and-shirley-wolf-teen-killers/.

Myers, N. S., and S. J. Llera (2020). "The role of child maltreatment in the relationship between social anxiety and dissociation: A novel link." *Journal of Trauma and Dissociation*. Vol. 21, issue 3: 319–336.

Myers, T. (2005). "Embodying delinquency: Boys' bodies, sexuality, and juvenile justice history in early-Twentieth-Century Quebec." *Journal of the History of Sexuality*. Vol. 14, issue 4: 383–414.

N

Näsi, M., M. Aaltonen, and J. Kivivuori (2016). "Youth hate crime offending: The role of strain, social control and self-control theories." *Journal of Scandinavian Studies in Criminology and Crime Prevention*. Vol. 17, issue 2: 177–184.

National Alliance on Mental Illness (NAMI) (2022). Schizophrenia: Overview. Retrieved from https://www.nami.org/About-Mental-Illness/Mental-Health-Conditions/Schizophrenia.

National Alliance on Mental Illness (NAMI) (n.d.). "Bipolar disorder." Retrieved from https://www.nami.org/About-Mental-Illness/Mental-Health-Conditions/Bipolar-Disorder.

National Association of School Resource Officers (NASRO) (n.d.). Frequently asked questions: How many school resource officers are there in the United States? Retrieved from https://www.nasro.org/faq/#:~:text=Because%20fewer%20private%20school%20than,have%20more%20than%20one%20officer.

National Association of Secondary School Principals (NASSP) (2006). "Tracking and ability grouping in middle level and high schools." Retrieved from https://www.nassp.org/tracking-and-ability-grouping-in-middle-level-and-high-schools/.

National Center for Drug Abuse Statistics (n.d.). Drug use among youth: Facts and Statistics. Retrieved from https://drugabusestatistics.org/teen-drug-use/.

National Center for Education Statistics (2021). "Students carrying weapons on school property and anywhere and students' access to firearms." *Condition of Education.* U.S. Department of Education Sciences. Retrieved from https://nces.ed.gov/programs/coe/indicator/a13.

National College Athletic Association (NCAA) Research (2020). Estimated probability of competing in college athletes. Apr. 8. Retrieved from https://ncaaorg.s3.amazonaws.com/research/pro_beyond/2020RES_ProbabilityBeyondHSFiguresMethod.pdf.

National Conference of State Legislatures (NCSL) (2018). "Teen pregnancy prevention." Report. Oct. 11. Retrieved from https://www.ncsl.org/health/teen-pregnancy-prevention#:~:text=Teen%20pregnancy%20is%20strongly%20linked,year%20of%20a%20child's%20birth.

National Conference of State Legislatures (NCSL) (2020). Congregate care, residential treatment, and group home state legislative enactments, 2014–2019. Q&A. Oct. 30. Retrieved from https://www.ncsl.org/research/human-services/congregate-care-and-group-home-state-legislative-enactments.aspx.

National Gang Center (NGC) (2015). *Parents' Guide to Gangs.* Washington, DC: Office of Juvenile Justice and Delinquency, U.S. Department of Justice.

National Gang Center (NGC) (2017). "A Law Enforcement Official's Guide to the OJJDP Comprehensive Gang Model." Washington, DC: Office of Justice Programs, U.S. Department of Justice. Retrieved from https://nationalgangcenter.ojp.gov/sites/g/files/xyckuh331/files/media/document/le-officials-guide-to-ojjdp-comprehensive-gang-model.pdf.

National Institute of Justice (NIJ) (2011). "Program profile: Multidimensional Treatment Foster Care—Adolescents." Office of Justice Programs, U.S. Department of Justice. June 10. Retrieved from https://crimesolutions.ojp.gov/ratedprograms/141.

National Institute on Alcohol Abuse and Alcoholism (NIAAA) (2021). Underage drinking. National Institution of Health. May. Retrieved from https://www.niaaa.nih.gov/publications/brochures-and-fact-sheets/underage-drinking.

National Institute on Alcohol Abuse and Alcoholism (NIAAA) (2022). Alcohol use in the United States. National Institute of Health. Mar.. Retrieved from https://www.niaaa.nih.gov/publications/brochures-and-fact-sheets/alcohol-facts-and-statistics.

National Institute on Alcohol Abuse and Alcoholism (NIAAA) (n.d.). "Understanding alcohol use disorder." National Institute of Health. Retrieved from https://www.niaaa.nih.gov/publications/brochures-and-fact-sheets/understanding-alcohol-use-disorder.

National Low Income Housing Coalition (NLIHC) (2019). "Gentrification and revitalization: What's the difference?" Apr. 5. Retrieved from https://nlihc.org/resource/gentrification-and-neighborhood-revitalization-whats-difference.

National Low Income Housing Coalition (NLIHC) (2019). Public housing history. Oct. 17. Retrieved from https://nlihc.org/resource/public-housing-history#:~:text=The%20federal%20public%20housing%20program,result%20of%20powerful%20grassroots%20organizing.

National Mental Health Association (NMHA) (2004). *Mental Health Treatment for Youth in the Juvenile Justice System: A Compendium of Promising Practices.* Chicago, IL: MacArthur Foundation.

National Mentoring Partnership (2021). "Report: Mentoring and Youth Violence Prevention." *Mentor.* Retrieved from https://files.eric.ed.gov/fulltext/ED614513.pdf.

National Public Radio (NPR) (2012). "Why millions of American have no government ID." Transcript. Feb. 1. Retrieved from https://www.npr.org/2012/02/01/146204308/why-millions-of-americans-have-no-government-id.

National Reentry Resource Center (2014). "Measuring and using recidivism data to inform policy, practice and resource allocation." The Council of State Governments Justice Center. July. Retrieved from https://csgjusticecenter.org/wp-content/uploads/2020/02/Measuring-and-Using-Juvenile-Recidivism-Data-to-Inform-Policy-Practice-and-Resource-Allocation.pdf.

National Sexual Violence Research Center (2014). An overview of adolescent sexual development. Retrieved from https://www.nsvrc.org/sites/default/files/2014-01/saam_2014_overview-of-adolescent-sexual-development.pdf.

Nation Master (2022). Crime stats: Compare key data on Taiwan and the United States. Retrieved from https://www.nationmaster.com/country-info/compare/Taiwan/United-States/Crime.

Native American Rights Fund (NARF) (n.d.). "Topic 8: Role of tribal courts." National Indian Law Library. Retrieved from https://narf.org/nill/documents/icwa/faq/role.html.

NBC Dallas Fort Worth, Channel 5 (2022). "Texas gunman warned of shooting grandmother, school in private Facebook messages." May 25. Retrieved from https://www.nbcdfw.com/news/national-international/texas-gunman-warned-of-shooting-grandmother-school-in-private-facebook-messages/2977774/.

Nelson, A. (2016). "Genuine struggle and care: An interview with Cleo Silvers." *American Journal of Public Health.* Vol. 106: 1744–1748.

Ness, C. D. (2010). *Why Girls Fight: Female Youth Violence in the Inner City.* New York: New York University Press.

Neubauer, I. L. (2014). "Australian child protection accused of repeating sins of 'Stolen Generations.'" *Time Magazine.* Mar. 11. Retrieved from https://time.com/19431/australian-child-protection-accused-of-repeating-sins-of-stolen-generations/.

New Mexico Children, Youth and Families Department (NMCYFD) (2022). JJS special programs. Retrieved from https://cyfd.org/jjs-special-programs.

Newport Academy (2021). How to deal with a rebellious teen. Sept. 24. Retrieved from https://www.newportacademy.com/resources/restoring-families/rebellious-teen/.

Nokali, N. E., H. J. Bachman, and E. Votruba-Drzal (2010). "Parent involvement and children's academic and social development in elementary school." *Child Development.* Vol. 81, issue 3 (May–June): 988–1005.

Nolo (n.d.). "Exceptions to confidentiality of juvenile court records." *Legal Encyclopedia.* Retrieved from https://www.nolo.com/legal-encyclopedia/exceptions-confidentiality-juvenile-criminal-records.html.

Novak, A., and K. Benedini (2020). "Sibling separation and self-reported offending: An examination of the association between sibling placement and offending behavior." *Child and Youth Services Review.* Vol. 111 (Apr.): 104830.

NYCourts.gov (n.d.). "Juvenile Delinquency." 7th Judicial District. Retrieved from https://ww2.nycourts.gov/courts/7jd/courts/family/case_types/juvenile_delinquency.shtml.

Nydegger, L. A., W. DiFranceisco, K. Quinn, and J. Dickson-Gomez (2017). "Gender norms and age-disparate sexual relationships as predictors of intimate partner violence, sexual violence, and risky sex among adolescent gang members." *Journal of Urban Health.* Vol. 94: 266–275.

O

Obama Foundation (2022). "A movement inspired by Trayvon Martin unleashes the power of communities to work together to solve problems for boys and young men of color." Retrieved from https://www.obama.org/mbka/eighth-anniversary/.

Obama Foundation (n.d.). "We are our brother's keepers." Retrieved from https://www.obama.org/mbka/.

Obama White House Archives (2016). "Fact sheet: My Brother's Keeper — Two years of expanding opportunity and creating pathways for success." Press release. Apr. 22. Retrieved from https://obamawhitehouse.archives.gov/the-press-office/2016/04/22/factsheet-my-brothers-keeper-%E2%80%93-two-years-expanding-opportunity-creating.

Obama White House Archives (2016). "My Brother's Keeper 2016 Progress Report: Two Years of Expanding Opportunity and Creating Pathways to Success." Retrieved from https://obamawhitehouse.archives.gov/sites/whitehouse.gov/files/images/MBK-2016-Progress-Report.pdf.

O'Donnell, J., J. D. Hawkins, R. F. Catalano, R. D. Abbott, and L. E. Day (1995). "Preventing school failure, drug use, and delinquency among low-income children: Long-term intervention in elementary schools." *American Journal of Orthopsychiatry.* Vol. 65, issue 1: 87–100.

Office for National Statistics (2020). Coronavirus and crime in England and Wales, August 2020: Impact of coronavirus (COVID-19) pandemic on crime and people's perceptions of crime during the April and May period of national lockdown. Government office, United Kingdom. Retrieved from https://www.ons.gov.uk/peoplepopulationandcommunity/crimeandjustice/bulletins/coronavirusandcrimeinenglandandwales/august2020.

Office for Victims of Crime (2014). Responding to transgender victims of sexual assault. Office of Justice Programs, U.S. Department of Justice. June. Retrieved from https://ovc.ojp.gov/sites/g/files/xyckuh226/files/pubs/forge/sexual_numbers.html.

Office of Justice Programs (OJP) (1998). "President's anti-gang and youth violence strategy." NCJ No. 193818. U.S. Department of Justice. Retrieved from https://www.ojp.gov/ncjrs/virtual-library/abstracts/presidents-anti-gang-and-youth-violence-strategy.

Office of Justice Programs (OJP) (2005). *Research in Brief: Co-Offending and Patterns of Juvenile Crime.* National Institute of Justice. Washington, DC: U.S. Department of Justice. Retrieved from www.ojp.gov/pdffiles1/nij/210360.pdf.

Office of Juvenile Justice and Delinquency Prevention (OJJDP) (1999). Report to Congress on Juvenile Violence Research. NCJ 176976. U.S. Department of Justice. July. Retrieved from https://ojjdp.ojp.gov/sites/g/files/xyckuh176/files/pubs/jvr/contents.html.

Office of Juvenile Justice and Delinquency Prevention (OJJDP) (2001). "Alternative schools." *Literature Review,* Model Programs Guide. U.S. Department of Justice. Retrieved from https://ojjdp.ojp.gov/model-programs-guide/literature-reviews/alternative_schools.pdf.

Office of Juvenile Justice and Delinquency Prevention (OJJDP) (2005). The National Hispanic Juvenile Delinquency Program of the Self-Reliance Foundation. Funding Award, 2005. Department of Justice Programs, U.S. Department of Justice. Retrieved from https://ojjdp.ojp.gov/funding/awards/2005-jl-fx-0141.

Office of Juvenile Justice and Delinquency Prevention (OJJDP) (2008). "Group homes: Literature Review." *Model Programs Guide.* Office of Justice Programs, U.S. Department of Justice. Retrieved from https://ojjdp.ojp.gov/model-programs-guide/literature-reviews/group_homes.pdf.

Office of Juvenile Justice and Delinquency Prevention (OJJDP) (2010). "Parent training." Literature Review, Model Programs Guide. Office of Justice Programs, U.S. Department of Justice. Retrieved from https://ojjdp.ojp.gov/model-programs-guide/literature-reviews/parent_training.pdf.

Office of Juvenile Justice and Delinquency Prevention (OJJDP) (2015). Literature review: Status Offenders. U.S. Department of Justice. Sept. Retrieved from https://ojjdp.ojp.gov/mpg/literature-review/status-offenders.pdf.

Office of Juvenile Justice and Delinquency Prevention (OJJDP) (2016). "Gun violence and youth." *Literature Review,* Model Programs Guide. U.S. Department of Justice. Retrieved from https://ojjdp.ojp.gov/mpg/literature-review/gun-violence-and-youth.pdf.

Office of Juvenile Justice and Delinquency Prevention (OJJDP) (2016). "Tribal youth in the juvenile justice system: Literature Review." *Model Programs Guide.* Office of Justice Programs, U.S. Department of Justice. Apr. Retrieved from https://ojjdp.ojp.gov/model-programs-guide/literature-reviews/tribal_youth_in_the_juvenile_justice_system.pdf.

Office of Juvenile Justice and Delinquency Prevention (OJJDP) (2017). "Intersection between mental health and juvenile justice system: Literature Review." *Model Programs Guide.* Office of Justice Programs, U.S. Department of Justice. July. Retrieved from https://ojjdp.ojp.gov/model-programs-guide/literature-reviews/intsection_between_mental_health_and_the_juvenile_justice_system.pdf.

Office of Juvenile Justice and Delinquency Prevention (OJJDP) (2017). "Intersection between mental health and the juvenile justice system." *Literature Review,* U.S. Department of Justice. July. Retrieved from https://ojjdp.ojp.gov/mpg/literature-review/mental-health-juvenile-justice-system.pdf.

Office of Juvenile Justice and Delinquency Prevention (OJJDP) (2018). "Improving juvenile reentry programs capacity for data collection, analysis, and reporting." Grant award, PBS Learning

Institute, Inc. Office of Justice Programs, U.S. Department of Justice. Nov/Dec. Retrieved from https://ojjdp.ojp.gov/funding/awards/2018-cz-bx-k001.

Office of Juvenile Justice and Delinquency Prevention (OJJDP) (2018). "Interactions between youth and law enforcement: Literature Review." *Model Programs Guide.* Office of Justice Programs, U.S. Department of Justice. Jan. Retrieved from https://ojjdp.ojp.gov/model-programs-guide/literature-reviews/interactions_between_youth_and_law_enforcement.pdf.

Office of Juvenile Justice and Delinquency Prevention (OJJDP) (2018). "Specialized responses to girls in the juvenile justice system." *Literature Review*, Model Programs Guide. June. U.S. Department of Justice. Retrieved from https://www.flcourts.gov/content/download/402743/file/Girls-in-the-Juvenile-Justice-System.pdf.

Office of Juvenile Justice and Delinquency Prevention (OJJDP) (2019). "Juvenile Justice Reform Act tribal provisions fact sheet." NCJ no. 254703. Office of Justice Programs, U.S. Department of Justice. July. Retrieved from https://www.ojp.gov/publications/jjra-tribal-provisions-fact-sheet.pdf.

Office of Juvenile Justice and Delinquency Prevention (OJJDP) (2020). "Research Central: Measuring what works in juvenile reentry." Office of Justice Programs, U.S. Department of Justice. Nov/Dec. Retrieved from https://ojjdp.ojp.gov/newsletter/ojjdp-news-glance-novemberdecember-2020/research-central-measuring-what-works-juvenile-reentry#:~:text=While%20national%20recidivism%20rates%20are,reconfinement%20rates%20averaged%2024%20percent.

Office of Juvenile Justice and Delinquency Prevention (OJJDP) (2022). "Five things about juvenile delinquency intervention and treatment." "Five Things" Series, National Institute of Justice. Mar. 22. Retrieved from https://nij.ojp.gov/topics/articles/five-things-about-juvenile-delinquency-intervention-and-treatment.

Office of Juvenile Justice and Delinquency Prevention (OJJDP) (2022). "Funding." Office of Justice Programs, U.S. Department of Justice. Retrieved from https://ojjdp.ojp.gov/funding#:~:text=In%20fiscal%20year%20(FY)%202021,youth%20and%20to%20deter%20delinquency.

Office of Juvenile Justice and Delinquency Prevention (OJJDP) (2022). OJJDP Statistical Briefing Book. Apr. 18. Retrieve from https://www.ojjdp.gov/ojstatbb/offenders/qa03301.asp#:~:-textViolent%20crimes%20by%20youth%20(ages,of%20school%20on%20school%20days.&textNote%3A%20Violent%20crimes%20include%20murder,%2C%20simple%20assault%2C%20and%20kidnapping.

Office of Juvenile Justice and Delinquency Prevention (OJJDP) (2022). "Racial and ethnic disparity in juvenile justice processing." *Model Programs Guide*, U.S. Department of Justice. Mar. Retrieved from https://ojjdp.ojp.gov/model-programs-guide/literature-reviews/racial-and-ethnic-disparity.

Office of Juvenile Justice and Delinquency Prevention (OJJDP) (2022). "Top story: Reentry programs offer resources to youth after residential placement." *OJJDP News @ a Glance.* Department of Justice. Retrieved from https://ojjdp.ojp.gov/newsletter/ojjdp-news-glance-marchapril-2022/top-story-reentry-programs-offer-resources-youth-after-residential-placement.

Office of Juvenile Justice and Delinquency Prevention (OJJDP) (n.d.). "About the Office." Office of Justice Programs, U.S. Department of Justice. Retrieved from https://ojjdp.ojp.gov/about#:~:text=%C2%A7%205601%20et%20seq.),has%20had%20on%20juvenile%20justice.

Office of Juvenile Justice and Delinquency Prevention (OJJDP) (n.d.). *Characteristics and Patterns of At-Risk Juveniles and Factors that Contribute to Violence Committed by or Against Juveniles.* Report to Congress, Juvenile Violence Research. Department of Justice Programs. Retrieved from https://ojjdp.ojp.gov/sites/g/files/xyckuh176/files/pubs/jvr/1.html.

Office of Juvenile Justice and Delinquency Prevention (OJJDP) (n.d.). "Enhancing law enforcement efforts and engagement with youth." Office of Justice Programs, U.. Department of Justice. Retrieved from https://ojjdp.ojp.gov/programs/enhancing-law-enforcement-efforts-and-engagement-youth.

Office of Juvenile Justice and Delinquency Prevention (OJJDP) (n.d.). Juvenile justice reform initiatives in the states, 1994–1996. U.S. Department of Justice. Retrieved from https://ojjdp.ojp.gov/sites/g/files/xyckuh176/files/pubs/reform2/ch2_c.html.

Office of Juvenile Justice and Delinquency Prevention (OJJDP) (n.d.). "Legislation." Office of Justice Programs, U.S. Department of Justice. Retrieved from https://ojjdp.ojp.gov/about/legislation.

Office of Juvenile Justice and Delinquency Prevention (OJJDP) (n.d.). "State compliance with JJDP Act core requirements." Office of Justice Programs, U.S. Department of Justice. Retrieved from https://ojjdp.ojp.gov/states/state-compliance-jjdp-act-core-requirements.

Office of Juvenile Justice and Delinquency Prevention (OJJDP) (n.d.). Statistical Briefing Book: Law enforcement and Juvenile crime, most serious offense, 2019. Retrieved from https://www.ojjdp.gov/ojstatbb/crime/qa05101.asp.

Office of Juvenile Justice, State of Louisiana (n.d.). Acadian a Center for Youth. Retrieved from https://ojj.la.gov/acadiana-center-for-youth/.

Office of the Attorney General, California (2020). Attorney General Becerra announces takedown of Riverside street gang. Press release. State of California Department of Justice. Jan. 17. Retrieved from https://oag.ca.gov/news/press-releases/attorney-general-becerra-announces-takedown-riverside-street-gang.

O'Hagan, K. P. (1995). "Emotional and psychological abuse: Problems with definition." *Child Abuse and Neglect.* Vol. 19, issue 4 (Apr.): 449–461.

Ohannessian, C. M., and A. Vannucci (2020). "Social media use and externalizing behaviors in early adolescence." *Youth and Society.* Vol. 53, issue 6: 871–893.

Okpala, C. O., A. O. Okpala, and F. E. Smith (2001). "Parental involvement, instructional expenditures, family socioeconomic attributes and student achievement." *Journal of Educational Research.* Vol. 95, issue 2: 110–115.

Oleson, J. C. (2016). *Criminal Genius: A Portrait of High-IQ Offenders.* Oakland, CA: University of California Press.

Oliverio, R., K. Katelina, and Z. M. Weil (2020). "Sex, drugs, and TBI: The role of sex in substance abuse related to traumatic brain injury." *Frontiers in Neurology.* Vol. 11 (Oct. 19). Retrieved from https://www.frontiersin.org/article/10.3389/fneur.2020.546775.

Olson, D. H., C. S. Russell, and D. H. Sprenkle (1982). "The circumplex model of marital and family systems, VI: Theoretical update." *Family Process.* Vol. 22: 69–83.

Olson, P., and L. Williams (2022). "Is video game addiction a real illness?" *Bloomberg.* Mar. 19. Retrieved from https://www.bloomberg.com/opinion/articles/2022-03-19/is-video-game-addiction-a-real-illness.

Olweus, D. (2012). "Cyberbullying: An overrated phenomenon?" *European Journal of Developmental Psychology.* Vol. 9, issue 5: 520–538.

O'Murphy, A. (2013). Preface. *School Resource Officers: Analysis of Law Enforcement in Schools*, ed. A. O'Murphy. Law, Crime, and Law Enforcement. New York: NOVA.

O'Neal, E. N., S. H. Decker, R. K. Moule, Jr., and D. C. Pyrooz (2014). "Girls, gangs, and getting out." *Youth Violence and Juvenile Justice.* Vol. 14, issue 1: 1–18.

Ongah, Y., N. Soetikno, F. I. R. Dewi, and M. J. Batobara-Yap (2021). "The role of child maltreatment and tendency to juvenile delinquency in late adolescents." *Advances in Heath Science Research.* Vol. 41: 296–301.

Opioid Affected Youth Initiative (OAYI) (n.d). "Our initiative." Office of Juvenile Justice and Delinquency Prevention (OJJDP), U.S. Department of Justice. Retrieved from https://www.opioidaffectedyouth.org/.

Oprea, C., and A. Stan (2012). "Adolescents' perceptions of online communication." *Procedia—Social and Behavioral Sciences.* Vol. 46: 4089–4091.

Orent Law Offices (2016). "Disturbing the peace—How the Arizona Justice System Looks at the Young Offender." Blog. Jan. 28. Retrieved from https://www.orentcriminallaw.com/blog/young-offenders-disturbing-the-peace/.

Origins Behavioral Healthcare (2019). "Is there a difference between emotional abuse and psychological abuse?" Feb. 20. Retrieved from https://www.originsrecovery.com/is-there-a-difference-between-emotional-abuse-and-psychological-abuse/.

Orlando Sentinel (2000). "Thai juvenile offenders state 2nd big breakout." *News.* Mar. 18. Retrieved from https://www.orlandosentinel.com/news/os-xpm-2000-03-19-0003200281-story.html.

Orozco, A. (2019). "Applying the CASA model on the juvenile justice system." Court-Appointed Special Advocates (CASA). Aug. 7. Retrieved from https://www.casadc.org/post/applyingthecasamodeltothejuvenilejusticesystem#:~:text=Court%20Appointed%20Special%20Advocates%2C%20or,or%20family%20at%20a%20time.

Ortiz, A. (2020). "Confidence in police is at record low, Gallup survey finds." *New York Times.* Aug. 20. Retrieved from https://www.nytimes.com/2020/08/12/us/gallup-poll-police.html.

Osgood, D., and J. M. Chambers (2003). Community correlates of rural youth violence. Office of Juvenile Justice and Delinquency Prevention, U.S. Department of Justice. May. Retrieved from https://www.ncjrs.gov/HTML/ojjdp/193591/page1.html#:~:text=Social%20dis-organization%20theory%20specifies%20that,strong%20systems%20of%20social%20relationships.

The Outsiders Fan Club (n.d.). Interview: S.E. Hinton. Retrieved from http://theoutsidersfanlub.weebly.com/exclusive-interview-with-se-hinton.html.

Owusa, D. N., K. O. Ansah, N. E. Y. Dey, H. O. Duah, P. Agbadi (2022). "Bullying and truancy among school-going adolescents in Timor-Leste: Results from the 2015 global school-based health survey." *Heliyon.* Vol. 8, issue 1: e08797.

Oyama, O., and N. A. Piotrowski (2022). "Depression." In *Magill's Medical Guide*, ed. B. C. Auday, M. A. Buratovich, and G. F. Marrocco. Ipswich, MA: Salem Press.

Özbay, Ö., and Y. Z. Özcan (2008). "A test of Hirschi's Social Bonding Theory." *International Journal of Offender Therapy and Comparative Criminology.* Vol. 52, issue 2: 134–157.

Ozer, M. M., and H. Akbas (2020). "The predictability of IQ on delinquency: A structural equation model (SQM)." *International Journal of Criminal Justice Science.* Vol. 15, issue 2: 283–297.

P

Panchal, N., R. Kamal, C. Cox, and R. Garfield (2021). The implications of COVID-19 for mental health and substance use. Kaiser Family Foundation.

Panezai, S., H. Panezai, A. A. Wassan, and S. E. Saqib (2019). "Exploring juveniles' delinquent behavior and associated factors: A cross-country comparison of Pakistan and Thailand." *Journal of Geography and Social Sciences.* Vol. 1, issue 1: 57–71.

Paquette, C. E., and R. A. Pollini (2018). "Injection drug use, HIV/HCVm and related services in nonurban areas of the United States." *Drug and Alcohol Dependence.* Vol. 188 (July): 239–250.

Parizek, R. A. (2021). "Health literacy does not protect against underage alcohol use during the COVID-19 pandemic." *Journal of Psychosocial Nursing and Mental Health Services.* Vol. 59, issue 12 (Dec.): Medline.

Parker, R. E., E. W. Burgess, and R. D. McKenzie (1967). *The City.* Chicago, IL: University of Chicago Press.

Parmar, R., and J. Lagoy (2021). "Is video game addiction a disorder?" *Psychiatric Times.* Vol. 38, issue 10. Retrieved from https://www.psychiatrictimes.com/view/is-video-game-addiction-a-disorder.

Parolin, Z., S. Collyer, and M. A. Curran (2022). Table 1: January 2022 Monthly Child Poverty Rates by Children's Race and Ethnicity, in "Absence of monthly tax credits lead to 3.7 million more children in poverty in January 2022." *Poverty and Social Policy Brief.* Center on Poverty and Social Policy, Columbia University. Vol. 6, issue 2. Retrieved from https://static1.squarespace.com/static/610831a16c95260dbd68934a/t/620ec869096c78179c7c4d3c/1645135978087/Monthly-poverty-January-CPSP-2022.pdf.

Paschall, M. J., J. W. Grube, and K. Kypri (2009). "Alcohol control policies and alcohol consumption by youth: A multi-national study." *Addiction.* Vol. 104, issue 11: 1849–1855.

Patterson, G. R., B. D. DeBaryshe, and E. Ramsey (1989). "A developmental perspective on antisocial behavior." *American Psychology.* Vol. 44: 329–335.

Patterson, G. R., J. B. Reid, and T. J. Dishion (1992). *Antisocial Boys: A Social Interactional Approach*, Vol. 4. Eugene, OR: Castalia.

Pennsylvania Coalition Against Domestic Violence (PCADV) (2022). Rural communities. Retrieved from https://www.pcadv.org/initiatives/underserved-populations/rural-communities/.

Pergola, J. (2014). "Music education in crisis." *School Band and Orchestra Magazine.* National Education Music Company. Retrieved from https://www.nemc.com/resources/articles/music-education-in-crisis.

Perr, I. N. (1979). "Comments on arson." *ASTM International.* Vol. 24, issue 4. Retrieved from https://www.astm.org/jfs10919j.html.

Peters, M. (2017). "A collection of anti-Nazi comic book covers from the 1940s is one of the most relevant books of the year." *Salon*. Aug. 17. Retrieved from https://www.salon.com/2017/08/17/a-collection-of-anti-nazi-comic-book-covers-from-the-1940s-is-one-of-the-most-relevant-books-of-the-year/.

Peterson, D. (2012). "Girlfriends, gun-holders, and ghetto-rats? Moving beyond narrow views of girls in gangs." In *Delinquent Girls: Contexts, Relationships, and Adaption*, ed. S. Miller, L. D. Leve, and P. K. Kerig. Switzerland: Springer International.

Peterson, D., T. J. Taylor, and F. Esbensen (2004). "Gang membership and violent victimization." *Justice Quarterly.* Vol. 21, issue 4 (Dec.): 793–815.

Petrosino, A., C. Turpin-Petrosino, and J. Buehler (2004). "Juvenile Awareness Programs for Preventing Juvenile Delinquency." *Campbell Systematic Reviews.* Vol. 2. Retrieved from https://onlinelibrary.wiley.com/doi/pdf/10.4073/csr.2004.2.

Petrosino, A., C. Turpin-Petrosino, M.E. Hollis-Peel, and J. G. Lavenberg (2013). " 'Scared Straight' and other juvenile awareness programs for preventing juvenile delinquency." *Cochrane Database of Systematic Review.* Vol. 2, issue 4 (Apr. 30): CD002796. Retrieved from https://www.cochranelibrary.com/cdsr/doi/10.1002/14651858.CD002796.pub2/full.

Petteruti, A. (2011). *Education Under Arrest: The Case Against Police in Schools.* Report. Washington, D.C.: Justice Policy Institute. Retrieved from https://justicepolicy.org/wp-content/uploads/2022/02/educationunderarrest_fullreport.pdf.

PEW Research Center (2014). Measuring juvenile recidivism: Data visualization. May 21. Retrieved from https://www.pewtrusts.org/en/research-and-analysis/data-visualizations /2014/measuring-juvenile-recidivism.

PEW Research Center (2017). The rise in dual-income families. June 15. Retrieved from https://www.pewresearch.org/ft_17-06-14_fathers_dual_income/.

Philbin, J. (2022). "Surviving social work burnout: Prevention strategies and advice." Student Training and Education in Public Service (Steps). May 11. Retrieved from https://www.publicservicedegrees.org/resources/surviving-burnout-social-work/.

Pimentel, D. (2012). "Criminal child neglect and the 'free range kid': Is overprotective parenting the new standard?" *Utah Law Review.* No. 947.

Pina, A. A., A. J. Polo, and S. J. Huey (2019). "Evidence-based psychosocial interventions for ethnic minority youth: The 10-year update." *Journal of Clinical Child and Adolescent Psychology.* Vol. 48, No. 2: 179–202.

Pioneer Valley Transit Authority (PVTA) (2019). Schedule, Holyoke. Retrieved from http://pvta.com/schedules.php.

Piotrowski, N. A., and L. V. Tischauser (2022). "Schizophrenia." In *Magill's Medical Guide*, ed. B. C. Auday, M. A. Buratovich, and G. F. Marrocco. Ipswich, MA: Salem Press.

Piquero, A. R. (2017). " 'No remorse, no repent': Linking lack of remorse to criminal offending in a sample of adolescent offenders." *Justice Quarterly.* Vol. 34, issue 2: 350–376.

Pitts, J. (1988). *Politics of Juvenile Crime.* Sage Contemporary Criminology Series. London, UK: Sage.

Plummer, M., and A. Cossins (2018). "The cycle of abuse: When victims become offenders." *Trauma, Violence, and Abuse.* Vol. 19, issue 3: 286–304.

Plutchik, R. (1982). "A psychoevolutionary theory of emotions." *Social Science Information.* Vol. 21, issues 4–5: 529–553.

Plutchik, R. (2001). "The nature of emotions: Human emotions have deep evolutionary roots, a fact that may explain their complexity and provide tools for clinical practice." *American Scientist.* Vol. 89, issue 4: 344–350.

Pompili, M., D. Harnic, X. Gonda, A. Forte, G. Dominici, M. Innamrati, K. H. Fountoulakis, G. Serafini, L. Sher, L. Janiri, Z. Rihmer, M. Amore, and P. Girardi (2014). "Impact of living with bipolar patients: Making sense of caregivers' burden." *World Journal of Psychiatry.* Vol. 4, issue 1 (Mar.): 1–12.

Popowski, A. (2022). "Dollar General employee stages robbery at store, Mobile police say." CBS 42. Jan. 28. Retrieved from https://www.cbs42.com/news/crime/dollar-general-employee-stages.

Population Reference Bureau (2022). Summary: Gang Involvement. KidsData. Retrieved from https://www.kidsdata.org/topic/73/gang-involvement/summary.

Potter, S. (2004). " 'Undesirable relations': Same-sex relationships and the meaning of sexual desire at the Women's Reformatory during the Progressive Age." *Feminist Studies.* Vol. 30, issue 2 (Summer): 394–415.

Pozueco, J. M. (2011). *Psicopatía, Trastorno Metnal y Crimen Violento: Aspectos Clínico-Forenses, Médico-Legales y Criminológicos* [Psychopathy, Mental Disorder: Clinical-Forensic Medico-Legal and Criminological Aspects]. Madrid, Spain: EOS.

Price, J. T. (2022). "More children die from gun violence than car crashes. Are school shootings to blame?" *News@Northeastern*. Northeastern University. June 3. Retrieved from https://news.northeastern.edu/2022/06/03/children-gun-violence/.

Price, P. (2009). "When is a police officer an officer of the law?: The status of police officers in schools." *Journal of Criminal Law and Criminology*. Vol. 99, issue 2 (Winter): 541–70.

Price-Robertson, R., L. Bromfield, and A. Lamont (2014). "International approaches to child protection: What can Australia learn?" *Child Family Community Australia*. CFCA Paper No. 23. Australian Institute of Family Studies, Australian Government. July. Retrieved from https://aifs.gov.au/cfca/sites/default/files/publication-documents/cfca-paper23.pdf.

Prithishkumar, I. J., and S. A. Michael (2014). "Understanding your student: Using the VARK model." *Education Forum*. Vol. 60, issue 2: 183–186.

Pronk, S., C. Kuiper, D. Smit, G. J. Stams, A. Popma, E. Mudler, and G. van den Berg (2020). "A meta-analysis on the outcomes of adolescents for school drop-out attending nonresidential alternative educational facilities." *Preventing School Failure*. Vol. 64, issue 2: 162–171.

Przbylski, A. K., and N. Weinstein (2019). "Violent video engagement is not associated with adolescents' aggressive behaviour: Evidence from a registered report." *Royal Society Open Science*. Feb. 13. London, UK: The Royal Society Publishing. Retrieved from https://royalsocietypublishing.org/doi/full/10.1098/rsos.171474.

Puzzanchera, C. (2020). Juvenile arrests, 2018. Juvenile Justice Statistics, *National Report Series Bulletin*. June. Washington, D.C.: U.S. Department of Justice, Office of Justice Programs.

Q

Quednau, J. (2021). "How are violent crime rates in U.S. cities affected by poverty?" *The Park Place Economist*. Vol. 28, issue 1. Retrieved from https://digitalcommons.iwu.edu/cgi/viewcontent.cgi?article=1530&context=parkplace.

Quigley, J., and the Committee on Substance Use and Prevention (2019). "Alcohol use by youth." *Pediatrics*. Vol. 144, issue 1: 1–6.

R

Rajalakshmi, J., and P. Thanasekaran (2015). "The effects and behaviours of home alone situation by latchkey children." *American Journal of Nursing Science*. Vol. 4, issue 4: 207–211.

Ramadas, S. (2008). "California youth and criminal law: 2007 juvenile justice reform and gang prevention initiatives." *Berkeley Journal of Criminal Law*. Vol. 13: 145–174.

Rand Corporation (2020). The effects of laws allowing armed staff in K-12 schools. Apr. 22. Retrieved from https://www.rand.org/research/gun-policy/analysis/laws-allowing-armed-staff-in-K12-schools.html#fn5.

Ranepa, Y. (2018). Juvenile delinquency in Russia: Causes and solutions. Conference paper, Problems of Management, Economy, Politics and Law in the Globalizing World. Rostov-on-Don, Russia. Apr. 16–19.

Ransley, J., and E. Marchetti (2018). "Medicalizing the detention of Aboriginal people in the Northern Territory: New/old regime of control?" *Social and Legal Studies*. Vol. 30, issue 1: 104–122.

Rapee, R. M., C. A. Schniering, and J. L. Hudson (2009). "The brain and behavior in childhood and adolescent anxiety disorders." In *Anxiety Disorders and Adolescents*, 2d ed., ed. W. K. Silverman and A. P. Fields. New York: Cambridge University Press.

Ravipati, S. (2017). "Report: Students with learning and attention issues three times more likely to drop out." Special Education, *The Journal*. May 17. Retrieved from https://thejournal.com/articles/2017/05/17/students-with-learning-and-attention-issues-three-times-more-likely-to-drop-out.aspx.

Raypole, C.; rev. T. J. Legg (2020). "Types of addiction and how they're treated." *Healthline*. Feb. 27. Retrieved from https://www.healthline.com/health/types-of-addiction.

Raywid, M. A. (1983). "Schools of choice: Their current nature and prospects." *Phi Delta Kappan*. Vol. 94, issue 10: 684–688.

Recovery Village (2021). "Where teens get illicit drugs," ed. C. Renzoni. Oct. 20. Retrieved from https://www.therecoveryvillage.com/teen-addiction/drug/how-teens-get-drugs/.

Reid, J. A., M. T. Baglivio, A. R. Piquero, M. A. Greenwald, and N. Epps (2019). "No youth left behind to human trafficking: Exploring profiles of risk." *American Journal of Orthopsychiatry*. Vol. 89, issue 6: 704–715.

Reinberg, S. (2019). "1 in 18 U.S. teens carries a gun to school: Study." *News*, WebMD.

Relva, I. C., O. M. Fernandes, and M. Alarcão (2017). "Dyadic types of sibling sexual coercion." *Journal of Family Violence*. Vol. 32: 577–583.

Renkoski, K. (2016). "School resource officers look to be more approachable with new, 'soft' uniforms." *Columbia Missourian*. Mar. 12. Retrieved from https://www.columbiamissourian.com/news/k12_education/school-resource-officers-look-to-be-more-approachable-with-new-soft-uniforms/article_7ad980f2-e7b4-11e5-9b13-1b33c1893169.html.

Rephann, T. J. (2009). "Rental housing and crime: The role of property ownership and management." *The Annals of Regional Science*. Vol. 43, issue 2: 435–451.

Reyes-Quilodran, C., M. C. Ruffolo, and S. Chang (2022). "Compassion fatigue among social workers in juvenile offender systems in Chile." *International Social Work*. May. https://doi.org/10.1177/00208728221088169

Reynolds, W. M. (1988). *Suicidal Ideation Questionnaire Professional Manual*. Odessa, FL: Psychological Assessment Resources.

Rhew, I. C., J. D. Hawkins, and S. Oesterle (2011). "Drug use and risk among youth in different rural contexts." *Health Place*. Vol. 17, issue 3 (May): 775–783.

Rhineberger-Dunn, G. and K. Y. Mack (2020). "Predicting burnout among juvenile detention and juvenile probation officers." *Criminal Justice Policy Review*. Vol. 31, issue 3 (Apr.): 335–355.

Rhone, N. (2021). Opinion: Mall culture and teens, already a strained relationship before Lenox curfew. *The Atlanta Journal-Constitution*. Sept. 15. Retrieved from https://www.ajc.com/life/opinion-mall-culture-and-teens-already-a-strained-relationship-before-lenox-curfew/WKIUVN5IUFEITNVPM2DRA7XHOA/.

Richards, K. (2011). "What makes juvenile offenders different from adult offenders?" Australian Institute of Criminology. *Trends and Issues in Crime and Criminal Justice*, No. 409. Updated Aug. 27, 2021.

Richmond, T. (2021). Explainer: Prosecutors play up Rittenhouse inexperience. Associated Press. Nov. 7. Retrieved from https://apnews.com/article/wisconsin-police-chicago-illinois-police-brutality-3df3e885caf039996246a4d9760859d4.

Riggs, M. (2017). "Why we fight and punish: A Q&A with Robert Sapolsky." *Reason*. Sept. 15. Retrieved from https://reason.com/2017/09/15/why-people-do-awful-things-a-qa-with-rob/#:~:text=Sapolsky%3A%20Juvenile%20justice%20is%20probably,that%20in%20three%20different%20rulings.

Rio.com (n.d.). A neighborhood full of surprises: Lapa. Retrieved from https://www.rio.com/practical-rio/lapa.

Rivera, F. I., P. J. Guarnaccia, N. Mulvaney-Day, J. Y. Lin, M. Torres, and M. Alegria (2008). "Family cohesion and its relationship to psychological distress among Latino groups." *Hispanic Journal of Behavioral Science*. Vol. 30, issue 3: 357–378.

Rivera-Calderón, N. (n.d.). "Arrested at the schoolhouse gate: Criminal school disturbances law and children's rights at school." National Lawyers Guild. Retrieved from https://www.nlg.org/nlg-review/article/arrested-at-the-schoolhouse-gate-criminal-school-disturbance-laws-and-childrens-rights-in-schools/.

Riverside Police Department (2018). "Operation 'Eastbound and Down.'" Press release, City of Riverside, California. Oct. 19. Retrieved from https://riversideca.gov/press/riverside-police-departments-operations-eastbound-down.

Rivinius, J. (2020). "New research reveals tremendous diversity in hate crime offenders' backgrounds and motivation." National Consortium for the Study of Terrorism and Responses to Terrorism. Department of Homeland Security Emeritus Center of Excellence University of Maryland. Oct. 26. Retrieved from https://start.umd.edu/news/new-research-reveals-tremendous-diversity-hate-crime-offenders-backgrounds-and-motivations.

Rizvi, S. F. I., and N. Najam (2014). "Parental psychological abuse toward children and mental health problems in adolescence." *Pakistan Journal of Medicine*. Vol. 30, issue 2 (Mar.-Apr.): 256–260.

Roberts, C. A. (1995). "Bilingual education program models: A framework for understanding." *Bilingual Research Journal.* Vol. 10, issues 3–4: 369–378.

Roberts, S., J. Kemp, A. Rathburn, R. E. Morgan, T. D. Snyder (2013). *Indicators of School Crime and Safety: 2013.* Bureau of Justice Statistics (BJS) and Institute of Education Sciences, National Center for Education Statistics.

Robins, L. N., H. Gyman, and P. O'Neal (1962). "The interaction of social class and deviant behavior." *American Sociological Review.* Vol. 27, issue 4 (Aug.): 480–492.

Robinson, P. L., W. J. Boscardin, S. M. George, S. Teklehaimanot, K. C. Heslin, and R. N. Bluthenthal (2009). "The effect of urban street gang densities on small area homicide incidences in a large metropolitan county, 1994–2002." *Journal of Urban Health: Bulletin of the New York Academy of Medicine.* Vol. 86, issue 4: 511–523.

Robles-Ramamurthy, B., and C. Watson (2019). "Examining racial disparities in juvenile justice." *Journal of the American Academy of Psychiatry Law.* Vol. 47, issue 1: Online. Retrieved from https://web.archive.org/web/20200319134851id_/http://jaapl.org/content/jaapl/early/2019/02/13/JAAPL.003828-19.full.pdf.

Rocca, G., A. Verde, and U. Gatti(2019). "Impact of alcohol and cannabis use on juvenile delinquency: Results from an international multi-city study (ISRD3)." *European Journal on Criminal Policy and Research.* Vol. 25, issue 3 (Sept.): 259–271.

Roff, J. D., and R. D. Wirt (1984). "Childhood aggression and social adjustment as antecedents of delinquency." *Journal of Abnormal Child Psychology.* Vol. 12: 111–126.

Roff, J. D., and R. D. Wirt (1985). "The specificity of childhood problem behavior for adolescent and young adult maladjustment." *Journal of Clinical Psychology.* Vol. 41, issue 4 (July): 564–571.

Rosenfeld, R. (2015). "Ferguson and police use of deadly force." *Missouri Law Review.* Article 11. Vol. 80, issue 4 (Fall): 1–23. Retrieved from https://scholarship.law.missouri.edu/cgi/viewcontent.cgi?article=4167&context=mlr.

Rosenthal, K. (2014). Banned books: Young adult novels. The University of Tulsa, Department of Special Collections and University Archives. Mar. 13. Retrieved from http://orgs.utulsa.edu/spcol/?p=3254.

Rosenthal, L. (2001). "Gang loitering and race." *Journal of Criminal Law and Criminology*, Northwestern University School of Law. Vol. 91 (2000–2001): 99–160.

Rovner, J. (2021). "Black disparities in youth incarceration." Sentencing Project. July 15. Retrieved from https://www.sentencingproject.org/publications/black-disparities-youth-incarceration/#:~:text=The%20Black%20youth%20placement%20rate,rate%20of%2072%20per%20100%2C000.

Rudd, R. A., L. J. Paulozzi, M. J. Bauer, R. W. Burleson, R. E. Carlson et al. (2014). "Increases in heroin overdose deaths — 28 states, 2010–2012." *Morbidity and Mortality Weekly Report.* Centers for Disease Control and Prevention (CDC). Vol. 63: 849–854.

Rural Health Information Hub (RHIhub) (2020). "Substance use and misuse in rural areas." Dec. 9. Retrieved from https://www.ruralhealthinfo.org/topics/substance-use.

Rural Health Information Hub (RHIhub) (2021). "Violence and abuse in the rural America." Mar. 26. Retrieved from https://www.ruralhealthinfo.org/topics/violence-and-abuse.

Rutten, A. X., R. R. J. M. Vermeiren, and C. Van Nieuwenhuizen (2017). "Autism in adult and juvenile delinquents: A literature review." *Child and Adolescent Psychiatry and Mental Health.* Vol. 11, issue 1: 1–12.

Ryan, E. (2012). "Changing perceptions of juvenile sex offending in society and the legal system." In *Juvenile Offenders: A Guide to Evaluation and Treatment for Mental Health Professionals*, ed. E. P. Ryan, J. A. Hunter, and D. C. Murrie. Oxford, UK: Oxford University Press.

Ryan, E. P. (2016). "Juvenile sex offenders." *Child and Adolescent Psychiatric Clinics North America.* Vol. 25, issue 1 (Jan.): 81–87.

Ryan, H. (2022). *The Women's House of Detention: A Queer History of a Forgotten Prison.* New York: Bold Type Books.

S

Sacca, L., S. C. Rushing, C. Markham, R. Shegog, M. Peskin, B. Hernandez, A. Gaston, M. Singer, N. Trevino, C. C. Correa, C. Jessen, J. Williamson, and J. Thomas (2021). "Empower sensitive conversations with American Indian and Alaska Native teens." *International Journal of Environmental Research in Public Health.* Vol. 18, issue 17 (Aug. 30): 9126.

Sacca, L., et al. (2021). "Assessment of the Reach, Usability, and Perceived Impact of 'Talking Is Power': A Parental Sexual Health Text-Messaging Service and Web-Based Resource to Empower Sensitive Conversations with American Indian and Alaska Native Teens." *Environmental Research and Public Health.* Vol. 18, issue 17 (Aug.): 9126. Open access at https://www.mdpi.com/1660-4601/18/17/9126.

Sai, K. G., R. Jalaja, A. Amutha, U. Venkatesan, F. M. Anjana, and R. Unnikrishnan (2021). "Psychological impact of COVID-19 in a social media group." *Journal of Diabetology.* Vol. 12, issue 2 (Jan.): 232–236.

Salk, R. H., J. S. Hyde, and L. Y. Abramson (2017). "Gender differences in depression in representative national samples: Meta-analyses of diagnoses and symptoms." *Psychology Bulletin.* Vol. 143, issue. 8 (Aug.): 783–822.

Salzberg, A. (2021). "French Culture: What is the legal drinking age in France and why?" *French Together.* July 19. Retrieved from https://frenchtogether.com/drinking-age-france/#:~:text=The%20legal%20drinking%20age%20in%20France%20is%2018%2C%20or%2016,a%20country%20of%20wine%2Dlovers.

Saminksy, A. (2010). "Preventing juvenile delinquency: Early interventions and comprehensiveness as critical factors." *Inquiries Journal.* Vol. 2, issue 1. Retrieved from http://www.inquiriesjournal.com/articles/165/preventing-juvenile-delinquency-early-intervention-and-comprehensiveness-as-critical-factors.

Sampson, R. J., and J. H. Laub (2005). "A life-course view of the development of crime." *Annals of the American Academy of Political and Social Science.* Vol. 602, issue 12: 12–45.

Sanchez, R. (2000). *My Bloody Life: The Making of a Latin King.* Chicago: Chicago Review Press.

Sanders, C. (2021). "State juvenile justice reforms can boost opportunities, particularly for communities of color." Center on Budget and Policy Priorities. July 27. Retrieved from https://www.cbpp.org/sites/default/files/7-27-21sfp.pdf. or https://www.cbpp.org/research/state-budget-and-tax/state-juvenile-justice-reforms-can-boost-opportunity-particularly-for.

Sanders, M. T., K. L. Beirman, B. S. Heinrichs (2020). "Longitudinal associations linking elementary and middle school contexts with student aggression in early adolescence." *Journal of Abnormal Child Psychology.* Vol. 48: 1569–1580.

San Francisco Probation Department (n.d.). Definition of terms—juvenile probation and court processing. Retrieved from https://sfgov.org/juvprobation/definition-terms-%E2%80%93-juvenile-probation-and-court-processing#:~:text=and%20Court%20Processing-,Referral,case%20is%20to%20be%20handled.

Sawyer, W. (2019). "Youth confinement: The whole pie in 2019." Press release. Prison Policy Initiative. Dec. 19. Retrieved from https://www.prisonpolicy.org/reports/youth2019.html.

Sawyer, W. (2020). "Visualizing the race disparities in mass incarceration." *Briefings,* The Prison Policy Initiative. July 27. Retrieved from https://www.prisonpolicy.org/blog/2020/07/27/disparities/?gclid=Cj0KCQjwmuiTBhDoARIsAPiv6L__SQQSqsRghc6LHV5OAG0QbaNttnZh-8bvRcGv7t_ta1IhVl9i0LZoaAqMOEALw_wcB.

Sax, L. (2017). *Why Gender Matters: What Parents and Teachers Need to Know About the Emerging Science of Sex Differences,* 2d ed. New York: Harmony Books.

Schaffer, H. R., and P. E. Emerson (1964). "The development of social attachments in infancy." *Monographs of the Society for Research in Child Development.*

Schulte, M. T., D. Ramo, and S. A. Brown (2009). "Gender difference in factors influencing alcohol use progression among adolescents." *Clinical Psychology Review.* Vol. 29, issue 6 (Aug.): 535–547.

Schwartz, I. M., M. W. Steketee, and J. A. Butts (2012). "Business as usual: Juvenile justice during the 1980s." *Notre Dame Journal of Law, Ethics, and Public Policy.* Vol. 5, issue 2: 377–396.

Seigel, E., N. Walsh, J. Weber (2014). *Core Principles for Reducing Recidivism and Improving Other Outcomes for Youth in the Juvenile Justice System.* Lexington, KY: Justice Center, Council of State Governments. Retrieved from https://csgjusticecenter.org/wp-content/uploads/2020/01/Juvenile-Justice-White-Paper-with-Appendices-1-1.pdf.

Semenza, D. C., A. M. Testa, D. B. Jackson, M. G. Vaughn, and N. C. Semenza (2020). "Criminal offending trajectories from adolescence through young adulthood and the risk of food insecurity: Evidence from the Add Health study." *Annals of Epidemiology.* Vol. 50: 20–26.e1.

Sentencing Project (2020). Fact sheet: Incarcerated women and girls. Nov. Retrieved from file:///Users/laurahansen/Downloads/Incarcerated-Women-and-Girls.pdf.

Sergel, C. (n.d.). *The Outsiders.* Book Adaptation. Woodstock, IL: Dramatic Publishing.

Serpico, D. (2021). "The cyclical return of the IQ controversy: Revisiting the lessons of the resolution on genetics, race and intelligence." *Journal of the History of Biology.* Retrieved from https://doi.org/10.1007/s10739-021-09637-6.

Sesso, G., G. E. Brancati, P. Fantozzi, E. Inguaggiato, A. Milone, and G. Masi (2021). "Measures of empathy in children and adolescents: A systematic review of questionnaires." *World Journal of Psychiatry.* Vol. 11, issue 10: 876–896.

Shader, M. (2003). Risk factors for delinquency: An overview. Office of Juvenile Justice and Delinquency Prevention (OJJDP), Office of Justice Programs, U.S. Department of Justice. Retrieved from https://www.ojp.gov/pdffiles1/ojjdp/frd030127.pdf.

Sharkey, J. D., S. Stifel, and A. Mayworm (2015; 2022). How to help me get out of a gang: Youth recommendations to family, school, community, and law enforcement systems. *OJJDP Journal of Juvenile Justice.* Pp. 64–83. *eScholarship,* University of California Santa Barbara. Retrieved from https://escholarship.org/content/qt2g45f1rx/qt2g45f1rx.pdf.

Shaw, D. (2019). "Reality check: Are more teenagers carrying knives?" *British Broadcasting Corporation News.* July 31. Retrieved from https://www.bbc.com/news/uk-46153257.

Sheehan, L. L., P. W. Corrigan, and M. A. Al-Khouja. (2017). "Stigma of Suicide: Stakeholder perspectives on the stigma of suicide attempt survivors." *Crisis: The Journal of Crisis Intervention and Suicide Prevention,* Vol. 38, issue 2: 73–81.

Sheley, J. F., and J. D. Wright (2000). "High school youth, weapons, and violence: A national survey of weapon-related experiences, behaviors, and concerns—Final Report." NCJRS, Document No. 181053. Feb. 18.

Shephard, R. E. (2007). Testimony before the Joint Committee on Healthy Families and Communities, Committee on Education and Labor, the Subcommittee on Crime, Terror, and Homeland Security, and Committee on the Judiciary. U.S. House of Representatives, 110th Congress. July 12. Washington, D.C.:U.S. Government Printing Office. Retrieved from https://www.govinfo.gov/content/pkg/CHRG-110hhrg36466/html/CHRG-110hhrg36466.htm.

Sheppard, D., H. Grant, W. Rowe, and N. Jacobs (2000). "Fighting juvenile gun violence." *Juvenile Justice Bulletin,* Office of Juvenile Justice and Delinquency Prevention (OJJDP). Sept. Retrieved from https://www.ojp.gov/pdffiles1/ojjdp/182679.pdf.

Shichor, D. (1983). "Historical and current trends in juvenile justice." *Juvenile and Family Court Journal.* Vol. 34, issue 3: 61–75.

Shieh, P., and T. Tsai (2022). "The prediction of perceived parenting style on mother-infant bonding." *Acta Psychologia.* Vol. 226 (June): 103573.

Shihadeh, E. S., and G. C. Ousey (1998). "Industrial restructuring and violence: The link between entry-level jobs, economic deprivation, and Black and White homicide." *Social Forces.* Vol. 77, issue 1: 185–207.

Shihadeh, E. S., and R. Barranco (2010). "Latino employment and black violence: The unintended consequences of U.S. immigration policy." *Social Forces.* Vol. 88, issue 3: 1393–1420.

Shjarback, J. A. (2019). "State-mandated transparency: A discussion and examination of deadly force data among law enforcement agencies in Texas." *Journal of Crime and Justice.* Vol. 42, issue 1: 3–17.

Shmeuli, B. (2014). "Corporal punishment of children in Jewish Law." *Jewish Law Annual.* Vol. 18: 137–212.

Short, J. F. (1990). "Delinquency and Society." NCJ No. 129399. Office of Justice Programs, U.S. Department of Justice. Retrieved from https://www.ojp.gov/ncjrs/virtual-library/abstracts/delinquency-and-society.

Sibley, M. (2001). "Beat the Heat: A youth program races to keep kids off the street." *Law and Order.* Vol. 49, issue 4 (Apr.): 60–63.

Sickmund, M. (2009). "Highlights: Girls and boys in the juvenile justice system: Are there differences that warrant policy changes in the juvenile justice system?" National Juvenile Justice Network. Retrieved from https://www.njjn.org/uploads/digital-library/Girls_and_boys_in_the_JJ_system_The_Future_of_Children_.pdf.

Siennick, S. E., A. O. Widdowson, and M. E. Feinberg (2020). "Youth with co-occurring delinquency and depressive symptoms: Do they have better or worse delinquent outcomes?" *Journal of Youth and Adolescence.* Vol. 49, issue 6: 1260–1276.

Sievers, F. L. (1963). Forward. *Guidance for Children in Elementary Schools*, H. M. Smith and L. O. Eckerson. Washington, DC: U.S. Department of Health, Education, and Welfare.

Silva, C. S., and M. M. Calheiros (2018). "Stop yelling: Interparental conflict and adolescents' self-representations as mediated by their perceived relationships with parents." *Journal of Family Issues*. Vol. 39, issue 7: 2174–2204.

Simon, H. A. (1982). *Models of Bounded Rationality*. Cambridge, MA: MIT Press.

Simon, H. A. (1990). "Bounded rationality." In *Utility and Probability*, ed. J. Eatwell, M. Milgate, and P. Newman. New York: Palgrave MacMillan.

Simons, R. L., C. A. Johnson, R. D. Conger, G. H. Elder (1998). "A test of latent trait versus life-course perspective on the stability of adolescent antisocial behavior." *Criminology*. Vol. 36: 217–244.

Simonton, S. (2014). "Report: Evidence shows community-based programs work better than incarceration." Retrieved from https://jjie.org/2014/06/25/report-evidence-shows-community-based-programs-work-better-than-incarceration/.

Siria, S., E. Echeburúa, and P. J. Amor (2020). "Characteristics and risk factors in juvenile sexual offenders." *Psicothema*. Vol. 32, issue 3: 314–321.

Sitnick, S. L., C. Galán, A. Chardée, and D. S. Shaw (2019). "Early childhood predictors of boys' antisocial and violent behavior in early adulthood." *Infant Mental Health Journal*. Vol. 40, issue 1 (Jan.): 67–83.

Sjödin, A., M. Wallinius, E. Billstedt, B. Hofvander, and T. Nilsson (2017). "Dating violence compared to other types of violence: Similar offenders but different victims." *European Journal of Psychology Applied to Legal Context*. Vol. 9, issue 2: 83–91.

Skewes, M. C., and V. M. Gonzalez (2013). "The Biopsychosocial Model of addiction." In *Principles of Addiction: Comprehensive Addiction Behaviors and Disorders*, Vol. 1, ed. P. Miller. Amsterdam, NL: Elsevier.

Skiba, R. J., and R. L. Peterson (2000). "School discipline at a crossroads: From zero tolerance to early response." *Exceptional Children*. Vol. 66, issue 3 (Spring): 335–347.

Skogan, W. (1990). *Disorder and Decline: Crime and the Spiral Decay in American Cities*. New York, NY: Free Press.

Slavin, R. E. (1990). "Achievement effects of ability grouping in secondary schools: A best-evidence synthesis." *Review of Educational Research*. Vol. 80: 471–499.

Slawson, N. (2021). "He was not in a gang": Lives and deaths of 30 London teenage homicide victims. *The Guardian*. Dec. 31. Retrieved from https://www.theguardian.com/uk-news/2021/dec/31/knife-rises-in-london-with-30-teen-homicides-in-2021.

Slomkowski, C., R. Rende, K. J. Conger, R. L. Simons, and R. D. Conger (2003). "Sisters, brothers, and delinquency; Evaluating social influence in early and middle adolescence." *Child Development*. Vol. 72, issue 1: 271–293.

Slotboom, A. M., J. Hendriks, J. Verbruggen (2011). "Contrasting adolescent female and male sexual aggression: A self-report study of prevalence and predictors of sexual aggression." *Journal of Sexual Aggression*. Vol. 17: 15–33.

Small, S. A., A. J. Reynolds, C. O'Connor, S. M. Cooney (2005). "What works, Wisconsin: What science tells us about cost-effective programs for juvenile delinquency prevention." Report, Wisconsin Governor's Juvenile Justice Commissions and the Wisconsin Office of Justice Assistance. University of Wisconsin-Madison. June. Retrieved from https://fyi.extension.wisc.edu/criminaljusticeandprevention/files/2012/04/whatworkswisconsin.pdf.

Smith, A. D., and R. Paternoster (1987). "The gender gap in theories of deviance: Issues and evidence." *Journal of Research in Crime and Delinquency*. Vol. 24: 140–172.

Soares-Weiser, K., N. Maayan, H. Bergen, C. Davenport, A. J. Kirkham, S. Grabowski, and E. E. Adams (2015). "First rank symptoms for schizophrenia." In *Cochrane Database of Systematic Reviews*. Cochrane Collaborative. Hoboken, NJ: John Wiley and Sons.

Sobel, R. S., and B. J. Osoba (2009). "Youth gangs as pseudo-governments: implications for violent crime." *Southern Economic Journal*. Vol. 75, issue 4: 996–1019.

Soderberg, L. (2018). "Writing the criminal child: Antebellum prison records, parenting manuals, and the rise of the incorrigible child." *Journal of Nineteenth-Century Americanists*. Vol. 6, issue 2: 307–334.

Solina, S. (2021). "After 2 decades away, Weed and Seed program is back to target crime in Chinatown." *Hawaii News Now*. Sept. 8. Retrieved from https://www.hawaiinewsnow.com/2021/09/09/after-2-decades-away-weed-seed-program-is-back-target-crime-chinatown/.

Spajic, D. J. (2022). "Piracy is back: Piracy statistics for 2022." DataProt. Feb. 9. Retrieved from https://dataprot.net/statistics/piracy-statistics/.

Spaulding, E. R. (1921). "Emotional episodes among psychopathic delinquent women." *Journal of Nervous and Mental Disease.* Vol. 54, issue 4 (Oct.): 293–323.

Springhall, J. (1999). *Youth, Popular Culture and Moral Panics: Penny Gaffs to Gangsta-Rap, 1830–1996.* London, UK: MacMillan Press.

Spruit, A., P. Hoffenaar, C. van der Put, E. van Vugt, and G. J. Stams (2018). "The effect of a sports-based intervention to prevent juvenile delinquency in at-risk adolescents." *Children and Youth Services Review.* Vol. 94: 689–698.

Sripada, K. (2017). " 'Beginning with the smallest intake': Children's brain development and the role of neuroscience in global environmental health." *Neuron.* Vol. 95 (Sept.): 1242–1245.

Stanley, S. M. (1996). "School uniforms and safety." *Education and Urban Society.* Vol. 28, issue 4: 424–35.

Stansfield, R., D. Semenza, and T. Steidley (2021). "Public guns, private violence: The association of city-level firearm availability and intimate partner homicide in the United States." *Preventative Medicine.* Vol. 148 (July): e106599.

State of Massachusetts (2019). *Charles E. Shannon Community Safety Initiative: Holyoke/Chicopee.* Boston, MA: Massachusetts Executive Office of Public Safety and Security.

Statista Research Department (2019). How many tattoos do you have? United States—Number of tattoos in 2019. Dec. 12. Retrieved from https://www.statista.com/statistics/721567/number-of-tattoos-united-states/.

Statista Research Department (2021). Moral stance towards gay or lesbian relations in the United States 2021. Aug. 12. Retrieved from https://www.statista.com/statistics/225968/americans-moral-stance-towards-gay-or-lesbian-relations/.

Statista Research Department (2021). Murder in the U.S.: Number of offenders in the United States 2020, by age. Statista Research. Oct. 7. Retrieved from https://www.statista.com/statistics/251884/murder-offenders-in-the-us-by-age/.

Statista Research Department (2021). Murder in the U.S.: Number of victims in the United States 2020, by age. Statista Research. Oct. 7. Retrieved from https://www.statista.com/statistics/251878/murder-victims-in-the-us-by-age/.

Statista Research Department (2022). "Russia: Which of the following problems of our society worry you the most and you consider most critical?" May 19. Retrieved from https://www.statista.com/statistics/1034365/russia-regions-with-most-youth-crimes/#:~:text=Magadan%20Oblast%20and%20the%20Republic,as%20co%2Dperpetrators%20 in%202021.

Stattin, H., D. Magnusson, and H. Reichel (1989). "Criminal activity at different ages: A study based on a Swedish longitudinal research population." *British Journal of Criminology.* Vol. 29, issue 4: 368–385.

Steffensmeier, D., J. S. Schwartz, H. Zhong, and J. Ackerman (2005). "An assessment of recent trends in girls' violence using diverse longitudinal sources: Is the gender gap closing?" *Criminology.* Vol. 43, issue 2: 355–406.

Steffensmeier, D., H. Zhong, J. Ackerman, J. Schwartz, and S. Agha (2006). "Gender gap trends for violent crimes, 1980 to 2003: A UCR-NCVS comparison." *Feminist Criminology.* Vol. 1: 72–98.

Steffes, T. L. (2012). *School, Society, and the State: New Education to Govern Modern America, 1890–1940.* Chicago, IL: University of Chicago Press.

Steinberg, A., and E. Nadworny (2022). "Community college enrollment is down, but skilled-trades programs are booming." National Public Radio (NPR). Mar. 28. Retrieved from https://www.npr.org/2022/03/28/1086454046/2-year-skilled-trades-programs-booming#::text=Two%2Dyear%20construction%20trades%20programs%20see%20spike%20in%20enrollment%20%3A%20NPR&text=Two%2Dyear%20construction%20trades%20programs%20see%20spike%20in%20enrollment%20Enrollment,in%20construction%20trades%20are%20booming.

Steinfels, P. (2009). "Despite a decade of controversy, the 'Faith-Based Initiative' endures." *The New York Times.* July 31. Retrieved from https://www.nytimes.com/2009/08/01/us/01beliefs.html.

Steketee, M., C. Aussems, and I. H. Marshall (2021). "Exploring the impact of child maltreatment and interparental violence on violent delinquency in an international sample." *Journal of Interpersonal Violence.* Vol. 36: 13–14.

Stephenson, S. (2015). *Gangs of Russia: From the Streets to the Corridors of Power.* Ithaca, NY: Cornell University Press.

Stephenson, Z., J. Woodhams, and C. Cooke (2014). "Sex differences in predictors of violent juvenile offending." *Aggressive Behavior.* Vol. 40, issue 2 (Mar.-Apr.): 165–177.

Stetina, A. (2022). "1,560 Belgian young offenders sent to community institutions in 2021." *Brussels Times.* July 8. Retrieved from https://www.brusselstimes.com/belgium/251339/1560-belgian-young-people-sent-to-community-institutions-in-2021.

Stevens, S. (2021). "The difference between gentrification and revitalization." *North Texas Daily.* May 4. Retrieved from https://www.ntdaily.com/the-difference-between-gentrification-and-revitalization/#:~:text=Revitalization%20is%20a%20positive%20approach,to%20important%20opportunities%20and%20resources.

Stiffman, A. R. (1989). "Physical and sexual abuse in runaway youth." *Child Abuse and Neglect.* Vol. 13: 417–426.

Stockman, F. (2000). "Kenya faces obstacles in aiding its poorest children." *Christian Science Monitor.* Vol. 92, issue 84: 7.

Stoloff, J. A. (2004). A brief history of public housing. Jan. Retrieved from https://www.researchgate.net/publication/228789405_A_brief_history_of_public_housing.

Stouthamer-Loeber, M., R. Loeber, D. L. Homish and E. Wei (2001). "Maltreatment of boys and development of disruptive and delinquent behavior." *Development and Psychopathology.* Vol. 13: 941–955.

Strello, A., R. Striethold, I. Steinmann, and C. Siepmann (2021). "Early tracking and different types of inequalities in achievement: Difference-in-differences evidence from 20 years of large-scale assessments." *Educational Assessment, Evaluation, and Accountability.* Vol. 33: 139–167.

Substance Abuse and Mental Health Services Administration (2003). *Results from the 2002 National Survey on Drug Use and Health: National Findings.* Rockville, MD: Office of Applied Studies.

Sui-Chu, E. H., and J. D. Willms (1996). "Effects of parental involvement on eighth-grade achievement." *Sociology of Education.* Vol. 69: 126–141.

Sukpanich, T. (2012). "Rising youth crime levels confound justice system." *Bangkok Post.* Jan. 22. Retrieved from https://www.bangkokpost.com/thailand/special-reports/276249/rising-youth-crime-levels-confound-justice-system.

Sukyirun, P. (2016). "Biosocial interaction and juvenile delinquency behaviors of Thai juvenile delinquents." *International Journal of Criminal Justice Science.* Vol. 11, issue 2: 100–113.

Sullivan, B. (2021). "Kyle Rittenhouse is acquitted of all charges in the trial over killing 2 in Kenosha." New England Public Radio. Nov. 19. Retrieved from https://www.npr.org/2021/11/19/1057288807/kyle-rittenhouse-acquitted-all-charges-verdict.

Sumner, J., D. Boisvert, and J. P. Andersen (2016). "The effects of stress and social support on externalizing behaviors among children in military families." *Deviant Behavior.* Vol. 37, issue 3: 246–262.

Sung, H., L. Richter, R. Vaughan, P. B. Johnson, and B. Thom (2005). "Nonmedical use of prescription opioids among teenagers in the United States: Trends and correlates." *Journal of Adolescent Health.* Vol. 37: 44–51.

Surarітthidham, C. (2020). "Juvenile crime in Thailand." Conference paper, 174th International Senior Seminar. United Nations Asia and Far East Institute for the Prevention Offenders (UNAFEI). Feb. Retrieved from https://www.unafei.or.jp/publications/pdf/RS_No111/No111_15_IP_Suraritthidham.pdf.

Sutherland, E. H. (1947). *Principles of Criminology.* Philadelphia: J. B. Lippincott.

Sutherland, E. H., and D. R. Cressey (1939). *Principles of Criminology.* Reprint 1992. Lanham, MD: AltaMira Press.

Sutphen, R. D., and J. Ford (2001). "The effectiveness and enforcement of teen curfew law." *Journal of Sociology and Social Welfare.* Vol. 28, issue 1 (Mar.): 55–78.

Sweatt, L. C., G. Harding, L. Knight-Lynn, S. Rasheed, and P. Carter (2002). "Talking about the silent fear: Adolescent's experiences of violence in an urban high-rise community." *Adolescence.* Vol. 37, issue 145: 109–121.

Sweeten, G., S. D. Bushway, and R. Paternoster (2009). "Does dropping out of school mean dropping into delinquency?" *Criminology.* Vol. 47, issue 1: 47–91.

Sykes, G. M., and D. Matza (1957). "Techniques of neutralization: A theory of delinquency." *American Sociological Review.* Vol. 22, issue 6: 664–670.

Sylvester, P. (2020). "12 Laws in Thailand: How to stay out of jail." *World Nomads.* Feb. 1. Retrieved from https://www.worldnomads.com/travel-safety/southeast-asia/thailand/a-travellers-guide-to-thailands-laws#drug-laws-in-thailand.

T

Tan, S. (2007). "Some Eden [high school] cheerleaders accused of shoplifting incident happened at Disney World." *Buffalo News.* Apr. 4. Retrieved from https://buffalonews.com/news/some-eden-cheerleaders-accused-of-shoplifting-incident-happened-at-disney-world/article_b4527063-c03a-5e57-9801-7a24514622f8.html#:~:text=Disney%20has%20a%20reputation%20for,can%20file%20the%20appropriate%20report.%22.

Tang, W., and C. Vandenbergh (2021). "Role overload and work performance: The role of psychological strain and leader-member exchange." *Frontiers in Psychology.* May 21. Vol. 12:e691207. Retrieved from https://www.ncbi.nlm.nih.gov/pmc/articles/PMC8176030/#:~:text=Role%20overload%20is%20a%20specific,understood%20through%20the%20COR%20lens.

Tanioka, I., and D. Glasier (1991). "School uniforms, routine activities, and social control of delinquency in Japan." *Youth and Society.* Vol. 23, issue 1 (Sept.): 50–75.

Taussig, H. N., J. Dmitrieva, E. F. Garrido, J. L. Cooley, and E. Crites (2021). "Fostering Health Futures prevention intervention for children in foster care: Long-term delinquency outcomes from a randomized controlled trial." *Prevention Science.* Vol. 22: 1120–1133.

Taylor, C. (2016). Review of the Youth Justice System in England and Wales. London, ENG: U.K. Ministry of Justice. May. Retrieved from https://assets.publishing.service.gov.uk/government/uploads/system/uploads/attachment_data/file/577105/youth-justice-review-final-report-print.pdf.

Taylor, K. (2019). "What we know about the Michelle Carter suicide texting case." *The New York Times.* July 9. Retrieved from https://www.nytimes.com/2019/07/09/us/michelle-carter-i-love-you-now-die.html.

Teachingcertificate.com (2022). "New Mexico substitute teaching license." Retrieved from https://www.teaching-certification.com/teaching/new-mexico-substitute-license.html.

Tener, D., E. Lusky, N. Tarshish, and S. Turjeman (2018). "Parental attitudes following disclosure of sibling sexual abuse: A child advocacy center intervention study." *American Journal of Orthopsychiatry.* Jan. 25. Retrieved from https://calio.org/wp-content/uploads/2017/08/Parental-Attitudes-Following-Disclosure-of-Sibling-Sexual-Abuse-A-Child-Advocacy-Center-Intervention-Study.pdf.

Texas Juvenile Probation Commission (1993). "Juvenile delinquency prevention in Texas." NCJ No. 142222. Office of Justice Programs, U.S. Department of Justice. Retrieved from https://www.ojp.gov/ncjrs/virtual-library/abstracts/juvenile-delinquency-prevention-texas#:~:text=Primary%20prevention%20is%20concerned%20with,in%20the%20juvenile%20justice%20system.

Textor, C. (2021). Number of young offenders in Taiwan 2010–2020. Statista. Jan. 6. Retrieved from https://www.statista.com/statistics/319872/taiwan-number-of-young-offenders/#:: text=In%202020%2C%20approximately%2010%2C226%20young%20offenders%20 had%20been%20recorded%20in%20Taiwan.

Thomas, S. (2022). "Impulse Control Disorders and substance abuse." American Addiction Centers. Mar. 15. Retrieved from https://americanaddictioncenters.org/co-occurring-disorders/impulse-control-disorder.

Thompson, M. (2022). "Carjackings soar by up to 500% in US cities." [U.K.] *Daily Mail.* Jan. 23. Retrieved from https://www.dailymail.co.uk/news/article-10433381/Carjackings-rise-500-large-cities-disturbing-spikes.html.

Thornberry, T. P. (1987). "Toward an interaction theory of delinquency." *Criminology.* Vol. 25, issue 4: 863–892.

Thornberry, T. P., A. J. Lizotte, M. D. Krohn, C. A. Smith, and P. K. Porter (2003). "Causes and consequences of delinquency." In *Taking Stock of Delinquency: An Overview of Findings from Contemporary Longitudinal Studies*, ed. T. P. Thornberry and M. D. Krohn. New York: Springer Publishing.

Thornberry, T. P., M. Moor, and R. L. Christenson (1985). "The effect of dropping out of high school on subsequent criminal behavior." *Criminology.* Vol. 23: 3–18.

Thoyibah, Z., N. Intansari, and D. W. Sumarni (2017). "Correlation between family communication patterns and juvenile delinquency in junior high school." *Belitung Nursing Journal.* Vol. 3, issue 4: 297–306.

Thrasher, F. M. (1949). "The comics and delinquency: Cause or scapegoat." *Journal of Educational Sociology.* Vol. 23, issue 4 (Dec.): 195–205.

Thulin, E. J., J. E. Heinze, P. Kernsmith, J. Smith-Darden, and P. J. Fleming (2021). "Adolescent risk of violence and electronic dating abuse: A latent class analysis." *Journal of Youth and Adolescence.* Vol. 50, issue 12 (Dec.): 2472–2486.

Tiihonen, J., M., M. Lehti, M. Aaltonen, J. Kivoivuori, H. Kautiainen, L. J. Virta, F. Hoti, A. Tanskanen, and P. Korhonen (2015). "Psychotropic drugs and homicide: A prospective cohort study from Finland." *World Psychiatry.* Vol. 14, issue 2: 245–247.

Tillyer, M. S., and R. Tillyer (2016). "Race, ethnicity, and adolescent violent victimization." *Journal of Youth and Adolescence.* Vol. 45: 1497–1511.

Toensing, G. C. (2018). "Akaka Bill gets Obama approval." *Indian Country Today.* Sept. 12. Retrieved from https://indiancountrytoday.com/archive/akaka-bill-gets-obama-approval.

Tomkins, D. M., and E. M. Sellers (2001). "Addiction and the brain: The role of neurotransmitters in the cause and treatment of drug dependence." *Canadian Medical Association Journal.* Vol. 164, issue 6: 817–821.

Tongkachok, K., A. Samati, and T. Tongkachok (2021). "Restorative juvenile justice system in the southeast border of Thailand." *Psychology and Education.* Vol. 58, issue 2: 2544–2556.

Transformative Justice Law Project of Illinois (n.d.). Quick guide to the criminalization of transgender and gender non-conforming people. Retrieved from https://www.prisonlegalnews.org/media/publications/Guide%20to%20Criminalization%20of%20Trans%20%26%20Gender%20Non-Conforming%20People%20Transformative%20Justice%20Law%20Proj.%20of%20IL.pdf.

Traylor, V. (2021). "What are the 5 developmental disabilities?" New Jersey Developmental Disabilities Council. Oct. 2. Retrieved from https://www.njddc.org/5-developmental-disabilities/.

Trujillo, D. (2022). "Mother issues warning after teen son dies by suicide over cyber blackmail." NBC Bay Area. Apr. 4. Retrieved from https://www.nbcbayarea.com/news/local/mother-issues-warning-after-teen-son-dies-by-suicide-over-cyber-blackmail/2854872/.

Tsai, T. M. (2002). "On Personal Victimization Features and Causes." Thesis, Department of Crime Prevention, Central Police University, Taiwan.

Tulviste, T., L. Toome, M. Männamaa, and H. Varendi (2020). "Language skills at corrected age 2; 0 are poorer in extremely and very preterm boys but not girls compared with their full-term peers." *Early Human Development.* Vol. 151: e105164.

Tunnell, K. D. (2006). "Socially disorganized rural communities." *Crime, Media, Culture.* Vol. 2, issue 3: 332–337.

Turner, A. (2017). "#FlashbackFriday—On this day in 1973, the APA removed homosexuality from the list of mental illnesses." Human Rights Campaign. Dec. 15. Retrieved from https://www.hrc.org/news/flashbackfriday-today-in-1973-the-apa-removed-homosexuality-from-list-of-me.

Twenge, J. M. (2000). "The Age of Anxiety? Birth cohort change in anxiety and neuroticism, 1952–1993." *Journal of Personality and Social Psychology.* Vol. 79, issue 6: 1007–1021. Available at https://www.apa.org/pubs/journals/releases/psp7961007.pdf.

Tygart, C. E. (1990). "Self-reported delinquency and natural parents-stepparent youth relations." *Journal of Divorce and Remarriage.* Vol. 13, issue 4: 89–99.

Tyler, T. R. (2015). "Why trust matters with juveniles." *American Journal of Orthopsychiatry.* Vol. 85, issue 6, suppl.: S93–S99.

U

Udris, R. (2016). "Cyber deviance among adolescents and the role of family, school, and neighborhood: A cross-national study." *International Journal of Cyber Criminology.* Vol. 10: 127–146.

Uggen, C. (2000). "Working as a turning point in life course of criminals: A duration model of age, employment, and recidivism." *American Sociological Review.* Vol. 65, issue 4: 529–546.

Ukris, D. (2001). Juvenile justice system in Thailand. 118 International Training Course. United Nations Far East Institute for Crime Prevention (UNFEI). July. Retrieved from https://www.unafei.or.jp/publications/pdf/RS_No59/No59_22PA_Ukris.pdf.

Umpierre, M. (2014). "Rights and responsibilities of youth, families and staff." In *Desktop Guide to Quality Practice for Working with Youth in Confinement*. Washington, D.C.: National Partnership for Juvenile Services and Office of Juvenile Justice and Delinquency Prevention.

Underwood, L. A., and A. Washington (2016). "Mental illness and juvenile offenders." *International Journal of Environmental Research and Public Health*. Vol. 13, issue 2 (Feb.): 228.

Unesco Institute for Statistics (2022). Kenya. Retrieved from http://uis.unesco.org/en/country/ke.

UNICEF (n.d.). Section 407: Juvenile justice system, Thailand. Legal age limits, State Party Report. Retrieved from https://www.unicef-irc.org/portfolios/documents/446_thailand.htm#:~:text=Thai%20law%20limits%20children's%20criminal,not%20liable%20to%20criminal%20punishment.

United Kingdom Government Services (n.d.). Selling, buying, and carrying knives: Basic laws on knives. Retrieved from https://www.gov.uk/buying-carrying-knives.

United Kingdom Legislation (2021). Firearms Act 1968. UK Public General Acts. July 14. Retrieved from https://www.legislation.gov.uk/ukpga/1968/27.

United Nations (UN) (n.d.). "Legal ban on violence against children." UN Special Representative of the Secretary-General on Violence Against Children. Retrieved from https://violenceagainstchildren.un.org/content/legal-ban-violence-against-children.

United Nations Women (2022). Facts and figures: Ending violence against women. United Nations. Feb. Retrieved from https://www.unwomen.org/en/what-we-do/ending-violence-against-women/facts-and-figures.

United States Attorney's Office (2018). "Weed and seed." Northern District of California, U.S. Department of Justice. Oct. 5. Retrieved from https://www.justice.gov/usao-ndca/weed-and-seed#:~:text=Weed%20and%20Seed%20is%20a,crime%20neighborhoods%20throughout%20the%20country.

United States Bureau of Alcohol, Tobacco, and Firearms (ATF) (2017). Youth Handgun Safety Act Notice. United States Bureau of Justice. July. Retrieved from https://www.atf.gov/firearms/docs/guide/atf-i-53002-%E2%80%94-youth-handgun-safety-act-notice/download#:~:text=(3)%20Federal%20law%20prohibits%2C,to%20a%20person%20under%2018.

United States Bureau of Justice Assistance (BJA) (n.d.). "Tribes: Hawaii. Walking on Common Ground." U.S. Department of Justice Programs, U.S. Department of Justice. Retrieved from http://walkingoncommonground.org/state.cfm?topic=20&fullstate=hawaii.

United States Bureau of Labor Statistics (BLS) (2020). "Comparing characteristics and selected expenditures of dual- and single-income households with children." *Monthly Labor Review*. U.S. Department of Labor. Sept. Retrieved from https://www.bls.gov/opub/mlr/2020/article/comparing-characteristics-and-selected-expenditures-of-dual-and-single-income-households-with-children.htm#:~:text=As%20shown%20in%20the%20figure,have%20two%20or%20more%20children.

United States Bureau of Labor Statistics (BLS) (2022). "Social Workers: Pay." *Occupational Outlook Handbook*. U.S. Department of Labor. Retrieved from https://www.bls.gov/ooh/community-and-social-service/social-workers.htm#tab-5.

United States Bureau of Labor Statistics (BLS) (2022). "Supplemental data measuring the effects of the coronavirus (COVID-19) pandemic on the labor market." Labor Force Statistics from Current Population Survey. U.S. Department of Labor. May 12. Retrieved from https://www.bls.gov/cps/effects-of-the-coronavirus-covid-19-pandemic.htm.

United States Department of Agriculture (USDA) (2022). Definitions of food insecurity. Apr. 22. Retrieved from https://www.ers.usda.gov/topics/food-nutrition-assistance/food-security-in-the-u-s/definitions-of-food-security/#:~:text=Food%20insecurity%E2%80%94the%20condition%20assessed,may%20result%20from%20food%20insecurity.

United States Department of Agriculture (USDA) (2022). Rural poverty and well-being. Mar. 7. Retrieved from https://www.ers.usda.gov/topics/rural-economy-population/rural-poverty-well-being/#demographics.

United States Department of Education (n.d.) Family Education Rights and Privacy Act (FERPA). Retrieved from https://www2.ed.gov/policy/gen/guid/fpco/ferpa/index.html.

United States Department of Health and Human Services (HHS) (1979). "The Belmont Report: Ethical Principles and Guides for the Protection of Human Subjects of Research." Apr. 18. Washington, DC: Department of Health, Education, and Welfare.

United States Department of Health and Human Services (HHS) (2014). "Office of Minority Health Minority Youth Violence Prevention Program: Grantee project summaries." Retrieved from https://minorityhealth.hhs.gov/omh/content.aspx?ID=10175.

United States Department of Health and Human Services (HHS) (2021). Federal law. Oct. 6. Retrieved from https://www.stopbullying.gov/resources/laws/federal.

United States Department of Health and Human Services (HHS) (2022). Laws, policies and regulation: State laws. Jan. 7. Retrieved from https://www.stopbullying.gov/resources/laws.

United States Department of Health and Human Services (HHS) (n.d.). "Grant fraud and the responsibilities of award recipients." Retrieved from https://www.grants.gov/learn-grants/grant-fraud/grant-fraud-responsibilities.html.

United States Department of Housing and Urban Development (HUD) (n.d.). Public housing: Image versus facts. Office of Policy Development and Research. Retrieved from https://www.huduser.gov/periodicals/ushmc/spring95/spring95.html#:~:text=Public%20housing%20contains%20a%20much,43%20percent%20of%20public%20housing.

United States Department of Justice (2005). "Massachusetts teen convicted for hacking into Internet and telephone service providers and making bomb threats to high schools in Massachusetts and Florida." Press Release, U.S. State Attorney's Office, District of Massachusetts. Sept. 8. Retrieved from https://www.justice.gov/archive/criminal/cybercrime/press-releases/2005/juvenileSentboston.htm#:~:text=A20Massachusetts%20juvenile%20pled%20guilty,high%20schools%20in%20Florida%20and.

United States Department of Justice (2021). Deprivation of rights under color of law. Civil Rights Division. May 31. Retrieved from https://www.justice.gov/crt/deprivation-rights-under-color-law.

United States Department of Justice (2021). "Justice Department announces investigation into conditions at five juvenile facilities in Texas." Press Release, Office of Public Affairs. Oct. 13. Retrieved from https://www.justice.gov/opa/pr/justice-department-announces-investigation-conditions-five-juvenile-facilities-texas.

United States Department of Justice (n.d.). "Juvenile" Defined. U.S. Department of Justice Archives. Retrieved from https://www.justice.gov/archives/jm/criminal-resource-manual-38-juvenile-defined.

United States Department of Justice Archives (2020). "Arresting Juveniles." *Criminal Justice Resource Manual*, CMR 118, U.S. Department of Justice. Jan. 20. Retrieved from https://www.justice.gov/archives/jm/criminal-resource-manual-118-arresting-juveniles.

United States Department of Labor (n.d.). Child labor: Children have rights. Retrieved from https://www.worker.gov/concerns/child-labor-wages/#:~:text=Federal%20child%20labor%20law%20generally,18%20in%20any%20hazardous%20occupation.

United States Department of Labor (n.d.). Parental exemption: Agricultural employment. Retrieved from https://www.dol.gov/general/topic/youthlabor/agriculturalemployment.

United States Department of Labor Statistics (2022). Education pays. U.S. Department of Labor. Sept. 8. Retrieved from https://www.bls.gov/emp/chart-unemployment-earnings-education.htm.

United States Food and Drug Administration (2021). *Tobacco 21*. Sept. 1. Retrieved from https://www.fda.gov/tobacco-products/retail-sales-tobacco-products/tobacco-21.

United States Government Accountability Office (GAO) (2021). "Juvenile Justice Grants: The Office of Justice Programs could improve the quality of a key fraud control." GAO-21-302. Mar. 31. Retrieved from https://www.gao.gov/products/gao-21-302.

United States Library of Congress (2008). Taiwan: Amendment to Firearms Law. Dec. 5. Retrieved from https://www.loc.gov/item/global-legal-monitor/2008-12-05/taiwan-amendment-to-firearms-law/.

United States Library of Congress (n.d.). Youth in the Civil Rights Movement. Civil Rights History Project, 2009. Retrieved from https://www.loc.gov/collections/civil-rights-history-project/articles-and-essays/youth-in-the-civil-rights-movement/.

United States Senate (1993). H.R. 3098—Youth Handgun Safety Act. 103rd Congress (1993–1994). Nov. 22. Retrieved from https://www.congress.gov/bill/103rd-congress/house-bill/3098/text#:~:text=3098%20%2D%20103rd%20Congress%20(1993%2D,Congress.gov%20%7C%20Library%20of%20Congress.

United States Supreme Court (1966). *Miranda v. Arizona*, 384 US 436. June 13. Retrieved from https://www.oyez.org/cases/1965/759.

United States Supreme Court (1968). *United States v. O'Brien*. 391 U.S. 367. May 27. Retrieved from https://scholar.google.com/scholar_case?case=12229836877065678192&hl=en&as_sdt=6&as_vis=1&oi=scholarr.

University of Central Florida (2022). "Juvenile probation officer: Salary, career outlook and requirements." UCF Online. Retrieved from https://www.ucf.edu/online/criminal-justice/news/juvenile-probation-office/.

University of Michigan (n.d.). Corporal punishment. Health Library, C.S. Mott Children's Hospital. Ann Harbor, MI. Retrieved from https://www.mottchildren.org/health-library/tm4923.

University of Western Alabama (n.d.). The Science of Emotions: Exploring the Basics of Emotional Psychology. UWA online. Retrieved from https://online.uwa.edu/wp-content/uploads/2019/04/Science-of-Emotion-Guide-UWA.pdf.

V

Vagins, D. J., and J. McCurdy (2006). *Cracks in the System: Twenty Years of Unjust Federal Crack Cocaine Law.* Washington, D.C.: American Civil Liberties Union (ACLU).

Vandiver, D. M., and G. Kercher (2004). "Offender and victim characteristics of registered female sexual offenders in Texas: A proposed typology of female sexual offenders." *Sexual Abuse.* Vol. 16: 121–137.

Van Dyke, N., and G. Tester (2014). "Hate crimes on college campuses." *Journal of Contemporary Criminal Justice.* Retrieved from https://www.researchgate.net/profile/Nella-Van-Dyke/publication/269598354_Dangerous_Climates_Factors_Associated_With_Variation_in_Racist_Hate_Crimes_on_College_Campuses/links/56faaa3a08ae8239f6dad24e/Dangerous-Climates-Factors-Associated-With-Variation-in-Racist-Hate-Crimes-on-College-Campuses.pdf.

VanLandingham, G. (2015). "Evidence trumps anecdote for 'Scared Straight' programs." PEW Research Center. Oct. 14. Retrieved from https://www.pewtrusts.org/en/research-and-analysis/blogs/stateline/2015/10/14/evidence-trumps-anecdote-for-scared-straight-programs.

Vasey, M. W., G. Bosmans, and T. H. Ollendick (2014). "The developmental psychopathology of anxiety." In *Handbook of Developmental Psychopathology*, ed. M. Lewis and K. Rudolph. Boston, MA: Springer.

Vaughan, J., J. A. Coddington, A. H. Ahmed, and M. Ertel (2017). "Separation anxiety disorder in school-age children: What health care providers should know." *Journal of Pediatric Health Care.* Vol. 31, issue 4 (July-Aug.): 433–440.

Vedantam, S., C. Benderev, T. Boyle, R. Klahr, M. Penman, and J. Schmidt (2016). "How a theory of crime and policing was born, and went terribly wrong." National Public Radio (NPR). Nov. 1. Retrieved from https://www.npr.org/2016/11/01/500104506/broken-windows-policing-and-the-origins-of-stop-and-frisk-and-how-it-went-wrong.

Victor, J. (1998). "Moral panics and the social construction of deviant behavior: A theory and application to the case of ritual child abuse." *Sociological Perspectives.* Fall. Retrieved from http://pascalfroissart.online.fr/3-cache/1998-victor.pdf.

Vincent, G. M. (2012). *Screening and Assessment in Juvenile Justice Systems: Identifying Mental Health Needs and Risk of Reoffending.* Washington, DC: Technical Assistance Partnership for Child and Family Mental Health.

Vitaro, F., M. Brendgen, and R. E. Tremblay (2000). "Influence of deviant friends on delinquency: Searching for moderator variables." *Journal of Abnormal Child Psychology.* Vol. 28, issue 4 (Aug.): 313–325.

Vogel, M., and S. F. Messner (2012). "Social correlates of delinquency for youth in need of mental health services: Examining the scope conditions of criminological theories." *Justice Quarterly.* Vol. 29, issue 4 (Aug.): 546–572.

Voth Shrag, R. J., L. G. Wood, and K. Wachter (2021). "Compassion fatigue among the intimate partner violence and sexual assault workforce: Enhancing organizational practice." *Violence Against Women.* Vol. 28, issue 1 (Jan.): 277–297.

Vu, H. (2021). "What happens when you get caught shoplifting at Disneyland?" Law Offices of Hieu Vu. May 28. Retrieved from https://vulawoffice.com/theft/shoplifting-at-disneyland/.

W

Wahyuni, H., Y. Riyanto, and I. K. Atmadja (2019). "The impacts of verbal violence by family members on children's social emotional aspects." *Advances in Social Science, Education and Humanities Research*. Vol. 387: 210–214.

Walgrave, L. (2002). "Juvenile justice in Belgium." In *Juvenile Justice Systems: International Perspectives*, ed. J. Winterdyk. Vancouver, B.C., CA: Canadian Scholars' Press.

Walker, S. W., and J. R. Herting (2020). "The impact of pretrial juvenile detention on 12-month recidivism: A matched comparison study." *Crime and Delinquency*. Vol. 66, issues 13–14: 1865–1887.

Wallace, K. (2013). "6-year-old suspended for kissing girl, accused of sexual harassment." CNN. Dec. 12. Available at http://www.cnn.com/2013/12/11/living/6-year-old-suspended-kissing-girl/.

Walsh, B. C., and D. P. Farrington (2009). "Early developmental prevention of delinquency and later offending: Prospects and challenges." *International Journal of Developmental Science*. Vol. 3, issue 3: 247–259.

Walters, A. C. (2018). "The forgotten children: Victims of domestic violence, victims of the system." *Albany Government Law Review*. Vol. 12: 286.

Walters, G. D. (2017). "Sibling delinquency as a risk factor for future offending: An exploratory analysis." *Youth Violence and Juvenile Justice*. Vol. 16, issue 4: 343–357.

Walters, G. D. (2020). "Prosocial peers as risk, protective, and promotive factors for the prevention of delinquency and drug use." *Journal of Youth and Adolescence*. Vol. 49 (Mar.): 618–630.

Walters, G. D. (2021). "Trajectories of bullying victimization and perpetuation in Australian school children and their relationship to future delinquency and conduct problems." *Psychology of Violence*. Vol. 11, issue 1: 19–27.

Walters, G. D., L. Runell, and J. Kremser (2021). "Social and psychological effects of the COVID-19 pandemic on middle-school students: Attendance options and changes over time." *School Psychology*. Vol. 36, issue 5: 277–284.

Ward, G. K. (2018). "Review Symposium: Rethinking the Pendulum Model of criminal justice history—Contention and the pendulum pivot: Weighting equal justice." *Law and Social Inquiry*. Vol. 44, issue 3: 806–813.

Ward, G. K., and A. Kupchik (2011). "Racial politics of juvenile justice policy support." *Race and Justice*. Vol. 1, issue 2: 154–184.

Warr, M. (2002). *Companions in Crime: The Social Aspects of Criminal Conduct*. Cambridge, UK: Cambridge University Press.

Wasserman, G. A., K. Keenan, R. E. Tremblay, J. D. Cole, T. I. Herrenkohl, R. Loeber, and D. Petechuk (2003). "Risk and protective factors of child delinquency." *Child Delinquency Bulletin Series*. Office of Juvenile Justice and Delinquency Prevention, Office of Justice Programs, U.S. Department of Justice. Apr. Retrieved from https://www.ojp.gov/pdffiles1/ojjdp/193409.pdf.

Wasserman, G. A., S. J. Ko, and L. S. McReynolds (2004). *Assessing the Mental Health of Youth in Juvenile Justice Setting*. Report. Washington, D.C.: Department of Justice, Office of Juvenile Justice and Delinquency Prevention.

Watt, B. D., K. Geritz, T. Hasan, S. Harden, and R. Doley (2015). "Prevalence and correlates of firesetting behaviours among offending and non-offending youth." *Legal and Criminological Psychology*, British Psychological Society. Vol. 10: 19–36.

Weber, M. (1922). "Bureaucracy." Reprint (2013) in *Economy and Society*, Vol. 2, ed. G. Roth and C. Wittich. Oakland: University of California Press.

Weintraub, M. J., D. Keenan-Miller, C. D. Schneck, M. F. Borlik, R. L. Suddath, S. E. Marvin, M. K. Singh, K. D. Chang, and D. J. Miklowitz (2022). "Social impairment in relation to clinical symptoms in youth at high risk for bipolar disorder." *Early Intervention in Psychiatry*. Vol. 16: 17–25.

Weisburd, D., and A. Petrosino (2004). "Experiments, criminology." In *Encyclopedia of Social Measurement*, ed. K. Kempf-Leonard. San Diego, CA: Elsevier.

Weissbourd, R., M. Batanova, J. McIntyre, and E. Torres (2020). "How the pandemic is strengthening fathers' relationships with their children." Making Caring Common Project, Graduate School of Education, Harvard University. June. Retrieved from https://static1.squarespace.com/static/5b7c56e255b02c683659fe43/t/5eeceba88f50eb19810153d4/1592585165850/Report+How+the+Pandemic+is+Strengthening+Fathers+Relationships+with+Their+Children+FINAL.pdf.

Weisz, J. R., A. Jensen-Doss, and K. M. Hawley (2006). "Evidence-based youth psychotherapies versus usual clinical care." *American Psychologist.* Vol. 61, issue 7 (Oct.): 671–689.

Welcome to Country (2022). History: Australia's brutal treatment of Aboriginal people. Jan. 2. Retrieved from https://www.welcometocountry.org/australias-brutal-treatment-of-aboriginal-people/#:~:text=Neck%20chains%20were%20used%20while,oppression%20continues%20today%20as%20well.

Welsh, B. C., N. E. Dill, and S. N. Zane (2019). "The first delinquency prevention experiment: A socio-historical review of the origins of the Cambridge-Somerville Youth Study research design." *Journal of Experimental Criminology.* Vol. 15: 441–451.

Welsh, E. (2017). "Note and Comment: The path of most resistance: Resisting gang recruitment as a political opinion in Central America's join-or-die gang culture." *Pepperdine Law Review.* Vol. 44: 1083.

Welsh, L. A., F. X. Archambault, M. D. Janus, and S. W. Brown (1995). *Running for Their Lives: Physical and Sexual Abuse of Runaway Adolescents.* New York: Garland.

Wernecke, D. C. (2022). "An Idiot's Guide to the American Upper Paleolithic." Lecture. Archeological Conservancy. Santa Fe, NM. June 22.

Wertham, F. (1948). "The psychopathology of comic books: A symposium." *American Journal of Psychotherapy.* Vol. 2, issue 3 (July): 472–490.

Westie, F., and A. T. Turk (1965). A Strategy for research on social classes and delinquency. *Journal of Criminal Law, Criminology, and Police Science.* Vol. 56 (Dec.): 454–462.

Weyns, T., K. Verschueren, G. Leflot, P. Onghena, S. Wouters, and H. Colpin (2017). "The role of teacher behavior in children's relational aggression development: A five-wave longitudinal study." *Journal of School Psychology.* Vol. 64: 17–27.

White House Archives (n.d.). "White House Faith-Based and Community Initiative." Retrieved from https://georgewbush-whitehouse.archives.gov/government/fbci/president-initiative.html#:~:text=The%20Initiative%20in%20Action,FBCOs%20in%20providing%20social%20services.

White House Briefing Room (2021). "FACT SHEET: President Biden Reestablishes the White House Office of Faith-Based and Neighborhood Partnerships." Statements and Releases. Feb. 14. Retrieved from https://www.whitehouse.gov/briefing-room/statements-releases/2021/02/14/fact-sheet-president-biden-reestablishes-the-white-house-office-of-faith-based-and-neighborhood-partnerships/.

Whiteman, S. D., A. C. Jensen, and J. L. Maggs (2013). "Similarities in adolescent siblings' substance use: Testing pathways of influence." *Journal of Studies on Alcohol and Drugs.* Vol. 74, issue 1 (Jan.): 104–113.

Whitney, N., and J. M. Froiland (2015). "Parenting style, gender, beer drinking, and drinking problems of college students." *International Journal of Psychology: A Biopsychosocial Approach.* Vol. 16: 93–109.

Whitt, C. (2021). A look at America's family farms. Report, *Farming, Research and Science.* July 29. Washington, DC: U.S. Department of Agriculture.

Wiemann, C. M., C. A. Agurcia, A. B. Berenson, R. J. Volk, and V. L. Rickert (2000). "Pregnant adolescents: Experiences and behaviors associated with physical assault by an intimate partner." *Maternal and Child Health Journal.* Vol. 4, issue 2: 93–101.

Wihbey, J. (2015). "Juvenile incarceration and its impact on high school graduation rates and adult jail time." *Journalist's Resource.* Shorenstein Center, Harvard Kennedy School, Harvard University. Feb. 4. Retrieved from https://journalistsresource.org/education/juvenile-incarceration-long-term-consequences/.

Wilkins, C., J. S. Romeo, M. Rychert, J. Prasad, and T. Graydon-Guy (2018). "Determinants of high availability of methamphetamine, cannabis, LSD and ecstasy in New Zealand: Are drug dealers promoting methamphetamine rather than cannabis?" *International Journal of Drug Policy.* Vol. 61 (Nov.): 15–22.

Willems, Y. E., C. V. Dolan, C. E. M. van Beijsterveldt, E. L. de Zeeum, D. I. Boomsma, M. Bartels, and C. Finkenauer (2018). "Genetic and environmental influences on self-control: Assessing self-control with the ASEBA Self-Control Scale." *Behavior Genetics.* Vol. 48: 135–146.

Willetts, M. (2022). "Teen under 'extreme pressure' from Instagram extortionist dies by suicide, MI cops say." *Kansas City Star.* Mar. 30. Retrieved from https://www.kansascity.com/news/nation-world/national/article259937105.html.

Williams-Butler, A. (2013). "Adolescent neglect, juvenile delinquency and the risk of recidivism." *Journal of Youth and Adolescence.* Vol. 42: 454–465.

Willison, J. (2016). "Characteristics of violent crime committed by female prisoners." *Violence and Victims.* Vol. 31, issue 3: 552–570.

Wilson, J. Q., and G. L. Kelling (1982). "Broken windows: The police and neighborhood safety." Originally published in *Atlantic Monthly*, Vol. 249, issue 3 (Mar.): 29–38. Retrieved from http://personal.psu.edu/exs44/597b-Comm&Crime/Wilson-Kelling-Broken%20Windows.pdf.

Winger, G., J. H. Woods, C. M. Galuska, and T. Wade-Galuska (2005). "Behavioral perspectives on the neuroscience of drug addiction." *Journal of Experimental Analysis of Behavior.* Vol. 84, issue 3 (Nov.): 667–681.

Winningham, R. D., M. R. Buetlich, D. E. Banks, T. C. B. Zapolski, and M. C. Aalsma (2019). "Substance use disorder and posttraumatic stress disorder symptomology on behavioral outcomes among juvenile justice youth." *American Journal on Addictions.* Vol. 28, issue 1 (Jan.): 29–35.

Wisconsin Legislature (n.d.). Chapter 948: Crimes against children. Retrieved from https://docs.legis.wisconsin.gov/statutes/statutes/948/60/2/a.

Wiseman, L. (n.d.). Historiography: Teenage attitudes of the 1950s. Theta Beta, Towson University. *Journal of Historical Studies.* Vol. 21. Retrieved from https://www.oc.edu/uploads/images/documents/Wiseman-Teenage-Attitude-of-the-1950s.pdf.

Wo, J. C. (2016). "Community context of crime: A longitudinal examination of the effects of local institutions on neighborhood crime." *Crime and Delinquency.* Vol. 62, issue 1: 1286–1312.

Wo, J. C. (2019). "Revisiting the crime control benefit of voluntary organizations: Organizational presence, organizational capacity, and crime rates in Los Angeles neighborhoods." *Crime and Delinquency.* Vol. 65, issue 7: 916–940.

Woldoff, R. A. (2002). "The effects of local stressors on neighborhood attachment." *Social Forces.* Vol. 81, issue 1: 87–116.

Wolf, J. P., and N. J. Kepple (2019). "Individual and county-level religious participation, corporal punishment and physical abuse of children: An exploratory study." *Journal of Interpersonal Violence.* Vol. 34, issue 19: 3983–3994.

Woodruff-Santos, M. (2015). "Telling young people they need a 4-year degree is a 'disservice.'" Opportunity Nation: The Forum for Youth Investment. June 17. Retrieved from https://opportunitynation.org/latest-news/media-highlights/telling-young-people-need-4-year-degree-disservice/.

Woolard, J. (2019). Waiver of counsel in juvenile court. No. 253015. National Criminal Justice Reference Service. June. Retrieved from https://www.ojp.gov/pdffiles1/nij/grants/253015.pdf.

World Health Organization (WHO) (2021). Violence against women: Key facts. Mar. 9. Retrieved from https://www.who.int/news-room/fact-sheets/detail/violence-against-women#:~:-text=Sexual%20violence%20is%20%22any%20sexual,the%20victim%2C%20in%20any%20setting.

World Population Review (2021). London population. Retrieved from https://worldpopulationreview.com/world-cities/london-population.

World Population Review (2022). Countries where prostitution is legal, 2022. Retrieved from https://worldpopulationreview.com/country-rankings/countries-where-prostitution-is-legal.

World Population Review (2022). Drinking age by country, 2022. Retrieved from https://worldpopulationreview.com/country-rankings/drinking-age-by-country.

World Population Review (2022). Most violent cities in America, 2022. Retrieved from https://worldpopulationreview.com/us-city-rankings/most-violent-cities-in-america.

Wright, J. D. (1995). "Ten essential observations on guns in America." *Society.* Vol. 32, issue 3: 63–68.

Wright, K. N., and K. E. Wright (1993). *Family Life and Delinquency: A Policymakers' Guide to the Literature.* Office of Juvenile Justice and Delinquency Prevention and National Institute of Justice. Washington, DC: U.S. Department of Justice.

X

Xuan, Z., J. G. Blanchette, T. F. Nelson, T. H. Nguyen, S. E. Hadland, et al. (2015). "Youth drinking in the United States: Relationships with alcohol policies and adult drinking." *Pediatrics.* Vol. 136, issue 1: 18–27.

Xuan, Z., T. F. Nelson, T. Heeren et al. (2013). "Tax policy, adult binge drinking, and youth alcohol consumption in the United States." *Alcoholism: Clinical and Experimental Research.* Vol. 37, issue 10: 1713–1719.

Y

Yamane, D. (2017). "The sociology of U.S. gun culture." *Sociology Compass.* Vol. 11: e12497.

Yang, A., and S. Dooley (2019). "Investigators in 'Slender Man' case discuss chilling interviews with 12-year-old attempted murderers." ABC News. Oct. 23. Retrieved from https://abcnews.go.com/US/investigators-slender-man-case-discuss-chilling-interviews-12/story?id=66320806.

Yates, A., L. E. Beutler, and M. Crago (1983). "Characteristics of young violent offenders." *Journal of Psychiatry and Law.* Vol. 11, issue 2 (June): 137–149.

Yeung, M. K., T. L. Lee, A. S. Chan (2021). "Negative mood is associated with decreased working memory in young adults." *Psychophysiology.* Vol. 58, issue 6: e13802.

Youth.gov (n.d.). "Reentry." Retrieved from https://youth.gov/youth-topics/juvenile-justice/reentry.

Youth Law Center (2018). Reenrollment of Juvenile Justice Youth. Nov. Retrieved from https://www.ylc.org/wp-content/uploads/2018/11/Reenrollment-of-Juvenile-Justice-Youth.pdf.

Yu, E. (2014). "Juvenile recidivism measurement inconsistent across states." Juvenile Justice Information Exchange. June 13. Retrieved from https://jjie.org/2014/06/13/juvenile-recidivism-measurement-inconsistent-across-states/.

Z

Zahn, M. A., R. Agnew, D. Fishbein, S. Miller, D. Winn, G. Dakoff, C. Kruttschnitt, P. Giordano, D. C. Gottfredson, A. A. Payne, B. C. Feld, and M. Chesney-Lind (2010). "Causes and correlates of girls' delinquency." In *Girls Study Group: Understanding and Responding to Girls' Delinquency.* Office of Juvenile Justice and Delinquency Prevention (OJJDP), Office of Justice Programs, U.S. Department of Justice. Apr. Retrieved from https://www.ojp.gov/pdffiles1/ojjdp/226358.pdf.

Zaliznyak, M., C. Bresee, and M. M. Garcia (2020). "Age at first experience of gender dysphoria among transgender adults: Seeking gender-affirming surgery." *Journal of the American Medical Association Network Open.* Vol. 3, issue 3 (Mar.): e201236.

Zamble, E., and E. Porporino (1988). *Coping Behavior and Adaptation in Prison Inmates.* New York: Springer-Verlag.

Zee, A. V. (2009). "The promotion and marketing of OxyContin: Commercial triumph, public health tragedy." *American Journal of Public Health.* Vol. 99, issue 2: 221-227.

Zimmer, S. (2021)."Dating violence and victimization." *Salem Press Encyclopedia.* New York: Salem Press.

Zimring, F. E. (2011). *The City That Became Safe: New York's Lessons for Urban Crime and Its Control.* Oxford, UK: Oxford University Press.

Zuckerman, D. (2022). "Youth violence in rural areas." National Center for Health Research. Retrieved from https://www.center4research.org/youth-violence-rural-areas/.

INDEX

G

S